survey of **Operating Systems**

Fourth Edition

Jane Holcombe
Charles Holcombe

SURVEY OF OPERATING SYSTEMS, FOURTH EDITION

Published by McGraw-Hill Education, 2 Penn Plaza, New York, NY 10121. Copyright © 2015 by McGraw-Hill Education. All rights reserved. Printed in the United States of America. Previous editions © 2012, 2006, and 2003. No part of this publication may be reproduced or distributed in any form or by any means, or stored in a database or retrieval system, without the prior written consent of McGraw-Hill Education, including, but not limited to, in any network or other electronic storage or transmission, or broadcast for distance learning.

Some ancillaries, including electronic and print components, may not be available to customers outside the United States.

This book is printed on acid-free paper.

1 2 3 4 5 6 7 8 9 0 RMN/RMN 1 0 9 8 7 6 5 4

ISBN 978-0-07-351818-3
MHID 0-07-351818-2

Senior Vice President, Products & Markets: *Kurt L. Strand*
Vice President, Content Production & Technology Services: *Kimberly Meriwether David*
Director: *Scott Davidson*
Senior Brand Manager: *Wyatt Morris*
Development Editor II: *Alan Palmer*
Senior Marketing Manager: *Tiffany Russell*
Director, Content Production: *Terri Schiesl*
Content Project Manager: *Jolynn Kilburg*
Buyer: *Laura Fuller*
Designer: *Lisa King*
Cover Image: © *Dave Cutler Studio, LLC*
Typeface: *10/12 Palatino LT Std*
Compositor: *MPS Limited*
Printer: *R. R. Donnelley*

Library of Congress Cataloging-in-Publication Data

Holcombe, Jane, author.
 Survey of operating systems / Jane Holcombe, Charles Holcombe. — Fourth
Edition.
    pages cm
  ISBN 978-0-07-351818-3 (alk. paper)
 1. Operating systems (Computers) I. Holcombe, Charles, author. II. Title.

QA76.76.O63H6465 2014
005.4'3—dc23
                    2013043699

The Internet addresses listed in the text were accurate at the time of publication. The inclusion of a Web site does not indicate an endorsement by the authors or McGraw-Hill Education, and McGraw-Hill Education does not guarantee the accuracy of the information presented at these sites.

About the Authors

JANE HOLCOMBE (MCSE, MCT, A+, Network+, CTT+, and Novell CNA) was a pioneer in the field of PC support training. In 1983, while working for a financial planning company, she moved the accounting and client-management operations to IBM PCs. This project included using three different operating systems to run the selected software and installing a local area network for sharing the accounting system and data. Although the network was not completely successful, this project showed the potential of networked PCs in business. Between 1984 and the mid-1990s she was an independent trainer, consultant, and course-content author, creating and presenting courses on PC operating systems nationwide and coauthoring a set of networking courses for the consulting staff of a large network vendor. In the early 1990s she worked with both Novell and Microsoft server operating systems, finally focusing on Microsoft operating systems. She achieved her Microsoft Certified Systems Engineer certification early, recertifying for new versions of Windows. Since 2000 she has worked primarily as a technical writer and technical editor.

CHARLES HOLCOMBE has a high-tech background in computing in the nuclear and aerospace fields. In his 15 years at Control Data Corporation, he was successively a programmer, technical sales analyst, salesman, and sales manager in the field marketing force. At corporate headquarters, he ran Control Data's Executive Seminar program, headed sales training for the corporation, was liaison to the worldwide university community, and was market development manager for the Plato computer-based education system. For the past 30 years, he has been an independent trainer and consultant. He has authored and delivered many training courses and is a skilled editor. Currently he is an independent editor for various clients and collaborates with Jane on writing projects. For a while, he claimed he was semi-retired, but, with his consulting and editing work, he cannot say that anymore.

Together the Holcombes have authored 11 books, beginning with the *MCSE Guide to Designing a Microsoft Windows 2000 Network Infrastructure* (Course Technology), both the *A+ Certification Press Lab Manual* and the *MCSE Certification Press Windows 2000 Professional Lab Manual* (McGraw-Hill/Osborne). They wrote *Using Windows 8* (McGraw-Hill) and the sixth, seventh, and eighth editions of the *CompTIA A+ Certification Study Guide* (McGraw-Hill). The book you are holding is their fourth edition of *Survey of Operating Systems*. The Holcombes also contributed chapters to four other technical books published by McGraw-Hill.

About the Contributors

This book was greatly influenced by the comments, suggestions, and feedback from the following group of dedicated instructors. To them we give our heartfelt thanks.

Technical Editors

Gerlinde Brady	*Cabrillo College*
Brenda Nielsen	*Mesa Community College*
Kevin Lee	*Guilford Technical Community College*
Tom Trevethan	*ECPI College of Technology*

Reviewers

David Barnes	*Penn State Altoona*
Gerlinde Brady	*Cabrillo College*
Menka Brown	*Piedmont Technical College*
Darren Denenberg	*Lee Business School*
Laura Hunt	*Tulsa Community College*
Kevin Lee	*Guilford Technical Community College*

Sue McCrory	*Missouri State University*
Gary Mosley	*Southern Wesleyan University*
Brenda Nielsen	*Mesa Community College*
Ruth Parker	*Rowan-Cabarrus Community College*
Theresa Savarese	*San Diego City College*
Donald Southwell	*Delta College*
Joyce Thompson	*Lehigh Carbon Community College*
Thomas Trevethan	*ECPI College of Technology*
David Wolfe	*Champlain College*
Kevin Wyzkiewicz	*Delta College*

Acknowledgments

After completing work on *Using Windows 8* we were looking for a little work-for-hire project. We called Alan Palmer, our development editor at McGraw-Hill, who asked if we wanted to write the fourth edition of our *Survey of Operating Systems*. Much has happened with operating systems and with personal computing since we wrote the first three editions, and we knew it would require a nearly complete rethinking of the content. Along with sponsoring editor Wyatt Morris and Alan, we wrote a survey that they sent to instructors—some of whom were still using the third edition. The results of this survey helped us create the outline for the fourth edition.

As with previous editions, knowledgeable peer reviewers scrutinized each chapter, giving us invaluable feedback on the relevancy and accuracy of the content. We can't imagine writing a book like this without these technical reviews.

We thank every member of the talented team of people at McGraw-Hill who ensured the book's integrity. They include Wyatt Morris, Alan Palmer, Jolynn Kilburg, Kayla Eisenbath, and Ruma Khurana from MPS Limited. We particularly want to thank Wyatt and Alan for their unstinting support, their continual cheerleading, and their professionalism.

We are thrilled with the updated design for this edition, and we greatly appreciate the expertise of the production group. They all worked hard to make the book look wonderful. Creating and laying out the many elements of this complex book design was a huge task, and they handled it with aplomb.

We truly appreciate all who worked hard to make this book what it is.

Thank you!

About This Book

Important Technology Skills

Information technology (IT) offers many career paths, leading to occupations in such fields as PC repair, network administration, telecommunications, Web development, graphic design, and desktop support. To become competent in any IT field, however, you need certain basic computer skills. This book will help you build a foundation for success in the IT field by introducing you to fundamental information about desktop operating systems, a needed basis for working with computers at any level.

Try This!
exercises reinforce the concepts.

Notes and Warnings
create a road map for success.

Engaging and Motivational!
Using a conversational style and proven instructional approach, the authors explain technical concepts in a clear, interesting way using real-world examples.

Makes Learning Fun!
Rich, colorful text and enhanced illustrations bring technical subjects to life.

Effective Learning Tools

The design of this colorful, pedagogically rich book will make learning easy and enjoyable and help you develop the skills and critical thinking abilities that will enable you to adapt to different job situations and troubleshoot problems. Jane and Charles Holcombe's proven ability to explain concepts in a clear, direct, even humorous way makes this book interesting and motivational, and fun.

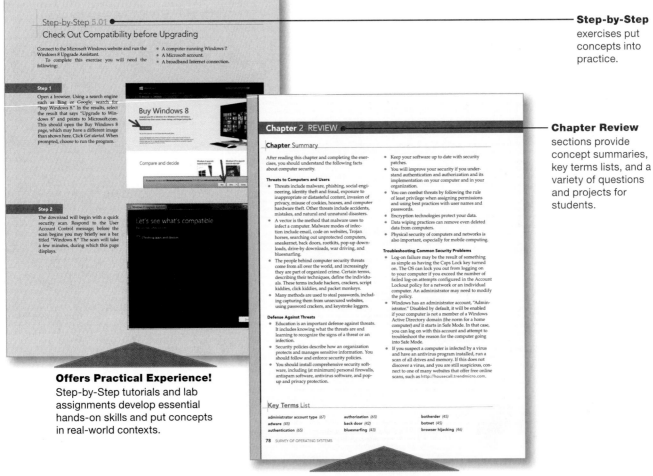

Step-by-Step exercises put concepts into practice.

Chapter Review sections provide concept summaries, key terms lists, and a variety of questions and projects for students.

Offers Practical Experience! Step-by-Step tutorials and lab assignments develop essential hands-on skills and put concepts in real-world contexts.

Robust Learning Tools! Summaries, key terms lists, quizzes, essay questions, and lab projects help you practice skills and measure progress.

Each chapter includes:

- **Learning Outcomes** that set measurable goals for chapter-by-chapter progress.
- **Four-Color Illustrations** that give you a clear picture of the technologies.
- **Step-by-Step Tutorials** that teach you to perform essential tasks and procedures hands-on.
- **Try This!** sidebars that encourage you to practice and apply the concepts in real-world settings.

- **Notes** and **Warnings** that guide you through difficult areas.
- **Chapter Summaries** and **Key Terms Lists** that provide you with an easy way to review important concepts and vocabulary.
- **Challenging End-of-Chapter Tests** that include vocabulary-building exercises, multiple-choice questions, essay questions, and on-the-job lab projects.

New to *Survey of Operating Systems*, Fourth Edition

General changes:

- Previous Chapter 5, *Windows XP Professional*, has been removed and replaced by Appendix A, *Securing and Troubleshooting Windows XP*.
- Previous Chapter 4, *Disk Operating System (DOS)*, has been replaced by Chapter 9, *The Command-Line Interface*, which explores the use of the command-line interface in Windows and OS X.
- New and revised chapters. All content has been reviewed and updated, as necessary.

Chapter 1 Introduction to Operating Systems

- Updated overview to include mobile devices.
- Renamed the section previously titled *Yesterday's Desktop Operating Systems* to *Yesterday's Operating Systems*. Updated the content of this section, as well as the timeline, which now runs from 1968 to 2013.
- Updated content of the section titled *Today's Desktop OSs*.
- Added a new section titled *Today's Mobile OSs* with an overview of modern mobile devices and a brief introduction to mobile operating systems: Google Android, Apple iOS, and Microsoft Windows 8 and Windows Phone 8.

Chapter 2 Computer Security Basics

- Updated chapter content.

Chapter 3 Desktop Virtualization

- Updated chapter content.

Chapter 4 Windows 7 (New Chapter)

- This chapter replaces Chapter 6, *Today's Windows—Windows Vista and Windows 7*. Windows Vista coverage is reduced, while focusing on Windows 7.
- This chapter describes several topics, including Windows 7 installation and features, customizing and managing Windows 7, and managing local security.

Chapter 5 Windows 8 (New Chapter)

- This new chapter begins with a description of Windows 8 features and editions, including the Windows 8.1 Update introduced in October 2013.
- The section on installing Windows 8 includes a discussion of the use of a Microsoft account, local account, or domain account with Windows 8 and the options for using the Web-Based Installer as well as the more conventional installation.

- This chapter includes explanations and examples of how to navigate the Windows 8 Start screen and Desktop GUIs as well as installing and updating apps from the Windows Store.
- The section on securing Windows 8 includes the new or modified security features of Windows 8, such as Windows Defender, options for administering local user accounts, Windows SmartScreen, and the use of Assigned Access to turn a Windows 8.1 computer into a secure kiosk.

Chapter 6 Under the Windows Desktop: Supporting and Troubleshooting Windows

- This chapter is an update to Chapter 7 in the third edition, with a more descriptive chapter name.
- Added coverage of Windows 8 Secure Boot and Fast Boot features and expanded the section on Troubleshooting to include Windows 8 recovery tools.

Chapter 7 OS X on the Desktop

- This chapter is an update to Chapter 9 in the third edition, with expanded coverage of OS X features.

Chapter 8 Linux on the Desktop

- This is a major revision of Chapter 8 in the third edition, with expanded coverage of GUI features.
- The section previously titled *Managing Files and Directories with Shell Commands* is replaced by a section titled *Linux Command-Line Interface*. The new section teaches basic skills for working at the Linux command-line interface using the terminal window.

Chapter 9 The Command-Line Interface (New Chapter!)

- This new chapter describes and compares the command-line interfaces in Windows (Command Prompt) and OS X (Terminal).

Chapter 10 Connecting Desktops and Laptops to Networks

- This chapter is a revision of Chapter 10 in the third edition, titled *The Client Side of Network*. The title change reflects the omission of mobile devices from this chapter. Chapter 11 will be devoted to mobile operating systems, including how to connect mobile devices to networks.
- We expanded coverage of IPv6 and removed some of the content and one Step-by-Step on configuring a dial-up connection.
- Removed coverage of advanced sharing for Windows and expanded coverage for sharing with HomeGroups. Updated the section on sharing the Public folder.

Chapter 11 Mobile Operating Systems (New Chapter)

- This new chapter first addresses the issue of employees bringing and using their own mobile devices at work. Then it describes how to configure accounts and wireless connections for mobile devices.

- Three mobile operating systems are compared in this chapter: Google Android, Apple iOS, and Windows Phone 8.
- Each topic is first introduced and then demonstrated in the different mobile OSs.

Appendix A: Securing and Troubleshooting Windows XP (New)

- At this writing Microsoft plans to end support for Windows XP in April 2014. Some industry analysts report that Windows XP is still on a large number of desktops, and this may influence Microsoft to extend this deadline. Therefore, we are including important information on securing and troubleshooting Windows XP in this appendix.

Appendix B: Windows Mouse and Keyboard Shortcuts (New)

- Many of us have used Windows for so long that we automatically use our favorite mouse and keyboard shortcuts to quickly move around, open files and select objects, open programs, and much more. This new appendix lists shortcuts we have tested in Windows 7 and Windows 8.

Contents

ABOUT THE AUTHORS   III

ABOUT THE CONTRIBUTORS   III

ACKNOWLEDGMENTS   IV

ABOUT THIS BOOK   V

NEW TO *SURVEY OF OPERATING SYSTEMS,*
FOURTH EDITION   VII

INTRODUCTION   XIV

1 | Introduction to Operating Systems   1

An Overview of Microcomputer Operating Systems 2

About Microcomputers   2
Functions of Microcomputer Operating Systems   5
How Much Memory Can an Operating System Use?   9

Yesterday's Operating Systems 10

UNIX—The OS for All Platforms   11
The Evolution of Desktop Operating Systems   12

Today's Desktop OSs 26

Microsoft Windows for the Desktop   26
Apple Mac OS X   28
Linux   28

Today's Mobile OSs 30

Mobile Devices   30
Connectivity   31
Mobile OS Features   31

CHAPTER 1 REVIEW 34

2 | Computer Security Basics   39

Threats to Computers and Users 40

Malware   40
Social Engineering   46
Identity Theft   48
Exposure to Inappropriate or Distasteful Content   49
Invasion of Privacy   49
Misuse of Cookies   50
Computer Hardware Theft   51
Accidents, Mistakes, and Disasters   51
Keeping Track of New Threats   52
The People Behind the Threats   52

Defense Against Threats 54

Education   54
Security Policies   55
Install Comprehensive Security Software   55
Firewalls   56
Antispam Software   60
Antivirus Software   60
Pop-Up Blockers   61
Privacy Protection and Cookies   61
Parental Controls   62
Content Filtering   63
Keep Up to Date   63
Authentication and Authorization   64
Passwords   65
Security Account Basics   66
Best Practices When Assigning Permissions   69
Best Practices with User Names and Passwords   69
Encryption   71
Data Wiping   73
Physical Security   74
Security for Mobile Computing   74

Troubleshooting Common Security Problems 74

Troubleshooting Log-On Problems   75
Using the Administrator Account in Troubleshooting   76
Troubleshooting a Suspected Malware Attack   76

CHAPTER 2 REVIEW 78

3 | Desktop Virtualization   83

Virtualization Overview 84

Virtualization Is Everywhere   84
Your (Great?) Grandfather's Virtual Machines   85
Today's Virtual Desktops   85

Virtual Machines on Windows Desktops 88

Microsoft Virtual PC 2007 for VMs on Old Versions of Windows   88
Windows XP Mode and Windows Virtual PC on Windows 7   93
Client Hyper-V on Windows 8   102
Oracle VirtualBox   105

Virtual Machines on Mac OS X 106

Apple Boot Camp—A Dual-Boot Option   106
Oracle VirtualBox   107

CHAPTER 3 REVIEW 113

4 | Windows 7   117

Installing Windows 7 118

Recommended System Requirements   118
Windows 7 Editions   118
Upgrade Paths   119
Preparing to Install Windows 7   120
The Installation   123
Post-Installation Tasks   128

Windows 7 Features 130

The Windows 7 Desktop   130
File System Support   136
Security   137
Program Compatibility   138
Recovery Tools   138

Customizing and Managing Windows 7 139

Computer Management   139
Preparing the Desktop for Users   140
Installing and Removing Applications   145
Managing Windows Components   146
Simple File Management   146

Managing Local Security in Windows 7 152

Administering Local User Accounts   152
Local Security for Files and Folders   155
BitLocker Drive Encryption   157
Windows Defender   159
Microsoft Security Essentials   159
Windows Firewall   159

CHAPTER 4 REVIEW 160

5 | Windows 8   165

Overview of Windows 8 Features and Editions 166

Windows 8 Features   166
Windows 8 Editions   169
Windows 8.1 Update   171

Installing Windows 8 171

System Requirements   172
Upgrade Paths   172
Preparing to Install Windows 8   173
The Installation   178

Postinstallation Tasks 183

Installing Drivers   183
Installing Updates   184
Virtual Machine Guest Additions   187
Remove Unnecessary Software   187
Create a Backup Image   187
Turn on File History   187
Shutting Down Windows 8   188

Navigating and Configuring Windows 8 189

The Lock Screen   189
The Start Screen   190
The Desktop   194
Managing Apps in Windows 8   197

Securing Windows 8 200

Windows Defender   200
Administering Local User Accounts   201
Windows SmartScreen   203
A Windows 8 Computer in a Kiosk   204

CHAPTER 5 REVIEW 205

6 | Under the Windows Desktop: Supporting and Troubleshooting Windows   211

Understanding the Registry 212

The Registry Defined   212
Automatic Registry Changes   212
Registry Files   213
Registry Hives   215
The Temporary Portion of the Registry   215
Viewing and Editing the Registry   215
Backing Up the Registry   217

Windows User and Power Options 220

User Options   221
Power Options   221
Windows 7 Startup Phases   222
Windows 8 Secure Boot and Fast Boot   225
Modifying System Startup   225

Installing and Managing Device Drivers 229

Installing Device Drivers   229
Managing Installed Devices   230

Using Windows Troubleshooting and Recovery Tools 235

When Windows Fails at Startup: The Windows Recovery Environment   235
Troubleshooting with Modified Startups   235
Troubleshooting Device Problems   245

CHAPTER 6 REVIEW 247

7 | OS X on the Desktop   253

OS X History and Versions 254

A Brief History of the Apple Operating Systems   254
OS X Versions   255

Installing and Upgrading OS X 257

Preparing to Install OS X   257
The Installation   259
Postinstallation Tasks   262

Navigating and Managing the OS X Desktop 263

The Desktop Menu Bar 263
File Management in Finder 264
Changing Settings in OS X 271
Launching and Switching between Apps with the Dock 272
Using the Heads-Up Program Switcher 272
View and Manage All Programs in Launchpad 273
Declutter the Desktop with Mission Control 274
Notification Center 275
Menu Extras 275
Printing in OS X 276
AirPlay 277

Managing Local Security in OS X 277

Check Out the OS X Firewall 278
Gatekeeper 278
Kernel ASLR 279
Digitally Signed and Sandboxed Apps 279
FileVault 279
Secure Virtual Memory 280
Keychain 280
Managing Local User Accounts 280

Troubleshooting Common Mac OS Problems 284

Where to Find Help 284
When to Quit 285
OS X Failure to Quit 285
Forgotten Password 285
Disappearing Sidebar Items 286
Useful System Utilities 287

CHAPTER 7 REVIEW 288

8 Linux on the Desktop 293

Linux Overview 294

Why Learn Linux? 294
The Evolution of Linux 294
Benefits of Linux 296
Drawbacks of Linux 298

Linux on Your Desktop 300

Acquiring Linux for the Desktop 300
Installing Linux or Using a Live Image 303

Exploring a Linux GUI 303

Logging In to Ubuntu Linux 303
The Ubuntu Unity Desktop 304
System Settings 309
Modify the Desktop 309
Ending a Linux Session from the GUI 311

Linux Command-Line Interface 312

The Terminal Window in Linux 312
Using Linux Shell Commands 313

Securing a Linux Desktop 320

Managing Users 320
File and Folder Permissions 324

CHAPTER 8 REVIEW 326

9 The Command-Line Interface 331

Introduction to the Windows Command Prompt 332

The Windows Command Prompt Is Not MS-DOS 332
The Windows Command Prompt Is Not Windows PowerShell 332
Opening Windows 7 Command Prompts 333
The Windows 8 Command Prompts 336

Success at the Windows Command Prompt 338

How Does the Command Prompt Use Letter Case? 338
How Does the Command Prompt Interpret a Command? 339
How Is a Program Found and Loaded? 340
Using Redirection Operators 341
Which Command Will Accomplish the Task? 341
What Is the Correct Syntax? 343
Batch Files at the Command Prompt 344
Working with Files and Directories 345

Using Terminal in OS X 351

Launch Terminal 352
Shell Commands in Terminal 353

CHAPTER 9 REVIEW 358

10 Connecting Desktops and Laptops to Networks 363

Configuring a Network Connection 364

Understanding the TCP/IP Protocol Suite 364
Transmission Control Protocol 365
Internet Protocol 365

Connecting to the Internet 376

Internet Service Providers 376
Computer-to-Internet versus LAN-to-Internet 376
Wired Connectivity Technologies 377
Wireless Connectivity Technologies 379
Using a Virtual Private Network 382

Using Internet Clients 383

Web Browsers 383
Email Clients 392
FTP Clients 396

Sharing Files and Printers 396

The Server Side of File and Printer Sharing 397
The Client Side of File and Printer Sharing 397
Sharing Files and Printers in Windows 7 and Windows 8 398

Troubleshooting Common Network Client Problems 402

    Built-In Network Diagnostics 402

    Testing IP Configurations and Connectivity 403

    Troubleshooting Connection Problems with tracert 407

    Troubleshooting DNS Errors Using ping, netstat, and nslookup 408

CHAPTER 10 REVIEW 409

11 | Mobile Operating Systems 415

From Luggable to BYOD 416

    Mobile Computing Then and Now 416

    Mobile Devices and BYOD 417

Configuring Accounts and Wireless Connections on Mobile Devices 419

    Your Mobile Device Account 419

    Connecting to Cellular Networks 421

    Connecting to Wi-Fi Networks 422

    Mobile Hotspots 423

    Tethering 424

    Connecting to Bluetooth Devices 424

    Connecting with Near Field Communications 425

    Airplane Mode 426

Email, Apps, and Synchronization 426

    Configuring Email 426

    Mobile Apps 429

    Synchronization 430

Securing Mobile Devices 434

    Security Software for Mobile Devices 434

    Patching and OS Updates 434

    Securing Lock Screens on Mobile Devices 434

    Location Settings 437

    Lost or Stolen Devices 439

CHAPTER 11 REVIEW 441

APPENDIX A SECURING AND TROUBLESHOOTING WINDOWS XP 445

APPENDIX B WINDOWS MOUSE AND KEYBOARD SHORTCUTS 467

GLOSSARY 471

PHOTO CREDITS 485

INDEX 487

Introduction

What Will You Learn?

The first two editions of this book were well received by instructors and students. This third edition updates the material and presents new information that is relevant to the topic of desktop operating systems, including Windows, Mac OS X, and Linux. We carefully revised every chapter as needed, with more illustrations and plenty of hands-on opportunities. We have added content throughout, while working to streamline the book in response to feedback we received from instructors.

How Will You Learn?

We don't want to simply give you an encyclopedia of information because it can feel like you're standing in front of an information fire hose, and we've been there ourselves many times in the past decades. Rather, keeping in mind that "less is more," we present just the key points about operating systems, and guide you in your own exploration of the specifics of the technology. One book simply can't give you everything you need to know about operating systems, but we do hope to empower you and to increase your ability to use widely available tools and resources to figure out the answers to your questions. Such tools as the Internet and the help program in your OS are aids you should turn to when you need to learn more about a topic, and when you want to enhance your skills in working with each of these operating systems—and with computers in general.

Each chapter uses many techniques to help you learn. We start by listing learning outcomes, follow that up with a lucid explanation of each topic, and support it with real-world experience and a liberal use of graphics and tables. To give you hands-on experience and to help you "walk the walk," each chapter contains detailed Step-by-Step tutorials and short Try This! exercises to reinforce the concepts. To build vocabulary to help you "talk the talk," each chapter contains computer term definitions, highlighted in a Key Terms List and compiled into a Glossary at the end of the book.

We've also included notes, which provide handy pieces of knowledge to use with your desktop OS. Warnings will help you prevent mishaps.

You can measure what you've learned with end-of-chapter Key Terms, Multiple-Choice, and Essay quizzes. In addition, Lab Projects challenge you to independently complete tasks related to what you've just learned.

Let's Get Down to Work

OK, enough of this introductory stuff. This is the last time in this book that you'll see so many words without illustrations. From now on it's downright exciting. Learn a lot and *have fun*!

Supplements

For teachers using this book in the classroom, a powerful collection of teaching tools written by the authors is available online at www.mhhe.com/holcombe4:

- An Instructor's Manual that maps to the organization of the textbook and provides additional instructor tips and activities to use with the book.
- A test bank for each chapter available online in either Word or EZ Test format.
- Engaging PowerPoint slides on the lecture topics, including key points and illustrations from the chapters.

Jane Holcombe

Charles Holcombe

Introduction to Operating Systems

"Physics is the universe's operating system."

—Steven R. Garman

"I do not fear computers. I fear lack of them."

—Isaac Asimov

"The computer was born to solve problems that did not exist before."

—Bill Gates

Understanding operating systems (OSs) is critical to your future success in life. It is. Just believe us. You don't? You say you drive a car just fine, but you don't understand its engine, transmission, or other systems? So why can't you just use your computer? Why do you have to even know it has an OS? If you can successfully operate a car, you actually know more about its internal workings than you realize. You turn on the ignition, shift to the correct gear, press the accelerator, and drive down the street without hitting anything. You stop it (in time, usually). You use your car to go somewhere, thus making the car your transportation tool. Having only superficial knowledge of the workings of your car is adequate if you never intend to repair your car or to explain to a mechanic the symptoms of a problem. And just as you can use a car without in-depth knowledge of how it works, you can use your computer to write a letter, send email, create a report, surf the Internet, participate in social networking, and much more without understanding operating systems. You only have to know how to turn it on, call up the application program you wish to use, do tasks, and turn it off.

Learning Outcomes

In this chapter, you will learn how to:

LO **1.1**   Describe the purpose and functions of operating systems.

LO **1.2**   Describe major events in the evolution of operating systems.

LO **1.3**   List and compare the common desktop operating systems in use today.

LO **1.4**   List the most common mobile OSs, the devices associated with them, and the features found in most of these devices.

But if you ever want to understand how your car actually works, you need to spend time studying it. And if you want to get the most out of the computers you use in your work, school, and private life, you need to understand how the most critical software component, the computer's operating system, works.

This chapter provides an overview of microcomputer operating systems—specifically, those commonly found on desktop and laptop computers and the personal mobile devices we use today. We'll begin with a brief look at microcomputers—their components and their general types. Then we'll explore the functions that operating systems perform, as well as describe the classic categories of operating systems. Finally, we introduce you to the OSs in all types of microcomputers including those in home and office computers as well as tablets and smartphones. 🌐

LO 1.1 | An Overview of Microcomputer Operating Systems

An operating system (OS) is a collection of programs that controls all of the interactions among the various system components, freeing application programmers from needing to include such functions in their programs. An application is software that allows a user to perform useful functions, such as writing a report, picking up email, editing graphics, calculating a budget, and much more. Microsoft Word is an application. Applications only need to send commands to the OS to interact with the hardware. This book explores the common operating systems used in microcomputers, but before we do, let's answer a few general questions you may have: What is a microcomputer? What types of microcomputers are in use today?

About Microcomputers

Our friend Brianna uses a PC at work and an Apple iMac at home, and she always has her smartphone handy. She will soon take night classes in which she will use either a tablet or laptop that she will carry to and from school. She wants to learn more about the computers she uses each day, beginning with the hardware.

To understand microcomputers, you need to learn a few technical terms, such as computer, integrated circuit, and microprocessor. A computer is a device that performs calculations. Early computers had many mechanical components, but a typical modern computer is an electronic device that can perform a huge number of useful tasks for its owner. Any computer, small or large, has a central processing unit (CPU) that performs the calculations, or processing for the computer.

A typical PC with components.
Product photo courtesy of Hewlett-Packard.

A microcomputer is a computer small enough and cheap enough for the use of one person. The CPU in a microcomputer is a microprocessor, although many still refer to it simply as a CPU or processor. This miniaturization of computer components became possible through the invention and development of many technologies. One of the most important of those inventions was the integrated circuit (IC), a small electronic component made up of transistors (tiny switches) and other miniaturized parts. These replaced the bulky vacuum tubes in older minicomputers and TVs and in mainframe computers, which were often huge, weighed tons, and used large amounts of power.

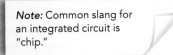

Note: Common slang for an integrated circuit is "chip."

Each computer that Brianna and the rest of us use consists of many components, some of which allow us to interact with it. In techie talk, we call interaction with a computer input/output (I/O). When we send something into the computer we call it input. For instance, you are inputting when you type on the keyboard or tap on a touch screen, and that makes a keyboard or a touch screen an input device. When something comes out of the computer, such as the text and graphics that displays on a screen, the printed results on paper, or music and other sounds, we call it output. That makes both the display screen, printer, and speakers output devices.

In a microcomputer the internal components include at least one microprocessor, random-access memory (RAM) that acts as the main memory for holding active programs and associated data, firmware (software resident in integrated circuits), and various other supporting circuitry, all installed onto a motherboard. This last is a circuit board on which the microprocessor, memory, and other components reside and connect to each other. It also has some form of storage, such as a hard drive. Additionally, it has at least one means each for input and output.

System firmware contains program code that informs the processor of the devices present and how to communicate with them. Firmware is an interface between the hardware and the operating system. The system firmware in PCs for most of the last three decades has been read only memory basic input output system (ROM BIOS), which has been replaced by a new standard for system firmware called Unified Extensible Firmware Interface (UEFI). UEFI supports modern computers, while ROM BIOS had many technical limits because it was designed to work with the original IBM PC. UEFI is faster and includes security features that protect the computer during that vulnerable time while an operating system is just starting up and not entirely in control.

Additionally, most components and peripheral devices that connect to a computer (such as the video and network adapters, USB ports, and digital cameras) have their own firmware, which is often limited to small programs for providing basic communication between the operating system and the component. Supplementing or replacing the firmware—even parts of the central system firmware—are device drivers. A device driver is a special program installed into an operating system. Each device driver contains code for controlling a component and it is an extension of the firmware, usually allowing much more control of a device than the small programs stored in that device's firmware.

> *Note:* Fortunately, you may never need to be concerned about device drivers because they install automatically in most operating systems.

Although you may never be aware of the firmware on your mobile devices, on an older PC or laptop you may see evidence of the system and other firmware as they perform tests of the hardware. The traditional system firmware test is known as the power on self-test (POST). Carefully watch the screen as you power up the computer, as shown in Figure 1–1 and if status and error messages display in plain text on a black background during startup, they are the result of the POST and the tests of additional firmware on the computer's components. More recent computers may show a message only if there is a serious problem with the computer.

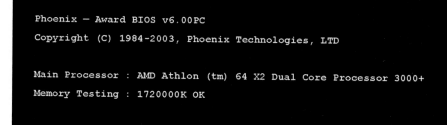

```
Phoenix — Award BIOS v6.00PC
Copyright (C) 1984-2003, Phoenix Technologies, LTD


Main Processor : AMD Athlon (tm) 64 X2 Dual Core Processor 3000+
Memory Testing : 1720000K OK
```

FIGURE 1–1 An example of a firmware start-up message on an older PC.

In general, consumers encountered their first microcomputers in 1977 with the introduction of Apple's Apple II, Radio Shack's TRS-80, and Commodore's PET. It was the Apple II that best combined the critical elements that make up what we considered a microcomputer at the time; these included a keyboard, a monitor, available peripherals, an operating system, desirable and useful applications, and a reasonable price tag.

What Types of Microcomputers Do You Use?

The miniaturization of computers led to computers being built into all types of machinery, including vehicles, aircraft, and appliances. And that is just the short list. Computers touch our lives 24/7, and each has some form of operating system. For our purposes, we will concentrate on the operating systems in desktops, laptops, and mobile devices. We will limit the mobile device OSs to those in tablets and smartphones. Another type of computer that you use less directly is a server. You connect to a server via your personal computers and devices. A server also uses microcomputer technology, but on a larger scale. We describe these types of microcomputers next.

A PC laptop.
Product photo courtesy of Toshiba.

A MacBook laptop.
Product photo courtesy of Apple.

Note: In this book we use the term **personal computer** (PC) for a desktop computer running Windows or Linux and **Mac** for the Apple iMac desktop computer as well as the MacBook laptop computer. Both types of Apple computers run Mac OS X.

Desktops and Laptops. A desktop computer is a computer designed to spend its useful life in one location—on a desk. A laptop computer has a flat screen and a keyboard, each integrated into a panel with a hinge holding the two together and allowing you to close the laptop and slip it into a case for easy portability. There are many sizes and types of laptop computers. Our discussion of operating systems in this book includes the most common operating systems that run on modern desktop and laptop computers as well as in those in consumer mobile devices. They include Microsoft Windows and Linux for PCs and laptops, and Apple's Mac OS X, which runs on Apple desktop and laptop computers. The same version of the Windows OS will run on a desktop, a compatible laptop computer, or a compatible tablet.

In the decades since the introduction of the IBM PC in 1981, the majority of desktop and laptop computers used in private and public organizations have used Microsoft operating systems, with computers running versions of Apple's operating systems a distant second. In recent years however, Apple desktop and laptop computers have made great gains in market share, but Apple's real advances have been in their mobile products.

Mobile Devices. Microcomputers today include a long list of devices that don't have *computer* in their name, including mobile devices that are often proprietary, comply with no, or very few, standards in their design, but are still microcomputers because they contain microprocessors. They use wireless technologies and include a wide variety of products ranging from simple handheld computers to multifunction mobile devices, such as those used in grocery stores to track inventory. Many mobile devices run proprietary OSs, while others run scaled-down versions of desktop OSs. A mobile device stores its OS in firmware, as an embedded OS.

The most popular mobile devices are smartphones. A smartphone works as a cell phone, but also lets you connect to the Internet, view your email, and install and run a variety of apps for entertainment, education, and work. Modern smartphones have high-quality touch screens. Examples of smartphones are Apple's iPhones, RIM's BlackBerry products, and various models by Motorola, Nokia, HTC, Samsung, LG, and others. Examples of operating systems designed specifically for use on smartphones include Google's Android,

Palm's webOS, Apple's iOS, and Windows Phone.

Another very popular type of mobile device is a tablet. A tablet has a touch screen, no integrated keyboard (usually), is larger than a smartphone, and is much more portable than a laptop. There are many lines of tablet products, including the Apple iPad, Microsoft's Surface and Surface Pro, Samsung Galaxy Tab, Nexus 7, Sony Xperia, Asus Transformer, Kindle Fire, BlackBerry Playbook, and HP Slate2. The tablet operating systems we will study in this book are Apple iOS, Google Android, and Microsoft Windows 8.

Servers. On a small network you can use a PC or Mac as a server, a computer that provides one or more services to other computers, which is why it is called a server. What services do servers provide? When we use a server to store data files for network-connected users, we call it a file server. If a server has one or more printers connected to it that it shares with users on the network, it is a print server. We call a server doing both tasks a file and print server; even though it sounds like two services, they combine into one service called a file and print service.

Other services include messaging services (email and fax), Web services, and many, many others. It takes specialized software to provide each type of server service, and complementary client software to request each type of service over a network. A server can offer multiple services at the same time while also being a client to other servers.

We call a computer on the user end of network services a client. Today's client computers include the PCs, laptops, tablets, and smartphones discussed in this book.

A desktop or laptop computer can act as a server for a few network clients. However, a server to which hundreds or thousands of clients must connect requires much more capable hardware to provide more storage, faster processing, and faster network access. Such a server also requires specialized software, beginning with the operating systems. There are versions of Windows, Apple Mac OS X, Linux, and UNIX especially designed for servers. The hardware for a high-quality server can run into the tens of thousands of dollars and upward, versus the much lower cost of a consumer-grade PC at a few hundred dollars.

Note: Nokia Corporation is the manufacturer of the popular Lumia line of Windows 8 phones. In September 2013 Microsoft Corporation and Nokia Corporation announced Microsoft's planned purchase of all of Nokia's Devices and Services business, as well as their planned licensing of Nokia's patents, and licensing and use of Nokia's mapping services. At this writing, the transaction is expected to close in the first quarter of 2014.

Note: The focus of this book is on using common desktop, laptop, and mobile operating systems. Therefore, it does not include details of server operating systems.

Functions of Microcomputer Operating Systems

When using her PC at work or her Mac at home our friend Brianna spends much of her time in a specific application, such as a word processor, a graphical drawing program, or a Web browser. However, she must also perform tasks outside of these applications, beginning with the simple task of logging onto the computer, launching an application, and managing files. But, because each of these different computers requires different ways of doing things, she wants to gain a better understanding of the OSs so that she can both perform better on the job and feel more comfortable while working on the various

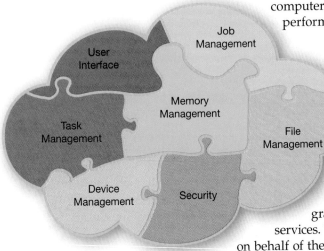

The functions of an operating system.

computers. She wants to learn what an OS is and what functions it performs, which we describe in the following sections.

An operating system is loaded (or "booted up," a derivation of the expression "lifting yourself by your own bootstraps") when a computer is turned on. Its main component, the kernel, remains in memory while the computer is running, managing low-level (close-to-the-hardware) OS tasks.

When a programmer, also known as a "developer," writes an application, he or she designs the application to interact with the operating system and to make requests for hardware services through the operating system. To do this, a programmer must write the program to use the correct commands to request operating system services. The operating system, in turn, interacts with the hardware on behalf of the application and fulfills the requests the application made. An operating system performs several functions. We'll study them next.

User Interface

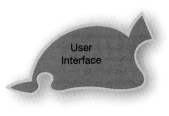

FIGURE 1–2 The DOS prompt.

The user interface (UI) is the software layer, sometimes called the shell, through which the user communicates with the OS. The UI includes the command processor, which loads programs into memory, as well as the many visual components of the operating system (what you see when you look at the display). On a computer running DOS (a legacy OS) or Linux (without a graphical shell), this visual component consists of a character-based command line that provides only sparse amounts of information. This is the command-line interface (CLI). Figure 1–2 shows the classic DOS prompt: white characters against a black screen, with a blinking cursor waiting for you to type a command at the keyboard. A cursor in a CLI is merely a marker for the current position where what you type on the keyboard will go. Further, only a limited set of characters can appear on the screen, each in its own little equal-sized grid of space.

To become proficient at working in a CLI, you must memorize the commands and their modifiers and subcommands. On the other hand, Apple's Mac OS, Microsoft's Windows, and even mobile operating systems each provides an information-rich graphical user interface (GUI), fully integrated into the operating system. It is through this GUI that you communicate with the OS and the computer. The GUI offers menus and graphical icons (small graphics) that allow you to use a pointing device to select programs to run and to perform many other tasks, such as opening a word processor file.

Although you do not have to memorize commands, working within a GUI does require learning the meaning of the various graphical pieces that make up the GUI and how to navigate among them to access your programs and data. In addition, you must learn how to activate a program (start it running) so that you can get your work or play done. Figure 1–3 shows a GUI screen. Notice the icons and other graphical components, such as the bar at the bottom containing the button showing the Microsoft logo and the arrow-shaped pointer in the open menu at left above the bar. In a GUI you move a graphical pointer around using a pointing device—usually a mouse, trackball, or touch pad. The pointer allows you to select or manipulate objects in the GUI to accomplish tasks. For example, to delete an item, you drag it into the recycle bin. By contrast, in a CLI, you would type a command such as "delete report.txt."

Note: Although Linux traditionally had a CLI, most current versions of Linux for the desktop come with both CLIs and GUIs.

Job Management

Job management is an operating system function that controls the order and time in which programs run. Two examples of programs that may take

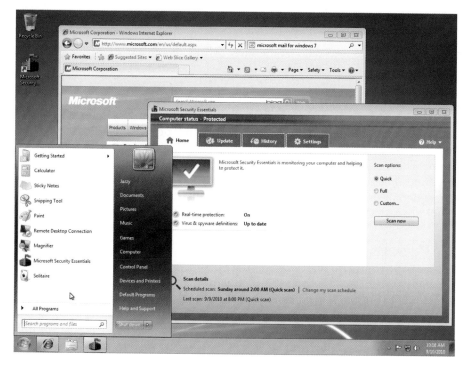

FIGURE 1–3 A typical GUI screen.

advantage of this function are a scheduling program that schedules other programs or batch files to run on a certain day and time, and a print program that manages and prioritizes multiple print jobs.

Task Management

Task management is an operating system function found in multitasking operating systems. Multitasking implies that a computer is running two or more programs (tasks) at the same time. In reality, a computer cannot simultaneously run more tasks than the number of processors that exist within the computer. Until recently, most microcomputers had only a single processor, so they accomplish multitasking through a scheme that makes order out of chaos by determining which program responds to the keystrokes and mouse movements. New processors can have multiple CPUs within a single chip, so they have true multitasking.

Task management controls the focus (where the system's attention is at any given moment). It also allows the user to switch between tasks by giving the focus to the application the user brings to the foreground. In most graphical operating systems, the foreground application runs in the current window, the window that is on top of other windows on the screen and the window that receives input from the keyboard when the user types. Any program or application may include many small components called processes when they are active in memory. The OS's task management function manages individual processes.

---

try this!

View Active Tasks in Windows or Mac OS X

You can see what tasks are running on your Windows or Mac OS X computer. Try this:

1. On a Windows computer with a keyboard, press CTRL-SHIFT-ESC to open Task Manager, a utility that lets you view tasks as running applications and their processes. Select the Processes tab and notice the large number of active processes.

2. On a Mac OS X computer press COMMAND+SPACEBAR to open the Spotlight search box, and then type "activity" and select Activity Monitor from the results list. Notice the list of processes in the column labeled Process Name.

Memory Management

Memory management is an operating system function that manages the placement of programs and data in memory, while keeping track of where it put them. Modern operating systems use a scheme for making optimal use of memory, even allowing more code and data to be in memory than what the actual physical system memory can hold. Using a memory management OS component called the virtual memory manager, operating systems move code and data, as necessary, to a portion of the disk defined as virtual memory, meaning that this disk space is used as if it were memory, not just disk storage space. The OS performs this transfer for code and data that are part of any program that currently does not have the user's attention because this now-unneeded information does not have to be kept in RAM for immediate use, so other programs that do need to use the memory can do so.

Note: The memory management function may not be included in every definition of an operating system, but it is a very important function, especially in the Windows, Macintosh, and Linux operating systems described in this book.

File Management

File management, also referred to as data management, is an operating system function that allows the operating system to read, write, and modify data, while managing the logical storage of the data. Each operating system has at least one scheme of logical organization, called a file system. A file system is the logical structure used on a storage device (hard disk, optical disc, thumb drive, etc.) for managing and storing files. The file system also includes the program within an operating system that allows the OS to store and manage files on a storage device. When an operating system uses a technique called formatting, it writes the logical structure to a storage device. The operating system maps the logical organization of the file system to physical locations on the storage device, most often a conventional hard disk drive or solid-state drive (SSD), so that it can store and retrieve the data. The logical structure of a file system stores metadata, which is data about the stored files.

Solid-state drives (SSDs) use integrated circuits, which the computer can write to and read from much faster than conventional hard disk drives and optical drives. We also call such storage solid-state storage. SSDs come in many forms, such as a tiny card installed inside the case of your tablet or smartphone, or a flat device, measuring about ¾ inch by 2 inches (or smaller) that you plug into a computer's USB connector. These are often called a thumb drive, jump drive, or flash drive.

Normally, a single storage device will have only a single file system, residing in a single area defined as a partition, but some operating systems allow a storage device to have more than one partition. A partition may be an entire drive volume or just a portion of a drive, and an operating system automatically assigns some identifier, such as C for the first hard drive recognized by DOS and Windows. These OSs follow the drive letter with a colon, so that a complete drive name may be C:. We call this a logical drive.

Within the logical structure of a file system, data is organized into entities called files that are saved to storage devices. File management also allows users to organize their files, using other special files that act as containers. One of these special files, called a folder or directory, can contain lists of files as well as other folders, along with the physical location of the files and folders.

Device Management

The device management function controls hardware devices by using special software called device drivers that are installed in the operating system. Device drivers are unique to the device, and the manufacturer of the device creates them to work with a specific operating system. For instance, a printer or video adapter will come with drivers for several different operating systems.

The device driver contains the commands understood by the device and uses these commands to control the device in response to requests it receives from the operating system. An operating system needs a component-specific device driver for each unique hardware component with which it interacts.

Security

The security function of an operating system provides password-protected authentication of the user before allowing access to the local computer and may restrict what someone can do on a computer. This protects the computer and the data it contains from unauthorized access. For example, Rachel is the accounting clerk in a small company. She has confidential information on her computer, and she doesn't want just anyone to be able to walk up to her computer and access the information stored there. Rachel can set up her computer so that anyone getting into it must log on with a user name and password from a user account. A user account is nothing more than a name and an associated password stored inside the PC. Security is a large topic—one that would take many books and weeks of your time to really master—but to go much farther in this book without addressing computer security would be foolish, so Chapter 2 is devoted to computer security basics. There you will learn about threats to computers, what security is built in to the operating systems discussed in this book, and the steps you can take to protect yourself from threats.

Security

How Much Memory Can an Operating System Use?

We call an operating system that can take advantage of the addressing and processing features of a processor an *x*-bit OS, referring to the number of bits the OS (using the processor) can manipulate at once. The original MS-DOS was a 16-bit OS, as was Windows 3.0 and its sub-versions. Windows 95, Windows 98, and Windows Millennium edition were really hybrids, with mostly 32-bit pieces but some 16-bit pieces for downward compatibility. Windows XP had a 64-bit version, but it was not widely used, and you are unlikely to encounter it. The Windows versions, Mac OS X, and Linux OSs we discuss in this book are available in both 32-bit and 64-bit versions.

All things being equal, the 64-bit version of an operating system will be faster than its 32-bit counterpart, but the biggest difference between the 32-bit and 64-bit versions of Windows is in the number of unique locations (the address space) a CPU can assign to both system RAM and other RAM and ROM in your computer. A 64-bit CPU can have a theoretical address space of 2^{64}, or 9.2 quintillion (nine followed by 18 digits). Windows does not use the maximum theoretical address space of a CPU, as shown in Table 1–1.

try this!

Are You Running 32-bit or 64-bit Windows?

If you have a Windows 7 computer handy, see if it is running a 32-bit or 64-bit version. Try this:

1. In the Start menu's Search box type "system."
2. In the search results list locate Control Panel and select "System." Do *not* select System Information.
3. This opens Control Panel to the System page.
4. The System Type field will say "32-bit Operating System" or "64-bit Operating System."

TABLE 1–1 Windows Memory Limits		
Edition	RAM Limit in 32-Bit Version	RAM Limit in 64-Bit Version
Windows 7 Ultimate/Enterprise/Professional	4 GB	192 GB
Windows 7 Home Premium	4 GB	16 GB
Windows 7 Home Basic	4 GB	8 GB
Windows 8	4 GB	192 GB

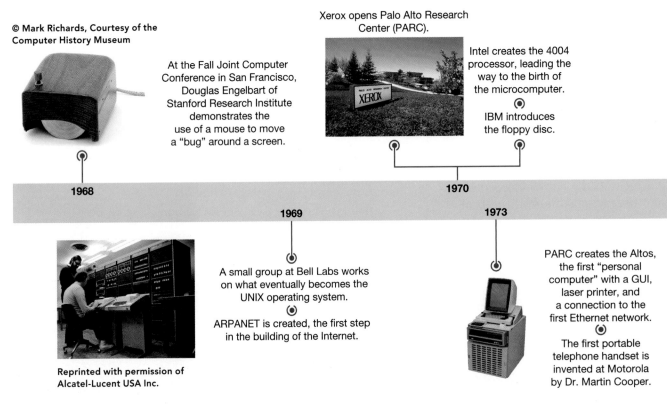

Find the operating system type in the System page of Control Panel.

A 64-bit operating system requires 64-bit drivers, and some 32-bit applications may not run, although Microsoft has offered ways to support older applications in each upgrade of Windows. If you purchase a new computer today with either Windows or the Mac OS preinstalled, it is most likely to be a 64-bit OS.

LO 1.2 | Yesterday's Operating Systems

Sometimes people think that they can simply take the newest and best computer or other gadget and make it work without understanding anything about how it came to be. Well, they probably can. But they probably can't fix

Note: The timeline running along the bottom of the next several pages shows highlights of computing history. Some are described in this chapter. Many are not.

© Mark Richards, Courtesy of the Computer History Museum

At the Fall Joint Computer Conference in San Francisco, Douglas Engelbart of Stanford Research Institute demonstrates the use of a mouse to move a "bug" around a screen.

Xerox opens Palo Alto Research Center (PARC).

Intel creates the 4004 processor, leading the way to the birth of the microcomputer.
◉
IBM introduces the floppy disc.

1968

1970

1969

1973

Reprinted with permission of Alcatel-Lucent USA Inc.

A small group at Bell Labs works on what eventually becomes the UNIX operating system.
◉
ARPANET is created, the first step in the building of the Internet.

PARC creates the Altos, the first "personal computer" with a GUI, laser printer, and a connection to the first Ethernet network.
◉
The first portable telephone handset is invented at Motorola by Dr. Martin Cooper.

it, modify it, or use it effectively without understanding how and why it came to be in the form it's in now. One really can't understand current PC technology without having a grasp of older PC technology. In other words, studying history is important to understand how we arrived at today. We'll begin with UNIX, arguably the oldest OS still in use today, with beginnings that predate microcomputers. Then we'll explore the history of computers leading to today's PCs and Mac desktop computers and the operating systems that evolved for each of these hardware platforms.

UNIX—The OS for All Platforms

UNIX has a longer history than any other popular operating system, and it is still in use today. In fact, Apple's Mac OS X is a certified UNIX operating system. UNIX grew out of an operating system developed for an early Digital Equipment Corporation (DEC) computer and went through several generations of changes before it emerged from the Bell Labs Computing Science Research Center (Bell Labs) as UNIX version 6 in 1975, a portable operating system for minicomputers and mainframe computers. A portable operating system is one that you can use on a variety of computer system platforms, with only minor alterations required to be compatible with the underlying architecture. Minicomputers and mainframe computers allowed multiple remote users to connect and use the computer's resources, and UNIX supported the time-sharing and multitasking features that made this possible.

The University of California at Berkeley licensed UNIX, modified it, and distributed it to other schools as Berkeley Software Distribution (BSD) version 4.2. Later versions followed. The schools paid licensing fees to Bell Labs. Students and others improved on and added to UNIX, freely sharing their code with each other. This tradition still prevails today with such versions of UNIX as Free BSD, Net BSD, Open BDS, and Open Solaris. Commercial versions of UNIX today include AIX, OpenServer (derived from SCO UNIX), and HP/UX.

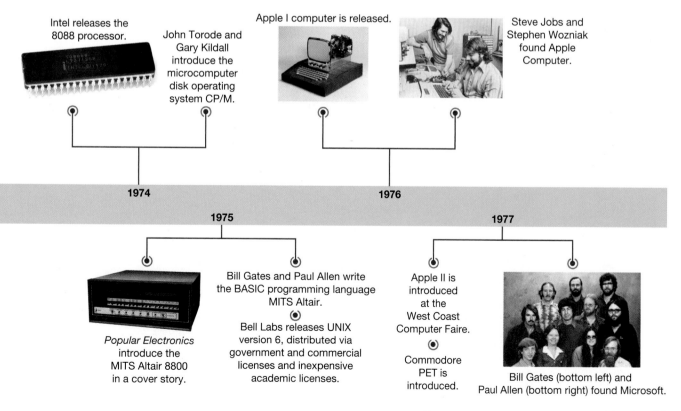

Intel releases the 8088 processor.

John Torode and Gary Kildall introduce the microcomputer disk operating system CP/M.

Apple I computer is released.

Steve Jobs and Stephen Wozniak found Apple Computer.

1974

1976

1975

1977

Popular Electronics introduce the MITS Altair 8800 in a cover story.

Bill Gates and Paul Allen write the BASIC programming language MITS Altair.

Bell Labs releases UNIX version 6, distributed via government and commercial licenses and inexpensive academic licenses.

Apple II is introduced at the West Coast Computer Faire.

Commodore PET is introduced.

Bill Gates (bottom left) and Paul Allen (bottom right) found Microsoft.

try this!

Research the History of UNIX

Read a history of the UNIX operating system.

Try this:

1. Enter **www.bell-labs.com/history/unix** into the address box of your Web browser.
2. Read the article "The Creation of the UNIX Operating System."
3. Read about the contributions of Dennis Ritchie and Ken Thompson.
4. Then point your browser to **www.unix.org/what_is_unix/history_timeline.html** to see a timeline of UNIX history.

Today UNIX is still used on very large computer systems (referred to as mainframes) and less commonly on Intel desktop systems, as well as on a variety of midsize computers. Versions of UNIX run on many of the world's Internet servers. Most versions of UNIX also offer several different user interfaces. Some use character mode, like the traditional shells, such as the Bourne shell and the C shell. Others use a graphical interface such as GNOME or KDE. As mentioned earlier, Apple's Mac OS X operating system is based on a version of UNIX, and it has a graphical user interface.

Even fierce UNIX advocates do not see UNIX taking over the desktop any time soon. However, it is very secure and stable. Versions of UNIX run on many of the world's Internet servers.

The Evolution of Desktop Operating Systems

The complex and powerful operating system like what you see on your desktop, laptop, or mobile devices didn't just magically pop into someone's head. An operating system as a separate entity didn't exist in the early years of digital computing (defined roughly as from World War II into the 1950s). Each computer was dedicated to a single purpose, such as performing trajectory calculations for weapons or mathematical analysis for a science lab, in addition to the system I/O functions. Loading a new program into a computer was a time-consuming process, and the software had to include system functions as well as the main purpose of the computer.

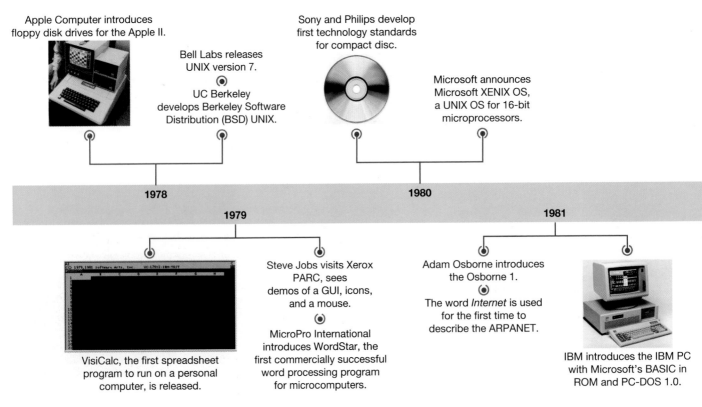

Apple Computer introduces floppy disk drives for the Apple II.

Bell Labs releases UNIX version 7.

UC Berkeley develops Berkeley Software Distribution (BSD) UNIX.

Sony and Philips develop first technology standards for compact disc.

Microsoft announces Microsoft XENIX OS, a UNIX OS for 16-bit microprocessors.

1978

1979

1980

1981

VisiCalc, the first spreadsheet program to run on a personal computer, is released.

Steve Jobs visits Xerox PARC, sees demos of a GUI, icons, and a mouse.

MicroPro International introduces WordStar, the first commercially successful word processing program for microcomputers.

Adam Osborne introduces the Osborne 1.

The word *Internet* is used for the first time to describe the ARPANET.

IBM introduces the IBM PC with Microsoft's BASIC in ROM and PC-DOS 1.0.

Operating systems evolved through many small steps over several decades, some in the form of technical advances and others in evolutionary changes in how people used computers, especially as they saw the need to use computers as multipurpose devices. The "user," at first a government agency, research institute, or large business, would define the computer's purpose at any given time by the program chosen to run. In the 1950s, some early "operating systems" managed data storage on tape for mainframe computers, but it was much more common for application programmers to write system I/O routines (the stuff of today's OSs) right into their programs. By the mid-1960s, as disk systems became more common on large computers, we needed operating systems to manage these disks and to perform other common system-level routines.

The computer enthusiasts who bought the earliest microcomputers of the 1970s, such as the MITS Altair 8800, were infatuated with the technology. What we now consider slow CPU speeds, very limited memory, clumsy I/O devices, and lack of software was exciting and new technology at the time. They would network with like-minded people, have informal meetings and discussions, and then gather in self-help groups and form clubs such as the Home Brew Computer Club in California's Silicon Valley. They shared their techniques for creating hardware and programming language software for these computers. Almost every one of these early microcomputers exceeded the expectations of their makers and users, but before long, and for a variety of reasons, most of the early entrepreneurial companies and their products disappeared.

Note: The MITS Altair 8800 was an important predecessor to the Apple II, TRS-80, and PET computers. Although featured in a cover article of the January 1975 issue of *Popular Mechanics*, it was not for ordinary people. Whether you bought the $395 kit or the fully assembled $495 version, the input method was switches that you flipped to program it, and the result of these efforts (the output) was a pattern of blinking lights. As a portent of the future, the Altair 8800 gave Bill Gates and Paul Allen their very first sale of the computer language of BASIC.

Software Versions

A software version is a unique level of an operating system. When a software publisher creates an entirely new OS, they give it a version number, usually 1.0. Software publishers constantly receive feedback from customers about problems and the need for particular additional features in each OS. In response,

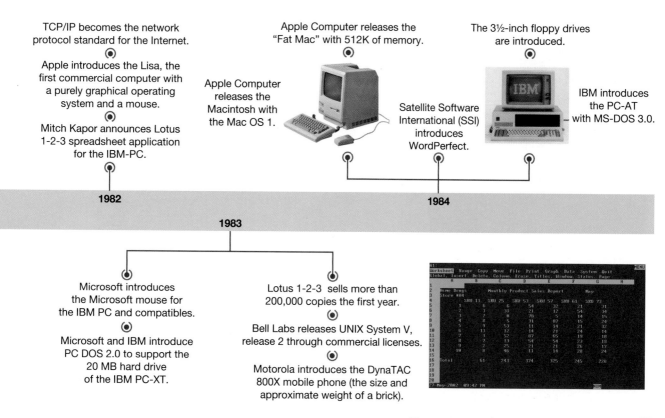

TCP/IP becomes the network protocol standard for the Internet.

Apple introduces the Lisa, the first commercial computer with a purely graphical operating system and a mouse.

Mitch Kapor announces Lotus 1-2-3 spreadsheet application for the IBM-PC.

Apple Computer releases the Macintosh with the Mac OS 1.

Apple Computer releases the "Fat Mac" with 512K of memory.

Satellite Software International (SSI) introduces WordPerfect.

The 3½-inch floppy drives are introduced.

IBM introduces the PC-AT with MS-DOS 3.0.

1982

1984

1983

Microsoft introduces the Microsoft mouse for the IBM PC and compatibles.

Microsoft and IBM introduce PC DOS 2.0 to support the 20 MB hard drive of the IBM PC-XT.

Lotus 1-2-3 sells more than 200,000 copies the first year.

Bell Labs releases UNIX System V, release 2 through commercial licenses.

Motorola introduces the DynaTAC 800X mobile phone (the size and approximate weight of a brick).

a publisher often introduces a modified version of the original product, in which case the number to the right of the decimal point will probably change (say, from version 1.0 to version 1.1—people often abbreviate *version* as simply "v"). An entirely new version number (2.0, 3.0, . . .) generally reflects an important change to an OS with major changes to the core components of the operating system as well as a distinctive and unifying look to the GUI.

The Killer App for PCs

For a microcomputer to truly become a successful, widely accepted product—used in businesses as well as by hobbyists—it had to be a tool that performed an important task; it had to have an application that many people needed enough to purchase a computer. We call that application a killer app.

One of these important tasks was spreadsheet calculations. Before microcomputers, people created spreadsheets manually, on large sheets of paper. They would enter a column of numbers—say, sales for one product in a drugstore—day-by-day for a month. Then they would add up the daily columns to get the total sales for that product for that month. The next column was for the next product, and so on. The process was tedious and error prone, but very valuable to the manager of the drugstore.

Thus, when VisiCalc, an electronic spreadsheet program, appeared it became a very successful application. It automated this thankless job, remembered the formulas for the calculations, and allowed people to recalculate a whole column of numbers after a single change was made. VisiCalc did more than this. It gave people a reason to want a personal computer. Many people were introduced to VisiCalc on the Apple II computer (running the Apple OS), and this contributed to the success of the Apple II in the late 1970s. However, as the 1980s arrived, Apple failed to come out with a successor to the Apple II in a timely fashion. So, when IBM introduced the IBM PC in 1981, the market was ready for a new microcomputer and VisiCalc was modified to run on the IBM PC.

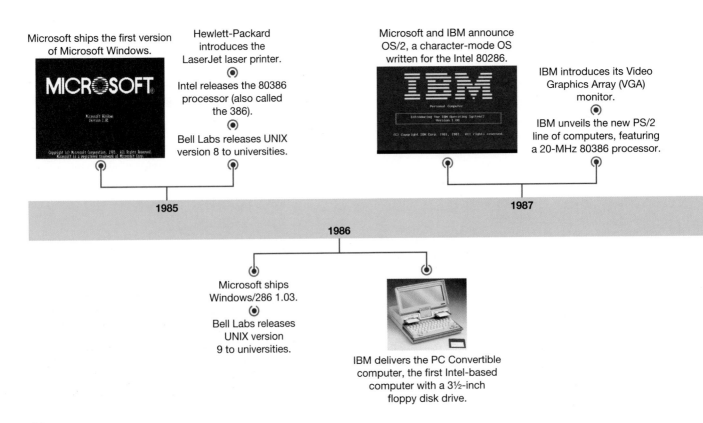

Microsoft ships the first version of Microsoft Windows.

Hewlett-Packard introduces the LaserJet laser printer.

Intel releases the 80386 processor (also called the 386).

Bell Labs releases UNIX version 8 to universities.

Microsoft and IBM announce OS/2, a character-mode OS written for the Intel 80286.

IBM introduces its Video Graphics Array (VGA) monitor.

IBM unveils the new PS/2 line of computers, featuring a 20-MHz 80386 processor.

1985

1986

1987

Microsoft ships Windows/286 1.03.

Bell Labs releases UNIX version 9 to universities.

IBM delivers the PC Convertible computer, the first Intel-based computer with a 3½-inch floppy disk drive.

The IBM PC Operating System

Another fateful series of events revolved around the choice of an OS for the IBM PC. IBM representatives came to Microsoft, then a fledgling software company, for the Microsoft BASIC interpreter, which other machines were using at that time. The result of that visit was that IBM licensed Microsoft's BASIC interpreter and installed it in the ROM of the IBM PC. The IBM folks also talked to Bill Gates about providing an OS; but he did not have one, and so he sent them to another company, Digital Research, the creators of the then-popular CP/M OS. Digital Research, however, refused to sign a contract with IBM, so the IBM guys went back to Bill Gates for the OS. Consequently, Microsoft bought an OS from another company, and this was the basis of the first versions of IBM PC DOS.

The IBM PC far exceeded IBM's sales forecast, which was for about a quarter of a million units during the predicted five-year lifetime of the product. According to one account, IBM took orders for half a million computers in the first few days after introducing the IBM PC. At first many enthusiasts bought it despite its roughly $5,000 price tag for a typical configuration. Additionally, the IBM name behind the product also inspired many business users to buy it because this name implied that it was a serious business computer.

The Second Killer App for PCs

Although many say that just having the letters *IBM* on the box was what sold that computer, the groundwork laid by VisiCalc left people ready for what was arguably the second

Note: Want to learn more about the early history of PCs? Our favorite book on the subject is *Fire in the Valley: The Making of the Personal Computer* (ISBN 0-07-135892-7).

try this!

Watch Old TV Commercials for the IBM PC and Lotus 1-2-3

It has been over 30 years since the introduction of the IBM PC in 1981 and the killer app Lotus 1-2-3 in 1983. See how these products were introduced to the public in TV advertisements. Try this:

1. Point your browser to http://mentalfloss.com/article/48627/lotus-1-2-3-three-decades
2. Read the article and watch the first two videos. Some of us can verify the accuracy of the portrayal of office workers at the time (except for the singing and dancing part).
3. The third video is a 30-minute Lotus 1-2-3 training video. Watch at least enough of the video to see some of the features in Lotus 1-2-3.
4. The fourth video reviews the history of Lotus 1-2-3 with great clips of the news coverage and events and people behind the product.

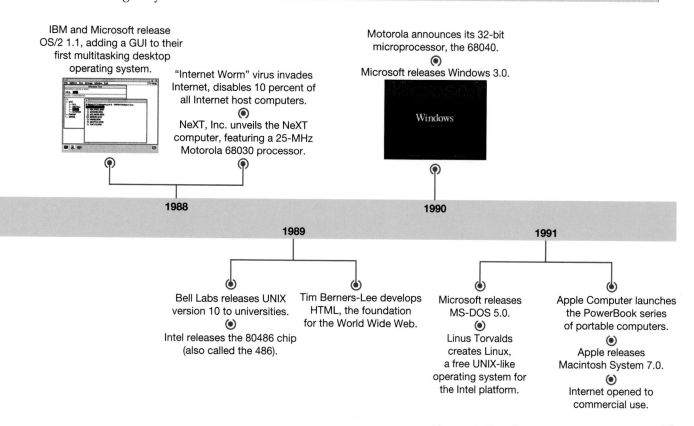

IBM and Microsoft release OS/2 1.1, adding a GUI to their first multitasking desktop operating system.

"Internet Worm" virus invades Internet, disables 10 percent of all Internet host computers.

NeXT, Inc. unveils the NeXT computer, featuring a 25-MHz Motorola 68030 processor.

Motorola announces its 32-bit microprocessor, the 68040.

Microsoft releases Windows 3.0.

1988

1990

1989

1991

Bell Labs releases UNIX version 10 to universities.

Intel releases the 80486 chip (also called the 486).

Tim Berners-Lee develops HTML, the foundation for the World Wide Web.

Microsoft releases MS-DOS 5.0.

Linus Torvalds creates Linux, a free UNIX-like operating system for the Intel platform.

Apple Computer launches the PowerBook series of portable computers.

Apple releases Macintosh System 7.0.

Internet opened to commercial use.

Note: Through the 1980s, PCs with DOS and a variety of DOS applications made great inroads into organizations of all sizes. In the decade after its introduction, thousands of applications were written for DOS, but Lotus 1-2-3, dBase (database management), and WordPerfect (word processing) were the de facto business standards at the end of that decade. All contributed to the mass adoption of PCs at work, at school, and at home.

killer app, Lotus 1-2-3 by Lotus Corporation. Introduced in 1983, this spreadsheet application ran on the DOS operating system and used all of the 640KB of memory available to software (OS plus application) on the IBM PC. Both the 1-2-3 program and the spreadsheet were in memory while the user worked. It was very fast compared to VisiCalc, which was written to run under the CP/M OS and designed to use much less memory. And 1-2-3 had additional features, including database functions and a program that could create and print graphs from the spreadsheet data. Lotus 1-2-3 was the real killer app, the software that made the IBM PC and PC DOS a must-have combination for people who worked all day crunching numbers and doing what-if calculations.

Apple OS

In 1976 Steve Jobs and Stephen Wozniak—two guys working out of a garage—founded Apple Computer, based on their first computer, the Apple I. Their real notoriety began in 1977 when they introduced the Apple II at the West Coast Computer Faire in San Francisco. This created interest in the brand, and the addition of disk drives in 1978 made it a sought-after product for the technically adventurous consumer. But the OS for the Apple computers at this point did not have a GUI interface—that showed up on the short-lived Apple Lisa computer.

In 1982 Apple introduced the Lisa, the first commercially available computer with a purely graphical operating system—and a mouse. However, this computer lacked something very important for consumers—applications. It was unsuccessful, and Apple's own Macintosh computer, released in 1984, overshadowed the Lisa and marked the beginning of consumer excitement and the near-cult following of the Apple computer products. The Macintosh came with Mac OS System 1, a GUI operating system that used a mouse. Apple improved the Mac OS over the years to include many easy-to-use features.

The final release of the classic Mac OS family was Mac OS 9, introduced in 1999. With its roots in the original 1984 OS, Apple revised and improved the operating system to support multiple users, but it was weak in memory

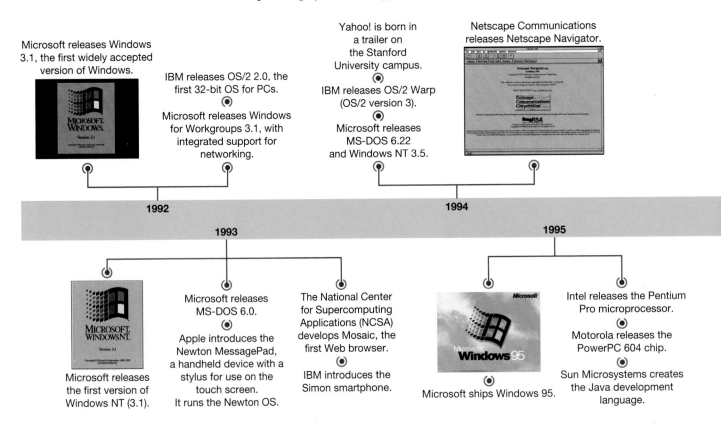

Microsoft releases Windows 3.1, the first widely accepted version of Windows.

IBM releases OS/2 2.0, the first 32-bit OS for PCs.

Microsoft releases Windows for Workgroups 3.1, with integrated support for networking.

Yahoo! is born in a trailer on the Stanford University campus.

IBM releases OS/2 Warp (OS/2 version 3).

Microsoft releases MS-DOS 6.22 and Windows NT 3.5.

Netscape Communications releases Netscape Navigator.

1992

1994

1993

1995

Microsoft releases the first version of Windows NT (3.1).

Microsoft releases MS-DOS 6.0.

Apple introduces the Newton MessagePad, a handheld device with a stylus for use on the touch screen. It runs the Newton OS.

The National Center for Supercomputing Applications (NCSA) develops Mosaic, the first Web browser.

IBM introduces the Simon smartphone.

Microsoft ships Windows 95.

Intel releases the Pentium Pro microprocessor.

Motorola releases the PowerPC 604 chip.

Sun Microsystems creates the Java development language.

management and full multitasking. In 2001 it was replaced by a completely new operating system—Mac OS X, based on UNIX. There is a brief overview of OS X later in this chapter and more detail on this OS in Chapter 7.

MS-DOS

DOS, which stands for "disk operating system," provides support for interaction, or input and output (I/O), between the memory and disk drives. It is a single-tasking OS with very limited memory support, no support for virtual memory, no native GUI, and no built-in security function. *MS-DOS* refers to the several versions of DOS developed by Microsoft and made available to non-IBM PC manufacturers. PC DOS is the version for IBM computers. Each major version of DOS was released to support new disk capacities. PC DOS 1.0 supported single-sided 5¼-inch floppies; PC DOS 1.1 added support for double-sided 5¼-inch floppies; and PC DOS 2.0, released with the IBM PC-XT, included support for the XT's 10MB hard drives. DOS 3.0 was released with the IBM PC-AT and included support for the larger AT hard drives. Support for 3½-inch floppies and the larger hard drives of the IBM PS-2 computers were added in DOS 4.0. MS-DOS 6.22 was the last widely used version of MS-DOS. Some forms of DOS are now available from third-party sources, but these sources are dwindling.

DOS has a text-mode command-line interface that requires users to remember cryptic commands and their subcommands to perform file management functions and to launch DOS applications. Figure 1–4 shows a good example of how cryptic DOS can be to the uninitiated.

Although you will not find DOS as the preferred OS on desktop computers, you might find a variation of it as the OS on some handheld devices that do not require a GUI interface. In the past, computer professionals often found DOS handy as a very small OS that fit on a floppy disk, to which they added various utilities for troubleshooting computers. This practice has all but disappeared today, as have floppy disks and floppy disk drives. Those same techs are now more likely to carry either optical discs or a flash drive loaded with specialized software for their work.

> *Note:* Many of us still open a command line interface (CLI) in Windows to use certain advanced troubleshooting tools. There are two that come with Windows: the Command Prompt and the Windows Power Shell. There's more on these CLIs, as well as the CLIs in Linux and OS X, in Chapter 9.

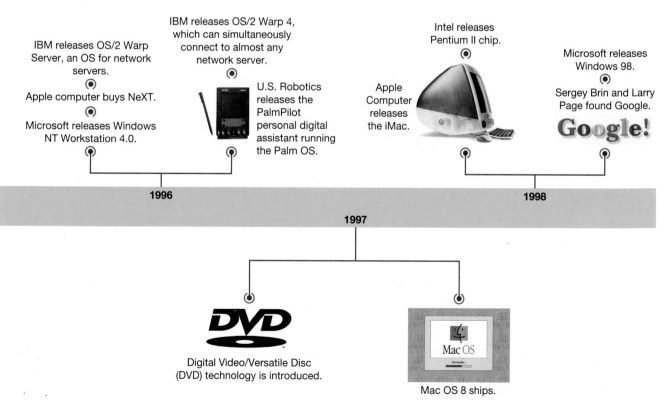

IBM releases OS/2 Warp Server, an OS for network servers.

Apple computer buys NeXT.

Microsoft releases Windows NT Workstation 4.0.

IBM releases OS/2 Warp 4, which can simultaneously connect to almost any network server.

U.S. Robotics releases the PalmPilot personal digital assistant running the Palm OS.

Intel releases Pentium II chip.

Apple Computer releases the iMac.

Microsoft releases Windows 98.

Sergey Brin and Larry Page found Google.

Google!

1996

1998

1997

DVD

Digital Video/Versatile Disc (DVD) technology is introduced.

Mac OS

Mac OS 8 ships.

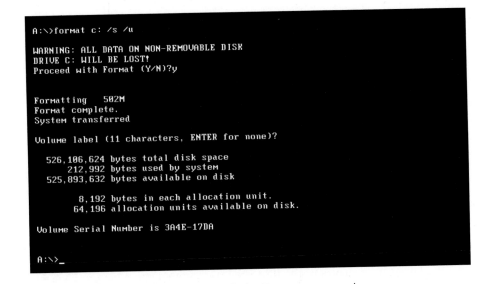

```
A:\>format c: /s /u

WARNING: ALL DATA ON NON-REMOVABLE DISK
DRIVE C: WILL BE LOST!
Proceed with Format (Y/N)?y


Formatting   502M
Format complete.
System transferred

Volume label (11 characters, ENTER for none)?

  526,106,624 bytes total disk space
      212,992 bytes used by system
  525,893,632 bytes available on disk

        8,192 bytes in each allocation unit.
       64,196 allocation units available on disk.

Volume Serial Number is 3A4E-17DA


A:\>_
```

FIGURE 1–4 The MS-DOS prompt with the Format command.

OS/2

In 1987, Microsoft and IBM introduced their jointly developed Operating System/2 (OS/2), intended to replace DOS. However, version 1.0 was written for the Intel 80286 processor, which had serious memory and operating limits. Despite the memory limits, it still required much more memory and disk space (2MB of memory and 8MB of disk space) than either PC DOS or MS-DOS. This was at a time when 2MB of memory and a 40MB hard drive (considered large in the late 1980s) cost several thousand dollars. Although the first version of OS/2 could multitask applications in memory, it did not have a GUI, and only one application could be visible on the screen at a time. Also, people had to write applications specifically for OS/2, because it had very limited support for DOS applications.

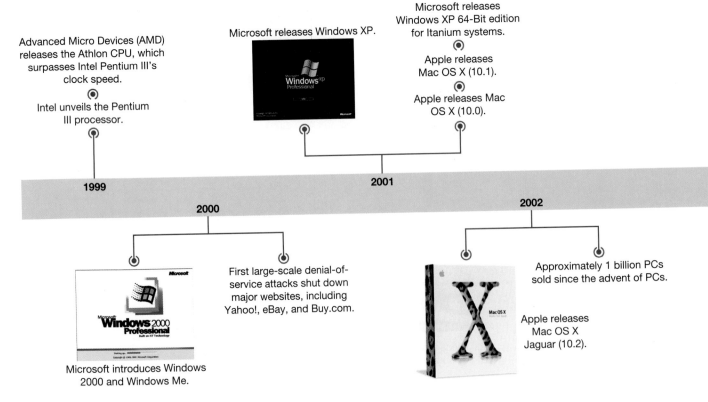

In the 1990s, IBM introduced OS/2 Warp, a greatly improved version of OS/2 with a very nice GUI. After about 18 months, however, IBM retreated from the battle for the desktop and targeted sales of OS/2 Warp to the high-end server market. It never rivaled Windows or UNIX in terms of sales. In 2003, IBM announced it would not develop any future versions of OS/2, and in December 2004 IBM sold its PC division to China-based Lenovo Group. In 2005 they discontinued support for OS/2.

Microsoft Windows

We'll begin our discussion of Windows by explaining Windows versions and editions, and then briefly go through the versions in chronological order.

Windows Versions and Editions. A Microsoft Windows version sometimes has a simple ordinal number, as in Windows 1 or Windows 2 (versions from the 1980s). Then some sub-versions appeared, such as Windows 3.1. In the mid-1990s, Microsoft moved away from the old convention and modified the names of several OSs to coincide with the calendar year of release, as in Windows 95, Windows 98, and Windows 2000. Then it created names such as Windows XP and Windows Vista, but underneath it all Microsoft still maintained a numeric version number, which resurfaced in the naming of Windows 7 and Windows 8. We will cover the Windows 7 and Windows 8 versions in detail in this book.

Then there is the issue of editions. In recent years, each version of Microsoft Windows included separate products, each called an edition. Just a sampling of edition names includes Windows XP Professional, Windows Vista Business, and Windows 7 Professional. The differences among the editions for the same version are in the features. The more feature-rich editions cost more. But we are getting ahead of ourselves. We'll start our discussion of yesterday's Windows versions with the first version and make our way to Windows XP. Then we will pick up the discussion of Today's Desktop OSs with Windows 7 and Windows 8.

Note: While OS/2 was not a success in terms of sales, an April 2, 2012, article by Harry McCracken, "25 Years of IBM's OS/2: The Strange Days and Surprising Afterlife of a Legendary Operating System" at techland.time.com reported that OS/2 was still used on some New York City subway system servers and on some supermarket checkout systems.

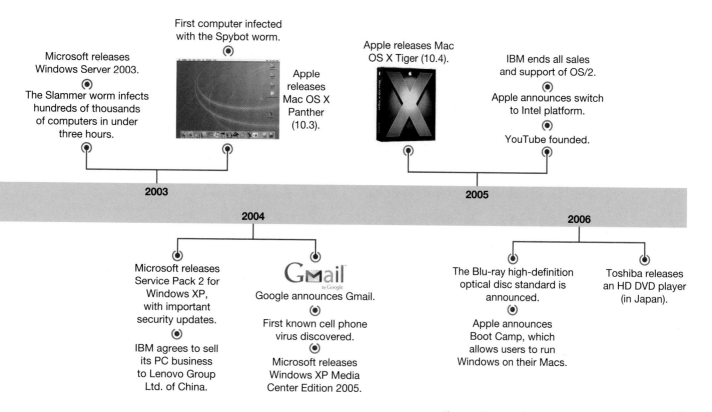

First computer infected with the Spybot worm.

Microsoft releases Windows Server 2003.

The Slammer worm infects hundreds of thousands of computers in under three hours.

Apple releases Mac OS X Panther (10.3).

Apple releases Mac OS X Tiger (10.4).

IBM ends all sales and support of OS/2.

Apple announces switch to Intel platform.

YouTube founded.

2003

2004

2005

2006

Microsoft releases Service Pack 2 for Windows XP, with important security updates.

IBM agrees to sell its PC business to Lenovo Group Ltd. of China.

Google announces Gmail.

First known cell phone virus discovered.

Microsoft releases Windows XP Media Center Edition 2005.

The Blu-ray high-definition optical disc standard is announced.

Apple announces Boot Camp, which allows users to run Windows on their Macs.

Toshiba releases an HD DVD player (in Japan).

Windows 1 through 3. In 1985, when the first version of Windows appeared, it was more smoke than OS. It consisted of a not-very-good GUI by today's standards, balanced precariously on top of MS-DOS. The GUI code was separate from the OS code. It was slow and had a flat look—you couldn't lay one graphic on top of another. The ability to overlap graphical elements, such as windows and icons, did not show up until a later version.

From 1985 to 1990, Microsoft continued to work on both Windows and DOS, but Windows was not much more than a pretty face until 1990 and Windows 3.0, which supported the three Intel processor modes of operation available at that time. Microsoft called these modes, as supported in Windows, Real mode, Standard mode, and 386 Enhanced modes. In Real mode, Windows 3.0 was just a GUI that ran on top of DOS. In the other two modes, it added functionality to DOS to take advantage of the 286 (Standard mode) and 386 (386 Enhanced mode) processor modes.

The most important feature of Windows 3.0 was better support for legacy DOS applications within Windows. This was possible in the 386 Enhanced mode. This meant that both DOS apps and Windows apps could run simultaneously. This version still had its quirks, but for the first time, IT managers saw a potential GUI replacement for DOS as the desktop OS of choice.

In the spring of 1992, Microsoft brought out a minor upgrade, Windows 3.1, which many organizations adopted as the standard desktop OS. The fact that Microsoft's entire suite of productivity applications was also available in versions for Windows 3.*x* helped encourage adoption.

Figure 1–5 shows the Windows 3.1 desktop. Notice that there is no task bar at the bottom of the screen, just the Program Manager window (the main window) with other windows nested in it.

Windows for Workgroups. DOS and Windows OSs through Windows 3.*x* included only the operating system functions. If you wanted to connect to

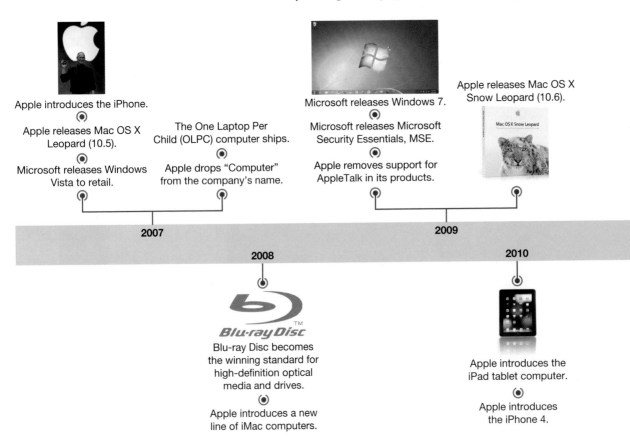

Apple introduces the iPhone.

Apple releases Mac OS X Leopard (10.5).

The One Laptop Per Child (OLPC) computer ships.

Microsoft releases Windows Vista to retail.

Apple drops "Computer" from the company's name.

Microsoft releases Windows 7.

Microsoft releases Microsoft Security Essentials, MSE.

Apple removes support for AppleTalk in its products.

Apple releases Mac OS X Snow Leopard (10.6).

2007

2009

2008

2010

Blu-ray Disc becomes the winning standard for high-definition optical media and drives.

Apple introduces a new line of iMac computers.

Apple introduces the iPad tablet computer.

Apple introduces the iPhone 4.

FIGURE 1–5 The Windows 3.1 desktop.

Note: Windows for Workgroups 3.1 was followed a year later by Windows for Workgroups 3.11, with the usual obligatory fixes and improvements including faster network and disk I/O operations. However, users were still working with a Windows OS that was running on top of DOS; that is, first DOS would start and then Windows. Windows depended on DOS, which had to be installed on the computer.

a network, you added a network operating system (NOS) on top of your installed OS. This separate network operating system might be from 3COM or Novell, or it might be Microsoft's LAN Manager NOS, developed in the late 1980s. You had to install the correct client software for the type of network and servers to which you connected.

Novell and LAN Manager were both network server operating systems that combined the operating system functions with the networking functions and also provided file and print sharing services to other computers. Additionally, to connect to a server, a client computer needed special client software so it could connect and request services from it.

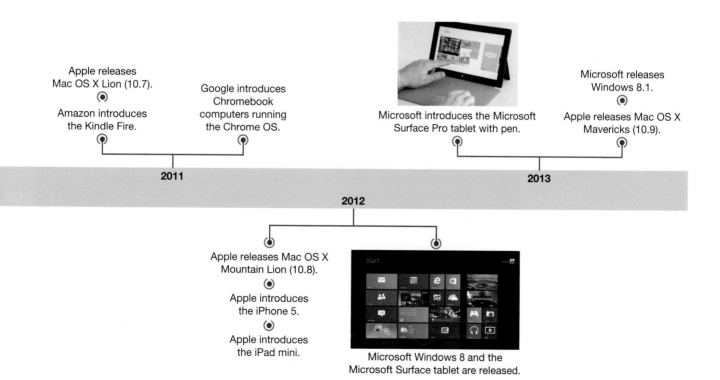

Apple releases Mac OS X Lion (10.7).

Amazon introduces the Kindle Fire.

Google introduces Chromebook computers running the Chrome OS.

Microsoft introduces the Microsoft Surface Pro tablet with pen.

Microsoft releases Windows 8.1.

Apple releases Mac OS X Mavericks (10.9).

2011

2013

2012

Apple releases Mac OS X Mountain Lion (10.8).

Apple introduces the iPhone 5.

Apple introduces the iPad mini.

Microsoft Windows 8 and the Microsoft Surface tablet are released.

However, beginning in October 1992 with Windows for Workgroups 3.1, Microsoft included both the client and server software in all of its Windows OS products. This enabled peer-to-peer networking, meaning desktop computers could act as servers to their peers. This worked well in a small work group environment of 10 or fewer computers.

Windows NT. Because it had the same user interface as Windows 3.1, Windows NT was introduced in 1993 as Windows NT 3.1. That was where the similarity ended. To begin with, it was a server operating system, which included server protocols in its integrated network support. Furthermore, unlike Windows 3.x and Windows for Workgroups, the GUI did not sit on top of DOS, but was an entirely new operating system.

With Windows NT Microsoft introduced the NTFS file system with an entirely new logical structure. It has unique security features that continue to be improved in each new version of Windows.

Windows NT was the first Microsoft OS to take full advantage of the capabilities of the special protected mode that Intel introduced in its processors manufactured after 1986. A major benefit of this was more stability and security in the OS. In fact, NT was so powerful that Microsoft decided to make two versions of NT: one designed mainly for servers, and another geared more toward individual user systems—what some folks call workstations. Thus, the next version, Windows NT 3.5, released in 1994, was also the first Windows OS to have separate editions: Windows NT Workstation and Windows NT Server. Both of these used the same kernel and interface, but the Server version had enhancements and components that were needed only on a network server. Microsoft configured the Workstation version as a robust desktop operating system targeted to corporate and advanced users. It had a higher price tag than Windows 95 (introduced in 1995), which was intended for consumers.

In 1996, Microsoft introduced Server and Workstation editions of Windows NT 4.0, which had a GUI similar to that of Windows 95 as well as other improvements and enhancements to the OS. Figure 1–6 shows the Windows NT desktop. Microsoft no longer sells or supports Windows NT.

Windows 95. Windows 95, released in 1995, predated Windows NT 4.0 Workstation. It was still a continuation of the Windows 3.x model with the graphical environment simply "sitting" on top of the DOS operating system. It did have some improvements in the operating system, including both 16-bit and 32-bit code. The greatest improvements were in the GUI, which made it the most popular microcomputer operating system up to that time.

Windows 98. Windows 98 was an evolutionary development in the Windows desktop operating system, including improvements in both visible and under-the-hood components. It offered more stability than its immediate predecessor, Windows 95, meaning that it was less likely to stop in its tracks just when you were about to complete that book order on Amazon. Although improved, Windows 98 was not as stable as the newer Windows OSs. Figure 1–7 shows the Windows 98 desktop. Its biggest drawback was lack of security. It did not have a local security accounts database for local authentication, and it lacked support for the NTFS file system for file and folder security.

Windows 98 offered new options for customizing the GUI, including tighter integration with Microsoft's Web browser, Internet Explorer (IE). Windows 98 came with drivers and support for devices, such as DVD drives,

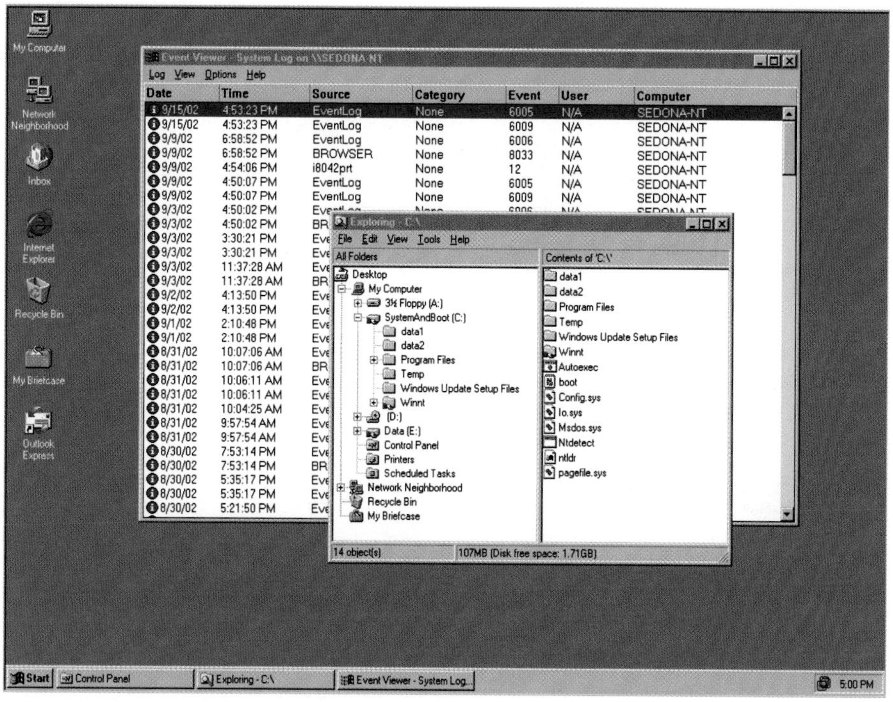

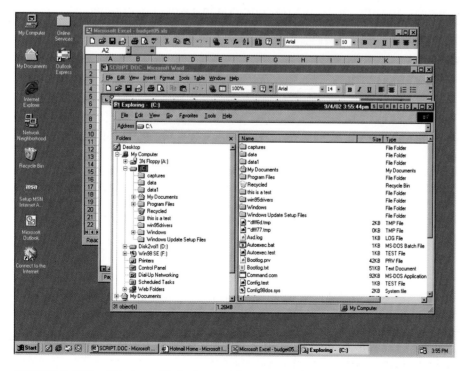

FIGURE 1–6 The Windows NT 4.0 desktop with open windows.

that were not included in Windows 95. As usual with an upgrade to an OS, Microsoft cleaned up existing problems and made the OS run faster.

Windows Me (Millennium Edition). Windows Me (Millennium edition), introduced in 2000, targeted the home market, especially the home game user. It was essentially Windows 98 with improved music, video, and home

FIGURE 1–7 The Windows 98 desktop with open windows.

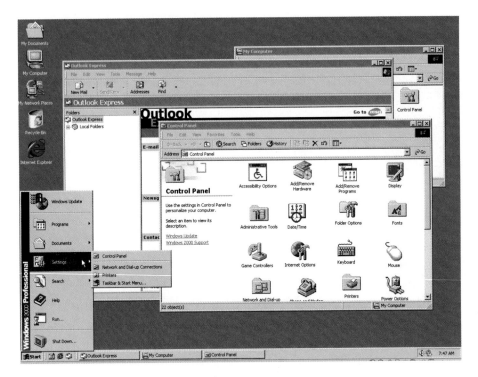

FIGURE 1–8 The Windows 2000 desktop.

networking support. The Windows Movie Maker allowed users to digitally edit, save, and share their home videos, and the Windows Media Player gave users a tool for organizing digital music and video. This was the last Microsoft OS based on the Windows 95 internals. Windows Me was installed on many computers that were sold to individuals, but it is not an OS that organizations adopted. You are not likely to encounter it in a work environment.

Windows 2000. In 2000, Microsoft introduced the Windows 2000 family of OS products, which brought together the best of Windows 98 (the GUI) and Windows NT. Windows 2000 was available in several editions that all shared the same kernel and covered OS needs from the desktop to the enterprise server. Figure 1–8 shows the Windows 2000 desktop.

Windows XP. With its Windows 2000 products, Microsoft brought all of its OSs together, building them on top of the same core internal piece (the kernel). Some of us, especially those whose jobs included support of both desktop and server computers, thought it would simplify our lives. We really liked that idea because we could learn just one OS for both the desktop and server. However, in 2001 Microsoft departed from that model when the company introduced Windows XP, intended only for the desktop or other consumer-type computer, not for the server environment. The new server products, introduced after Windows XP, began with Windows Server 2003.

There were several Windows XP editions, but the three most common were Windows XP Home edition, Windows XP Professional, and Windows XP Media Center. All were 32-bit OSs, had the same improved GUI, and shared many of the same features, but only Windows XP Professional included several important network- and security-related features. Additionally, Microsoft offered Windows XP 64-bit edition, which supported only 64-bit software and was limited to computers with the Intel Itanium processors.

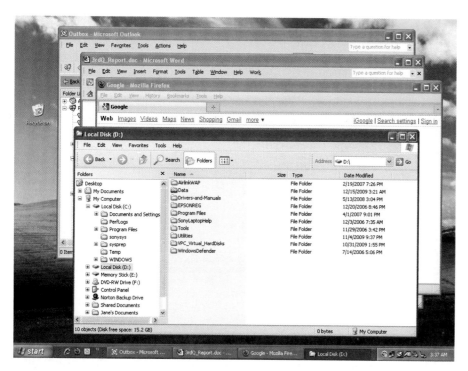

FIGURE 1–9 The Windows XP desktop with open windows.

The Windows XP desktop was very different from that of its main predecessor, Windows 98, in that by default the recycle bin (where deleted files go) was the only icon on the desktop. Figure 1–9 shows the Windows XP desktop with several open windows. Microsoft redesigned and reorganized the Start menu, shown here.

The last service pack for the 32-bit version of Windows XP was SP 3, and October 22, 2010, marked the last day you could buy a new PC with Windows XP preinstalled. This date was one year after the introduction of Windows 7. Support for Windows XP Service Pack 2 (SP2) ended July 13, 2010. If you are still using Windows XP, ensure that you have Service Pack 3 installed. Microsoft will support Windows XP with Service Pac 3 (SP3) until April 2014. Service pack 3 is for 32-bit Windows XP; there was no Service Pack 3 for 64-bit Windows XP. Support for the 64-bit version of XP SP 2 also ends in April 2014. This is Microsoft's published policy, called the Microsoft Support Lifecycle.

Windows Vista. Microsoft released the first retail edition of Windows Vista early in 2007. Seen more as an upgrade of Windows XP, it included improvements in how Windows handles graphics, files, and communications. The GUI had a new look compared to previous versions of Windows (see Figure 1–10). It also had a feature called Aero, which included translucent windows, live thumbnails, live icons, and other enhancements to the GUI. Windows Vista was not widely adopted due to problems with speed on older hardware as well as high hardware requirements. Mainstream support for Windows Vista ended in April 2012.

The Windows XP Start Menu.

try this!

Learn About the Microsoft Support Lifecycle

The Microsoft Lifecycle fact sheet describes the types of support Microsoft provides for its products and how long each support type will be available. Learn more about it. Try this:

1. Point your browser to support.microsoft.com/lifecycle
2. On the Microsoft Support Lifecycle page there are links to general information on the Support Lifecycle Policy and to the life cycle of specific products.
3. Explore this Lifecycle information for Microsoft products you use.

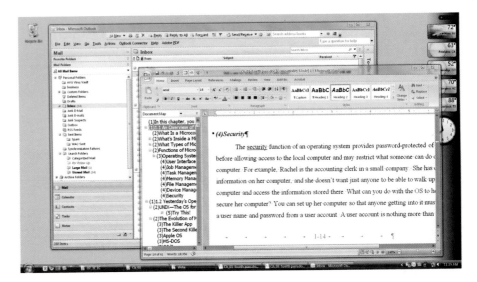

FIGURE 1–10 The Windows Vista desktop.

LO 1.3 | Today's Desktop OSs

Today's desktop microcomputer operating systems include Windows 7, Windows 8, Mac OS X, and Linux. The latest versions of all of these OSs are multiuser/multitasking operating systems, with support for virtual memory and security, and each comes in versions that support either 32-bit or 64-bit processors.

Table 1–2 summarizes the current desktop OSs covered in later chapters of this book, listing the publisher, platform, and types of applications that you can run natively on each OS. All of these OSs can run virtualization software that will run other OSs, and therefore other types of applications, but we will defer discussion of virtualization to Chapter 3.

What follows is a brief description of these OSs, with more detail in the chapters devoted to each OS.

Microsoft Windows for the Desktop

Today's Windows for the desktop include both Windows 7 and Windows 8. Whereas many organizations have or are transitioning to Windows 7, Windows 8 is meeting some resistance, discussed in the Windows 8 section.

Windows 7

Released in October 2009, Windows 7 includes several improvements correcting the shortcomings that kept Windows Vista from being widely accepted. Windows 7 is faster than Windows Vista in several ways, from starting up, to going into and out of sleep mode, to recognizing new devices when you connect

Desktop/Laptop OS	Company	Platform	Applications Supported
TABLE 1–2 Summary of Current Desktop/Laptop OSs			
Windows 7	Microsoft	Intel/Microsoft	DOS, 16-bit Windows, 32-bit Windows, 64-bit Windows applications
Windows 8	Microsoft	Intel/Microsoft	DOS, 16-bit Windows, 32-bit and 64-bit Windows applications for the Desktop and for the new Windows 8 GUI, available only through the Windows Store.
OS X	Apple	Apple Mac	Macintosh applications
Linux	Various	Intel/Microsoft	UNIX/Linux applications

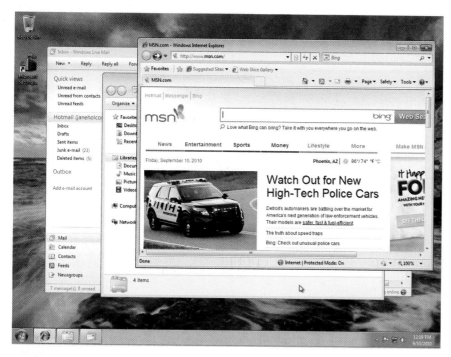

FIGURE 1–11 The Windows 7 desktop.

them. Windows 7 has many new features. The short list includes a redesigned desktop (see Figure 1–11) with a new taskbar that has many new features of its own, such as jump lists. Learn more about Windows 7 in Chapter 4.

Windows 8

Like many technically minded people, we worked with prerelease versions of Windows 8 for many months previous to its final availability in October 2012, so we were able to become familiar with Windows 8 before it was released. Predictably, it is faster than previous versions and includes better security and improved wireless connectivity. It includes support for some newer hardware, such as USB 3.0 ports and improved touch screen support that includes recognition of simultaneous multiple touches and gestures.

The most controversial changes to Windows 8 are to the GUI, or rather GUIs. The default GUI, centered around the Start screen shown in Figure 1–12,

FIGURE 1–12 The Windows 8 Start screen.

FIGURE 1–13 The Windows 8 desktop.

Note: One frustration for us is that Microsoft does not have an official name for this GUI, and refers to it only as "Windows 8." This is also the name of the version and the name of a unique edition of Windows 8.

is a departure from the Windows 7 desktop with its three-dimensional look. Objects in this new GUI appear flat, without shading and borders so that they do not take up unnecessary screen space. This is necessary because Windows 8 is intended to run on a wide range of computing devices: PCs, laptops, and tablets. The new Windows 8 GUI inherited much of its look from the Metro user interface found in the Microsoft Windows Phone 7.5 OS. The Windows 8 Start screen contains tiles that represent apps. Each tile can show active contents, such as newsfeeds, stock quotes, slideshows, and more, depending on the tile's app.

The second Windows 8 GUI, a modified version of the Windows 7 desktop, without the Start menu, also has a very flat look to it in spite of having overlapping windows. Figure 1–13 shows the Windows 8 desktop. Learn more about Windows 8 on Desktops and Laptops in Chapter 5, and Windows 8 on mobile devices in Chapter 11.

Apple Mac OS X

Whereas the Linux and Microsoft OSs are available to install on hardware from many manufacturers, the Apple Inc. strategy has been to produce proprietary hardware and software for better integration of the OS and the hardware. They do not license Mac OS X to run on other manufacturers' computers. This has historically resulted in a higher price for a Mac than for a comparable PC. For several years, beginning in the mid-1990s, Macintosh computers used the Motorola PowerPC chip with an architecture enhanced for graphics and multimedia. Since 2005 the Apple Mac line of computers are Intel-based.

The Mac OSs in common use today are versions of Mac OS X (X is the Roman numeral for 10). OS X is a revolutionary change from the previous Mac OS 9 because Apple based OS X on NextStep, an OS with a UNIX kernel. Until Mac OS X, the Macintosh OSs were strictly GUI environments, with no command-line option. Mac OS X, with its UNIX origins, gives you the option of a character-based interface, but most users will happily work solely in the GUI (see Figure 1–14). OS X v10.8 (aka Mountain Lion) is current as of this writing, but OS X v10.9 (Mavericks) was announced and will be available in the fall of 2013. Chapter 7 is devoted to Mac OS X.

Linux

Linux is an operating system modeled on UNIX and named in honor of its original developer, Linus Benedict Torvalds. He began it as a project in 1991

FIGURE 1–14 Macintosh OS X GUI.

while a student at the University of Helsinki in his native Finland. He invited other programmers to work together to create an open-source operating system for modern computers. They created Linux using a powerful programming language called C, along with a free C compiler developed through the GNU project called GNU C Compiler (GCC). Linux has continued to evolve over the years, with programmers all over the globe testing and upgrading its code. Linus Torvalds could not have predicted in 1991 how well accepted the new operating system would be over 20 years later.

Linux is available in both 32-bit and 64-bit distributions, and it can be modified to run on nearly any computer. A distribution or "distro," is a bundling of the Linux kernel and software—both enhancements to the OS and applications, such as word processors, spreadsheets, media players, and more. The person or organization providing the distribution may charge a fee for the enhancements and applications, but cannot charge a fee for the Linux code itself. Many distributions are free or very inexpensive.

Linux natively uses a command-line interface, and Figure 1–15 shows an example of a Linux directory list at the command line. Windows-like GUI environments, called shells, are available that make it as accessible to most users as Windows or Mac OS X. We'll discuss selecting a Linux distribution in Chapter 8 along with other Linux-specific details.

```
[cottrell@localhost ppp]$ ls -l
total 56
-rw-------   1 root     root        78 Feb 27 17:09 chap-secrets
-rw-r--r--   1 root     root       927 Apr 14 12:38 firewall-masq
-rw-r--r--   1 root     root       825 Apr 14 12:38 firewall-standalone
-rw-r--r--   1 root     root         0 Apr  8 09:08 ioptions
-rwxr-xr-x   1 root     root       310 Dec 26  2000 ip-down
-rwxr-xr-x   1 root     root      3564 Mar 20 22:17 ip-down.ipv6to4
-rwxr-xr-x   1 root     root       362 Dec 26  2000 ip-up
-rwxr-xr-x   1 root     root      5745 Mar 11 17:42 ip-up.ipv6to4
-rwxr-xr-x   1 root     root       918 Mar 11 17:43 ipv6-down
-rwxr-xr-x   1 root     root       918 Mar 11 17:43 ipv6-up
-rw-r--r--   1 root     root         5 Feb 27 17:09 options
-rw-------   1 root     root        77 Feb 27 17:09 pap-secrets
drwxr-xr-x   3 root     root      4096 Jul  5 15:02 peers
-rw-r--r--   1 root     root        93 Apr 14 12:38 pppoe-server-options
[cottrell@localhost ppp]$
```

FIGURE 1–15 A Red Hat Linux directory listing (the ls command).

LO 1.4 | Today's Mobile OSs

Mobile computing today has followed the trajectory of all computing, thanks to the miniaturization of components and new technologies. And like PCs, mobile devices became more desirable thanks to apps. However, don't look for a single "killer app" for mobile devices. Rather, the most popular mobile devices are those with a large number of compelling apps. Also, unlike the early PCs, which were seen more as office productivity tools, today's mobile devices are very personal devices used for communicating and entertainment as well as for work- and school-related tasks.

Of the three mobile OSs featured in this book, Apple licenses iOS only for use on Apple mobile devices, Microsoft charges manufacturers licensing fees for each device on which they install a Windows OS, adding to the cost of each device. Only Google does not charge manufacturers licensing fees for using Android, at least not on smartphones. They license it for free under the Android Open Source Project. This helps hold down the cost of Android smartphones, but this is changing because several companies hold patents on the technology in mobile devices and some of them have successfully sued manufacturers of Android devices for patent licensing fees, in some cases, collecting fees of $5 per device.

Mobile Devices

There are many manufacturers of mobile devices, but the ones we will focus on are those that use the Apple iOS, Android, or Windows operating systems. Two things they all have in common is support of a variety of wireless technologies and the ability to customize them with a variety of apps. Table 1–3 gives a summary of these OSs and the devices that use them. Following is a brief description of the hardware features of these devices.

In general, mobile devices today include these hardware features:

- Network adapters for various types of wireless networks.
- Great high-quality color touch screens that allow the OS to respond to several types of touch gestures.
- One or two (front and back) digital cameras.
- Built-in speakers and/or speaker ports for external speakers.
- Rechargeable batteries with battery life to get you through a normal day of use.
- An accelerometer that detects the physical tilt and acceleration of the device.
- Solid-state drives (SSDs).

Note: Manufacturers are expected to ship over 1 billion smartphones globally in 2014. This is according to a research report by Nokia Corporation cited in an article published on *The Wall Street Journal* website on February 19, 2013, titled "The Smartphones, the Networks, and the Suppliers: The Mobile Triumvirate—Research Report on Nokia Corporation, Ericsson, Juniper Networks, Inc., Alcatel Lucent, and Corning."

Note: The iPod Touch also runs iOS, but we are not covering this device. With its small (4-inch) screen and NO cell phone support, it is simply a digital music player with tablet features.

TABLE 1–3 Summary of Current Mobile OSs and Related Devices Featured in This Book

Mobile OS	Source of OS	Smartphones/Tablets	Sources for Apps
Apple iOS	Apple	Apple iPhone and iPad	Apple Apps Store
Android	Google	Smartphones and tablets from various manufacturers	Apps from Google and many other sources
Windows Phone 8	Microsoft	Smartphones from various manufacturers	Microsoft App Store
Windows 8	Microsoft	Tablets from many sources	Apps from the Microsoft software store—both Windows 8 (Metro) and Desktop apps—and many other sources for Desktop apps

Connectivity

The "smart" in smartphone comes from the computing ability that makes it a tool for work, home, and school. The "phone" in smartphone recognizes the ability to connect to a cellular network for voice communication. Typically you purchase a smartphone from a cellular provider, and connect the phone to the provider's network as your first ownership task. The cellular network is a form of wide area network (WAN), allowing you to make and receive voice calls as well as giving you a data connection to the Internet—both for a price. Your cellular plan usually separates usage by voice (connection time during voice calls), data (quantity of data downloaded from the Internet), and text. These plans can be very expensive depending on how you use your smartphone.

Many tablets also have cellular network support for which you pay a premium—both for the cellular hardware in the tablet and for the cellular service. Most tablets with cellular support only offer data connections. We once wrote, "Imagine holding a tablet up to your ear to make a voice call." You don't have to imagine it because there are now tablets that offer voice as well as data cellular connections.

To help control the cost of cellular data plans, we are fortunate to also have Wi-Fi connectivity in virtually all smartphones and tablets. Wi-Fi is a type of local area network (LAN), and on its own, it allows you to connect to a wireless network covering a small area, such as a house, office building, or small campus. But most Wi-Fi networks, such as those in coffee shops, offices, and homes, connect to a router that in turn connects to the Internet. Therefore, if you enable Wi-Fi on your smartphone, you can save on your cellular data usage by connecting to an Internet-connected Wi-Fi network.

Another common wireless option is Bluetooth, a wireless networking technology for connecting over very short distances (a few yards or meters). Bluetooth is used to connect a mobile device to other computers and to wireless devices, such as keyboards and printers.

We will discuss how to enable and configure different types of network connections for mobile devices in Chapter 11.

Mobile OS Features

When discussing mobile OSs it is difficult to separate the OS from the hardware, so the OS features we describe are closely tied to the previously listed hardware features of the mobile device.

Touch Screen and Virtual Keyboard Support

A mobile OS supports the touch screen by interpreting the various screen gestures we make. It also supports a feature called virtual keyboard. When you touch an area of screen that requires input from a keyboard, the OS will display the virtual keyboard, an on-screen image of a keyboard with labeled keys that you can tap. Figure 1–16 shows the virtual keyboard on an iPad. Many mobile devices will optionally connect to an external keyboard—usually via a Bluetooth wireless connection. Learn more about these features in Chapter 11.

Screen Rotation

Mobile operating systems take advantage of the hardware accelerometer by rotating the image on the screen to accommodate the position and allow you to read the screen. This feature is called screen rotation or screen acceleration. Figure 1–17 shows the screen of an iPad tablet running in "portrait" orientation,

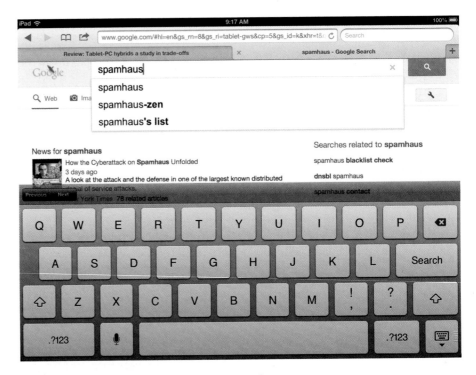

FIGURE 1–16 The virtual keyboard on an iPad.

FIGURE 1–17 An iPad home screen in portrait orientation.

and Figure 1–18 shows the screen of the same tablet in "landscape" orientation.

Updateable

As with desktop operating systems, the ability to update a mobile OS is important to the usability and security of the mobile device. While Microsoft's OSs are updateable during their clearly-defined life span, that is not quite as clear with mobile operating systems. In general, you can update an OS depending on the constraints of the hardware and limits imposed by the manufacturer. In Chapter 11 we will describe the differences in how and when you can update mobile OSs.

Availability of Apps

As we stated earlier, today's devices sell in part because of the number of useful apps, making the availability of a large selection of compelling apps more important than a single killer app that millions desire. All of the mobile OSs in this book have a large number of quality apps available to them, as well as many trivial and nonessential apps. Each mobile OS has one or more online sources, such as the Windows Store, shown in Figure 1–19, for Windows 8 apps. In Chapter 11 we describe and compare sources of apps for your mobile devices.

Security

Mobile devices are targeted by the same security threats that target other computers. Being able to

FIGURE 1–18 An iPad home screen in landscape orientation.

update the OS is only part of what you need to do to protect yourself and your data. Third-party solutions are available for some mobile OSs, and all of them come with some built-in security features. We will explore the security options for the various mobile operating systems in Chapter 11.

Synchronizing Data

Data synchronization is an important feature supported by mobile OSs, especially for people who use multiple devices and wish to access the same data across all devices. For instance, you can access your contacts list and other data from anywhere with whatever device you are using. We will examine the synchronization options for mobile devices in Chapter 11.

FIGURE 1–19 Microsoft Store for Windows 8 apps.

Chapter Summary

After reading this chapter and completing the exercises, you should know the following facts about operating systems.

An Overview of Microcomputer Operating Systems

- An operating system is a collection of programs that controls all of the interactions among the various system components, freeing application programmers from needing to include such functions in their programs.
- A computer is a device that calculates. A central processing unit (CPU) is the component that performs the calculation for a computer.
- A microcomputer is a computer small enough and cheap enough for the use of one person. The integrated circuit (IC) is one of the inventions that made microcomputers possible.
- Interaction with a computer is called input/output (I/O).
- The CPU in a microcomputer is a microprocessor, which, along with several other important components (memory, firmware, and more), is installed onto a motherboard.
- System firmware contains the program code that informs the CPU of the devices present and how to communicate with them.
- Read only memory basic input output system (ROM BIOS) is a type of firmware used since the first IBM PC (circa 1981), and recently replaced by firmware that complies with a new standard, Unified Extensible Firmware Interface (UEFI). It is faster and includes security features.
- A device driver is a special program installed into an operating system containing code for controlling a component.
- Common microcomputers in use today include desktops, laptops, tablets, and smartphones.
- The same version of the Windows or Linux OS will run on a desktop and compatible laptop computer. The same is true of Mac OS X and the iMac desktop and MacBook laptop models.
- A server is a computer that provides one or more services to other computers.
- Smartphones and tablets are the two most popular mobile devices.
- Operating systems provide these functions:
  - User interface
  - Job management
  - Task management
  - Memory management
  - File management
  - Device management
  - Security
- Today's popular operating systems for desktops and laptops come in versions for 32-bit and 64-bit processing. The biggest advantage of a 64-bit OS over a 32-bit version of the same OS is that a 64-bit OS supports a much greater amount of memory.

Yesterday's Operating Systems

- UNIX is the oldest popular operating system and comes in versions for very large computers, as well as microcomputers. It is a portable OS that is usable on a variety of computer system platforms, with only minor alterations required for the underlying architecture.
- The complex and powerful OSs we now use evolved over many decades and how people used computers changed.
- Early microcomputers included the MITS Altair 8800, the Apple I and Apple II, Radio Shack's TRS-80, and the Commodore, all introduced in the 1970s. The Apple computers came with the Apple OS.
- Software is created in versions, and some versions come in separate editions, products with bundled capabilities.
- Certain "killer apps," notably VisiCalc and Lotus 1-2-3, made microcomputers appeal to organizations and ordinary people who were attracted to programs that automated formerly manual tasks.
- IBM introduced the IBM PC in 1981, and its sales far exceeded the expectations of IBM with Microsoft BASIC in ROM. They offered PC DOS for computers with a floppy disk drive.
- Microsoft made MS-DOS available to third-party PC manufacturers and no longer supports or sells MS-DOS. Other sources continued the development of non-Microsoft DOS.
- OS/2 was first developed in a joint effort between Microsoft and IBM, and IBM soon continued development of it without Microsoft, bringing out OS/2 Warp, a GUI version. IBM discontinued support for OS/2 in 2005.
- Microsoft Windows evolved from the first version in 1985 to Windows 8, introduced in 2012. Each of

the newer versions comes in multiple products, called editions.

- The Apple Mac computer, introduced in 1984, came with the MAC OS System. This OS line continued through Mac OS 9, introduced in 1999, and phased out after Mac OS X was introduced 2001. OS X v10.8 (aka Mountain Lion) is current as of this writing.

Today's Desktop Operating Systems

- Today's desktop operating systems include Windows 7, Windows 8, Mac OS X, and Linux.
- Windows 7, released in 2009, included many improvements over Windows Vista, convincing many businesses to migrate their desktops to this OS.
- Windows 8 was introduced in October 2012 with two GUIs: the new Metro-style GUI and a Desktop GUI that is a modified version of the Windows 7 desktop, without the Start menu. It is faster and includes more security features than Windows 7.
- Apple's Mac OS X, based on NextStep, an OS with a UNIX kernel, runs only on Apple Mac desktop and laptop computers.
- Linus Torvalds developed Linux as a collaborative effort beginning in 1991. It is available in both 32-bit and 64-bit distributions and can run on nearly any computer. It natively uses a command-line interface, but GUI shells are available for most distributions.

Today's Mobile OSs

- People use mobile devices for communicating and personal entertainment as well as for work- and school-related tasks.
- Apple's iOS runs on Apple's iPhone and iPad products (as well as on the iPod touch). Apps are only available from the Apple Apps Store.
- Google's Android OS runs on smartphones and tablets from many manufacturers. Apps are available from Google and from many other sources.
- Windows Phone 8 runs on smartphones from several manufacturers with apps available from the Microsoft App Store.

- Windows 8 runs on tablets from many sources with apps available from the Microsoft App Store and many other sources.
- Features in mobile devices include:
  - Multiple types of wireless network adapters.
  - High-quality color touch screens.
  - One or two (front and back) digital cameras.
  - Built-in speakers and/or speaker ports.
  - Rechargeable batteries with battery life sufficient for a normal day of use.
  - An accelerometer that detects the physical tilt and acceleration.
  - Solid-state drives (SSDs).
- Smartphones and some tablets support cellular connections and are usually bought through a cellular provider who usually charges for voice usage by connection time and data usage by amount of data downloaded from the Internet.
- Smartphones and tablets also offer Wi-Fi connections, which give you a cheaper option for accessing the Internet with the device.
- Bluetooth is a wireless networking technology for connecting over very short distances (a few yards or meters) that is used to connect a mobile device to other computers and to wireless devices, such as keyboards and printer.
- A mobile OS interprets screen gestures and displays a virtual keyboard when you touch an area of screen that requires input from a keyboard.
- A mobile OS takes advantage of the hardware accelerometer in a device by rotating the image on the screen to accommodate the position of screen so that it is readable to you.
- Most mobile operating systems can be updated to some degree.
- Popular mobile OSs have a large number of apps available to them.
- All mobile OSs have security features, and third-party solutions are available for some mobile OSs.
- It is important to have good options for synchronizing data across all devices used by an individual.

Key Terms List

accelerometer *(30)*

application *(2)*

central processing unit (CPU) *(2)*

client *(5)*

command-line interface (CLI) *(6)*

computer *(2)*

cursor *(6)*

device driver *(3)*

device management *(8)*

directory *(8)*

distribution *(29)*

edition *(19)*

embedded OS *(4)*

file management *(8)*

file system *(8)*

firmware *(3)*
folder *(8)*
formatting *(8)*
graphical user interface (GUI) *(6)*
input/output (I/O) *(2)*
integrated circuit (IC) *(2)*
job management *(6)*
kernel *(6)*
Mac *(4)*
memory *(3)*
memory management *(8)*
microcomputer *(2)*
microprocessor or processor *(2)*

motherboard *(3)*
multitasking *(7)*
operating system (OS) *(2)*
partition *(8)*
personal computer (PC) *(4)*
portable operating system *(11)*
processes *(7)*
random-access memory (RAM) *(3)*
read only memory basic input output system (ROM BIOS) *(3)*
screen acceleration *(31)*
screen rotation *(31)*
security *(9)*

server *(5)*
smartphone *(4)*
solid-state drive (SSD) *(8)*
tablet *(5)*
task management *(7)*
Unified Extensible Firmware Interface (UEFI) *(3)*
user interface (UI) *(6)*
version *(13)*
virtual keyboard *(31)*
virtual memory *(8)*

Key Terms Quiz

Use the Key Terms List to complete the sentences that follow. Not all terms will be used.

1. A/an _____ takes care of the interaction between a program and a computer's hardware, freeing application programmers from the task of including such functions in their programs.

2. The _____ is the main component of an OS that always remains in memory while the computer is running, managing low-level OS tasks.

3. If you save confidential data on your local hard drive, you should be using an operating system that includes a/an _____ function, which protects the computer and the data it contains from unauthorized access.

4. An operating system that uses _____ will allow you to simultaneously run more programs than the physical memory of the computer will hold.

5. When you run several applications at once and switch between them, you are experiencing the _____ feature of an operating system.

6. Interaction with a computer involving getting data and commands into it and results out of it is called _____.

7. The role of a _____ is to provide services to other computers on a network.

8. Software that allows the operating system to control a hardware component is a/an

   _____.

9. A/an _____ is a hardware component in a mobile device that an OS uses when it rotates the image on the screen so that it is readable in its current position.

10. The _____ function of an OS includes the visual components as well as the command processor that loads program into memory.

Multiple-Choice Quiz

1. Which of the following operating systems cannot be licensed for a PC?
   a. Mac OS X
   b. Windows Vista
   c. Windows 7
   d. Linux
   e. Windows 8

2. Which of the following is a small electronic component made up of transistors (tiny switches) and other miniaturized parts?
   a. Peripheral
   b. Integrated circuit (IC)

   c. Tablet
   d. Mouse
   e. Vacuum tube

3. Introduced in 1983, this application program became the "killer app" that made the IBM PC a must-have business tool.
   a. Microsoft Word
   b. VisiCalc
   c. BASIC
   d. PC DOS
   e. Lotus 1-2-3

4. Which of the following is not available as a desktop operating system?
   a. Windows 8
   b. Macintosh OS X
   c. Windows 7
   d. Linux
   e. iOS

5. Which of the following is a computer input device? Select all correct answers.
   a. Mouse
   b. Printer
   c. Keyboard
   d. RAM
   e. ROM

6. On a network, the purpose of this type of computer is to allow end users to connect over the network to save and access files stored on this computer, as well as to print to printers connected to this computer.
   a. Desktop computer
   b. File and print server
   c. Tablet
   d. Laptop
   e. Smartphone

7. Which desktop OS now has a GUI optimized for touch screens with screen objects that appear flat and borderless so that they take up less screen space?
   a. Linux
   b. UNIX
   c. Mac OS X
   d. Windows 8
   e. Windows 7

8. Max OS X is built on NextStep, an OS based on what kernel?
   a. Linux
   b. UNIX
   c. DOS
   d. Windows
   e. BASIC

9. In the early 1950s, a typical computer end user would have been a _____.
   a. computer gamer
   b. medical doctor
   c. politician
   d. government agency
   e. secretary

10. An operating system is to a computer as a _____ is to a department.

    a. salesman
    b. spreadsheet
    c. steering wheel
    d. ignition
    e. manager

11. Which of the following accurately describes the overall trend in computing during the past 60-plus years?
    a. Toward physically larger, more powerful computers.
    b. Toward physically larger, less powerful computers.
    c. Toward physically smaller, less powerful computers.
    d. Toward physically smaller, more powerful computers.
    e. Toward physically smaller, single-use computers.

12. When working with a mobile device, if you touch an area of screen that requires input from a keyboard, the OS will display this for your use.
    a. Help screen
    b. Virtual keyboard
    c. A Bluetooth button so that you can connect a keyboard.
    d. CLI
    e. Screen gestures

13. Using this type of wireless network connection when browsing the Internet with a smartphone or tablet can save you data fees.
    a. Bluetooth
    b. Wi-Fi
    c. USB
    d. Cellular
    e. Ethernet

14. This type of chip contains the basic input/output system for a computer.
    a. Microprocessor
    b. IC
    c. RAM
    d. ROM BIOS
    e. Floppy disk

15. What is the very first thing a user must do to gain access to a secure computer?
    a. Back up all data.
    b. Connect to the Internet.
    c. Log on with a user name and password.
    d. Double-click the Start menu.
    e. Reboot.

Essay Quiz

1. Describe the interactions you have had with computers in the past 24 hours.

2. If you use both a desktop computer and mobile device, describe some of the similarities and differences you have noticed in working with the GUI on each device. If you do not use both types of computers, find someone who does (classmate or other) and interview that person to answer this question.

3. Describe virtual memory and list an OS described in this chapter that does not use it.

4. Linux comes in distributions from many sources. Define the term *distribution* in this context.

5. In general terms, describe a mobile OS's use of a device's accelerometer.

Lab Projects

LAB PROJECT 1.1

To understand the relative cost of each of the desktop operating systems you are studying and the availability of each, research the price of each of the operating systems listed in the table below. You are not bargain hunting, so you don't need to look for the lowest price; just find the relative cost of the operating systems, packaged with an optical disc, if possible. Some are only available as downloads. You will also find

that some are not available as new retail products, although you may find them at other sources. We have listed the full retail versions separately from the upgrade versions. You can install the full versions on a computer that does not have a previous version of Windows installed. The upgrade versions are cheaper than the full versions, but will not install without a previous version of Windows. In Table 1–4, enter the cost of each product.

TABLE 1–4 Price and Availability Comparison

Operating System	Cost	Operating System	Cost
Windows 7 Professional Full Version		Windows 8 Pro Upgrade	
Windows 7 Professional Upgrade		Windows 8 Pro OEM Full Version	
Windows 7 Ultimate Full		Windows 8 Pro Pack—Download	
Windows 7 Ultimate Upgrade		Ubuntu Linux—Download	
Windows 8 OEM Full Version		Mac OS X Mountain Lion Upgrade	

LAB PROJECT 1.2

In studying the common operating systems, you have considered the availability of software that runs on each OS and the general reasons you may choose one over the others. Put yourself in the position of an information technology professional in a new company that will open its doors on day one with

50 employees who will need computers on their desks connected to a corporate network and will need to work with standard business applications. What are some other practical considerations that you can think of that must come into play when making this decision? Your answer does not need to specify a particular OS.

chapter

2 Computer Security Basics

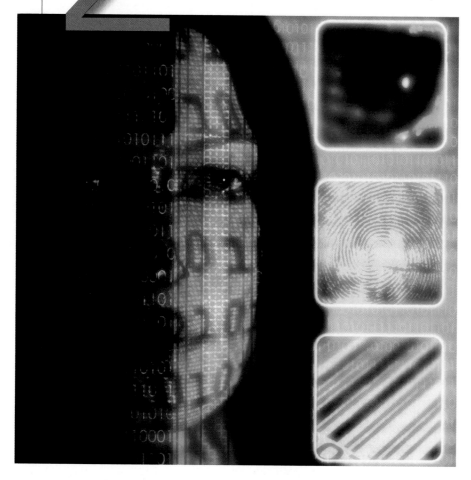

"If you think technology can solve your security problems, then you don't understand the problems and you don't understand the technology."

—Bruce Schneier
Security technologist and author

Why do operating systems have a long list of security features? Why do we need to apply security patches to operating systems? Why has computer security become a multibillion-dollar business worldwide? Why? Because it's dangerous out there! And, as you will learn in this chapter, "out there" seems to be everywhere, because no place or technology is safe from threats. That includes the Internet, corporate extranets, desktop and laptop computers, and even your cell phone, tablet, or other mobile devices. Here you'll learn about the threats, and the methods, practices, and technologies for protecting your computer systems.

In this chapter we first attempt to instill a healthy dose of paranoia in your mind, and then we identify methods for securing a computer, such as authentication and authorization, encryption, firewalls, antispam, antivirus, anti-popup, privacy protection, and other types of protections. Then, in later chapters, you will learn how to implement OS-specific security.

Learning Outcomes

In this chapter, you will learn how to:

LO **2.1** Describe security threats and vulnerabilities to computers and users.

LO **2.2** Identify methods for protecting against security threats.

LO **2.3** Troubleshoot common security problems.

LO 2.1 | Threats to Computers and Users

What are you risking if your computer or mobile device is not secure? The short answer is that you risk your identity, the work you have created, your company's integrity, and your own job if you are responsible for loss of the company's equipment or data. Today, government regulations, such as the Sarbanes-Oxley Act or the Health Insurance Portability and Accountability Act (HIPAA) require that organizations protect certain personal information, such as health and personal financial data. The consequences to an organization that does not comply with these regulations, or that experiences a breach of security involving such data, can be very severe. In the extreme, malicious software can cause death when it infects critical national defense software or software in computers onboard an airplane or in a train switching system.

We'll begin the long answer with an overview of common threats and how they gain access to computers. Many of the threats described are severe enough to be considered cybercrimes. A cybercrime is illegal activity performed using computer technology.

Malware

We call software threats malware, a shortened form of "malicious software." This term covers a large and growing list of threats, including many that you no doubt know about, such as viruses, worms, Trojan horses, or spam. But have you heard of pop-up downloads, drive-by downloads, war driving, bluesnarfing, adware, spyware, back doors, spim, phishing, or hoaxes? Read on and learn about the various types of malware and their methods of infecting computers and networks.

Malware development has become a huge industry that targets all computing devices, with perhaps the greatest growth in malware targeting mobile devices. As reported by Kaspersky Lab, in 2011 they detected approximately 5,300 new malware programs targeting all mobile operating systems, but by 2012 the number of new malware programs was over six million.

Zero-Day Exploit

We also call a malware attack an exploit because it takes advantage of some vulnerability in our computers or networks. Experts are constantly discovering these vulnerabilities and attempting to stay ahead of the bad guys with appropriate defense techniques. However, sometimes someone finds a software vulnerability in an operating system or application such as those we study in this book that is unknown to the publisher of the targeted software, and someone devises a way to exploit that vulnerability. We call this unknown exploit (often a virus) a zero-day exploit, and it is very difficult to protect against such a threat.

Vectors

A vector is a method that malware uses to infect a computer. While some malware may use just a single vector, multivector malware uses an array of methods to infect computers and networks. Let's look at a few well-known vectors.

Social Networking. Social networking is the use of social media, which is any service (Internet-based or other) that provides a place where people can interact in online communities, sharing information in various forms. Community members generate social-media content. A social networking site is a website that provides space where members can communicate with one another and share details of their business or personal lives. Facebook is a

Note: Malware continues to evolve with variations on the types of malware described in this chapter. A short list of such variations includes logic bombs, pharming, vishing, whaling, appender infection, and swiss cheese infection.

Note: Members of the Chinese People's Liberation Army hacked into Facebook and many other American companies and government agencies, stealing vast amounts of data. However, in what may be ironic justice, some of the hackers were later identified because they accessed Facebook (presumably with their personal accounts) from the same network from which they carried out the hacking attacks.

very popular social networking site. Like all popular social media sources, Facebook has a membership requirement, and each member creates a password-protected account and provides personal information. LinkedIn is a social media site targeted to professionals who use it for business contacts. Twitter allows users to send and receive short text messages of up to 140 characters.

We see social media as a vector for malware and social engineering (defined later in this chapter) as well as a rich source of personal information on individuals. We are horrified to see the personal details that people reveal on their Facebook and Twitter sites.

try this!

More About Social Media

Check out the latest in social media. Try this:

1. Open your favorite search engine, such as Google.com or Bing.com.
2. Enter the key words "social media."
3. Browse through the results and create a list of at least 10 social-media sites.
4. Return to the search engine and enter "social media security."
5. Browse through the results and look for recent articles on social media security concerns. Read some of the articles and discuss them with your classmates.

Email Vectors. Some malware infects computers via email. You may have believed it was always safe to open email as long as you didn't open attachments, but the simple act of opening an email containing the Nimda virus can infect a computer, depending on the software you are using to read the message. This was true with Microsoft's Outlook Express email client included with Windows XP. Microsoft released a patch to close this vulnerability. This is an argument for keeping your software updated with security patches.

Regardless of the email client you use, clicking on a link in an email message can launch malware from a website.

Code on Websites. Some malware infects computers by lurking in hidden code on websites. An unsuspecting user browses to a site and clicks on a link that launches and installs malware on her computer.

Trojan Horses. A Trojan horse, often simply called a Trojan, is both a type of malware and a vector. The modern-day Trojan horse program gains access to computers much like the ancient Greek warriors who, in Homer's famous tale (the epic poem *The Iliad*), gained access to the city of Troy by hiding in a large wooden horse presented as a gift to the city (a Trojan horse). A Trojan horse program installs and activates on a computer by appearing to be something harmless, which the user innocently installs. It may appear as just a useful free program that a user downloads and installs, but it is a common way for malware to infect your system.

While it is hard to fit all threats into tidy categories, we consider threats similar to the "Complete a Quick Survey" exploit to be a Trojan because it appears to be something harmless, tempting you to comply. If you complete the survey it may take some action, such as pretending to scan your computer for problems, but the results will be bogus, offering to fix the problems it claims to find and asking for payment to support charities. This type of threat states that you must complete the survey or it will delete critical files. We call this type of threat scareware.

Searching for Unprotected Computers. Still other malware searches throughout a network for computers with security flaws and takes advantage of the flaws to install itself.

Sneakernet—The Oldest Vector. Yet another vector is as old as PCs. In the days when it was uncommon for computers to connect to any network, users

Trojan horse
Carol and Mike Werner/Alamy

WARNING!

Many messages associated with threats contain bad spelling and poor grammar. However, not all are so obvious, but the scare tactics should be a tip off.

WARNING!

Malware often infects our computers because we unwittingly invite it in via a Trojan. For instance, in 2012, the Flashback Trojan, masquerading as an installer for Adobe's Flash Player browser plugin, was reported to have infected hundreds of thousands of Apple computers whose users unwittingly installed the malware from websites that hosted this Trojan. Once installed, it locates usernames, passwords, and personal data and sends this information back to a server.

shared data between computers by carrying a floppy disk containing data or programs from one computer to another. The slang for this practice is sneakernet. Sometimes, the floppy disk contained malware, making sneakernet the oldest vector for PCs. Sneakernet still exists, but the storage device used today is the flash drive, and the computers are usually also connected to a network, which extends the risk when malware infects a single computer. In August 2010 the U.S. Deputy Defense Secretary declassified the information that a flash drive, inserted into a U.S. military laptop in 2008 on a military post in the Middle East, was the vector for malicious code that caused a significant breach of military computers.

Back Doors. In computing, a back door is a way in which someone can gain access to a computer, bypassing authentication security. Sometimes a program's author installs a back door into a single program so she can easily access it later for administering and/or for troubleshooting the program code. Or an attacker may create a back door by taking advantage of a discovered weakness in a program. Then any program using the back door can run in the security context of the invaded program and infect a computer with malware. The security context of the program encompasses the privileges granted to the logged-on user or to the program itself when it was installed. In one well-known situation, the Code Red worm took advantage of a specific vulnerability in Microsoft's Internet Information Server (IIS) Web server software to install a back door. The result was that the worm displayed a message on every Web page on the IIS server. The message included the phrase, "Hacked by Chinese." Then the Nimda worm took advantage of the back door left by the Code Red worm to infect computers.

Rootkits. A rootkit is malware that hides itself from detection by anti-malware programs by concealing itself within the OS code or any other program running on the computer. Someone who has administrator (root) access to the computer installs a rootkit, giving an attacker administrator privileges to the computer. Once installed, he can then run any type of malware to quietly carry out its mission. "Rootkit" also refers to the software components of a rootkit.

Pop-Up Downloads. A pop-up is a separate window that displays (pops up) uninvited from a Web page. The purpose of a pop-up may be as simple as an advertisement, but a pop-up can be a vector for malware. A pop-up download is a program downloaded to a user's computer through a pop-up page. It requires an action on the part of a user, such as clicking on a button that implies acceptance of something such as free information, although what that something may actually be is not clear. The program that downloads may be a virus or a worm.

Drive-By Downloads. A drive-by download is a program downloaded to a user's computer without consent. Often the simple act of browsing to a website, or opening an HTML email message, may result in such a surreptitious download. A drive-by download may also occur when installing another application. This is particularly true of certain file-sharing programs that users install to allow sharing of music, data, or photo files over the Internet. Some drive-by downloads may alter your Web browser home page and/or redirect all your browser searches to one site. A drive-by download may also install a virus, a worm, or even more likely, adware or spyware (which we describe later in this chapter).

War Driving. We should secure all Wi-Fi networks with the latest standard of Wi-Fi security and require passwords to access the network. A Wi-Fi network that connects to the Internet through a router is a hotspot. Someone who

Windows Wardriving Street Hacking

Dannozz 1 videos ☒ | Subscribe

Just watched | Up next

↻ Replay

👍 Like

↱ Share

wardriving session 3 a

From gigarello
views :3542

2:00

Top 100 Network Sec | WLAN Infosendung, | NetStumbler | Bruce's wardriving

Suggestions

wardriving session 3 a
by gigarello
31,542 views

Top 100 Network Security Tools
by JohnConnor9
3,867 views

WLAN Infosendung, Networkstumbler, Ethereal
by JustVBlog
7,217 views

NetStumbler
by Xafique
12,403 views

Bruce's wardriving equipment
by bblacklaws99
4,095 views

Wardriving Documentary
by seinman
22,602 views

▶ 🔊 4:14 / 4:14   360p   ⬒ ↗ ⛶

Dannozz | June 29, 2008
A quick wardrive in Holland :D   4,082 views

👍 Like 👎 | Save to ▾   ✉ Share   <Embed> ⚑

Online videos show examples of war driving.

detects an unprotected hotspot can access the Internet for free. If they do this without the hotspot owner's permission they are using Internet access illegally, riding on the subscription of the hotspot owner. Further, the reason we see this as a vector is that they also can capture keystrokes, email, passwords, and user names from the wireless traffic, giving them ways to send malware to connected users or use the information they gather to steal users' identities.

Some people actively seek out unsecured Wi-Fi networks, a practice called war driving. A war driver moves through a neighborhood in a vehicle or on foot, using a mobile device equipped with Wi-Fi wireless network capability and software that identifies Wi-Fi networks. There are also simple and inexpensive Wi-Fi sensors available from many sources.

If the individual computers on the wireless network, or other networks connected to it, are unprotected, unauthorized people may access those computers, making this a vector for malware. Hotspots are frequently intentional, and more and more hotspots are available for free or for a small charge by various businesses, such as coffee shops, bookstores, restaurants, hotels, truck stops, and even campgrounds.

Using an unsecured hotspot can expose you to threats unless your computer is secure. If you need to be inspired to secure your Wi-Fi network, check out the Internet where tons of websites describe how to war drive, as well as how to protect your data from theft. There are even many war driving videos on YouTube, as shown above.

Bluesnarfing. Similar to war driving, bluesnarfing is the act of covertly obtaining information broadcast from wireless devices using the Bluetooth standard, a short-range wireless standard used for data exchange between desktop computers and mobile devices. Bluetooth devices have a range of from 10 centimeters to 100 meters, depending on the power class of the device. Using a smartphone, a bluesnarfer can eavesdrop to acquire information, or even use the synchronizing feature of the device to pick up the user's information—all without the victim detecting it.

Stealing Passwords

A password is a string of characters that you enter, along with an identifier, such as a user name or email address, to authenticate yourself. If someone steals your passwords they can gain access to whatever you thought you were protecting with the password. We first considered calling this section "Discovering Passwords," but that phrase is far too innocent sounding—as if the perpetrator was innocently walking along and "discovered" your password lying on the sidewalk. What really happens is theft with intent to break into computers and networks. It is stealing, so let's call it that! People use many methods to steal passwords.

Stealing Passwords Through Websites. There are numerous programs and techniques for stealing passwords. One commonly used technique is to invade an unsecured website to access information unwitting users provide to the site, such as user names and passwords, and such personal information as account numbers, Social Security numbers, birth dates, and much more.

Stealing Passwords with Password Crackers. Another technique used for discovering a password is a program called a password cracker. Some password crackers fall into the category of "brute-force" password crackers, which simply means the program tries a huge number of permutations of possible passwords. Often, because people tend to use simple passwords such as their initials, birth dates, addresses, etc., the brute-force method works. Other password crackers use more sophisticated statistical or mathematical methods to discover passwords.

Stealing Passwords with Keystroke Loggers. Another method for discovering passwords, as well as lots of other information, is the use of a keystroke logger, also called a keylogger. This is either a hardware device or a program that monitors and records every keystroke, usually without the user's knowledge. In the case of a hardware logger, the person desiring the keystroke log must physically install it before recording and then remove it afterward to collect the stored log of keystrokes. For example, the Spytech keystroke logger is a USB device the size of a flash drive that installs between the keyboard cable and a USB connector on the computer. There are also hardware keystroke loggers for PS/2 keyboard connectors. They are all very unobtrusive when connected to the back of a PC; one keystroke logger can hold a year's worth of keystroke data in flash memory and comes with software for reading the specially formatted data files.

A software keystroke logger program may not require physical access to the target computer but simply a method for downloading and installing it on the computer. This could occur through one of the vectors described earlier in this chapter. Once installed, such a program can send the logged information over the Internet via email, or using other methods, to the person desiring the log.

Some parents install keystroke loggers to monitor their children's Internet activity, but such programs have the potential for abuse by people with less benign motivations, including stalking, identify theft, and more. A simple Internet search of "keystroke logger" will yield many sources of both hardware and software keystroke loggers. The latter are now the more common.

Viruses

While, in the broadest sense, "virus" is a term used for all malware, technically, a virus is one class of malware: a program installed and activated on a computer without the knowledge or permission of the user. Viruses usually attach themselves to a file, such as a Microsoft Word document, and replicate and spread as you copy or share the infected file. At the least, the intent is mischief, but most often the intent is to be genuinely damaging. Like a living

Two hardware keystroke loggers.
Product photo courtesy of www.keycobra.com

Note: Advanced keystroke loggers may also capture screenshots of all activity on a computer.

virus that infects humans and animals, a computer virus can result in a wide range of symptoms and outcomes. Loss of data, damage to or complete failure of an operating system, or theft of personal and financial information are just a few of the potential results of computer virus infections. If you extend the range of a virus to a corporate or government network, the results can be far-reaching and even tragic. There are thousands of viruses "in the wild" today.

Note: "In the wild" is a term frequently used to describe the overall computing environment, including private networks, and Internet and all other public networks. "In the Zoo," refers to a controlled and isolated environment where viruses can be analyzed during the development of patches. This type of environment is also called a "sandbox."

Worms

Like a virus, a worm is a program installed and activated on a computer without the knowledge or permission of the user. But a worm replicates itself on the computer, or throughout a network. In other words, a worm is a network-aware virus that does not require action from the unwitting user to replicate, and it can have a similar range of outcomes. In recent years the Netsky and MyDoom worms caused chaos and loss of productivity just in the amount of network traffic they generated. The typical worm resides in a single file that it replicates onto multiple machines. However, the Nimda worm changed all that by inserting its code into other executable files on the local drive of each machine to which it replicated itself, making it hard to locate and remove the worm.

Botnets and Zombies

A botnet is a group of networked computers that, usually unbeknown to their owners, are infected with programs that forward information to other computers over a network (usually the Internet). A bot, short for robot, is a program that acts as an agent for a user or master program, performing a variety of functions—both for good and evil. An individual computer in a botnet is a zombie because it mindlessly serves the person who originated the botnet code. Most often affecting home computers, botnets have grown to be one of the biggest threats on the Internet. A botherder is someone who initiates and controls a botnet.

Spyware

Spyware is a category of software that runs surreptitiously on a user's computer, gathers information without the user's permission, and then sends that information to the people or organizations that requested it. A virus may install Internet-based spyware, sometimes called tracking software or a spy-bot, on a computer. Spyware can be used by companies to trace users' surfing patterns to improve the company's marketing efforts; it can be used for industrial espionage; it can be used by law enforcement to find sexual predators or criminals (with appropriate legal permissions); and it can be used by governments to investigate terrorism.

Adware

Adware is a form of spyware that collects information about the user in order to display targeted advertisements to the user, either in the form of inline banners or pop-ups. Inline banners are advertisements that run within the context of the current page, just taking up screen real estate. Pop-ups are a greater annoyance, because they are ads that run in separate browser windows that you must close before you can continue with your present task. Clicking to accept an offer presented on an inline banner or a pop-up may trigger a pop-up download that can install a virus or worm.

Browser Hijacking

We received a call the other day from Dave, a finance officer at a large farm implement company. Every time he opened Internet Explorer, the home page pointed to a site advertising adware removal software. This is an example of **browser hijacking**, a practice that has been growing. Some unscrupulous people do this so that their website will register more visitors and then they can raise their rates to advertisers.

Dave was able to reverse this by changing the default page in Internet Options, but it was very annoying. He was lucky; sometimes hijackers make it very difficult to defeat the hijack by modifying the registry (a database that stores configuration settings in the Windows OS) so that every time you restart Windows or your Web browser the hijack reinstates. Or you may even find that a registry change makes Internet Options unavailable.

Spam and Spim

Spam is unsolicited email, often called junk email. This includes email from a legitimate source selling a real service or product, but if you did not give the source permission to send such information to you, it is spam. Too often spam involves some form of scam—a bogus offer to sell a service or product that does not exist or tries to include you in a complicated moneymaking deal. If it sounds too good to be true it is! We call spam perpetrators spammers, and spam is illegal. Spam accounts for a huge amount of traffic on the Internet and private networks, and a great loss in productivity as administrators work to protect their users from spam and individuals sort through and eliminate spam. Some corporate network administrators report that as much as 60 percent of the incoming email traffic is spam.

Spim is an acronym for spam over instant messaging, and the perpetrators are spimmers. A spimmer sends bots out over the Internet to collect instant-messaging screen names, and then a spimbot sends spim to the screen names. A typical spim message may contain a link to a website, where, like spam, the recipient will find products or services for sale, legitimate or otherwise.

Social Engineering

Social engineering is the use of persuasion techniques to gain the confidence of individuals—for both good and bad purposes. People with malicious intent use social engineering to persuade targeted people to reveal confidential information or to obtain something else of value. Social engineering is as old as human interaction, so there are countless techniques. Following are just a few categories of computer security threats that employ social engineering.

Fraud

Fraud is the use of deceit and trickery to persuade someone to hand over money or other valuables. Fraud is often associated with identify theft (discussed later), because the perpetrator will falsely claim to be the victim when using the victim's credit cards and other personal and financial information.

Phishing

Phishing is a fraudulent method of obtaining personal and financial information through Web page pop-ups, email, and even paper letters mailed

Take a Phishing Test!

It is often difficult to discern which emails are legitimate and which are "phish." To complete this test, you will need a computer or mobile device with an Internet connection.

Step 1

Use your Web browser to connect to the phishing test at www .sonicwall.com/phishing/. If this URL no longer works, use a search engine to find a phishing test.

Step 2

After reading the instructions and helpful hints, start the test.

Step 3

You will be presented with 10 messages and you must decide whether each is legitimate or phish.

Step 4

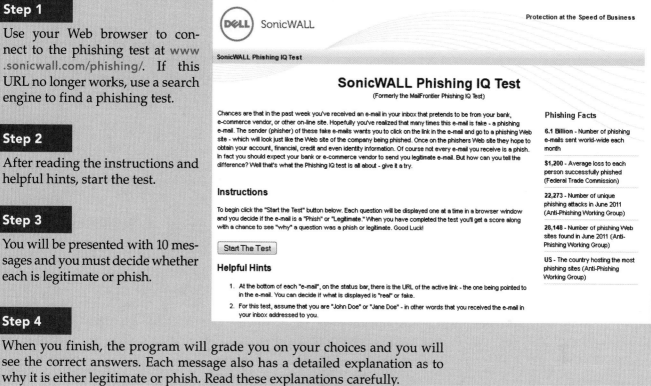

When you finish, the program will grade you on your choices and you will see the correct answers. Each message also has a detailed explanation as to why it is either legitimate or phish. Read these explanations carefully.

via the postal service. Think of the metaphor of a fisherman preparing and casting his bait in an ocean full of fish. Even if only one in a hundred fish take the bait, he is statistically likely to have many successes. We'll concentrate our discussion on Web page pop-ups and email. A phishing message ("bait") purports to be from a legitimate organization, such as a bank, credit card company, retailer, and so on. In a typical phishing scenario, the email or pop-up may contain authentic-looking logos, and even links to the actual site, but the link specified for supplying personal financial information will take recipients (the "phish") to a "spoofed" Web page that asks them to enter their personal data. The Web page may look exactly like the company's legitimate Web page, but it's not at its site. A common practice is for a phisher to use the credit information to make purchases over the Internet, choosing items that are easy to resell and having them delivered to a destination address to which the phisher has access, such as a vacant house.

While the typical phishing attack casts a wide net by sending out millions of messages, some phishing attacks are more targeted. We call these spear phishing, and the target of a spear-phishing attack is usually one that has a high probability of delivering a very valuable return. Such an attack may come in the form of a message with a greeting that includes your name and content that includes some of your personal information. If you work in a large organization, the attack may have language that seems to come from a colleague, detailing department information or referring to a recent (perhaps unnamed) meeting. The source of the message may actually be your colleague's valid address if the attacker managed to hijack the email account. Or it may appear to be your colleague's valid address, but in reality, it is a forged email address. Someone forges an email address by modifying the sender's address in the email message's header—the information that accompanies a message but does not appear in the message. We also call this type of forgery email spoofing.

Be very suspicious of email requesting personal or financial information. Legitimate businesses will never contact you by email and ask you for your access code, Social Security number, or password. Phishing (and spear phishing) are just old-fashioned scams in high-tech dress.

Hoaxes

A hoax is a deception intended either for amusement or for some gain with malicious intent. Hoaxes take many forms. One example is an email message appearing to be from someone you know claiming she took an unplanned trip to London where she was mugged in the subway. The email address looks legitimate, but when you respond, you receive a message from someone else stating that your friend is now in jail and needs bail money. Sounds outlandish? We received such a message, but we were suspicious and called our friend who reported that she was safe at home and that several other of her friends had responded to the message and received the plea for money.

Hoaxes take many forms.
Henrik Kettunen/Alamy

Enticements to Open Attachments

Social engineering is also involved in the enticements to open attachments to emails. Called "gimmes," you find these enticements either in the subject line or in the body of the email message. Opening the attachment then executes and infects the local computer with some form of malware. A huge number of methods are used. Sadly, enticements often appeal to the less noble human characteristics such as greed (via an offer too good to be true), vanity (physical enhancement products), or simple curiosity (with a subject line that appears to be a response to an email from you). More tragic, these enticements may appeal to people's sympathy and compassion by way of a nonexistent charity or by fraudulently representing a legitimate charity.

Identity Theft

Identify theft occurs when someone collects personal information belonging to another person and uses that information to fraudulently make purchases, open new credit accounts, and even obtain new driver's licenses and other forms of identification in the victim's name. They may not even be interested in actual financial information; simply obtaining your Social Security number and other key personal information may be enough to steal your identity. There are many ways not directly involved with computers for thieves to steal your identity. Identity theft is a huge business involved in the theft of large numbers of persons' data from large databases. These criminals sell such identity information for pennies per record. Several websites maintained by the U.S. government offer valuable information for consumers who wish to protect themselves from identify theft. A starting place is the website www.idtheft.gov,

The FTC Identity Theft Web page.

by the President's Task Force on Identity Theft; it has links to other websites where you can learn more and report incidents of identity theft. Alternatively, enter a search string, as suggested in the Try This, that will take you directly to a page with helpful information at a government agency.

Exposure to Inappropriate or Distasteful Content

The Internet, and especially the World Wide Web, is a treasure trove of information. It is hard to imagine a subject that cannot be found somewhere on the Internet. However, some of this content may be inappropriate or distasteful. To some extent, only an individual can judge what is inappropriate and distasteful; however, circumstances in which certain content is harmful to some individuals—such as young children—is considered a threat and thus is inappropriate.

Invasion of Privacy

One can also view many of the threats discussed so far as invasions of privacy. Protecting against privacy invasion includes protecting your personal information at your bank, credit union, both online and bricks-and-mortar retail stores, athletic clubs, or almost any organization in which you are a customer,

try this!

Learn More About Identity Theft

Learn more about identity theft in general, how to protect yourself, and how to report suspected identity theft. Try this:

1. Open your browser and use a search engine to search on the key words "FTC id theft." (Omit the quotation marks.)

2. In the search results select the site identified as the U.S. government's central website for information about identity theft.

3. At the Federal Trade Commission's ID theft website, explore the various links from this page to learn more about identity theft and related topics.

4. If it is available, watch the video on identity theft. You may be surprised at how easy it is to be a victim of identity theft.

member, or employee. All steps you take to make your computer more secure also contribute to the protection of your privacy.

Invasion of privacy by shoulder surfing.
Troy Aossey/Digital Vision/Getty Images

Misuse of Cookies

A more subtle form of privacy invasion involves the misuse of something called cookies. Cookies are very small files an Internet browser saves on the local hard drive at the request of a website. The next time you connect to that same website, it will request the cookies saved on previous visits—often giving you the convenience of automated log-ins to each site. Cookies are text files, so they cannot contain viruses, which are executable code, but they may contain the following:

- User preferences when visiting a specific site.
- Information you may have entered into a form at the website, including personal information.
- Browsing activity.
- Shopping selections on a website.

The use of cookies is a convenience to a user who does not have to reenter preferences and pertinent information on every visit to a favorite website. In fact, users are not overtly aware of the saving and retrieving of cookies from their local hard disk, although most good websites clearly detail whether or not they use cookies and what they use them for. You can find this information in the privacy statement or policy of the site. Cookies are only accessible by the website that created them, or through some subterfuge of the website creator. A cookie contains the name of the domain that originated that cookie. A first-party cookie is one that originates with the domain name of the URL to which you directly connect. A third-party cookie refers to a cookie that originates with a domain name beyond the one shown in your URL. An ad embedded in a Web page—often called banner ads—can use cookies to track your Web surfing habits, and third-party cookies play a part in this type of tracking, making third-party cookies less desirable than first-party cookies.

WARNING!

From now on, when you browse the Web, look for links to the privacy statement or site policy at each website you visit.

Computer Hardware Theft

Of course security includes something as simple as locking doors, keeping hardware locked away from prying eyes and sticky fingers. That's obvious. What may not be obvious to you, especially if you use a laptop as your principal computer, is what happens if someone steals your computer. You would be astonished at how many computers, especially laptops and mobile devices, are stolen each year, and unless your computer has been properly secured, and all the data backed up, there goes your business information, your data files, your financial information, your address book, everything! Although a large percentage of computer thefts occur just so the thief can sell the hardware quickly and get some quick cash, an increasing number of thieves are technically sophisticated and will go through your hard drive looking for bank account, credit card, and other financial data so they can steal your identity.

Guard against computer theft.
Image Source/Getty Images

Accidents, Mistakes, and Disasters

Accidents and mistakes happen. We don't know of anyone who hasn't accidentally erased an important file, pressed the wrong button at the wrong instant, or created a file name he can't remember. Disasters also happen in many forms. Just a few are fires, earthquakes, and weather-induced disasters such as tornadoes, lightning strikes, and floods. Predicting such events is imperfect at best. The principal way to protect against accidents, mistakes, and disasters is to make frequent, comprehensive backups. You can make backups of an entire hard drive using programs that make an image of the drive, or you can use programs that back up your critical data files on a periodic basis. Organizations that have a lot of valuable data even make multiple

Computer accidents.
R and R Images/Photographer's Choice/Getty Images

FIGURE 2–1 The FTC Bureau of Consumer Protection website.

backups and keep copies off-site. Then, in case of fire, flood, earthquake, or other natural disaster that destroys not only the on-site backups but also the computer, they can still recover.

Keeping Track of New Threats

We cannot begin to cover all the methods currently used to victimize computer users. However, various organizations work to keep track of these threats, counter them, and inform the public. The Federal Trade Commission (FTC) Bureau of Consumer Protection is one such organization. It maintains a website (www.ftc.gov/bcp/), shown in Figure 2–1, containing a list of documents about various consumer issues and threats. These documents are worth reviewing from time to time to learn about new threats. This site also gives interesting information on threats.

The People Behind the Threats

The people behind computer security threats are as varied as are their motivations. They come from all walks of life and are scattered all over the globe. Organized crime is a growing source of these threats. Organized crime cartels exist in every major country in the world, with certain areas notorious for their homegrown crime organizations. Online banking and online shopping are just two areas where billions of dollars exchange every day, and these cartels work to exploit weaknesses. Organized crime specialists work at stealing bank account login information and also are the source of many fraud attempts and money laundering via online shopping.

As any group of people engaged in similar endeavors grows and matures, it develops a set of terms and participant competency rankings. For years, the term "hacker" has been used, particularly by the press, to mean someone who uses sophisticated computer programming skills to invade private computers and networks to cause havoc, steal passwords, steal identities and money, and so on. But the people who work to invade others' systems actually fall into several classifications describing their action—classifications defined by the people within that community themselves or by those who work to bring them to justice.

Although these levels of competency are worth understanding, from the standpoint of someone trying to protect systems against invasion, it doesn't much matter what level of attacker you are facing. The point is to protect systems against attack. So, for the purposes of this book, and because the term is widely understood, we'll use hacker to mean any attacker.

Hackers

A hacker is an expert programmer with sophisticated skills who is also a networking wizard. Hackers are highly trained, fluent in a number of programming languages, and motivated by the challenge of solving complex problems. They belong to a community, a shared culture, which traces its history back decades. The members of this culture originated the term "hacker," and they were involved in building the Internet, making the UNIX operating system what it is today, running Usenet, and making the World Wide Web work. Although in the past some hackers were involved in damaging attacks, in general, genuine hackers are involved in solving complex problems and contributing to the computing community. However, in most articles you will read on malware, the term "hacker" refers to the malevolent hacker. To distinguish the good guys from the bad guys, some use the term "white-hat hackers" to describe hackers who hack for good, searching for vulnerabilities in software and disclosing it to the source of the software so that they can correct the problem.

Hacker.
Comstock/Getty Images

Crackers

A cracker is a member of a group of people who proudly call themselves hackers, but aren't. These are mainly adolescents who get a kick out of causing damage after breaking into computers and making phone systems do things they aren't supposed to do (the latter is called phone phreaking). Real hackers call these people "crackers" and want nothing to do with them. Real hackers mostly believe that being able to break security doesn't make you a hacker any more than being able to hot-wire a car makes you an automotive engineer. The basic difference is this: Hackers build things, crackers break them. They are both harmful!

Script Kiddies

A script kiddie is someone who usually lacks the knowledge to personally develop a security threat, but uses scripted tools or programs created by others to break into computer systems to cause damage or mischief. The name implies enough knowledge to run computer scripts or programs, even from a command line.

Click Kiddies

A click kiddie is similar to a script kiddie, but with even less knowledge than a script kiddie, requiring a GUI to select and run a hacking tool. A click kiddie browses the Web, searching for sites that make it even easier by providing forms the click kiddie can fill out, enter a target IP address, and click to initiate an attack. Such sites provide the additional benefit of anonymity to the perpetrator.

Packet Monkeys

Packet monkeys are similar to script kiddies and click kiddies in that they need to use programs created by others to perform their attacks. They typically have little understanding of the harm they may cause, and their exploits are often random and without a purpose other than the thrill of trying to get away with something. Hackers call packet monkeys "bottom feeders."

Packet monkeys create denial-of-service attacks by inundating a site or a network with so much traffic (data packets) that the network is overwhelmed and denies service to additional traffic. Their attacks may be on a broad scale which makes it more difficult to trace the identity of the packet monkey.

LO 2.2 | Defense Against Threats

No simple solutions exist to the damaging and mischievous threats that lurk on the Internet and on private networks, but doing nothing is not an option. We need to make our best efforts to thwart these threats, even if we cannot deter a determined and skilled invader. Most people do not have the necessary skills, motivation, or access to sophisticated tools, so implementing basic security will keep the majority out. Here are some basic defensive practices that you can apply in operating systems to avoid being a victim. Often you will need to install a third-party program (free or commercial) to add protection your operating system does not provide.

Education

This chapter may be just the beginning of your education about how threats, such as viruses, get access to computers and networks and how our own behavior can make us vulnerable to such threats as identity theft. Beyond understanding how these things can happen, also be actively alert to signs of a virus or that someone is using your credit. Then you can take steps to defend against threats and recover from damage from threats.

Be suspicious of anything out of the ordinary on your computer. Any unusual computer event may indicate that a virus, some sort of browser hijack, or other form of spyware, adware, and so on has infected your computer. Signs to look for include:

- Strange screen messages.
- Sudden computer slowdown.
- Missing data.
- Inability to access the hard drive.

Similarly, unusual activity in any of your credit or savings accounts can indicate that you are a victim of identity theft, including:

- Charges on credit accounts that you are sure you or your family did not make.
- Calls from creditors about overdue payments on accounts you never opened.

artpartner-images.com/Alamy

- Being rejected when applying for new credit for reasons you know are not true.
- A credit bureau reports existing credit accounts you never opened.

Along with education about threats comes paranoia. However, if you use a computer at home, work, or school, and are on a network and/or the Internet, a touch of paranoia is healthy. Just don't let it distract you from your day-to-day tasks. Take proactive, responsible steps, as we outline here.

Security Policies

Every organization should have a set of established security policies describing how they protect and manage sensitive information. Security policies define data sensitivity and data security practices, including security classifications of data, and who (usually based on job function) may have access to the various classes of data. For instance, a security policy may state, "Only server administrators and advanced technicians may access the server room, and must not give access to any other individuals." Security policies should also describe the consequences of breaking policy rules.

Security policies should exist in both document form and software form. For instance, at work or school, if you are logging into a network with a central login, such as a Microsoft domain, administrators may configure the servers to enforce a password policy that accepts only strong passwords. How they define a strong password depends on the settings selected, such as minimum password length or complexity. Complexity requirements may say the characters must include a combination of lowercase alphabetical characters, uppercase alphabetical characters, numerals, punctuation characters, and math symbols. In addition, they may require that you create a new password every month, and that you cannot repeat any of the previous 10 passwords.

Windows has security policies implemented from the domain level on the computers as well as on the users that log on to the domain. Windows also has a local security policy that affects the local computer and users, but can be overridden by domain policy when the computer and user are logged on to a Windows domain. The Local Security Policy console shown here allows an administrator to set local security policy. This is a very advanced task.

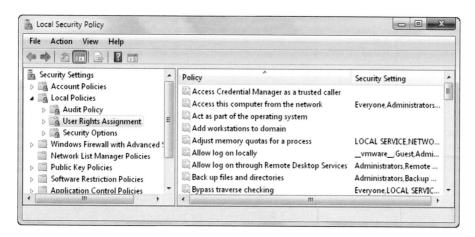

The Windows Local Security Policy console.

Install Comprehensive Security Software

A logical progression through the appropriate defense against computer security threats would have us look at authentication and authorization at this point. However, because we include activities that require that you access the Internet, we will first talk about the comprehensive security software that

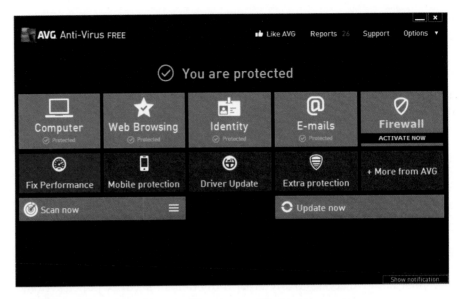

FIGURE 2–2 Security software with many bundled components.

should be in place before you connect to the Internet. This does not mean that security software is more important than authentication and authorization. They are all important pieces of every security defense strategy.

Comprehensive security software may come in one bundle of software from one source, or it can be separate software from many sources. The pieces should include (at minimum) a personal firewall, antivirus software, anti-spam software, and an email scanner. Figure 2–2 shows the console for AVG Internet Security with both the security components and various tools for managing the security package, such as the Update Manager that automatically checks the AVG site for updates and then downloads and installs them. The following sections will describe some of these security components.

Firewalls

A **firewall** is either software or a physical device that examines network traffic. Based on predefined rules, a firewall rejects certain traffic coming into a computer or network. The two general types of firewalls are network-based hardware firewalls and personal firewalls that reside on individual computers. We recommend that you always have a reliable personal firewall installed, even if your computer is behind a hardware firewall. An attack can be from another computer behind the firewall, and that is when your personal firewall becomes your last line of defense between your computer and the world. Let's look at these two general types of firewalls.

Network-Based Firewalls

A network-based firewall is a hardware device designed to protect you against the dangers of having an unprotected connection to the Internet. It sits between a private network and the Internet (or other network) and examines all traffic in and out of the network it is protecting. It will block any traffic it recognizes as a potential threat, using a variety of techniques. Table 2–1 lists some of the most common technologies normally included in a firewall, although some of these are not strictly firewall technologies. Your ISP and most corporations employ hardware firewalls, expensive and specialized computers manufactured by companies such as Cisco, 3COM (now owned by Cisco), Netgear, and others, and these sophisticated firewalls require highly

TABLE 2–1 Firewall Technologies

Technology	Description
IP packet filter	An IP packet filter inspects (or filters) each packet that enters or leaves the network, applying a set of security rules defined by a network administrator. Packets that fail inspection may not pass between the connected networks.
Proxy service	Sometimes referred to as an application-layer gateway, a proxy service watches for application-specific traffic. For example, a Web proxy only examines Web browser traffic. Acting as a stand-in (a proxy) for internal computers, it intercepts outbound connection requests to external servers and directs incoming traffic to the correct internal computer. You can configure a proxy service to block traffic from specific domains or addresses.
Encrypted authentication	Some firewalls require external users to provide a user name and password before they can open a connection through a firewall. Since the authentication information (user name and password) must pass over the Internet, it is important to encrypt it. This authentication involves the use of one of several encryption protocols. Encrypted authentication is a security service that is not limited to firewalls and is not always implemented on a firewall.
Virtual private network (VPN)	Not a true firewall technology, a virtual private network (VPN) is a virtual tunnel created between two endpoints over one or more physical networks, done by encapsulating the packets. Other security methods usually applied include encryption of the data and encrypted authentication. When set up in combination with properly configured firewalls, a VPN is the safest way to connect two private networks over the Internet.

trained people to manage them. Such a firewall probably protects the network at work or at school.

At home or in a small office, most people have a consumer-grade hardware firewall that comes in a small device that performs many of the same functions performed by a more professional-grade firewall. The most common name for these devices is broadband router or cable/DSL router. They combine the function of a firewall, a router (a device that "routes" traffic from one network to another), an Ethernet switch, and even a wireless access point all in one tiny box. These inexpensive devices can handle the traffic of just a few computers, while the more serious devices employed by ISPs and large organizations can handle thousands of simultaneous high-speed transmissions. These consumer-grade devices now come with the "one button" configuration that automatically configures a simple connection to the Internet, with the latest security turned on. You can also access the built-in Web page to make manual changes to the settings. Figure 2–3 shows the security page of a Cisco Wireless-N Router, which includes support for all the technologies

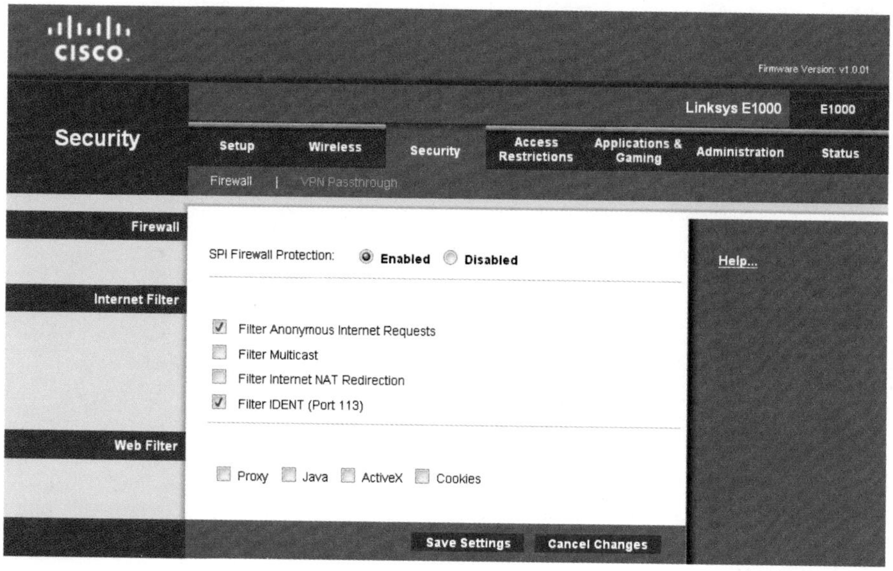

FIGURE 2–3 The Security page from a Cisco Wireless-N Router's configuration utility.

listed in Table 2–1 and many more features, including support for the 802.11N standard for Wi-Fi communications and security. The setting labeled "Firewall" is just one option for securing your home network. Even with this device, you would need to research the impact of the various settings before changing from the default settings.

The firewall administrator configures a firewall to allow traffic into the private network or prohibit traffic from entering the private network based on the types of computers residing within the private network, and how they will interact with the Internet. If all the computers on a private network are desktop computers that connect to the Internet to browse Web pages and access FTP sites, the firewall protecting the network has a simple job. It simply blocks all in-bound traffic that is not the result of a request from a computer on the internal network; it matches incoming traffic with previous outgoing traffic that made requests that would result in incoming traffic. Then, when you connect to a website, outgoing traffic from your computer to the website requests to see a page. That page comes to you as incoming traffic and a firewall will allow it through based on your initial request.

But if the private network includes servers that offer services on the Internet, then the firewall must allow initiating traffic to come through, but it does not allow all incoming traffic through. In this case, you configure a firewall to allow incoming traffic of the type that can only communicate with the internally based servers. The various types of traffic include email, Web, FTP, and others. Each type of traffic has a certain characteristic the firewall can recognize. Figure 2–4 shows a firewall protecting a network containing both servers and desktop computers (shown as clients).

A network professional would look at the simplified example of a firewall shown in Figure 2–4 and immediately talk about setting up a DMZ, named for a wartime demilitarized zone. In networking, a DMZ is a network between a private (inside) network and public (outside) network. An organization puts any servers that it wishes to have offer services to the Internet in the DMZ.

Note: A server created as a decoy to draw malware attacks and gather information about attackers is called a **honey pot**. A honey pot may be located outside a corporate firewall, within a DMZ, or inside the corporate network.

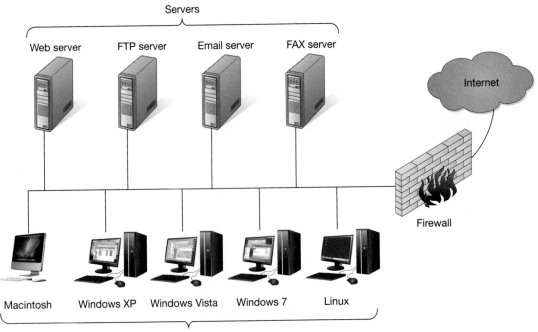

FIGURE 2–4 A private network protected by a firewall.

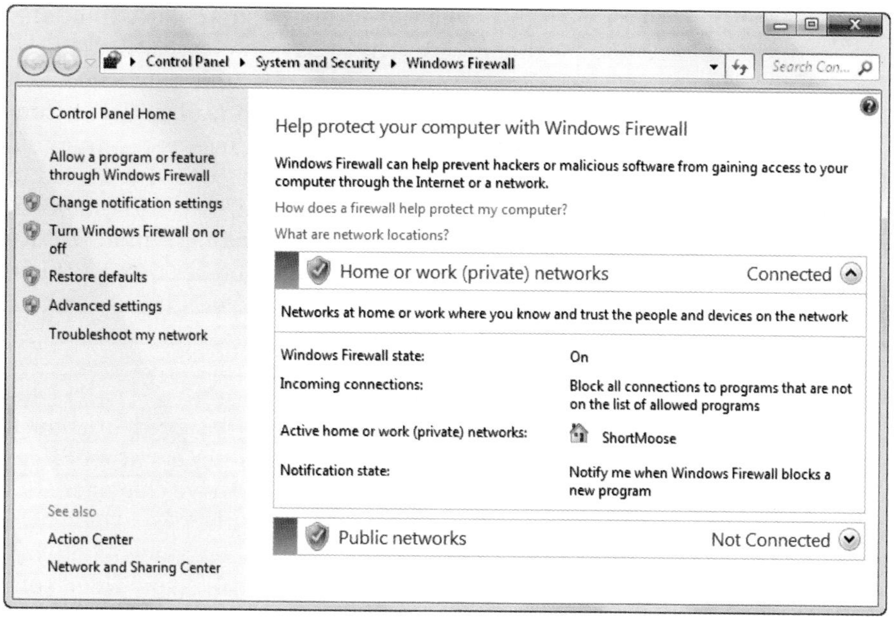

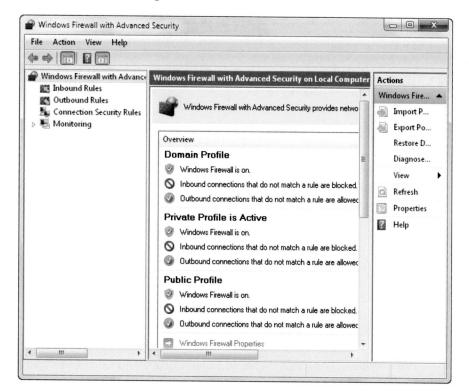

FIGURE 2–5 The Windows Firewall Control Panel.

Personal Firewalls

Because many attacks come from within a private network, personal firewalls have become standard. The Windows Firewall is included in Windows. Mac OS X comes with a firewall, and there are many third-party firewalls for Windows, Mac OS X, and Linux. There are two places where you can configure the Windows Firewall. One is the Windows Firewall Control Panel, shown in Figure 2–5. Using the links in the pane on the left, you can make changes to the Firewall. A more advanced configuration tool is Windows Firewall with Advanced Security, a Microsoft Management console shown in Figure 2–6. You can access both in Windows 7 by entering "windows firewall" into the Search box and selecting the tool.

Note: Zone Labs (www.zonelabs .com) offers many excellent security products, including Zone Alarm, a personal firewall.

FIGURE 2–6 Windows Firewall with Advanced Security console.

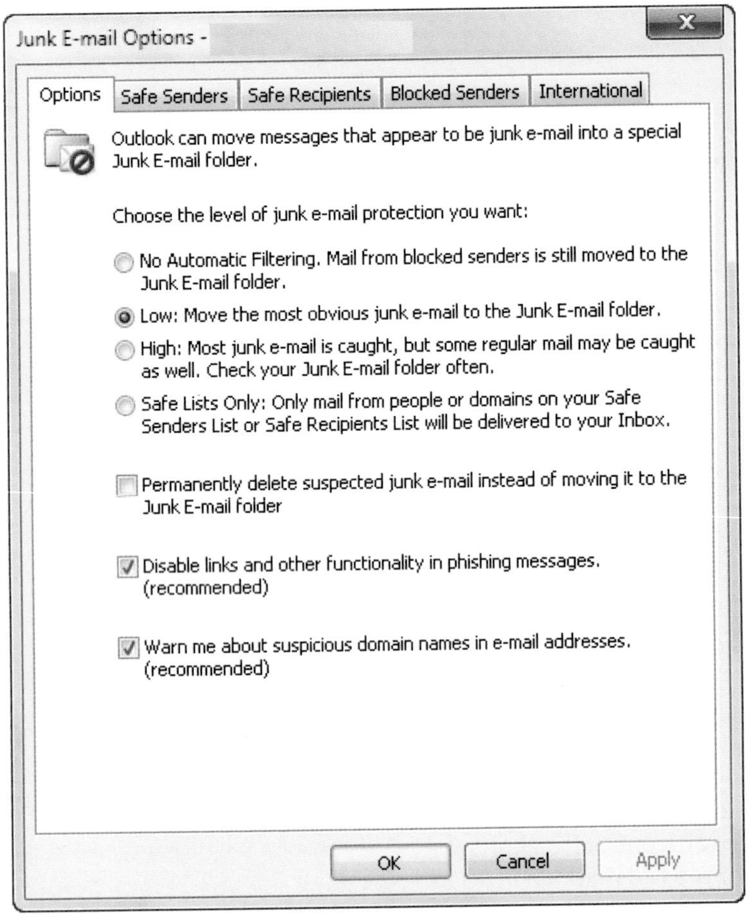

FIGURE 2–7 The Windows Junk Email Options page.

If you have installed a third-party firewall—either separately or as part of a security suite—the Windows Firewall will be turned off. Opening the Windows Firewall applet in Control Panel will show you a message stating that your computer is unprotected and you need to turn on Windows Firewall. This informational message may simply mean that Windows Firewall is disabled because you are using a third-party firewall.

Antispam Software

A **spam filter** is software designed to combat spam by examining incoming email messages and filtering out those that have characteristics of spam, including certain identified keywords. In an organization with centralized network and computer management, spam filter software installed on central mail servers can remove spam before it gets to a user's desktop. Other network administrators use Internet-based spam filtering services that block spam before it reaches the corporate network.

Individuals connected to the Internet from home or in small businesses are often on their own when it comes to eliminating spam. Luckily, many email clients, such as Microsoft Outlook, now offer spam filtering. Without a spam filter you must sort through your own email to find and delete the spam. Spam filters are not perfect—they often filter out legitimate messages, while allowing some spam messages through. For this reason, most spam filters require some configuration on the part of the user using rules or filters that will automate the process of removing spam from known sources. And the user will still often need to review a list of suspected spam messages. Figure 2–7 shows the Microsoft Outlook Junk Email Options dialog box with several tabbed pages of settings that allow you to configure the spam filter.

Antivirus Software

An antivirus program can examine the contents of a storage device or RAM looking for hidden viruses and files that may act as hosts for virus code. Effective antivirus products not only detect and remove viruses, but they also help you recover data that has been lost because of a virus. To remain current, they require frequent updating as to the virus threats to watch for. An antivirus program includes an antivirus engine (the main program) and a set of patterns of recognized viruses, usually contained in files called definition files. Retailers of antivirus software commonly charge an annual fee for updates to the antivirus engine and the definition files. There are excellent free services for home users. One example is AVG antivirus from GRIsoft. Software companies that offer free security software usually also offer a feature-rich commercial version to which you can upgrade for a fee. The free version gives you a chance to see if you like using it before you put out any money. Once installed, most antivirus programs will automatically connect to the manufacturer's website and check for these updates.

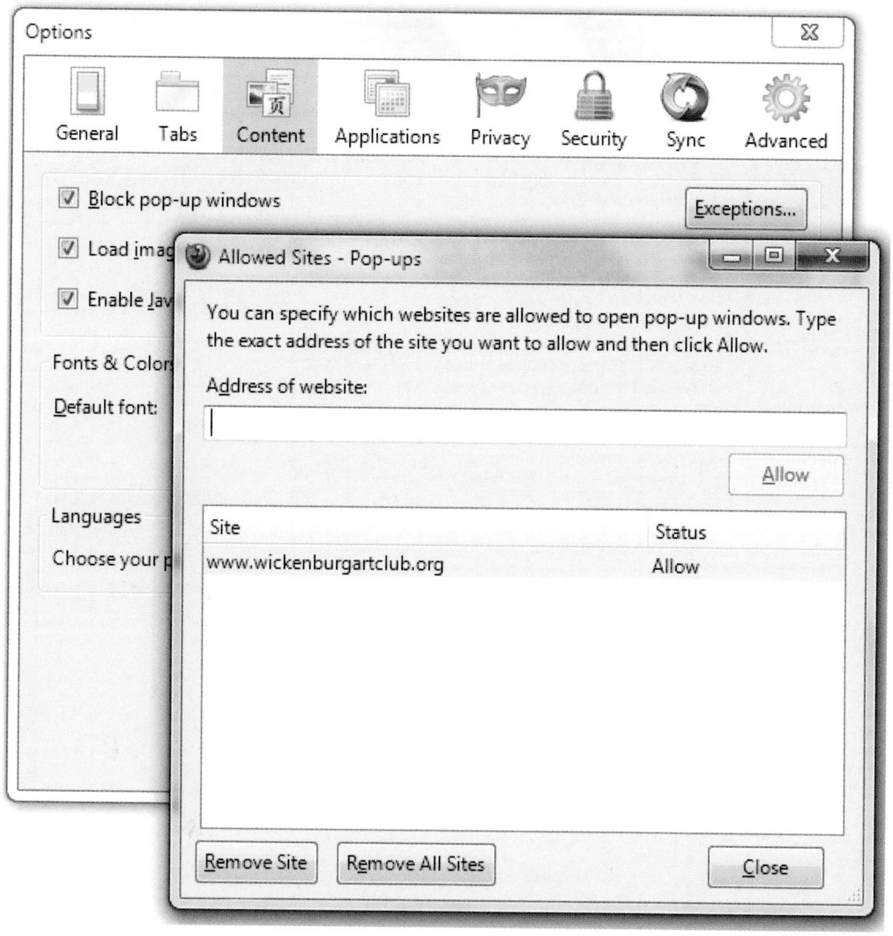

FIGURE 2–8 The Firefox Pop-Up Blocker Exceptions page.

Pop-Up Blockers

Many free and commercial programs are available that effectively block various forms of adware, especially pop-ups, which are the easiest to block and the most annoying because a pop-up advertisement appears in its own window and must be closed or moved before you can see the content you were seeking. A program that works against pop-ups is a **pop-up blocker**, and all major Internet browsers now have built-in pop-up blockers. You can configure a pop-up blocker so that it will block pop-ups quietly, but you can also configure one to make a sound and/or display a message allowing you to choose to make a decision on each pop-up or to automatically and quietly block all pop-ups. We have found a few websites where blocking all pop-ups has blocked much of the content we were seeking. In that case, we may configure the pop-up blocker to make an exception for that site. You can enable the pop-up blocker feature on the Privacy page of the Internet Options dialog box for Internet Explorer. Once enabled, click the Settings button to open the Pop-up Blocker Settings page.

To configure the pop-up blocker in Firefox, open Options and select the Content tab, where you will find the setting to turn the pop-up blocker off or on. You can also open the Exceptions dialog for Firefox, shown in Figure 2–8, and add any website where you wish to enable pop-ups.

Privacy Protection and Cookies

Web browsers and security programs offer privacy protection options. In Microsoft Internet Explorer, you can configure privacy settings, including the pop-up blocker, through the Internet Options dialog box, accessible

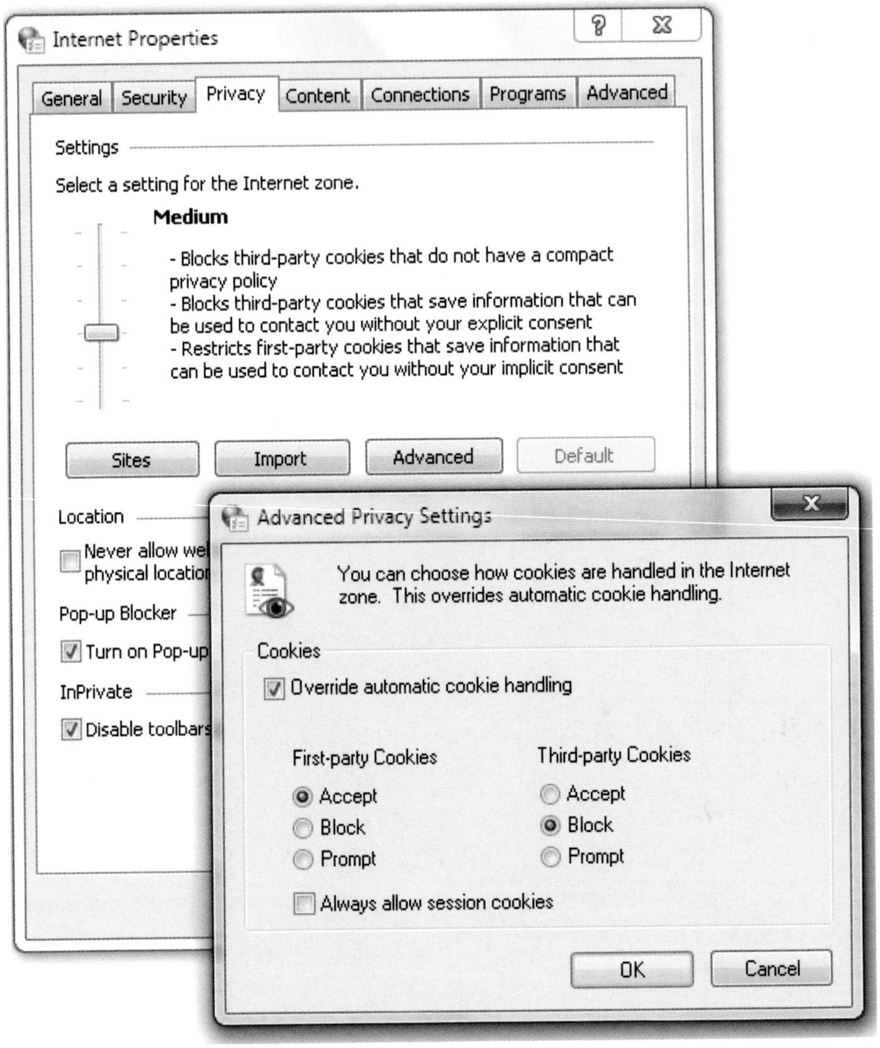

FIGURE 2–9 Use the Advanced Privacy Settings in Internet Options to control the use of cookies.

from either the Control Panel or the Tools menu in Internet Explorer. This is also where you determine how Internet Explorer handles cookies. The settings range from "Block all cookies" to "Allow all cookies," with a variety of settings in between. Experiment with the settings by choosing one and then spending some time browsing the Internet. The balance here is between the convenience of cookies for automated login to frequently accessed sites and the risk of an invasion of privacy. The Sites button in Internet Explorer will block specific sites; you will see a list of known bad sites listed here. The Advanced button allows you to customize the handling of cookies, as shown in Figure 2–9. We recommend that you allow first-party cookies for the convenience (explained earlier) and block third-party cookies because the tracking methods often associated with third-party cookies are an invasion of privacy.

Parental Controls

Parental Controls, accessed from the Content tab in Internet Options, is a feature in Internet Explorer. It allows parents to protect their children from harm by setting specific Parental Controls for a child's user account. Only someone using a password-protected administrator account can enable and configure

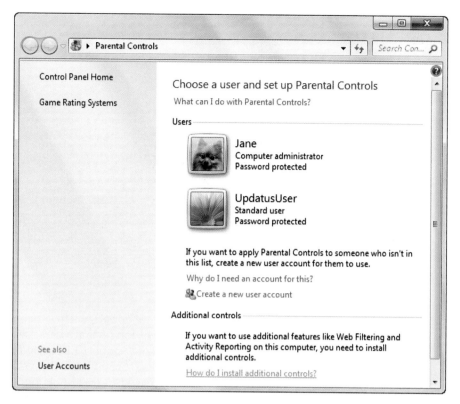

FIGURE 2–10 The Parental Controls Control Panel.

Parental Controls, and there must be an existing standard account for the child. The parent can then set time limits, game limits, and software restrictions. If you have Internet Explorer 10 installed, access Parental Controls by first opening Internet Options, selecting the Content tab, and then clicking the Family Safety button. This will then show the Parental Controls Control Panel, as you can see in Figure 2–10.

Content Filtering

You can use software that blocks content, called a content filter, to enable protection from inappropriate or distasteful content. A common type of content filter used on the Internet is a Web content filter, a software program designed to work with a Web browser to either block certain sites or to allow only certain sites. As with most types of software, you can find both free and commercial versions of Web content filters on the Internet. In fact, you may already have a Web content filter in your Web browser that you only need to enable and configure.

Note: To learn more about content filters, use your favorite search engine to search on the key words "Web content filter."

Many services are available on the Internet to evaluate website content and give each site ratings based on such parameters as language, nudity, sex, and violence. A content filter may use one or more of these rating services, and allow the administrator to choose the rating level to permit or exclude. Not all websites are rated, so if you enable a Web content filter, you will also have to decide what it should do in the event the user connects to an unrated site.

Keep Up to Date

You should be sure to keep your operating system and applications up to date with security patches, especially if you are running Windows. Microsoft

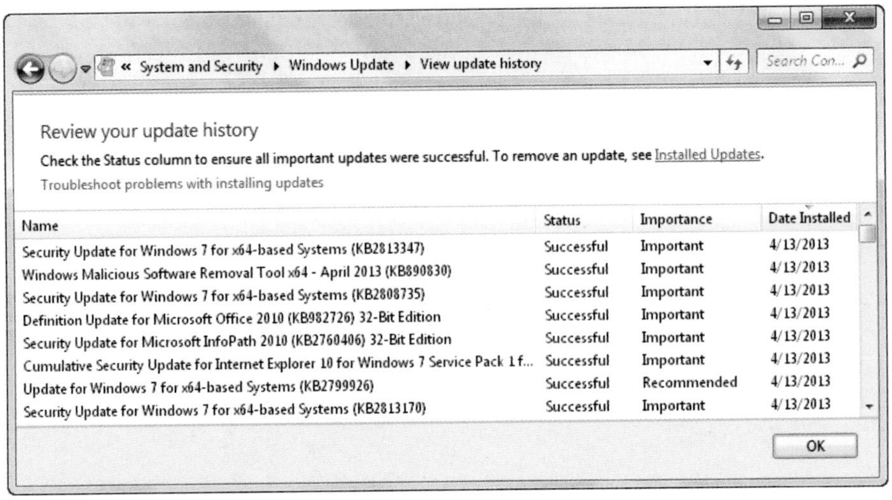

FIGURE 2–11 Windows Update maintains a list of updates.

try this!

View the Windows Update History

You can see the update history on your Windows 7 or Windows 8 computer. Try this:

1. Open Control Panel and locate Windows Update.
2. Tap or click on the Windows Update link in Control Panel to open it.
3. In the task pane (on the left) in Windows Update click or tap View Update History.
4. This opens the View Update History control panel where you can scroll through the list of installed updates.

continues to update each version of Windows for several years (see the Microsoft Support Lifecycle at www.microsoft.com), and the versions discussed in this book automatically check for the updates that plug security holes that malware perpetrators exploit. Windows keeps a list of all the updates, as shown in Figure 2–11.

Authentication and Authorization

One of the first defenses against threats is authentication and authorization by a security system built into the operating systems on your local computer and on network servers. With the exception of DOS, the desktop OSs surveyed in this book support authentication and authorization. In fact, Linux, Windows, and Mac OS X require it.

After you, as the administrator, have set up an account for Rachel in accounting she must enter her username and password when she logs on to her computer. Before giving her access to the computer, security components of her operating system will verify that she used a valid user name and password. This validation of the user account and password is authentication.

A recently hired part-time clerk, Kirsten, works at night entering accounts payable information into Rachel's computer. To allow Kirsten to also log on to Rachel's computer, you can create a new user account for Kirsten. Although only Rachel and Kirsten can log on to this computer, Rachel does not want Kirsten to be able to access the payroll information, also stored there, because this is private information. What might you do to help Rachel with this problem? One thing you could do (if her operating system supports it) is to set up Rachel's computer so that she can assign special permissions to the files and folders on her hard disk, giving each user account the level of permission it needs. For instance, one of Kirsten's tasks is to add accounting information to the accounts payable files, so you could give Kirsten's account the authorization that will allow her to write to the files in the accounts payable folder. You will not give Kirsten's account access to any of the other folders, and you will give Rachel's account full control of only the folders that she needs to use.

Right about now you're thinking that we're wrong about Windows and Mac OS X requiring authentication. Your computer is running the latest version of Windows or Mac OS X, but you don't have to enter a username or password to access your desktop and all your personal settings and data. So, obviously, you are not authenticated. Right? Wrong! Windows, Mac OS X, and Linux always require authentication, but each has a feature called automatic login that the OS installation program system turns on under certain circumstances, such as when you bring home a PC or Mac that you just bought in a retail store. Automatic login authenticates anyone who powers up your computer using the same credentials, and they have access to everything that you normally do. You should never enable automatic login on a computer at school or at work.

Authentication

Authentication is the verification of who you are. Authentication may be one-factor, two-factor, or even three-factor. One-factor authentication is your use of a user name and password as you log on to your computer. In this case, you are authenticated based on something you know—your user name and password. Two-factor authentication involves the use of something you know plus something you have, referred to as a token. If you use a cash card at an ATM, you are familiar with two-factor authentication, because the something you know is your PIN (personal identification number) code, while the token is your cash card. For even more security, consider three-factor authentication, adding biometric data, such as a retinal scan, voice print, or fingerprint scan to the token and password.

Authorization

Authorization determines the level of access to a computer or a resource (files, folders, printers, and so on) to an authenticated user. Authorization includes authentication, plus verification of your level of access to a computer or resource, including permissions and/or user rights. When you connect to a shared folder on your LAN, the security system of the computer hosting the folder will perform authorization, authenticating you, and verifying that your account has some level of access to the folder. This level of access is called a permission. Permission describes an action that you may perform on an object. An example of a permission found on a file system is the read permission that allows reading of the contents of a file or folder, but by itself it does not allow any other action on that file, such as deleting or changing it. Another component that affects level of access is a user right. A user right defines a system-wide action that a user or group may perform such as logging on to a computer or installing device drivers.

Passwords

The most common method of authentication is the use of a password and identifier, such as a user name. A password is an important piece of the security puzzle. Don't take your password for granted. In fact, password should be plural, because you should not use the same password everywhere, and you should put a great deal of thought into creating passwords that truly help you protect yourself. This is important because, unless you deal strictly in cash and do all your transactions in person at the bank, secure authentication is your basic defense against an invasion of your privacy, and your password is central to having secure authentication. Passwords are a very important part of any security system. Most experts recommend using passwords that are at least eight characters long and that contain a mixture of numbers, letters

> **WARNING!**
>
> A blank password (literally no password) or one written on a sticky note and kept handy near a computer provides no security. Always insist on nonblank passwords, and do not write down your passwords and leave them where others can find them.

(both uppercase and lowercase), and nonalphanumeric characters. It's easy to guess passwords that use common words—such as the name of a pet—and therefore they offer little in the way of real security.

Establish a method for creating strong passwords—whether it is some scheme that you think up or software that helps you create these passwords. Begin by thinking of a phrase that is easy to remember such as: "I love the Boston Red Sox." Then take the first letter of each word in that phrase and string the letters together. In our example, the result is: iltbrs. Now turn it into a more complex password by capitalizing some of the alpha characters and inserting numbers and other symbols between the letters: i-l,T.b+r-s. If this meets the minimum password requirements you have a password. Now, the trick is to remember this password without the use of sticky notes!

Security Account Basics

A security account is an account that can be assigned permission to take action on an object (such as a file, folder, or printer) or the right to take some action on an entire system, such as install device drivers into an operating system on a computer. A security account may identify a single entity (individual or computer) or a group of entities. Security accounts exist in security databases, such as those maintained by Novell servers, UNIX or Linux systems, Mac OS X desktop and server OSs, and Windows server and desktop operating systems (excluding the old Windows 9x family).

User Accounts

All operating systems discussed in this book have robust security that begins with using user and group accounts and the requirement to log in to the computer with a user account. The most common type of security account is an individual account, called a user account, and assigned to a single person. In the security database, a user account contains, at minimum, a user name and password used to authenticate a user. Depending on the structure of the security accounts database, a user account may contain additional identifying information. Typically, a user account will include the user's full name, a description, and a variety of other fields including email address, department, phone numbers, and so on. User accounts exist in all Windows security accounts databases.

Built-In User Accounts

Each OS has a very special, very privileged built-in account—a super user—that can perform virtually all tasks on a computer, from installing a device driver to creating other security accounts. In Windows this privileged built-in user is Administrator, and it is disabled by default. In those operating systems with their ancestry in UNIX—Mac OS X and Linux—root is the most powerful user account, as it is in UNIX. We'll discuss these accounts in the appropriate chapters.

At the other end of the privilege spectrum, we have a guest account, found in Windows, Mac OS X, and Linux. This account is the least privileged and is disabled by default in Windows. If this account is enabled, a stranger can log in with the account (usually with no password), but cannot see anyone else's files and cannot make changes to the system.

Account Types: Standard Versus Administrator Accounts. Linux and the versions of Windows and the Mac OS featured in this book all have the notion of types of user accounts. In Windows Vista, Windows 7, and Windows 8 a standard user account (previously called a limited account in Windows XP) is

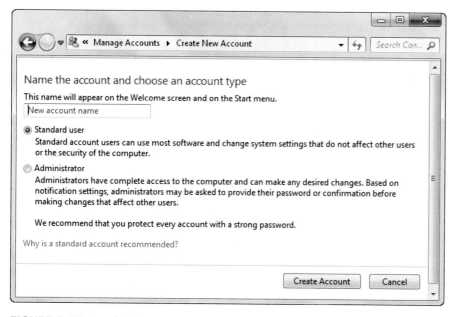

FIGURE 2–12 An administrator account may create accounts of either type.

for an "ordinary" user without administrator status. A user logged on with a standard account can change her password and other personal settings, but cannot change computer settings, install or remove software and hardware, or perform other systemwide tasks. In contrast, a user logged on with an account that is an administrator account type can perform systemwide tasks that affect the overall operating system and other users. For example, an administrator can create new users, change user settings, install applications and operating system components, install hardware (and the drivers for that hardware), and access all files on a computer. Ignoring the built-in, but disabled, Administrator account, the first account created in any of these systems must be an administrator account type, and then you may use this account to create additional accounts. Figure 2–12 shows the Windows dialog box for creating a Standard User account.

In Mac OS X, there is a check box in the Accounts dialog for a user: the "Allow user to administer this computer" check box. If this is checked, the user account is an administrator account; if it is unchecked the account is a standard account. As with the Windows administrator accounts, a Mac OS X administrator account can install programs and do a range of systemwide tasks. A Mac OS X standard user is limited much as a Windows standard user is.

The administrator type of account in Linux includes the all-powerful root, and some other accounts, but the standard account type is not as clear. For instance, "standard user" is the term used to describe the long list of accounts some distributions will create automatically if you choose a special installation. Since this includes the root account and others with a wide range of permissions, it is not the same as the standard type of account used in Windows and Mac OS X.

Group Accounts

A group account is a security account that contains one or more individual accounts, and, in some security accounts databases, may contain other groups. Group accounts allow us to manage resources for multiple users and make administration of accounts much easier. Group accounts exist in the security accounts databases of all the OSs discussed here—some are built in and privileged users can create others. We will concern ourselves only with those

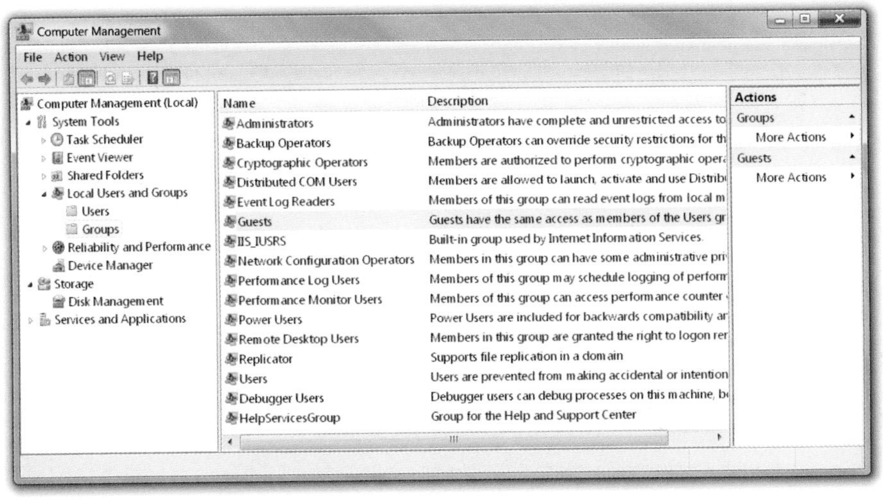

FIGURE 2–13 The Local Users and Groups node in computer management shows all groups on the local computer.

groups that exist in the security accounts database on a desktop computer and not with the security accounts that exist on a network server, such as a Windows Domain Controller. We call the accounts on a desktop computer local user and group accounts. The built-in local groups in Windows include Administrators, Users, and Guests, but other groups are created for various services and applications as they install into Windows. Figure 2–13 shows the Local Users and Groups node of the Computer Management console, an advanced tool for managing users and groups in Windows.

Computer Accounts

Computers (and sometimes devices) may also have security accounts within a security accounts database maintained by a network server, such as in a Microsoft Windows Active Directory domain. This means your computer actually joins a domain before you, as a user, can log on to the network. When this occurs, new group accounts appear in the accounts database on your desktop Windows computer as it integrates into the domain. The details of this relationship are beyond the scope of this book, but be aware that this is the case if your computer is part of a Windows Active Directory Domain. How could this affect you? If you bring your personal laptop to the office, you will not be able to log on to the corporate network in the same way that you do from your desktop until an administrator makes your computer a member of the domain. If it's not desirable to join your personal laptop to the network there are other methods to give you access to the corporate network.

User Account Control

Before Windows Vista, if you wanted to make changes to your system such as installing a new device or program, you had to log on as an administrator. This meant, if you were already logged on with an account that did not have administrative access, you would have to log off and log on again with an administrator account before you could perform a major system task. To avoid this annoyance, many people stayed logged on all day every day using an account with administrator access. This meant that if malware infected your computer, it would have full control over your computer because it would have the same level of access as the logged-on user. To prevent this, Microsoft introduced User Account Control (UAC) in Windows Vista to prevent unauthorized changes to Windows. With UAC enabled, there are two scenarios.

In the first scenario, a user logged on with a privileged account with administrative rights only has the privileges of a standard account, until the user (or a malicious program) attempts to do something that requires higher privileges. At that point, UAC makes itself known, graying out (dimming) the desktop, and displaying the Consent Prompt, as shown here. You must click Yes to continue or No to cancel the operation.

In the second scenario, a user logs on with the privileges of a standard user and attempts to do something that requires administrative privileges. In this case, UAC displays the Credentials Prompt shown here, requiring the user name and password of an account with administrative privileges. If you provide these, the program or task will run with these elevated privileges, but you will return to the standard user privileges for all other activities. In either case, if you do not respond in a short time, UAC will time out, cancel the operation, and return the desktop to you.

The Windows 7 consent prompt.

By default, UAC is turned on in Windows Vista, Windows 7, and Windows 8. Microsoft made changes beginning in Windows 7 that reduced the number of prompts you will see because it changed the number of Windows programs that require approval to run. Even with UAC turned off, Windows still may not allow you to perform all tasks and you will see a message such as "The requested operation requires elevation" when you attempt to perform certain functions.

Mac OS X also has a function similar to Windows UAC, but it is more subtle. Certain dialog boxes have a lock symbol on the lower left. It will appear locked in some instances and unlocked in others. If you are in a dialog box, such as Accounts, you will find that when the lock symbol shows it is locked you can still make certain changes, such as changing your own picture, without a problem, but unlocking the lock reveals more settings that only an administrator may change. If you wish to access the advanced settings, you simply double-click on the lock and enter the user name (it will default to the currently logged-on user) and password of an administrator account, as shown in Figure 2–14. So, even if you have logged on

The Windows 7 credentials prompt.

with an account with administrator privileges, it acts like Windows UAC by requiring you to take an extra step before making systemwide changes.

Best Practices When Assigning Permissions

The most important practice in assigning permissions to accounts in any operating system is to use the rule of least privilege. Give permissions to each user or group that allows each user the amount of access required to complete assigned tasks, but do not give users more access than required. Thus, the user has the least privileges necessary to function.

Best Practices with User Names and Passwords

You may actually have habits that make you vulnerable to identity theft or another type of attack on your computer, data, or personal information. Consider the following questions:

- Do you have too many passwords to remember?
- When you have an opportunity to create a new password, do you use your favorite password—the one that you use everywhere?

FIGURE 2–14 Unlock a dialog box in Mac OS X to access advanced settings.

- At school or work, do you have your password written on sticky notes or your desk calendar?
- Have you used the same password for more than a few months?

If you can answer yes to any of these questions, you are at risk! And the risk is not only with your password. Because many websites allow you to provide a user name to use when you log in, you may also be reusing the same user name and password combination. Now a hacker doesn't even have to guess your account name.

Don't Give Away Your User Name and Password

If you use the same user name and password at your bank as you do at a website where you took what seemed like a harmless personality test, you may have put your bank account and your other financial assets at risk. Perhaps someone created the website to surreptitiously gather just such personal information, or it may have an innocent mission, but simply employ weak security practices. Either way, the outcome may be the same—someone now has information that could allow access to your bank account. "But," you say, "I didn't provide them with my bank account information." Are you sure? If you provided any personal information to the website, they may be able to use it to search online databases (some containing information illegally gathered), and to discover, or guess, which bank you use. Then, even though the bank has much better security practices than the website you went to, you have just given someone the key (so to speak) to your assets.

Create Strong Passwords

A strong password is one that meets certain criteria, and these criteria change over time as hackers create more techniques and tools for discovering passwords. The National Institute of Standards and Technology describes a strong password as one containing no fewer than 12 characters. This was adopted as a standard by the U.S. government in 2007. However, an administrator should have a password that is a minimum of 15 characters long. Additionally, a strong password includes a combination of letters, numbers, and other symbols, as allowed by the security system accepting the password. Common sense requires that your personal password should be easy for you to remember, but difficult for others to guess.

Note: Learn more about protecting your computer with passwords. Use an Internet search engine to search on "strong passwords." You will find great tips on how to create complex passwords that are easy to recall, but hard for others to crack.

Always use strong passwords for the following types of accounts:

- Banks, investments, credit cards, and online payment providers.
- Email.
- Work-related accounts.
- Online auction sites and retailers.
- Sites where you have provided personal information.

Never Reuse Passwords

Every account should have a unique name (if possible) and a unique password (always). Many websites require your email address as the user name, so these will not be unique.

Avoid Creating Unnecessary Online Accounts

Many websites ask that you create an account and join, but what are the benefits of joining? Why do they need information about you?

Don't Provide More Information Than Necessary

Avoid creating accounts with websites that request your Social Security number and other personal and financial information. Avoid having your credit card numbers and bank account information stored on a website. Although it's not easy to do online, you can do this with a merchant in person: If asked for your Social Security number, ask these four questions:

try this!

Get Help Creating Passwords

There are programs that will help you create passwords. While we strongly recommend that you come up with your own method to create and remember strong passwords, it is helpful to see some strong passwords. Try this:

1. Open your browser and connect to your favorite search engine. Search on "random password generator" (without the quotation marks).
2. Select a password generator from the results list and experiment.
3. For instance, the Secure Password Generator on the PC Tools website (www.pctools.com/guides/password/) allows you to define the password rules and then, after you click the Generate Password button, it will generate a password that complies with the rules.
4. Try creating a password, but do not use one you generated in this fashion. Rather, devise your own scheme for creating secure passwords. Then you are more likely to remember your password.

1. Why do you need it?
2. How will you protect it?
3. How will you use it?
4. What happens if I don't give it to you?

You may have to make a decision as to whether to do business with that merchant if you don't receive satisfactory answers.

Encryption

Encryption is the transformation of data into an unreadable format (cipher text) that you can decrypt only by using a secret key or password. A secret key is a special code used to decrypt encrypted data. You can encrypt data you are sending over a network. In addition, you can encrypt data files that are stored on a local computer or network server. Encryption protects sensitive or valuable data and only someone who knows the password or holds the secret key can decrypt the data back to its original state. The secret key may be held in a digital certificate (also called a security certificate, or simply a certificate), which is a file stored on a computer.

Encrypting Network Traffic

Without being aware, you participate in encrypting network traffic when you do online banking or shopping. Look at the address line and you will see the protocol prefix "http" replaced by "https." This means that you are now using Secure HTTP (HTTPS), which encrypts the communications between you and the bank or e-commerce server. HTTPS uses the Secure Sockets Layer (SSL) security protocol. For this encryption method, the user certificates contain identifying information used for verifying the holder of the certificate (your bank or the online retailer) including the holder's public key for use in encrypting a message for the user. Only the user holds the private key to decrypt the message. Your Web browser and its security protocols manage it all for you. If the browser detects a problem with a certificate as a page is loading, you will receive a warning that a website's security certificate is invalid. You should not continue loading the page and should block this website via your browser's security settings.

Windows Encrypting File System

Encryption is very useful for data stored on a laptop or in professional settings, where data theft is a concern. The Microsoft NTFS file system allows you to encrypt selected files and folders (not an entire drive) through a feature called Encrypting File System (EFS). Turn on encryption through the Advanced button of the Properties dialog box of a folder residing on an NTFS volume, and then all files created in that folder become encrypted. Figure 2–15 shows the Advanced Attributes dialog that opens from the Advanced button on the Properties of a folder named Ch_02_Security. Clicking the check box labeled Encrypt Contents To Secure Data will turn on encryption for this folder. Anyone who is logged on with your credentials has access to EFS encrypted data. If you copy or move an encrypted file to another NTFS-formatted volume, the encryption is maintained. If you do this to a volume that is not formatted with NTFS, the file is saved without encryption.

Encrypting with Windows BitLocker

BitLocker Drive Encryption is a feature of the Ultimate and Enterprise editions of Windows Vista and Windows 7 and Windows 8 Pro and Ultimate. It allows you to encrypt an

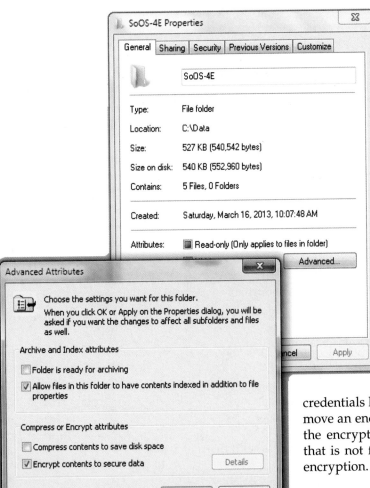

FIGURE 2–15 Turn NTFS encryption on or off using the Properties of a folder.

entire drive. You or anyone else who is logged on with your credentials has access to the encrypted drive. When using BitLocker in Windows 7 Ultimate or Enterprise or in Windows 8 Pro or Enterprise, you can use a feature called BitLocker to Go to encrypt external hard drives and flash drives. When you create a BitLocker to Go volume, you select the method for unlocking. Because this is a portable drive, you can assign a password or a smart card to unlock the drive.

Older versions of Windows cannot create a BitLocker to Go volume, but they can read them, provided the user has the means to unlock the volume, owing to the program BITLOCKERTOGO.EXE, a BitLocker to Go Reader, that is installed on each BitLocker to Go volume. You will still need to unlock the drive, using a password or smart card.

Encrypting with Mac OS X FileVault

Mac OS X has a feature called FileVault that began life as an encryption tool for all the files in your Home folder, and it has been improved in recent versions. Figure 2–16 shows the Security dialog box in which you can enable OS X FileVault. Someone logged on with your credentials can access the encrypted files.

Data Wiping

When you move computers from user to user or remove a computer from service within an organization and sell it or give it away, you should remove the data on the computer. This goes beyond a simple delete operation, because there are many methods for "undeleting" such files. To be sure that a determined person will not access your old files, you must remove them completely. The permanent removal of data from a storage device is data wiping.

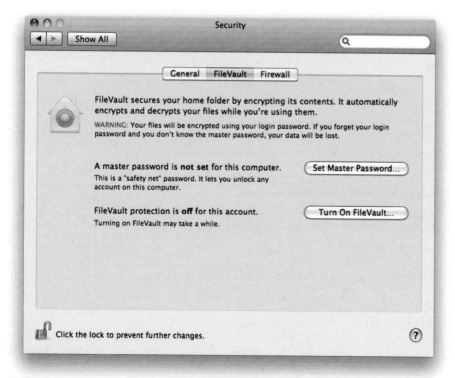

FIGURE 2–16 Configuring FileVault in Mac OS X.

A reformat of the hard drive is one method, but it's not truly very secure, and it's a problem if you wanted to keep the operating system and programs on the disk. Another method is to use data wiping software that uses an algorithm for writing over an entire drive volume, or just those portions of a drive that contain data—whether it has been deleted or not. You can perform data wiping on any storage media that is rewritable, including hard drives, optical drives, and solid-state storage. Both free and commercial data wiping programs will do the trick for most purposes. Such programs are available for all storage types. Those written for hard drives can take advantage of a government-approved ability built in to newer hard drives—Secure Erase. You cannot recover data once you have used such a data-wiping program.

Physical Security

Physical security of computers and networks is yet another huge topic that we can only touch on here. Physical security for desktop computers and networks includes limiting who has access to the building or room in which the desktop computers or network servers reside. Physical security is part of a school or other organization's security policy, and that policy must define its implementation. Small organizations often simply rely on the trustworthiness of their employees—with mixed results—while larger organizations implement formal physical security protection. This can include a mode of identifying someone trying to get entry to a building or room. This mode can be a guarded entrance with confirmation of a person's credentials, key card access, or a variety of other methods depending on the security needs of the organization. Securing laptops and other mobile devices has its own challenges, addressed next.

Security for Mobile Computing

In addition to the practices outlined above as defenses against threats, special considerations are required when traveling with laptops or other mobile computing devices. We will discuss specific security options for mobile devices in Chapter 11. Following are a few general tips.

Be Extra Wary of the Danger of Theft

The very portability of laptops and other mobile computing devices obviously makes them more susceptible to physical theft, so you should be alert to that threat and never leave them unattended while traveling.

Encrypt Sensitive and Confidential Data

In addition to applying permissions, you should further protect any sensitive data on a mobile device with encryption, if available for that device.

LO 2.3 | Troubleshooting Common Security Problems

Most apparent problems have a simple cause, and that is as true with security problems as it is with most computer-related problems. Therefore, when troubleshooting any problem, you should first ask yourself, "What is the simplest (dumbest?) thing that could cause this problem?" This will keep you from going off in a panic looking for a high-tech solution before at least considering one or more simple solutions. In this section we discuss some common security problems we have encountered and our recommended solutions.

Troubleshooting Log-On Problems

There are certain nearly universal log-on problems. They include the following.

Caps Lock Key Turned On

Everyone does it! You're in a hurry, and when you type in your user name and password, you don't notice the placement of your hands and one or both of them are incorrect. You receive an error message indicating that the user name or password is incorrect, as in Figure 2–17. No problem; you type it in again, but don't notice that you have the caps lock on. Some operating systems, including Windows Vista and Windows 7, will warn you of this, but other operating systems will not. Therefore, be careful about the placement of your hands and ensure that Caps Lock is off before entering your user name and password.

Too Many Log-On Attempts

On a bad day, like your first day back at work after a vacation, you may try several times before you enter the password correctly. If you're logging on to a corporate network, it is counting all these tries and you may exceed a limit on the number of log-on attempts. This limit is part of account policies, which you learned about earlier in this chapter. Exceeding the number of log-on attempts (account lockout threshold) may result in your user account being locked out of the computer and the network for a period of time (account lockout duration), and you will see a message similar to that in Figure 2–18. There is usually a third parameter used for account policy: the period of time after which the counter for the number of log-on attempts resets to zero.

If a message like this appears when you are trying to log on to a network at school or work, you will have to call an administrator for help. An

FIGURE 2–17 Log-on error message.

FIGURE 2–18 Log-on lockout message.

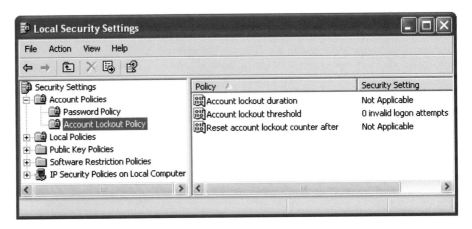

FIGURE 2–19 The Account Lockout policy with values set for lockout duration, threshold, and a period of time after which the counter resets.

administrator may be able to override the lockout so that you can try again. Type carefully this time!

If no administrator is available, you will have to wait for the account lockout time to expire. An administrator configures these settings, usually to comply with a company's security standard (see Figure 2–19). So, it could be a matter of minutes, or it could even be days! Although at the time it can be a huge inconvenience, this is your protection against password crackers, who may need to make many tries before they guess the correct password.

In the unlikely event that you receive a lockout message when attempting to log on to a stand-alone or work group Windows computer, someone will have to log on with an account that is a member of the administrators' group and modify the account lockout policy, or you will have to wait out the lockout duration period.

Using the Administrator Account in Troubleshooting

Windows has an administrator account, cleverly named Administrator. It is disabled by default, as shown in Figure 2–20. The Administrator account is enabled if your computer starts in Safe Mode and if the computer is not a member of a Windows Active Directory domain. In this case, you can log on with this account and attempt to troubleshoot the reason for the computer going into Safe Mode.

Troubleshooting a Suspected Malware Attack

If you suspect a computer is infected by a virus and you have an antivirus program installed, first use it to run a scan of all drives and memory to see if you can discover and remove the virus. If this does not discover a virus but you are still suspicious, or if you do not have an up-to-date antivirus program installed, you can connect to one of many websites that offer free online scans. An online virus scanner does not fully install, so it should not conflict with your installed security software. Just one example of such a scanner is Housecall, found at housecall.trendmicro.com. This scanner is by Trend Micro, which also offers a commercial security suite at www.trendmicro.com.

FIGURE 2–20 The Properties dialog box for the Administrator account shows it is disabled by default in Windows 7.

Perform an Online Virus Scan

Try one of the online virus scanners. All you need is a Windows computer with a Web browser and a connection to the Internet. Use the online scanner at Trend Micro, or search the Internet for another one to use.

Step 1

Open your browser and connect to http://housecall.trendmicro.com.

Step 2

On the Trend Micro HouseCall page, select the link to download the latest version of HouseCall for your operating system.

Step 3

Answer any questions, but be careful that you do not purchase or download the full version of Trend Micro (unless you intend to do so).

Step 4

When prompted, choose to run the HouseCall program, responding to any User Account Control prompt.

Step 5

Accept the terms of the license agreement.

Step 6

Follow the on-screen instructions to run the scan.

Step 7

When finished, close all open windows.

Chapter Summary

After reading this chapter and completing the exercises, you should understand the following facts about computer security.

Threats to Computers and Users

- Threats include malware, phishing, social engineering, identity theft and fraud, exposure to inappropriate or distasteful content, invasion of privacy, misuse of cookies, hoaxes, and computer hardware theft. Other threats include accidents, mistakes, and natural and unnatural disasters.

- A vector is the method that malware uses to infect a computer. Malware modes of infection include email, code on websites, Trojan horses, searching out unprotected computers, sneakernet, back doors, rootkits, pop-up downloads, drive-by downloads, war driving, and bluesnarfing.

- The people behind computer security threats come from all over the world, and increasingly they are part of organized crime. Certain terms, describing their techniques, define the individuals. These terms include hackers, crackers, script kiddies, click kiddies, and packet monkeys.

- Many methods are used to steal passwords, including capturing them from unsecured websites, using password crackers, and keystroke loggers.

Defense Against Threats

- Education is an important defense against threats. It includes knowing what the threats are and learning to recognize the signs of a threat or an infection.

- Security policies describe how an organization protects and manages sensitive information. You should follow and enforce security policies.

- You should install comprehensive security software, including (at minimum) personal firewalls, antispam software, antivirus software, and pop-up and privacy protection.

- Keep your software up to date with security patches.

- You will improve your security if you understand authentication and authorization and its implementation on your computer and in your organization.

- You can combat threats by following the rule of least privilege when assigning permissions and using best practices with user names and passwords.

- Encryption technologies protect your data.

- Data wiping practices can remove even deleted data from computers.

- Physical security of computers and networks is also important, especially for mobile computing.

Troubleshooting Common Security Problems

- Log-on failure may be the result of something as simple as having the Caps Lock key turned on. The OS can lock you out from logging on to your computer if you exceed the number of failed log-on attempts configured in the Account Lockout policy for a network or an individual computer. An administrator may need to modify the policy.

- Windows has an administrator account, "Administrator." Disabled by default, it will be enabled if your computer is not a member of a Windows Active Directory domain (the norm for a home computer) *and* it starts in Safe Mode. In that case, you can log on with this account and attempt to troubleshoot the reason for the computer going into Safe Mode.

- If you suspect a computer is infected by a virus and have an antivirus program installed, run a scan of all drives and memory. If this does not discover a virus, and you are still suspicious, connect to one of many websites that offer free online scans, such as http://housecall.trendmicro.com.

Key Terms List

administrator account type (67)	authorization (65)	botherder (45)
adware (45)	back door (42)	botnet (45)
authentication (65)	bluesnarfing (43)	browser hijacking (46)

content filter (63)	identity theft (48)	social networking (40)
cookies (50)	keylogger (44)	social networking site (40)
cybercrime (40)	keystroke logger (44)	spam (46)
data wiping (73)	limited account (66)	spam filter (60)
digital certificate (72)	malware (40)	spear fishing (47)
DMZ (58)	Parental Controls (62)	spim (46)
drive-by download (42)	password (43)	spyware (45)
email spoofing (48)	password cracker (44)	standard user account (66)
Encrypting File System (EFS) (72)	permission (65)	third-party cookie (50)
encryption (71)	phishing (46)	token (65)
exploit (40)	pop-up (42)	Trojan horse (41)
FileVault (73)	pop-up blocker (61)	user account (66)
firewall (56)	pop-up download (42)	User Account Control (UAC) (68)
first-party cookie (50)	rootkit (42)	user right (65)
forged email address (48)	scareware (41)	vector (40)
fraud (46)	secret key (71)	virus (44)
group account (67)	Secure HTTP (HTTPS) (72)	war driving (43)
guest account (66)	Secure Sockets Layer (SSL) (72)	worm (45)
header (47)	security account (66)	zero-day exploit (40)
honey pot (58)	social engineering (46)	zombie (45)
hotspot (42)	social media (40)	

Key Terms Quiz

Use the Key Terms List to complete the sentences that follow. Not all terms will be used.

1. A/an _____ defines what a user or group can do to an object such as a file or folder.

2. Programs on a website may send very small text files called _____ to a Web browser, along with a request that the Web browser save the file to disk.

3. Unsolicited email, usually sent to market a service or product (legitimate or otherwise), is called _____.

4. _____ occurs when someone collects personal information belonging to another person and uses that information fraudulently to make purchases, open new credit accounts, or even obtain new driver's licenses and other forms of identification in the victim's name.

5. In Windows, a/an _____ defines a systemwide action a user or group may perform, such as logging on to a computer or installing device drivers.

6. _____ includes authentication, plus determination of a person's level of access to a computer or a resource.

7. The EFS feature in Windows NTFS and the Mac OS X FileVault feature are both examples of _____ at the file system level.

8. _____ is verification of who you are.

9. A parent wanting to protect a child from inappropriate Web content may use _____.

10. A person or program with administrative access can install malicious code or a/an _____, which hides itself from detection within the operating system or other program code on a computer.

Multiple-Choice Quiz

1. What is the name for the defining rules and practices for protecting and managing an organization's sensitive information?
   a. Firewalls

   b. Security policies
   c. Comprehensive security software
   d. Content filtering
   e. Antivirus

2. This type of annoyance appears uninvited in a separate window when you are browsing the Web and can provide a vector for malware infections.
   a. Inline banner
   b. Pop-up
   c. Spam
   d. Adware
   e. Back door

3. With this Windows Vista/7 feature turned on (as it is by default) a logged-on user only has the privileges of a standard account, even if that user is an administrator, and must provide credentials to perform most administrative tasks.
   a. Account lockout threshold
   b. EFS
   c. Lockout policy
   d. UAC
   e. Account lockout duration

4. This term describes unsolicited messages received via instant messaging.
   a. Spam
   b. Spyware
   c. Zombie
   d. Spim
   e. Bot

5. You open your browser and, rather than pointing to your home page, it opens to a Web page advertising adware removal or antivirus software. You reconfigure the browser to point to your home page, but when you restart the browser, it again points to the wrong Web page. This behavior is a symptom of what type of malware?
   a. Spyware
   b. Worm
   c. Browser hijacking
   d. Keystroke logger
   e. Trojan horse

6. What type of malware installs on a computer without the knowledge or permission of the user, and replicates itself on the computer or throughout a network?
   a. Virus
   b. Utility
   c. Worm
   d. Scam
   e. Spim

7. What term is used for a seemingly harmless program that has malicious code hidden inside?
   a. Worm
   b. Trojan horse
   c. Antivirus
   d. Optimizer
   e. Cookie

8. What utility or feature of a browser is used to inhibit the annoying windows that open when you are browsing the Web?
   a. Content filter
   b. Firewall
   c. Antivirus
   d. Spam filter
   e. Pop-up blocker

9. Strange screen messages, sudden computer slowdown, missing data, and inability to access the hard drive may be symptoms of what?
   a. War driving
   b. Spam
   c. Encryption
   d. Virus infection
   e. Fraud

10. This device sits between a private network and the Internet (or other network) and examines all traffic in and out of the network it is protecting, blocking any traffic it recognizes as a potential threat.
    a. Router
    b. Firewall
    c. Bridge
    d. Worm
    e. Keystroke logger

11. After several failed log-on attempts, a message appears stating that your account was locked out. This is the result of exceeding this setting in Account Lockout policy on a Windows computer.
    a. Password length
    b. Account lockout threshold
    c. Account lockout duration
    d. Maximum password age
    e. Password complexity requirements

12. This type of malware is also a vector, concealing itself within the OS code and giving someone administrative access to a computer.
    a. Rootkit
    b. Pop-up download
    c. Drive-by download
    d. Worm
    e. Hoax

13. What is the term used to describe the use of persuasion to gain the confidence of individuals?
    a. Hoax
    b. Fraud
    c. Phishing
    d. Social engineering
    e. Enticement

14. What term describes the action of a password cracker who simply tries a huge number of permutations of possible passwords?
    a. Keystroke logging
    b. Brute force

c. Statistical analysis
d. Mathematical analysis
e. Phishing

15. This firewall technology inspects each packet that enters or leaves the protected network, applying a set of security rules defined by a network administrator; packets that fail are not allowed to cross into the destination network.
    a. Proxy service
    b. VPN
    c. IP packet filter
    d. Encrypted authentication
    e. DMZ

Essay Quiz

1. Explain automatic log-in and why you should not allow it in a situation in which you require security.

2. Consider the following statement: User Account Control limits the damage that someone can do who accesses your computer when automatic log-in is enabled. Elaborate on this statement, describing why it is true, and why there is still a great risk.

3. Why should you disable the Guest account?

4. In your own words, describe why the use of Internet cookies can be an invasion of privacy.

5. Differentiate between permission and user right.

Lab Projects

These Lab Projects ask you to research various topics. In your answers, please provide links to websites you discovered that support your essay or project responses.

LAB PROJECT 2.1

Research identity theft/fraud to answer the following questions.

1 What is the estimated cost of identity theft/fraud in the United States in a recent year? What is the trend compared to previous years?

2 Identity theft can involve computers, but in many cases, computers play only a small part in identity theft. Find a recent article on an identity theft ring and describe how the thieves operated.

3 Share your findings with others in your class and compare the information you found.

LAB PROJECT 2.2

Research the latest malware threats. Many organizations, including antivirus vendors and security services, post information on the Internet about the latest malware threats. Use an Internet search engine to research the latest threats, which you may find at one of the top security software manufacturers, such as McAfee or Symantec. Using the information from one of these sites, make a list of five current threats and research each to learn more about it. Briefly describe each threat and how you will use security software or behavior to defend your computer from each one.

LAB PROJECT 2.3

Organizations require trained specialists to keep their computers and networks secure. One way prospective employers can determine how much someone knows about security is by requiring job applicants to hold certain appropriate security certifications that require study, experience, and passing exams. Find and research a security certification and give a brief description of this certification, including the organization that is behind this certification, who should seek it, what domains (topics) are included in the exam, and the job titles this certification would apply to.

chapter

3 Desktop Virtualization

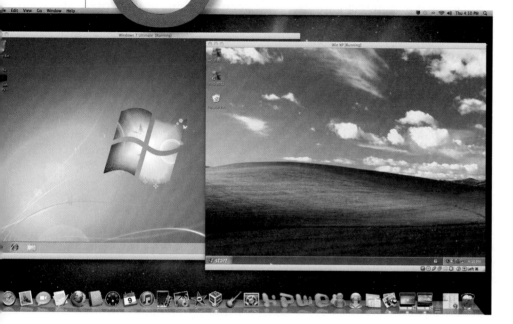

"The machine invades me all day."

—Sharon Atkins

U.S. receptionist. As quoted in Working, book 2, by Studs Terkel (1973)

In the 1990s if you wanted to test a new version of Windows or try a Linux distribution, you had to dedicate an entire computer to this task. Similarly, in the mid-1990s when preparing to teach classes on the latest Windows server OSs, a Microsoft Certified Trainer (MCT) needed several computers to create the same mix of desktop computers and servers the trainer would encounter in the classroom. Likewise, in the mid-1990s, classes for Novell administrators and engineers required that you pair a server and client computer at each desk, so students could experience setting up a server and configuring a client to connect to that server.

As the 1990s ended and the new millennium began, virtualization of operating systems evolved, allowing us to simultaneously run multiple operating systems on a single computer. The student experience changed, as instructors configured classes in which each participant worked with servers and clients—all on a single PC. Today, all you need in addition to specialized virtualization software is a computer with the processing power and enough RAM and hard drive space to support the number, and types, of OSs you wish to run. You also need appropriate licenses for all the software you run, including the OSs running in the virtual machines.

In this chapter we explore the exploding phenomenon of OS virtualization, and prepare you to install the desktop OSs described in this book into virtual machines (VMs). This will save you the cost and physical desktop space of working with multiple physical computers. 🟤

Learning Outcomes

In this chapter, you will learn how to:

LO **3.1** Describe the various types of virtualization used in everyday computing and ways you might use desktop virtualization.

LO **3.2** Select and install a desktop virtualization option for a Windows desktop host computer.

LO **3.3** Select and install a desktop virtualization option for a Mac OS X host computer.

LO 3.1 | Virtualization Overview

In this section, we define virtualization and many of the terms associated with it, describe its background, and discuss how it has led to the virtualization of desktop operating systems.

Virtualization Is Everywhere

Virtualization is the creation of an environment that seems real, but isn't, and today it seems like virtualization is everywhere in the computing world. There are many types. You can spend time in a virtual world, such as Second Life (see Figure 3–1). A virtual world often lets a user select an animated computer-generated human, an avatar, to represent him or her within it. People use virtual worlds in online training, marketing of products, and in games of many types. When this virtual world includes three-dimensional images and involves other senses, giving the participant a feeling of actually being present in that time and space, we call it virtual reality.

Many organizations use storage virtualization in which client computers can utilize many networked hard drives as though they are one. Network engineers work with network virtualization involving a network addressing space that exists within one or more physical networks, but which is logically independent of the physical network structure. Then there is server virtualization, in which a single machine hosts multiple servers, each of which performs tasks as independently from the others as separate physical machines would. Companies that provide low-cost web hosting services can create a separate virtual web server for each customer.

With only a small leap from these we come to desktop virtualization, the virtualization of a desktop computer into which you can install an operating system, its unique configuration, and all the applications and data normally used by a single person. This virtual desktop may reside on a server, allowing a user to access it from a computer with specialized client software, or it may exist on the local computer.

Each individual virtual environment in both server virtualization and desktop virtualization is a virtual machine—the software emulation of all hardware with which an operating system must interact. But wait, there's more! There is application virtualization, in which a user connects to a server and accesses one

FIGURE 3–1 An avatar (at center bottom) walks on a London street in Second Life.

or more applications rather than an entire desktop environment. This chapter is devoted to today's desktop virtualization, but first we will look at the past.

Your (Great?) Grandfather's Virtual Machines

Today's virtual machines have a long pedigree: They can trace their roots back to the 1960s when mainframe computer manufacturers, such as IBM, routinely created multiple discrete environments on a single computer. A user connected using a dumb terminal that was little more than a keyboard and display with a connection to a host computer (mainframe or minicomputer), but it had little or no native processing power (hence the term *dumb*).

A dumb terminal would connect to the host computer, sending keystrokes, and displaying the keystrokes and responses on the display. During a single terminal session, a user would connect to a discrete area on the host called a partition. The partition to which each user connected was not like today's virtual machines, but was an area where the user had access to programs and data. After the advent of the IBM PC in the 1980s, a PC configured to emulate a dumb terminal often replaced the dumb terminal.

For years, this model prevailed for those organizations that wished to have a centralized system where all the programs and data resided, with the individual users connecting from whatever served as a terminal. The 1990s implementation of this model included servers or minicomputers running terminal services to which users connected nearly seamlessly to partitions from their desktop PCs using terminal client software. These were not, however, virtual machines because the entire hardware and operating system environment was not part of the partition to which users connected. They did not have a fully configurable desktop operating system, such as Windows, to work with beyond their application and data.

A 1970s-era computer terminal.

Today's Virtual Desktops

In the past decade or so, many large organizations have adopted the thin client for their desktop users. A thin client is a dedicated terminal or software installed on a PC. In either case, a thin client usually lacks such common peripherals as expansion slots and optical drives. The purpose of a thin client is to connect to a server, allowing the user to work in a server-hosted environment. When that environment provides the entire OS experience and the working applications it becomes a virtual desktop, or a full virtual machine. This virtual machine may reside on a server and be accessed by a client computer (thin or not), or it may reside on a desktop computer. This allows the interactive user (the one sitting in front of that computer) to switch between the host OS, the operating system installed directly on the computer, and one or more guest OSs, the operating systems running within a virtual machine.

The term used today for hosting and managing multiple virtual desktops on network servers is virtual desktop infrastructure (VDI). The term is attributed to the VMware company in distinguishing its virtual desktop server products from the products offered by competitors, specifically Citrix and Microsoft, products that did not provide a full desktop environment. Today VDI applies to any server product that provides the full virtual desktop support.

Type I and Type II Hypervisors

Note: Microsoft Hyper-V Server and VMware vSphere are examples of competing Type 1 hypervisors used on servers.

A hypervisor, also called a virtual machine monitor (VMM), is the software layer that emulates the necessary hardware on which an operating system runs. The hardware virtualization allows multiple operating systems to run simultaneously on a single computer, such as a network server. Each hypervisor normally emulates a computer separate from the underlying computer, but it must use a virtual processor compatible with that of the underlying machine—mainly either an Intel processor or an AMD processor. There are two types of hypervisors, Type I and Type II. A Type I hypervisor—sometimes called a bare-metal hypervisor—can run directly on a computer without an underlying host operating system. A Type II hypervisor requires a host operating system.

Type I hypervisors first appeared on high-powered servers. At the time, desktop computers lacked the hardware support required for virtualization of some hardware. Of course, that was not a big hurdle, and now bare-metal hypervisors are available from the major hypervisor manufacturers—notably Citrix and VMware. Both companies offer a selection of products that centrally manage desktop virtual machines, delivered to the desktop (laptop or PC) over a network. Learn more at www.citrix.com and at www.vmware.com.

Most of the hypervisors we use in our examples in this chapter are Type II hypervisors requiring an underlying operating system. Whatever hypervisor you use, you will find more and more organizations deploying server-based virtual machines that are the users' everyday work environment. The reason for this is easier central management of the operating systems and user environment.

Note: If your computer's documentation indicates that the processor supports virtualization but a hypervisor requiring this fails to install due to lack of support, look in the documentation for instructions on enabling this feature.

You have several choices for Type II hypervisors for desktops, but today some of these run only on computers with hardware-assisted virtualization features, which means they require a computer with either the Intel Virtualization Technology for x86 (Intel VT-x) or AMD Virtualization (AMD-V) architecture extensions, which improve the performance of virtual machines on the host. Some hypervisors, such as the one that comes with Windows 8, requires even newer features. You can install a Type II hypervisor on your desktop and test another operating system without the expense of a separate computer. Figure 3–2 shows Windows 7 running in a virtual machine on a Mac OS X OS.

FIGURE 3–2 A Windows 7 client OS running in a virtual machine in OS X on an Apple computer.

There are several choices of desktop Type II hypervisors, depending on both the hosting OS and the desired guest OSs. The ones we will discuss in this chapter all have several things in common; they are the tasks required to create a virtual machine, the order in which you do them, and how the host and guest OSs share the mouse and keyboard.

1. Prepare the host computer:
   - If this is the first time you have installed this hypervisor, select a computer that is not important for your everyday work.
   - Confirm that the computer's hardware and operating system meet the minimum requirements for hosting the hypervisor you intend to install.
   - Back up your hard drive in case something goes wrong.
   - Remove any conflicting software.
   - If you decide to install two or more different hypervisors on a single host system, know that you cannot run different hypervisors at the same time, although you can have multiple virtual machines active in the same hypervisor.

2. Install the hypervisor, such as Oracle's VirtualBox hypervisor (see Figure 3–3).

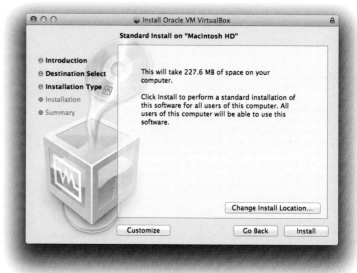

FIGURE 3–3 Installing a hypervisor.

3. Install a virtual machine, selecting from a list of guest OSs that the hypervisor supports. Each hypervisor has default settings for each OS, based on the minimum requirements of the guest OS. Installation of a virtual machine creates a number of files on the host. One is a virtual machine file containing all the settings; another is a virtual hard drive file containing all the operating system files, installed program files, and data created from within the virtual machine and appearing as a hard drive (usually drive C:) when the virtual machine is running. Other files, such as log files, may be created at this time.

4. Install the guest OS. This normally requires the full retail version of the OS on disc, although there are exceptions. One exception is that you can bring in compatible precreated virtual machines. You must have a legal license or a trial version for each guest OS.

5. Install appropriate utilities for the guest OS. The hypervisor publisher provides these utilities, and they include special software for making a virtual machine work better for the guest, especially the GUI. Depending on the hypervisor in use, it may prompt you to install the guest utilities the first time you run each guest OS, and you may be notified of updates to the installed guest utilities.

6. Finally, once you have an OS installed into a virtual machine, you need to realize that the guest OS and host OS are sharing the same physical hardware, and certain things aren't easy for a user to share. The keyboard and mouse are good examples of hardware that can serve only one master at a time. Normally, you give a VM control of a mouse by moving the pointer into the VM and clicking inside the guest window. The virtual machine captures the mouse and keyboard, giving the VM the focus. To release the mouse and keyboard, there is a host key, which varies in each hypervisor. In VirtualBox on a Mac, it is the left Command key, while in Virtual PC it is the right Alt key. You will normally see a message about the host key during the installation or the first time you run the guest OS. Make sure you write down what key or key combination is the host key and keep the information handy. Practice using it right away.

Major Hypervisor Sources

The major hypervisor manufacturers are Citrix, VMware, Parallels, Microsoft, and Oracle. There are many other players in the field, described in articles and reviews in technical publications and websites.

LO 3.2 | Virtual Machines on Windows Desktops

You have several options—both paid for and free—for running Linux, DOS, or Windows on a Windows desktop computer. At this writing you cannot run any version of Mac OS X in a VM on a PC, due more to licensing issues than technical issues. The hypervisors we describe here for Windows hosts are free. Three are from Microsoft (Virtual PC 2007, Virtual PC, and Client Hyper-V) and one is from Oracle (VirtualBox).

Microsoft does not require that you register with it to acquire a free Microsoft Windows desktop hypervisor. However, the installation program will verify that your host OS is a legitimate version of Windows before the Microsoft virtualization products will install.

Microsoft Virtual PC 2007 for VMs on Old Versions of Windows

Microsoft Virtual PC 2007, as its name implies, is an older version of Microsoft's hypervisor. It will install and run on certain editions of Windows XP, Windows Server 2003, and Windows Vista. You can create VMs and install other versions of Windows, Linux, and DOS. An important distinction between Microsoft Virtual PC 2007 and its successor, Windows Virtual PC (discussed next), is that the former does not require a CPU that supports hardware virtualization, while Windows Virtual PC does require this support.

If you are interested in using Microsoft Virtual PC 2007, browse to the Virtual PC 2007 page in the Microsoft Download Center and check out the system requirements. The requirements list uses the term *x64* (or *x86-64*) to refer to a PC (processor, motherboard, and other components) that conforms to the 64-bit architecture required to run 64-bit operating systems and applications. If you are unsure of the edition of Windows or the system type of your computer (32-bit or 64-bit), open the Start menu, right-click on Computer, and select Properties. The System Type will tell you if it is a 32-bit or 64-bit operating system.

try this!

Download Microsoft Virtual PC 2007

You can download Virtual PC 2007 from the Microsoft site. This requires a high-speed broadband connection, but the 30 MB file should take only a minute or two to download. Try this:

1. Use a search engine to locate the Microsoft download page for Windows Virtual PC 2007.
2. Select the appropriate architecture version for your operating system (32-bit or 64-bit), and begin the download (find this information in the System Control Panel applet).
3. Verify that you saved the file, presently named "setup.exe," to the Downloads folder or to the location you selected.
4. You are ready to install Virtual PC 2007 on your Windows computer.

The Try This! describes the steps for downloading Microsoft Virtual PC 2007.

Step-by-Step 3.01 will walk you through installing Microsoft Virtual PC 2007 on a Windows XP or Windows Vista computer.

Step-by-Step 3.01

Installing Microsoft Virtual PC 2007 into Windows XP or Windows Vista

Using the file you downloaded in the Try This! or a file provided to you by your instructor, install Microsoft Virtual PC 2007 on your Windows XP or Windows Vista computer. For our example, we will use Windows Vista. To complete this exercise you will need the following:

- A computer running Windows Vista with a minimum of 2 GB of RAM installed.
- The username and password of an administrator account for this computer.
- A broadband Internet connection.

Step 1

Locate and double-click the installation program (setup.exe). This will start the Microsoft Virtual PC 2007 Wizard.

Step 2

Click Next on the Welcome page and follow the instructions on the following page, including accepting the License Agreement.

Step 3

Enter the Username (this does not need to match your user account name) and Organization information in the Customer Information page. Notice that Microsoft automatically entered the Product Key on this page and grayed it out, so you cannot change it.

Step 4

Click Next on the Customer Information page. On the Ready to Install the Program page, notice the location in which the program will install. You will normally allow it to install in the default location, but if you need to change this, click the Change button and browse to another location. When you are ready to have the installation begin, click the Install button.

Step 5

The Installing Microsoft Virtual PC 2007 page shows the status of the installation with a progress bar. When the installation is complete, the Next button will become active; click it to proceed to the Installation Complete page.

Step 6

Click the Next button when the progress bar shows that the installation is complete. On the Installation Complete page, click Finish.

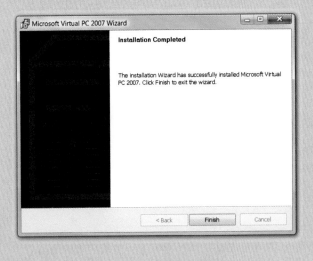

Step 7

Verify that Microsoft Virtual PC 2007 was installed by clicking Start | All Programs. Microsoft Virtual PC will be highlighted as a new program.

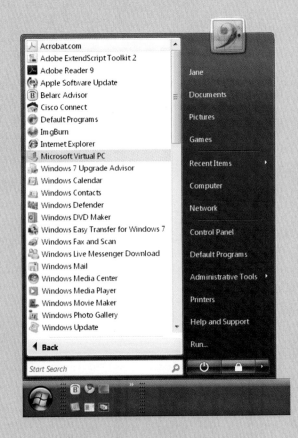

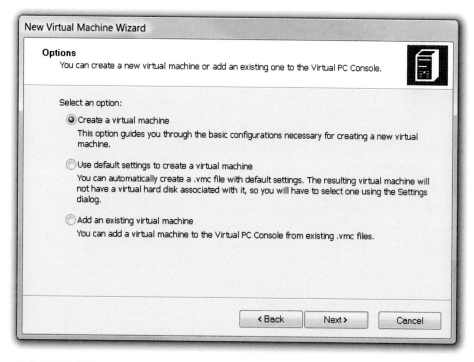

FIGURE 3–4 Select the correct option.

Once you have installed Virtual PC 2007, the next step is creating a virtual machine appropriate for the first operating system you wish to install. Begin by launching Virtual PC 2007 from Start | All Programs. This launches the New Virtual Machine Wizard. On the Welcome page click the Next button. On the Options page, there are three choices, as shown in Figure 3–4. The first choice lets you create a virtual machine, allowing you to customize the configuration beyond the bare minimum for the operating system you will install. This includes both the virtual machine (saved in a .vmc file) and the virtual hard disk (saved in a .vhd file). We prefer to use this when creating a virtual machine. The second option is quicker; however, it creates a virtual machine with the default settings, but no virtual hard disk. You would choose this if you wanted only a minimally configured virtual machine and will use a previously created virtual hard disk. The third option lets you add a preexisting virtual machine, which means you need an existing .vmc file.

If you select the first option to create a virtual machine and click Next, the Virtual Machine name and Location page appears. Enter a meaningful name—such as the name of the OS you plan to install, as shown in Figure 3–5. Use the Browse button only if you want to specify a location other than the default location. Click Next, and in the Operating System page, select the operating system you plan to install. Figure 3–6 shows this page with the drop-down box open and displaying the list of supported Guest OSs. Select Other if you wish to install DOS or Linux.

After you select an OS, click Next to proceed to the Memory page where you may either keep the default setting for the selected OS or choose to adjust the amount of RAM used by the virtual machine and click Next to move to the Virtual Hard Disk Options page. Select the option to create a new virtual hard disk and click Next.

On the Virtual Hard Disk Location page, keep the indicated disk location, unless you wish to move it to a drive with more space. Then click Next to continue. The Completing the New Virtual Machine Wizard page displays a summary of the choices you made. Double-check the choices and if they are

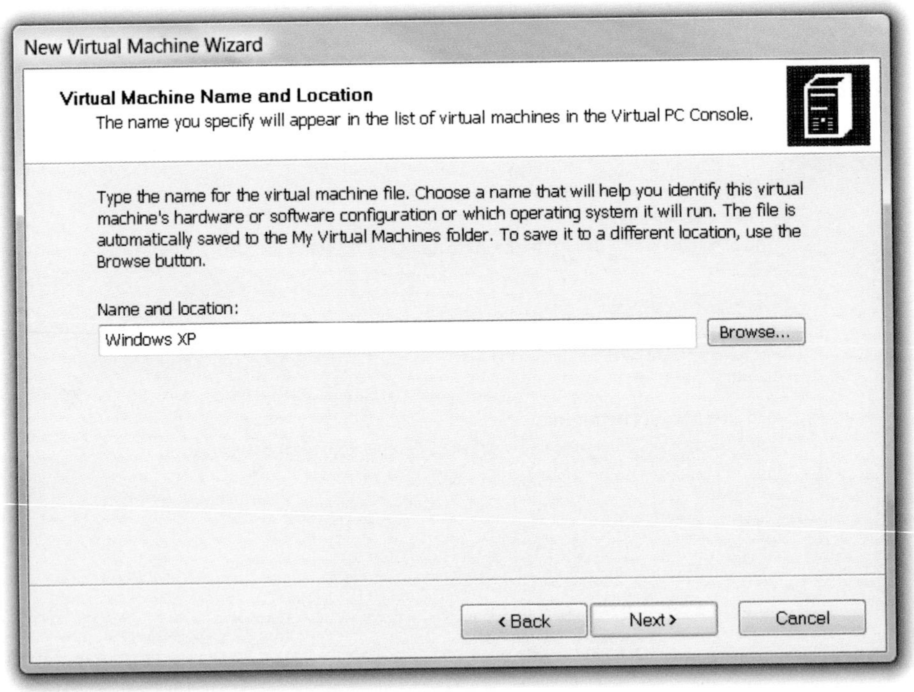

FIGURE 3–5 Enter a name for the virtual machine.

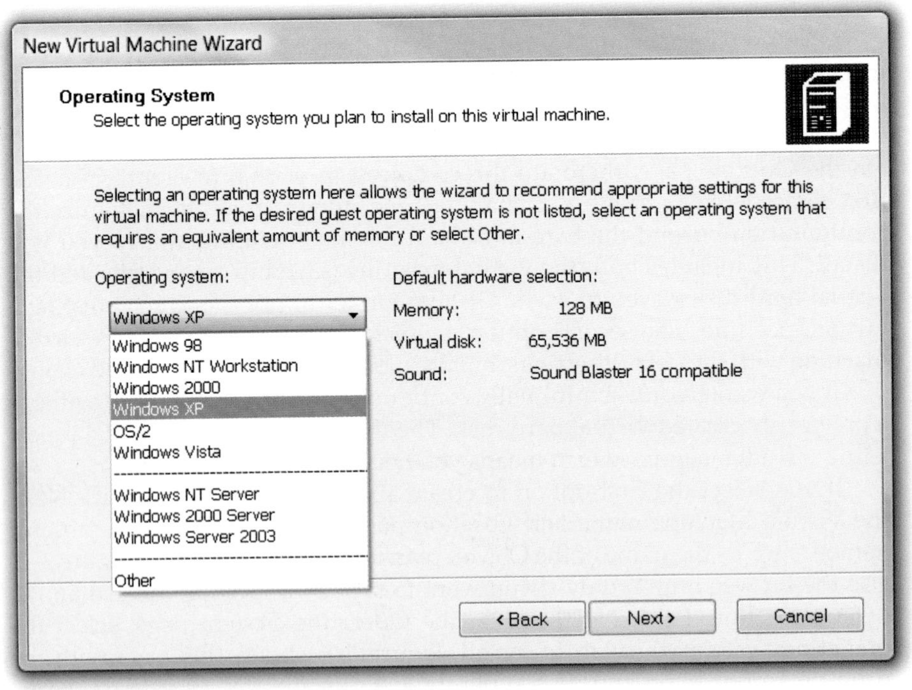

FIGURE 3–6 Select from the list of supported OSs.

OK, click Finish. You can configure several virtual machines—even before you begin installing the guest operating systems. The Virtual PC Console will list all the virtual machines, as shown in Figure 3–7.

Once you have configured a virtual machine, you are ready to install an OS into it. You will need the distribution disc for the OS you wish to install. You can also provide the file in ISO form. Let's assume you have the disc. Before beginning, place this disc in the host computer's optical drive.

FIGURE 3–7 The Virtual PC Console with four virtual machines.

To start an OS installation, open Virtual PC from the Start menu which now opens the Virtual PC Console. Select the virtual machine for your OS and then click the Start button. This is the equivalent of turning on your PC. A window will open, and at first the background will be black while it loads the virtual system BIOS. This generally happens so fast that you cannot even read what displays there. It will then boot from your disc, starting the OS installation. From there, you install the OS just as you would on a physical machine, following the instructions in the setup program.

Windows XP Mode and Windows Virtual PC on Windows 7

Microsoft provides both Windows XP Mode and Windows Virtual PC as free, optional components of Windows 7. The main purpose of Windows XP Mode for Windows 7 is to run legacy Windows XP applications that will not run well in Windows 7. It uses a runtime version of Windows Virtual PC. You can install Windows XP Mode and/or Windows Virtual PC. Once installed, these features appear on the Start menu, as shown in Figure 3–8.

Microsoft recommends Windows XP Mode and Windows Virtual PC for small and midsize businesses with Windows 7 desktops. For larger organizations Microsoft recommends Microsoft Enterprise Desktop Virtualization (MED-V), which is a server-based, centrally managed desktop virtualization.

With Windows Virtual PC you can also create VMs to run other guest systems, including Windows Vista, Windows 2000, and most versions of Linux. Once installed, it is so well-integrated into

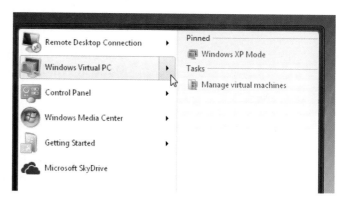

FIGURE 3–8 The Start menu showing Windows Virtual PC and Windows XP Mode.

The Windows Features Control Panel showing Windows Virtual PC available, but not enabled.

try this!

See if Windows Virtual PC or Windows XP Mode is enabled on your computer. Try this:

1. In the Start menu's Search box enter "windows features."

2. In the search results list select Turn Windows Features on or off. This opens the Windows Features dialog box.

3. In the Windows Features dialog box, the features list alphabetically. Scroll down to see if Windows Virtual PC is listed. If it is not, you will need to connect to the Microsoft site and install it. If it is listed but not checked, you will need to check it to initiate the installation. Then follow the instructions.

Windows 7 that you can start programs installed in the Windows Virtual PC VM from Start menu shortcuts of the host OS. Beyond that, if you have a certain data-file type that you prefer to run in a program that is in the VM, you can assign that file type to the program in the host. Then, double-clicking on such a data file will launch the VM and the program within it.

Only three editions of Windows 7 support Windows Virtual PC and Windows XP Mode. They are Windows 7 Professional, Enterprise, and Ultimate. You may only need to enable them in the Windows Features Control Panel, shown here. The Try This! will show you how to locate this dialog box and determine if Windows Virtual PC is listed. We will look at Windows XP Mode and Virtual PC separately.

Downloading and Installing Windows XP Mode in Windows 7

If you cannot start the installation of Windows XP Mode from the Windows Features dialog, you will need to connect to the Windows XP Mode Download page at Microsoft.com. Step-by-Step 3.02 describes how to do this.

Using Windows XP Mode

When Windows XP Mode launches for the first time you will see a security warning stating that you need to install an antivirus. However, before you can do that, you may need to update the Internet Explorer browser, as shown by this message in Internet Explorer. Follow the instructions to do so.

Downloading and Installing Windows XP Mode

Complete this exercise using a computer running one of the supported versions of Windows 7: Professional, Enterprise, or Ultimate.

Step 1

Open your browser and use a search engine, such as Google or Bing, to search on "windows xp mode download." Select the link to the correct download page at the Microsoft Download Center.

Step 2

Look for the words "Validation Required," and below that under Quick Details, click the Continue button to download and install the validation program to confirm that you are running a legal copy.

Step 3

This will take you to the Genuine Windows Validation page with two numbered steps. Click the green Continue button under step 1.

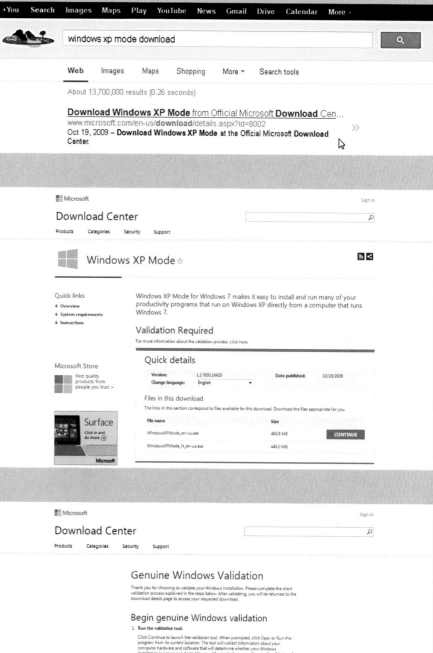

Step 4

You will then see a dialog in which you can click the Save File button to save the GenuineCheck. exe file that will then download to your Downloads folder.

Opening GenuineCheck.exe

You have chosen to open:

📄 **GenuineCheck.exe**

    which is a: Binary File (1.5 MB)

    from: http://download.microsoft.com

Would you like to save this file?

Save File   Cancel

Step 5

When it is complete, open the folder and double-click on the file named GenuineCheck. An Open File—Security Warning dialog box will open. Click the Run button. If your software is legal, you will see a message like this with a validation code. Click the Copy to Clipboard button and return to the Genuine Windows Validation page.

Windows Genuine Advantage

Copy and paste or type this code into the box in Step 2. Then click Validate. Once the code has been accepted, close this Window.

83GP7PTV   Copy to Clipboard

Step 6

Click in the Validate box (see illustration in step 3), right-click, and from the context menu select Paste, which will insert the validation code in the box.

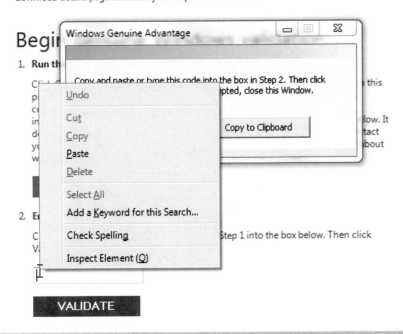

Genuine Windows Validation

Thank you for choosing to validate your Windows installation. Please complete the short validation process explained in the steps below. After validating, you will be returned to the download details page to access your requested download.

Begin

1. **Run th**

    C   this

    p

    c

    in   low. It

    d   tact

    y   bout

    w

Windows Genuine Advantage

Copy and paste or type this code into the box in Step 2. Then click ...epted, close this Window.

Undo

Cut

Copy

Paste

Delete

Select All

Add a Keyword for this Search...

Check Spelling

Inspect Element (Q)

Copy to Clipboard

2. **E**

    C   Step 1 into the box below. Then click

    V

VALIDATE

Step 7

Once the code is in the box, click the Validate button.

2. Enter your validation code.

Copy and paste or type the code provided in Step 1 into the box below. Then click Validate.

5B3HVBG6

VALIDATE

Step 8

The Windows XP Mode Download page displays once again and shows the title "Genuine Microsoft Software" in place of "Validation Required." You can now download XP Mode. Notice the two Download buttons: one for the United States English version (WindowsXPMode_en-us.exe) and one for the United Kingdom English version (WindowsXPMode_N_en-us.exe). Click the Download button by the correct version of XP Mode for your system.

Step 9

When you see the prompt shown here, click the Save File button. This will download and copy the file to your Downloads folder. If may take several minutes if you have a slow Internet connection.

Opening WindowsXPMode_en-us.exe

You have chosen to open:

WindowsXPMode_en-us.exe

which is a: Binary File (470 MB)

from: http://download.microsoft.com

Would you like to save this file?

Save File   Cancel

Step 10

If you open the Downloads folder and see two files with names that begin with "WindowsXPMode" and one has zero bytes, then the download has not completed. Wait until one of the files disappears and the other shows the size indicated on the Downloads page. Then double-click on the file to launch.

Step 11

In the Security Warning dialog box, click the Run button. The files will then extract and the Windows XP Mode Setup wizard will display. Click the Next button and accept the defaults for the location, clicking Next.

Step 12

The wizard now installs the virtual hard disk file and, at this point, if User Account Control is enabled, you will see a User Account Control dialog box. Respond to this with a Yes (Consent box) or with credentials (Credentials box) to continue. When setup is finished, you will see the Setup Completed page of the wizard. Click Finish.

Step 13

However, it is not really finished. Yes. If this is the first time Windows XP Mode has been installed on this computer, you will see the License Agreement page. Click to place a check in the box labeled "I accept the license terms," and click the Next button.

Step 14

In the Installation folder and credentials page enter and confirm a password for the XPMUser and leave a check in the box labeled "Remember credentials (Recommended)." Click Next.

In the Help Protect Your Computer page leave the first button checked to turn on Automatic Updates for this installation of Windows XP. Click Next.

On the page titled "Setup will share the drives on this computer with Windows XP Mode" click the Start Setup button. Then Windows XP Mode Setup will continue in earnest, displaying a progress bar at the bottom of a window with messages about Windows XP Mode.

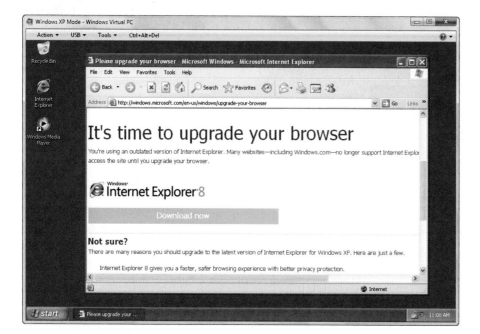

Upgrade Internet Explorer.

Once you have upgraded Internet Explorer, browse to a site where you can download and install an antivirus. We suggest installing the free Microsoft Security Essentials (MSE), which you can find by searching on the name in a search engine and selecting the download site at Microsoft.com. Follow the instructions to install MSE. After you install an antivirus, open Security Center in Windows XP Mode, and it should look like Figure 3–9. Windows XP Mode is now ready for you to install apps.

Removing Windows XP Mode

To remove Windows XP Mode open the Programs and Features Control Panel, locate Windows XP Mode in the list of programs and double-click on it. It will delete the XP Mode virtual hard disk and all data saved to the disk. It will not delete data you saved on the host drive.

If you also installed the full Windows Virtual PC, removing Windows XP Mode will not remove the hypervisor.

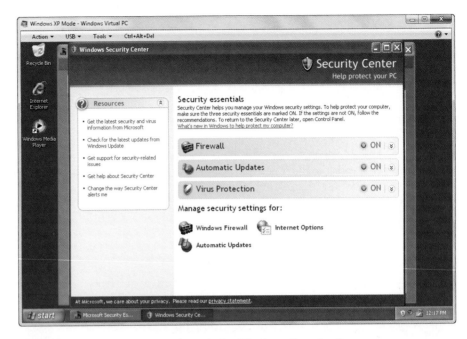

FIGURE 3–9 Windows XP Mode with the Windows Security Center open.

Installing Windows Virtual PC in Windows 7

If you cannot initiate Windows Virtual PC through the Windows Features dialog, connect to the Windows Virtual PC page in the Microsoft Download Center (shown in Figure 3–10). Click the Continue button and follow the instructions to validate your Windows software, which are identical to steps 3 through 7 in Step-by-Step 3.2.

After you successfully validate your version of Windows, you will return to the download page, which now says "Genuine Microsoft Software" in place

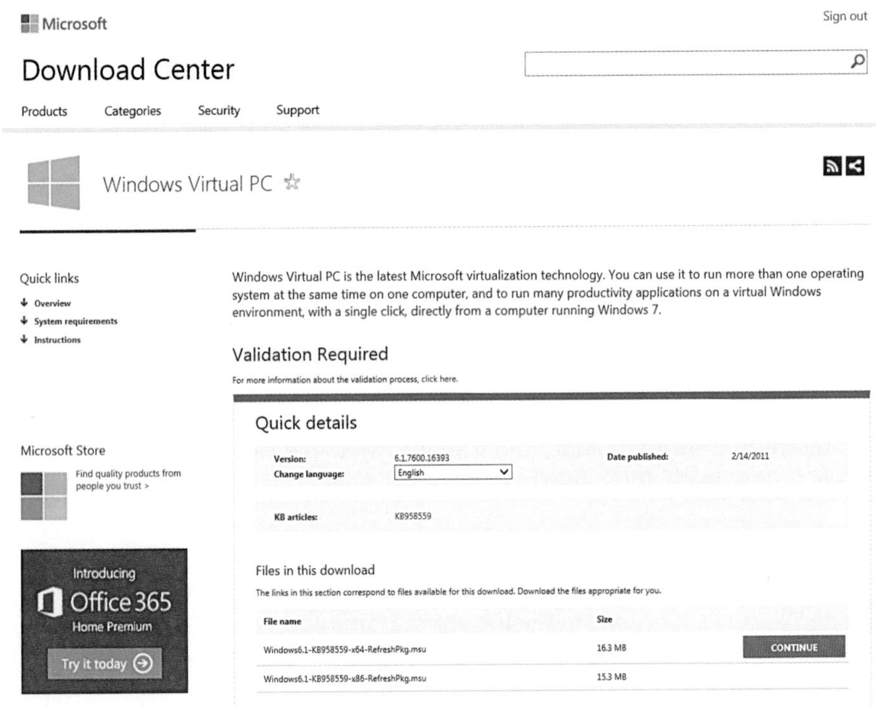

FIGURE 3–10 The Windows Virtual PC Download page with Validation Required.

of "Validation Required." Now locate the correct file. If you are running 64-bit Windows 7, select the file with "x64" in its name. If you are running 32-bit Windows 7, select the file with "x86" in its name. Click the Download button by the correct file.

A dialog box will give you the choice of opening or saving the file. Select Open and click OK. Follow the prompts after that, including allowing the system to restart. After it restarts, go to the Start menu, where Windows Virtual PC is listed. Click it and the Virtual Machines folder will open with a bar that includes a button (shown here) labeled Create Virtual Machine.

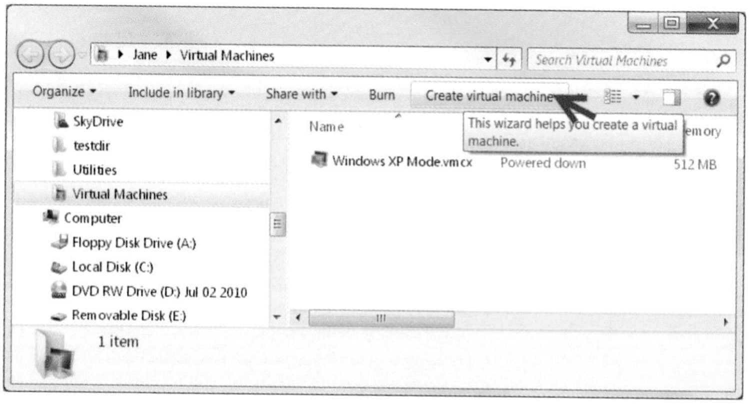

Click the Create Virtual Machine button to open the Create Virtual Machine Wizard. On the first page, enter the name for the new virtual machine. In this example, we use a name that identifies the OS we plan to install. Leave the location as is and click the Next button.

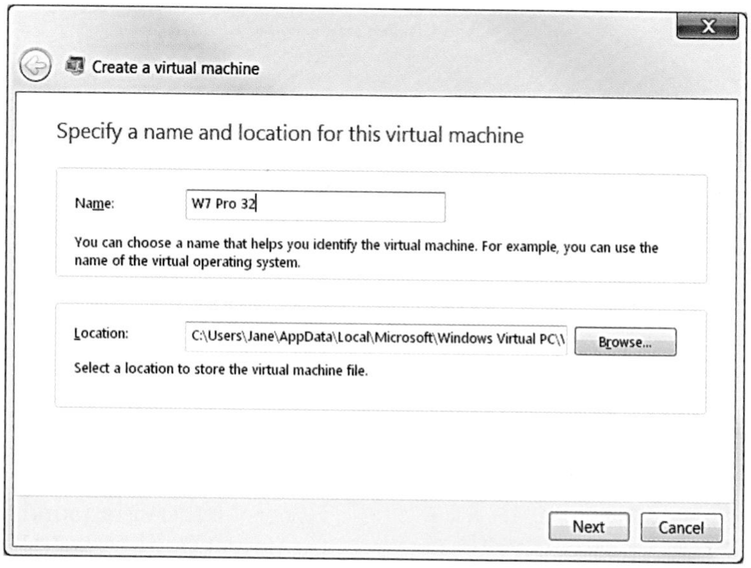

On the next page, enter the amount of memory required and whether you want the VM to use the computer network connections. On the Add a Virtual Hard Disk page select the first option and click Create. It creates a virtual machine and you are now ready to install a new OS into the virtual machine. It lists the virtual machines you create in the Virtual Machines folders. Figure 3–11 shows the Virtual Machines folder with several virtual machines listed. You can launch one of these virtual machines by double-clicking it.

Click the Create Virtual Machine button.

Enter a name for the new virtual machine.

Removing Windows Virtual PC

Windows Virtual PC is installed as an update to Windows 7, so to remove it, you must go into the Programs and Features Control Panel, select View Installed Updates, and then in the Installed Updates page scroll down to the Microsoft Windows category, as shown in Figure 3–12. Double-click Windows

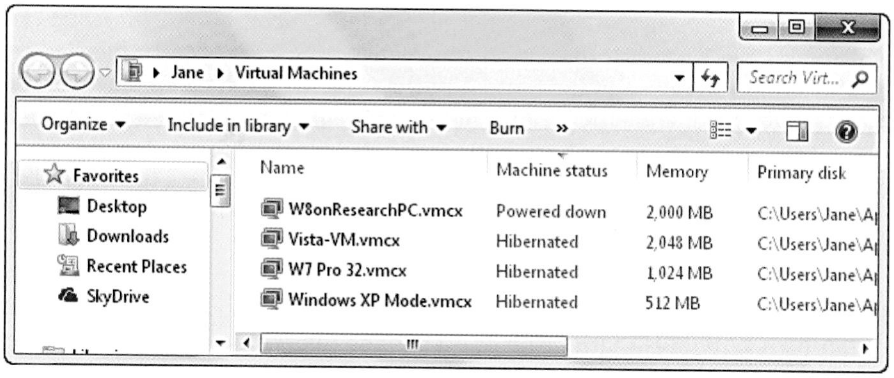

FIGURE 3–11 The Virtual Machines folder with several VMs.

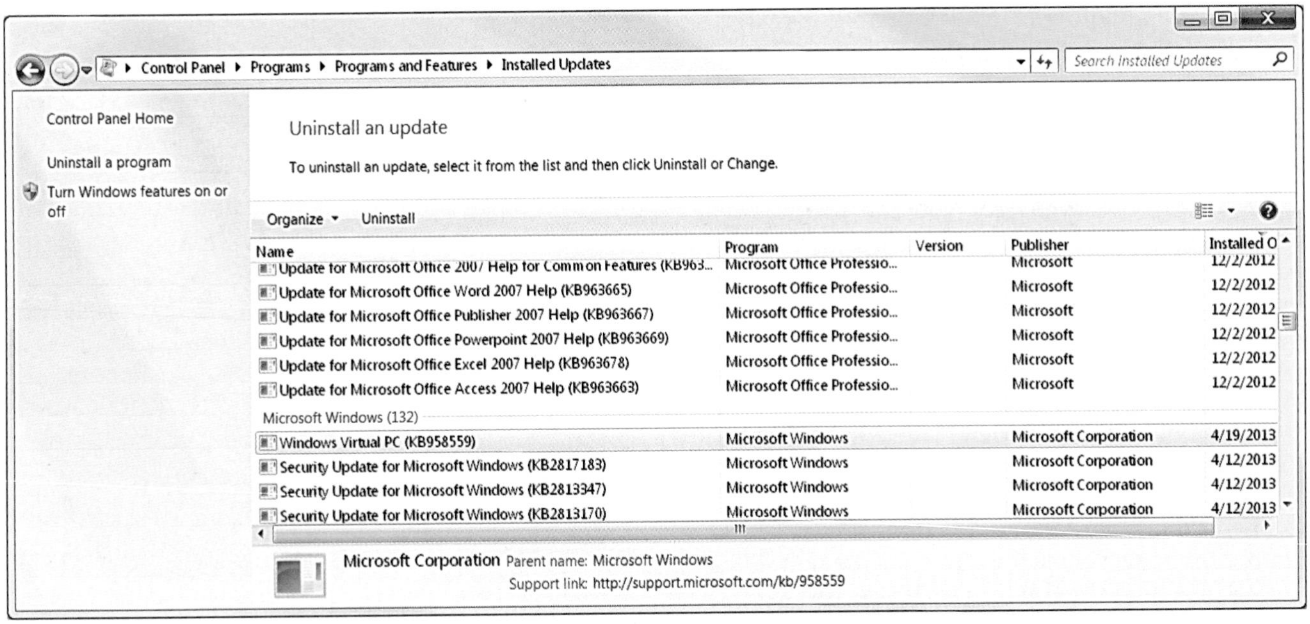

FIGURE 3–12 To remove Virtual PC double-click Window Virtual PC (KB958559).

Virtual PC (KB958559). When the Uninstall an Update prompt appears, click the Yes button. When prompted to restart the computer, close all open Windows and then click the Restart Now button.

Client Hyper-V on Windows 8

The hypervisor in Windows 8, Client Hyper-V, is a Type I (bare metal) hypervisor. It does not include a Windows XP Mode virtual machine. It is based on the Hyper-V hypervisor found on Windows Servers. It includes the Windows To Go Virtual Hard Disk (VHD) feature that allows you to create a virtual hard disk (VHD) on a USB drive, take it to another computer and boot from it.

Hyper-V is only available on Windows 8 Pro or Enterprise editions. It has more rigorous hardware requirements than other desktop hypervisors, requiring at least 4 GB of RAM (more is better) and a CPU with the **Second-Level Address Translation (SLAT)** feature found in many newer Intel and AMD CPUs.

Note: At this writing the Intel Core i3, i5, and i7 CPUs support SLAT. AMD uses many different model names for their SLAT-compliant CPUs. Therefore, to see a list of AMD CPUs that support SLAT, enter the search string "amd hyper-v" in a search engine and select results at amd.com.

Enabling Hyper-V

First you need to determine if your computer running Windows 8 Pro or Windows 8 Enterprise has hardware support for Hyper-V. Open Search and type "sys" while watching the Results list on the left. Select System Information. This opens the System Information console. With System Summary selected on the left, scroll down to the bottom of the contents pane where, if Hyper-V is not yet enabled, you will see four items that begin with "Hyper-V." All four items have a value of "yes" as shown here. If Hyper-V or another hypervisor is already installed, these four items will be replaced with this message: "A hypervisor has been detected, Features required for Hyper-V will not be displayed."

To enable Client Hyper-V, open the Windows 8 Control Panel and open Programs and Features. Then, in the left pane of Programs and Features click or tap Turn Windows Features on or off to open the Windows Features dialog box (Figure 3–13). Locate the Hyper-V node and expand it so that you can see the two components of Client Hyper-V: Hyper-V Management Tools and

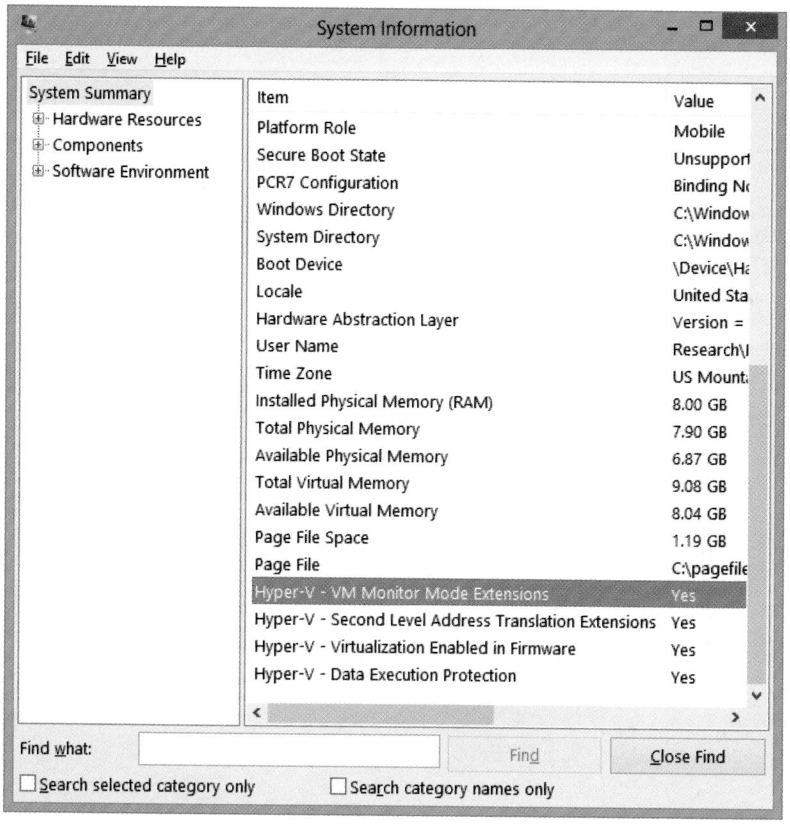

System Information shows that Hyper-V is supported on this computer.

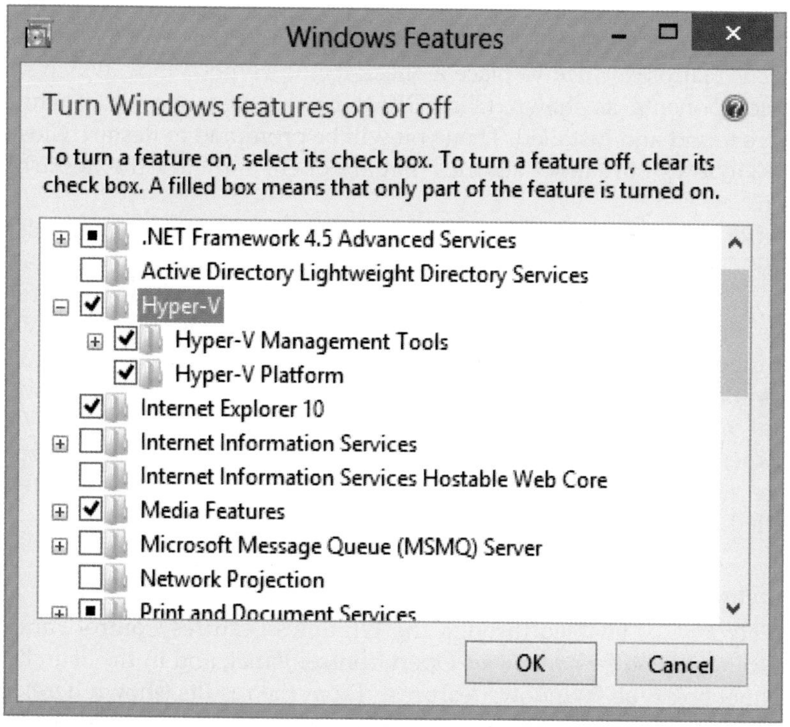

FIGURE 3–13 Click to place a check in the Hyper-V box. This will also select the two Hyper-V components.

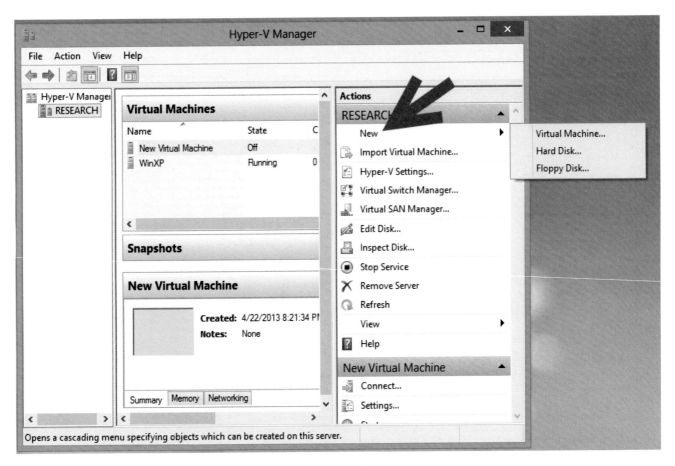

FIGURE 3–14 Create and manage virtual machines using Hyper-V Manager.

Hyper-V Platform. Click to place a check in the Hyper-V box, which selects both components, as shown. Click OK; there will be a short wait while the files are found and installed. Then you will be prompted to Restart. Close any open windows, save any data files that are open, and click the Restart Now button.

After installing Hyper-V, two new tiles will display on the Start screen: Hyper-V Virtual Machine Connection and Hyper-V Manager. Click or tap the Hyper-V Manager to create and manage virtual machines. Figure 3–14 shows Hyper-V Manager with the New menu open. Selecting Virtual Machine from this menu will start the New Virtual Machine Wizard, which will walk you through creating a virtual machine. Figure 3–14 shows two virtual machines listed in Hyper-V Manager, one named New Virtual Machine, which is the default name the wizard will use if you do not specify a more meaningful name. The second is WinXP, for the operating system we installed into the virtual machine.

Removing Hyper-V

Since Hyper-V is enabled through the Windows Features Control Panel you need to remove it the same way. Open Control Panel, and in the Search Control Panel box type "windows features." From the results (shown here) select "Turn Windows features on or off." This opens the Windows Features Control Panel. Locate the Hyper-V node and click to clear the check box, and then click OK. The Windows Features dialog box will display progress information

The Hyper-V tiles on the Start screen.

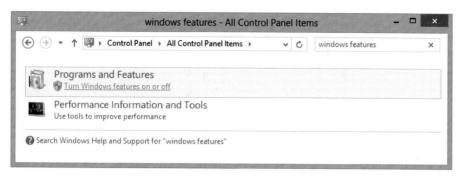

Select Turn Windows features on or off.

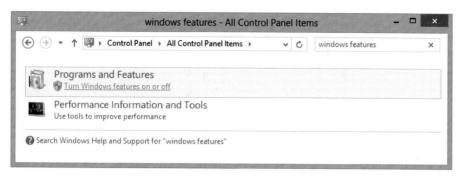

FIGURE 3–15 Click Restart Now to complete the removal of Hyper-V.

while it initiates the change, and then it will display the message shown in Figure 3–15 stating that it needs to restart to complete the changes. Click the Restart Now button, and it will make changes as it shuts down and again when it restarts Windows 8.

Oracle VirtualBox

Oracle VirtualBox is a versatile free hypervisor that comes in versions for a variety of host operating systems, such as Windows, Linux, and Mac OS X. It will run guest versions of Windows, Linux, and DOS. And like Microsoft's Virtual PC 2007, Oracle VirtualBox will run on hardware that does not support virtualization, so it is yet another choice for older computers without hardware virtualization support. It is available for download at **www.virtualbox.org**. Because it runs on a Mac OS X host, we will use it in the next section when we discuss Virtual Machines on Mac OS X.

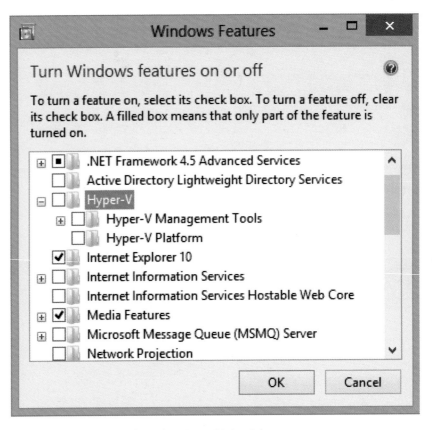

In Windows Features, clear the Hyper-V check box.

LO 3.3 | Virtual Machines on Mac OS X

You may want to use virtualization software on a Mac to test a distribution of Linux or a version of Windows or to run certain Windows apps that aren't available for the Mac OS. There are several options for doing this, including Apple Boot Camp (not really a virtualization tool), VirtualBox, and Parallels. Apple Boot Camp is a multiboot solution, but VirtualBox and Parallels offer virtualization on the Apple desktop. Parallels Desktop by Parallels is a commercial product, and you can learn about it at www.parallels.com/products/desktop/.

Apple Boot Camp—A Dual-Boot Option

Apple Boot Camp is available with Mac OS X. It is a dual-boot option, meaning it allows you to install Windows onto a separate disk partition, and then you can choose to boot into either OS. This is an either-or situation; you need to restart to change from one OS to the other. The advantage of a dual-boot solution is performance—each OS is running directly on the Mac with no performance loss from being in a virtual machine. However, today's hypervisors, when used on a recent Apple computer running Mac OS X, perform well enough to discourage us from dedicating the disk space to a multiboot solution like Apple Boot Camp.

Boot Camp comes with Mac OS X 10.6 and later versions. Before running the Boot Camp Assistant to configure your computer and install Windows, back up your Mac because the first step requires that you create a new

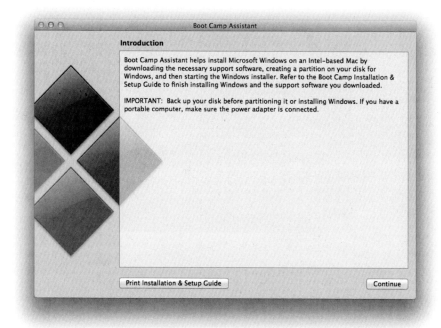

FIGURE 3–16 Print the Installation and Setup Guide before proceeding.

partition for the Windows OS. You will also need the installation disc or an ISO file for a full version of Windows (not an update).

Boot Camp installs only on an internal hard drive, so if you only have one drive with a single partition, Boot Camp Assistant will repartition that drive to create a new partition. Those of us with decades of experience working with hard drives cringe at partitioning an already fully partitioned drive containing data, but it works.

Run Boot Camp Assistant from the Applications Utilities folder. Notice that the first page, seen in Figure 3–16, gives you the option to print the Installation and Setup Guide for Boot Camp. This is an excellent idea. Print it out and read it before continuing. Then, if you still want to install and use Boot Camp, return to this screen, click Continue, and follow the instructions to prepare the disk and install Windows.

If you do continue, you should decide how big a partition you wish to have for your Windows OS. Remember that you will be installing applications into Windows, so you will need a bigger partition than the minimum recommended for the version of Windows you plan to install. For instance, when installing Windows 7 on an iMac with a 500 GB hard drive, we considered the minimum requirements for the OS itself (16 GB for 32-bit or 20 GB for 64-bit) and then we considered the requirements of the various applications we wish to install and the data we will generate (unless you are saving it to a server). Considering these needs, and the overall hard drive space, we decided to create a partition of 100 GB.

Oracle VirtualBox

The free version of Oracle VirtualBox will run on a variety of host operating systems including Windows, Linux, and Mac OS X. It supports as guest OSs versions of Windows, Linux, and DOS. It will also run on hardware that does not support virtualization. Figure 3–17 shows Windows 8 running in VirtualBox in OS X.

FIGURE 3–17 Windows 8 running in VirtualBox in OS X.

Point your browser to the VirtualBox download page, shown in Figure 3–18. Click on the VirtualBox link for OS X hosts, shown under VirtualBox platform packages. This is the core software required for VirtualBox. You will also need to download the VirtualBox Extension Pack, also shown on this page.

Once you have downloaded the disk image file, when you are ready to install VirtualBox, simply open the Downloads folder and double-click on VirtualBox. Step-by-Step 3.03 describes how to install Oracle VirtualBox.

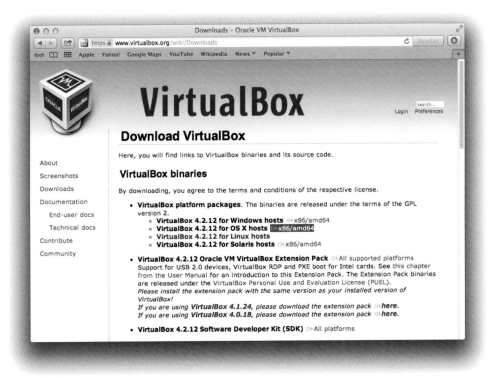

FIGURE 3–18 Download the OS X version from the VirtualBox Download page.

Step-by-Step 3.03

Installing Oracle VirtualBox

Using the file you downloaded or a file provided to you by your instructor, install Oracle VirtualBox. The instructions provided are for installing it into Mac OS X and you begin with a disk image file (.dmg). To complete this exercise you will need the following:

- A computer running the version of Mac OS X supported by the latest version of VirtualBox. You can find older versions on the VirtualBox Website, if necessary.

- A computer that meets the hardware requirements for the version of VirtualBox you will install.

- The user name and password of an administrator account for this computer (even if you have logged on as an administrator, you will need these credentials to install new software).

- A broadband Internet connection.

Step 1

Locate and double-click the VirtualBox disk image. It will be on the desktop or in the Downloads folder in Finder. This will open the VirtualBox drive. If you wish to read the documentation, open the UserManual.pdf file. Also, note that the VirtualBox Uninstall tool is located here, for when you decide you do not need this program.

Step 2

To start the VirtualBox installation, double-click on the VirtualBox.pkg icon. The VirtualBox installation wizard runs. At first it runs a test to verify that the computer can support VirtualBox. Follow the instructions and proceed through the pages, including reading and accepting the software license agreement, after which you can either accept the defaults for a standard install or select a different destination and installation type.

Step 3

In a very short time the installation is complete, and you will find VirtualBox listed in Applications. Launch VirtualBox and then open the Machine menu at the top of the screen. Select New.

Step 4

The New Virtual Machine app will guide you through the creation of a virtual machine. This process does not require the guest OS, but you do need to know which OS you will install into the virtual machine you are creating. You are simply configuring the machine to accept the guest OS. When prompted to name the virtual machine, use a meaningful name, such as the name and version of the OS you plan to install. Then select the OS you will install and continue.

Step 5

On the Memory size page select the amount of base memory, initially accepting the default and continuing.

Step 6

On the Hard Drive page select Create a Virtual Hard Drive Now and press Create. On the Hard Drive File Type page select the first type, unless you have a reason for selecting another type. Then press Continue.

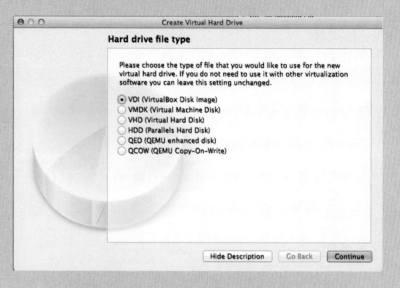

Step 7

On the Storage on Physical Hard Drive page select Dynamically Allocated and click Continue.

Step 8

On the File Location and Size page the name will match the name you gave to the virtual machine. Accept the defaults for name, location, and size on this page and click Create. On the next page you will see a summary of the virtual disk settings. Confirm that these are correct and click the Done button to complete the creation of the virtual disk. Then you will see another summary page for all the settings for this virtual machine. Confirm the settings and click Done.

The console will appear with your new virtual machine, ready for the installation of the OS. The console shown here includes several virtual machines.

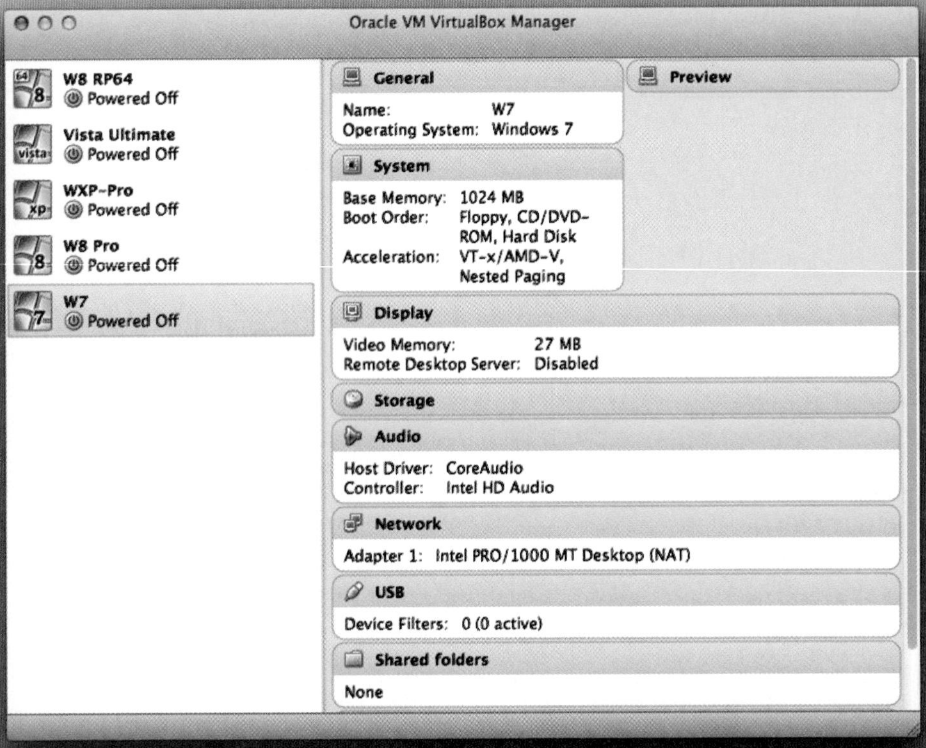

When you are ready to install an operating system, double-click on a virtual machine. This will launch the First Run Wizard, which will guide you through the process of beginning the installation of your OS. Install the VirtualBox Extension Pack that you previously downloaded from the VirtualBox Download page.

Secure the virtual machine. Assign a strong password to any user account you create within the guest OS, then update the OS with all security updates, and install antivirus and other security software.

Chapter Summary

After reading this chapter and completing the exercises, you should understand the following facts about desktop virtualization.

Virtualization Overview

- There are many types of virtualization today, such as virtual worlds, virtual reality, storage virtualization, network virtualization, server virtualization, and desktop virtualization—the subject of this chapter.
- Virtualization had its roots in the dumb-terminal/mainframe systems of the 1960s and the terminal service/terminal client systems of the 1990s.
- You can host today's virtual desktops on network servers or on PCs.
- A hypervisor, or virtual machine monitor (VMM), is the software that emulates the necessary hardware on which an operating system runs.
- A Type I hypervisor (a "bare-metal hypervisor") runs directly on a computer without an underlying host operating system.
- A Type II hypervisor requires a host operating system.
- The major sources of hypervisors are Citrix, VMware, Parallels, Microsoft, and Oracle.

Virtual Machines on Windows Desktops

- There are both commercial and free hypervisors for running Linux, DOS, or Windows on a Windows desktop computer.
- Microsoft Virtual PC 2007 is free and will run on any computer running Windows XP or newer versions of Windows, and it supports Windows, Linux, and DOS guests without requiring hardware-assisted virtualization.
- Windows XP Mode is a free hypervisor that installs on a Windows 7 host with a Windows XP guest OS preinstalled. It does not require hardware-assisted virtualization.
- Download Windows XP Mode from the Microsoft Website and install it.

- Remove Windows XP Mode through Windows from the Programs and Features Control Panel.
- The free Windows Virtual PC requires both Windows 7 and hardware-assisted virtualization.
- Download and install Virtual PC from the Microsoft website. It installs as an update, so to remove it you will need to uninstall it from the Installed Updates Control Panel.
- Client Hyper-V is the Type I hypervisor that is included with Windows 8 Pro and Windows Enterprise editions.
- Client Hyper-V has more rigorous hardware requirements than other desktop hypervisors, requiring at least 4 GB of RAM and a CPU with the Second-Level Address Translation (SLAT) feature.
- Enable Client Hyper-V through the Windows Features Control Panel.
- Remove Hyper-V by deselecting it in the Windows Features Control Panel.
- Oracle VirtualBox is free and runs on several hosts including versions of Windows, Linux, and Max OS X, and it will run on hardware that does not support virtualization.

Virtual Machines on Mac OS X

- You have several choices for hypervisors for Mac OS X that will run versions of Windows and Linux.
- Apple Boot Camp is not actually a hypervisor but a dual-boot option that allows you to dual boot between Mac OS X and Windows. This gives each OS full use of the hardware, but only one can be loaded at a time.
- Oracle VirtualBox is a free hypervisor and will run versions of Windows, Linux, and DOS on hardware that does not support virtualization.

Key Terms List

application virtualization *(84)*

avatar *(84)*

desktop virtualization *(84)*

dumb terminal *(85)*

guest OS *(85)*

host key *(87)*

host OS *(85)*

hypervisor *(86)*

network virtualization *(84)*

Second-Level Address
      Translation (SLAT) (102)
server virtualization (84)
storage virtualization (84)
terminal client (85)
terminal services (85)

thin client (85)
Type I hypervisor (86)
Type II hypervisor (86)
virtual desktop
      infrastructure (VDI) (85)
virtual machine (84)

virtual machine monitor (VMM) (86)
virtual reality (84)
virtual world (84)
virtualization (84)
Windows XP Mode (93)

Key Terms Quiz

Use the Key Terms List to complete the sentences that follow. Not all terms will be used.

1. The software layer that emulates the necessary hardware on which an operating system runs in a virtual machine is a/an _____.

2. A/an _____ is a discrete area of a mainframe computer devoted to a single terminal session.

3. Many organization use _____ in which many networked hard drives are seen as one to the client computers.

4. _____ is the creation of an environment that seems real.

5. When you run one desktop OS within another operating system, it is called _____.

6. In the 1960s, a/an _____ was the very simple interface device to a mainframe computer.

7. In the 1990s, people often used _____ software on a PC to connect to a specialized server or minicomputer.

8. A/an _____ is a low-cost PC, usually without such common peripherals as expansion slots, and optical drives, and is used to connect to a special environment on a server that could be simply a partition or a virtual machine.

9. In desktop or server virtualization, the software emulation of all hardware with which an operating system must interface is a/an _____.

10. Second Life is an example of a/an _____.

Multiple-Choice Quiz

1. In which type of virtualization does a user connect to a server and work within a program, without an entire virtualized desktop environment?
   a. Storage virtualization
   b. Application virtualization
   c. Terminal service
   d. Thin client
   e. Virtual world

2. What term describes the hosting and management of multiple virtual desktops on network servers?
   a. Thin client
   b. Terminal services
   c. Minicomputers
   d. Virtual desktop infrastructure (VDI)
   e. Partitioning

3. Which of the following does not require a host OS?
   a. Type II hypervisor
   b. Type I hypervisor
   c. Microsoft Virtual PC 2007
   d. Windows Virtual PC
   e. Windows XP Mode

4. What hypervisor, described in this chapter, is a "bare metal" hypervisor?
   a. Microsoft Virtual PC 2007
   b. Windows Virtual PC
   c. Windows XP Mode
   d. Oracle VirtualBox
   e. Client Hyper-V

5. What type of hypervisor would you install on a Windows host OS?
   a. Type II
   b. Type I
   c. Boot Camp
   d. A bare-metal hypervisor
   e. A dual-boot hypervisor

6. If you wanted to run Windows 7 on an iMac running OS X 10.8, which option would give you the best performance, but would not run Windows in a virtual machine?
   a. Windows XP Mode
   b. Microsoft Virtual PC 2007
   c. Oracle VirtualBox

d. Parallels

e. Apple Boot Camp

7. Which free hypervisor, studied in this chapter, runs on Windows, Mac OS X, and Linux OSs?

a. Microsoft Virtual PC 2007

b. Windows Virtual PC

c. Oracle VirtualBox

d. Apple Boot Camp

e. Windows XP Mode

8. You upgraded your four-year-old PC to Windows 7 and you would like to install a hypervisor so that you can run and test Linux applications. A test shows that your computer does not support hardware-assisted virtualization. Which of the following can you install on the PC that will work for your purposes?

a. Windows XP Mode

b. Client Hyper-V

c. Microsoft Virtual PC 2007

d. Boot Camp

e. VDI

9. Which of the following solutions should you select if you wish to run a Windows guest on Mac OS X 10.8, but you need frequent access to both the host and guest OSs?

a. Windows XP Mode

b. Windows Virtual PC

c. Oracle VirtualBox

d. Boot Camp

e. Microsoft Virtual PC 2007

10. Which of the following will release the mouse from the control of a virtual machine?

a. Guest key

b. Host key

c. Host OS

d. VDI

e. Terminal service

11. Which of the following is synonymous with hypervisor?

a. Terminal service

b. Bare metal

c. Virtual hard drive

d. Virtual machine

e. Virtual machine monitor (VMM)

12. Your PC has an AMD processor installed that includes AMD-V technology and the motherboard fully supports this processor. Which is the most capable version of a Microsoft hypervisor you can install on this machine, provided the computer meets all the requirements?

a. VirtualBox

b. Client Hyper-V

c. Windows XP Mode

d. Boot Camp

e. Parallels Desktop

13. What legal issue must you consider when installing a guest OS into a hypervisor?

a. Copyright of guest OS

b. Antivirus

c. Licensing of guest OS

d. Guest key

e. Supplying security credentials

14. After downloading VirtualBox to an iMac with Mac OS X 10.6, which of the following is the name of the object you should double-click to install VirtualBox on your computer?

a. VirtualBox.pkg

b. VirtualBox.iso

c. VirtualBox.exe

d. VirtualBox.pdf

e. VM.bat

15. Which of the following is a multiboot option for running Windows as a second OS on a Mac OS X 10.6 computer?

a. VirtualBox

b. Windows Virtual PC

c. Windows XP Mode

d. Boot Camp

e. Parallels

Essay Quiz

1. What is the purpose of each of the two most important files created by a Type II hypervisor when preparing a new virtual machine?

2. Describe a feature of Client Hyper-V that allows you to take a virtual machine to another computer on a common small handheld device.

3. Explain why an IT person would want to use a hypervisor on a desktop computer.

4. Why is there (at this writing) no hypervisor for running Mac OS X on a Windows PC?

5. You have Windows XP Mode installed on your Windows 7 computer, and you would like to do a side-by-side comparison of Windows XP Mode and Windows XP in a VirtualBox VM. What precautions should you take and how many computers are required for this comparison?

LAB PROJECT 3.1

Find out how virtualization is being used in an organization in your area. Arrange an interview with an IT manager, network engineer, or other knowledgeable IT staff person from an organization in your area. Consider approaching someone at a regional hospital or medical clinic because privacy laws require that they meet certain minimum standards in IT, and they often have the best IT staff in a community. Ask if they are using virtualization, and if so, what type? What are their future plans for virtualization? Report your findings to your classmates.

LAB PROJECT 3.2

If you installed a hypervisor on your computer, find another one that will run on your OS. Uninstall the first one without removing the virtual machines created for that hypervisor; install the second one. Compare the similarities and differences. Will the new hypervisor work with the virtual machines you created with the first one? Decide which one you prefer working with. If it is the second, then keep it; if you preferred the first one, uninstall the second and reinstall the first.

LAB PROJECT 3.3

Find out the latest about Type I and Type II hypervisors. Browse the Internet using the keyword *virtualization* and watching for recent articles and news releases. Consider turning on Google alerts with the key term *virtualization*. Watch the number of alerts you receive over just a period of a few days.

4

Windows 7

"One of the favorite things that the development team did during the course of building Windows 7 is create this thing in one of the R&D buildings that they called the Wishing Wall. And on the Wishing Wall, they collected and put up just a ton of customer feedback. Things that they called technical feedback, emotional feedback, to try to really bring alive in the physical world all of that information that we were getting back in the virtual world to help us tune the product."

—Steve Ballmer

Microsoft CEO, during the Windows 7 Launch in New York on October 22, 2009

This book has limited coverage of Windows Vista because it was not widely adopted in the years following its release in 2007. The resistance to moving to Windows Vista was so strong that Microsoft prolonged the life of Windows XP, allowing sales of new PCs with OEM (original equipment manufacturer) Windows XP installed up until October 2010. This was one year after the release of Windows Vista's successor, Windows 7, and nine years since the introduction of Windows XP. When it comes to installing and working with Windows Vista versus Windows 7, the steps are nearly identical. Therefore, this chapter is about Windows 7, with very light treatment of Windows Vista as we consider the issues of installing and configuring Windows, followed by an overview of Windows 7 features and the basics of managing an installed OS. Finally, we'll explore issues for configuring local security in Windows.

Learning Outcomes

In this chapter, you will learn how to:

LO **4.1** Install and configure Windows 7.

LO **4.2** Use the features of Windows 7.

LO **4.3** Manage Windows 7.

LO **4.4** Configure local security in Windows 7.

LO 4.1 | Installing Windows 7

Many of us are finding that our old desktop and laptop computers continue to serve us well even after more than five years of use. Therefore, moving to a new operating system does not have to involve purchasing a new computer. Once you have made the decision to move to a new OS on your existing computer, you need to decide how you will do that. In this section we will explore the options you have for installing a new version of Windows.

Each new version of Windows has included improvements in how the OS installs. In this section we'll first identify the upgrade paths available should you decide to install Windows 7 on an existing Windows desktop or laptop, answering such questions as, "Can I upgrade from Windows XP to Windows 7?" and "Can I upgrade from Windows Vista to Windows 7?" Then we will describe your options for moving your data and settings to a new installation of Windows 7 and detail the actual steps for doing a clean installation of Windows 7, following by important post-installation tasks.

Recommended System Requirements

The recommended system requirements for Windows Vista and Windows 7 are nearly identical. When Microsoft introduced Windows Vista, people gave the hardware requirements as a reason they did not upgrade their Windows XP computers to Windows Vista. However, in the years since then, hardware has continued its trend toward more power for less money, and today these same requirements seem very reasonable. It's almost as if Microsoft had reduced the hardware requirements. Further, Microsoft designed Windows 7 to provide better performance and to be more reliable on the same hardware required by Windows Vista. Windows 7 boots faster than Windows Vista and takes up less memory. Table 4–1 shows the Windows 7 minimum requirements.

All versions of Windows have memory maximums—the maximum amount of memory the OS can use. The Windows 7 and Windows 8 memory limits are listed in Table 1–1 in Chapter 1. In brief, the maximum RAM for 32-bit Windows 7 is 4 GB, and the maximums for the 64-bit versions vary by edition between 8 GB and 192 GB. Windows 8 (see Chapter 5) has the same 32-bit limit of 4 GB and a 192-GB limit for the 64-bit version.

Windows 7 Editions

As with earlier versions of Windows, Microsoft offers Windows 7 as several separate products, called editions. Keep in mind that all editions of a single version of Windows have the same kernel and other core components. The differences among editions are mainly in the included components, targeted to specific types of users, and the more features the more expensive the edition. Microsoft sells

WARNING!

If you plan to run Windows XP Mode, Microsoft recommends a PC with Intel-VT or AMD-V enabled in the CPU, plus you will need a minimum of 2 GB of memory and an additional 15 GB of free disk space.

TABLE 4–1 Windows 7 Minimum Requirements

	Windows 7 32-bit Editions	Windows 7 64-bit Editions
Processor	1 GHz 32-bit ×86	1 GHz 64-bit ×64 processor
System memory	1 GB	2 GB
Available hard drive space	16 GB	20 GB
Support for DirectX 9 graphics with WDDM 1.0 or higher driver (DirectX 10 required for certain games)	X	X
Graphics memory (to support Aero)	128 MB	128 MB
Audio output (if desired)	X	X
Internet access (for keeping the OS updated)	X	X

some Windows editions at retail, meaning you can buy a package containing the Windows DVD. Other Windows editions are bundled with hardware as OEM Windows (with or without the accompanying DVD), while the Enterprise edition of any version of Windows is not available at retail, but sold only to customers of the Microsoft Software Assurance plan, a distribution channel for bulk licensing to organizations. The Enterprise editions have added features desirable to a large enterprise. These features include support for mass distribution, linking with enterprise security, compliance, collaborative productivity, and more.

Windows 7 also comes in two scaled-down editions called Starter and Home Basic. The Starter edition is an OEM edition that has many features removed or disabled, including the ability to change the desktop wallpaper or join a Windows domain. The Home Basic edition targets emerging markets and is not available in the United States, most of Europe, the Middle East, Australia, New Zealand, and Japan. Windows 7 comes in three retail editions: Home Premium, Professional, and Ultimate.

Upgrade Paths

The only in-place installation you can do from an earlier version of Windows to Windows 7 is from Windows Vista to Windows 7. In some cases, you can also do an easy upgrade from a lesser Windows 7 edition to an edition of Windows 7 with more features, which we describe below.

From Windows Vista to Windows 7

An upgrade of an operating system, also called an in-place installation, is an installation of a newer operating system directly over an existing installation. An upgrade has the benefit of saving you the trouble of reinstalling all your programs and re-creating all your preference settings, which are tasks you would have to do when you start with a new computer with Windows 7 preinstalled.

An upgrade also has its risks, since you end up with a new OS on an old computer with all the problems of the old installation as far as unnecessary installed programs, old hardware, and possible data loss or permission problems.

Table 4–2 lists the direct upgrade paths to Windows 7. Blank fields indicate that you must do a clean install. You cannot directly upgrade from Windows XP or older versions to Windows 7.

Note: An upgrade installation is different in two ways from the full Windows 7 retail product. The first is in how you install it, and the second is really a licensing issue; The upgrade product is cheaper than the full product because it is intended to replace the previously installed licensed Windows. You can actually do a clean installation of a retail Windows 7 upgrade, as long as you have the disc from the previous version and the product code from the packaging. It is then illegal to continue to run the previous version on another computer.

Windows 7 Anytime Upgrade Discontinued

Originally, Windows 7 Home Basic, Home Premium, or Starter editions came with the Anytime Upgrade option, listed under All Programs on the Start menu. When you ran this, you would follow the prompts to either enter an upgrade key you had previously purchased or you would connect to Microsoft online and purchase an upgrade key. Then Windows Anytime Upgrade would add the features of the upgraded edition to your installation of Windows 7. After the release of Windows 8, Microsoft discontinued the sale of the upgrade key for all but the upgrade from Home Premium to Professional.

TABLE 4–2 Upgrade Paths to Windows 7

Windows Vista Edition (with SP1 or SP2)	Windows 7 Home Basic	Windows 7 Home Premium	Windows 7 Professional	Windows 7 Enterprise	Windows 7 Ultimate
Business			X	X	X
Enterprise					X
Home Basic	X	X			X
Home Premium		X			X
Ultimate					X

When we checked with Microsoft in the spring of 2013, the Anytime Upgrade from Home Premium was "out of stock." However, we found many heavily discounted Windows 7 Anytime Upgrades at e-commerce sites.

Preparing to Install Windows 7

The preparation steps for installing Windows 7 vary based on whether you are doing an upgrade from Windows Vista, a side-by-side multiboot installation, or a clean installation. Here is a brief overview of each of the installation types:

- An upgrade, also called an in-place installation, installs directly into the folders in which the previous version of Windows installed. Windows 7 setup manages to preserve the old settings, while removing the old OS before installing the new OS, thus avoiding inheriting any problems in the old OS. You can only upgrade from a Windows Vista edition that is upgradeable to the edition of Windows 7 you plan to install (see Table 4–2). However, if you simply aren't quite ready to break all ties with your old installation of Windows, then consider the next option.

- A multiboot installation leaves an old OS in place, installing a new OS in a separate partition or hard disk. This allows you to select the OS you wish to boot into every time you start the computer, and this is what we did on Jane's computer because she still wanted an installation of Windows Vista for screen shots and comparison while writing about both Windows Vista and Windows 7. She also decided to multiboot to have access to a few programs the Upgrade Advisor flagged as incompatible for Windows 7. This was a temporary arrangement, because she soon found replacements for the programs, or found upgrades to them that worked better in Windows 7. To install Windows 7 to multiboot, you do a clean installation on a separate partition or hard disk, which means you will select the Custom installation choice. Windows 7 setup will preserve the earlier version of Windows and create a Windows Boot Manager menu, as Figure 4–1 shows, which will display for a short period at every restart. We often refer to a multiboot configuration with just two choices of operating system as a dual-boot configuration.

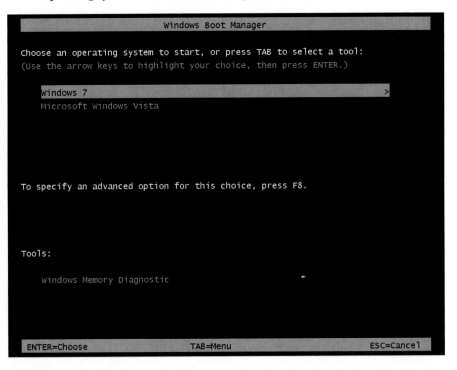

FIGURE 4–1 The Windows Boot Manager menu showing two choices: Windows 7 and Windows Vista.

- A clean installation is an installation of an OS onto a completely empty hard disk or one from which all data is removed during the installation. It takes the least amount of disk space and is a new beginning for the new OS installation. You most often do a clean installation on a totally clean hard drive, although, in the case of a multiboot installation, you can direct Windows 7 setup to install as a clean installation on a different partition or drive from that of the existing OS. To start a clean installation you will select the Custom installation choice. To automate a clean installation onto many desktops, organizations use other, more advanced methods, such as hands-free, scripted install, or they use an image, which is an exact duplicate of the entire hard drive contents, including the OS and all installed software. The use of images is very popular in medium-to-large organizations that have dozens, hundreds, or thousands of desktop computers. You create a custom image for a large number of users by installing the OS and applications on a reference computer identical to those on which you will eventually place the images. Then you use imaging software to copy the image of the hard drive. Products for enterprises centrally distribute images over a network out to the desktops.

Regardless of the type of installation you plan to do, you must ensure the hardware minimums are met, verify hardware and software compatibility, determine how to boot into the Windows setup program, and decide if you will activate immediately or later and if you wish to register the product with Microsoft. You can verify that your computer meets the recommended minimums by comparing the system configuration with Table 4–1.

Note: IT professionals use scripted installations or some type of imaged installations. These methods often take a great deal of preparation and knowledge and are best used when you must install an OS on many computers, using identical configurations as in a classroom or computer lab.

Registration versus Activation

At some point, Windows setup will prompt you to register your product and to activate it. Many people confuse activation with registration. These are two separate operations for Microsoft software, although we have seen other popular software that combines these two functions, requiring that you give an email address and other information before the program is considered "legal" and activated.

Registration is when you inform Microsoft who the official owner or user of the product is and provide contact information, such as name, address, company, phone number, email address, and so on. Registration is generally optional with Microsoft products. Activation of Microsoft products is called Microsoft Product Activation (MPA), and is an antipiracy tool, meaning that Microsoft wishes to ensure that you are using your software per the software license, which normally limits its use to a single computer.

Microsoft Product Activation does not scan the contents of the hard disk, search for personal information, or gather information on the make, model, or manufacturer of the computer or its components, and it sends no personal information about you as part of the activation process.

Activation is mandatory for retail versions of Windows and you must do it within 30 days of installing the software. You can do it during installation of Windows, or delay it for a later time. When prompted to activate during the installation, if you choose to activate at that time you enter a product key code from the Windows packaging. The activation program communicates with Microsoft (you must have an Internet connection to do this online), and generates a product ID from the product key code and then combines it with a value that represents your hardware components to create an installation ID code. The activation program sends this code to Microsoft, which returns a 42-digit product activation code. Activating automatically online is the best way to do this.

If you do not have an Internet connection when you try to activate, or if the activation program detects a problem, you will see a message telling you to

Note: If you know that you will make major changes to the hardware in the first 30 days of using the new Windows installation, then do not activate during installation, but wait until you have made the changes. This is because major hardware changes trigger the activation process again. Major hardware changes include: upgrading of the motherboard, CPU, hard drive, network interface card (NIC), graphics card, or RAM.

call Microsoft. While sitting by the computer, dial the number provided. You will need to read the installation ID to a representative and enter the resulting 42-digit activation code in the Activate Windows By Phone dialog box.

How Will Windows Update?

Before you begin the Windows installation program you need to give some thought to how you want Windows to acquire the necessary updates that may improve its performance and make it more secure. During Windows installation you will configure Windows Update, a Windows utility that can automatically connect to the Microsoft site and download and install updates. If you own the computer in question, then we recommend that you choose to have the updates downloaded and installed automatically. If the computer is part of a corporate or school network, then you need to ask your instructor or the IT staff how they want to handle updates.

Run Windows Upgrade Advisor

If you are preparing to upgrade Windows Vista to Windows 7, first run the Windows 7 Upgrade Advisor, a compatibility checker that you can download from the Microsoft website and install. You will need administrative access to install it, and after you run it the result will be a report of any hardware or software incompatibilities found, as shown here. Read the report carefully, because it will suggest actions to take, such as searching for updated drivers for a device or disabling a program just for the duration of the installation.

try this!

Checking Compatibility before an Upgrade

Download and run the Windows 7 Upgrade Advisor. Try this:

1. Enter www.microsoft.com in your browser's address box, and then search on "download upgrade advisor." Navigate to the download page for the Windows 7 Upgrade Advisor.
2. Download the Upgrade Advisor. Once you have downloaded it, open the folder in which you saved it and run the installation program.
3. After the Upgrade Advisor installs, start it from a shortcut on the desktop or on the Start menu. It will take a few minutes to complete, and then it will display a report.
4. Print out the report and take any suggested action before installing Windows 7.

Prepare to Transfer Settings and Data

Unless you are doing an in-place installation to Windows 7, you will want a way to transfer your data, email, and settings for the Windows desktop and your applications. Microsoft provides a utility that will do this for you, whether you plan to dual-boot

FIGURE 4–2 Windows Easy Transfer for Windows 7.

between an older version of Windows and Windows 7, do a clean installation, or purchase a new computer with Windows 7 preinstalled. You can download this utility, Windows Easy Transfer (WET), from the Microsoft site where you will find versions for transferring files and settings from Windows XP or Windows Vista (both 32-bit and 64-bit editions).

From your Windows XP or Windows Vista computer connect to www.microsoft.com and download the correct version of Windows Easy Transfer. Before you run it, make sure you have an appropriate location where you want to transfer the files. This can be directly to a new computer, providing you have a special cable to use or a network connection between the two computers. However, you are most likely to do this using an external hard drive or USB flash drive. Just make sure you are prepared to provide this information, and that the location has plenty of free space for the files you will transfer. After you select the location, the next page asks "Which computer are you using now?" You will click the choice labeled "This is my old computer."

Then, when you have your Windows 7 computer ready, you run the Windows Easy Transfer utility, which you can find by entering "easy transfer" in Start | Search programs and Files. You will need to enter the location of the files into Windows Easy Transfer, and then identify your computer by selecting "This is my new computer." Then follow the instructions to transfer the files. Figure 4–2 shows the Welcome screen to Windows Easy Transfer, describing the types of data that it can transfer.

The Installation

When you start the Windows 7 setup program the Windows Preinstallation Environment (PE) starts. This is a scaled-down Windows operating system. Much like the old Windows setup program, it has limited drivers for basic hardware support for 32-bit and 64-bit programs. Windows PE supports the Windows setup GUI, collecting configuration information. Both Windows Vista and Windows 7 installation programs require very little user input near the beginning and the end of the process. Step-by-Step 4.01 will walk you through the steps for performing a clean installation.

Installing Windows 7

In this step-by-step exercise, you will do a clean installation of Windows 7. To complete this exercise, you will need the following:

- A Microsoft/Intel standard personal computer (desktop or laptop) compatible with Windows 7, with at least the recommended minimum hardware and configured to boot from DVD, and an unpartitioned hard disk (disk 0, the first hard disk) or a virtual machine you have prepared before beginning the Windows 7 installation (see Chapter 3).

- The Windows 7 DVD.
- The Product ID code. If you are using a retail version, look for this on the envelope or jewel case of your Windows 7 DVD. If you are not using a retail version, your instructor will provide a Product ID code or other instructions.
- A 15-character (or less) name, unique on your network, for your computer.
- A strong password for the user account created during setup.

Step 1

Insert the Windows DVD and boot the computer. Watch the screen for instructions to boot from the optical drive. A plain black screen will briefly flash, followed by a black screen with the message: "Windows is loading files . . ." while Windows Preinstallation Environment is loaded and started. The Starting Windows screen signals that Windows PE is starting and will soon load the GUI for Windows 7 setup.

Step 2

On the first Install Windows page, select a language, time, currency format, and keyboard input methods and select Next.

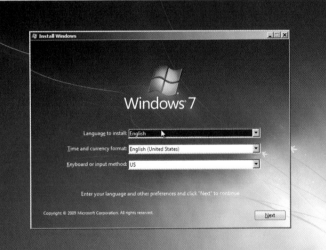

Step 3

At the center of the next screen is the Install Now button, but you should notice two important links on the bottom left. One is labeled "What to know before installing Windows." Click on it to see if you have overlooked a preparation step. The second link, labeled "Repair your computer," is an important one to remember. If, after you install Windows 7 your system will not start, pull out your Windows 7 DVD, boot from it, and select this option.

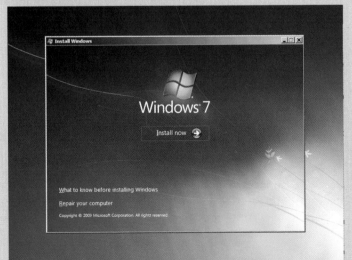

Step 4

On the license page read the Microsoft Software License Terms, then click to place a check in the box labeled "I accept the license terms" and click the Next button.

Step 5

On the next page you are asked, "Which type of installation do you want?" Select Custom to perform a clean installation.

Step 6

On the next page, you need to select the target drive for the installation. On most systems, this page will show a single disk, and you will simply click Next. In this illustration, although it is not obvious, the target is a virtual hard drive in a virtual machine, and it is smaller than we would normally choose for Windows 7 if we were installing it on a user's desktop computer.

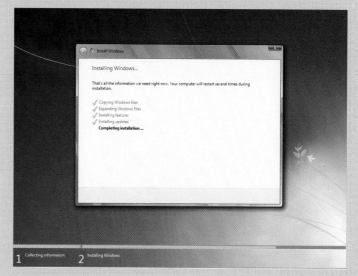

Step 7

Now relax while Windows 7 setup goes through the installation phases, restarting several times and returning to this page that displays progress with a green check by each completed phase.

Step 8

When it reaches the Completing Installation phase, the message "Setup will continue after restarting your computer" displays. After this, as Windows 7 restarts, the message "Setup is checking video performance" displays. Then you will need to enter a user name for the first user account (a Computer Administrator type, although that detail is not mentioned) and a name for the computer.

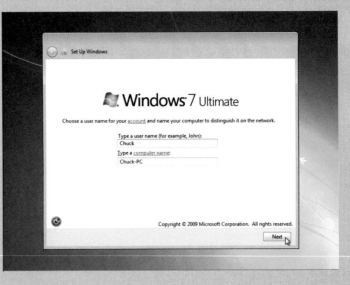

Step 9

Next create the password for the user account, entering it twice, and type a password hint that will help you to recall the password but not reveal it to others. The password hint will display anytime you enter an incorrect password when logging on.

Step 10

On the next page you will need to enter the 20-character Product Key. Notice the check box labeled "Automatically activate Windows when I'm online." Already checked by default, this means it will activate automatically if your computer connects to the Internet. You must activate Windows within 30 days of installation. If not activated within 30 days, Windows will stop functioning. Click Next to continue the final configuration steps.

On the next page configure the Automatic Update Settings. Unless your instructor tells you otherwise, click the first option: "Use recommended settings." Windows setup will then continue. On the next page select your time and date settings, and click Next.

Now select your computer's current location. If you are at home, select Home Network; if you are at school or work, select Work Network; if your computer has mobile broadband or you are using a public Wi-Fi network, select Public Network. There will be a short delay while Windows connects to the network and applies settings.

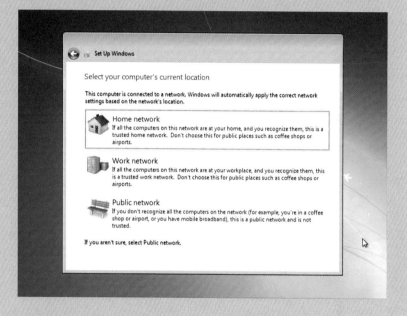

The Welcome page displays, followed by a message: "Preparing your desktop . . ." Soon the desktop displays and, depending on the setting you selected for updating and whether you have an Internet connection, you will see a message that Windows is downloading and installing updates. Some updates require restarting Windows to complete installing the update.

Post-Installation Tasks

After you install Windows 7, perform the necessary post-installation tasks. They include verifying network access (assuming you connected to a network) and installing at least the critical updates, including Service Packs. You should complete these tasks before moving on to customizing the desktop for yourself or another user and performing other desktop management tasks.

Verifying Network Access

Once you have completed the installation, look for the network status icon on the taskbar. If it does not show a red *x* then you have a network connection. If it shows a yellow exclamation mark, you have a local network connection, but do not have a connection to the Internet, although a router is present. Hover the mouse cursor over the icon. In the example shown here, the icon indicates a connection to a network named "ShortMoose" as well as to the Internet. If the network has no name, the top line would simply say "Network." In reality "ShortMoose" is the name of a wireless broadband router to which this computer connects via Ethernet. In Chapter 10 you will learn more about connecting to a private network as well as to the Internet.

The network status icon.

Installing Security Software

It's difficult to say which is more important: downloading and installing the all-important updates or installing a security package. We opt to install the security program before completing all the updates. If you do not have another program available to use, consider the free Microsoft Security Essentials, shown in Figure 4–3, available at www.microsoft.com/security_essentials. It includes general malware protection and free, automated updates. If you do not have another preferred security program, download and install this easy-to-use package as soon as possible.

Installing Updates

Now that you have verified that the computer has network access and installed security software, your next task is to install updates. Although some updates do install at the end of the Windows Vista and Windows 7 installation, you will need to ensure that additional updates install. How you actually obtain updates will depend on the organization (school or business) where you install

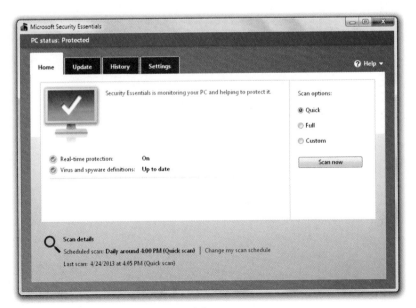

FIGURE 4–3 Microsoft Security Essentials.

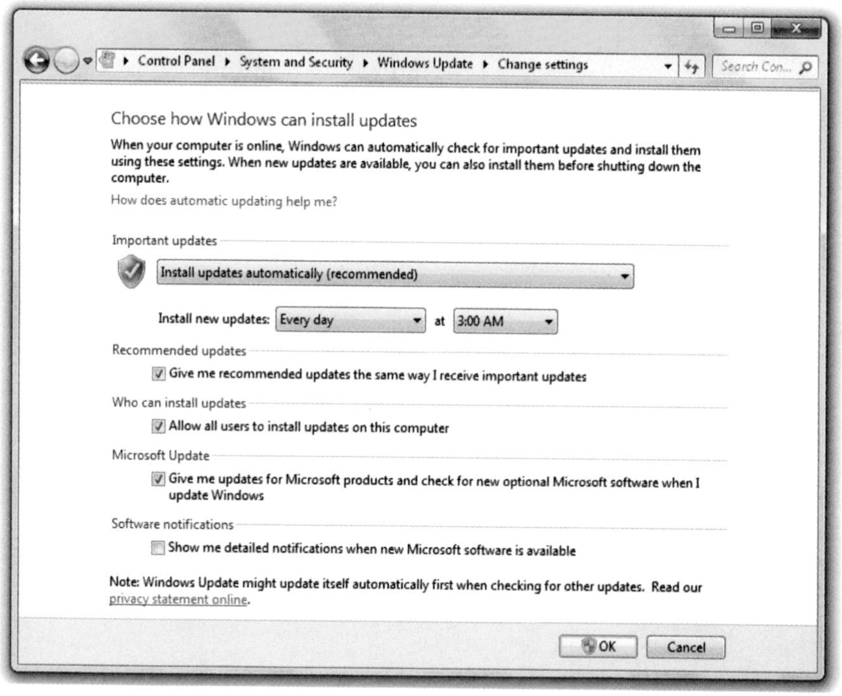

FIGURE 4–4 Options for Windows Update.

Windows. In some organizations, the IT department may distribute updates for new installations on CD even before connecting a computer to a network. Other organizations may make them available on a shared folder on the private network. In most cases, if you have an Internet connection, you will configure Windows Update to automatically download and install updates. Figure 4–4 shows the options for configuring Windows Update.

try this!

Configure Windows Update

If you are logged on as an administrator you can make changes to Windows Update. To configure Windows Update, try this:

1. Open the Start menu, in the Search Programs and Files box type "Windows Update," and select Windows Update from the results list.
2. In the task pane of Windows Update click Change Settings.
3. Using the drop-down lists and the check boxes, select the desired settings.
4. Click OK to close the Windows Update Change Settings box. Close Windows Update.

If, during setup, you configured updates to download and install automatically, you can let nature take its course. In addition we like to be more proactive, because it can take Windows Update a few days before it downloads and installs all the updates for a new installation, especially as Microsoft continues to create more updates for a maturing Windows version. Therefore, even with automatic update configured, we recommend you use the Windows Update program to manually access the updates immediately after upgrading or installing Windows. This will still take several iterations, but you will bring it up-to-date sooner this way.

Virtual Machine Additions

If you installed Windows 7 into a virtual machine, be sure to install the virtual machine additions for Windows. Whatever hypervisor you are using will remind you to do this, usually when you start the newly installed OS in the virtual machine. Each hypervisor product has a different name for these additions, and you may simply need to respond to a pop-up window or you may need to look in one of the menus on the window surrounding your virtual machine to initiate the installation of the additions.

LO 4.2 | Windows 7 Features

This section offers an overview of Windows 7, including the separate Windows 7 products and some key features offered in Windows 7. Table 4–3 lists Windows 7 features and the editions in which each feature is included. We will examine just a few of these features in the following sections.

The Windows 7 Desktop

A shortcut.

The Windows 7 Desktop is only an evolutionary, not revolutionary change from that of its predecessors. For instance, the Windows 7 GUI can contain shortcuts in various locations, such as the desktop. A shortcut is an icon that represents a link to one of many types of objects. Double-clicking on a shortcut has the same results as taking the same action directly on the linked object. An object can be a folder, a data file, a program, or any other type of object an icon can represent in Windows. Shortcuts are often, but not always, distinguished by a small bent arrow, as seen here on the shortcut Mozilla Firefox. Shortcuts on the Start menu, such as the five shown on the left in Figure 4–5, typically do not have the bent arrow.

Two areas of improvement on the desktop are enhancements to Aero and the use of Jump Lists and pinning on the Start menu and taskbar.

Aero

Windows Aero is Microsoft's name for a group of GUI desktop features and visual themes introduced in Windows Vista and improved somewhat in Windows 7 that include transparent windows (referred to as "Glass"), Windows animations, and Flip 3D.

FIGURE 4–5 Shortcuts (at left) on the Start menu.

TABLE 4–3 Features in the Windows 7 Retail Editions

	Home Premium	Professional	Ultimate
Improved desktop navigation features such as Shake, Peek, and Snap.	✓	✓	✓
Improved Instant Search organized into categories, searches external hard drives, networked PCs, and libraries.	✓	✓	✓
Internet Explorer 8 (Upgrade this to Internet Explorer 10 for more improvements.)	✓	✓	✓
Windows Media Center (It requires a TV tuner and other hardware required for some functions.)	✓	✓	✓
HomeGroup for easy file-and-print sharing on a home network (HomeGroup requires a network and PCs running Windows 7.)	✓	✓	✓
Windows XP Mode for running Windows XP programs not compatible with Windows 7.		✓	✓
Windows Touch (requires a touch-sensitive screen)	✓	✓	✓
Domain Join wizard for joining a Windows domain		✓	✓
Backup to a home or business network		✓	✓
BitLocker			✓
Switch among 35 languages			✓

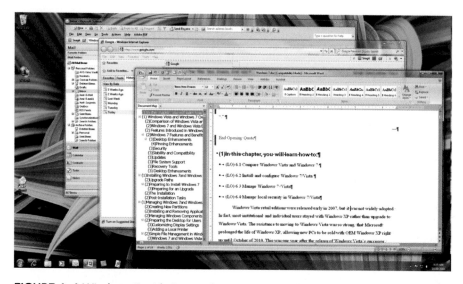

FIGURE 4–6 Windows 7 with Aero enhancements, including transparent Glass.

FIGURE 4–7 Using Flip 3D in Windows 7.

Flip 3D lets you switch through your open windows as if they were a stack of cards or photos. Figure 4–6 is an example of the Windows 7 desktop with Aero enabled. Use the WINDOWS KEY+TAB combination to use Flip 3D, as shown in Figure 4–5. Windows Aero is not in the Starter edition and has some capabilities disabled in Windows 7 Home Basic edition. It also requires a video card that supports (at minimum) DirectX 9.0 and Shader Model 2.0. Although not written as an acronym with all caps, Aero purportedly stands for Authentic, Energetic, Reflective, and Open. Figures 4–6 and 4–7 also show one of the desktop themes available with Windows 7.

New features introduced in Windows 7 include Aero Snap and Aero Shake. Aero Snap lets you manipulate windows quickly. For instance, to maximize a window, drag it until its title bar touches the top edge of your display. Restore a maximized window by dragging it away from the top of the display. Aero Shake lets you quickly minimize all but one window by giving that window a quick shake.

> *Note:* In our testing we have found that some app windows, when shaken, do not trigger Aero Shake, although when another app that works with Aero Shake is shaken, the uncooperative app's window will close, along with all other open windows.

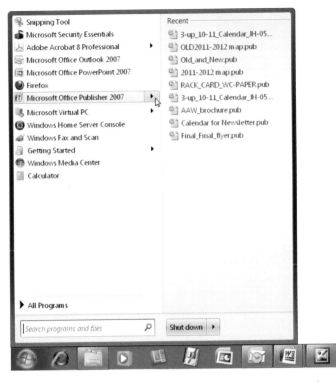

FIGURE 4–8 A Jump List (in the right column) for Microsoft Office Publisher.

Jump Lists and Pinning

Windows 7 improves the Start menu and taskbar with the Jump Lists and pinning features. The old pinned area of the Start menu is still available, and programs are often pinned there, but you can also pin items on the taskbar. When you right-click on a program shortcut on the Start menu or taskbar, a Jump List displays, as in Figure 4–8. This is a list of recently opened items such as files, folders, and websites. It automatically lists only the recently opened items, but you can select an item and "permanently" pin it to a Jump List. Practice pinning items in Step-by-Step 4.02.

Pinning replaces the Quick Launch toolbar. It allows you to place icons for applications and destinations on the taskbar and Start menu. Once pinned, an item's icon remains on the toolbar regardless of whether the program is open or closed. Simply click it to open the application or destination. When a program is running, its icon appears as a square button on the toolbar, as demonstrated by the Microsoft Outlook button on the toolbar in Figure 4–9, which shows a portion of a Windows 7 taskbar with the various icons labeled.

Figure 4–10 shows the Jump List for Microsoft Word that includes both Word documents and other types of files, such as the recently embedded TIF files in Word documents.

Pin a program and then use that program's Jump List to pin several data files to the one program. When you pin a program to the taskbar, you use that one icon to open the program and switch to the program, and then you can select an item from the program's Jump List, which, like most pinned items, carries an automatically generated list of recently opened files for that item, but you can also add items to this list. There are several ways to pin programs. Learn more about pinning and Jump Lists in Step-by-Step 4.02.

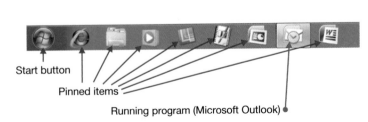

FIGURE 4–9 Pinned items on a taskbar, along with the button for a running program.

FIGURE 4–10 Right-click a pinned item to view its Jump List.

Pinning Items

Practice pinning programs and then pinning files within a program's Jump List. In this step-by-step exercise, you will need the following:

● A computer with Windows 7 installed—either a conventional installation or an installation in a VM.

Step 1

Start a program, such as Microsoft Word. Then right-click the program's taskbar icon and select Pin This Program To Taskbar. The running icon will appear the same, but when you close the program, a pinned icon will remain.

Step 2

You can also pin a program to the taskbar by dragging it. Open the Start menu and browse through the All Programs menu until you locate the icon for a program you wish to pin. Then drag and drop the program icon onto the taskbar.

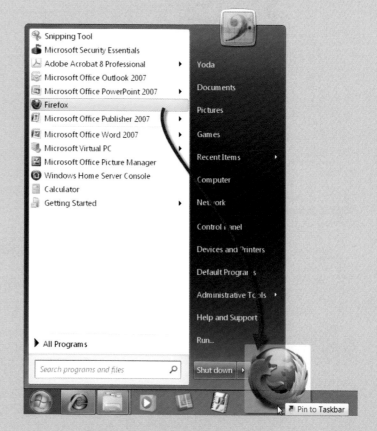

Step 3

Windows 7 automatically generates Jump Lists, but you can ensure that an item stays on a Jump List by pinning it. To pin an item, right-click an icon on the Start menu to display the Jump List. Then hover the mouse cursor over an item in the list until the push-pin icon displays. Click the pushpin icon to pin the item.

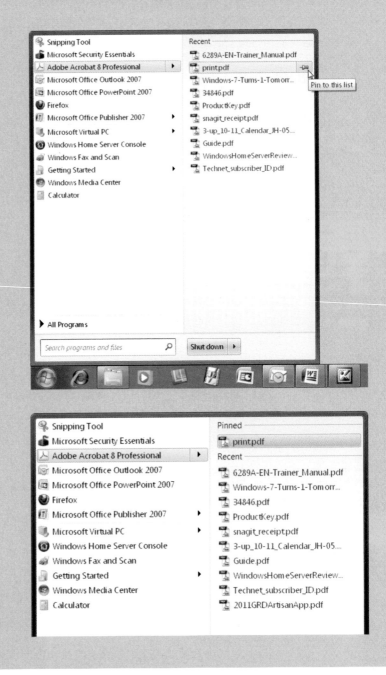

Step 4

Now you can see the distinction between the items Windows 7 automatically pins to the Jump List and those you choose to pin.

The hidden status icons revealed by clicking the Show hidden icons button.

Notification Area

The notification area, also called the system tray, is not new in Windows 7, but it is greatly improved over that of previous versions of Windows. The notification area holds status indicators and pop-up menus for a variety of devices and programs installed on your computer. It is so handy that many installation programs—both by Microsoft and by other software publishers—insert their own handy icons here. Before Windows 7, this practice resulted in clutter that detracted from the value of this feature. Windows 7 changed all that. To begin with, it does not display as many icons here itself, and best of all, it changed how icons appear and behave. Further, all those additional status icons are tucked away, but readily available with a click on the Show Hidden Icons button, as you see here.

Figure 4–11 identifies the objects in the notification area. The Network icon shown indicates an Ethernet (wired) network, whereas an icon with five

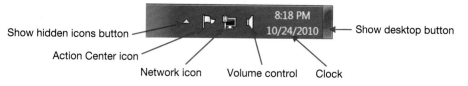

Show hidden icons button

Action Center icon

Network icon   Volume control   Clock

Show desktop button

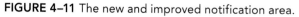

FIGURE 4–11 The new and improved notification area.

vertical bars in graduated sizes indicates a wireless network. If the network adapter is disconnected, a red X will appear on the icon. If there is another problem with the network, it will have a yellow triangle with a black exclamation mark. Hover the mouse cursor over an icon to see a brief description; right-click to display a context menu, and click on the icon to open the related program.

Action Center

The Windows Action Center, represented by the small flag icon, will briefly display a message balloon when there is a problem with your security programs or backup. Then it will quietly sit there with a white X against a red circle until you resolve the problem. A single click opens a message box, as shown here, and to open Action Center (see Figure 4–12) either click on the Open Action Center link in the message box or double-click the Action Center icon.

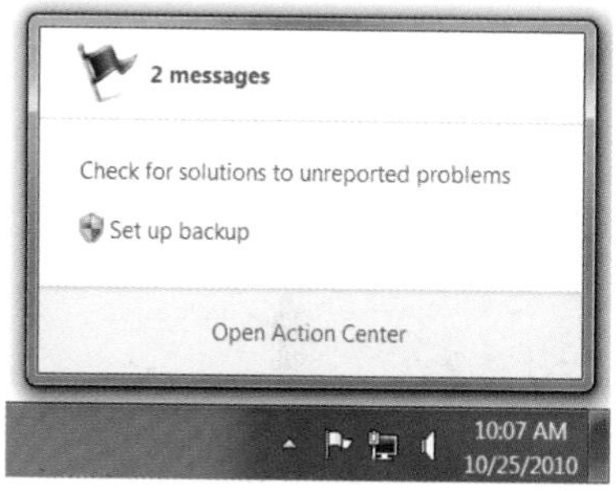

Libraries

Windows 7 has a new feature called libraries. A library looks like a file system folder, but it is not. Even though the four default libraries in Windows 7 carry the names of special folders in Windows Vista: Documents, Music, Pictures, and Videos. While a folder is a container for files and other folders (called subfolders), a library; only contains links to the locations of files and folders.

A library stores information about the locations of folders and files, displaying them as if they were all in one location, thus making it easier for you to find related information or types of files. For instance, in our example, the Documents library shows two default locations: My Documents (in this case D:\Yoda\Documents) and Public Documents (D:\Users\Public\Documents), as shown in Figure 4–13. Locations can be on the local computer or on shared locations on a network.

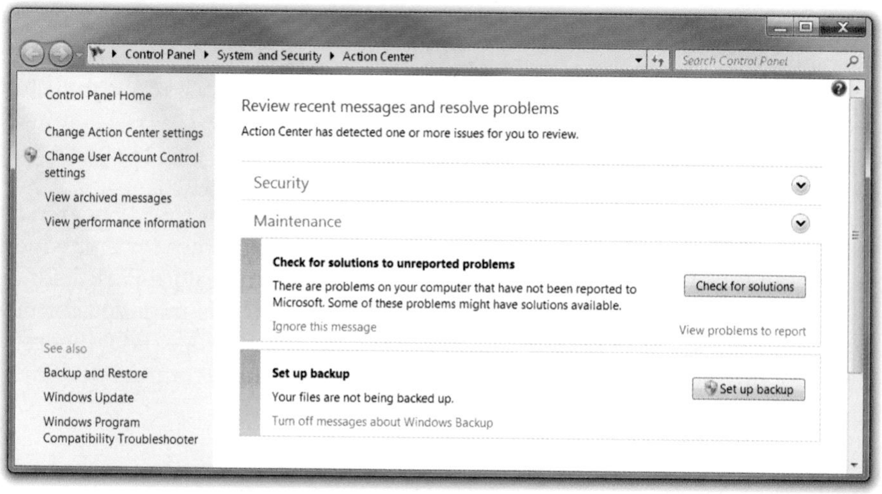

The Action Center message box appears after a single click of the Action Center icon.

FIGURE 4–12 Open the Windows 7 Action Center by clicking on the Action Center link in the message box.

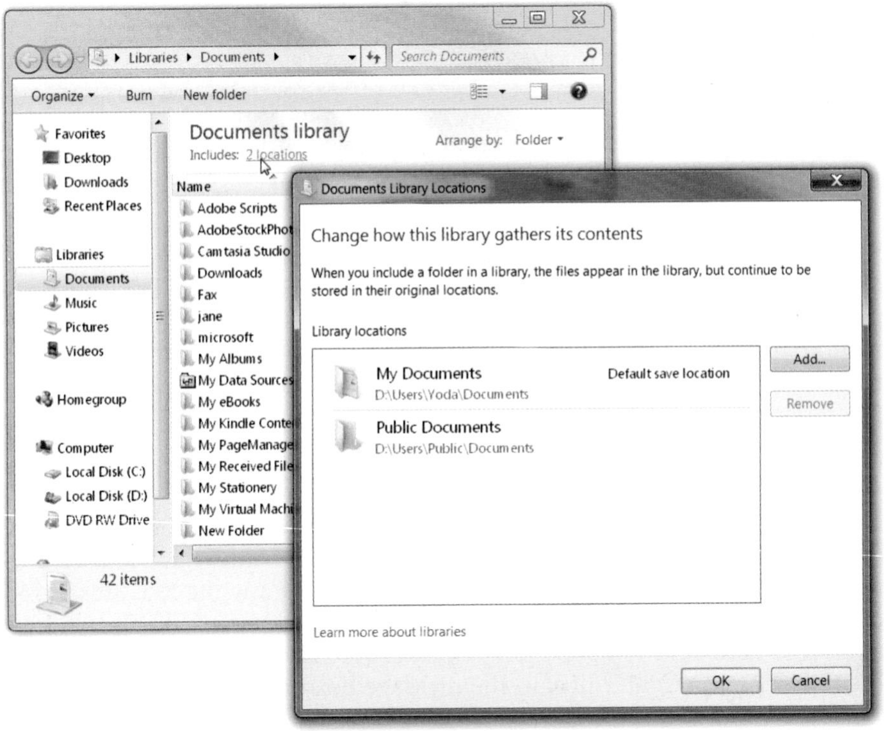

FIGURE 4–13 The two default locations for the Documents library.

File System Support

Regardless of the file system used on a disk or disc, what you see in Windows Explorer remains the same: folders and files. Windows 7 supports the file systems previously supported in Windows Vista. They are described below.

FAT File Systems

The FAT file systems include FAT12, FAT16, FAT32, and exFAT. Each has a logical structure that includes a file allocation table (FAT)—hence the name of the file system—and a directory structure. The file allocation table enables the OS to allocate space for files, while a directory gives the OS a place for identifying information about each file. The FAT file system used many years ago by Microsoft's MS DOS operating system on hard disks is now called the FAT16 file system.

The FAT32 file system was introduced in Windows 95 OEM Service Release version 2. The FAT32 file system can use larger partitions than FAT16 and allocates space more efficiently. Windows OSs only use the FAT12 file system when formatting a floppy disk, and floppy disk drives have all but disappeared from modern computers. Apple OS X supports FAT32, as well as exFAT (discussed next), so consider using one of these on a flash drive that you intend to use in both a Windows and Apple OS X computer.

The Extended File Allocation Table (exFAT) file system first appeared in Microsoft's Windows Embedded CE 6.0, a version of Windows for embedded applications, and later it was added to Windows Vista in Service Pack 1. Since then, all versions of Windows support this file system. It is intended for use with solid-state storage devices, such as flash drives. While exFAT theoretically supports volume sizes up to 64 zettabytes (ZBs), the recommended maximum is 512 terabytes (TBs).

Windows NTFS File Systems

The NTFS file system is available in all versions of Windows beginning with Windows NT, but excluding the Windows 95, Windows 98, and Windows Me versions. The main NTFS logical structure is a master file table (MFT) that is expandable, and therefore can be modified In future versions. Windows uses a transaction processing system to track changes to files, adding a measure of transaction-level recoverability to the file system, similar to what your bank uses to track transactions, and it will roll back incomplete transactions.

Over the years Microsoft improved NTFS. From the beginning, the NTFS file system provided file and folder security not available on FAT volumes. Today, in addition to file and folder security and transaction processing capability, NTFS supports many features. The short list includes file compression, file encryption, and an indexing service. NTFS is the preferred file system for hard drives in Windows and the default created when you install Windows.

File Systems for Optical Discs

Optical discs require special Windows file system drivers. The CD-ROM File System (CDFS) allows Windows OSs to read CD-ROMs and to read and write to writable CDs (CD-R) and rewritable CDs (CD-RW). The Universal Disk Format (UDF) is a file system driver required for Windows to read DVD ROMs and to read and write DVD-R and DVD-RW.

In addition to the traditional method for writing to optical drives (basically, a write once method), Microsoft introduced a new file system for optical drives in Windows Vista, which allows you to write to an optical disc, notably the DVD-RW and CD-R optical discs, adding files at any time, as long as the disc has room. Learn how to select between these two methods in the section titled "Managing Windows."

Security

In Windows 7, Microsoft improved existing security features such as User Account Control, BitLocker, and Windows Defender.

Improved User Account Control

User Account Control, introduced in Windows Vista, is less annoying in Windows 7, with fewer tasks requiring user intervention and use of an elevation prompt. Additionally, if you log on with an account with administrative privileges, you can adjust the User Account Control elevation prompt behavior.

Note: BitLocker and BitLocker To Go will encrypt an entire volume, regardless of the file system (NTFS, FAT, or exFAT).

BitLocker and BitLocker To Go

BitLocker, introduced in Windows Vista Enterprise and Ultimate editions, is also limited to the Enterprise and Ultimate editions in Windows 7. In Windows 7, as in Vista, you can encrypt the boot volume, but you can also encrypt any internal hard drive. Further, a feature called BitLocker To Go lets you encrypt external drives, such as flash drives. Later in this chapter you will learn how to secure use BitLocker in Windows 7.

AppLocker

You can use AppLocker, a new feature in Windows 7, to control which applications each user can run, reducing the chance of malware running on the user's computer. You administer AppLocker with Group Policy, which you can centrally manage through a Windows Active Directory domain.

Windows Defender

Introduced in Windows Vista, Windows Defender is an improved free built-in antispyware utility integrated into the Windows 7 Action Center where you can configure spyware scanning and updates.

Program Compatibility

- If you need to run an old application that does not work well in Windows 7, open Help and Support from the Start menu, search on "compatibility," and check out the recommendations there. One recommendation is to run the Program Compatibility Troubleshooter (called the Program Compatibility Wizard in Windows XP). This will walk you through creating settings that may help your program to run better. Or you can do this manually by tweaking the compatibility settings for that application in the Properties for the application or its shortcut.
- If the application still will not run, download and install Windows XP Mode, as described in Chapter 3. Install the application into the Windows XP VM. Windows 7 will even allow you to create a shortcut on the Start menu to an application installed in Windows XP Mode.

Recovery Tools

With each version of Windows, Microsoft has enhanced the recovery tools for repairing damage to the operating system. One of the most venerable of these tools is Task Manager, which has been in Windows through several versions and was extensively improved along the way. Task Manager is a Windows utility that allows you to see the state of individual processes and programs running on the computer, and to stop errant programs, when necessary.

You can access some of these tools while Windows is up and running, but in case a serious problem prevents Windows from starting, you can access an entire menu of tools by booting your system from the Windows Vista or Windows 7 disc. Choose the language settings, click Next, and click the option Repair Your Computer. Select the OS you want to repair (if you installed more than one), click Next, and the System Recovery Options menu will display (see Figure 4–14). The following tools are available from this menu:

- Startup Repair will scan for problems with missing or damaged system files and attempt to replace the problem files.

> *Note:* Task Manager has abilities beyond managing tasks. If your Windows computer seems unusually slow, open Task Manager and select the Performance tab to determine if CPU or memory usage is high. Select the Networking tab to see state and speed of your network connections.

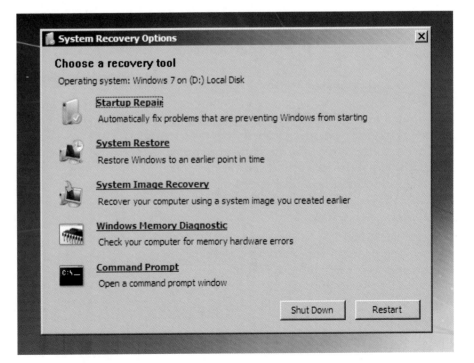

FIGURE 4–14 The Windows 7 System Recovery Options.

- **System Restore** will allow you to create a restore point, which is a snapshot of Windows, its configuration, and all installed programs. Many restore points are also created automatically when you make changes to your system. If your computer has nonfatal problems after you have made a change, you can use System Restore to roll it back to a selected restore point.

- **System Image Recovery** will let you restore a complete PC Image backup, providing you created one. This is a replacement for the Automated System Recovery (ASR) tool previously found in the Windows XP Backup program.

- **Windows Memory Diagnostic Tool** tests the system's RAM because RAM problems can prevent Windows from starting normally. If this tool detects a problem, replace the RAM before using any other recovery tool.

- **Command Prompt** replaces the Recovery Console found in Windows XP. It provides a character mode interface in which you can use command-line tools to resolve a problem.

LO 4.3 | Customizing and Managing Windows 7

Once you have installed Windows 7, configured the OS to work with your network, and installed updates and service packs, it's time to customize Windows for the user. In this section, you will practice some of the common procedures for customizing and managing Windows 7, using Computer Management tools for a variety of tasks, installing and removing applications, managing Windows components, and preparing the desktop for users, including modifications to display settings and adding a printer.

Computer Management

After you installed Windows 7, if you add a new hard drive to your computer and need to partition it or do any other maintenance, open the Computer Management console and expand the Disk Management node. Figure 4–15 shows the disks on our Windows Vista/Windows 7 dual-boot computer. Windows Vista is installed on Disk 0 (drive C:) and Windows 7 is installed on Disk 1 (drive D:).

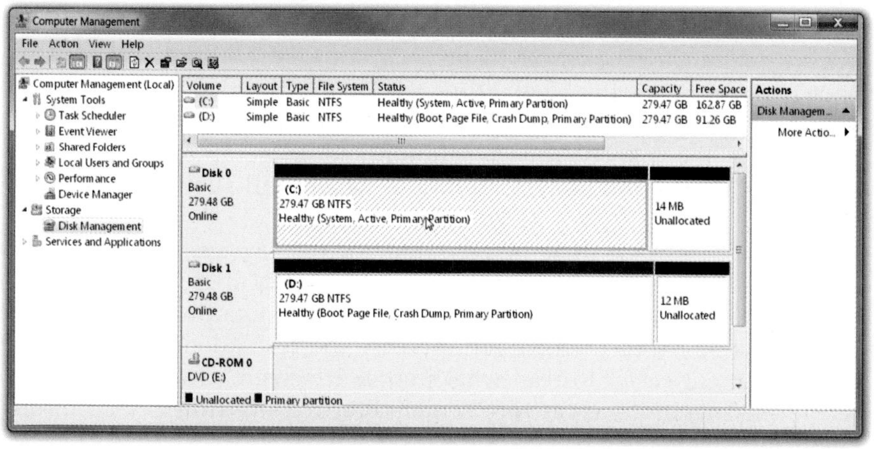

FIGURE 4–15 The Disk Management node in the Computer Management console.

If you add a hard drive—internal or external—use Disk Management to partition and format the drive, if necessary. New external drives often come pre-formatted with FAT32, which does not provide security and cannot automatically repair damage to the disk. Therefore, open Computer Management, and reformat your new drives if you wish to use the NTFS file system. This will destroy all data on the target partition. There is also a method for converting a FAT partition to NTFS from the command prompt, which it will do without losing data. Although the danger of data loss is small, we recommend backing up your data before converting a FAT partition. To do this conversion, open a command prompt and enter **convert *d*: /fs:ntfs,** where *d:* is the letter of the target partition you wish to convert to NTFS.

Preparing the Desktop for Users

In the decades we have worked with PCs running Windows OSs, we have noticed one phenomenon: A user who would have to have someone show him or her the location of the on/off button will quickly figure out how to personalize the desktop. It seems like one day we help unpack the PC and a week later we come back to see dozens of shortcuts arrayed over desktop wallpaper of a child's crayon drawing. Whenever possible, we encourage such personalization because it means the person is making the computer his or her own and learning how to move around in Windows at the same time. So, whether you are preparing a PC for yourself or another user, there are some items to do after you complete the immediate post-installation tasks and before you install the necessary everyday applications. These include customizing the display settings—mainly the resolution—and adding a local printer.

Customizing Display Settings

After installing Windows 7 you may need to customize the display settings for resolution and (if you are lucky) for multiple displays.

Display Resolution. The Windows 7 installation program is very good at quickly installing Windows, but we still find that we need to tweak the display resolution settings because, during installation, Windows setup may install a generic display driver that might leave the display adapter at a lower resolution than it should be set to. This is especially true when you install it into a virtual machine. In that case, you will install the virtual machine additions appropriate for the hypervisor and installed version of Windows, which will include better video adapter support. Then you will be able to select a higher resolution for the virtual display.

When you have installed Windows 7 on a desktop computer with a flat-panel display, if it installed the appropriate driver for the video adapter and the display, then resolution should be appropriate. A flat-panel display has one native resolution, which will show as the recommended resolution.

A related issue is that because today's display systems (the video adapter and display combined) are capable of very high resolution, you may need to enlarge icons and other objects to make them more visible on the desktop. In fact, when you increase the resolution, it will prompt you to "Make it easier to read what's on your screen." This is where you change the size of items on your screen. Practice adjusting screen resolution in Step-by-Step 4.03.

Step-by-Step 4.03

Adjusting the Display Resolution

In this step-by-step exercise, you will familiarize your-self with the Windows 7 Appearance and Personalization applet and make a few changes to the desktop. These Windows 7 steps are very similar to those for Windows Vista. To complete this task, you will need the following:

- A PC with Windows 7 installed.

Step 1

First change the screen resolution. A quick way to open the Screen Resolution page of the Appearance and Personalization applet is to right-click on an empty area of the desktop and select Screen Resolution from the context menu.

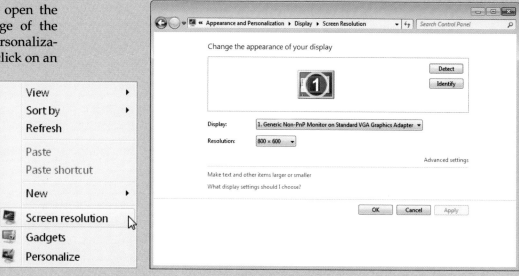

Step 2

Click on the down arrow in the drop-down list labeled Resolution, look for a recommended resolution, and select it. Click OK.

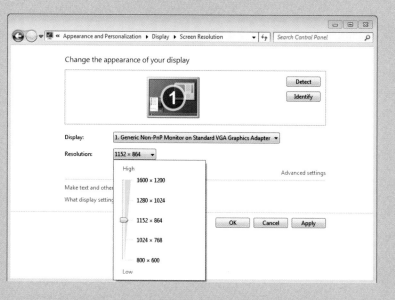

If you have increased your resolution, you will see this page, on which you can select the size of the text and other screen objects. This page is also available from the Screen Resolution page by clicking the link labeled "Make text and other items larger or smaller." Watch the Preview as you select a different size.

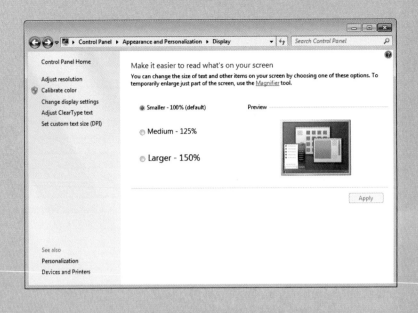

If you changed the text and object size, you will need to log off and then log on again for the change to take effect.

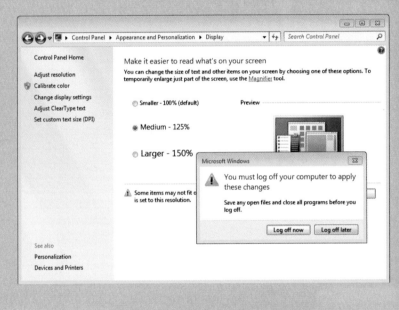

Multiple Displays. Although most PCs today only have a single display, more and more jobs require the increased screen real estate of multiple displays. Windows has supported multiple displays for several versions. All you need to add more display space to a typical desktop PC is a dual-headed video adapter and a second display. For most laptops the only cost is for a second display, because laptops usually come with a display connector for an external display that you can use simultaneously with the built-in display. We have worked with dual displays for over a decade on our computers and we found that it can be a bit weird to work with displays of different sizes. Therefore, the ideal situation is to use identical displays.

When you have multiple displays, you can configure how Windows uses these displays on the Screen Resolution page. Our preferred mode is "Extend these displays," which leaves the taskbar on the primary display (labeled 1 in Figure 4–16) and extends the desktop to the secondary display. It is great to have a document open on one display and an Internet browser open on

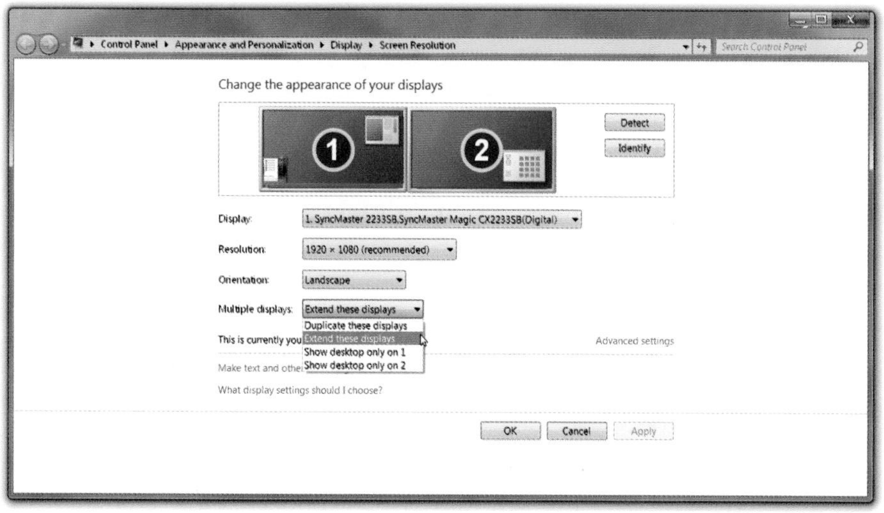

FIGURE 4–16 Select how you want the desktop to appear on multiple displays.

FIGURE 4–17 When you click the Identify button a numeral will appear briefly on each display.

the other, for instance. The setting "Duplicate these displays" shows the same desktop on both displays. You might use this if your laptop connects to a projector on which you wish to show the desktop. The remaining setting, "Show desktop only on 1" and "Show desktop only on 2" will leave the display you do not select blank.

Click the Identify button to have a number display on each physical display (see Figure 4–17) so that you can confirm that you have the displays oriented left to right as they are in the Screen Resolution page. If they are not, click and drag the display images on the Screen Resolution page to place them in the correct order.

> *Note:* Figure 4–17 is a screenshot captured on a dual-display with a window positioned to overlap both displays. It is one continuous image captured on two physically separate displays.

Desktop Gadgets

Windows Vista had a feature called the Sidebar in which you could configure one or more small programs called gadgets. The Sidebar is gone from Windows 7, but the gadgets remain; now you can position them anywhere you wish on the desktop. Each gadget performs some small function—usually involving keeping information handy in a small screen object. This information can be the date or time, stock quotes, weather in a certain city, and much more.

Gadgets have proven to be a potential security hole. We no longer use them or recommend them, but if you should decide to try them, check out the article titled "Safety tips for using Windows gadgets," found in the Microsoft Safety and Security Center at http://www.microsoft.com/security/pc-security/gadgets.aspx.

Adding a Local Printer

Installing a new printer in Windows should be a nonevent because Windows is a plug-and-play OS, and new printers are plug-and-play. Therefore, you simply follow the setup guide for the new printer. In many cases, Windows will already have the printer driver and will install it without requiring a DVD from the manufacturer, but there can be another reason to run a setup program from the printer manufacturer. A new printer, especially one that includes other functions—primarily document scanning, copying, and faxing—will also include special software beyond the standard printer driver. Most common is software for scanning and organizing your documents.

Before connecting a printer, be sure to read the printer's setup guide—usually a hard-to-miss oversized sheet of paper with the basic instructions for setting up the printer. Often, a printer setup guide will instruct you to install the printer's software before connecting it, especially if it connects via USB. It will also guide you through making both the power connection and the connection to the computer. How will your printer connect to the computer? The most common wired printer interface is USB, but some printers also use IEEE 1394 (FireWire).

If a printer uses a cable (USB or IEEE 1394) you will first connect the printer, and then turn it on. If it connects via a wireless method, you will turn on the printer and establish the wireless connection. Once Windows detects a printer, it installs the driver and configures the printer for you. It will be added to the Devices and Printers applet, shown in Figure 4–18, and be available to all applications that can use a printer. The printer with the white check mark on a green circle is the default printer that Windows will use unless you select a different printer. Double-click on a printer icon to open the printer page with status information and links to the printer properties, print queue, and other pages for managing and controlling the printer and its features.

Connecting to a Network Printer

If you are installing a Bluetooth or Wi-Fi printer, or if a printer is available on your school or corporate network, and an administrator has configured it

Note: In the example in Figure 4–18, not all devices in the Printers and Faxes categories are physical printers or faxes. Some are software "printers" such as Adobe PDF and Snagit 9, which take files from one format (a Word document or a graphic file) and "print" it to a file in a new format, such as Adobe PDF, a file format commonly used for electronic document exchange that does not require users to have the same software that was used to create these documents, just software that can read them.

FIGURE 4–18 The Devices and Printers Control Panel.

with appropriate permissions so that you can connect and print to it, you can do just that. To do so, open Devices and Printers and click Add a printer. In the Add Printer wizard select "Add a network, wireless or Bluetooth printer." It will take time to search for all available network printers and then display them in the box. Select the Printer Name of the printer you wish to connect to, click Next, and follow the instructions. This will install the appropriate printer driver on your computer so that Windows can format each print job for that printer before sending it to the network printer.

Installing and Removing Applications

By now, you are ready to install applications into Windows to make your computer the tool you need for work, home, or school. If you purchased a computer with Windows preinstalled, you may also need to remove some of those preinstalled applications you have no desire or need to use.

Installing Applications

Today, each mainstream application comes with its own installation program that will walk you through the installation process. Some offer just a few options, installing with very little user input, while others will give you the option to do a custom install, in which you select the components to install and the location for the installed files. These programs copy the application files and make necessary changes to Windows, such as associating one or more file types with the application so that when you double-click on, say, a file with a DOCX extension, it knows to open Microsoft Word.

After completing an application installation, you should make sure to update the application. If you have an Internet connection, most applications will check for updates. This is very important today when malware targets our business productivity software. If your applications are from Microsoft, you can update them through Windows Update, which will list updates under Optional Updates, as shown in Figure 4–19.

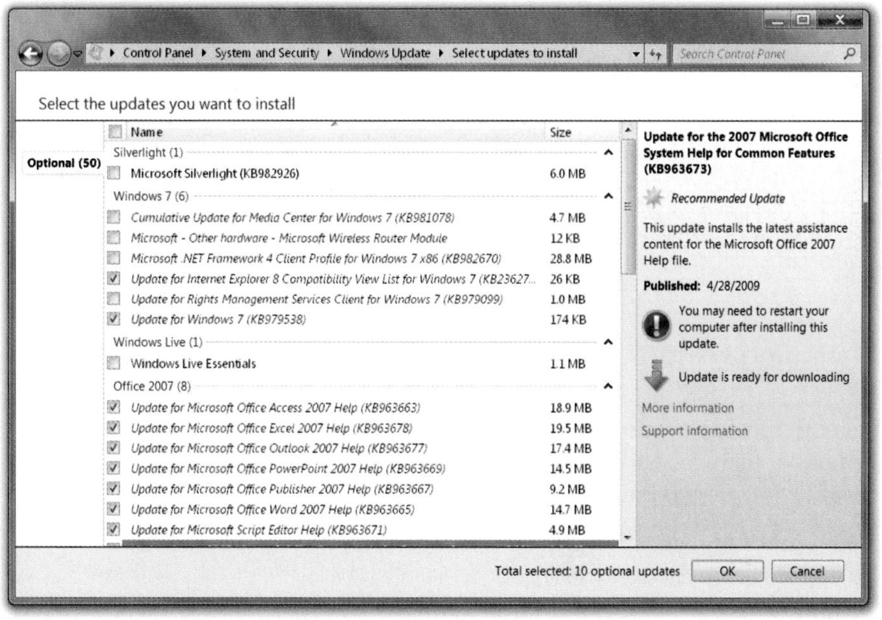

FIGURE 4–19 Update Microsoft Applications through Windows Update.

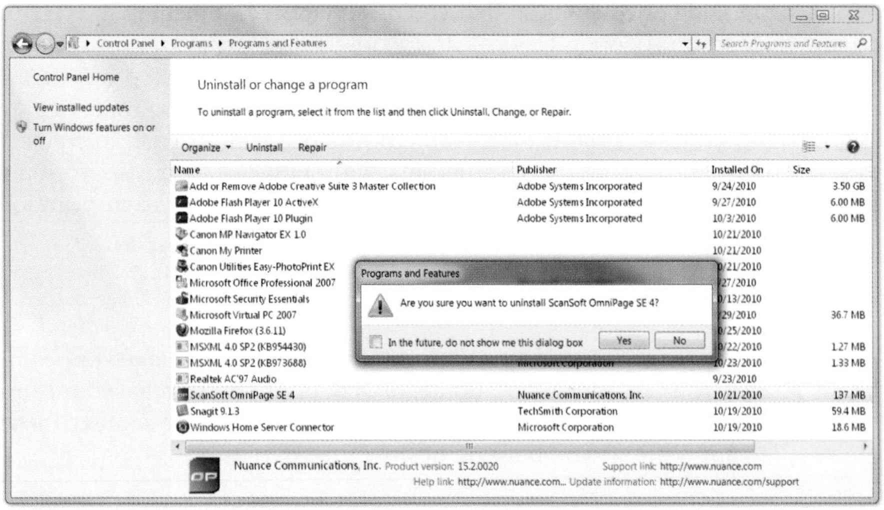

FIGURE 4–20 Uninstall unwanted programs.

try this!

Use Add or Remove Programs

Become familiar with the list of programs installed on your computer. In addition to applications, the Programs and Features applet lists the installed Windows updates. Try this:

1. Open the Control Panel. Under Programs, click on Uninstall A Program. Wait for the list to display. Browse through the list of Currently Installed Programs.
2. If you find a program that you want to remove, click the program, and then click the Uninstall button in the bar above the list to begin the uninstall process. Sometimes you must provide the installation CD before you can remove the program.
3. In the task list on the left, click View Installed Updates to see a list of installed Windows updates. If you have a good reason to uninstall an update, this is the place to do it. We don't recommend uninstalling updates unless you are sure it is necessary.
4. When you have finished exploring, close the open windows. If you uninstalled an application, you may need to allow the uninstall program to restart the computer.

Removing Applications

When it comes time to remove an application, you should first look for an uninstall program for the application. If the application has a submenu off the Start menu, it may include the uninstall program, which is usually the best choice for uninstalling. You can also search the folder in which the application installed for an uninstall program. If you cannot find such a program for an application you wish to uninstall, open Control Panel, locate Programs, and click Uninstall A Program. It may take a few seconds for the list of installed programs to display in the Programs and Features page. Locate the program you wish to uninstall and double-click it. You will see a warning, as shown in Figure 4–20. Follow the instructions to complete the operation.

Managing Windows Components

Windows 7, like previous versions, includes many Windows components beyond the basic operating system files. You can view them by opening Windows features in Control Panel. Simply click a check box to turn individual features on or off, as shown on page 147.

Simple File Management

As with any operating system, file management in Windows Vista and Windows 7 is mainly about organizing data files so that you can easily find the files you need when you need them. Windows provides a set of folders for just this purpose. Before you use them, get a basic understanding of the default file hierarchy in whatever version of Windows you are using. Then learn how to work with not just files and folders, but also the libraries that Windows 7 introduced. Finally, learn about the Windows file systems for optical discs and the ones that allow you to copy files to CD or DVD as easily as you copy them to a hard drive or flash drive.

Windows 7 Default File Hierarchy

All versions of Windows create one set of folders for the operating system, another set for application program files, and an additional set, personal folders, for each user account to hold user data files. The 32-bit and 64-bit distributions of Windows differ only in the location in which they store programs. The 32-bit distributions of Windows 7 stores all programs in the Program Files folder, while the 64-bit distributions store only 64-bit programs in this folder and store 32-bit programs in the folder named Program Files (x86). Figure 4–21 shows the folder hierarchy for a 64-bit installation of Windows 7. The default location for the majority of the Windows operating system files is in C:\Windows.

The default location for user data is C:\Users\<username> where <username> is the log-on user name. In Figure 4–22, note the folder for the user Jade. Within this folder are the personal folders created by Windows to hold various types of data or, as in the case of the Desktop folder, to hold files from a certain location. The Downloads folder holds files you download with your Internet browser.

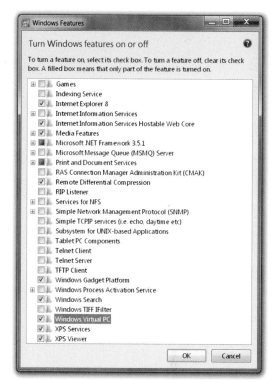

Use the check boxes to turn Windows features on or off.

Navigating Windows Explorer

There are several ways to manage your files in Windows. The primary tool for saving files is the individual application you use to create and modify files of a certain type: for instance, a word processing program, spreadsheet program, photo editing program, or other application. When you issue the command within an application to save a file, you can navigate to the location of your choice and either save the file in an existing folder or create a new folder before saving. Similarly, when you decide to open an existing file from within an application, you can navigate to a location and open the desired file.

Although you can also do many file management tasks within an application, the primary tool for copying, moving, renaming, and deleting files is Windows Explorer. Microsoft has added some new features to the Windows Explorer folder windows, which we will highlight here. Figure 4–23 shows the anatomy of a Windows Explorer folder window. By default, the Menu bar appears only when you press the ALT key, and you can use the Organize button and other buttons on the toolbar to modify the appearance and functionality of the Windows Explorer folder windows.

Navigate through Windows Explorer with mouse operations. When you hover the mouse over the navigation pane, small clear triangles appear next to each folder object that can be expanded. Click the triangle

try this!

Explore Windows Folders

If you are sitting at a computer with Windows Vista or Windows 7, explore the folder hierarchy. Try this:

1. Click Start | Computer.
2. In Windows Explorer double-click the icon for the Local Disk (C:). Note the folders in the root of drive C:.
3. Double-click the icon for Program Files and note the folders under Program Files. If you have a 64-bit installation of Windows, double-click the icon for Program Files (x86) and note the folders in this folder.
4. Now browse to the Users folder and open the folder for the account with which you logged on and explore the contents of this folder.

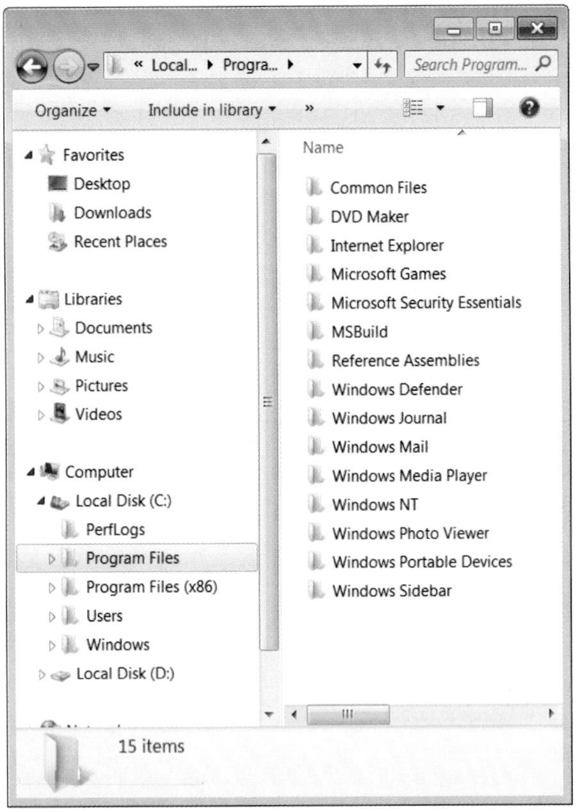

FIGURE 4–21 The Windows 7 64-bit default folder hierarchy.

FIGURE 4–22 Windows 7 personal folders for the user Jade.

and it turns solid black and points down to the right in the navigation pane at the now-visible objects contained in the original folder. Click an object's icon in the navigation pane to open it in the contents pane. If you wish to open objects (folders, files, etc.) in the contents pane, you double-click on the object. You can move files and folders from one location to another by dragging and dropping the object you wish to move. Right-click on an object to access other possible operations.

Libraries

Recall what you learned earlier in this chapter about libraries. A library points to one or more locations. Familiarize yourself with libraries by clicking the libraries pinned icon on the taskbar (it looks like a bunch of folders in a stand) and clicking on any library in the navigation pane. For instance, when you do this to the Documents pane, its contents appear in the contents pane and above that pane is the Library pane. The word *Includes* appears in the Library pane, and after that appears the number of locations. But this is also a link—click it to open the Documents Library Locations window.

You can add locations to a library and create libraries of your own. This is very handy if you want to organize all the files related to a project but those files are stored in folders in various locations on your local hard drive, external hard drives, or network servers. You can back up data in a library as if it were stored in one location. To add a location to the

Note: Open Windows Explorer quickly by pressing the Windows key and "e" key together.

Note: By default, Windows Explorer hides extensions for known file types, an inconvenience for power users. To make file extensions visible, open Windows Explorer and press Alt-T to open the Tools menu, select Folder Options, then click the View tab. In Advanced Settings clear the check box labeled Hide extensions for known file types. Click OK to close Folder Options.

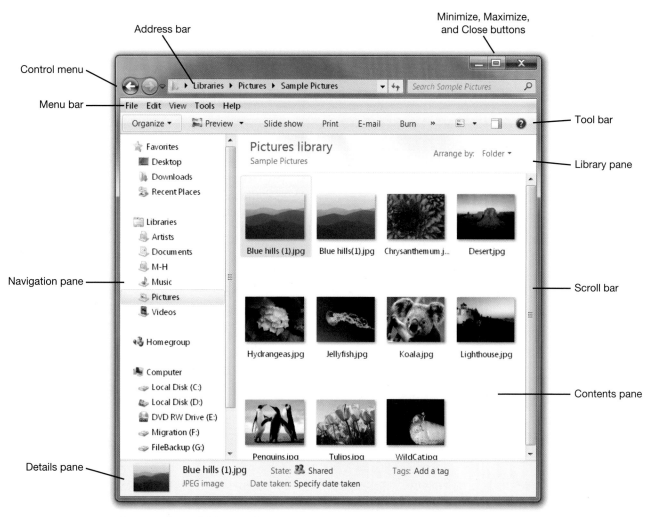

Control menu

Address bar

Minimize, Maximize, and Close buttons

Menu bar

Tool bar

Library pane

Navigation pane

Scroll bar

Contents pane

Details pane

FIGURE 4–23 A Windows Explorer folder window.

Documents library, simply click the Add button, which opens the Include Folder in Document window. Use this to browse to the folders you wish to add, select the folder, and click the Include Folder button. Windows then adds the new location to the library.

Notice the words *Default save location*. When you save files into this library, you are putting them in the default location for saving files. To change the default save location, first you need more than one save location in a library. Then all you need to do is right-click the desired location and select "Set as default save location."

To create a new library, first click on Libraries in the navigation pane, then notice the New Library tool that appears on the toolbar. Click New Library, which will create a new library folder, ready for a name and locations. If you missed entering the name when you created it, right-click on the New Library, select rename, enter the name, and press Enter. With the new library selected in the navigation pane, the contents pane will indicate that the library is empty. Click the "Include a folder" button to begin adding locations to this new library. You can continue to add locations. Figure 4–24 shows a new library named M-H with two locations—one on a network server named HTC-SERVER.

Working with Optical Discs

Even most inexpensive consumer-grade PCs come with optical drives capable of burning (writing data, music, or videos to disc), and optical discs are great for those files you wish to remove to make more room on the computer's hard

FIGURE 4–24 A new library, M-H, with two locations, Manuscripts and Screenshots.

drive. Whatever your need for burning CDs or DVDs, you should first understand the two formats Windows 7 uses when it burns discs: the ISO Mastered format and the Universal Disk Format (UDF) Live File System.

Use the Mastered format when you want to be able to use a CD or DVD in a conventional CD or DVD player or in any computer (older Apple Macs or PCs). The trouble with using this format is that each item you select to copy to the PC is stored temporarily in available hard disk space (in addition to the space used by the original file) until you finish selecting all you wish to copy, and then they are copied in one operation. This makes it difficult to copy files from a hard drive when you have very little free hard drive space on any hard drive in your computer.

Use the Live File System to burn a disc when you will only use the disc on newer Apple Macs and newer PCs (Windows XP and newer support it, but older PCs may not). Using Live File System you can directly copy items to the drive without requiring extra hard drive space. You can copy items individually, over time—either by leaving the disc in the drive or reinserting the disc multiple times. If all the systems in which you plan to use a disc are newer PCs or Macs, then keep the default setting, which uses the Live File System. Step-by-Step 4.04 will walk you through copying files to an optical disc using the Live File System format.

Step-by-Step 4.04

Burning a CD or DVD

In this step-by-step exercise, you will burn a DVD using the Live File System, which allows you to copy files much as you would to any hard drive or flash drive. To complete this exercise, you will need the following:

- A computer with a DVD/CD drive and with Windows 7 installed—either a conventional installation or an installation in a VM.
- A blank CD or DVD.

Step 1

Insert a blank disc into the optical drive. When the Autoplay dialog opens, select Burn Files to Disc.

Step 2

In the Burn a Disc dialog, provide a title for the disc (the default is the current date), enter a name, and then click Next.

Live File System format

Mastered format

Burn a Disc

How do you want to use this disc?

Disc title: OS Project

○ **Like a USB flash drive**
Save, edit, and delete files on the disc anytime. The disc will work on computers running Windows XP or later. (Live File System)

○ **With a CD/DVD player**
Burn files in groups and individual files can't be edited or removed after burning. The disc will also work on most computers. (Mastered)

Which one should I choose?

Next   Cancel

Step 3

Windows formats the disc.

Formatting (0 bytes)

Formatting (0 bytes)

on **DVD RW Drive (E:)**
Preparing to format

Step 4

After the disc is prepared, this message displays. You can now copy files to the disc from Windows Explorer—either click the button labeled "Open folder to view files" (just one way to open Windows Explorer), or close the box and continue working, copying files to the disc as you would normally copy files to a hard disk or USB drive.

AutoPlay

DVD RW Drive (E:) OS Project

General options

Open folder to view files
using Windows Explorer

View more AutoPlay options in Control Panel

Step 5

For instance, you can drag and drop folders and files to the disc, as we have done here with the folder titled "06-A+SG_7E." When you use the Live File System, you can continue to add files to the disc as long as it has available space. You can do that now, or add files to it later.

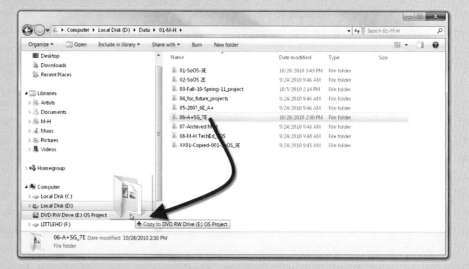

151

LO 4.4 | Managing Local Security in Windows 7

If your Windows computer is on a corporate network, the company will centrally manage it, including the security issues. A computer that is not part of a corporate network depends on the knowledge of the user for its security. Security implemented solely on a desktop or laptop computer is local security. Here we will look at administering local user accounts, local security for files and folders, Windows BitLocker drive encryption, Windows Defender antispam protection, and Windows Firewall.

Administering Local User Accounts

Local user accounts reside in the local accounts database on a Windows computer. You use a local account to give someone access to the Windows computer and local data. More than one person can log on to a Windows desktop computer as an interactive user (the one sitting at the keyboard), through a feature called Switch Users, but only one person at a time can physically use that Windows desktop computer's mouse, keyboard, and display. Typically, only one interactive user uses a desktop computer. Therefore, most users have little or no experience managing local accounts other than their own, and those same users rarely need to make any changes to their own account. This section gives you a chance to create and manage a local user account.

User Accounts Applet

The primary tool for administering local user accounts is User Accounts, a Control Panel applet. Either browse to it from Start | Control Panel or enter "user accounts" in the Start menu Search box and select User Accounts from the list of results. In the example shown here, the user Yoda is an Administrator and the account is password protected.

Working with User Accounts in Windows

You must log on with an account that is a member of the Administrators group to see all the local user accounts on your computer. Then open User Accounts and click Manage Another Account. The Manage Accounts window

The User Account Control Panel.

will show the existing accounts. In the example shown there are only two accounts: Yoda and Guest; the Guest account is off, which is the default for this account.

Windows 7 also has a local account built-in named Administrator, disabled by default during a clean installation or an upgrade. The exception to this is when you upgrade a Windows Vista installation that only has the Administrator and has no other active local account that is a member of the local Administrators group, which would be a rare occurrence. In that case, the local Administrator account is enabled, so it would be visible in Local Users when an administrator selects Manage Another Account.

When you are performing an upgrade to Windows 7 on a Vista PC in a Microsoft Active Directory Domain, it will disable the local Administrator account regardless of the contents of the local accounts database. You can enable this account after installation, but we strongly recommend that you not do it because *this* account is all-powerful and immune to the User Account Control (UAC) security feature, whereas other accounts that are simply members of the local Administrators group are not immune to UAC.

Therefore, while the built-in Administrator account is logged on, the computer is more vulnerable to a malware attack. So it's good practice to not enable the Administrator account for everyday use, as you may never need this account.

Step-by-Step 4.05

Creating a New Account in Windows 7

In this step-by-step exercise, you will create a new Standard user account. To complete this exercise, you will need the following:

- A computer or virtual machine with Windows 7 installed. You may use Windows Vista, keeping in

mind that the screens will not exactly match the illustrations in the steps.

- To log on using an Administrator account (not necessarily *the* Administrator account).

Step 1

Open User Accounts, using one of the methods described earlier. In the User Accounts window, click Manage Another Account. Enter a name for the account, read the descriptions of the Standard user and Administrator user account types, but leave Standard user selected and click Create Account.

Step 2

The Manage Accounts window opens with the new user added.

Step 3

The new account does not have a password. To password protect the account, you can either allow the user to log on and create a password, or you (as an Administrator) can create a password that the user will need to use when logging on. To create a password for this account, double-click on the account icon and click Create a Password.

Step 4

In the Create Password window, enter the new password twice in the New password and Confirm new password boxes. It is optional to enter a password hint, and we recommend you do that. Then click the Create Password button.

Step 5

The new user account appears in User Accounts as a Standard user account and is password protected. Close all open windows. Notice the other changes you can make to this account. When you are finished, close User Accounts.

User Account Control

Recall from Chapter 2 that User Account Control (UAC), introduced in Windows Vista and improved in Windows 7, is designed to protect the computer from having malware installed. In Vista or Windows 7, even if you log on as an Administrator, UAC will inform you that a program is trying to perform something for which it needs elevated permissions (administrator).

Windows 7 has eliminated many of the events that would have triggered a UAC prompt in Windows Vista. For instance, if you are logged on with an Administrator type account you will not see the Consent Prompt appear for certain advanced administrative tasks, such as opening the User Account Control Settings window. A Standard user will need to provide credentials.

Local Security for Files and Folders

Windows 7 supports the use of permissions to protect files and folders on local NTFS volumes. Additionally, it offers encryption on NTFS volumes, allowing you to turn on encryption for a folder, as described in Chapter 2. In this section, we will look at applying permissions on local NTFS volumes.

File and Folder Permissions

The NTFS file system allows you to control who has access to specified files and folders by assigning permissions. These permissions restrict access to local users and groups as well as to those who connect to these resources over the network. However, in the case of those connecting over a network, the share permissions (not related to NTFS permissions) take effect first and may block access to the underlying files and folders. Only NTFS volumes allow you to assign permissions to files and folders directly. In this section, we will focus on the security features of NTFS, including file and folder permissions.

On a volume formatted with the NTFS file system, each folder and file has a set of security permissions associated with it using the following mechanism. Each file and folder on an NTFS volume has an associated Access Control List (ACL), which is a table of users and/or groups and their permissions to access the file or folder. Each ACL has at least one Access Control Entry (ACE), which is like a record in this tiny ACL database that contains just one user or group account name and the permissions assigned to this account for that file or folder. An administrator, or someone with Full Control permission for the file or folder, creates the ACEs.

To view the ACEs in an ACL for a file or folder, open the Properties dialog box and select the Security tab. Figure 4–25 shows the Security page for a folder named Jade, which is the top-level personal folder automatically created by Windows the first time the user Jade logged on. Notice the list of permissions for the user Jade. This is an ACE. These are the default permissions set by Windows on the user's personal folders.

Change the permissions on a folder or file by opening its Security page and clicking the Edit button to reveal the page shown here where you can add a user or group, remove a user or group, and specify the permissions assigned to the file or folder for each user or group. Table 4–4 compares the standard permissions on folders versus those on files.

Modify the permissions for the folder named Jade.

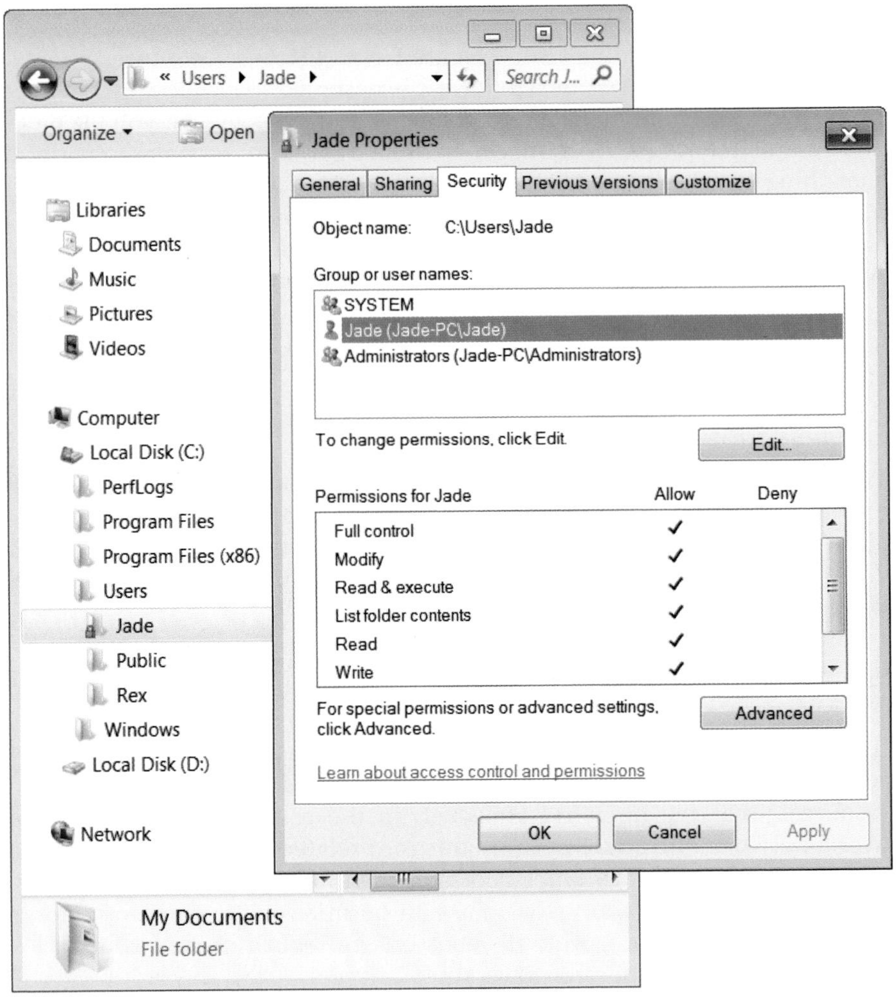

FIGURE 4–25 The list of permissions Windows creates on a user's personal folder.

TABLE 4–4 Comparison of Folder and File Standard Permissions	
Standard Folder Permissions	**Standard File Permissions**
Full control	Full control
Modify	Modify
Read and Execute	Read and Execute
Read	Read
Write	Write
List Folder Contents	

These permissions apply to files and folders on an NTFS volume and protect those resources from both locally logged-on users and those who may connect over a network. Windows only assigns network shares to folders, so you must assign the permissions to the shared folder. This entirely different set of permissions is applied before a network user accesses the NTFS folder and file permissions. We will explore sharing files on a network and setting share permissions in Chapter 10.

NTFS Permission Inheritance

The folders and files on a volume are in a hierarchy, with the drive itself at the top, followed by the root folder and subfolders. Every subfolder and its contents inherits these permissions. If you wish one of the subfolders to have different permissions, you must first navigate to it and open its Properties dialog to explicitly set those permissions on the Security page. When you view permissions on a file or folder, the permissions inherited from the parent are visible but unavailable, as shown by the gray checks and lack of boxes, and you will not be able to modify those permissions at that level. New permissions can be assigned, but inherited permissions cannot be altered. You can modify them in the folder in which they originated or you can choose to block inheritance on a folder or file to which you wish to assign different (usually more restrictive) permissions. To do this, you must access the Advanced Security Settings, then click the Change Permissions button, and deselect the check box labeled Include inheritable permissions from this object's parent.

Inherited permissions are grayed out.

BitLocker Drive Encryption

If you have very high security needs and have either the Ultimate or Enterprise version of Windows Vista or Windows 7, consider enabling BitLocker Drive Encryption. Microsoft introduced it in Windows Vista as an optional feature for encrypting only the drive on which the Windows OS resides. It was enhanced in Windows 7 to include drives beyond the system drive, including internal hard drives and externally attached drives. This last feature is called BitLocker To Go.

BitLocker is off by default. When you enable it, BitLocker encrypts the entire contents of a drive, storing an encryption and decryption key in a hardware device that is separate from the encrypted hard disk. To do this, the computer must have either a chip with Trusted Platform Module (TPM) version 1.2 or higher or a removable USB memory device (a USB flash drive will do). When you use TPM, the drive and computer are married because the chip resides in the computer.

To encrypt the drive on which Windows is installed, BitLocker requires a hard drive with at least two partitions: one that contains Windows (the "system" partition), and a second partition (the "boot" partition) created by BitLocker and not directly usable by the user. When you perform a clean installation of Windows 7 it creates the hidden boot partition. This partition is critical to booting up your computer and without it, Windows cannot be started from the encrypted partition.

In Windows 7, when you wish to encrypt a drive—either internal or external—you simply open Windows Explorer, right-click a drive, and select BitLocker from the context menu, as shown here. The existence of this choice on the menu indicates that the selected drive supports BitLocker.

BitLocker To Go may be the BitLocker feature most ordinary folks will use because many people carry flash drives, and when they have confidential information, such as medical records, it is important to protect that data. However, you will be able to access the data only on the drive on the computer on which you encrypted it or on a computer where you can make the keys available, which is limited to computers running Windows 7.

Right-click a drive and look for the option Turn on BitLocker.

try this!

View the BitLocker Status of All Drives at Once

Quickly view and manage the BitLocker status of your drives on a Windows 7 computer. Try this:

1. Select Start | Control Panel | System and Security | BitLocker Drive Encryption or simply enter "bitlocker" in the Start | Search box.
2. Click the link labeled TPM Administration to see if your computer supports TPM.
3. If you have a flash drive and have permission to do so, insert it into your computer and turn on BitLocker for the drive.

The tool for managing Bit-Locker for all your drives is the BitLocker Drive Encryption Control Panel shown here. Notice the lock and key on the encrypted drive, named Cruzer. Once you encrypt a drive with BitLocker, Manage BitLocker becomes a choice on the context menu for that drive in Windows Explorer, so you can access the management options for the drive from either location. You can also open the BitLocker Drive Encryption Control Panel by entering "manage bitlocker" in the Start menu's Search box or from within the main Control Panel window.

BitLocker is turned on for Drive H:.

Windows Defender

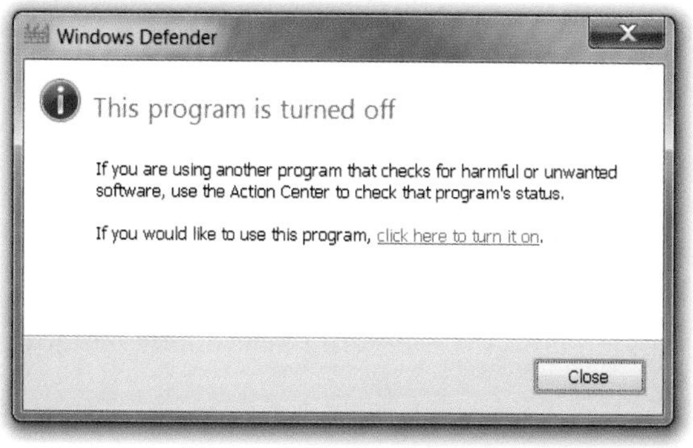

Windows Defender is free antispyware software included with Windows 7. This version protects only against spyware and does not protect against malware infecting your system. To see if Windows Defender is running on your computer click Start, type "defender," and select Windows Defender from the results list. If you see this message, Windows Defender is off, and if no other security software enabled, click the link "Click here" to turn it on. However, if you have Microsoft Security Essentials (mentioned earlier in this chapter, and described next), or almost any full-featured third-party security software installed, it will include antispyware software.

Windows Defender is turned off.

Microsoft Security Essentials

Whereas Windows Defender in Windows 7 protects only against spyware, Microsoft Security Essentials (MSE) offers much broader real-time protection against malware as well as scheduled scans. MSE is available for Windows 7 and earlier versions as a free download from Microsoft. When you install MSE, Windows Defender is disabled because it is not necessary.

Note: The Windows 7 version of Microsoft Security Essentials (MSE) will not run in Windows 8, but they do include a replacement that is nearly identical to MSE and renamed Windows Defender! Learn more about this in Chapter 5.

Windows Firewall

We strongly recommend that you use a personal firewall on your PC if it connects to any network. Most security software suites come with a personal firewall. Windows Firewall has been a feature of Windows since Windows XP Service Pack 2. Windows Vista and Windows 7 added their own enhancements to this personal firewall. So there is really no excuse for not using a personal firewall on your PC.

To open the Windows Firewall enter "windows firewall" into the Start Search box. The example shown in Figure 4–26 is on a computer connected to a private network. Notice that it shows we are not connected to a public network, which refers to an open Wi-Fi network like you would encounter if you used your laptop in an airport terminal or at your favorite coffee shop. The computer in question actually is connected to the biggest public network in the world—the Internet—but a firewall on a router guards our connection to the Internet.

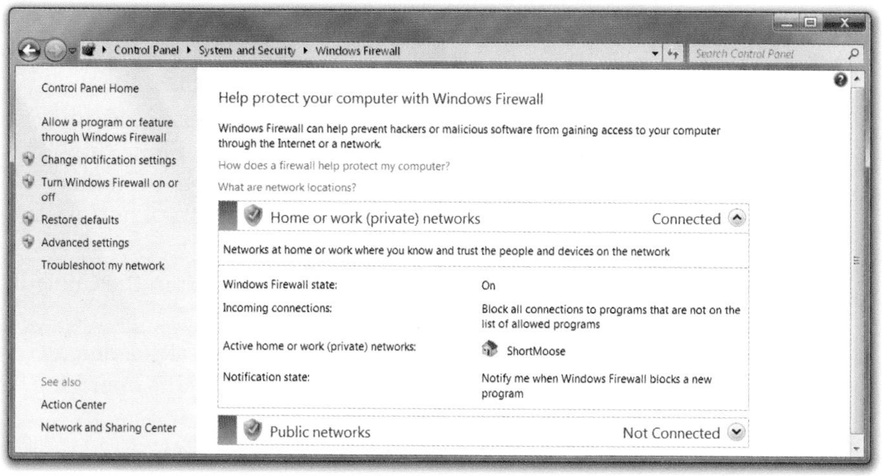

FIGURE 4–26 On this page "Public networks" refers to public Wi-Fi networks and other untrusted public networks.

Chapter 4 REVIEW

Chapter Summary

After reading this chapter and completing the Step-by-Step tutorials and Try This! exercises, you should understand the following facts about Windows 7.

Installing Windows 7

- The Windows 7 system requirements are nearly identical to the requirements for Windows Vista, but while the requirements described an upscale computer at the introduction of Widows Vista, by the time Windows 7 was introduced the same system requirements described a common, affordable computer.

- As with Windows Vista, Windows 7 is bundled as several products called editions—each with a set of features. Two scaled-down editions, Starter and Home Basic, are not considered mainstream editions. Windows 7 has three retail editions: Home Premium, Professional, and Ultimate.

- You cannot directly upgrade Windows XP to Windows 7, and the ability to upgrade from Windows Vista to Windows 7 depends on the editions involved in the upgrade—both for Windows Vista and for Windows 7.

- You must decide on the type of installation: upgrade, multiboot, or clean installation. You achieve the latter two by using the Custom option in the Windows setup program.

- Retail editions of Windows must be activated, a process that confirms you are using a legal product, not a pirated copy.

- Decide how you want the Windows Update program to download and install updates because Windows 7 setup will query you about this.

- Before installing Windows 7 on an existing Windows computer run the Windows 7 Upgrade Advisor, a compatibility checker that will create a report of any hardware or software incompatibilities.

- Unless you are doing an in-place installation to Windows 7, run a program, such as Windows Easy Transfer (WET) in the old installation to gather the settings and data you want to transfer to your new Windows installation. Then, after installing Windows 7, run the WET utility from the new installation to complete the transfer.

- The Windows 7 startup program runs a special scaled-down Windows OS, Windows PE.

- Immediately after installing Windows, verify network access, install security software, and finish updating Windows. If you installed Windows into a VM, run the virtual machine additions for the hypervisor.

Windows 7 Features

- Windows Vista introduced Windows Aero; Windows 7 improved on it. The desktop is enhanced with such features as Jump Lists and pinning.

- Windows 7 supports several file systems: FAT, exFAT, NTFS, and files systems for optical discs.

- Security features such as User Account Control, BitLocker, and Windows Defender are improved in Windows 7, and BitLocker To Go and AppLocker have been added.

- If an old app does not run in Windows 7, first use the Program Compatibility Troubleshooter. If it does not solve the problem, download and install Windows XP Mode.

- Windows 7 has enhanced or added new recovery tools, including Startup Repair, System Restore, System Image Recovery, and Windows Memory Diagnostic Tool.

Customizing and Managing Windows 7

- Familiarize yourself with the tools in the Computer Management console, especially the Disk Management node, which will allow you to perform a variety of tasks on disks.

- If necessary, adjust the display resolution, and change the text and object size.

- If a computer has multiple displays, use the Display Resolution control panel to configure the displays for the way the user will use them.

- Install and uninstall a program using the program's own installation program. Some programs do not come with an uninstall option. In that case, use the Programs applet in the Control Panel to uninstall the program.

- Turn Windows features on and off in the Control Panel Programs applet.

- During installation, Windows creates a default folder hierarchy into which it installs operating system files and program files.

- The first time a user logs on, Windows creates the user's personal folders under the Users folder at the root of the drive on which Windows installed.

If this is an NTFS volume, Windows will set permissions for the user's personal folders.

- Libraries appear to be folders when viewed in Windows Explorer, but a library is not a folder—it is an object that keeps track of one or more locations where certain folders and files are stored. There are four default libraries in Windows 7, and you can create custom libraries.

- If you burn an optical disc with the Mastered format you will be able to use it in a conventional CD or DVD player, or in any computer, including older Apple Macs or PCs, but the burn process for this format requires hard drive space to temporarily store the files before burning to disc.

- If you burn an optical disc with the Live File System you will only be able to use the disc on newer Apple Macs and newer PCs (Windows XP and newer support it, but older PCs may not). This format allows you to directly copy items to the drive without requiring extra hard drive space. You can also add files to a disc formatted with the Live File System.

Managing Local Security in Windows 7

- Local user accounts reside in the local accounts database on a Windows computer, and the User Account Control Panel applet is the primary tool for managing these accounts.

- You must log on as an Administrator to see all the local user accounts on your computer.

- User Account Control (UAC) has been improved in Windows 7 with fewer events that trigger UAC prompts.

- As with previous versions, Windows 7 supports the use of permissions on local NTFS volumes, as well as folder encryption.

- Each folder and file on an NTFS volume has a set of security permissions, Access Control Entries (ACEs), stored in an Access Control List (ACL). These permissions are inherited through the folder hierarchy.

- BitLocker Drive Encryption in Windows Vista can only encrypt the boot volume (the volume on which Windows resides). In Windows 7, it can encrypt other disk volumes, as well as external disks. This last feature is called BitLocker To Go.

- Windows Defender is a built-in antispam utility. Microsoft Security Essentials (MSE) is a broader antimalware program that is free from Microsoft. Windows Firewall is a personal firewall that comes with Windows.

Key Terms List

Access Control Entry (ACE) *(155)*

Access Control List (ACL) *(155)*

Action Center *(135)*

activation *(121)*

Add Printer wizard *(145)*

Aero Shake *(131)*

Aero Snap *(131)*

AppLocker *(137)*

Automated System Recovery (ASR) *(139)*

BitLocker *(137)*

BitLocker To Go *(137)*

clean installation *(121)*

dual-boot *(120)*

FAT file systems *(136)*

Flip 3D *(131)*

gadget *(143)*

image *(121)*

Jump List *(132)*

library *(135)*

Live File System *(150)*

local security *(152)*

Mastered *(150)*

master file table (MFT) *(137)*

Microsoft Product Activation (MPA) *(121)*

Microsoft Security Essentials (MSE) *(128)*

multiboot *(120)*

NTFS *(136)*

personal folders *(147)*

pinning *(132)*

Program Compatibility Troubleshooter *(138)*

restore point *(139)*

shortcut *(130)*

Startup Repair *(138)*

System Image Recovery *(139)*

System Restore *(139)*

Task Manager *(138)*

upgrade *(120)*

Upgrade Advisor *(122)*

Windows Aero *(130)*

Windows Defender *(137)*

Windows Easy Transfer (WET) *(123)*

Windows Explorer *(148)*

Windows Memory Diagnostic Tool *(139)*

Windows Preinstallation Environment (PE) *(123)*

Windows Update *(122)*

Key Terms Quiz

Use the Key Terms List to complete the sentences that follow:

1. Each file or folder on an NTFS volume has a/an _____ associated with it, containing security permissions.

2. _____ is the name for a group of GUI desktop features and visual themes in Windows Vista and Windows 7.

3. _____ is a feature that lets you switch through your open windows as if they were a stack of cards or photos.

4. A _____ folder contains pointers to multiple locations on your local computer and network, allowing you to work with these files as if they were all stored in a single location.

5. _____ is a scaled-down Windows operating system that supports the Windows setup GUI.

6. A/an _____ is a small program that performs some small function, usually displaying information in a small screen object.

7. Use the _____ format when you burn a disc to be used in a conventional CD or DVD player or in any computer including old Apple Macs or PCs.

8. Use the _____ to burn a disc when you will use the disc only on newer Apple Macs and newer PCs.

9. _____ is a new feature in Windows 7 that allows you to encrypt a removable drive.

10. When you right-click on a program shortcut on the Windows 7 Start menu or taskbar, a _____ displays containing recently opened items and items you may have pinned there.

Multiple-Choice Quiz

1. What *retail* edition of Windows 7 includes BitLocker?
   a. Enterprise
   b. Home Basic
   c. Home Premium
   d. Professional
   e. Ultimate

2. What is the name for the desktop feature in Windows 7 that allows you to quickly minimize all but the current window with a simple mouse movement?
   a. Aero Snap
   b. Flip 3D
   c. Aero Shake
   d. AppLocker
   e. UAC

3. This Windows Vista and Windows 7 feature requires a video card that supports (at minimum) DirectX 9.0 and Shader Model 2.0.
   a. BitLocker
   b. Windows Aero
   c. Instant Search
   d. Windows Defender
   e. Windows XP Mode

4. What alternative term correctly describes an upgrade of an operating system?
   a. Clean installation
   b. In-place installation
   c. Multiboot
   d. Optional installation
   e. Managed installation

5. After you complete a multiboot installation, you will see this special menu at every restart.
   a. Select OS
   b. F8
   c. System
   d. Windows Boot Manager
   e. Computer Management

6. You have Windows Vista Ultimate edition and want to upgrade to Windows 7. Which of the following editions is your only choice for doing an in-place installation of Windows 7?
   a. Ultimate
   b. Home Premium
   c. Home Basic
   d. Enterprise
   e. Business

7. What installation type should you choose in Windows setup if you want to do either a multiboot or clean installation?
   a. Upgrade
   b. Custom
   c. Dual-boot
   d. In-place
   e. Advanced

8. The Disk Management node exists in this console utility.
   a. Administrative Tools
   b. Control Panel
   c. Windows Explorer
   d. Computer Management
   e. System and Security

9. If you are setting up a multimonitor system, which Display option will let you put different windows and other objects on each multiple display, giving you more work space?
   a. Landscape
   b. Extend these displays
   c. Show desktop only on 1
   d. Duplicate these displays
   e. The recommended resolution

10. Clock, Weather, Calendar, and CPU Meter are all examples of what types of desktop programs in Windows 7?
    a. Sidebar
    b. Widgets
    c. Gadgets
    d. Taskbar
    e. Multimedia

11. What new feature of Windows 7 appears to be something it isn't, but allows you to organize and work with data from various locations as if they were together in one place?
    a. Windows Aero
    b. BitLocker To Go
    c. Library
    d. Notification Area
    e. Instant Search

12. What all-powerful user account built into Windows is disabled by default?
    a. Administrator
    b. Standard
    c. Local
    d. Guest
    e. Parental

13. During Windows setup one account is created for the user of that computer, and you provide a name and password for it. What type of account is this?
    a. Standard
    b. Administrator
    c. Parental
    d. Local
    e. Guest

14. What is the term used in the Windows Firewall Control Panel in Windows 7 to refer to Wi-Fi networks at coffee shops and other retail locations?
    a. Private networks
    b. Work networks
    c. Home networks
    d. Public networks
    e. Internetworks

15. What antispyware program comes bundled with Windows 7?
    a. Microsoft Security Essentials
    b. UAC
    c. BitLocker
    d. BitLocker To Go
    e. Windows Defender

Essay Quiz

1. Describe Flip 3D, including what it does and how to use it.

2. Your Windows XP computer is a newer PC that is more than adequate for Windows 7. You would like to do a clean installation of Windows 7, discarding your old Windows XP installation, but after running Windows 7 Upgrade Advisor you found that while all the hardware is compatible, one critical old application is incompatible and will not run in Windows 7. What is your best option for continuing to use this old application on a Windows 7 computer until you find a compatible replacement? Describe both the best solution and one other option, including the type of installation of Windows 7 required for each, and any other requirements beyond the minimums.

3. Windows setup now includes updating Windows. Does the inclusion of this step mean that you will not have to update immediately after installing Windows? Your answer must be more than a yes or no. Include why your answer is true.

4. Describe how you would use a new feature in Windows 7 to keep track of all the files you are

using for a project called Management Training, even though some of those files are on your local PC and some are on a network server. Name the feature, describe the general steps you would take to set this up, and explain your answer.

5. Describe how UAC works to protect your computer from malware.

Lab Projects

LAB PROJECT 4.1

Using a computer with Windows 7 installed, open an app, pin the app to the taskbar, and repeat this for the three or four apps you use the most. Close all the apps, and then open each again from the pinned shortcut on the taskbar. Open two or more files in each app so that the file names appear on the Jump List for each app. Write a few sentences about how this did or didn't work for you compared to launching these apps from the Start menu.

LAB PROJECT 4.2

How successful is Windows 7? What is the latest information on the global operating system market share for Windows 7? Is Windows 7 more successful or less successful than Windows XP? Research the answers to these questions and write about your findings.

LAB PROJECT 4.3

Use the Internet to research the conditions under which you read a flash drive on a Windows XP PC after the flash drive has been encrypted with BitLocker To Go on a Windows 7 computer, then test it: Prepare the flash drive as necessary. Copy data onto the flash drive. Then use BitLocker To Go to encrypt the drive, using the option to create a password (be sure to remember the password). Then take the flash drive to a Windows XP computer and insert the drive. Are you prompted to supply a password? Are you able to access the data on the drive? Describe how you prepared the flash drive and the results.

chapter

5

Windows 8

With Windows 8, Microsoft is standardizing the look of Windows across all types of devices from PCs to tablets. Windows 8 comes with a new multitouch-enabled GUI modeled on the Metro interface of the Windows Phone OS. Windows Phone 8 is a separate operating system for smartphones with the same Metro GUI. Windows 8 also includes an updated desktop GUI that looks much like Windows 7 without the Start menu. This is where the old-style Windows apps run.

Microsoft does not officially use the term "Metro" to describe the Windows 8 GUI. They now use the term "Modern UI," or simply "Modern" to describe the new GUI. For clarity, in this book we use the term "Modern" to refer to the new Windows 8 GUI, and "Desktop" to refer to the Windows 8 version of the traditional Windows desktop.

In Chapter 4 we began our discussion of Windows 7 with installation, but Windows 8 presents a change in how we work with Windows. So, organizing a chapter about Windows 8 in the same way we organized the Windows 7 chapter is not appropriate.

Learning Outcomes

In this chapter, you will learn how to:

LO **5.1** Select a Windows 8 edition for a type of user based on an analysis of the Windows 8 features and editions.

LO **5.2** Select the method of installation, and then install and configure Windows 8.

LO **5.3** Perform appropriate postinstallation tasks to prepare Windows 8 for everyday use.

LO **5.4** Practice working with the new features of the Windows 8 GUI.

LO **5.5** Configure local security in Windows 8.

You really need to know something about the new features of this operating system before you decide to buy a new Windows 8 computer, laptop, or tablet or before installing Windows 8 on an existing computer or laptop. Then you need to consider the support for entirely different hardware architectures and the different features offered in the retail editions of Windows 8, so we begin this chapter with an overview of Windows 8 features and editions as well as significant changes in the Windows 8.1 Update. Finally we examine your options for installing Windows 8, detail recommended configuration actions, practice file management tasks, and configure Windows 8 security features.

This chapter is not all you need to know to be productive in Windows 8, but it is a beginning. We hope to set you on the right path to learning more about Windows 8 on your own.

LO 5.1 | Overview of Windows 8 Features and Editions

In this section we begin with a brief look at Windows 8 features and editions. Then we give an overview of features added in the Windows 8.1 update.

Windows 8 Features

The most obvious Windows 8 features are the two GUIs, which we mentioned in Chapter 1 and above. There are also many internal improvements in the areas of security and performance, but we begin with a short list of other Windows 8 features we believe are significant to most users and important to know before you decide to move to Windows 8. Because some features are included only in certain editions, this section describes features common to all editions. Later, we'll describe the Windows 8 editions and the differences in the features supported by the separate editions.

Windows 8 Is Faster and Smaller

While Windows 7 was faster and smaller than previous versions, Windows 8 is even faster and uses less memory, leaving more room for your programs. If you used any previous version of Windows, you will see the difference in how fast the OS starts up when you power on your computer each day. In Chapter 6 learn how Windows 8 manages to start up faster than earlier versions of Windows.

Separate Products for Two Architectures

Windows 8 comes in editions (described later) for either the traditional Intel/AMD computer architecture or the ARM architecture. A company named ARM Holdings licenses this architecture to manufacturers such as NVIDIA, Qualcomm, and Texas Instruments, who use it in mobile devices. ARM uses 32-bit CPUs that require very little power and therefore do not require fans to dissipate heat. The power-draw disparity between the ARM chips and Intel and AMD chips is narrowing as these manufacturers work to create more efficient low-power chips for mobile devices.

A New GUI Optimized for Touch Devices

You can use touch gestures anywhere in Windows 8, even in your old windowed desktop apps, but the Windows 8 Modern GUI and its apps are optimized for touch devices (especially touch screens) that support multitouch. **Multitouch** is the ability of a multitouch-enabled screen, mouse, or touchpad to interpret

FIGURE 5–1 The Start screen with live tiles and circles indicating 10 simultaneous touches.

multiple simultaneous touch gestures, such as the pinching gesture in which fingers first touch the device at separate locations and then pinch together. The reverse of this gesture also has a special meaning in Windows 8, and there are many unique gestures with names such as tapping, swiping, panning, and zooming. Multitouch support has been included with Windows since Vista, but this support is better integrated in the Windows 8 operating system code and enhanced by a GUI designed for multitouch.

The new GUI is anchored by a home screen called the **Start screen**, shown in Figure 5–1. Notice the circles indicating ten simultaneous finger touches. In order to take this screenshot, we were careful not to touch the screen in a way that would be interpreted as a gesture by the OS. It also took four hands: two to press on the screen and two to press Windows key+PrtScn to send a screenshot to the Pictures folder.

Overlapping windows and shortcuts are still available in the Windows 8 Desktop GUI. Missing from this GUI is the Start menu, perhaps because it is not very touch friendly. The first release of Windows 8 also came minus the Start button, but Microsoft added it back in with the first major update, Windows 8.1, described later in this chapter. You can navigate both the Desktop and Modern GUIs using the more conventional keyboard and mouse (see Appendix B).

Corners and Edges. While many touch gestures and mouse actions occur in the main area of the screen, some important mouse gestures begin in the corners, while their touch counterparts originate at the edges. We will remind you of this difference, as we introduce relevant touch and mouse actions.

Live Tiles. The Start screen contains rectangular tiles with which you launch apps by a tap of a finger (on touch devices) or a click of a mouse.

These tiles replace the old desktop shortcuts and are called live tiles. A live tile displays active content related to the app without requiring you to launch the app. With live tiles, a glance at the Start screen may tell you the local weather, how many new emails you have received, current news headlines, and much more. Some of the tiles in Figure 5–1 show active content; the tile for the News app has active content turned off.

Windows Store Applications. From the Start screen you can launch both the new full-screen Windows Store applications (Modern apps) and traditional

Note: While the **mouse**, a pointing device that you move with your hand on a level surface to manipulate objects on the screen, is still common in some form on most desktop PCs, the typical laptop has a touchpad integrated into the keyboard area. A **touchpad** is a pointing device that responds to finger touch gestures; newer touchpads respond to multitouch input. Touchpads also come as separate wireless or USB devices. Similarly, a **touch mouse** responds to touch gestures on the surface of the mouse, in addition to the typical mouse features.

Note: With the release of Windows 8.1, we essentially have two releases of Windows 8, with some differences. Therefore, when we wish to make a distinction between these two releases, we will use the term Windows 8.0 for the first release and Windows 8.1 for the second release. When speaking of features that are generally available in both releases, we will simply use the term Windows 8.

FIGURE 5–2 On a touch screen, the on-screen keyboard displays when you need to enter alphanumeric data into Windows 8.

Note: Some Microsoft documentation refers to the apps designed for the new Windows 8 GUI as Windows Store apps; in this book, we call them Modern apps.

windowed desktop apps (if they have a tile on the Start screen). When you tap or click the tile for a desktop app, the desktop opens. A Modern app runs full screen, without overlapping windows. The only exception to the one-app-on-the-screen-at-a-time rule for Modern apps is a simple screen-sharing feature called Snap that allows you to display two Modern apps or one Modern app and the desktop on the screen, side-by-side with a vertical division, but no overlap. More on Snap later in this chapter.

The On-Screen Keyboard. An on-screen keyboard, much like those seen on smartphones, displays when you need to enter alphanumeric characters on a touch-screen device that lacks a hardware keyboard. On a touch-screen device that also has a keyboard, the on-screen keyboard displays when you touch a text box, rather than typing from the keyboard. Figure 5–2 shows the on-screen keyboard open for typing into the Search box, which is contained in the Search bar that opens on the right of the screen whenever you start typing at the Start screen.

While the on-screen keyboard is a necessary feature on devices without a keyboard, it is not entirely new to Windows. It was available in previous versions of Windows as an accessibility option, and you can use it in that way in Windows 8—even on a computer with a keyboard and without a touch screen. You can enable it from the Accessibility button on the bottom left of the Sign-in screen. Simply click this button to open the Accessibility Menu, shown in Figure 5–3. Then you can select the on-screen keyboard to sign in. When you open this menu, the Narrator will dictate the menu items to you.

Keyboard Shortcuts. All versions of Windows have keyboard shortcuts. A keyboard shortcut is a key combination that performs an assigned action, saving you several mouse, keyboard, and (now) touch actions. The old keyboard shortcuts continue to work in Windows 8, and new ones have been added. We provide special notes, pointing out some of our favorite Windows 8 keyboard shortcuts. Many keyboard shortcuts take advantage of the WINDOWS KEY (⊞) located near the bottom left of most keyboards labeled with a Windows symbol and/or the word "Start." The Microsoft Touch Mouse has a button that performs the same function.

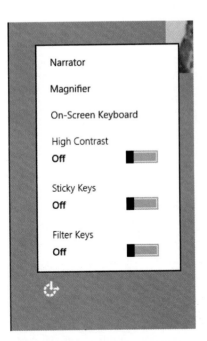

FIGURE 5–3 Enable the on-screen keyboard from the Ease of Access menu.

Support for Special Hardware in Mobile Devices

All editions of Windows 8 include support for hardware in mobile devices. Examples of this are the new Connected Standby power-saving mode as well as support for various sensors common in mobile devices.

Connected Standby. Windows has long had various power-saving modes, mainly targeted at laptops. Moving to support features of mobile devices that are almost never powered off, Microsoft added a new power-saving mode in Windows 8, called Connected Standby. In this mode, Windows 8 allows specially designed apps to perform small tasks, such as email and notifications, in background while the device is sleeping. Therefore, it is connected while in Standby mode.

Windows 8 and Sensor Devices. Tablets and smartphones include hardware devices that sense different aspects of the environment in which they operate. In response to input from various sensors, Windows 8 can dim or brighten a screen or rotate a screen so that it remains readable after you turn it 90 degrees. If a GPS sensor is present, Windows 8 will work with your mapping apps to let you plan a route and even follow your progress turn by turn. Another type of sensor goes beyond sensing screen rotation, sensing more types of movements than those required for screen rotation, such as tilt and the 360-degree turns required for a game controller in flight simulation.

Tap to Send. Yet another feature targeted to mobile devices is Tap to Send. If a device includes a Near Field Communication (NFC) chipset, described in Chapter 11, Windows 8 can wirelessly send data to another compatible device when the two devices touch or are very close to one another.

Note: Windows Phone 8, a separate operating system, is available on smartphones and features this Modern GUI.

Note: In the United Kingdom and other countries, some banks and transit systems are using NFC to allow their customers to make payments from their mobile devices.

Windows 8 Editions

Windows 8 comes in three retail editions: Windows RT, Windows 8, and Windows 8 Pro. It also comes in a Windows 8 Starter edition, only available in emerging markets, and Windows 8 Enterprise, available to large corporate customers through Microsoft's Windows Software Assurance volume licensing program. If you purchase a packaged retail edition with discs, it will include a card containing the product key, as shown in Figure 5–4. In the following sections we describe the three retail editions.

Windows RT for the ARM Architecture

Windows RT comes preinstalled on tablets based on the ARM processor architecture. Presently, you cannot buy this edition as a separate software product at retail. Windows RT only runs apps written for the new GUI (discussed later) and is incompatible with all desktop apps from previous versions of Windows. Windows RT comes with a special software bundle,

FIGURE 5–4 Look for a card containing the product key when you purchase the packaged Windows 8 discs.

Microsoft Office Home and Student 2013 RT, which runs on the Windows RT Desktop. This bundle and other built-in apps are the only apps that will run on the Windows RT Desktop. This version of Office uses a special Touch Mode. The only source of software for Windows RT (Modern or Desktop) is the Windows Store, an online retail site that sells Windows 8 and Windows 8 apps. Windows RT can use a maximum of 4 GB of RAM and up to 2 CPUs.

Windows 8 and Windows 8 Pro for the Traditional PC Architecture

There are two Windows 8 editions designed for the traditional Intel/AMD computer architecture found on the majority of PCs and laptops. The official names of these two editions are Windows 8 and Windows 8 Pro. However, simply saying "Windows 8" when referring to the first of these two editions seems confusing, as that is the name of the version. Therefore, in this book we will call this basic edition "Windows 8 *Basic*," although it is not the official name for this edition. Both of these editions can run apps for the Modern GUI as well as traditional Windows Desktop apps. The only source of Modern apps is the Windows Store, while traditional Windows desktop apps are available at both the Windows Store and other retail sources. Let's look more closely at these two Intel/AM computer-architecture-based editions.

Windows 8 Basic. The Windows 8 *Basic* edition is comparable to Windows 7 Home or Home Premium, containing the features that typical home users need on a PC, laptop, or tablet with only a single CPU. The GUI features of Windows 8 *Basic* are identical to the other Windows 8 editions, but it lacks certain features, such as BitLocker and BitLocker to Go, Client Hyper-V, and Encrypting File System that a more advanced or business user would need. You can install both new Modern and traditional Desktop apps into this edition.

Windows 8 *Basic* has limited support for Remote Desktop, a group of features in some editions of Windows that allows a user at one computer to connect to another computer and see and work in that remote computer's desktop—displayed either full screen or in a window—on the local computer. The remote computer must include the ability to host Remote Desktop, while the local computer must include support to be a client. Windows 8 *Basic* only includes the Remote Desktop client allowing it to connect to a Remote Desktop host (such as Windows 7 Professional, Business, or Ultimate; Windows 8 Pro; or Windows Server).

Another difference between this edition and Windows 8 Pro is the media it can play. With the included Windows Media Player (WMP) app you can play several types of digital media files, burn music CDs, rip media from CDs, sync digital media files to a portable device, and shop online for digital media. Windows Media Player does not play DVDs. If you wish to watch movies on DVDs, you will need to add software to Windows 8 *Basic*. You can search for a third-party app or consider Microsoft's Windows Media Center (WMC), an app with all the features of Windows Media Player and more, including the ability to play DVDs that was available in some editions of Windows 7. Although Windows Media Center does not install directly into this edition, you can purchase the Windows 8 Pro Pack ($99.99), which upgrades Windows 8 *Basic* to Windows 8 Pro and installs Windows Media Center. There are other commercial and free programs with the abilities of Windows Media Center.

The 32-bit version of this edition is able to use up to 4 GB of RAM, while the 64-bit version can use up to 128 GB. Windows 8 *Basic* supports up to two physical CPUs.

Windows 8 Pro. Windows 8 Pro, like Windows 7 Professional and Windows 7 Ultimate, is aimed at individuals with more advanced needs, at home or in a small office. It comes with the features that came with Windows 7 Ultimate edition, with improvements, and you can install traditional desktop apps into this edition. The 32-bit version of this edition can use up to 4 GB of RAM, while the 64-bit version can use up to 512 GB. Windows 8 Pro supports up to two CPUs.

In addition to the features of Windows 8 *Basic,* Windows 8 Pro includes the following features not found in the lesser edition:

Note: During development of the Windows 8.1 update, Microsoft's internal name for it was "Windows Blue."

- Domain Join, a feature that allows a Windows computer to join a Microsoft Active Directory Domain.
- Support for Group Policy, the Domain's central policy–based management system implemented as a set of configuration settings that are applied to each computer as it signs in as well as to each user at sign-in.
- Support for both Remote Desktop host as well as the Remote Desktop client supported in Windows 8 *Basic.*
- BitLocker and BitLocker To Go, as described in Chapter 4.
- The ability to add Windows Media Center by purchasing the Windows 8 Media Center Pack for $9.99 from the Windows Store.

Windows 8.1 Update

At this writing, Microsoft has announced an update to all editions of Windows 8 named Windows 8.1. Available for free through Windows Update beginning October of 2013, this update is Microsoft's response to feedback from Windows 8.0 users concerning the Modern and Desktop GUIs. The final Windows 8.1 update is not available to us at this time. The majority of the screenshots in this chapter were made using Windows 8.1 Preview, with a few screenshots of the final release added just before publication.

FIGURE 5–5 Hold a finger on the Start button until a square appears, then release to open the Power User menu.

While there are many new features in 8.1, one small item, the addition of a Start button on the Desktop taskbar, was the most anticipated, although it did not return the old Start menu to the desktop. Click or tap the Start button in Windows 8.1 to return to the Start screen. At the Start screen the Start button appears when you move the cursor to the bottom-left corner.

Windows 8.1 includes an improved Power User menu (also called the Win-X menu or the Power Tools menu). This menu opens at the bottom left of the screen and gives you access to many handy Windows utilities for power users and IT professionals. To open this menu, press ⊞+X or move the cursor to the bottom-left corner and right-click. To open it with a touch gesture, hold a finger on the Start button until a small square appears (Figure 5–5), then immediately lift your finger and the Power User menu will appear. Figure 5–6 shows the Power User menu in Windows 8.1. The most important addition to this menu is something almost all users will welcome: Shut down, shown with its menu open. Now you can open the Power User menu, select Shut down, and quickly select one of the Shut down options. This placement of the Shut down options is where experienced Windows users expect to find them. On page 189 we compare several methods of shutting down Windows 8.

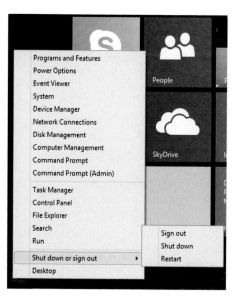

FIGURE 5–6 The Power User menu with the Shut down menu open.

LO 5.2 | Installing Windows 8

Before you can install any new OS you need to make sure your computer meets the system requirements. If you wish to upgrade from an older version, you will need to know what upgrade paths are available to you and determine ahead of time if the hardware and apps are compatible with Windows 8. Armed with this much information you can then move on to preparing for and performing the installation. Afterward, perform some postinstallation tasks. We describe all this next.

System Requirements

The minimum hardware requirements to install Windows 8 on an Intel/AMD architecture computer are nearly identical to that of Windows 7, with the exception of a minimum screen resolution. However, you will want much more RAM and more disk space than the minimum described if you plan to install many programs and store data locally. Today, even budget-level computers come with faster processors, much more RAM, very large hard drives, and great video adapters and displays, which seems to make the requirements irrelevant. But just for the record, the minimums are:

- 1 GHz or faster processor.
- 1 GB RAM (32-bit) or 2 GB RAM (64-bit).
- 16 GB available hard disk space (32-bit) or 20 GB (64-bit).
- DirectX 9 graphics device with Windows Display Driver Model (WDDM) driver.
- 1024 × 768 minimum screen resolution (1366 × 768 recommended).
- Broadband Internet connection for synchronizing settings and files from one Windows 8 PC to another.

Further, a multitouch-capable display, touchpad, or touch mouse is required if you wish to take advantage of Windows 8's multitouch support. A multitouch-capable screen or other device allows Windows 8 to interpret many simultaneous touch points. Multitouch hardware certified by Microsoft as Designed for Windows 8 must support a minimum of five simultaneous touches. Look for this on tablets, laptops, displays screens, touchpads, and devices similar to the Microsoft Touch Mouse.

Upgrade Paths

The upgrade paths depend on the edition. For instance, Windows RT comes on certain tablets, and supports entirely different hardware architecture than was supported by previous versions of Windows. As such, you cannot upgrade to Windows RT from any previous version of Windows, so the upgrade paths are only available for the Intel/AMD computer architecture. If you have a PC or laptop with Windows 7, you may have a direct upgrade path. You can upgrade to Windows 8 *Basic* and Windows 8 Pro from certain editions of Windows 7, as Table 5–1 shows.

Note: You can upgrade Windows 7 using either an upgrade version or a full version of Windows 8.

TABLE 5–1 Upgrade Paths to Windows 8 *Basic* and Windows 8 Pro.

Upgrade from Windows 7 Edition	Upgrade to Windows 8 *Basic*	Upgrade to Windows 8 Pro
Starter	X	X
Home Basic	X	X
Home Premium	X	X
Professional		X
Ultimate		X

Preparing to Install Windows 8

Activating a Retail Product

Before installing Windows 8, understand the new rule concerning activation of a retail edition. Activation is no longer something you can delay for 30 days. It occurs early in the installation process and requires the product key. If you purchase the Windows 8 retail package (either edition) with discs, the product key will be on a small card in the packaging, as shown back in Figure 5–4. When you purchase Windows 8 as a download, you will also receive a product key, which you should save. You must manually enter this product key when you install the purchased software from disc or from the download file. The product key only works with one instance of the Windows 8 product. If you use the Windows 8 Web-based Installer, the product key will be entered automatically.

Purchasing Online from Microsoft

If you plan to purchase Windows 8 online from the Windows Store, you will need a Microsoft account, previously called a Windows Live ID. A Microsoft account is simply an account with Microsoft that gives you access to Microsoft services, such as Hotmail, Messenger, SkyDrive, Windows Phone, Xbox LIVE, and Outlook.com. A Microsoft account is free, as are many of the services. Fees apply when you upgrade services, such as increasing your maximum storage on SkyDrive.

How Will You Sign In to Windows 8?

You can sign in to Windows 8 with a local account that only exists on the Windows 8 computer, a Microsoft account, or a Windows Active Directory account if your computer is a member of a Windows Active Directory domain (at work or school). Learn more about these accounts next.

Signing In with a Local Account. When you install Windows it creates a local account, but you can sign in using either that local account or a Microsoft account. If you use a local account, you will need to sign in separately to any Microsoft services. Figure 5–7 shows a Sign-in screen for a local account. This

> *Note:* If you do not enter a password when you create a local account, sign in will not require a password, and the Sign-in screen will not show the password box. We strongly recommend that you create a password for your local account unless you are the only person with physical access to your computer.

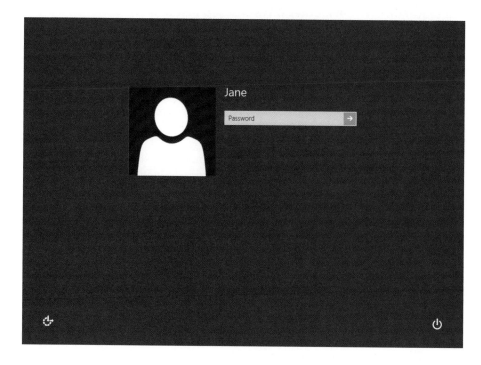

FIGURE 5–7 The initial Sign-in screen for a local account.

account has not yet been customized with a picture, which you can do after you install Windows 8.

Signing In with a Microsoft Account. If you use a Microsoft account, it is associated with a local account, although the Sign-in screen will display the name and the email address associated with your Microsoft account. The one sign-in gives you access to the local computer as well as to your Microsoft services. Then you can access all your data across other devices and services, and you can synchronize your settings on other Windows 8 computers that use the same sign-in. We prefer to use the Microsoft Account sign-in.

Presently, you can acquire a Microsoft account from several different locations on Microsoft websites. For instance, simply use a search engine, such as Google or Bing, and enter "Microsoft account sign-up." From the results select a likely location. At this writing, you can do this at live.com, hotmail.com, and skype.com. You can also wait and create a Microsoft account during Windows 8 installation, if you choose to configure Windows 8 with a Microsoft account sign-in. You will need an email address (any legitimate email address, not just a Hotmail address) and a password. Select a password for use with the Microsoft account only. A Microsoft account is required for some Modern apps, such as Calendar, Mail, Messaging, and People, as well as Xbox Music, Xbox Video, and Xbox LIVE Games.

Signing In with a Domain Account. If your computer is running Windows 8 Pro or Windows 8 Enterprise, it can join a Microsoft Active Directory Domain (based on Windows Server), and you will be required to sign in using a domain user account. In this case, you may not be involved in the installation or selection of the account at all but have a fully configured computer delivered to your desk. Alternatively (and there are several alternatives), the computer will show up on your desk, and the first time you turn it on you will go through the last portion of the installation (described later as the "Out of Box Experience." You will then enter your domain credentials, as instructed by a domain administrator, and log in to both Windows 8 and the Active Directory Domain.

Understanding the Windows 8 Web-based Installer

If you purchase Windows 8 online you have the option of installing after the fact from a downloaded file or by using the online install process available through the Microsoft website. This Web-based Installer saves you extra steps during an upgrade from Windows 7, especially since it enters your product code without your help (thus activating Windows) and includes the functions of both the Upgrade Advisor (now called the Upgrade Assistant) as well as the migration of settings and data. We described both of these in Chapter 4.

Although you will not need to enter the product key manually if you install using the Web-based Installer, you should still store it in a safe place just in case you reinstall Windows 8 or need to reactivate your installation of Windows 8.

Running Upgrade Assistant before Purchasing Windows 8

Whether you plan to use the Web-based Installer or the more traditional Windows 8 setup from DVD, you can connect to the Microsoft website and run Upgrade Assistant, as described in Step-by-Step 5.01. This will prepare you for the changes you may need to make due to hardware or software incompatibility. You may need to find updated device drivers. It is unlikely that you will have a problem running a program that ran well in Windows 7.

Step-by-Step 5.01

Check Out Compatibility before Upgrading

Connect to the Microsoft Windows website and run the Windows 8 Upgrade Assistant.

To complete this exercise you will need the following:

- A computer running Windows 7.
- A Microsoft account.
- A broadband Internet connection.

Step 1

Open a browser. Using a search engine such as Bing or Google, search for "buy Windows 8." In the results, select the result that says "Upgrade to Windows 8" and points to Microsoft.com. This should open the Buy Windows 8 page, which may have a different image than shown here. Click *Get started*. When prompted, choose to run the program.

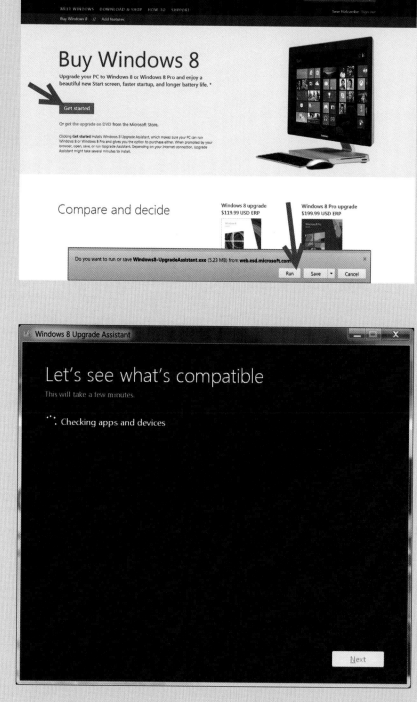

Step 2

The download will begin with a quick security scan. Respond to the User Account Control message; before the scan begins you may briefly see a bar titled "Windows 8." The scan will take a few minutes, during which this page displays.

When the scan is complete, you will see a screen with a statement summarizing the number of compatible devices and apps and a note concerning the items about which you will need to make a decision.

At this point, if you wish to see the details (recommended), select the link labeled "See compatibility details."

Windows 8 Upgrade Assistant

Here's what we found

You can get more info about each app and device in compatibility details.

✔ 23 of your apps and devices are compatible

✖ 4 items for you to review

See compatibility details

▢ I want to help make Windows 8 Upgrade Assistant better

Next

The compatibility report displays. You will have different results from those shown here. If you want a printed copy of this report select the Print button (at bottom), and if you wish to save the report as an HTML file, click Save. You can do both. Also notice the link under each item. Click one of these to learn more about a compatibility issue. When done reviewing the compatibility details, click the Close button to return to the Upgrade Assistant.

Windows 8 Upgrade Assistant

Compatibility details

If you decide to install Windows 8, we'll help you take care of the things that need your attention later.

For you to review

Install an app to play DVDs
You may need to install an app to play DVDs in Windows 8.
More info

Secure Boot isn't compatible with your PC
Your PC's firmware doesn't support Secure Boot so you won't be able to use it in Windows 8.
More info

Microsoft Security Essentials
Microsoft Corporation
✖ Go to the app website for help

Canon MP Navigator EX 1.0
⚠ Update available

Compatible

Add or Remove Adobe Creative Suite 3 Master Collection
Adobe Systems Incorporated

Adobe Flash Player 11 ActiveX
Adobe Systems Incorporated

Adobe Flash Player 11 Plugin
Adobe Systems Incorporated

Why are some apps and devices not listed?

Print   Save   Close

Close the window to exit and you are finished.

If, after running the Upgrade advisor, you close the Compatibility Details window and click Next in the Windows 8 Upgrade Assistant, it opens a page that initiates a migration tool, shown here. When we ran this on a Windows 7 Ultimate computer, we chose the first item, indicating that we wanted to keep Windows settings, personal files, and compatible apps. It then recommended an upgrade to Windows 8 Pro. When we chose just personal files or nothing, the Upgrade Assistant recommended either Windows 8 Pro or Windows 8.

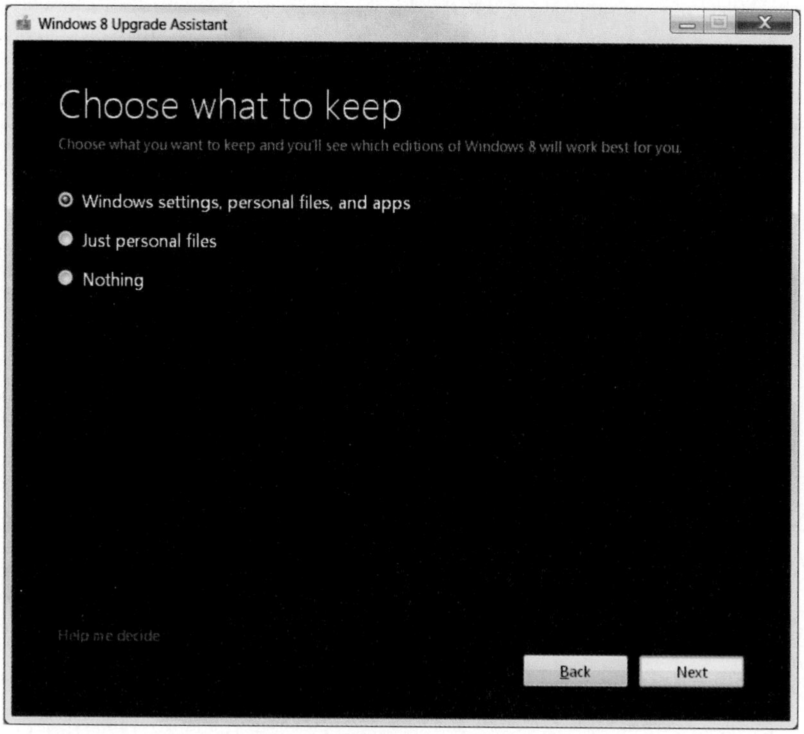

Select what you want to keep when you upgrade.

This page displays when we choose "Just personal file" or "Nothing." If you select either "order" button, it will continue to process the order.

On the page labeled "Review your order," you can choose just the download option or add an order for the DVD for an additional cost. If you proceed, you will go to the Checkout page. You can also change your mind at this point by clicking the Back button.

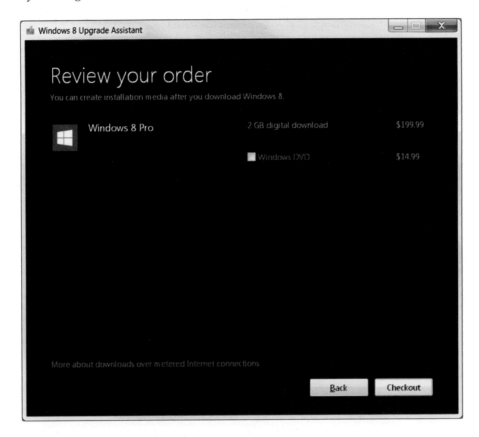

Acquiring Updated Drivers for Hardware

One of the incompatibilities you may discover using the Upgrade Assistant is that Windows 8 does not have drivers for some of your hardware so you may need to contact the manufacturer of your computer or of the specific incompatible component. You can usually do this on their website, and, if they have a new driver, download it ahead of time and have it available on a disc or USB drive. This is especially important if the Upgrade Assistant reported an incompatibility with the network interface card (NIC) because it is critical that you have the correct NIC driver installed so you can search the Web for Windows 8 drivers for less critical hardware.

If no updated driver is available for a component reported as incompatible, you may still want to wait until after installing Windows 8 to discover if a generic driver from Windows 8 takes care of the problem. Be prepared to replace any component that becomes unusable after the update.

The Installation

As described on page 173, you can purchase Windows 8 as a download from the Windows Store, from other online retailers, or at a bricks-and-mortar store. If purchasing online to upgrade from Windows 7, you can either do a Web-based install or a more conventional Windows setup install.

Web-Based Setup

If you purchase Windows 8 online, you have the option of doing a Web-based setup, which is quick and combines the more traditional Windows setup program with the features of the Windows Upgrade Advisor and the settings and data migration tools described in Chapter 4, which were separate from Windows setup. Web-based setup requires very little interaction and is very fast. If downloading, follow the on-screen instructions to install it.

Traditional Windows Setup

Windows setup is the traditional program for installing and upgrading Windows. To install Windows 8 using this program, you must have the Windows 8 setup files on bootable media.

Acquiring Bootable Media. If you purchase the retail package you will have boot media in the form of DVDs. Use the appropriate disc (32-bit or 64-bit) for your computer.

If you purchase Windows 8 online and choose the option *Install later by creating Media,* you have the options to download to a USB drive or to an ISO file. If you install it to a USB drive, it creates a bootable USB setup drive.

If you choose ISO, it will download an ISO image, which is a file containing a copy of the entire contents of a disc. After downloading it to a Windows 7 computer, simply double-click the file and the Windows Disc Image Burner dialog will display. Click Burn and it will create the disc.

Beginning Windows Setup. Once you have the media, you can either boot your computer from it (clean install) or if upgrading, simply insert the media into your Windows 7 computer after signing in. If it does not automatically run setup, browse to the disc in Windows Explorer and double-click the Setup file.

Windows 8 setup closely resembles the Windows 7 setup described in Step-by-Step 4.01 in Chapter 4. One important change is that you must enter the product key and activate Windows 8 during installation. You no longer have the 30-day grace period to activate that was possible with previous versions. The page for doing this, shown in Figure 5–8, appears very early, whereas in Windows 7 setup this page is near the end of Windows setup. Notice that you

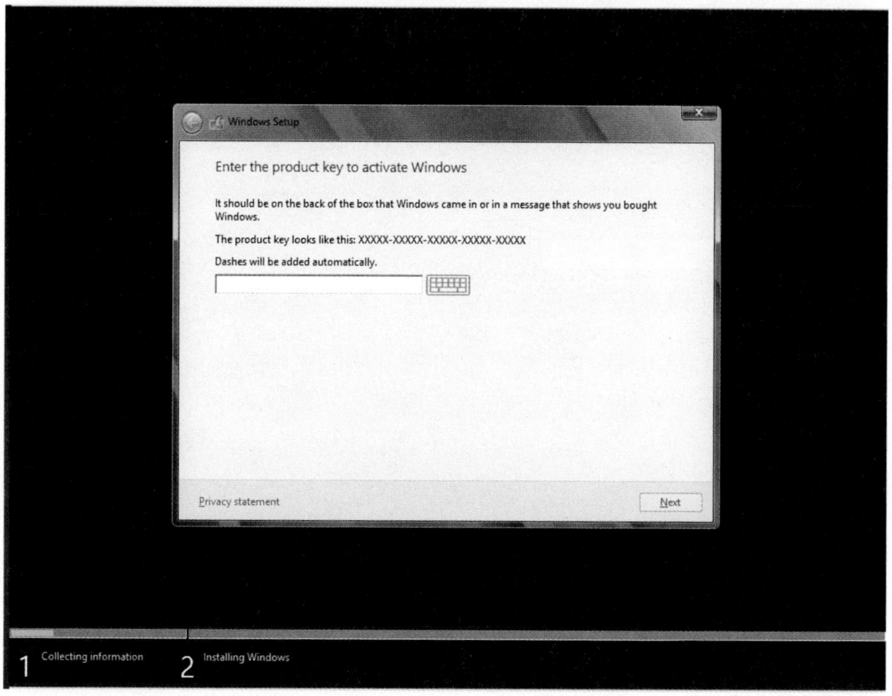

FIGURE 5–8 You must enter the product key before Windows setup will proceed.

must enter the product key to continue. At this point in the Windows 7 setup, you could deselect an option labeled "Automatically activate Windows when I'm online," which would give you the 30-day grace period.

In Windows 8 setup, after you enter the correct product key and click Next, you proceed to the License terms page. Accept the terms of the licensing agreement and proceed to the page where you select the type of installation, Upgrade or Custom, followed by other pages similar to those in Windows 7 setup. Setup will copy files and reboot. This type of restart, in which the operating system is restarted without a hardware power-down–power-up cycle, is called a warm boot. During a warm boot, apps are closed, the currently signed-in user or users are signed out, the current operating system settings are written into the registry files (the registry is described in Chapter 6), the operating system stops functioning, and the computer is powered down. We call the action of bringing a computer and operating system up from such a no-power state by turning on the power switch, a cold boot. The restarts performed during setup are warm reboots.

After a reboot, the Out of Box Experience begins, as described next.

The Out of Box Experience (OOBE)

Both the traditional Windows setup and the Web-based Installer end with the Out of Box Experience (OOBE) in which you customize your installation. The Out of Box Experience (OOBE) gets its name from the fact that when you buy a new computer with Windows 8 preinstalled, and you take it out of the box and turn it on, you will be greeted with this last phase of Windows installation where you personalize the GUI and configure how you will sign in.

Personalize Windows 8. The Personalize page (Figure 5–9) signals the beginning of the OOBE. This is where you can select the color for the screen and name the PC. The Settings page, shown in Figure 5–10, follows the Personalize

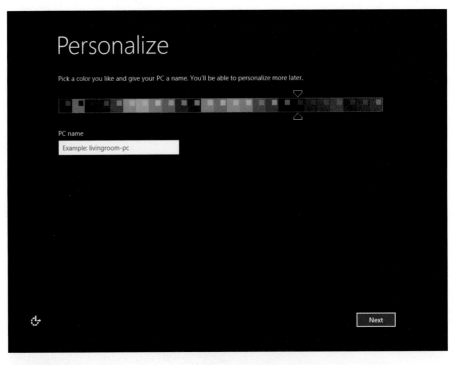

FIGURE 5–9 The Personalize page marks the beginning of the Out of Box Experience (OOBE).

FIGURE 5–10 The bulleted list shows the settings used if you click the *Use express settings* button.

page. We recommend reviewing the bulleted list of settings, and if these will work for you, click the "Use express settings" button. If you want different settings click Customize.

Selecting How to Sign In. Next, choose the type of account you will use to sign in. While you must make a decision during setup, you can change your choice any time after setup. The Sign in screen, shown in Figure 5–11, offers a

> *Note:* If your computer is offline (not connected to the Internet) during installation, OOBE will not display the option of using a Microsoft account. If that is the case, and you want to use the Microsoft account sign in, you can do it after-the-fact when you can connect the computer to the Internet. At that time, open the Users panel in the PC Settings screen (PC Settings is discussed later in this chapter) and select *Switch to a Microsoft account.*

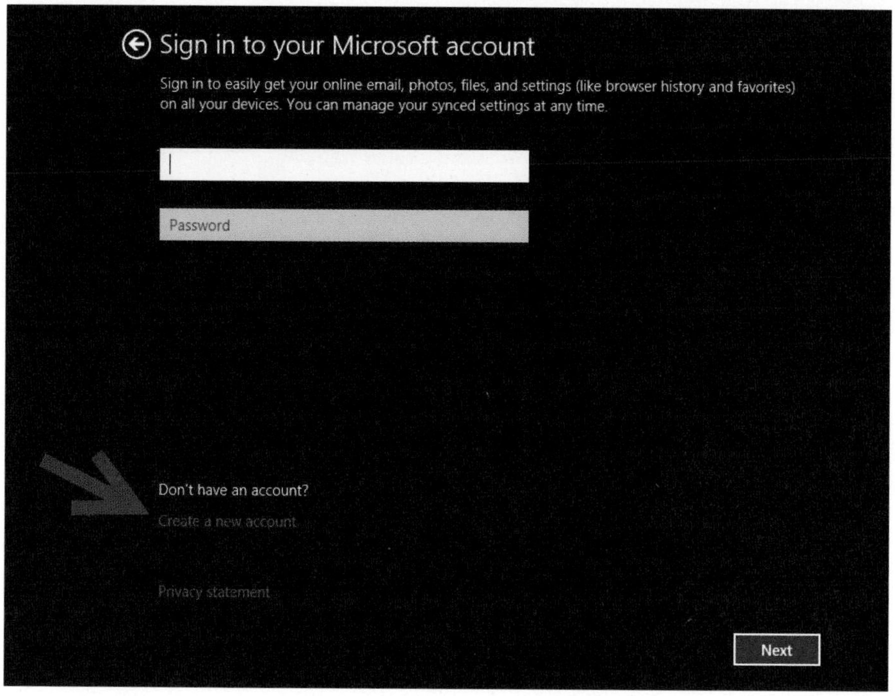

FIGURE 5–11 To sign in with a local account choose the link labeled *Create a new account.*

Note: If you have enabled two-step verification for signing in with your Microsoft account, you will need to first enter your email address and password, and then enter a one-time security code that is immediately sent to you by email, text, or phone call. Enable or disable two-step verification online in your Microsoft account settings.

choice between a Microsoft account and a new account. If you have a Microsoft account and wish to use it, enter the email address and password and click Next. Windows setup will create a local administrator type of account and associate it with your Microsoft account. If you do not have a Microsoft account and want to create one, select the link shown in Figure 5–11 labeled *Create a new account,* indicated by an arrow. Enter the required information on the next page (Figure 5–12).

When you sign in with a Microsoft account you enter your Microsoft account credentials (email address and password). In a sense you have a dual identity, giving you access to your local computer and to your Microsoft services. If you use this same account on multiple Windows 8 computers, you can choose to synchronize your data and settings.

If you do not want to use a Microsoft account for this installation, click the link labeled *Create a new account,* indicated by the arrow in Figure 5–11. When you choose that option, setup displays the page shown in Figure 5–12. Select the link labeled Sign in without a Microsoft account. This opens the page, shown in Figure 5–13, where you type in a user name and password (twice), as well as a password hint for the new account. If this is an upgrade from Windows 7, you will have a *Skip* button in addition to the *Finish* button. Selecting Skip tells setup to use your old local account.

Note: The ⊞ key returns you to the Start screen from anywhere in Windows 8. On a touch screen swipe in from the right edge and select Start.

Several more pages will display while Windows setup finishes configuring your installation and installs the default apps into Windows 8. Finally the Start screen displays, as Figure 5–14 shows. This is your home base and launching pad. Whenever you want to return to the Start screen, either swipe in from the right side of the screen to open the Charms bar and select the Start charm, press the ⊞ key on the bottom left on your keyboard, or touch or click the Start button at the bottom left of the Desktop screen.

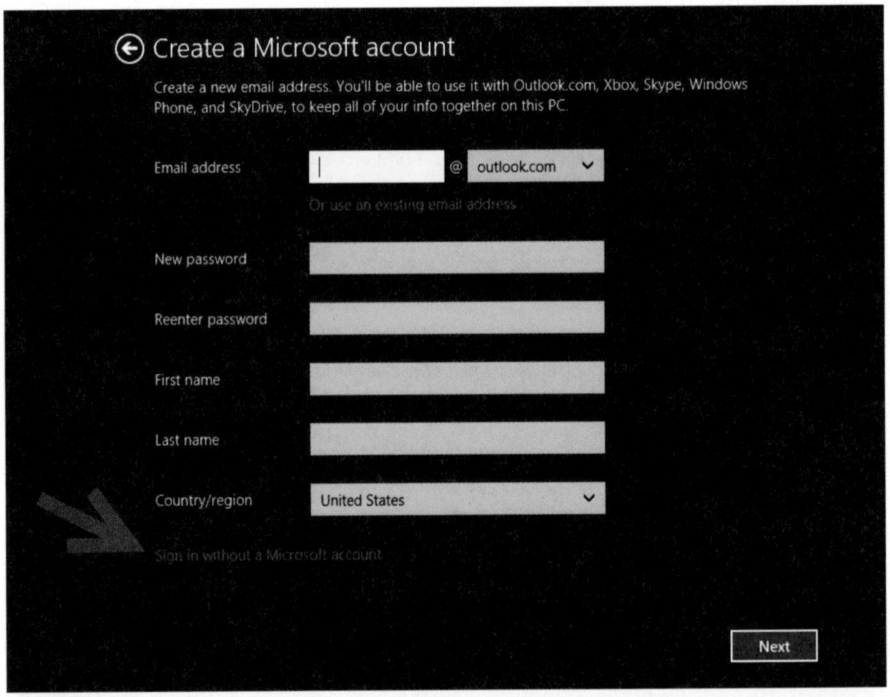

FIGURE 5–12 Complete this page to create a new Microsoft account. If you want to create a local account, click *Sign in without a Microsoft account.*

FIGURE 5–13 Enter a user name and password (twice), as well as a password hint.

FIGURE 5–14 The Windows 8 Start screen.

LO 5.3 | Postinstallation Tasks

You will need to do some tasks immediately after installing Windows 8. In previous versions of Windows we would have recommended you install security software at this point, but Windows 8 comes with a new and improved Windows Defender. It includes antivirus and antispyware. We will look at Windows Defender later in this chapter. Your postinstallation tasks should include installing drivers, if necessary, and running Windows Update.

Installing Drivers

If setup detected a device that would not work with one of the available drivers, you may have been prompted to provide the driver files. Setup may have simply installed a generic driver that works with a device but doesn't take advantage of all its features. Or, you may have a noncritical device that simply does not work after Windows 8 is installed. Therefore, one postinstallation task is to install updated drivers. You have some choices for this which we will explore next.

On a touch screen, touch and hold until a small square appears, then release to display the context menu.

The desktop context menu.

Note: Virtually all displays in use are flat panels as opposed to the old bulky CRT displays. A flat-panel display, which uses some variation of LCD or LED technologies, has just one physical resolution, and Microsoft shows that as the Recommended resolution in Screen Resolution.

Note: Windows Update categorizes driver updates as "optional updates." Step-by-Step 5.02 gives an example of this.

Use Updated Drivers from Manufacturers

If you were prepared to install new drivers during setup but did not have an opportunity to install them, then immediately after setup check for problems with the installed drivers in the form of error messages or a component not functioning properly. If you see such symptoms, install the drivers you prepared ahead of time. In most cases, when manufacturers supply a compatible driver, it comes as an executable. If you have the driver file on an external device, open **File Explorer** (the new name for the updated version of the Windows file management tool, Windows Explorer), locate the file, and double-click it to run the driver setup.

Check Display Driver

If the display does not seem to be functioning properly, check to see if the correct video driver was installed by looking at the Screen Resolution setting. To do that, from the Start screen click or tap the Desktop tile. This opens the Windows Desktop where you right-click to open the context menu, shown here. On a touch screen press on an empty area of the Desktop and hold until a small square appears, as shown in the illustration at the bottom of page 183, then immediately release. When the context menu displays select *Screen resolution.*

In the Screen Resolution dialog the resolution on a flat-panel display should be at the maximum resolution of the display. To confirm this, the resolution should have the word "Recommended" in parenthesis, as shown in Figure 5–15 where the resolution is 1,366 × 768. If your setting is something other than the recommended, look for a compatible driver.

One way to give Windows 8 a chance to automatically resolve any remaining driver problems is to run Windows Update, which we explain next.

Installing Updates

Although Windows installation includes some updating of the Windows code, and Windows 8 is configured for automatic updates by default, you should manually trigger updates soon after the installation because it can take several days for Windows Update to bring your installation completely up to date.

Windows Update will download and install updates it categorizes as "important." These are mostly security updates and updates to critical Windows components. However, you should also check out other updates available through Windows Update. Additionally, we recommend configuring Windows Update to update all your installed Microsoft software, not just Windows components.

Windows Update comes in a Modern version as well as a Desktop version nearly identical to that in Windows 7. Step-by-Step 5.02 walks through the steps for using Windows Update, showing how you may work in both versions. In the process, you will learn about the Windows 8 PC Settings panels, use Windows Update to download and install both important and optional updates, and learn how to configure Windows Update to update other Microsoft software.

FIGURE 5–15 The resolution should be set at the Recommended resolution for the display.

Using and Configuring Windows Update

Windows Update in Windows 8 comes in both the Modern GUI and the traditional Control Panel GUI. Sometimes while working in the Modern GUI you will make a choice that opens the Desktop GUI. We expect this jumping between GUIs to eventually change, but for now, that's how it is, and this exercise will help you to work with Windows Update in both GUIs.

- A computer running Windows 8 or Windows 8 Pro.
- You should be signed in with an administrator account or have the user name and password of an administrator account for the computer.
- A broadband Internet connection.

Step 1

To run the Modern version of Windows Update you will need to first open the Windows 8 Settings bar. You can do this with a swipe from the right edge of the screen to open the Charms bar, shown here, which contains small graphic objects called charms. A charm acts as a shortcut to important systemwide tasks.

Step 2

Select the *Settings charm* to open the Settings bar. Or go directly to the Settings bar with the ⊞+I keyboard shortcut. The Settings bar slides out along the right side of the screen in both the Desktop and the Start screen. Click or tap *Change PC settings* at the bottom of the Settings bar.

The PC Settings screen contains several panels for configuring some Windows 8 settings. Scroll to the bottom of the list and select *Update & Recovery.* The Update and Recovery page displays. Assuming you do this immediately after installing Windows 8.1, the update information is current. However, click *Check now* to see what happens. Often additional updates are ready.

If Windows Update finds updates for your computer, it will display them in a list. If so, click the Install button and respond to any dialog boxes for User Account Control, agreements, and to restart the computer. If your computer restarts, sign in and return to the Updates and Recovery page. Move on to the next step.

In order to configure Windows Update to include both Windows components and other Microsoft programs, select the *Choose how updates get installed* option on the Windows Update page. This opens a page where you can select how important updates, recommended updates, and updates for other Microsoft products (think Microsoft Office) are installed. For most users we recommend the settings shown here.

When you are finished, return to the Start screen using one of the following methods. Using a mouse, point the cursor in the far left corner until the Start button displays, and then click; using a keyboard, press the Windows key; or on a touch screen swipe in from the right edge to open the Charms bar, and then tap the Start charm.

Virtual Machine Guest Additions

If you installed Windows 8 into a virtual machine, an important postinstallation task is to install the software into the virtual machine that will make it run better. The name for this software and how it installs vary by hypervisor. You may have already seen a message pop-up in Windows 8 in your virtual machine with instructions. Or look for an option in the hypervisor window surrounding the virtual machine, as we did when we installed Windows 8 into VirtualBox on an iMac, opening the VirtualBox Devices menu, shown in Figure 5–16. We selected the option *Install Guest Additions*.

Remove Unnecessary Software

If you purchase a computer with Windows 8 preinstalled, the first time you turn it on you will go through the personalization tasks in the Out of Box Experience, described earlier. When you finally arrive at the Start screen you may discover that the manufacturer installed a security package, along with lots of other software often called bloatware (one of the more civil terms for this software). Bloatware has been around since long before Windows 8, so it is not just a Windows 8 problem. We have found most of the bloatware to be more like "annoyware," or like the scareware discussed in Chapter 2. We find it unnecessarily time-consuming to sort out what is useful and what was just installed to convince us to buy something else.

For instance, our new touch-screen laptop from a major PC manufacturer came with a 30-day free trial of a security package. Every time we sign in, a reminder pops up asking us to connect and upgrade from the trial to the $60/year package. After a few days, we decided that the $5 savings for the 30 days was not worth being annoyed. We temporarily disabled our Internet connection, then opened the *Uninstall or change a program* page in Control Panel (open the Power menu and select Control Panel) and removed the trial software. Then we opened Windows Defender (described later in this chapter). It soon became active, guarding against attacks, and when we enabled the Internet connection Windows Defender updated, and began a scan.

In addition to the security software, this computer came with two Modern apps from the manufacturer, as well as five windowed apps. One app connects directly to their store, others are diagnostic or utilities that replace or supplement some that come with Windows.

Create a Backup Image

Most new computers do not ship with installation or recovery discs, so you should look for some program from the manufacturer for creating an image of the factory-installed software in case you need to return the computer to its original state. Locate this software, create backup media, and put it in a safe place.

Turn on File History

Since the most important files on your computer are your data files, you should also plan for data backup. File History is a new and easy way to automatically back up files in your Documents, Music, Pictures, and Videos folders. File History is not turned on by default; if you have a spare external drive connected to your computer or a network location, turn on File History and point to the location to

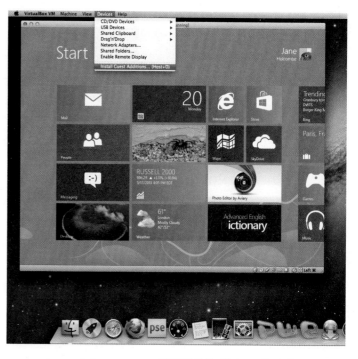

FIGURE 5–16 Installing Guest Additions in VirtualBox.

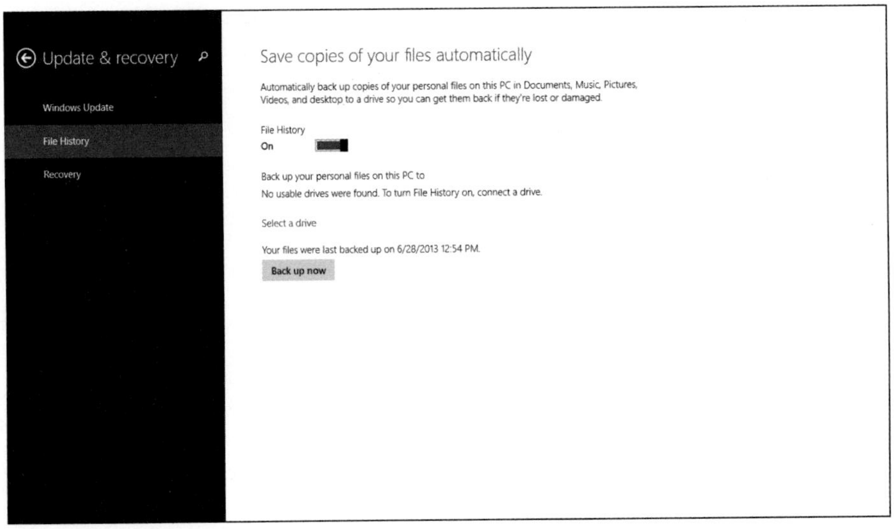

FIGURE 5–17 Open File History in Update and Recovery.

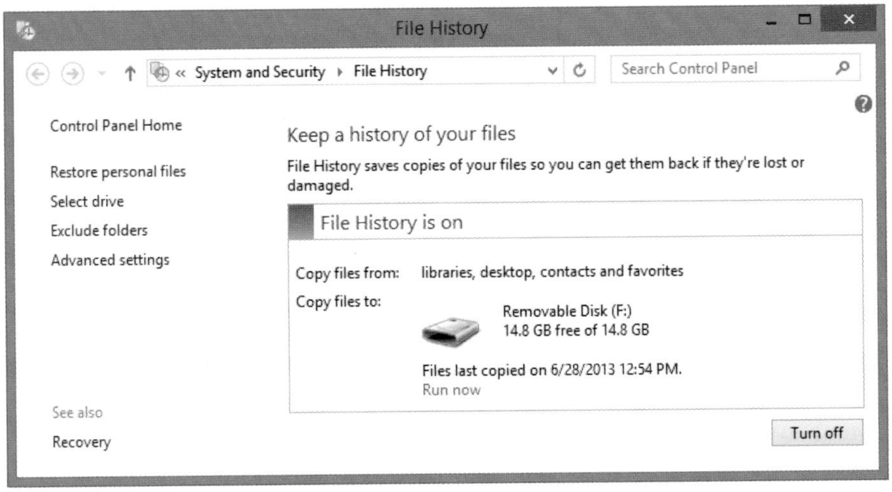

FIGURE 5–18 For more File History settings, open File History in the Control Panel.

use—either any external drive or network location. Turn on and configure File History using the Desktop Control Panel or with the File History page in PC Settings added in Windows 8.1. Figure 5–17 shows the PC Settings page where you can turn File History on or off, select a drive, and initiate a backup, although once File History is turned on it works automatically.

To make more changes, open File History in the Control Panel, shown in Figure 5–18. Here you can turn it on or off and select a location, as you can from the File History page. You can also add backup locations, exclude folders (from those within the default locations), and choose how often to save files and how long to keep saved versions (yes, File History saves versions of files).

Shutting Down Windows 8

What do you do when you are done working at your computer? Do you press your computer's power button? Do you sign out or shut down from a menu in Windows?

If you press the power button, what happens depends on how the Power Options are configured in the Control Panel. On a laptop, pressing the power button will usually put the computer to sleep, saving the current state (all open programs and data files) so that the next time you press this button it will immediately wake up.

We prefer to close all our apps and data and open a menu that includes the option *Shut Down*. This signs out the currently signed in user and turns off the computer. There are several methods for accessing a menu to shut down Windows 8.

Using a Keyboard to Quickly Shut Down

A quick method for shutting down Windows 8.1 is to open the Power User menu (WINDOWS KEY + x), and then press u twice. Flip back to Figure 5–6.

Another not-so-quick method is to press CTRL-ALT-DELETE, which opens the CTRL-ALT-DELETE screen (of course!). This very plain screen displays four options in the middle: Lock, Switch user, Sign out, and Task Manager. It also has two buttons: the Accessibility button on the left and the Power button on the right. Select the Power button to open the Power menu from which you can select Sleep, Shut down, or Restart. Select Shut down from the Power menu to Shut down.

Using a Mouse or Touch to Open the Power Menu

Alternatively, if you have not upgraded to 8.1, first open the Charms bar (shown in step 1 of Step-by-Step 5.02) by moving your mouse from the bottom-right corner of the screen or by swiping in from the right edge. Click the Settings charm to open the Settings Bar, shown earlier in step 2 of Step-by-Step 5.02. Then click or tap the Power charm. This opens a small menu of power states, shown here. The states available will depend on how your computer is configured. They may include *Sleep, Shut down, Restart* (or the option *Update and Restart* if updates are ready to install), and Hibernate. This example shows three choices. Hibernate is not a choice by default.

The Power menu options depend on the configuration.

LO 5.4 | Navigating and Configuring Windows 8

Customizing and managing Windows 8 begins by understanding the two GUIs of Windows 8, and learning where you will find the tools for these tasks. If you followed along in the earlier sections of this book and did the Try This! and Step-by-Step exercises, you practiced working with several tools in both GUIs, including the PC Settings screen in the Modern GUI. You also became familiar with several features of the Start screen. We'll begin with the Lock screen and continue with more Start screen basics and configuration tasks, followed by an overview of the desktop and the File Explorer file management tool.

The Lock Screen

By default, the Lock screen displays under certain conditions including: when you first start up your computer, after a period of inactivity, when you choose Lock from the User tile, or when you use the ⊞+L shortcut. The Lock screen is a screen that prevents you from accidentally triggering some action on a touch screen and causing something you did not intend to happen. The classic example is "pocket dialing" someone on a smartphone while the phone is in your pocket. That is not the typical scenario on a touch-screen tablet where you are more likely to accidentally launch a program from the Start screen. To

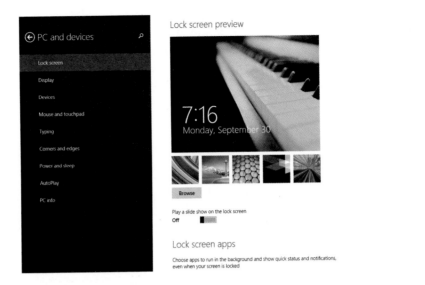

The Lock screen settings page.

Note: Press [⊞]+L to lock your Windows computer before walking away from your desk at work or school. This will keep your current apps and data open, but require unlocking the screen and signing in (if your computer is configured for a sign in).

return to Windows 8 from the Lock screen press any key or simply swipe on a touch screen to close the Lock screen and access the Sign-in screen.

To customize the Lock screen open PC Settings | PC and devices | Lock Screen, shown above. Select a background (even one of your own photos) or a slide show, and decide what apps can run in background and display status and notifications and what apps can show alarms.

The Start Screen

The Start screen features highlighted to this point include live tiles, charms, Charms bar, Power charm, Settings bar, on-screen keyboard, and the Power User menu. We also described the screen-sharing Snap feature. Here we describe more details of the Start screen.

Start Screen Anatomy

Figure 5–19 shows the anatomy of the Start screen. Notice the various tiles. When Windows 8 was first introduced in Fall 2012 it had only two sizes of

FIGURE 5–19 The Start screen and its components.

tiles on the Start screen—what we now know as Medium and Wide. The Windows 8.1 update, released in late 2013, added two more sizes: Small and Large. Figure 5–19 includes the four sizes of tiles. The eight smallest tiles on the screen are Small, the tiles that are approximately four times the size of the Small tiles are Medium, the tiles twice the size of Medium tiles are Wide, and the largest tile shown is an example of (what else?) Large.

Navigating and Customizing the Start Screen

The horizontal scroll bar appears at the bottom of the Start screen when it contains more tiles than it can display at one time on the screen. Move the bar with your mouse or use a swiping touch motion to look at the additional tiles.

Drag a tile around with your mouse or finger to change its position on the Start screen. Arrange tiles in groups that work for you. Beginning in Windows 8.1 you can name these groups (or not), as shown in Figure 5–19 where we named three groups, but did not name the fourth. If you drag a tile to the space on either side of a group, without overlapping the group, pause, and a gray vertical bar appears. Release and Windows 8.1 creates a new group and a gray horizontal box opens above the new group labeled *Name Group.* Enter a name for the group and then click or tap outside the name box. If you do not wish to name this group, click anywhere on the background of the Start screen and the boxes will disappear and just the names you have created will appear above groups.

In order to move entire groups around, you must shrink the Start screen tiles on the screen. In the bottom right of the Start screen is a zoom button that you click to shrink the Start screen. On a touch screen use a pinching motion. When the Start screen is zoomed out (reduced in size), you can manipulate the groups of tiles (but not individual tiles), moving them around so that the ones you use the most are grouped together. This zoom feature is called semantic zoom, and it works within apps that support it.

try this!

Zoom the Start Screen

Use the mouse or touch actions to zoom the Start screen and rearrange the tile groups. Try this:

1. From the Start screen, use a pinching action or move the mouse to the bottom-right corner and click the Zoom button.
2. While the Start screen tiles are small, use your mouse or touch actions to rearrange the groups.
3. When you are ready to return the Start screen tiles to full size click or tap on the background.

Shrink the tiles (zoom out) and drag a group of tiles to rearrange the groups.

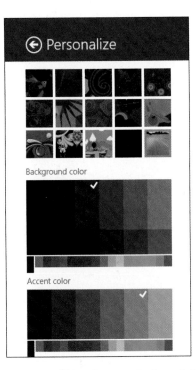

Background color

Accent color

The Personalize bar in Windows 8.1

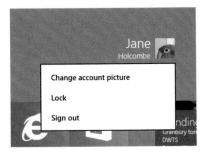

Jane
Holcombe

Change account picture

Lock

Sign out

The User menu.

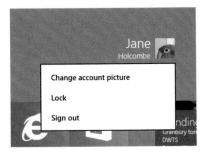

Apps by name ∨

Alarms NEW	eBay	Mail	Photos	Travel	CyberLink Media Suite
Amazon	Finance	Maps	Reader	Video	CyberLink LabelPrint 2.5
Amazon	Food & Drink NEW	Microsoft Solitair... NEW	Reading List NEW	Weather	CyberLink Med Suite Essentials
Calculator NEW	Games	Movie Maker	Scan NEW	Windows 8 Cheat Keys	CyberLink Power2Go 8
Calendar	Health & Fitness NEW	Music	SkyDrive	Windows Media Player	CyberLink PowerDirector
Camera	Help & Tips	News	Skype		CyberLink PowerDVD 10
Dell	Getting Started with...	Intel(R) WiDi	PC settings	Sound Recorder NEW		Desktop Burnin Gadget
Dell Shop	Internet Explorer	People	Sports		ISO Viewer
Desktop	Kindle	Photo Gallery	Store		Virtual Drive

FIGURE 5–20 The Apps screen shows all installed apps.

Customizing Tiles from the Apps Screen. Beginning in Windows 8.1 an Apps button on the bottom left of the Start screen opens the Apps screen, Figure 5–20, where you can customize app tiles and even remove apps from your computer.

Changing the Start Screen Background. Previous to Windows 8.1 you would do some Start screen customization from the Personalize page in PC Settings (open Charms bar, select Setting, Change PC Settings). In Windows 8.1 the Settings bar has a Personalize option that opens yet another bar on the right edge, the Personalize bar, shown here, where you can change the patterns, background color, and accent colors.

Beginning in Windows 8.1 you can configure the same background on the Desktop and the Start screen. Make this change from the Desktop by right-clicking on the Taskbar, selecting Properties, and then in the Taskbar and Navigation properties dialog box, select the Navigation tab. Click to place a check in the box labeled *Show my desktop background on Start*.

Changing the User Tile Picture. On the top right of the Start screen is the User tile displaying your account name and an image. You can choose a custom picture. Click or tap the User tile to open the menu shown here. From this menu you can Change your account picture, Lock the screen, or Sign Out. The Try This! describes how to change your account picture in Windows 8.1. The instructions are slightly different for Windows 8.

try this!

Change Your Account Picture

Would you like to personalize your account picture? You can easily use an existing photo or take a new picture with your computer's camera. Try this:

1. Click or tap the User tile and select *Change account picture*.
2. This opens the Accounts pane in PC Settings. From there you can browse to a location of an existing picture, select the Camera to take a picture, or open the People app to find a picture.
3. Once you select a picture, you return to the Personalize pane with your new picture. This will display on the Start screen and on the Sign-in screen.

Moving between Apps

What you cannot see at first glance in both the Start screen and the Windows Desktop is also significant and discoverable, such as screen corners and edges, which make it easier to switch between apps. Mouse gestures activate the corner, and the edges respond to **edge gestures**, touch motions that begin close to the bezel of the screen.

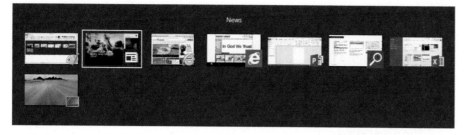

FIGURE 5–21 Windows Flip displays as a horizontal bar with a thumbnail of each running app.

After opening one or more apps, switch between running apps with a swiping gesture from the left bezel. Each swipe slides out one open app at a time. Repeat, and eventually you will cycle through all running apps. Or, if using a mouse, point it at the top-left corner to display the Back tip in that corner. A Back tip is a thumbnail (a small graphic image representing a larger object) that shows a tiny image, as shown here. Click the Back tip to display the app on the screen. Repeat to bring previous apps to the screen, one at a time. A shortcoming of using either the swipe gesture or the Back tip to cycle through open apps is that Windows 8 treats the desktop as one app, no matter how many apps are open on the desktop.

But wait! There are even more ways to switch tasks. Press and hold the ALT KEY while tapping the TAB KEY. This opens Windows Flip, a visually flat version of Flip 3D (described in Chapter 4). Windows Flip displays a rectangle across the middle of the screen that shows all running apps, including individual Desktop apps. The app with the white outline in Figure 5–21 will open on the screen if you release the ALT KEY. If you continue holding the ALT KEY and tapping the TAB KEY, Windows Flip will cycle through the running apps.

Windows Flip is not a new feature in Windows 8, we just neglected to mention it in Chapter 4, choosing instead to talk about its fancier sibling, Flip 3D. Since Windows 8 has a flatter look, Flip 3D is not supported, and the keyboard shortcut for Flip 3D (WINDOWS KEY+TAB) now opens the Switcher, a black bar with a thumbnail for each running app. Press and hold the Windows key and tap the Tab key to open the Switcher. To cycle through the running apps, continue to hold the Windows key while tapping the Tab key. Like Windows Snap, Switcher identifies the app it will open with an outline, as shown here. However, like the Back tip and the swipe from the left edge, Switcher lumps all your running Desktop apps into one thumbnail.

To open the Switcher with a mouse, point the mouse at the bottom-left corner and move it up the left edge (do not drag it) until the Switcher appears. Open Switcher with an edge gesture, sliding a finger a short distance from the left edge of the screen and then quickly moving it back—a quick left-right gesture from the left bezel.

Windows 8 Search

Windows 8 has an improved Search function for finding files, apps, and settings, and in Windows 8.1 the Search function also searches the Internet using the Bing search engine. It centers on the Search bar shown back in Figure 5–2. Using a keyboard, open the Search bar from the Start screen by typing the first characters of the key word you want to use in a search. Open the Search bar from anywhere in Windows 8 with ⊞+Q, or by opening the Charms bar with a swipe from the right bezel and tapping the Search charm. In Windows 8.0, you had to select a search category. Search in Windows 8.1 is improved and, unless you are in a searchable Modern app such as People or Store, it will default to searching everywhere. Press Esc to close Search.

The Back tip displays in the upper-left corner.

The Switcher displays along the left side of the screen.

Note: ⊞+Q opens the Search bar from anywhere in Windows 8.

Note: As with previous versions of Windows, the Alt+F4 keyboard shortcut closes open Desktop windows and apps.

Note: Press ⊞+D to open the Desktop from anywhere in Windows 8.

The Desktop

You will find yourself working on the desktop if you use any of the pre-Windows 8 versions of Microsoft productivity tools, such as Microsoft Office. You will also gravitate here for many of the administrative tools, such as Control Panel and Computer Management until Microsoft improves on the new Windows 8 GUI tools.

Desktop Overview

From the Start screen tap or click the Desktop tile (or press ⊞+D) to open the Desktop GUI. Open a Desktop app and then right-click on its Taskbar icon and select *Pin this program to taskbar*. After that, you can open the app from the Taskbar. Figure 5–22 shows the Windows 8 Desktop with two app windows open. It looks much like the Windows 7 Desktop, except that Windows 8 had no Start button and neither Windows 8 nor Windows 8.1 has the Start menu. The Start screen replaces the Start menu. As mentioned earlier, the Windows 8.1 Desktop, shown in Figure 5–22, includes the Start button that returns you to the Start screen. Notice that even the Desktop has lost the three-dimensional look of Windows 7. The Desktop windows and buttons have crisp corners and there is just the hint of shading around the current open window, the only nod to the third dimension.

Desktop-Centric Options in Windows 8.1

In Windows 8.1, in addition to adding the Start button, Microsoft also added options desired by people who work primarily with Desktop apps. These options are under *Start Screen* on the Taskbar and Navigation page of the Taskbar and Navigation Properties and dialog box, shown in Figure 5–23. One way to access this page is to first open Control Panel from the Power User Menu, enter "task" in the Search box, and select *Taskbar and Navigation* from the results. The one setting in this group not targeted at the Desktop crowd specifically is labeled *Always show Start on my main display when I press the Windows logo key.* This is for people with dual-displays, so that they can control where the Start screen displays. We explain the other Start screen settings next.

Open the Desktop at Startup. Select *When I sign in or close all apps on a screen, go to the desktop instead of Start.* If you do not want to start your day at the Start

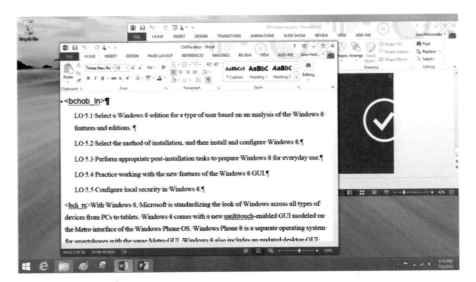

FIGURE 5–22 The Windows 8.1 Desktop with two application windows open.

screen because you still use many Desktop apps. If you only select this, you can still go to the Start screen from the Start button.

Use the Same Background on the Desktop and the Start Screen.
To do this, select *Show my desktop background on Start.* Then the background you configure in the Personalization Control Panel will show on both the Desktop and the Start screen.

Replace Start Screen with the Apps View. Select *Show the Apps view automatically when I go to Start.* This replaces the Start screen with the Apps view. In addition, selecting this also selects the normally unavailable option, *Search everywhere instead of just my apps when I search from the Apps view.* Because you have effectively disabled the Start screen, this second option gives you the default Search behavior (search everywhere) you would normally have from the Start screen.

List Desktop Apps First in Apps View. If you would like Desktop Apps to be listed first in Apps view, select this option. Then, when you open Apps view, click on the button at the top next to Apps and select *by category* to have the apps sorted by category. Notice that you can sort apps by name, date installed, most used, or category.

File Explorer for File Management

Click or tap the folder icon on the Desktop Taskbar to open File Explorer, shown in Figure 5–24. File Explorer (the new name for Windows Explorer) is the same file management tool that you used in Windows 7, with some changes to the GUI. For one thing, the Quick Access toolbar at the left of the Title bar shows the return of the Control button (the folder icon on the far left) that disappeared in Windows 7. Clicking the Control button opens a menu of options to control the File Explorer window itself: Restore, Move, Size, Minimize, Maximize, and Close. To the right of the Control button is the Properties button (ALT+ENTER) that opens the Properties dialog for the item selected

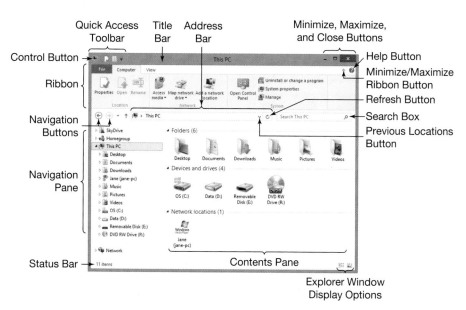

FIGURE 5–24 The Windows 8.1 File Explorer window.

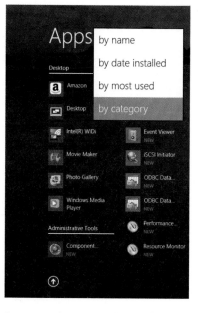

FIGURE 5–23 The Taskbar and Navigation Properties dialog box.

Sort apps by name, date installed, most used, or category.

in File Explorer. Next is the New Folder button (Ctrl+Shift+N) that creates a new folder in the current location. The last default item on the Quick Access toolbar is a button that opens the Customize Quick Access Toolbar drop-down menu for adding or removing buttons on this toolbar.

On the far right of the File Explorer window are the Minimize, Maximize, and Close buttons with some of the actions also found on the Control Button menu. On the bottom left of the window is the Status bar that shows the status of the currently selected item. For instance, in the example, This PC is selected and it contains 11 items. On the far right are buttons for changing the display options for the Contents Pane.

The more obvious difference between Windows Explorer in Windows 7 and File Explorer on the Windows 8 Desktop is the ribbon, a horizontal area below the title bar containing links to tools and options. The ribbon is similar to that found in recent versions of Microsoft Office. If the ribbon is not visible, click the Minimize/Maximize Ribbon button on the right of the menu bar below the Title bar.

The appearance of the ribbon changes based on the focus of File Explorer window, bringing up tools and features you might need and sparing you the task of digging around in multilevel menus for those same features. While navigating File Explorer, take time to notice all that is available on the ribbon as it changes with the file and folder location selected.

Further, File Explorer opens special contextual tabs that appear in the top bar. These tabs open based on the type of file or folder selected in File Explorer. Watch for these special tabs as you browse files. They include: Picture Tools, Music Tools, Disk Tools, and Application Tools. Figure 5–25 shows File Explorer focused on the Pictures folder, with the Picture Tools tab and its related ribbon.

Restoring Deleted Files

Most files on your hard drive are not permanently deleted when you use the Delete command or Del key in File Explorer. Files deleted in this way are moved to the Recycle Bin, a special folder. To restore a file, open the Recycle Bin, select the file and then click or tap the button in the Recycle Bin Tools

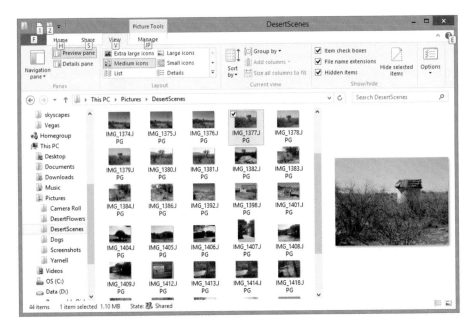

FIGURE 5–25 File Explorer with the Picture Tools tab and its related ribbon.

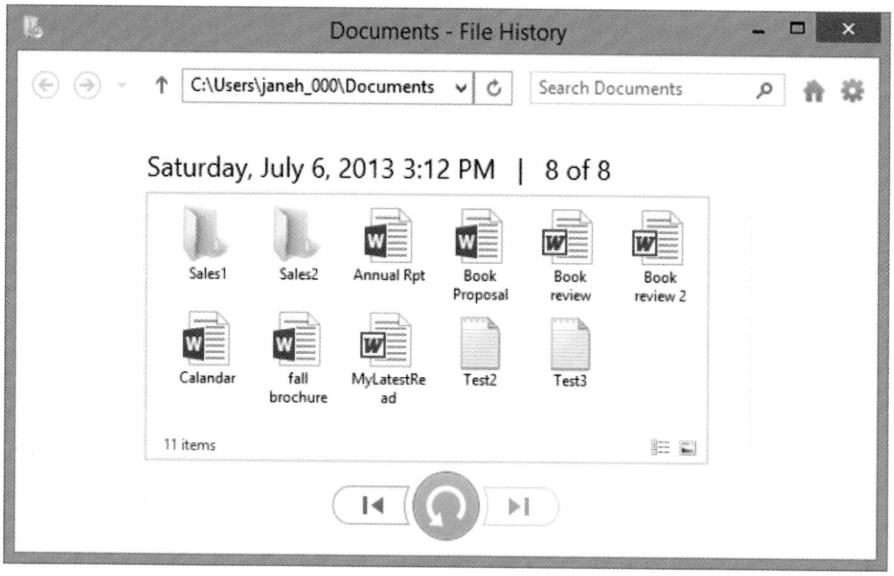

FIGURE 5–26 Select a file to restore in File History.

ribbon labeled *Restore the selected items.* The item is then restored to its original location.

If you delete a file permanently you cannot restore it from the Recycle Bin. That's when you need File History. If you turned on File History and if the file you deleted was in a location backed up by File History, you can open File History in File Explorer, locate your file (even a certain version of the file) and restore it. On the Home ribbon, click or tap the History button to open File History for that folder, as shown in Figure 5–26. Click the green button at the bottom of the window and your file is restored.

Managing Apps in Windows 8

The reason we have computers is to use apps for fun, school, or work. Therefore it is important to know how to acquire, install, update, and remove apps. Desktop apps will install and behave much as they did in Windows 7, only now you can launch a Desktop app from the Start screen, the Apps screen, or from a pinned icon on the Desktop taskbar.

Launch Modern apps from the Start screen or from the Apps screen. Windows 8 comes with some Modern productivity apps, such as People, Mail, Photos, Messaging, and Maps. Internet Explorer comes in two GUIs—Modern and Desktop. Installing and updating your Modern apps is all done through the Windows Store.

In the first release of Windows 8 newly installed apps are automatically given tiles on the Start screen, but in Windows 8.1 you get to decide if you want an app on the Start screen. With the Apps screen now so easy to access from the Start screen, you may not want to create Start screen tiles for an app you use infrequently.

Installing Apps from the Windows Store

The Windows Store is your only source of Modern apps, but you can still find Desktop apps from other sources, as well as at the Windows Store. You will need a Microsoft account to use the Windows Store. Click or tap the Store tile (the shopping bag) on the Start screen to connect to the Windows Store and the Store page will open with a dynamically changing selection of apps and categories as shown here.

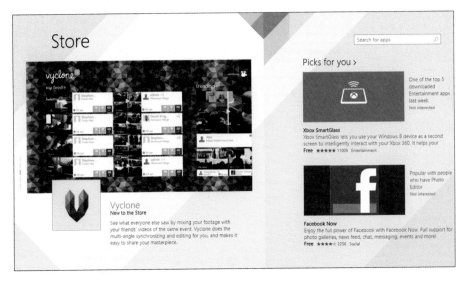

Find apps at the Windows Store.

Browse through the store by scrolling the screen, or use the Search box in the Store to search for an app. Click or tap on a tile to learn more about an app, as shown in Figure 5–27, which opened when we tapped on the tile for Adobe Reader Touch. If you decide to install an app, click the Install button. When you return to the Start screen, open the Apps page (click or tap the down arrow button on the bottom left) and look for the new app. Right-click on the app tile to open the Apps bar at the bottom of the screen. In the Apps bar, you can pin or unpin an app's tile, uninstall an app, and customize it. Figure 5–28 shows the App bar open for the Adobe Reader Touch app. Notice the button labeled "Find" in Start. Click this button, and the Start screen will open with the tile for the selected app visible. You can then move the tile to a group on the Start screen.

try this!

Install a Free App from the Windows Store

If you have an Internet connection, use the Store to browse for free apps at the Windows Store. Try this:

1. From the Start screen tap or click the Windows Store tile.
2. Enter a search string into the Search box or scroll through the selections and click those that interest you. Look for a free or free trial app.
3. Follow the on-screen instructions to download and install the app.

FIGURE 5–27 Read the details about an app before deciding to purchase and install it.

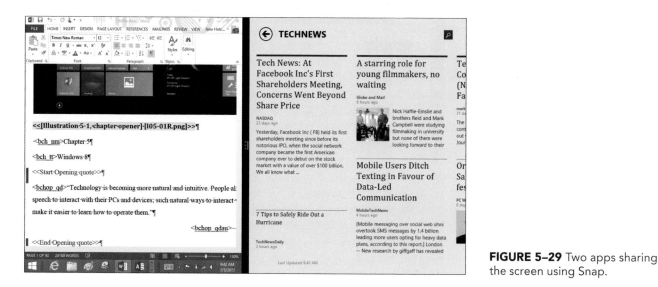

FIGURE 5–28 Use the Apps bar to configure, pin or unpin an app, uninstall it, find it on the Start screen, and customize the app.

Updating Apps from the Windows Store

Microsoft updates Windows 8 apps from the Windows Store. The Store tile on the Start screen will let you know when updates are available for your Modern apps. The example shown here indicates that 16 apps have updates ready. Click on the tile to connect to the Windows Store and open the App updates page. On this page, select which apps to update and then click the *Install* button to install the updates.

Using Snap

To use the Windows 8 screen-sharing feature, Snap, first open two Modern apps and/or one Modern app and the Desktop (with or without a Desktop app open). Then, if using touch, touch the left edge and drag your finger a short distance of about an inch until you see a thumbnail image for the second app and a vertical bar. If using a mouse, drag the pointer a short distance from the upper-left corner. Release the mouse button or lift your finger and the second app will appear in a vertical space next to the app that previously occupied the entire space. This takes practice. Previous to Windows 8.1, one app could only occupy a narrow vertical area on one side or the other, while the other app occupied the bulk of the screen. Beginning with 8.1, you can adjust the vertical divider to any position on the screen (Figure 5–29).

The Store tile shows the number of updates available for installed apps.

FIGURE 5–29 Two apps sharing the screen using Snap.

LO 5.5 | Securing Windows 8

As with previous versions of Windows, securing Windows 8 involves using security software to protect against malware and spyware, using a personal firewall, enabling automatic updates, and using a secure sign-in. These security features are enabled by default during Windows installation.

As with Windows 7, Windows Firewall is turned on by default, and the Windows Firewall Control Panel looks and works almost exactly like that in Windows 7 (shown in Figure 4–26). By default, Windows Update automatically downloads and installs important updates, which include security updates. You learned earlier how to configure Windows Update to update your other Microsoft software, which also helps to keep your system more secure. In this section, learn about new security features in Windows 8 and how you can use them. We begin with a discussion of the improved Windows Defender, followed by a short description of bloatware (also a security issue), and then describe what is new in administering user accounts in Windows 8.

Windows Defender

Securing your Windows 8 computer has become easier, because it comes with antispyware and antimalware protection in the form of Windows Defender. Now, rather than having to find and install a security package, Windows Defender comes installed and ready to go to work for you. Figure 5–30 shows Windows Defender's home page with minimal status information. It will automatically check for updates to virus and spyware definitions. Use the Update tab if you want to initiate a manual update. The History tab will describe suspected malware code that has been quarantined (isolated) so that it cannot become active and do harm. The History page also describes all detected items and any items allowed because you configured Windows Defender to allow them. This last you configure through options on the Settings tab: *Excluded files and locations* and *Excluded file types*.

Figure 5–31 shows the Advanced options on the Settings tab set to the defaults. For a higher level of security select *Scan removable drives*. If you select the option *Create a restore point*, then before Windows Defender quarantines a file it will create a restore point. If Windows or important software becomes unstable after files are quarantined, this allows you to restore your computer to the prequarantined state.

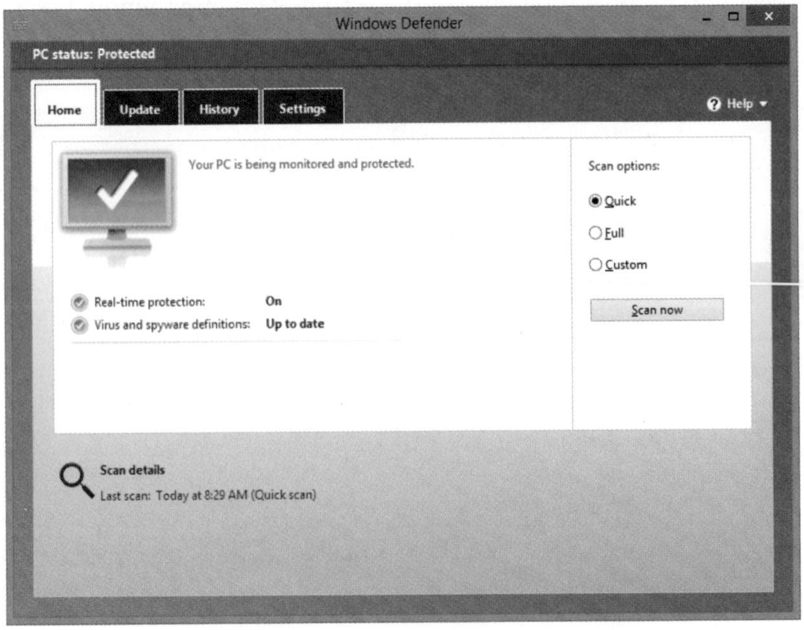

FIGURE 5–30 The Windows Defender home page.

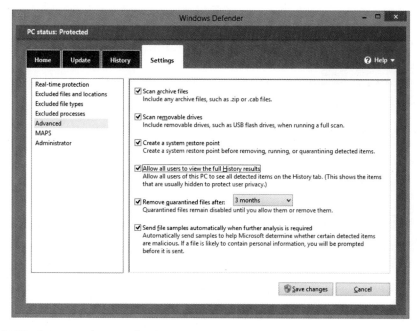

FIGURE 5–31 Windows Defender settings.

This is questionable, since you could be restoring your computer to an infected state if the files were, indeed, infected. It does make sense to select the option *Remove quarantined files after.* You configure the time period. A quarantined file is not allowed to run, so if some program requires a quarantined file, that program will not run at all or will issue error messages. Providing a time period before deleting the file gives you time to notice if the quarantined file was needed. The best action to take if quarantining a file disables an important program is to reinstall the program, provided it is first scanned for malware.

Administering Local User Accounts

As with Windows 7 (and many versions previous to it), local user accounts reside in the local accounts database on a Windows 8 computer, and use of a local account gives someone access to the computer and to local data. You can create multiple user accounts on a computer that is used by multiple people, with different permissions assigned to each user for accessing local files, folders, and printers.

Administer user accounts using the traditional Desktop tool, User Accounts Control Panel, which has not significantly changed since Windows 7. There is also a new Windows 8 GUI tool. In Windows 8.0, this tool was the Users panel in the PC Settings page. In Windows 8.1 it is the Accounts page in PC Settings, shown in Figure 5–32. In both releases, this tool allows you to do simple user management tasks. We will begin there.

Administering User Accounts

The Accounts page in PC Settings in Windows 8.1 has three panes. When the *Your account* pane is open it will resemble Figure 5–32 if you are signed on with a Microsoft account, and your email address will display under your name.

Options on Your Account Pane. If you are signed in with a local account, no email address will display, only the words *Local Account.* When signed in with a Microsoft account, the button labeled *Disconnect* lets you switch to signing in with a local account, at which point you will lose the benefits of the Microsoft account. If you are signed in with a local account, this button is replaced by one labeled *Connect to a Microsoft* account.

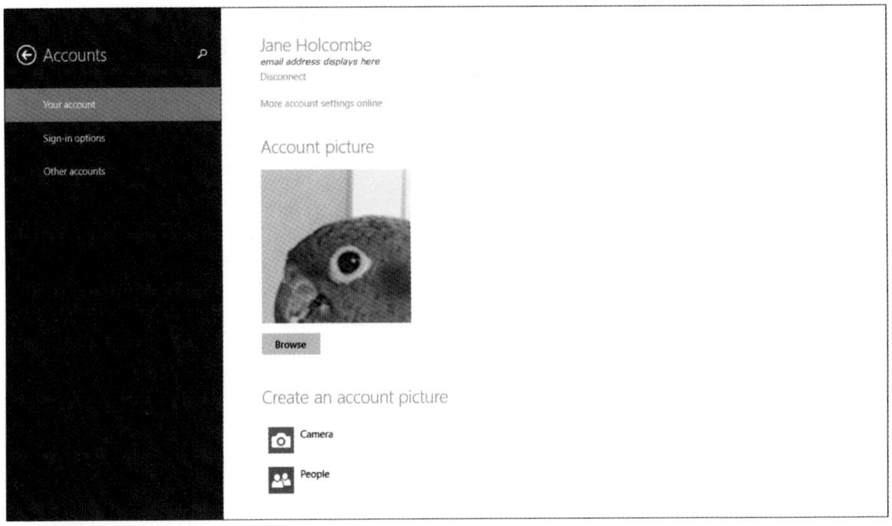

FIGURE 5–32 If you are signed in with a Microsoft account, the Your account pane in Accounts will show these choices with your account picture.

The link *More account settings online,* only available for a Microsoft account, connects to your account settings online. You will need to enter your Microsoft account password before you can access your account settings. This is to protect you from someone using your unattended computer after you've signed in to connect and modify your settings. For both a Microsoft account or a local account, the only other options shown in the *Your account* pane in Windows 8.1 are for changing your account picture.

Sign-In Options Pane. The *Sign-in options* pane is where you change your password, and create or change a Picture password, create or change a PIN (a four-digit number) for signing in, or change the Password policy so that any user with a password doesn't need to enter it when waking the PC, or the opposite, requiring a password.

Adding Users. If you are signed in with an administrator account, you can add other users to your computer by selecting *Other accounts* on the Accounts page. In the *Other accounts* pane, click the + button labeled *Add an account.* The next page, shown in Figure 5–33, includes choices for signing in with a Microsoft account, creating a new Microsoft account, or , signing in with a

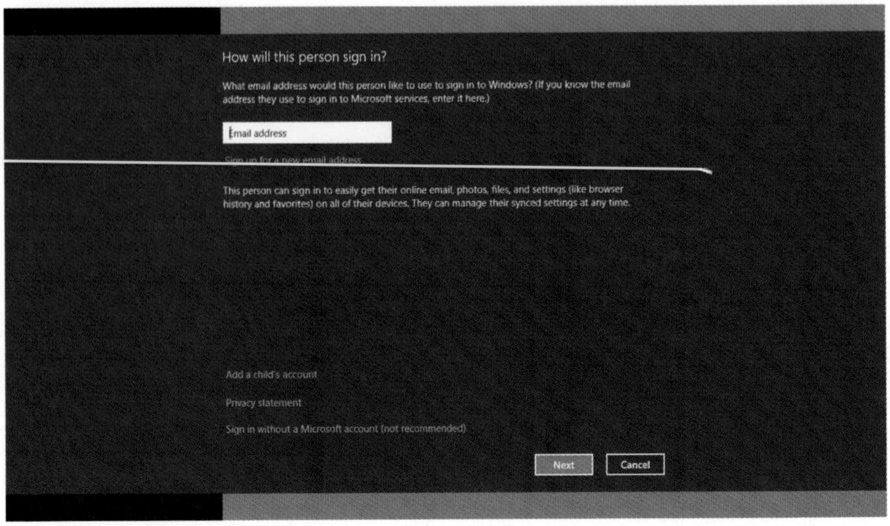

FIGURE 5–33 Select how a user will sign in.

local account. Experience portion of Windows installation. To have the new user sign in with a local account if you choose the last option, *Sign in without a Microsoft account.*

Not so obvious is the fact that creating a new account using this tool creates a standard account (nonadministrator), and if you decide to change that you will need to take extra steps after the account is created, using the Users Account Control Panel.

Adding an Account for a Child and Enabling Family Safety. Monitor a child's use of a computer using a Windows 8 feature called Family Safety. In Windows 8.0 you would enable Family Safety after creating an account. In Windows 8.1, you can create an account with Family Safety turned on by selecting the link labeled *Add a child's account* near the bottom of the screen shown in Figure 5-33. This opens the screen shown here where you can choose to create a Microsoft account for the child or create a local account using the link at the bottom of the screen.

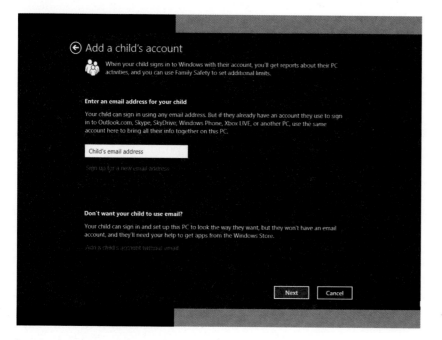

When you create a child's account in Windows 8.1 Family Safety will monitor that account's usage.

Now manage your Family Safety settings. In Control Panel, open Family Safety shown in Figure 5–34. Click the link to *Manage settings on the Family Safety website.* Sign in with your Microsoft account, and access the Activity Reporting page where you can turn on activity reporting, and view activity reports.

Windows SmartScreen

SmartScreen was introduced in Internet Explorer 9 to prevent downloading of suspicious programs during Web browsing. In Windows 8, Microsoft introduced a more powerful feature, Windows SmartScreen that improves on the original. No longer just part of the Internet Explorer browser, Windows SmartScreen runs at the OS level so that it protects against malicious downloads from any source, such as browsers, email, and even your local network or locally attached drives. SmartScreen uses special sensing features, as well as an online service to determine if software is malicious or from a source.

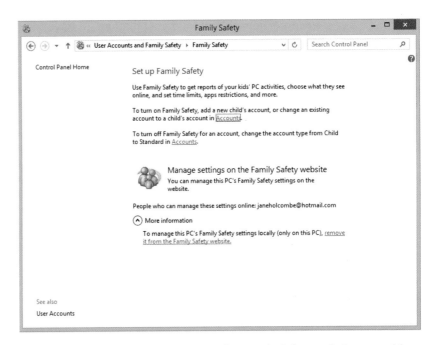

FIGURE 5–34 Select *Manage settings on the Family Safety website* to enable or disable activity reporting and view activity reports.

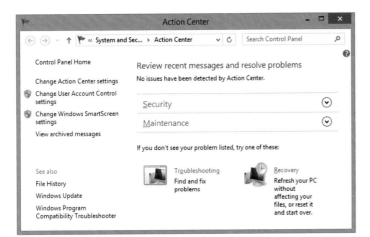

Open Action Center and select *Change Windows SmartScreen settings* (on left).

You can turn Windows SmartScreen off or on (it is on by default) for Windows Store apps (just part of the SmartScreen function). In Windows 8.1, open PC Settings and select Privacy. On the Privacy page select General, and the third choice is labeled *Turn on SmartScreen Filter to check web content (URLs) that Windows Store apps use.* You will find other settings for Windows SmartScreen in the Action Center Control Panel, shown here. Open it from the Desktop by clicking or tapping the Action Center icon (a small flag) on the Taskbar, then click or tap Open Action Center.

Select the link labeled *Change Windows Smart-Screen settings.* This opens the Windows Smart-Screen dialog box, shown in Figure 5–35, with just a few options. The default, as shown, is the most secure option.

A Windows 8 Computer in a Kiosk

Assigned Access is a feature added in Windows 8.1 that allows an administrator to assign a single user account to run just one app. This is done through the Users page in Settings. You can use this feature to turn a PC into a kiosk computer, meaning you could place the computer in a public place, configured to automatically sign in a user with limited permissions who can only run a single app. Imagine a physically secured touch-screen tablet in a mall kiosk running an app that helps visitors find the various businesses in the mall, but does not allow them to access any other files or programs on that computer.

FIGURE 5–35 The default SmartScreen setting.

Chapter 5 REVIEW

Chapter Summary

After reading this chapter and completing the exercises, you should know the following facts about Windows 8.

Overview of Windows 8 Features and Editions

- Windows 8 is faster and smaller than previous versions.
- Windows 8 comes in separate products for two architectures: ARM and Intel/AMD computer architecture.
- Windows 8 has two GUIs: the Modern GUI optimized for touch devices with features such as live tiles and the Desktop GUI much like that of Windows 7. The first release did not include the Start button, which was added in Windows 8.1, but still no Windows 7-style Start menu.
- Windows 8 supports multitouch, which is the ability of a multitouch-enabled screen, mouse, or touchpad to interpret multiple simultaneous touch gestures.
- The new GUI is anchored by a home screen called the Start screen, which contains the live tiles used for launching apps. A live tile displays active content related to its associated app without requiring you to launch the app.
- The Modern GUI does not contain overlapping windows. All Modern apps are full screen. The only exception is a simple screen-sharing feature called Snap that allows two Modern apps or one Modern app and the Desktop to share the screen with a vertical divide.
- Overlapping windows are only supported within the Desktop GUI.
- An on-screen keyboard is available for use on touch screens within keyboards, or as an accessibility option on systems with a keyboard.
- The Connected Standby power mode in Windows 8 allows specially designed apps to perform small tasks while a device is sleeping.
- Windows 8 supports a variety of sensor hardware in mobile devices, responding by dimming or brightening the screen, rotating the image on a screen, using GPS location information, and turning a mobile device into a game controller.
- The Tap to Send feature allows Windows 8 to take advantage of special hardware (if present) to wirelessly send data to other compatible devices with a single tap on a special area on the exterior of the device.
- Windows comes in three retail editions: Windows RT, Windows 8 *Basic* and Windows 8 Pro. Windows RT runs only on the ARM architecture while Windows 8 *Basic* and Windows 8 Pro run on the Intel/AMD computer architecture.
- Windows 8 Enterprise is an edition not available at retail, sold to large corporate customers through Microsoft's Software Assurance volume licensing program.
- The Windows 8 Starter edition is available only in emerging markets.
- Windows RT will run Modern apps and special Desktop apps provided by Microsoft through the Windows Store. It comes with a special software bundle of Microsoft Office 2013 RT. It does not run traditional Windows apps.
- Windows *Basic* and Windows Pro run both the Modern apps only available through the Windows Store and traditional Windows apps available from Microsoft and other sources.
- Windows 8 *Basic* includes Remote Desktop client, allowing it to connect to a Remote Desktop host computer, but it does not include the Remote Desktop host.
- Windows 8 Pro includes both the Remote Desktop client and the Remote Desktop host.
- Windows Media Player, available in both Windows 8 *Basic* and Windows 8 Pro, plays several types of digital media files, burns music CDs, rips media from CDs, syncs digital media files to a portable device, and lets you shop online for media files. It does not include the ability to play DVDs.
- Windows Media Center, which you can purchase and add to Windows 8 Pro for $9.99, is a full-feature media app, plus it will play DVDs.

Installing Windows 8

- Minimum requirements for the Intel/AMD computer architecture are nearly identical to those for Windows 7, with the exception of a minimum screen resolution of 1024 × 768 (1366 × 786 recommended) for Windows 8, but most recently manufactured computers far exceed this minimum.

- Windows RT supports an entirely different architecture called ARM, and as such is not available as an upgrade.
- Upgrade paths are limited to the Intel/AMD computer architecture and certain editions of Windows 7 to certain editions of Windows 8 (see Table 5–1).
- Before installing Windows 8, understand the new rule concerning activation of a retail edition. Activation is no longer something you can delay for 30 days. It occurs early in the installation process and requires the product key.
- If you purchase Windows 8 from the Microsoft Store, you will need a Microsoft account, previously called a Windows Live ID. This account is free, as are many of the services. Fees apply when you upgrade services, such as increasing your maximum storage on SkyDrive.
- Decide ahead of time how you will sign in to Windows 8. Your choices are: local account, Microsoft account, and Microsoft Active Directory Domain account.
- The Windows 8 Web-based Installer is a new and improved installation method for a retail edition purchased through the Microsoft Store. It combines many tasks and automatically enters your product code (although you should still record and save the product code).
- If you plan an upgrade—whether you plan to use the more conventional Windows setup or the Web-based Installer, run the Upgrade Assistant ahead of time to be prepared for incompatibility issues. This may include acquiring updated drivers.
- To run the traditional Windows setup you will need bootable media in the form of discs purchased at retail, a disc created from a downloaded ISO image file, or a bootable USB drive also created from a downloaded image.
- Both the traditional Windows setup and the Web-based Installer end with the Out of Box Experience (OOBE) in which you customize your installation.

Postinstallation Tasks
- If updated drivers did not all install during installation, take steps to install them afterward. Use driver update programs from manufacturers and/or Windows Update.
- Check that the correct display driver is installed by opening the Screen Resolution dialog in the Control Panel.
- Run Windows Update several times to bring all the Windows components up to date.
- Configure Windows Update to automatically update other Microsoft software in addition to Windows components.
- If you installed Windows 8 into a virtual machine, install the Guest Additions into the virtual machine so that Windows 8 will run better. How you do this, and the name for this software, varies by hypervisor.
- On a computer with factory-installed Windows 8 look for bloatware, the extra software the manufacturers often install. Some of it is useful, like a utility to create an image of the factory installed software in case you need to return the computer to its original state. Some programs that manufacturers install are simply trial versions of programs, and you will need to pay a fee to continue using them past the trial period.
- Shut down Windows 8 by opening the Charms bar, selecting the Settings charm, and then from the Power charm, select Shut down.

Navigating and Configuring Windows 8
- Windows 8 has settings based in both GUIs: the new Windows 8 PC Settings page and the familiar Control Panel in the Desktop GUI.
- The Lock screen is designed especially for touch-screen devices to prevent you from accidentally triggering some action. By default, it appears when you first start up your computer, choose Lock from the User tile, or after a period of inactivity triggers the screen saver.
- Start screen features include live tiles, charms, Charms bar, Power charm, User tile, scroll bar, and zoom button,
- Point the mouse at the bottom-left corner to display the Start tip, showing either the last active app or the Start screen (when in an app).
- When several apps are open, a swipe gesture from the left edge of the screen will switch among the open apps one at a time. A swipe gesture that begins at the left edge and almost immediately goes back to the edge reveals the Switcher, a bar containing thumb nails of all open app.

- When using a mouse, moving the mouse from the lower-left corner (or upper-left corner) along the left side reveals the Start tip, a thumbnail of the most recently opened app.
- Use Windows 8 Search to find files, apps, and data. Open the Search bar when a Modern app is open and do a search related to the app.
- Change the User tile to a custom picture in the Personalize page in PC Settings.
- Zoom the Start screen out so that you can rearrange the groups of tiles.
- Open the Desktop from the Desktop tile on the Start screen.
- The Desktop resembles that of Windows 7, minus the Start button (Windows Orb). Therefore, there is also no Start menu; it was replaced by the Start screen.
- File Explorer (the new name for Windows Explorer) is the same file management tool that you used in Windows 7, with some changes to the GUI, including a menu ribbon similar to that in Microsoft Office.
- The Windows Store is your source of Modern apps as well as the updates to those apps.

Securing Windows 8

- Securing any version of Windows involves using security software to protect against malware and spyware, using a personal firewall, enabling automatic updates, and using a secure sign in. These features are enabled and configured by default in Windows 8.
- Windows Defender is included in Windows 8 for antispyware and antimalware protection.
- Do simple administration of local user accounts in the Users panel of PC Settings. Any users you add here will be standard users. If an account will be used by a child, you can enable Family Settings to monitor the child's activities.
- SmartScreen was introduced in Internet Explorer 9 to prevent downloading of suspicious programs during Web browsing. An expanded version of this, Windows SmartScreen, in Windows 8 improves on the original feature by running at the OS level so that it protects against malicious downloads from any source, such as browsers, email, and even your local network or locally attached drives.
- If you need to run a Windows 8 computer in a public area, such as a kiosk, use the Assigned Access feature added in Windows 8.1 to create a user with limited access that is assigned to run just one program.

Key Terms List

Assigned Access (204)

Back tip (193)

bloatware (187)

charm (185)

Charms bar (185)

cold boot (180)

Connected Standby (169)

Domain Join (171)

edge gestures 172)

File Explorer (184)

Group Policy (171)

ISO image (179)

keyboard shortcut (168)

live tile (167)

Lock screen (189)

Microsoft account (173)

Microsoft Store (170)

mouse (167)

multitouch (166)

on-screen keyboard (168)

Out of Box Experience (OOBE) (180)

PC Settings screen (186)

Power User menu (189)

Remote Desktop (170)

Remote Desktop client (170)

Remote Desktop host (171)

ribbon (196)

Search bar (168)

semantic zoom (191)

Settings bar (185)

SmartScreen (203)

Snap (168)

Start button (171)

Start screen (167)

Switcher (193)

Tap to Send (169)

thumbnail (193)

touch mouse (167)

touchpad (167)

warm boot (180)

Web-based Installer (174)

Windows 8.1 (171)

Windows 8 *Basic* (170)

Windows 8 Pro (171)

Windows Flip (193)

Windows key (168)

Windows Media Center (WMC) (170)

Windows Media Player (WMP) (170)

Windows RT (169)

Windows setup (179)

Windows SmartScreen (203)

Windows Store (170)

Key Terms Quiz

Use the Key Terms List to complete the sentences that follow. Not all terms will be used.

1. Search, Share, Start, Devices, and Settings are all _____ on a bar that slides out from the right when you swipe in from the right edge of a touch screen.

2. A/an _____ is a rectangular object on the Start screen that acts as a shortcut to open an app, but can also display active content related to that app at the Start screen.

3. You can sign in to a Windows 8 computer using a Microsoft Active Directory Domain account, a local account, or a _____.

4. The _____ is your only source for Windows 8 Modern apps.

5. The _____ edition only runs on devices with the ARM computer architecture.

6. If you need to configure a Windows 8 computer for a public space where it will run only a single app, use the _____ feature added in Windows 8.1.

7. Both the Windows setup and Web-based Installer end in the _____, in which you customize your installation of Windows.

8. When you use _____ at the Start screen you can rearrange the groups of tiles by dragging them around.

9. A/an _____ is a file containing a copy of the entire contents of a disc.

10. The _____ contains several panels for configuring Windows 8 settings.

Multiple-Choice Quiz

1. Which of the following represents the computer architecture supported by Windows RT?
   a. 64-bit
   b. Intel/AMD
   c. ARM
   d. Texas Instruments
   e. UEFI

2. A Windows 8 computer configured with default settings will start up to this screen.
   a. Sign-in
   b. Lock
   c. Settings
   d. Users
   e. Start

3. Your personal computer at home is running Windows 7 Professional and you want to do an in-place upgrade to Windows 8. Which edition of Windows 8 should you purchase?
   a. Ultimate
   b. Windows 8
   c. Windows RT
   d. Windows 8 Pro
   e. Home Premium

4. A Windows 8 Modern app normally runs full screen. What Windows 8 feature allows two Modern apps or one Modern app and the Desktop to share the screen?
   a. Charms
   b. Live tiles
   c. Start tip
   d. Semantic zoom
   e. Snap

5. Swipe from the left side of the screen to cycle through open apps, or use a mouse to point at the top left corner to open a _____ showing a thumbnail of the last open app.
   a. Charms
   b. Live tile
   c. Back tip
   d. Semantic zoom
   e. Snap

6. Previously only included in Internet Explorer 9, this improved and slightly renamed security feature works at the OS level in Windows 8 to guard against malicious downloads from any source.
   a. Windows SmartScreen
   b. Connected Standby
   c. Group Policy
   d. Lock screen
   e. Domain Join

7. This power-saving feature of Windows 8 allows specially designed apps to perform small tasks—such as email and notifications—in background while the device is sleeping.
   a. Windows SmartScreen
   b. Connected Standby
   c. Group Policy

    d. Lock screen

    e. Domain Join

8. Use this key to return to the Start screen in Windows 8.

    a. ALT

    b. CTRL

    c. ESC

    d. RETURN

    e. WINDOWS

9. What is the updated file management tool that runs on the Windows 8 Desktop?

    a. File Manager

    b. File Explorer

    c. Windows Explorer

    d. Ribbon

    e. Windows Manager

10. What is the name for the antivirus/antispyware software that is included in Windows 8?

    a. Windows Defender

    b. Microsoft Security Essentials

    c. OOBE

    d. Windows SmartScreen

    e. Assigned Access

11. You want to configure a Windows 8.1 computer to install in a kiosk in your school's lobby and run just one program that helps visitors find various offices. What feature will you use to limit visitor's access on that computer?

    a. Windows Defender

    b. Microsoft Security Essentials

    c. OOBE

    d. Windows SmartScreen

    e. Assigned Access

12. What do you "experience" the first time you power on a new computer with a factory installation of Windows 8?

    a. Windows Defender

    b. Microsoft Security Essentials

    c. OOBE

    d. Windows SmartScreen

    e. Assigned Access

13. Where will you find the Power charm?

    a. Scroll bar

    b. Switcher

    c. Settings bar

    d. Search bar

    e. Charms bar

14. This Windows 8 Feature, if enabled, automatically backs up certain folders, even tracking file versions, so that you can restore files after they are permanently deleted.

    a. Charms bar

    b. Recycle bin

    c. Settings bar

    d. Search bar

    e. File History

15. If you are using Windows 8.1 on a computer with a keyboard, use these keystrokes to quickly shut down Windows and the computer.

    a. CTRL-ALT-DELETE

    b. CTRL+SHIFT+N

    c. WINDOWS KEY + X

    d. WINDOWS KEY + X, u, u

    e. WINDOWS KEY+TAB

Essay Quiz

1. You plan to do a clean install of Windows 8 Pro onto a computer that currently is running Windows 7, and you plan to reinstall the Windows apps that are currently on that computer. Describe what steps you will take to see if your existing hardware and applications are compatible with Windows 8 and to prepare for any incompatibilities.

2. Describe how you would open the context menu on the Windows 8 Desktop on a touch-screen device without a keyboard.

3. Briefly explain the two computer architectures supported by Windows 8 and the edition or editions available for each architecture.

4. Describe a shortcoming of both the swipe and Back tip for use in cycling through open apps.

5. Describe how you are alerted that updates are available for your Windows 8 Modern apps.

Lab Projects

LAB PROJECT 5.1

The authors had to pick and choose what to present in a single chapter. One big topic that we could not cover is the specifics of working with the installed Modern apps and how well they share data. Pick two apps, such as Mail and People, and test them, even if you need to create a temporary Hotmail account with Microsoft and enter fictitious names and data into the People app. Or try the Music, Video, and Pictures apps and describe how they share data. Then describe what you did and how the two apps you selected share data.

LAB PROJECT 5.2

The authors have done their best to prepare you for working with Windows 8, but this operating system continues to evolve. Consider the features described in this chapter and compare them with your experiences with the latest update to Windows 8. What feature was added that helps you the most (if any)? What would you like to see added or removed from Windows 8?

LAB PROJECT 5.3

In addition to the three account types, you can also choose to sign in using a picture password or a PIN. Research these options and pick one and write a description of how you enable it and your opinion of the value and weakness of that option.

6

Under the Windows Desktop: Supporting and Troubleshooting Windows

"Computing is not about computers any more. It is about living."

—Nicholas Negroponte
Founder and chairman emeritus, Massachusetts Institute of Technology's Media Lab and founder of the One Laptop per Child Association

When IBM introduced the IBM PC in 1981, the computer had a mostly open architecture, and although the PCs of today have evolved to be much more powerful computers than those of three decades ago, they still have an open architecture that includes improvements made along the way. This open architecture enables each of us to transform a personal computer into the tool we need by adding the right mix of software and hardware. To many, a PC is an office automation tool with office productivity software, a printer, an Internet connection, and maybe a scanner. Another person will make a PC a video workstation with the addition of elaborate video editing and movie production components. Or a PC may be the uniting component in a music studio; and in entirely different environments, it may run manufacturing equipment, or auto-test equipment.

For the PC to be such a versatile machine, it must first have a hardware architecture that allows you to add your choice from a huge variety

Learning Outcomes

In this chapter, you will learn how to:

LO **6.1** Define the role of the registry in Windows, and back up and modify the registry when needed.

LO **6.2** Describe the Windows user options and power options, and, given a scenario, select appropriate startup options.

LO **6.3** Install and manage device drivers.

LO **6.4** Troubleshoot common Windows problems.

of hardware components. Then, it also must have an operating system that you can configure to control all the devices you choose to plug in. And you probably want a visually pleasing, easy-to-use GUI operating system, along with GUI applications that are compatible with the OS and that complement your master plan for the PC.

Windows is just such a configurable operating system—but there is a price to pay for having so much potential in an operating system: complexity. Much of that complexity is hidden, so in this chapter we look under the Windows desktop at some of that complexity, including the registry, the device drivers, the Windows power options and startup procedure, and methods for troubleshooting common Windows problems. ✹

LO 6.1 | Understanding the Registry

The registry, introduced in Windows 95, is one of several technical features that has made Windows easier to configure and support than the earlier Microsoft operating systems. Ironically, it is also one of the most complicated and least understood features of Windows. The structure of the registry in Windows 8 is the same as that of Windows Vista and Window 7. In this section you'll learn about the registry—its role in Windows and how to modify it when needed.

The Registry Defined

The Windows **registry** is a database of all configuration settings in one installation of Windows. It includes settings for:

- Device drivers
- Services
- Installed application programs
- Operating system components
- User preferences

Windows creates the registry during its installation, and it continues to make modifications to it as you configure Windows and add applications and components. During startup, Windows depends on the registry to tell it what services, drivers, and components to load into memory, and how to configure each component. The registry remains in memory while Windows is active.

Note: Remember that the registry contains only settings, not the actual device drivers, services, or applications to which the settings apply. Windows will not work as you expect it to if these other components are damaged or not available.

Automatic Registry Changes

The Windows registry will automatically change when:

- Windows starts up or shuts down.
- Windows Setup runs (which occurs more often than you may think; e.g., each time Windows gets updated).
- Changes are made through a Control Panel applet or a Windows 8 PC Settings tool.
- A new device is installed.
- Any changes are made to the Windows configuration.
- Any changes are made to a user's desktop preferences.
- An application is installed or modified.
- Changes are made to user preferences in any application.

Registry Files

Although considered only a single entity, the registry is actually stored in a number of binary files on disk. A binary file contains program code. The Windows registry files include the following:

- BCD
- default
- ntuser.dat
- sam
- security
- software
- system

The Windows developers named the portion of the registry represented in one of these registry files a hive. Hive files are the permanent portions of the registry, with all the changes saved from use to use. With the exception of ntuser.dat and BCD, these registry files are in a disk folder named config, located below C:\Windows\System32. Figure 6–1 shows the contents of the config folder in Windows 7. Look for the files that match the list above (except ntuser.dat and BCD). Notice that the registry files listed in the config folder have file names without file extensions. If you have Windows Explorer (Windows Vista or Windows 7) or File Manager (Windows 8) configured to show hidden

try this!

View Hidden Files and Extensions in Windows Explorer/File Explorer

By default Windows hides hidden files and extensions in the GUI. Make them visible in Windows Explorer/File Explorer. These steps work in Windows 7 and Windows 8. Try this:

1. Open the **Start** menu (Windows 7) or **Power User** menu (Windows 8) and select **Control Panel**.
2. In **Control Panel** search on "folder options" and open **Folder Options** from the results.
3. In Folder Options select **View**.
4. On the View tab enable the radio button labeled **Show hidden files, folders, or drives**.
5. Ensure that there is *no* check in the box labeled **Hide extensions for known file types**.
6. Click or tap the OK button.
7. Open Windows Explorer/File Explorer and browse to the **config** folder. Extensions and hidden files are now visible.

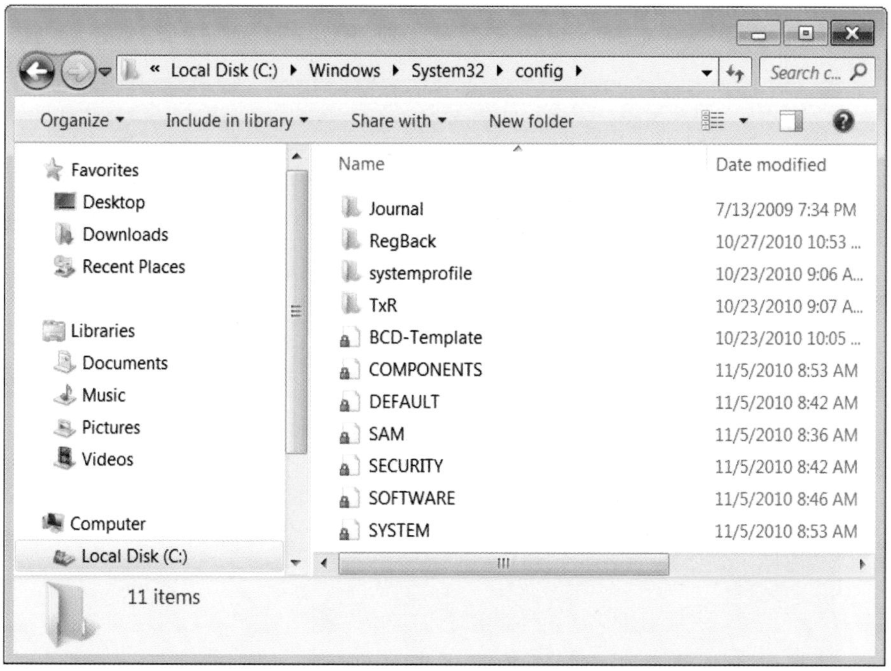

FIGURE 6–1 This view of the Windows 7 config folder shows the location of the registry files.

files, you will see other files, including files with log extensions that have file names that match the registry files. The operating system uses LOG files for logging transactions to the registry files. Other hidden files with matching file names and SAV extensions are backup copies of registry files created at the end of the text mode stage of setup. In Windows 8, the registry files are in the same location.

BCD

The BCD file resides in the Boot folder in the hidden system partition. As with other registry files, it is a binary file. It contains the Boot Configuration Database (BCD) store used by Windows during the bootloader phase of startup, providing the bootloader with information it needs to locate and load the operating system files.

DEFAULT

The default hive contains user desktop settings, called a user profile, used when there is no logged-on user. You do need desktop settings for the GUI even before you log on. You'll see evidence of this profile in the desktop settings used for the Logon screen shown in Figure 6–2.

NTUSER.DAT

The ntuser.dat hive file contains the user profile for a single user. These settings include application preferences, screen colors, network connections, and other personal choices. Each user who logs on to the computer has a separate ntuser.dat file. During startup, Window uses the other registry hives to load and configure the operating system. One of the last tasks of the operating system at startup is to request a user logon. When a user logs on, the settings from that user's ntuser.dat file apply and become part of the current registry. The first time a user logs on to a computer, Windows uses the ntuser.dat file from the C:\Users\Default folder to create the initial profile for the user. It saves the ntuser.dat file in the top-level personal folder for that user, and it is a hidden file so it is only visible if your Folder Options are set to Show hidden files, folders, and drives.

Note: We described personal folders in Chapter 4.

FIGURE 6–2 The default user profile used until a user logs on.

SAM

The sam hive contains the local security accounts database; sam is an acronym for Security Accounts Manager.

SECURITY

The security hive contains the local security policy settings for the computer, including rules for password complexity and for how the system will handle numerous failed attempts at entering a password.

SOFTWARE

The software hive contains configuration settings for software installed on the local computer, along with various items of miscellaneous configuration data.

SYSTEM

The system hive contains information used at startup, including device drivers to load as well as the order of their loading, and configuration settings, instructions for the starting and configuring of services, and various operating system settings.

Registry Hives

Previously you learned about the files used to store portions of the registry and their locations on disk. Table 6–1 shows the registry hive files and where their data is located in the registry. With Regedit, use this table to browse to the locations in the registry for each of these hives.

The Temporary Portion of the Registry

The information stored in HKEY_LOCAL_MACHINE\HARDWARE is temporary information, gathered during the hardware detection process of the detect-and-configure-hardware phase of Windows startup. Windows does not save it to disk in a file, as it does other portions of the registry.

Viewing and Editing the Registry

You view and edit the hierarchical structure of the registry using the Registry Editor utility, Regedit. Its executable file, regedit.exe, is located in the folder in which the operating system is installed (by default that is C:\Windows), but it does not have a shortcut on the Start menu. This is for a very good reason: It should not be too handy. When you need it, start it from the Windows 7 Start Search box, the Windows 8 Search Settings. In all Windows versions in this book you can start it from the Run box. It will aid your understanding of the registry if you open the Regedit program now and refer to it as you read the following descriptions of the registry components.

WARNING!

Do not directly edit the registry with a tool like Regedit unless it is absolutely necessary; there are many safer ways to make a change to the registry. For example, when you change settings in a Control Panel applet, that applet in turn modifies the registry because that is where it maintains and uses the settings.

TABLE 6–1 Locations of the Hives within the Registry

Hive File	Registry Location
BCD	HKEY_LOCAL_MACHINE\BCD00000000
default	HKEY_USERS\.DEFAULT
ntuser.dat (of the currently logged on user)	HKEY_CURRENT_USER and HKEY_USERS
sam	HKEY_LOCAL_MACHINE\SAM
security	HKEY_LOCAL_MACHINE\SECURITY
software	HKEY_LOCAL_MACHINE\SOFTWARE
system	HKEY_LOCAL_MACHINE\SYSTEM

Note: Describing a registry location is similar to the way we describe file and folder locations on disk; we use a notation that shows the path from a root key down through the subkeys: HKEY_LOCAL_MACHINE\SYSTEM\CURRENTCONTROLSET\CONTROL.

The first time Regedit runs on a computer, it looks like Figure 6–3. Each folder represents a **key**, an object that may contain one or more settings as well as other keys. Each of the top five folders is a **root key** (also called a subtree in Microsoft documentation). Each root key is at the top of a hierarchical structure containing more keys. Each key may contain one or more settings as well as other keys. A key that exists within another key is a **subkey**. Each setting within a key is a **value entry**. When you click on the folder for a key, it becomes the active key in Regedit, its folder icon "opens," and the contents of the key show in the right pane, as you see in Figure 6–4. Table 6–2 gives an overview of the information stored within each root key of the registry.

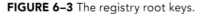

FIGURE 6–3 The registry root keys.

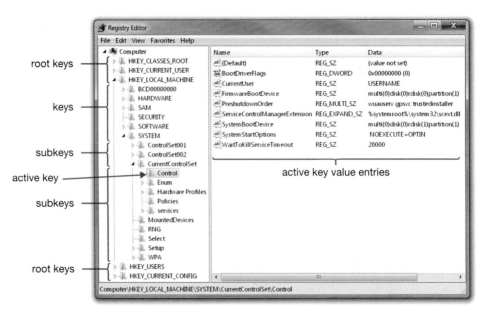

FIGURE 6–4 Registry components.

TABLE 6-2 Contents of Registry Root Keys

Root Key	Description
HKEY_CLASSES_ROOT	Shows relationships (called associations) between applications and data file types defined by file extension. Thanks to the information in this key, you can double-click on a data file and the correct application will open and load the file. This root key is actually all the information located in HKEY_LOCAL_MACHINE\SOFTWARE\Classes.
HKEY_CURRENT_USER	Contains the user profile for the currently logged-on user, storing all the user settings that affect the desktop appearance and the default behavior of installed applications.
HKEY_LOCAL_MACHINE	Contains the system information, including detected hardware, application associations, and information for hardware configuration and device drivers.
HKEY_USERS	User profiles for all local user accounts, including the profile of the currently logged-on user (also shown under HKEY_CURRENT_USER), the default profile, and profiles for special user accounts used to run various services. Except for the default profile, each is labeled with a security ID (SID), a unique string of numbers preceded by S-1-5 that identifies a security principal (an entity that can be authenticated) in a Windows security accounts database, including users and groups.
HKEY_CURRENT_CONFIG	Contains configuration information for the current hardware profile, which is a set of changes (*only* changes) to the standard configuration in the Software and System subkeys under HKEY_LOCAL_MACHINE.

TABLE 6-3 Windows Registry Data Types (The Short List)

Data Type	Description
REG_BINARY	Raw binary data. It shows some hardware data in binary. Ironically, it shows binary data in hexadecimal and might look like this: ff 00 ff ff 02 05.
REG_DWORD	A 4-byte-long number (32 bits), stored in binary, hexadecimal, or decimal format. It may look something like this in hexadecimal: 0x00000002.
REG_EXPAND_SZ	A single string of text including a variable, which is a value that an application will replace when called. An example of a common variable is *%systemroot%*, which, when Windows uses it, is replaced by the path of the folder containing the Windows system files. Example: a registry entry containing *%systemroot%*\regedit.exe becomes c:\windows\regedit.exe.
REG_MULTI_SZ	Multiple strings of human-readable text separated by a special NULL character that it does not display. Example: wuauserv gpsvc trustedinstaller
REG_SZ	A sequence of characters representing human-readable text. It may use this data type when the data is quite simple, such as a string of alphanumeric characters—for example, ClosePerformanceData—or to represent an entire list: comm.drv commdlg.dll ctl3dv2.dll ddeml.dll.

In Regedit, each value entry appears in three columns labeled: Name, Type, and Data. The Type column shows a label that describes the format of the data in that registry value, also called data type. There are many data types in the registry; take a few minutes to study Table 6–3, which shows just a few registry data types, to give you an idea of how diverse the data in the registry can be.

Backing Up the Registry

It is very important to remember that the last thing you should consider doing, even if your best friend or brother-in-law insists you do it, is to directly edit the registry using Regedit or a third-party registry editing tool. We are even more than a little squeamish about the registry cleaning tools promoted all over the Internet. But even though you should rarely if ever edit the registry, you should know how to back up the registry in case you decide that you have no choice but to use Regedit. Here are two methods for backing up the registry. The first, using System Restore, is a very broad approach that backs up the entire registry and more. The second method, backing up a portion of the registry with Regedit, is a more targeted approach.

Creating a Restore Point

Our favorite method is to simply create a restore point using System Restore. While Windows creates restore points on a regular basis, you can create one

Creating a Restore Point

In this step-by-step exercise you will create a restore point. For this exercise you will need a computer running Windows 7 or Windows 8. The steps are written for both versions, although the illustrations are from Windows 7. In both cases, you will need to respond to a User Account Control (UAC) prompt. If you logged on as a standard account, you will need to enter an administrator password. This exercise does not work with Windows RT.

Step 1

In Windows 7 or Windows 8 press ⊞+R and in the Run box type "sysdm.cpl." Do not type the quotation marks! Click OK.

Step 2

This brings up the System Properties dialog. Select the System Protection tab. Then click the Create button.

Step 3

Type a descriptive name for the restore point. Then press the Create button.

Step 4

It will take a minute or two, during which a progress message will display in the System Protection box. When Windows has created the restore point, this message will display. Click the Close button.

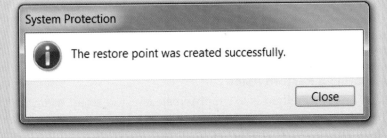

The System Properties dialog box will remain open. To see the restore points, click the System Restore button. If a page displays with a recommended restore point, click Choose a different restore point. Then click the Next button. If a simpler page without the recommended restore point displays, as shown here, simply click Next.

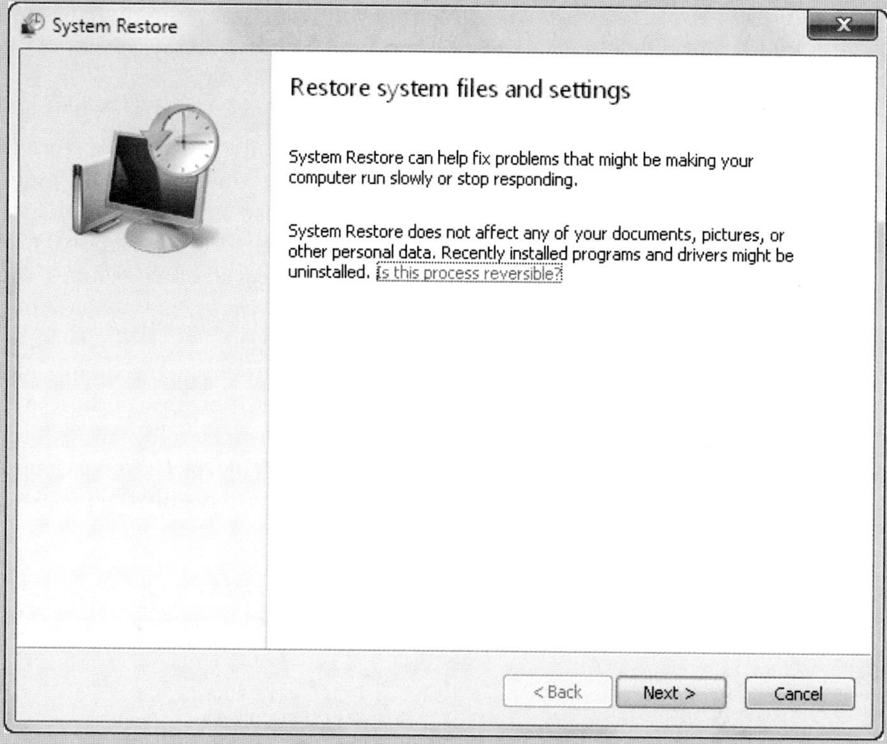

System Restore

Restore system files and settings

System Restore can help fix problems that might be making your computer run slowly or stop responding.

System Restore does not affect any of your documents, pictures, or other personal data. Recently installed programs and drivers might be uninstalled. Is this process reversible?

< Back   Next >   Cancel

Caution: you want to view only the existing restore points—you do not want to actually roll back to a previous restore point. Simply view the list of restore points, noticing the descriptions. In the example, the top one is the only one we manually created. Windows created the others and gave an appropriate description at the same time. Press Cancel to exit from System Restore. Press Cancel again in the System Properties dialog.

System Restore

Restore your computer to the state it was in before the selected event

How do I choose a restore point?

Current time zone: GMT-7:00

Date and Time	Description	Type
5/7/2013 7:50:41 PM	Before_editing_reg	Manual
5/4/2013 3:33:30 PM	Windows Update	Critical Update
4/29/2013 4:05:18 PM	Windows Update	Critical Update
4/24/2013 9:39:41 PM	Windows Update	Critical Update
4/24/2013 10:16:35 AM	Installed Oracle VM VirtualBox 4.2.12	Install
4/23/2013 4:45:12 PM	Windows Update	Critical Update
4/22/2013 1:37:06 PM	Installed Windows XP Mode	Install

☑ Show more restore points   Scan for affected programs

< Back   Next >   Cancel

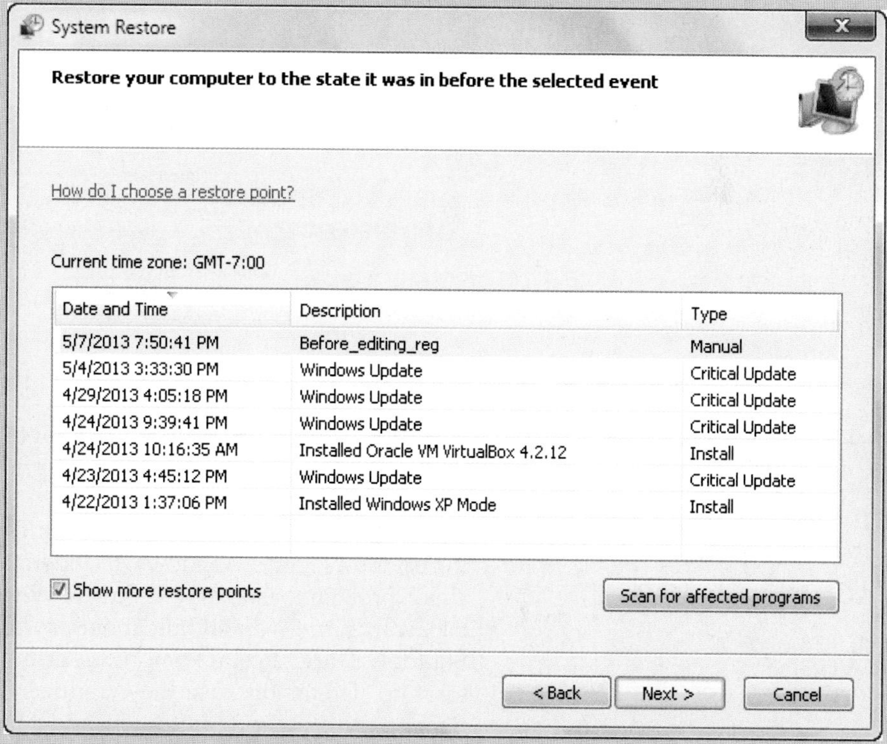

any time you want, knowing that you will have a snapshot of Windows at that point in time. Step-by-Step 6.01 will walk you through this process.

Use Regedit to Back Up the Registry

Despite knowing the danger of directly editing the registry, you might find yourself in a position in which editing the registry is the only way to solve a problem. This may be the case when an administrator or help desk person has given you specific instructions for virus removal or some other necessary change. Do this only after attempting all other avenues, including using system restore to restore your computer to a previous state or doing a total restore of your computer from a complete backup set. But if all else fails, and you know the exact change that you must make to the registry, then before you attempt to edit the registry, use Regedit to back up the portion of the registry you plan to edit. To back up a registry key, right-click on the folder for the key in Registry Editor and select Export, as shown here. Provide a location and name for the file, and Regedit will create a .reg file. If you need to restore the file, simply double-click on it.

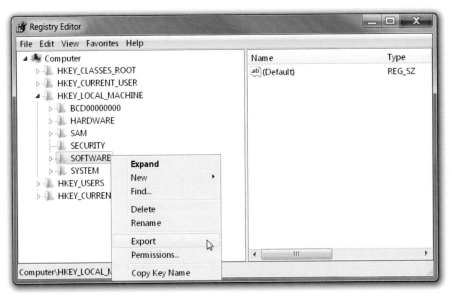

Back up a registry key and all its subkeys and values.

LO 6.2 | Windows User and Power Options

Windows 7 combined both the user options and power options on one menu, while Windows 8 separates these options. We will examine both types of options so that you understand how to use them. As part of the discussion on power options, we will also describe the shutdown and startup procedures for Windows 7 and Windows 8. Understanding these can help you to troubleshoot problems that may occur as Windows starts up. It may seem a little backwards, but we will talk about power options, including Sleep, Hibernate, Shutdown, and Restart before describing how Windows 7 and Windows 8 start up. This is because the Windows 8 Fast Boot, its default startup mode, depends on a Hybrid Shutdown, and it helps to understand Hybrid Shutdown before learning about Fast Boot.

The Windows 7 Shutdown button has a smaller button alongside it, and when you click it, the Shutdown options menu appears, shown in Figure 6–5. It includes *Switch user, Log off, Lock, Restart,* and *Sleep*. We call the first three options user options and the last two, *Restart* and *Sleep*, power options.

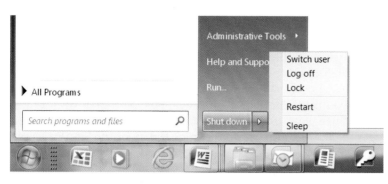

FIGURE 6–5 The Windows 7 Shutdown options menu shown here includes Switch user, Log off, Lock, Restart, and Sleep.

User Options

Windows 8 has moved the user options to the User menu (tap or click the User tile) on the Start screen. In Windows 7, selecting *Switch user* keeps the current user's session in memory without closing any programs, and presents the logon screen. Another user can then log on and run in a separate user session with her own user profile, seeing her files, but not accessing the first user's open session.

In Windows 8, although the user options menu does not include *Switch user* it does allow you to switch users. If there is another user account on that computer, that user name and profile picture will display on the User menu, shown in Figure 6–6. In this example, the other user is Chrissy. Selecting Chrissy saves the current user's session in memory and shows the Sign-in screen ready (in this case) for Chrissy to provide her password.

Where Windows 7 provides *Log off* and *Lock* on the Shutdown options menu, Windows 8 offers *Sign out* and *Lock* on the User menu.

Power Options

While Windows 7 offers Restart, Sleep, and (in some cases) Hibernate from the Shutdown options menu, Windows 8 offers these choices from the Power menu, shown here, which you can access from the Settings bar or Sign-in screen. In both Windows 7 and Windows 8, Hibernate is not a default option but you can enable it. We will describe the difference between Sleep and Hibernate next.

Sleep

If you select the Sleep option, the computer stays on in a very-low-power mode; the system state and user session (applications and data) are saved in RAM, but the screen turns off. Wake up your computer (resume) by clicking a mouse button, tapping a touch screen, or pressing keys. On some computers, you may press the power button to bring Windows out of Sleep mode, but try these other actions first. When the computer resumes from Sleep, you may need to enter your password before you are back in Windows with all your apps open and data intact.

When should you use Sleep? A common scenario is when you must interrupt your work on a laptop or tablet, as when you board a plane. Select Sleep mode before boarding, and when you have settled in your seat, resume and continue working.

Do not use Sleep for a lengthy period of time because when the battery runs down, Sleep mode ends. Microsoft has safeguards built in, but we have never been comfortable using Sleep for an extended period of time.

FIGURE 6–6 The Windows 8 User menu opens when you click or tap the User tile on the Start screen. It contains user options.

The Power options menu.

Hibernate

If you select the Hibernate option, Windows saves to disk an image of the contents of RAM, including the OS, open apps, and all the associated data, in a file named hiberfil.sys, and then the OS sends the command to power down the computer.

When should you use Hibernate? If it is available, you may want to use it when you would use Sleep, except that Hibernate does not require power. To resume, press the power button, and the Lock screen or the Sign-in screen will greet you.

The Windows 7 Shutdown

When you select *Shutdown* from the Windows 7 Start menu, several events occur. Windows does the following:

1. Sends messages to all running apps to save data and settings.
2. Closes the session for each logged-on user.
3. Sends a shutdown message to all running services and then shuts them down.
4. Sends a shutdown message to all devices.
5. Closes the operating system's session.
6. Writes pending data to the system drive.
7. Sends a signal to power down the computer.

Windows 8 Hybrid Shutdown

When you select *Shutdown* from the Windows 8 Power menu it does a Hybrid Shutdown, during which Windows does the following:

1. Sends messages to all running apps to save data and settings, and then shuts down the apps.
2. Closes the session for each logged-on user.
3. Hibernates the Windows session and saves it in a file. It does not hibernate the User session.

Because the hibernate process saves an image of the system session to disk, the operating system does not have to reassemble all its parts every time it starts up. Next we will look at the Windows 7 and Windows 8 startup procedures.

Restart

When you select the *Restart* option, both Windows 7 and Windows 8 do a full shutdown and a full system start up. This is important to know because a Restart will seem slower on a Windows 8 computer than a cold boot does, and that is because it will not do the Hybrid shutdown described above, nor the Windows 8 Fast Boot, described later.

Windows 7 Startup Phases

The Windows 7 startup has several phases on a typical desktop PC. These include:

1. Power-on self-test
2. Initial startup
3. Bootloader
4. Hardware detection and configuration
5. Kernel loading
6. Logon

In the first two phases, the hardware "wakes up" and system firmware searches for an operating system. Through the remaining phases, the operating system builds itself, much like a building, from the ground up, with more levels and complexity added at each phase.

Power-On Self-Test

When you power on your computer, the CPU loads firmware programs into memory. Firmware is software installed in nonvolatile memory chips. This memory may be read-only memory (ROM), erasable programmable read-only memory (EPROM), or a similar technology. All computing devices contain firmware. The common traditional name for the firmware in computers is ROM-BIOS, as defined in Chapter 1, but newer computers come with much more sophisticated firmware that complies with a specification called Unified Extensible Firmware Interface (UEFI), also described in Chapter 1.

Among the first firmware programs that run are those that perform the power-on self-test (POST)—a series of tests of the system hardware that determines the amount of memory present and verifies that devices required for OS startup are working. The POST most often only displays a brief black screen before Windows loads.

Initial Startup

During the initial startup the firmware bootstrap loader program uses hardware configuration settings stored in nonvolatile memory, commonly called CMOS, to determine what devices can start an OS and the order in which the system will search these devices while attempting to begin the OS startup process. The order may be optical drive or USB drive, then hard drive. On a computer with UEFI with Secure Boot turned on, this will normally be drive C only, unless you modify firmware settings, which is an advanced task. The bootstrap loader then looks in the location specified for Windows OS startup code, called the bootloader, and loads it into memory.

Bootloader

Bootmgr is the bootloader file that begins the loading of OS components for Windows Vista, Windows 7, and Windows 8. Once bootmgr loads, the OS starts the file system, reads the Boot Configuration Database (BCD) file to learn the location and names of the remaining Windows OS files to load into memory at startup. Then it starts the winload.exe program, which is the OS loader boot program. Together, bootmgr and winload.exe manage the startup phases that follow.

Note: Windows 8 has the same startup procedures and its files have the same names and roles as those used in Windows 7. But Windows 8 startup is made more secure by Trusted Boot and starts much faster when it uses Windows 8 Fast Boot. We describe both later.

Detect and Configure Hardware

The Detect and Configure hardware phase includes a scan of the computer's hardware and creation of a hardware list for later inclusion in the registry.

Kernel Loading

During the kernel loading phase, the Windows kernel ntoskrnl.exe loads into memory from the location indicated in the BCD. Hardware information passes on to the kernel, and the hardware abstraction layer (HAL) file for the system loads into memory. The system hive of the registry loads, and components and drivers listed in the registry as required at startup are now loaded. All of this code is loaded into memory, but is not immediately initialized (made active).

Once all startup components are in memory, the kernel (ntoskrnl.exe) takes over the startup process and initializes the components (services and drivers) required for startup. Then the kernel scans the registry for other components that were not required during startup but are part of the configuration. It then loads and initializes them.

The kernel starts the session manager, which creates the system environment variables and loads the kernel-mode Windows subsystem code that switches Windows from text mode to graphics mode.

The Session manager then starts the user mode Windows subsystem code (csrss.exe). Just two of the session manager's other tasks include creating the virtual memory paging file (pagefile.sys) and starting the Windows logon service (winlogon.exe), which leads us to the next phase.

Logon

More things happen during the logon phase than simply authenticating the user, and they happen simultaneously. They include the following:

User Logon. The key player in this phase is the Windows Logon service, which supports logging on and logging off, and starts the service control manager (services.exe) and the local security authority (lsass.exe). At this point, depending on how your computer was configured, you may not be required to actually enter a user name and password. Figure 6–7 shows just one possible logon screen that you may see in Windows 7, in which you simply enter a password for the user name shown.

Program Startup. During program startup, logon scripts (if they exist) run, startup programs for various applications run, and noncritical services start. Windows finds instructions to run these programs and services in many locations in the registry.

Plug-and-Play Detection. Plug-and-play detection uses several methods to detect new plug and play devices, and when it detects a new device, it allocates system resources (memory and other OS resources) to the devices and installs appropriate device drivers.

Note: The actual screen or dialog box that appears before you log on varies with the configuration of your computer.

FIGURE 6–7 Log on to Windows 7.

Windows 8 Secure Boot and Fast Boot

On a Windows 8 computer, all you may see during startup may be the manufacturer's logo and, after a brief pause, the Lock screen. Windows 8 system code is not much different from that of Windows 7, so it must go through a process similar to that of Windows 7 startup to assemble all the pieces of the OS along with settings, drivers, services, and apps. In view of what you learned earlier in this chapter about how Windows 7 starts up, you may wonder how Windows 8 can get all of this done so quickly. We explain that mystery now.

Firmware Startup

When you turn on your computer, the CPU loads firmware into memory and the power-on-self-test occurs regardless of the OS installed, because it occurs before the OS is in control. If you have installed Windows 8 on an older computer with ROM-BIOS, the startup may be a bit longer than Windows 8 on a UEFI-compliant computer, but it should be faster than previous versions of Windows on that same computer. Computers that come with Windows 8 preinstalled must have UEFI firmware and must have security features of UEFI enabled by default to protect Windows 8 during the startup process. Secure Boot is the UEFI firmware feature that loads only trusted operating system bootloaders. From there, as with the Windows 7 startup process described previously, the Windows components take over, with the addition of Windows Trusted Boot, described later.

While Windows proceeds with the phases of startup, up to the point when antimalware software loads, a UEFI firmware feature called Measured Boot logs the process, and antimalware software can analyze this log to determine if malware is on the computer or if the boot components were tampered with. In an enterprise environment with Windows Active Directory servers, Windows 8 can send this log to a trusted server that can assess the PC's startup and track the security and health of the PC.

Trusted Boot

Trusted Boot is a Windows 8 feature that examines each of the system files required for the boot process before it loads into memory. Another security component, called Early Launch Anti-Malware (ELAM) does the same for all device drivers before they load into memory, thus preventing suspicious drivers from loading.

> **Note:** During Windows 8 startup, as part of Trusted Boot, each operating system file is examined before it is loaded into memory. If one appears to have been altered, an unmodified version of the file is used.

Fast Boot

While the security features described above add complexity to the Windows 8 startup, Windows 8 actually starts up very rapidly. The reason for this is a feature called Fast Boot, which takes advantage of the hibernated kernel of the Windows 8 Hybrid Shutdown, described earlier in this chapter. Fast Boot simply brings the hibernated system session out of hibernation, saving all the work of the Kernel Loading phase. Additionally, on a computer with multiple CPU cores, the cores work in parallel when processing the hibernation file. Hybrid Shutdown is the default when you select the Shutdown option, and Fast Boot is the default when you power up your computer.

Modifying System Startup

You can modify the system startup on your Windows computer in many ways. First, determine if you can make the change you want through the GUI, such as the Advanced System Settings page. As a last resort, you can directly edit these settings using the correct tool for the version of Windows in question.

> **Note:** Learn about special startup modes for troubleshooting later in this chapter.

We'll look at modifying system startup for Windows 7 and Windows 8 including the settings for choosing the default OS started on a multiboot system and the length of time the selection menu displays.

Modifying System Startup for Windows 7 and Windows 8

In Windows 7 and Windows 8, the Boot Configuration Database is actually a hidden part of the registry, stored in a registry file named BCD, located in a hidden partition. The basic information stored in BCD provides locale information, the location of the boot disk and the Windows files, and other information required for the startup process. View the contents of BCD using the BCDedit program, a utility that needs to run from a Command Prompt with elevated privileges, meaning that it runs with the privileges of a local administrator, as described in Step-by-Step 6.02.

To change Windows startup settings, the safest method is to use the Startup and Recovery page of System Properties. Step-by-Step 6.02 will walk you through making a change to BCD using the Startup and Recovery page, and then you will use BCDedit to view the changes made to the BCD file.

Step-by-Step 6.02

Modifying Windows System Startup

In this step-by-step exercise you will modify the system startup for Windows 7 or Windows 8 using the Startup and Recovery page of System Properties. The steps work in Windows 7 or Windows 8. The images are from Windows 8, but these are nearly identical to what you will see in Windows 7.

Step 1

In Windows 7 or Windows 8 press ⊞+R to open the Run box. In the Run box, type "sysdm.cpl" (do not type the quotation marks). Click OK. In System Properties click the Advanced tab.

On the Advanced tab of System Properties, locate the Startup and Recovery section near the bottom and click the Settings button to open the Startup and Recovery page. If your computer is a multi-boot computer you can choose the default operating system that it will select if you do not respond to the menu during the time that it displays the list of operating systems. Notice the time selected is 30 seconds.

Startup and Recovery

System startup

Default operating system:

Windows 8

☑ Time to display list of operating systems: 30 seconds

☐ Time to display recovery options when needed: 30 seconds

System failure

☑ Write an event to the system log

☑ Automatically restart

Write debugging information

Automatic memory dump

Dump file:

%SystemRoot%\MEMORY.DMP

☑ Overwrite any existing file

OK   Cancel

Step 3

Change the selected time to 35 seconds and click OK to close the Startup and Recovery page. Click OK again to close System Properties. Windows will save the changes in a file named BCD, and they will take effect the next time Windows starts.

Step 4

To see the changes you made you will need to run BCDedit, an editor that will let you see the contents of BCD. If you are using Windows 7, go to step 5. If you are using Windows 8, skip to step 6.

Step 5

In Windows 7, open Start Search and type **cmd**. Then right-click **cmd**, and select *Run as administrator* from the context menu, as shown here. Respond to the User Account Control (UAC) prompt (if required). The Command Prompt will then open. The Title bar of the window should say Administrator: Command Prompt. If it doesn't, carefully repeat this step. With the Command Prompt window open, skip to step 7.

In Windows 8 open the Search bar, type **cmd**, and then locate **Command Prompt** in the results and right-click on it. This opens the **App bar** for Command Prompt at the bottom of the screen. Select **Run as Administrator** from the App bar. Respond to the User Account Control (UAC) prompt (if required). The Command Prompt window should open. The Title bar of the window should say: Administrator: Command Prompt. If it doesn't, then carefully repeat this step.

```
Administrator: Command Prompt

Microsoft Windows [Version 6.2.9200]
(c) 2012 Microsoft Corporation. All rights reserved.

C:\Windows\system32>_
```

At the command prompt type "bcdedit" and press Enter. The result should look something like the example here. Windows 8 usually has more entries in BCD than does Windows 7. Notice the Timeout setting, which you changed in the earlier steps.

```
Administrator: Command Prompt

Microsoft Windows [Version 6.2.9200]
(c) 2012 Microsoft Corporation. All rights reserved.

C:\Windows\system32>bcdedit

Windows Boot Manager
--------------------
identifier              {bootmgr}
device                  partition=\Device\HarddiskVolume1
path                    \EFI\Microsoft\Boot\bootmgfw.efi
description             Windows Boot Manager
locale                  en-US
inherit                 {globalsettings}
integrityservices       Enable
default                 {current}
resumeobject            {01002782-ae41-11e2-903f-f01faf007d96}
displayorder            {current}
toolsdisplayorder       {memdiag}
timeout                 35

Windows Boot Loader
-------------------
identifier              {current}
device                  partition=C:
path                    \Windows\system32\winload.efi
description             Windows 8
locale                  en-US
inherit                 {bootloadersettings}
recoverysequence        {bdef0164-ae5d-11e2-80bd-f01faf007d96}
integrityservices       Enable
recoveryenabled         Yes
isolatedcontext         Yes
allowedinmemorysettings 0x15000075
osdevice                partition=C:
systemroot              \Windows
resumeobject            {01002782-ae41-11e2-903f-f01faf007d96}
nx                      OptIn
bootmenupolicy          Standard

C:\Windows\system32>
```

To close the Command Prompt windows type Exit and press Enter.

LO 6.3 | Installing and Managing Device Drivers

A huge number of devices work in Windows. There are the ones we take for granted, such as hard drives, flash drives, video adapters, network interface cards, displays, sound cards, and printers, as well as keyboards, mice, and other pointing devices. Then there are others, such as cameras, scanners, video capture cards, and game controllers. In this section we learn about installing device drivers and managing installed device drivers.

Installing Device Drivers

All devices need device drivers, and the latest versions of Windows come with huge caches of device drivers. Both Windows and virtually all devices for PCs are plug and play. Plug and play is the ability of a computer and OS to automatically detect and configure a hardware device. To work, the computer, the device, and the OS must all comply with the same plug-and-play standard. Therefore, when you connect a device, Windows recognizes it, and then finds and installs the appropriate driver.

But there are exceptions. For example, in some cases, even though the device is plug and play, you need to install the driver (and with it the companion software) before connecting the device. There is also the issue of when you should power on an external device. Some require that you power up the device before connecting it to the PC, while others require that you connect the device, and then power it up. The supreme authority for each device is the manufacturer, so you really need to read the manufacturer's quick-start guide or user manual before connecting a new device.

Permissions

Regardless of how easily a device driver installs, you need administrator privileges to install or uninstall a device. In Windows Vista, Windows 7, and Windows 8 you can install a device driver while logged on as either a computer administrator or a standard user. When logged on as an administrator you will simply need to click Yes in the UAC Consent Prompt, whereas a standard user will need to provide computer administrator credentials in the Credentials Prompt.

Fortunately, unplugging a device does not uninstall the driver from your computer—it just gives the device a status of "not present." Therefore, once a device is installed, any local users may disconnect and reconnect the device without restriction and it will operate.

Working with Signed versus Unsigned Device Drivers

Because a device driver becomes a part of an operating system, a poorly written device driver can be a vector for malware and cause problems, including system crashes. For this reason bad device drivers have long been the top cause of operating system instability. Windows has features that help users avoid badly written program code.

One of the latest additions to protections against bad device drivers is the Early Launch Anti-Malware (ELAM) during Windows 8 startup, described previously in this chapter. But one of the long-standing central features that protects against all types of bad program code is code signing, the use of a digital signature provided by Microsoft as its seal of approval on program code. A digital signature is encrypted data placed in the signed file. Windows decrypts the digital signature by a process called file signature verification. The digital signature includes information about the file so that the operating system can detect any alterations to the file. Driver signing is simply code signing of device drivers that indicates the integrity of the file or files and that the device driver has passed Microsoft's test for compatibility. This does not mean all nondigitally signed device drivers are bad. What it does mean is that Microsoft has provided a process that manufacturers can choose to use to have their device drivers tested and signed by Microsoft. This is part of the process of having a device added to Microsoft's compatibility list.

If you attempt to install a program that contains unsigned code, you may get a warning. It is then up to you if you want to continue using the unsigned code. If you trust the source, continue. By default, you cannot install unsigned drivers in 64-bit Windows 7 or in Windows 8; the installation will simply fail.

Managing Installed Devices

Devices and Printers in Windows 7 and in Windows 8 as well as the PC Settings Devices page in Windows 8 are simple tools for managing devices. The Device Manager Control Panel, available in all versions of Windows, is a more advanced tool. Learn about each of these.

Devices and Printers

You can manage many devices through the user-friendly Devices and Printers Control Panel applet, found in both Windows 7 and Windows 8 (see Figure 6–8). Open Devices and Printers in Windows 7 from the Start menu; open it in Windows 8 by searching in Settings. This gives you an overview of the most obvious devices attached to your computer. From here you can access the Properties dialog and other appropriate applications and actions by double-clicking on the device (for the default action) or right-clicking and selecting an action from the context menu. For instance, double-clicking on

FIGURE 6–8 The Devices and Printers page.

the Fax object will open Windows Fax and Scan. If you have installed special faxing and scanning software from the manufacturer, that software will open in place of Windows Fax and Scan.

In Figure 6–8, the Canon inkjet printer has a round green icon with a white check mark indicating it is the default printer that will be used unless you select a different printer when you select the Print command in an app. To change the default printer right-click on a printer's icon and then select *Set as Default Printer* from the context menu, shown in Figure 6–9.

Expect newer devices to have a special "home page" that is part of Windows 7's new Device Stage feature. For instance, in previous versions of Windows, double-clicking a printer's icon brought up the printer's print queue. That still happens in Windows 7—only if your installed printer does not have the Device Stage feature. If it has Device Stage, double-clicking on it will bring up a new page from which you can make many choices for managing the device, including a link to open your printer's print queue. Figure 6–10 shows the Device Stage page for a printer.

FIGURE 6–9 Set the default printer.

Windows 8 PC Settings

In Windows 8 the Devices page of PC settings lists printers and other devices (See Figure 6–11). From this page you can add a Plug-and-Play device that Windows did not automatically detect and install by clicking the *Add a device* button.

Using Device Manager to Manage Device Drivers

Device Manager is a tool that allows an administrator to view and change device properties, update device drivers, configure device settings, uninstall devices, and roll back a driver update. Rollback is quite handy for those times when you find the new device driver causes problems. Device Manager has been in the last several versions of Windows and is still available in the Windows 8 Desktop. Our favorite method for opening Device Manager is by entering "device manager" in the Windows 7 Start Search box or in Windows 8, Search Settings. But when you are working with Device Manager repeatedly on the same computer, consider making a desktop shortcut, as described in Step-by-Step 6.03.

Note: At this writing, you can only add or remove devices in PC Settings in the Windows 8 or 8.1 Modern GUI. For more management tools, go to the Windows Desktop and use the same tools you used in Windows 7: Devices and Printers and Device Manager.

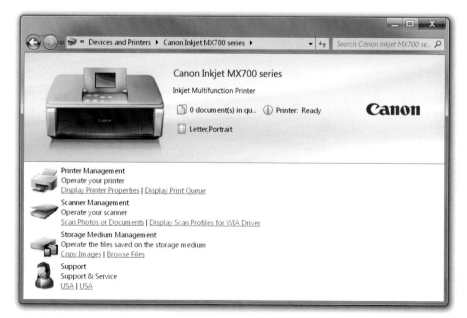

FIGURE 6–10 The Devices Stage page for a printer.

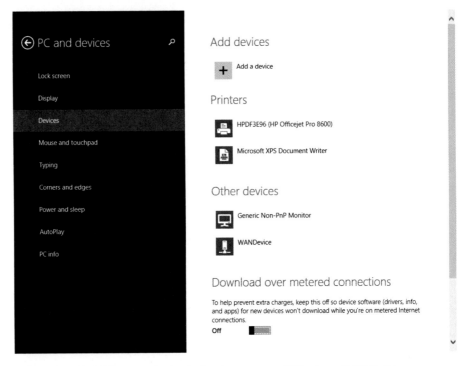

FIGURE 6–11 Add a new device in Devices page of Windows 8 PC Settings.

Getting to Know Device Manager

In this step-by-step exercise you will create a shortcut to Device Manager on the desktop to make it more convenient to open. You'll then examine the information shown in Device Manager. Although we wrote this exercise for Windows 7 or Windows 8, it also works in Windows Vista. The screen shots are from Windows 8. You will need a computer running one of these versions of Windows, and you need to either be logged on with an administrator account or be prepared with the credentials of an administrator on that computer.

Step 1

Right-click on an empty area of the Desktop; select New | Shortcut.

In the Create Shortcut wizard, a text box prompts you to enter the location of the item. Simply enter the file name and extension for the Device Manager console: devmgmt.msc. Double-check your typing. Click the Next button.

Create Shortcut

What item would you like to create a shortcut for?

This wizard helps you to create shortcuts to local or network programs, files, folders, computers, or Internet addresses.

Type the location of the item:

`devmgmt.msc`   Browse...

Click Next to continue.

Next   Cancel

On the following page of the Create Shortcut wizard, in the text box labeled "Type a name for this shortcut," type "Device Mgr," and click the Finish button.

Create Shortcut

What would you like to name the shortcut?

Type a name for this shortcut:

`Device Mgr`

Click Finish to create the shortcut.

Finish   Cancel

Locate the new shortcut on the desktop.

Test your new shortcut by double-clicking on it to open Device Manager. Use the View menu to experiment with various ways of changing how it can display information—you have two options for viewing devices and two options for viewing resources, which you can choose from the View menu. You will normally view devices by type because this approach is simpler and more understandable. Another option allows you to view hidden devices, which is handy when you want to remove a device driver for a device that is no longer connected or installed in the computer.

When viewing devices by type, there is a node for each device type, such as Audio inputs and outputs, Batteries, Bluetooth, Computer, Disk drives, and so on. Familiarize yourself with Device Manager by opening the nodes. Notice that the buttons on the button bar change as you click on the top node (the computer itself), then click on a type node (such as Display adapters), and then double-click on a device under a type node.

Double-clicking a device opens its Properties dialog box, where the Driver tab lets you manage a device (some of these actions are available from the button bar). Do not make any changes, and when you are finished, close all open windows. You will use other features of Device Manager in the troubleshooting section of this chapter.

LO 6.4 | Using Windows Troubleshooting and Recovery Tools

A short list of the handiest and most effective tools for troubleshooting Windows problems and recovering from virus infections includes the various Startup options, the System Configuration utility, and Device Manager. Explore these tools in this section.

When Windows Fails at Startup: The Windows Recovery Environment

In Chapter 4 we described the Windows Preinstallation Environment (Windows PE), the scaled-down Windows operating system that supports the Windows Setup GUI. This environment is available for Windows Vista, Windows 7, and Windows 8. It has limited drivers for basic hardware and support for the NTFS file system, networks, and programs. However, this is still a very robust and specialized operating system, and when needed, it supports a powerful group of diagnostics and repair tools called the Windows Recovery Environment (Windows RE). Computer manufacturers who preinstall Windows have the option of adding their own repair tools to Windows RE.

If your Windows Vista, Windows 7, or Windows 8 computer fails at startup, if the damage is not too extensive, Windows RE will start and load the Windows Error Recovery page with the options: Launch Startup and Repair (Windows RE's built-in diagnostics and recovery tool), and Start Windows Normally. It is always worth trying the second option to see if the cause of the problem was something transient. Then, if it still doesn't start up normally, select the Launch Startup Repair and follow the instructions on the screen.

In situations where Windows starts up but you notice problems, you may want to use modified startups to troubleshoot and recover from the problem. We will look at them next.

Troubleshooting with Modified Startups

As you work with Windows computers, you may run into computers that fail to start normally or that behave oddly after startup. Windows offers a number of methods for starting with certain components disabled. Some of these are available through a special menu of startup options; others (including some of the same methods) are available through the System Configuration utility.

The Advanced Boot Options Menu in Windows Vista and Windows 7

To access a list of startup options in versions of Windows previous to Windows 8, restart the computer and press F8 before the graphical Windows start screen appears. This will bring up a special menu of startup options entitled "Advanced Boot Options Menu" in Windows Vista and Windows 7. Figures 6–12 and 6–13 show these menus as they appear in Windows Vista and Windows 7, respectively. Following are brief descriptions of these options.

Repair Your Computer (Windows 7). If you select this option, Windows PE (the environment used by Windows setup) loads and first requires that you supply a keyboard input method, then requires that you log on, and finally displays the Windows RE System Recovery Options menu shown in Figure 4–14 in Chapter 4. From here you can select one of the following recovery tools, also described in Chapter 4:

- Startup Repair
- System Restore
- System Image Recovery
- Windows Memory Diagnostic
- Command Prompt

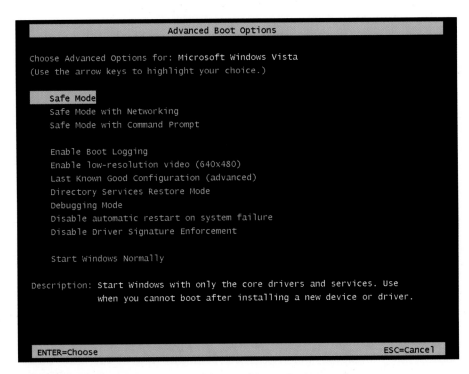

FIGURE 6–12 The Windows Vista Advanced Boot Options menu.

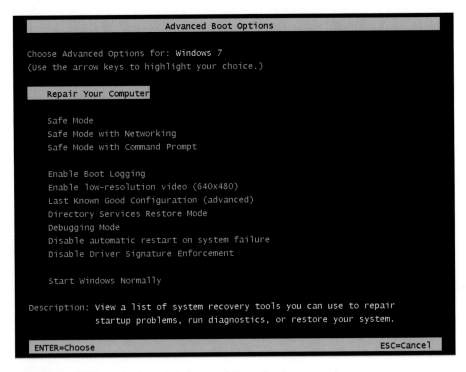

FIGURE 6–13 The Windows 7 Advanced Boot Options menu.

Safe Mode. Safe Mode is a mode for starting Windows with certain drivers and components disabled. Access Safe Mode from the Advanced Options Menu in Windows Vista or Windows 7, as shown in Step-by-Step 6.04. In Windows 8 access it from the Advanced Startup option on the General page of PC Settings, which we will describe later. Safe Mode does not disable Windows security. You are required to log on in all variants of Safe Mode, and you can access only those resources for which you have permissions. If Windows will not start normally but starts just fine in Safe Mode, use Device Manager within Safe Mode to determine if the source of the problem is a faulty device. Run System Restore while in Safe Mode and roll back the entire system to a restore point from before the problem occurred.

Three Safe Mode variants are available:

- **Safe Mode** starts without using several drivers and components that it would normally start, including the network components. It loads only very basic, non-vendor-specific drivers for mouse, video (loading Windows' very basic vga.sys driver), keyboard, mass storage, and system services.

- **Safe Mode with Networking** is identical to plain Safe Mode, except that it also starts the networking components. Use the following debug sequence with Safe Mode with Networking:

  - If Windows will not start normally but starts OK in plain Safe Mode, restart and select Safe Mode with Networking.

  - If it fails to start in Safe Mode with Networking, the problem area is network drivers or components. Use Device Manager to disable the network adapter driver (the likely culprit), then boot up normally. If Windows now works, replace your network adapter driver.

  - If this problem appears immediately after upgrading a network driver, use Device Manager while in Safe Mode to roll back the updated driver. When an updated driver is available, install it.

- **Safe Mode with Command Prompt** is Safe Mode with only a command prompt as a user interface. In a normal startup, Windows loads your GUI desktop, but this depends on the program explorer.exe, the GUI shell to Windows. In place of this GUI shell, Safe Mode with Command Prompt loads a very limited GUI with a command prompt (cmd.exe) window. This is a handy option to remember if the desktop does not display at all. Once you have eliminated video drivers as the cause, corruption of the explorer.exe program may be the problem. From within the command prompt, you can delete the corrupted version of explorer.exe and copy an undamaged version. This requires knowledge of the command line commands for navigating the directory structure, as well as knowledge of the location of the file that you are replacing. You can launch programs, such as the Event Viewer (eventvwr.msc), the Computer Management console (compmgmt.msc), or Device Manager (devmgmt. msc) from the command prompt.

Enable Boot Logging. While boot logging occurs automatically with each of the three Safe Modes, selecting Enable Boot Logging turns on boot logging and starts Windows normally. Boot logging causes Windows to write a log of the Windows startup in a file named ntbtlog.txt and save it in the systemroot folder. This log file contains an entry for each component in the order in which it loaded into memory. It also lists drivers that were not loaded, which alerts an administrator to a possible source of a problem.

Enable Low-Resolution Video (640×480). Titled "Enable VGA Mode" until Windows Vista, this option starts Windows normally, except the video mode is changed to the lowest resolution (640×480), using the currently installed video driver. It does not switch to the basic Windows video driver. Select this option after making a video configuration change that the video adapter does not support and that prevents Windows from displaying properly.

Last Known Good Configuration. Last Known Good (LKG) Configuration is a startup option that will start Windows normally and select the configuration that existed at the last successful user logon (the "last known good configuration"), ignoring changes made after the last logon. This works if you made changes that caused obvious problems. On the very next restart, selecting this option will discard the changes. But if you have logged on since the changes occurred, those changes will be part of the last known good configuration, so this recovery option won't work. This rather crude system restore method only works if you did not restart and log on since making the change. Windows 7 is the last version to offer this option.

Directory Services Restore Mode. This option only works on Windows Servers acting as domain controllers.

Debugging Mode. This is a very advanced, (dare we say) obsolete, option in which Windows starts normally, and information about the Windows startup is sent over a serial cable to another computer that is running a special program called a debugger.

Disable Automatic Restart on System Failure (Windows Vista and Windows 7). The default setting for Windows is for it to restart after a system crash. However, depending on the problem, restarting may simply lead to another restart—in fact you could find yourself faced with a continuous loop of restarts. If so, press F8 at the next restart and select the Disable automatic restart on system failure option. Windows will attempt to start normally (just once for each time you select this option) and may stay open long enough for you to troubleshoot. Do not attempt to work with any data file after restarting with this option because the system may be too unstable. If you are not able to solve the problem, then you will need to restart in Safe Mode to troubleshoot.

Disable Driver Signature Enforcement (Windows Vista and Windows 7). If you are unable to install a driver due to Driver Signing, and you trust the manufacturer, select this option, which will start Windows normally, disabling driver signature enforcement just for that startup.

Start Windows Normally. Use this option to start Windows normally with no change in behavior. You would use this after using F8 to view the Advanced Options menu and deciding to continue with a normal startup. It does not restart the computer.

Return to OS Choices Menu (Multiboot Only). Selecting this option on a multiboot computer will return to the OS Choices Menu (OS Loader menu).

Step-by-Step 6.04

Using Windows 7 in Safe Mode

In this step-by-step exercise you will start Windows in Safe Mode. Although we show Windows 7 screen shots, you can use Windows Vista. The screen will not be identical, but you can experience Safe Mode in any of these OSs. Be prepared to provide credentials to access Safe Mode because security is still in place when you access Safe Mode. Once in Safe Mode you can run most Windows troubleshooting tools just as you would after a normal start.

Step 1

Restart the computer, pressing F8 as soon as the power down completes and before the splash screen appears. On the Advanced Boot Options menu use the up and down arrows to move the cursor around. Position the cursor on Safe Mode and press Enter.

Step 2

When prompted, provide credentials. Safe Mode loads with a black desktop background and the words *Safe Mode* in the corners of the screen. It also opens Windows Help and Support to the page on Safe Mode. Browse through the help information and click on the link labeled "Diagnostic tools to use in safe mode."

Step 3

On the resulting page, locate links to start several very handy tools in Safe Mode. In the following steps, practice opening some of these utilities.

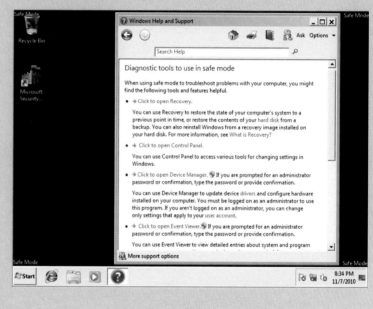

Step 4

Click the link labeled *Click to open Recovery*. On the Recovery page notice the links to other tools. Click the button labeled *Open System Restore*. On the page labeled *Restore files and settings* click Next to see a list of the restore points on your computer. Click Cancel to leave System Restore and close the Recovery windows to return to Help and Support.

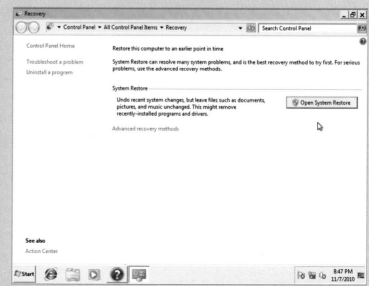

Next use the link that will open Control Panel. You can open most tools you would need from this page.

When you are finished exploring Safe Mode, close all open windows, and either shut down or restart Windows, allowing it to start normally.

The Advanced Startup Options in Windows 8

Previously in this chapter you learned that if your Windows computer fails at startup and the damage is not too extensive, Windows RE will start and load the Windows Error Recovery page. Another option is to boot from the Windows installation DVD disc, but if Windows 8 was preinstalled on your computer and UEFI boot is in effect, you may not be able to boot from disc unless you modify the UEFI settings, disabling Safe Boot security. How you do that differs from manufacturer to manufacturer.

The options you access from the Windows Error Recovery page are those that you can also access from the Windows 8 Advanced Startup options, available through the General page of Windows 8 PC Settings. It is good to practice trying the Windows 8 Advanced Startup options before you really need them for troubleshooting or recovery of the operating system. Step-by-Step 6.05 will walk you through a tour of the Windows 8 Advanced Startup options.

Note: Yet another way to access the Advanced Startup Options in Windows 8 is to open the Power menu from the Sign in screen or the Settings bar. Then hold down the Shift key while clicking or tapping Restart. After the restart the Choose an Option screen displays, as shown in Step 2 of Step-by-Step 6.05 and you can continue from there as described in the remaining steps.

Step-by-Step 6.05

Exploring Windows 8 Advanced Options

If you have access to a computer running Windows 8.1 and can sign in with an administrator account for that computer, you can do this exercise.

Step 1

Open the Charms bar, select Settings, and then from the Settings bar select *Change PC Settings*.

Windows 8.0, from the PC Settings screen select *General*, and then scroll down to *Advanced startup*. Select *Restart now*. Skip the next paragraph and move to Step 2.

In PC Settings in Windows 8.1 select *Update and Recovery*, and then select *Recovery*. Then select *Restart now*.

Update and recovery

Windows Update

File History

Recovery

Refresh your PC without affecting your files

If your PC isn't running well, you can refresh it without losing your photos, music, videos, and other personal files.

Get started

Remove everything and reinstall Windows

If you want to recycle your PC or start over completely, you can reset it to its factory settings.

Get started

Advanced startup

Start up from a device or disc (such as a USB drive or DVD), change Windows startup settings, or restore Windows from a system image. This will restart your PC.

Restart now

Windows Recovery Environment (Windows RE) launches. The resulting screen will resemble this, but will normally have more options showing. To restart in a troubleshooting mode, select Troubleshoot.

On the Troubleshoot screen, you will see these options, plus you may see one or more of the others added by the manufacturer of your computers. We will discuss the options labeled *Refresh your PC* and *Reset your PC* later. Do not select one of them at this time. From this screen select *Advanced options*.

Again, the Advanced Options screen shown here may look different on your computer, especially on a computer with UEFI in place of legacy BIOS. This screen is from Windows 8.0. In Windows 8.1 the Automatic Repair option is named Startup Repair. From this screen select *Startup Settings*.

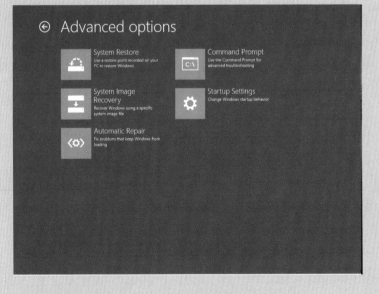

Step 5

This screen shows the options you will have after the next screen, so select the Restart button to move on.

Step 6

After a brief pause, the second Startup Settings screen displays with real choices. This is the Windows 8 replacement for the Advanced Boot Options menu. Press the 4 key to start in Safe Mode.

Step 7

At this point, you will see a normal sign-in screen. Enter your credentials to sign in and Windows 8 will start in Safe Mode. Safe Mode starts in the Desktop view with one window open: Windows Help and Support.

Step 8

Spend a few minutes exploring the options available to you in Safe Mode. Open the Power User menu on the Safe Mode Desktop to access tools, such as Control Panel, Device Manager, Event Viewer, and System. When you have finished restart Windows 8.

Windows 8 Refresh Recovery Option. If you flip back to the illustration with step 3 in Step-by-Step 6.05, you will see an option labeled Refresh your PC. It refreshes the operating system without affecting your files. This is more involved than a system restore, but it is less drastic than some other measures you could take (such as the next option on the Troubleshoot page). Refresh is a very quick solution to a scenario that previously required advanced tasks and much time. For instance, in the past, if Windows had unexpected fatal errors in which a blue screen appeared one solution was to reinstall Windows, but then you would have to restore your data and reinstall all your apps.

The Refresh option saves your user accounts, personal files, personal settings, all your installed apps that came with Windows 8, as well as any apps purchased through the Windows Store, and your important settings. Then it reinstalls Windows 8 and reinstalls all the saved apps. However, PC system settings are changed back to the defaults, apps installed from disc or websites other than the Windows Store are removed, and a list of all removed apps will be saved on the desktop.

To begin Refresh from the Troubleshoot screen of Windows RE, click or tap the *Refresh your PC* option. After a short delay while Windows prepares your PC, a screen displays where you select an account to use for the sign-in. Enter your password and follow the prompts on the screen (See Figure 6–14). If asked, provide your Windows installation or recovery media on disc or flash drive. It will then take several minutes, showing progress messages. Finally, the Start screen displays after Refresh is complete.

Windows 8 Reset your PC Option. The Windows RE Troubleshoot screen (See step 3 in Step-by-Step 6.05) also includes the much more drastic Reset your PC option. It removes everything and reinstalls Windows, requiring that you enter a product key code. You would choose this option if you no longer plan to use this computer—maybe you are giving it away, because if you want to keep the computer, you will need to reinstall everything that does not come with Windows. As with Refresh, Reset may require the Windows installation or recovery media.

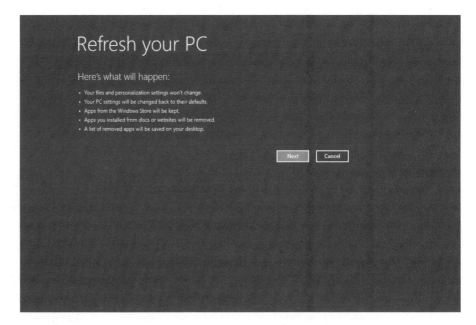

FIGURE 6–14 To complete a Refresh, follow the prompts on the screen.

If Windows came preinstalled on your computer, you may want to use the manufacturer's restore option. This may be available from the same menu, but it may require that you previously created a set of backup discs.

Troubleshooting with the System Configuration Utility (MSCONFIG)

The System Configuration Utility, more commonly known by its executable name, MSCONFIG, is a GUI tool for temporarily modifying system startup. It allows you to modify and test startup configuration settings without altering the settings directly. It gives you access to settings that are buried within the registry through a moderately friendly user interface, and it allows you to make the changes temporary or permanent (see Figure 6–15).

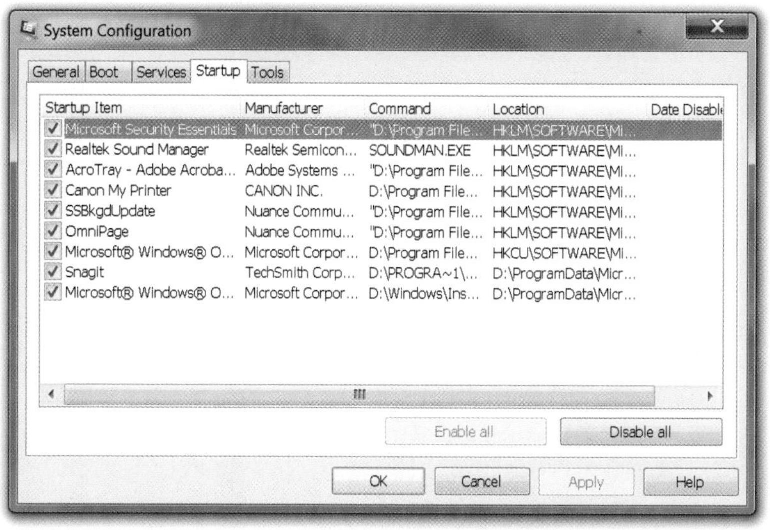

This utility is a great way to test startup "what if" scenarios. For instance, use it when you need to stop a program from launching at startup but do not want to search all the possible locations for starting programs and you are not yet ready to uninstall. Temporarily disabling a program that normally starts with the OS is one way to see if that program is the source of a problem. Similarly, you can temporarily stop a service from starting. Further, if you are having a problem restarting a Windows Vista or Windows 7 computer in Safe Mode because you are unable to access the startup options menu, you can configure MSCONFIG to start Windows in Safe Mode.

While System Configuration is listed in Administrative Tools, this menu is, by default, buried in the Windows GUI, or optionally on the Start menu. Therefore, we prefer to launch this program from the Run box by simply typing "msconfig."

FIGURE 6–15 System Configuration (MSCONFIG) lets you test startup scenarios.

> **WARNING!**
>
> If you select the Safe option on the Boot page, it will also change settings on the General page. Therefore, any time you make changes, note the changes and be aware that before the system will restart normally, you will need to return to the General page and select Normal startup.

Troubleshooting Device Problems

You will quickly learn if Windows detects a problem with a device when you open Device Manager. You will see an expanded device type, and the problem device will have an exclamation mark in a yellow triangle on the icon, as Figure 6–16 shows. The problem may be with the device itself, its device driver, or the ability of the operating system to automatically configure it. In Figure 6–16, Windows has placed the problem device under Other devices because it does not have enough information about it. This usually means that there is no installed device driver.

If you see the exclamation symbol on a device, double-click the device icon to open its Properties dialog box. You will see more

try this!

> **Explore MSCONFIG**
>
> Open MSCONFIG and explore the option pages. These steps will work in Windows Vista and Windows 7. In Windows 8 open the Run box by selecting it from the Power User menu (right-click on the left bottom corner of the screen). Try this:
>
> 1. Open the Run box and type "msconfig" and press the Enter key or click or tap OK.
> 2. Explore the five tabs (General, Boot, Services, Startup, and Tools) of the System Configuration dialog box.
> 3. If you make any changes, make sure you remember them. Click Apply, then OK, and click the Restart button in the final message box.
> 4. After testing a modified restart, open MSCONFIG again and be sure to select Normal startup before restarting.

FIGURE 6–16 Device Manager indicates a problem with a device.

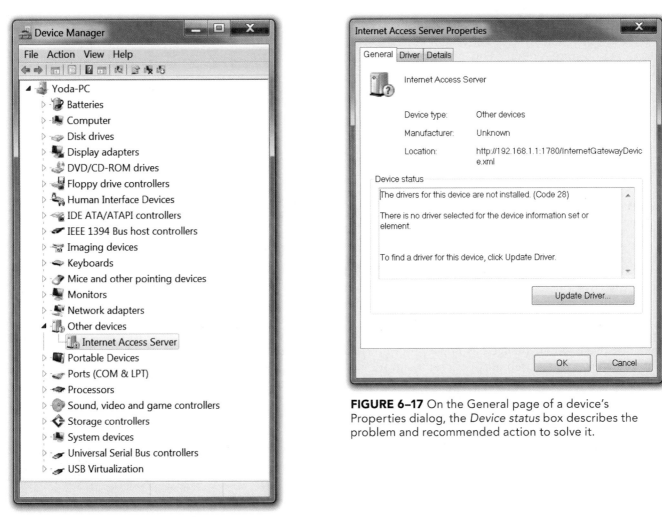

FIGURE 6–17 On the General page of a device's Properties dialog, the *Device status* box describes the problem and recommended action to solve it.

information, as shown in the Windows 7 example in Figure 6–17. Follow the instructions in the Device Status box. In the example, it recommends running Update and provides the Update button (not normally shown on this page). Clicking update opened the Update Driver Software page with two choices: Search automatically for updated driver software and Browse my computer for driver software. Select the second one if you have the driver disc or have the driver on your local computer or on a network share. Select the first choice to have Windows search on the Internet. In the scenario shown, we selected the first choice and it found the driver, downloaded it, and installed it with no more interaction from us. In our example, the device was recognized and placed under the Network Infrastructure Devices category, as shown in Figure 6–18.

For other Device problems, open Device Manager and check out the Driver page of the Properties for the device. For instance, if you update a device driver, and then find that the device fails or is not working as well as before the update use the Roll Back Driver button on the Driver page to remove the updated driver and return to the previously installed driver. This button is active only after you have updated a driver, as shown in Figure 6–19. You can also use this page to update a driver, disable it, or uninstall it. You might disable a driver to see if it relates to another problem. Uninstall it if you do not need a device or if you believe there was a problem with the installation and plan to reinstall the driver.

WARNING!

If you are logged in to Windows 7 or Windows 8 as a standard user you will not be able to make changes to any settings in Device Manager, but it is still a good tool to use to see the status of devices. You can then report problems to a help desk if you are at school or work.

FIGURE 6-18 After installing the device driver, Windows places the device under the Network Infrastructure Devices category.

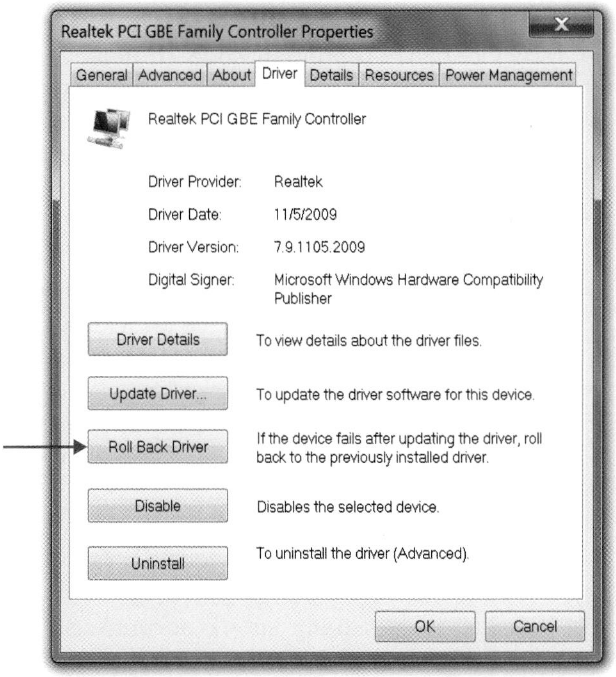

FIGURE 6-19 The *Roll Back Driver* button is active only after a driver update.

Chapter Summary

After reading this chapter, and completing the Step-by-Step tutorials and Try This! exercises, you should understand the following facts about what is under the Windows desktop:

Understanding the Registry

- The registry is a database of all configuration settings in Windows. Avoid directly editing the registry because you can cause severe damage. The Control Panel applets provide a safe way to edit the registry.

- Windows creates the registry during setup and modifies it any time a setup or installation program runs after that and during startup and shutdown. Windows also modifies it any time it installs a device driver and whenever it configures any application, Windows component, or device.

- Most of the registry is in several files, called hives. They include system, software, security, sam, default, and ntuser.dat. These are the permanent portions of the registry.

- You view the registry in a hierarchical folder structure in Registry Editor.

- A key is a folder object that can contain one or more sets of settings as well as other keys.

- There are five top-level keys, or root keys.

- A key that exists within another key is a subkey.

- Settings within a key are value entries. Each value entry has a name, type, and data.

The Windows Startup Process

- The phases of the Windows startup process are
  - Power-on self-test
  - Initial startup
  - Bootloader
  - Detect and configure hardware
  - Kernel loading
  - Logon

- If necessary, modify system startup using the Startup and Recovery page in System Properties. You can also modify the BOOT.INI (Windows XP) and BCD (Windows Vista/Windows 7) files directly to modify startup, but only very advanced techs should do this.

Installing and Managing Device Drivers

- A device driver is program code, created by the device manufacturer, which allows an OS to control the use of a physical device. Look for device drivers on the disc that comes with a device or at the website of the manufacturer.
- You need Administrator privileges to install any device driver in Windows.
- Once a device is installed, a standard user may disconnect and reconnect the device without restriction—the driver will not be uninstalled.
- Code signing exists to avoid problems caused by badly written code. It involves a digital signature, provided by Microsoft, as a seal of approval of program code.
- Always read the manufacturer's documentation and follow the instructions before attempting to install a device driver, whether it is plug and play or not.
- When an administrator installs or connects a plug-and-play device to a Windows computer, the computer will automatically detect the device and install and configure the driver with little or no interaction from the user, except to provide the device driver disk if requested.

- Plug-and-play devices connected to USB or IEEE 1394 (Firewire) can be disconnected without restarting Windows, but you should use the Safely Remove Hardware applet before disconnecting.
- Device Manager is the Windows tool for managing and troubleshooting device problems.

Troubleshooting Windows Problems

- Windows offers a variety of startup options, and some are well suited for troubleshooting. These include the Advanced Boot Options menu and the System Configuration utility. Both allow you to select from several options for restarting Windows.
- Device Manager is the primary tool for troubleshooting device problems. A yellow exclamation mark on a device in Device Manager indicates a problem. Open the properties dialog box to see an explanation.
- Use Device Manager to uninstall, update, and remove device drivers. You can also use it to disable a device without removing the driver.

Key Terms List

binary file *(213)*

bootloader *(223)*

bootstrap loader *(223)*

code signing *(229)*

Consent Prompt *(229)*

Credentials Prompt *(229)*

data type *(217)*

Device Manager *(231)*

Device Stage *(231)*

digital signature *(229)*

driver signing *(229)*

Early Launch Anti-Malware (ELAM) *(225)*

Fast Boot *(225)*

file signature verification *(229)*

Hibernate *(222)*

hive *(213)*

Hybrid Shutdown *(222)*

key *(216)*

Last Known Good (LKG) Configuration *(237)*

logon phase *(224)*

Measured Boot *(225)*

MSCONFIG *(245)*

plug and play *(229)*

power-on self-test (POST) *(223)*

registry *(212)*

root key *216)*

Safe Mode *(236)*

Secure Boot *(225)*

security ID (SID) *(217)*

Sleep *(221)*

subkey *(216)*

Trusted Boot *(225)*

value entry *(216)*

Windows Recovery Environment (Windows RE) *(235)*

Key Terms Quiz

Use the Key Terms List to complete the sentences that follow.

1. A/an _____ is a portion of a registry, containing a hierarchy of keys, that is saved in a registry file.

2. _____ is a new feature in Windows 7 that provides a special home page for a device. This home page contains many choices for managing the device.

3. When viewed with a registry editor, a/an _____ is a registry key located at the top level.

4. Many things occur during some of the startup phases. For instance, during the _____ programs start and plug-and-play devices are detected.

5. _____ is the use of a digital signature provided by Microsoft as its seal of approval on program code.

6. _____ is the ability of a computer and OS to automatically detect and configure a hardware device.

7. A/an _____ contains program code.

8. The _____ utility is very handy for troubleshooting startup problems, allowing you to temporarily disable programs you suspect are causing problems.

9. _____ is a startup mode for starting Windows with certain drivers and components disabled.

10. A/an _____ is a unique string of numbers preceded by S-1-5 that identifies a security principle in a Windows security accounts database.

Multiple-Choice Quiz

1. Which of the following will you not find in the registry?
   a. Device driver settings
   b. Services settings
   c. User data files
   d. User preferences
   e. Application program settings

2. Any change to Windows or an installed application results in a change to this special database.
   a. Microsoft SQL Server
   b. Microsoft Excel
   c. ntuser.dat
   d. Registry
   e. Default

3. Most of the Windows registry files are stored in this location.
   a. *systemroot*\System32\config
   b. D:\Windows
   c. *systemroot*\System32\Registry
   d. *systemroot*\Windows
   e. *systemroot*\WINNT

4. If you select this option from the Power menu in Windows 8, both the system state and the user session are saved in memory, requiring a small amount of power.
   a. Fast Boot
   b. Hibernate
   c. Hybrid Shutdown
   d. Sleep
   e. Measured Boot

5. During this phase, programs start and plug-and-play devices are detected.
   a. Kernel loading
   b. Logon
   c. Initial startup
   d. POST
   e. Bootloader

6. Which statement is true?
   a. Only the Administrator may disconnect or reconnect an installed device.
   b. Only members of the Administrators group may disconnect or reconnect an installed device.
   c. Only members of the Guests group may disconnect or reconnect an installed device.
   d. Any member of the local Users group may disconnect or reconnect an installed device.
   e. No one may disconnect or reconnect an installed device.

7. What UEFI security feature loads only trusted operating system bootloaders?
   a. Fast Boot
   b. Secure Boot
   c. Measured Boot
   d. Trusted Boot
   e. Early Launch Anti-Malware (ELAM)

8. Which of the following is a Device Manager feature only available after an installed driver updates?
   a. Uninstall
   b. Roll back driver
   c. Disable
   d. Update driver
   e. Remove driver

9. What registry hive does the bootloader use during startup to locate the operating system files it must load?
   a. BCD
   b. winload.exe
   c. bootmgr
   d. ntoskrnl.exe
   e. winlogon.exe

10. What page in a Windows Desktop GUI utility would you open to modify the length of time the OS selection menu displays during Windows startup?
    a. Startup and Recovery
    b. Device Manager
    c. BCDedit
    d. Local Security Policy
    e. Computer Management

11. What choice on the Windows 7 Advanced Boot Options menu gives you a selection of tools that includes Startup Repair, System Restore, System Image Recovery, Windows Memory Diagnostic, and Command Prompt?
    a. Safe Mode with Command Prompt
    b. Debugging Mode
    c. Directory Services Restore Mode
    d. Last Known Good Configuration
    e. Repair Your Computer

12. Which of the following Windows 7 startup options will not do you any good if you have restarted and logged on after making a change that caused problems in Windows?
    a. System Restore
    b. Repair Your Computer
    c. Enable Boot Logging
    d. Safe Mode with Command Prompt
    e. Last Known Good Configuration

13. When Windows 8 does this, it hibernates the Windows session and saves it in a file but does not save the user session.
    a. Sleep
    b. Hybrid Shutdown
    c. Switch user
    d. Restart
    e. Hibernate

14. You upgraded a device driver, and Windows immediately failed and restarted. The problem is that it seems to be in a continuous restarting loop. What boot startup option will restart normally and give you an opportunity to try to troubleshoot the problem after a normal reboot?
    a. Debugging mode
    b. Enable boot logging
    c. Safe Mode with command prompt
    d. Disable automatic restart on system failure
    e. Safe Mode with networking

15. Which of the following is the executable name for the GUI utility that allows you to temporarily modify system startup?
    a. SYSCON
    b. MSCONFIG
    c. SYSEDIT
    d. regedit
    e. BCDedit

Essay Quiz

1. Describe at least five actions that will automatically change the Windows registry.

2. Your Windows 7 computer is having display problems when starting. You suspect that the cause is a video driver update that you installed. You managed to log on at the first restart after the update, despite being barely able to see the distorted logon dialog box. Then you found that, even though you had logged on, it was hopeless to try to work with the GUI. Describe how you would confirm that the problem is the video adapter and how you will correct the problem.

3. Describe and contrast two tools for modifying Windows startup in Windows 7: the Advanced Boot Options menu and System Configuration.

4. A fellow student asked for your help in diagnosing a problem with a Windows computer. He believes there is a problem with the network adapter. He works in a small office and does not know the credentials for the Administrator account on that computer. The person who does know is out of town and is unwilling to give him the password until he can convince her that there truly is a problem. He wants to use Device Manager to see the status of the network adapter. What advice can you give him?

5. Describe what boot logging does and how you would use it as a troubleshooting tool.

Lab Projects

LAB PROJECT 6.1

Your Windows 7 computer will not start, and you believe the cause is a network card you recently installed.

1. Describe the steps you will take to isolate the problem.
2. Demonstrate the steps to your instructor.

LAB PROJECT 6.2

A fellow student asked for your help because his Windows 8 computer seems to be unstable. He is considering using either Refresh your PC or Reset your PC. Describe the differences, and if possible do a refresh of a Windows 8 computer. Be sure you have permission to do this, and do not use a production computer. After the refresh, go into Windows 8 and describe any changes you found.

LAB PROJECT 6.3

You are having a problem with your Windows computer that is isolated to a single graphics editing program that you use every day in your work. When you described the problem to the customer service support person for this product, she told you that the only fix for it is to edit a key under HKEY-LOCAL_MACHINE\SOFTWARE. She has assured you that this fix will work without causing any problems, but you are wary of doing this.

1. Describe the steps you will take before making the suggested registry changes.
2. Demonstrate only the steps you would take before modifying the registry. Do not actually modify the registry.

7

OS X on the Desktop

"Steve had this perspective that always started with the user's experience; and that industrial design was an incredibly important part of that user impression."

—John Sculley
Former CEO of Apple discussing Steve Jobs in an October 2010 interview by Leander Kahney, editor and publisher of Cult of Mac (www.cultofmac.com)

So far we have discussed operating systems in general, security for operating system, virtualization of desktop operating systems, and the Windows operating system. Now we change our focus to OS X from Apple.

In this chapter, you will explore the OS X operating system, beginning with an overview, learning how to install it, managing the desktop, and troubleshooting common OS X problems. You'll learn the basics of local security in OS X on the desktop. There are 800-page tomes written about using OS X, so we won't pretend to give you more than a survey of the OS and key facts and features.

Learning Outcomes

In this chapter, you will learn how to:

LO **7.1** Describe the important events in the history of Apple operating systems and the versions of OS X; determine what version of OS X is installed on an Apple computer.

LO **7.2** Prepare and implement an OS X upgrade or installation, and list the postinstallation tasks.

LO **7.3** Navigate and manage OS X on the desktop, including describing the Home folder, using Finder, performing file management tasks, and working with features and settings.

LO **7.4** Manage local security in OS X.

LO **7.5** Troubleshoot common OS X problems.

LO 7.1 | OS X History and Versions

In this overview, we explore the history of Apple's operating systems and the versions of the current line, OS X.

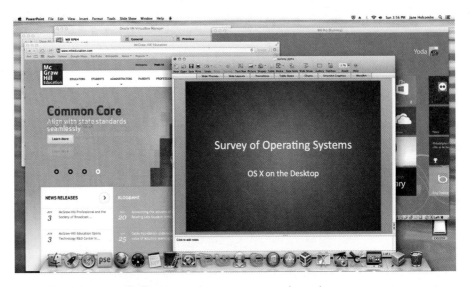

Personalize an OS X desktop to suit your tastes and needs.

A Brief History of the Apple Operating Systems

Apple Computer (now officially Apple Inc.) was founded April 1, 1976, by Stephen Wozniak, Steven Jobs, and Ronald Wayne. They developed and manufactured their first product, the Apple I computer, in a garage in Los Altos, California. The following year, the Apple II version debuted at a local trade show. The Apple II was the first personal computer to be in a plastic case and include color graphics, although it didn't have a graphical user interface. In 1983, Apple launched the Lisa, the first production computer to use a graphical user interface (GUI), and in 1984 the company launched the Macintosh 128k, the first *affordable* personal computer with a GUI. The Macintosh brought with it a new operating system, and Apple shortened the name to Mac in later computer models.

These earliest incarnations of the Apple computers popularized the personal computer beyond the world of techies, leading to today's popular iMac, Mac Pro, MacBook, MacBook Pro, MacBook Air, and other models, not to mention the iPod, iPhone, and iPad. Apple computers have had a profound impact on the computer industry and have inspired a strong community of proponents.

For many years the microprocessors and chipsets in Apple computers were different from those used in standard PCs that ran Windows, and therefore Apple computers would not run Windows. Apple abandoned this strategy around 2006 when they adopted Intel-compatible microprocessors and chipsets; now you could configure a new Mac to dual-boot between Windows and OS X using Apple Boot Camp, as described in Chapter 3.

As for the operating system, the Mac OS, or "System," was born along with the Macintosh in 1984 and went through many changes to the original code over the years until Apple introduced **Mac OS X Server** 1.0 in 1999 and the desktop version, OS X 10.0 in 2000. OS X is a very different OS from the earlier Mac OS. OS X has a UNIX core, known as **Darwin**, that was originally a product of the open-source community.

Note: As with the differences between Windows Server and desktop products, Mac OS X Server began as the same OS, but with many enhancements and services required for its role as a server. Previously, it came preinstalled on Apple's server computers, which Apple discontinued in 2011. Today it is not a standalone operating system. You must already have OS X installed before you can install OS X Server as an add-on. The good news is that it only costs $19.99. But in this chapter we discuss only the desktop versions of OS X.

OS X Versions

Apple has issued several major releases of OS X (referred to as "OS ten") beginning with the initial release for the desktop, 10.0, code-named Cheetah during its development. Although Apple did not publicly use this code name for 10.0 and 10.1, for each subsequent version they tied the code name to the product and used it heavily in marketing and packaging. Apple continued to name OS X versions for species of big cats until 10.9, Mavericks.

Between the major releases Apple has made minor releases (10.8.1, 10.8.2, etc.). Each major release has added hundreds of improvements and new features—both minor and major. The last few versions include features first introduced by Apple in their iOS operating system for their popular portable devices, the iPod, iPhone, and iPad. With OS X 10.8 Mountain Lion, Apple dropped the "Mac" from in front of the name of the OS, to make their desktop OS increasingly like the mobile OS, although the GUIs of OS X and iOS are still separate operating systems.

As you may notice while comparing the illustrations in this book to OS X on your lab computer, you always have the ability to customize the look so that no two installations need to be identical. The screenshots you see in this chapter all use either one of the backgrounds that comes with OS X or a white background for ease of viewing the captured windows and message boxes. Table 7–1 lists the major releases, their names, and release date.

OS X has had many versions and minor releases since its introduction in 2001, and Apple has manufactured a variety of desktop and laptop computers running OS X. It is important to know both the version of OS X and the vintage of your computer before you make a decision to upgrade to a new version of OS X because the latest versions do not run on the older Macs, nor can you upgrade directly from some older versions of OS X to the latest version.

Whenever a new version is available, connect to the Apple website at www.apple.com and search on the product name of the new upgrade. Go to the Web page and select Tech Specs. This will list the requirements, including the OS X version, amount of memory and free disk space, the supported Apple computer models, and the requirements for special features of the new version.

To help you prepare for the next OS X upgrade, Step-by-Step 7.01 walks you through the process of checking out the OS X version and Mac hardware-vintage information.

Note: Most of the OS X screen shots in this book are from OS X version 10.9, Mavericks.

TABLE 7–1 Release Dates of Major OS X Versions

Major OS X Release	Release Date
10.0 Cheetah	March 2001
10.1 Puma	September 2001
10.2 Jaguar	August 2002
10.3 Panther	October 2003
10.4 Tiger	April 2005
10.5 Leopard	October 2007
10.6 Snow Leopard	August 2009
10.7 Lion	July 2011
10.8 Mountain Lion	July 2012
10.9 Mavericks	October 2013

Checking Version and Hardware Information in OS X

It is simple to check the installed version of OS X, as well as the model information for a Mac. This exercise will walk you through the steps for checking out this information and more. You need:

- An Apple desktop or laptop computer running OS X.
- The user name and password of an administrator account for this computer.

Step 1

Log on to an Apple Mac computer running OS X.

Step 2

Click the Apple menu in the top-left corner of your desktop and select *About This Mac*. The screen that pops up displays the version of the installed OS X. You can also run Software Update by clicking the button, shown here.

Step 3

Click the *More Info . . .* button to see information about the computer itself, including the model name and the date of manufacture, the processor, the amount of installed RAM memory, the type of Graphics card, and the serial number.

In OS X Lion (10.7) or later, click the *System Report* button to open a detailed list of the installed hardware and software, as well as the network configuration. The example here shows the hardware list; simply scroll down in the left pane to see network and software information. Keep this window open on your computer while you continue into the next section, because you will need to check the hardware information.

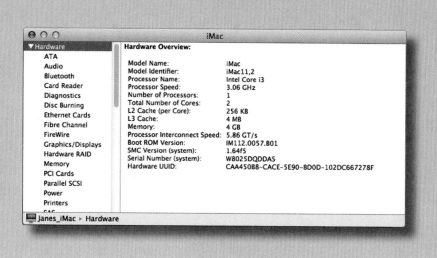

LO 7.2 | Installing and Upgrading OS X

This section details the process of installing and configuring OS X, including the minimum hardware and software requirements, the installation process, and the postinstallation task of updating software. If you purchase a new Apple computer with OS X preinstalled, the OS will need to be personalized for you. In that case, the first time you power up your new computer the OS X Setup Assistant prompts you for the user preferences information, including the user name and password you will use for logging on to this computer.

Preparing to Install OS X

A new Apple Mac computer has OS X preinstalled, but people with existing Macs will often upgrade to a new version of OS X, so we begin by discussing the minimum hardware requirements for upgrading to OS X.

Access a Fast Internet Connection

At this point, the latest OS X upgrade required downloading a file that was over 4 GB in size and may take a while to download. If your Internet connection is slow, or if you have a metered connection, meaning you pay for a certain amount of data usage per month, then you may want to take your computer to an Apple store and take advantage of their free fast Internet access to download the upgrade.

> *Note:* When you exceed the data usage limit in a metered connection, you are billed at a higher rate for the additional data.

Back Up Your Computer

Before installing or upgrading OS X be sure to do a full backup. The best way to do this is to use an external hard drive and Time Machine, the backup software included with OS X since Snow Leopard (10.6). Time Machine requires a dedicated drive that is always available whenever the computer is on. This can be an external USB, FireWire, or Thunderbolt hard drive, an Apple Time Capsule (an Apple product that serves as a networked hard drive), an internal hard drive (in addition to the startup drive), or a separate partition on a drive. If you have one of these drives available and connected to your computer, open the Time Machine preferences in System preferences, turn on Time Machine and follow the instructions.

Check the Computer Model and OS X Version before Upgrading

Before upgrading to the latest version of OS X, verify the version of the Mac OS already installed as well as the model (and vintage) of the computer, using the instructions in Step-by-Step 7.01. If your Mac computer is too old you may not be able to upgrade its OS. If the OS is too old you will not be able to directly upgrade. You may need to first upgrade to an interim version before upgrading to the latest version. Even if you have an upgradable version, run Software Update from the Apple menu, a drop-down menu that appear when you click the Apple icon on the far left of the menu bar. Running Software Update will bring your OS up to the latest incremental update before you upgrade.

Other Hardware Requirements

Ensure that you have adequate memory and disk space. Presently, you need 8 GB of free space and 2 GB of RAM to install the latest version. However, you will want much more of both for running programs and storing data. As we write this, OS X 10.9 Mavericks is the latest version available, and there may be an even newer version of OS X when you read this because, as Table 7–1 shows, Apple releases new versions at intervals of one to two years.

Check the Firmware Version before Upgrading

Finally, check to see if your computer requires a firmware update. Read the article "EFI and SMC firmware updates for Intel-based Macs" at http://support.apple.com/kb/HT1237, which explains that firmware updates "may not be displayed automatically using Software Update," and describes how to find your firmware version and how to determine if a firmware update is available. Scroll down in that document to see the firmware list (Figure 7–1), which is regularly updated. Locate your computer model in the list, and then check to see if a firmware update is available. The Hardware report, shown in step 4 of Step-by-Step 7.01 displays the version of firmware installed on your computer on the lines beginning with "Boot ROM Version" and "SMC Version."

Disable Disk Encryption

FileVault disk encryption has been included with OS X since Snow Leopard (10.6). If you have encrypted your files with either FileVault or a third-party program, temporarily disable it or turn it off. This is just a precaution to avoid any possible incompatibilities during the upgrade process or delays caused by the process of unencrypting. After a successful upgrade, enable encryption, unless you are using a third-party program that the new OS X version no longer supports.

Decide Where to Install OS X

Normally, you install OS X as an upgrade over a previous version. However, if you have installed another hard drive into your Mac and wish to install the new version onto that drive, you must first format it using the

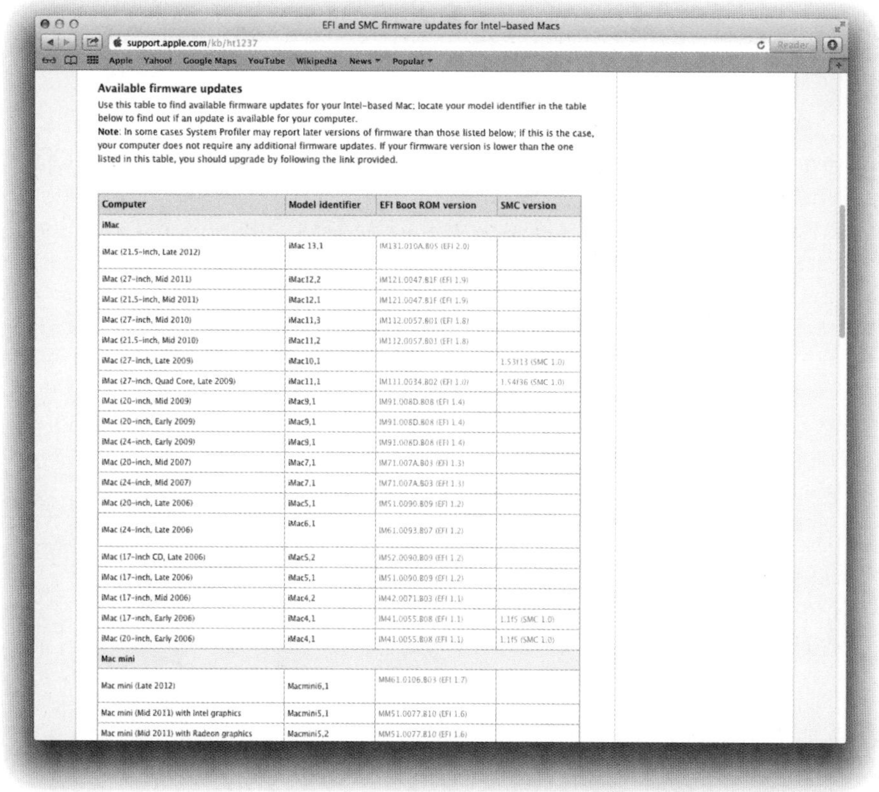

Available firmware updates

Use this table to find available firmware updates for your Intel-based Mac; locate your model identifier in the table below to find out if an update is available for your computer.

Note: In some cases System Profiler may report later versions of firmware than those listed below; if this is the case, your computer does not require any additional firmware updates. If your firmware version is lower than the one listed in this table, you should upgrade by following the link provided.

Computer	Model identifier	EFI Boot ROM version	SMC version
iMac			
iMac (21.5-inch, Late 2012)	iMac 13,1	IM131.010A.B05 (EFI 2.0)	
iMac (27-inch, Mid 2011)	iMac12,2	IM121.0047.B1F (EFI 1.9)	
iMac (21.5-inch, Mid 2011)	iMac12,1	IM121.0047.B1F (EFI 1.9)	
iMac (27-inch, Mid 2010)	iMac11,3	IM112.0057.B01 (EFI 1.8)	
iMac (21.5-inch, Mid 2010)	iMac11,2	IM112.0057.B01 (EFI 1.8)	
iMac (27-inch, Late 2009)	iMac10,1		1.53f13 (SMC 1.0)
iMac (27-inch, Quad Core, Late 2009)	iMac11,1	IM111.0034.B02 (EFI 1.0)	1.54f36 (SMC 1.0)
iMac (20-inch, Mid 2009)	iMac9,1	IM91.008D.B08 (EFI 1.4)	
iMac (20-inch, Early 2009)	iMac9,1	IM91.008D.B08 (EFI 1.4)	
iMac (24-inch, Early 2009)	iMac9,1	IM91.008D.B08 (EFI 1.4)	
iMac (20-inch, Mid 2007)	iMac7,1	IM71.007A.B03 (EFI 1.3)	
iMac (24-inch, Mid 2007)	iMac7,1	IM71.007A.B03 (EFI 1.3)	
iMac (20-inch, Late 2006)	iMac5,1	IM51.0090.B09 (EFI 1.2)	
iMac (24-inch, Late 2006)	iMac6,1	IM61.0093.B07 (EFI 1.2)	
iMac (17-inch CD, Late 2006)	iMac5,2	IM52.0090.B09 (EFI 1.2)	
iMac (17-inch, Late 2006)	iMac5,1	IM51.0090.B09 (EFI 1.2)	
iMac (17-inch, Mid 2006)	iMac4,2	IM42.0071.B03 (EFI 1.1)	
iMac (17-inch, Early 2006)	iMac4,1	IM41.0055.B08 (EFI 1.1)	1.1f5 (SMC 1.0)
iMac (20-inch, Early 2006)	iMac4,1	IM41.0055.B08 (EFI 1.1)	1.1f5 (SMC 1.0)
Mac mini			
Mac mini (Late 2012)	Macmini6,1	MM61.0106.B03 (EFI 1.7)	
Mac mini (Mid 2011) with Intel graphics	Macmini5,1	MM51.0077.B10 (EFI 1.6)	
Mac mini (Mid 2011) with Radeon graphics	Macmini5,2	MM51.0077.B10 (EFI 1.6)	

FIGURE 7–1 Locate your computer model in the list, and then check to see if a firmware update is available.

Mac OS Extended format and the drive must be empty when you begin the installation.

Prepare to Purchase the Upgrade Online

Buy the latest version of OS X at the online App Store. Step-by-Step 7.02 includes instructions for accessing the App Store and purchasing the upgrade. Beginning with OS X 10.8 Mountain Lion, you can no longer order it on DVD; you must do an online upgrade or download the installation image and burn it to a DVD or USB flash drive if you want to do a clean installation.

Note: Before creating passwords, review the information on creating strong passwords in Chapter 2.

The Installation

There are rarely surprises with an OS X installation—mainly because the installation is usually an upgrade; one can legally license this OS only on Apple Mac computers. If you do an upgrade, then at the end of the upgrade, you should only need to log in with the account you used before the upgrade.

Even when you buy a new Apple computer, which always has the OS pre-installed, you get to experience the final stages of the installation the first time you start the computer. That is when the Setup Assistant appears, and you will need to answer a few questions, including providing a user name and password.

Note: In Step-by-Step 7.02 and other exercises we mention an OS X feature called the Dock. The **Dock** is a screen object resembling a floating tray usually located at the bottom of the desktop window. Like the Windows Taskbar, the Dock holds icons for commonly used programs, as well as for open applications. Click an icon to open a program. Learn how to configure the Dock later in this chapter.

Upgrading OS X

This exercise describes the steps for upgrading OS X. If you have an Apple Mac that meets the hardware requirements but is not using the latest version, you can perform an upgrade during this exercise.

- An Apple Mac that meets or exceeds the hardware requirements.
- An Apple ID for purchasing the update.
- A broadband Internet connection.

Step 1

Begin an upgrade by first updating your current installation of OS X. Do this from the Apple Menu's Software Update option or by connecting directly to the App Store. To connect to the App Store, double-click on the App Store icon on the Dock.

Step 2

At the App Store, select Updates. When upgrading from Mountain Lion to Mavericks we signed into the store and downloaded the updates to Mountain Lion before upgrading to Mavericks.

Step 3

While the update is downloading, an icon will display on the Dock with a progress bar.

Step 4

After downloading and installing all updates to the last version, select the new version. In our example, it is OS X Mavericks. After it downloads the *Install OS X* window displays. Click *Continue*.

Step 5

Read the license agreement and click the *Agree* button to accept the terms of the license agreement.

Step 6

On the next screen, you will normally see only one location for installing the upgrade. If you decide to select another drive, click *Show all disks*. Otherwise, click *Install* to continue.

Step 7

This screen displays for a short time, and then the computer reboots and you see an Install OS X message box (against a plain background) with progress bar. After this, the message changes to *Install Succeeded* and it reboots again. What happens next depends on whether you did an upgrade over an older version of OS X or installed onto a clean hard drive.

Step 8

If you did an upgrade over an older version of OS X your apps will be intact, as will your settings, including your local user account. So after the restart the logon screen displays where you log in and meet the new version of OS X.

Step 9

f you did a clean install onto an empty hard drive you have more work to do. The Setup Assistant runs and you will need to answer screens of questions to complete the configuration of your computer, including a new user name and password.

Postinstallation Tasks

A benefit of Apple's requirement that you purchase OS X through the online App Store is that the installation image you download includes the latest updates to OS X. This requirement began with Mountain Lion, and eliminates the need to update OS X immediately after an upgrade or install. If you install OS X from an image you created days or weeks ago, you will need to check updates, as described earlier. Other postinstallation tasks include installing apps into a clean installation, updating apps, and enabling disabled components.

Installing Apps

If you did a clean install, you will need to install all your apps and personalize your computer to your own preferences.

Updating Apps

Apple does not include updates for your apps in the image, so you should check out available updates. An easy way to do this is by simply checking to see if a number appears on the top right of the App Store icon. When that happens, double-click the icon, the App Store window will open, and you can initiate the download and install the update from there.

Alternatively, when you do not see a message or indication of an update but want to see if any are available, open the Apple menu and select *Software Update*, which will also open the App Store window and check for updates.

In yet another scenario, you open an app and a message displays stating that an update is available. We had that occur recently with Microsoft Word. We responded to messages to start the download, including one allowing incoming network connections from the Microsoft Word update program. Then a message box from Microsoft AutoUpdate displayed, giving choices to accept or reject individual updates and to start the install. The message in Figure 7–2 displayed while the update was downloading, After the download completed, we had to respond to more messages to continue, to accept the license terms, to select a destination drive, and finally to install the update.

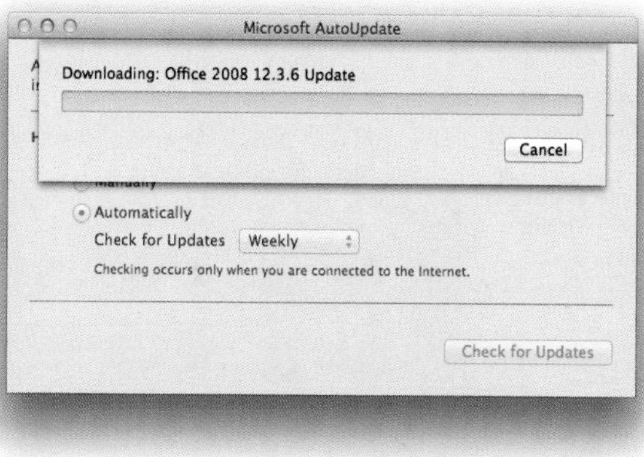

FIGURE 7–2 Progress information display while an app is downloading and updating.

Enable Disabled Components or Apps

If you disabled any components, such as FileVault, before upgrading OS X, enable them after completing the upgrade. We describe FileVault later in this chapter.

try this!

Install Software Updates
It is simple to install updates. Try this:
1. Click the Apple menu in the top-left corner of your desktop and click Software Update.
2. In the Software Update box, see if any updates are available and respond to any messages to begin the Install.
3. Click Agree on any License Agreement page that displays (if you agree, of course). There may be several.
4. Click Restart, if requested.
5. It can take several minutes for the updates to install.

LO 7.3 | Navigating and Managing the OS X Desktop

Navigating in OS X is much like it is in the Windows desktop. You move around by clicking graphical objects that have parallels in the Windows GUI. Tasks include customizing the desktop, installing and removing applications, and adding a printer. You will learn how to set up system preferences, manage files, print, and create and manage user accounts. We also describe the features you use for your everyday work on a Mac, including launching programs and working with the newer OS X features.

The Desktop Menu Bar

One of the biggest differences between the OS X GUI and the Windows desktop is that Windows has a Taskbar at the bottom of the screen with general functions and notifications, and each app has its own menu bar at the top of its window. But OS X has a menu bar across the top of the screen with general functions and which also contains drop-down menus for the current app, and a notification area on the far right that serves some of the same functions as the right end of the Windows Taskbar. Depending on how OS X is configured, the notification area displays the day and time and contains icons for features

Note: The window for an app in OS X does not contain the menu bar, but it does contain buttons for accessing many of the same features available through the menu bar and the round window control buttons in the upper left corner for minimizing (orange), maximizing (green), and closing (red) the window.

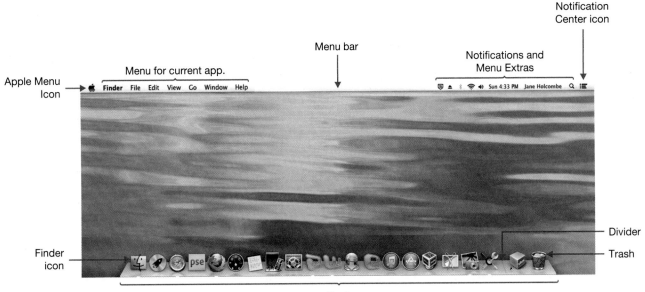

Figure 7-3 Key features of the OS X desktop.

Labels in figure:
- Apple Menu Icon
- Menu for current app.
- Menu bar
- Notifications and Menu Extras
- Notification Center icon
- Divider
- Trash
- Finder icon
- Dock

FIGURE 7–3 Key features of the OS X desktop.

FIGURE 7–4 The Apple menu.

such as the Spotlight search feature that searches local files and folders. Spotlight is also at the top of every Finder window. Figure 7–3 shows the OS X desktop with key features labeled. COMMAND+SPACE BAR opens the Spotlight search box. Spotlight presents results as soon as you start typing because Spotlight does a live search.

Click on the Apple icon on the left of the menu bar to open the Apple menu shown in Figure 7–4. This where you find the version information (and details of the hardware and software), initiate a Software Update, connect to the App Store, open System Preferences to configure settings, put the computer into Sleep mode, restart the computer, shut down, and log out.

File Management in Finder

Like the classic Windows desktop, the OS X desktop has a file manager, Finder, as its foundation. When you launch OS X, Finder owns the desktop, as evidenced by the Finder menus at the top of the screen, but a Finder window is not open by default. Apple is gradually replacing this focus on files in OS X by a focus on apps, which we discuss more in the sections on the Dock and Launchpad. However, Finder is your file management tool in OS X, and in the following sections we look at the Finder views, then practice creating folders, and learn other file management tasks.

Home Folder

Each person who logs on to an OS X computer has his or her own Home folder. When you open a Finder window, the Home folder for the currently logged-on user is identified in the Sidebar, the panel on the left of the Finder window, by an icon representing (what else?) a house. The house icon also displays at the top of the window. Any time you want to open the Home folder, click on it in an open Finder window or simply press SHIFT+COMMAND+H. Several folders are created in the Home folder by OS X. They include Desktop, Documents, Downloads, Movies, Music, Pictures, and Public. You can also create custom folders to help you organize your files. The Documents folder is the default location that many apps use when saving your data files.

Note: SHIFT+COMMAND+H opens the Home folder. SHIFT+COMMAND+D opens the Desktop folder that contains files and folders that appear on your OS X Desktop.

The Home folder has a house icon and displays the user's name.

The Finder menus—Finder, File, Edit, View, Go, Window, and Help—offer a variety of file management and power-on or -off tools. The Finder menu, shown here, lets you manage Finder itself, as does the menu in this position for any open app. The About Finder menu gives its version number. Since Finder is part of the OS, it has the same version number as the OS, but when you open the About menu for an app that is not part of the OS you will see a different version number, and often, much more information about the app. The Window menu arranges window views, and the Go menu offers shortcuts to folders used for storage both on the computer and out on a network.

The Finder menu.

Finder Views

Finder has four views or ways of displaying objects: Icon, List, Column, and Cover Flow. Finder saves the preferred view of the first folder or disk opened in a new Finder window. The unifying factor in all four viewing modes in OS X is the ability to navigate the file and folder structure of your disks and to open files and folders by double-clicking them. If you are sitting at a Mac, follow the instructions in the Try This exercise, and then, while reading the following paragraphs describing the four views, experiment with the different views. You can set view options from the View menu, or from the View buttons, which we labeled in Figure 7–5.

Note: The Finder in OS X Mavericks includes Finder Tabs, which act much like the tabs in Safari and other browsers. This reduces clutter by allowing you to have multiple tab pages in one window.

FIGURE 7–5 Change the view from the Finder View menu or by clicking one of the View buttons on the toolbar.

try this!

Explore Finder Views

Open Finder and browse through it while reading about the different types of views. Try this:

1. Open a Finder folder by clicking the Finder icon on the Dock.
2. Click each object in the left pane and then settle on one object that displays many files and folders in the right pane.
3. Locate the View buttons on the Finder window toolbar.
4. As you read through the description of Finder views, select the appropriate View button to select a view.

Icon View. In Icon view you simply see the icon for each object in the selected location. This example shows the Applications folder open in Icon view. OS X stores application executables in this folder; double-click an icon to launch its app. We describe other methods for launching apps later in this chapter.

Note: SHIFT+COMMAND+A opens the Applications folder.

The Finder window with the Applications folder open in Icon view.

List View. List view displays content in an indented outline format that allows you to see the contents of enclosed folders. This is a powerful means of viewing and organizing your folders and files without having to open new windows for each subfolder, a process that can make your virtual desktop as messy as a real one!

To expand a folder, click the triangular icon to the left of the folder icon. To close the folder, simply click the icon again to hide the contents of that folder. The List view offers a wealth of information about folders and files such as date modified, size, and kind (for example, application or file). If you double-click a folder, that folder opens either in the same folder window or in a new window, as in the other two view options.

Sorting Files in List View

In List view, four columns offer information about your files: Name, Date Modified, Size, and Kind. The default view is an alphabetical sort by name. You can change that order. Try this:

1. Open a Finder folder by clicking the Finder icon on the Dock.
2. Double-click a folder or hard disk.
3. Click the title of any of these columns, and you will see your files sorted by that attribute. Sorting based on the size and data columns is useful when you want to recover hard disk space. Look for big, obsolete files this way.
4. Click the same title again to see the files sorted by that attribute in reverse order. Used most often with the Date column, this technique is effective when you want to search for recently changed or out-of-date files.

The Finder window in List view.

Column View. In Column view, when you select a file by clicking it once, the file's icon or a preview of its contents, either text or graphics, is displayed in a column to the right. If you click on a folder, the contents display in the column to the right, and if you click on a subfolder, yet another column opens with that folder's contents. When a window is in Column view, you can change the size of columns by dragging the bottom of the column divider. This image shows a Finder window in Column view showing the songs located in Documents\ChrissyBackup\music backup July 2008\ Allison Kraus.

The Finder window in Column view.

Cover Flow View. Cover Flow view opens a pane containing small images of each object in the currently selected folder. Below this pane is a list pane. Select a file or folder in this list and it will appear in the center of the Cover Flow.

The Finder window in Cover Flow view.

Creating Folders in the Finder

Organize your documents and applications in the contents pane. Create a new folder to contain copied or moved files or folders by choosing New Folder from the File menu in the Finder or by right-clicking an area of the contents pane and selecting New Folder. Practice creating a new folder in Step-by-Step 7.03.

Copying, Pasting, and Deleting Files and Folders

Copy and paste files and folders into local or network locations.

- To copy, select the item and choose Copy from the Edit menu (or press COMMAND+C).

- To cut, select the item and choose Cut from the Edit menu (or press COMMAND+X).

- To paste, first either copy or cut a file or folder. Then open the destination location and select Paste from the Edit menu (or press COMMAND+V).

- To delete, choose Delete from the Edit menu (or press COMMAND-DELETE). This moves the file or folder into the Trash. To empty the Trash, select Empty Trash from the Finder menu (or press COMMAND+SHIFT+DELETE).

- If you drag a file or folder and drop it onto a different drive, that operation is a copy, meaning that you have copied the file or folder to the new location and the original remains in the old location. To copy a file or folder onto the same drive with a drag operation, hold down the OPTION key as you let go of the file or folder. Otherwise, it will be a move (discussed next).

The Finder Edit menu.

Moving and Renaming Files and Folders in Finder

If you drag a file or folder and drop it in a different folder on the same drive, that operation is a move; meaning that it is first copied to the new location and then automatically deleted from the old location. When you cut and paste a file or folder, it results in a move regardless of the locations. In Step-by-Step 7.03 you create a folder, and then drag files into the new folder.

Renaming Files and Folders in Finder

Open Finder and locate the file or folder you want to rename; click on it once to select it, and then after a short pause click again. This will highlight the name of the item and you will be able to edit the file name without changing the extension. (You should almost never change a file's extension.) When you are ready to save the item with the new name, either click away from the item or press RETURN.

> **WARNING!**
>
> When you rename files, be careful not to change the file extension. This can keep the operating system from recognizing a file type and the OS would not know which program to use to open the file.

Creating a New Folder and Organizing Files

In this exercise, you will create a folder within an existing folder, rename it, and move files into it. To complete this exercise, you will need the following:

- A Mac computer with OS X installed.

- A user name and password that will allow you to log on to your computer.
- Files in at least one of the folders of your home directory.

Step 1

Open Finder by clicking its icon (the rectangular, blue icon with a face image) on the Dock. Click on your Home folder in the left pane to see its contents on the right.

Step 2

Create a new folder. Press COMMAND+ SHIFT+N or select New Folder from the Finder's File menu. A new folder, called "untitled folder," will appear in the list of files and folders.

Step 3

Type a new name for the folder and press ENTER to save it. Or click the folder once, pause, and then click it a second time to highlight its name, and then type a new name and press ENTER to save the file with the new name.

Step 4

Double-click on the new folder so that the contents pane opens on the empty folder.

Step 5

On the menu bar, select File, New Finder Window. Position the new window next to the window for the new folder. In the newly opened window, navigate to a folder containing files or folders you wish to move to the new folder.

Select a file or folder that you want to place into this folder by clicking it once and then dragging it to the window containing the new folder. If you want to select multiple files or folders, hold down the COMMAND key while clicking each file until you have selected all the files.

When you are finished selecting items, drag them together to the contents pane for the new folder you created and then let go. The files move into the new folder.

Changing Settings in OS X

Open System Preferences from the Apple menu or from the Dock where its icon is a gray box filled with gears. This is the OS X equivalent of the Windows Control Panel, and Apple's "preferences" are like Window's "settings." Figure 7–6 shows the main System Preferences window. Notice the *Show All* button in the title bar; this will always return you to the main System Preferences window. The icons are in rows by category. The actual icons in each row depend on the installed features and devices. While any logged-on user can change some settings, some can only be changed by an administrator, and some can be configured to be changed by either type of user. We describe the System Preferences categories below.

The System Preferences icon on the Dock. In iOS on mobile devices this icon is labeled "Settings."

- **Personal**—Desktop, security, and privacy settings for the currently logged-on user.

FIGURE 7–6 System Preferences organized by category. This screenshot from OS X 10.8 Mountain Lion shows the category names, which were removed in OS X 10.9 Mavericks, although the icons are still organized in these same rows.

- **Hardware**—Settings for hardware devices. Some of these are obviously associated with a single device, but Energy Saver controls the conditions under which different components are put into a low-power sleep mode and/or awakened.
- **Internet and Wireless**—Settings that apply to any form of network available to the computer and to certain services that rely on networking.
- **System**—Nonhardware settings that apply to all users of the computer.
- **Other**—Settings that apply to miscellaneous services and devices that do not quite fit into the other categories.

If you have trouble with the default organization of the System Preferences icons, you can sort them in alphabetical order by clicking the View menu (in the Menu bar at the top of windows) and selecting *Organize Alphabetically*. This is helpful when you know the name of a Preference pane but do not recall its category. As we describe selected features of OS X we describe where you can change settings for these features in System Preferences.

> *Note:* Press OPTION+COMMAND+D to hide the Dock. Press it again to unhide the Dock.

Launching and Switching between Apps with the Dock

While early versions of Mac OS used the Finder as a task switcher, OS X delegates the task of launching frequently used apps and switching between open apps to the Dock, shown in Figure 7–3. A subtle line "engraved" in the Dock separates program icons from icons representing disks, folders, and documents. A single click on an icon on the Dock launches the program.

When you launch a program, a small dot appears under the app's icon on the Dock; simply click on one of these icons to quickly switch between tasks. The Trash icon sits on the Dock, waiting for you to drag unwanted files, folders, and apps into it. Add a file, folder, application, or Internet bookmark to the Dock by simply dragging it there. If you want to remove something from the Dock, just drag it off and onto the desktop and release the mouse button. The icon disappears in a puff of smoke. An icon on the Dock behaves like a Windows shortcut, but it is simply pointing to a file, program, or location. Therefore removing it from the Dock only removes the icon.

try this!

Add an Icon to the Dock

Add a shortcut icon to the Dock. Try this:

1. Open the Application folder in Finder and select something you would like to call up quickly from the Dock.
2. Click the item's icon and drag it onto the Dock. Before letting go of the mouse button, move the icon over the Dock to position it between existing Dock icons. Depending on the type of icon, you will be able to position it to the right or left of the divider.
3. Release the mouse button when you are satisfied with the position of the icon.
4. To reposition the Dock on the screen, click the Apple menu and select Dock. From the Dock menu click to select one of the position options. Notice the change in the appearance of the Dock as well as the orientation of the icons.
5. To remove the icon, drag it to the Trash icon.

> *Note:* Press and hold COMMAND while tapping TAB to open the heads-up switcher. Repeat until you have selected the desired app.

Using the Heads-Up Program Switcher

There are several ways to switch among open apps, but we find using the Dock, as described above, and using the Heads-Up Program Switcher to be the methods we use the most. Simply press and hold the COMMAND key and tap the TAB key. The heads-up display of open app icons appears in the middle of the screen. Keep the COMMAND key down while you repeatedly tap the Tab key to cycle through the app icons. When the app you want is selected release the Command key.

The Heads-Up Program Switcher.

View and Manage All Programs in Launchpad

Launchpad, a new feature in OS X Mountain Lion, resembles the home screen on Apple iOS devices (Shown in Chapter 11). Click the Launchpad "rocket" icon on the Dock to open Launchpad. With Launchpad open, the menu bar at the top of the screen and objects on the desktop disappear, but the Dock remains visible. Now you can view all the existing apps on your computer and launch one with a single click. If you have more program icons than will fit on a page, scroll to see additional pages, just as in iOS.

Figure 7–7 shows Launchpad open with one page of app icons, and two dots positioned just above the Dock. These dots represent the Launchpad pages; the white dot shows the current page. Click a dot or swipe to move to another page. Customize Launchpad by clicking on an icon and holding the mouse button until all the icons in Launchpad start jiggling. Then drag the selected icon to different positions on the pages. If you drag an icon on top of another program icon (without releasing it), a horizontal band opens in the middle of the screen. Drop the icon into this band to group it into a folder with the other icon. When we dragged a Microsoft Word icon on top of a Microsoft PowerPoint icon the band opened with the suggested folder name of "Production." When we dropped the Word icon, it created the folder and showed it above the band, as shown in Figure 7–8.

> *Note:* Launchpad, like the Windows 8 Apps screen, displays all installed apps.

FIGURE 7–7 The Launchpad contains app icons.

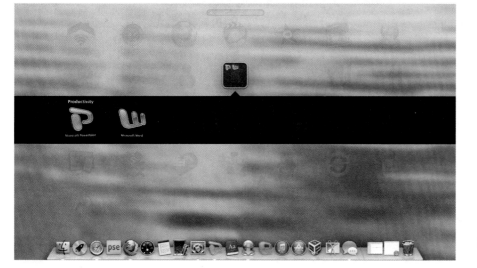

FIGURE 7–8 Creating a folder in Launchpad.

Declutter the Desktop with Mission Control

Mission Control is a window-management program that combines the functions of the Exposé, Dashboard, and Spaces features. "Exposé" was the term Apple previously used to refer to the feature that let you view all open windows on the screen at once. Dashboard is a screen containing small applets that act somewhat like Windows widgets. A Space is a virtual screen; OS X supports up to 16 Spaces. Use Spaces for separating work, play, and school projects into virtual desktops. Or open an app full screen and place it in its own Space. OS X Mountain Lion introduced full-screen apps.

Open the Mission Control screen to manage these features. Discover the keystroke or key combination to open Mission Control in the Mission Control preferences pane, shown here. On our iMac, the documented Mission Control shortcut is CTRL+UP ARROW, but the F3 key, formerly assigned to Exposé, also works. It may be different on your computer, but once you find the shortcut, notice that it is a toggle: Use it once to open Mission Control. Use it again to close Mission Control.

Change Mission Control settings in this preferences pane.

Note: To see a list of all keyboard shortcuts for OS X open the Shortcuts tab of the Keyboard pane in System Preferences.

When you open the Mission Control screen, notice that the pile of open windows on your desktop are organized and represented by thumbnails. You start out with two Spaces: one containing the Dashboard and the other containing the initial desktop, represented by the first two thumbnail images on the top row in Figure 7–9. Move the cursor to the upper right of the screen until a box with a plus sign appears, also shown in Figure 7–9. Click this to open a new space, such as the thumbnail labeled Desktop 2. You can drag apps onto one of the desktop spaces. In our example we have two Word documents open and two PowerPoint documents open—all in separate windows on the same desktop. Mission Control grouped them together. This is a gentle suggestion for organizing your spaces by type of app. You can drag the grouped apps to one of the spaces. Switch between spaces by selecting a space within Mission Control or by simply using the CTRL+RIGHT ARROW key or CTRL+LEFT ARROW key.

Note: Press CTRL+RIGHT ARROW key or CTRL+LEFT ARROW key to switch between Spaces.

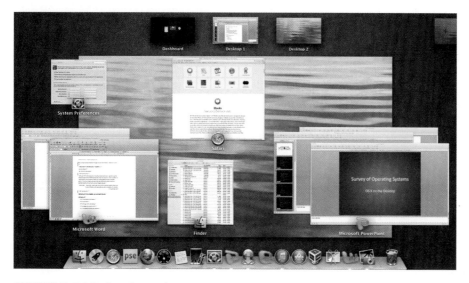

FIGURE 7–9 Mission Control.

Notification Center

The Notification Center displays important status messages, notifying you of events, such as a new email or text message or the availability of a new update. These messages pop down on the top right of the Desktop, as shown in Figure 7–10. To open the Notification Center itself, click on its icon to the right of the Spotlight (magnifying glass) icon that opens OS X's search feature. In Notification Center, shown in Figure 7–11, you can see all your messages at once. Click the tiny icon in the bottom-right corner of the open Notification Center to open the Notifications preferences window (also shown in Figure 7–11) where you can configure settings for notifications. Alternatively, open Notifications preferences from System Preferences.

FIGURE 7–10 A notification on the Desktop.

Menu Extras

The OS X menu bar has a variety of icons on the right side—some open up menus, while others, like the speaker icon, open controls. These icons that give you quick access to some System Preferences settings are called Menu Extras. Add Menu Extras to the Menu bar through the individual preferences panes in System Preferences. For instance, the day and time are visible on the Menu bar because of a setting enabled on the Clock page of the Date & Time preferences pane. This setting is *Show date and time in menu bar*. Similarly, the Volume Control is on the menu bar because of a setting titled *Show volume in menu bar*.

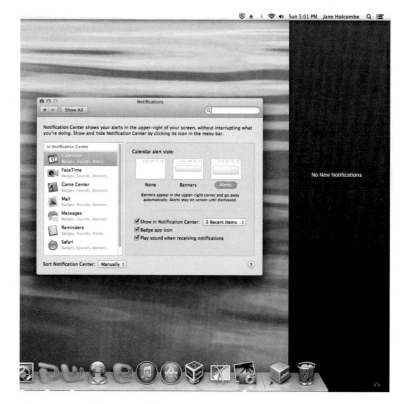

FIGURE 7–11 The Notifications preferences window.

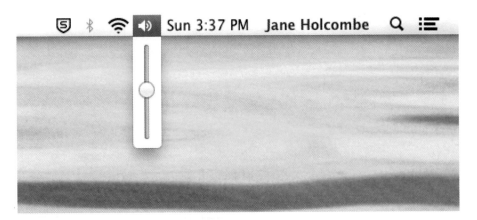

Some Menu Extras have menus; others have controls, like the Speaker icon that has a slider control for volume.

Printing in OS X

No matter what type of printer you have, almost every OS X application manages the printing process in the same way, including giving you the ability to create an Adobe PDF document from any Print menu.

Installing a Printer

Installing a printer in OS X is a nonevent. You simply connect the printer, power up, and it installs without any fuss or obvious activity. OS X quietly goes searching for the driver, downloading it from the Internet if the computer has an Internet connection.

To verify that the printer did install, open Printers and Scanners in System Preferences. With the Print tab selected, installed printers are listed on the left. If your new printer is not listed, click the plus (+) button under the list (shown in Figure 7–12) and use the disc that was packed with the printer or, if you do not have a disc, contact the manufacturer for help finding a driver.

Most of your printer interaction takes place in the Print dialog box within applications. During printing, the Print Center icon appears in the Dock, allowing you to view, hold, or delete jobs.

Setting Printing Options

A printer has a variety of configurable options, which you may modify from the Print menu in any application's File menu (or the Print and Scan preferences pane). These options are specific to the printer model. You should explore these options for your own printer so that you are aware of its capabilities and can plan to take advantage of them.

Where to Find the Print Queue

When you are ready to send a job to the printer, simply open the Print menu in the application, select the printer, and if you need to change paper

> *Note:* While Menu Extras is the official term for these little menus and controls, some users call them *menulets*.

> *Note:* Previous to OS X Snow Leopard (10.6), OS X kept a large cache of printer drivers on the local hard drive, taking up a good deal of space. Snow Leopard and newer versions no longer do that.

FIGURE 7–12 Click the plus (+) at the bottom of the list to add a new printer.

size, orientation, or scale, click the Page Setup button and make those changes. When you are ready to print, click the Print button. While a job is printing, an icon displays on the Dock, and if you're fast, you can open it in time to see the print queue, which closes when the print job is finished. Otherwise, you can find the Print Queue for an individual printer by calling up the Print and Scan preferences pane. Select a printer from the list on the left and double-click on any printer or click the *Open Print Queue* button to view its print queue, check the ink or toner level, print a test page, or open a printer utility that will let you do certain printer maintenance and testing.

AirPlay

Apple added AirPlay, a feature that was first introduced in iOS, to OS X in Mountain Lion. Use AirPlay to connect to an Apple TV, which acts as an intermediary device for sending your iTunes songs, video, pictures, and other data from your computer to a high definition (HD) TV via Wi-Fi.

LO 7.4 | Managing Local Security in OS X

When we purchased an iMac at an Apple Store three years ago we were told that Macs don't need third-party security software. While most malware attacking desktop computers target Microsoft Windows, OS X is not impregnable, and anyone who connects to a network, plugs in a flash drive, or inserts an optical disc in their computer is vulnerable—not to mention the threats you can encounter browsing the Web and even in the messages you receive.

Apple is aware of the threats and has built in many security features that are on by default. Make sure you have updated your software, as described earlier in this chapter. It also doesn't hurt to add an antivirus to your Mac. However, the greatest threats may be from scams and frauds, and your best defense against them is self-education and skepticism (even paranoia) when faced with messages that ask for information or require that you click on a link. In this section we examine the OS X security features that do a pretty good job of protecting you from everything but social engineering.

Apple's Website includes a page describing the security features of OS X. It also includes a box titled "More ways to keep your Mac safe." Their recommendations include:

Note: We use a third-party antivirus, Sophos. Do your own research and make your own decision about this. Enter "antivirus for Mac" into a search engine and see what others think about this issue.

- Turn on a firewall to prevent other machines from accessing services running on your Mac.
- Control access to your Mac by locking your screen after a period of inactivity.
- Securely delete outdated sensitive files with the Secure Empty Trash command.
- Set up secure file sharing.

So where do you begin? Start your relationship with your Mac by exploring the security features of OS X and ensuring that you are using every security option available to you. We explore enabling regular updates, managing local user accounts, and installing antivirus protection.

try this!

What Does Apple Say about Security Today?

Find out what Apple says about OS X security today. Try this:

1. Point your Internet browser to https://ssl.apple.com/osx/what-is/security.html. If the page is no longer at this address, do a search of the site on "OS X security."
2. Read the contents of the resulting page.
3. Look for a link to a recent security brief, and retrieve and read it.
4. Draw your own conclusions about the security of your Mac and discuss it with classmates.

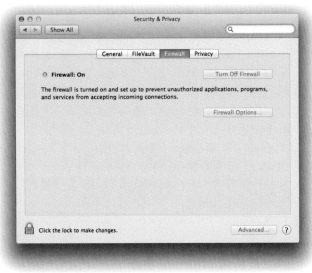

FIGURE 7–13 Firewall is on.

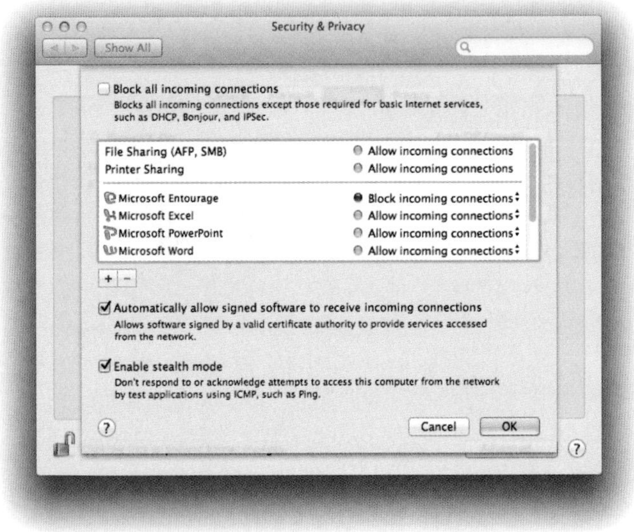

FIGURE 7–14 Incoming connections are allowed for sharing and for certain apps.

WARNING!

Anytime you unlock a settings pane, be sure to lock it again when you finish.

Note: Gatekeeper is very effective at what it does, but it only guards against downloading unsafe software; it does not protect against programs from other sources, such as from jump drives and from CD or DVD discs.

Check Out the OS X Firewall

How does your Mac connect to the Internet? Is it through a broadband router at home, or through a Wi-Fi hotspot at the school cafeteria or the local coffee shop? However your computer connects—whether it is a network you trust (at home or school) or an untrusted network, such as many of the public Wi-Fi hotspots, you need to ensure that you have the OS X Firewall turned on. While the most recent versions of OS X turn it on by default, you should check it out and familiarize yourself with it.

To view and modify Firewall settings, open the Security and Privacy pane in System Preferences and click on Firewall. Ensure that the firewall is on. If it is not, turn it on. You may need to click on the lock icon on the lower left of the window to unlock the settings, in which case you will need to provide a password. Then click the button labeled **Turn on Firewall**. Figure 7–13 shows the Firewall turned on.

After ensuring that the firewall is on, click the Firewall Options button to view the settings. Figure 7–14 shows this page. This requires some explanation. You could block all incoming connections if all you are doing is simple Web browsing and sending and receiving email. During these operations you initiate the connection to a Web server or mail server. The traffic that comes to your computer because of these actions is not seeking to initiate a connection to your computer; it is simply responding to your request for Web pages or email messages. Therefore, you could block all incoming connections, but still browse the Internet and send and receive email.

Our example in Figure 7–14 is more complicated because we have enabled sharing services on the Mac. If you install or enable services on your Mac that require incoming traffic (not initiated from within), it will configure the Firewall to allow this type of traffic. However, if you do not plan to do any type of sharing and have not enabled any service requiring incoming traffic, Firewall will block all incoming connections and it will turn on stealth mode, which it will gray out so that you cannot disable it. If you later wish to use a sharing service, the installation will change the setting to allow incoming connections for that service.

Gatekeeper

Gatekeeper, a feature introduced in OS X Mountain Lion, limits the online sources from which you can download programs. You will not find an icon labeled Gatekeeper, but you can configure Gatekeeper settings by selecting one of the options labeled *Allow applications downloaded from* on the General page of the Security & Privacy preferences pane. Here is a description of each of those settings (shown in Figure 7–15):

1. **Mac App Store**: Only install apps from the App Store. The most restrictive setting.

2. **Mac App Store and identified developers**: Download and install apps that include a Developer ID signature as well as apps from the Apps Store. Less restrictive.

3. **Anywhere**: Download and install apps from any location, as long as other security features of OS X allow this action. The only restrictions will be from other security components. This turns Gatekeeper off.

Kernel ASLR

Using a security feature called address space layout randomization (ASLR), OS X Mountain Lion and newer OSs load the core operating system code, the kernel, into random locations in memory, rather than loading into the same memory addresses every time. This prevents malware from accessing operating system functions based on their known location in memory.

Digitally Signed and Sandboxed Apps

All apps available through the App Store are digitally signed. A digitally signed app will issue a warning if its code is modified. In addition, each app available through the App Store is sandboxed, meaning that it cannot access any code or device it is not authorized to access. It is in a virtual sandbox where it can only play with those "toys" it is permitted to access.

FileVault

FileVault is OS X's file and disk encryption feature. Earlier versions only encrypted the Home folder, but in recent versions of OS X, FileVault encrypts everything on your startup drive every time you log out. With FileVault disk encryption turned on, your files are accessible only while you are logged on. Unless someone has access to your password, or you walk away from your computer without logging out, no one can open the encrypted files. An administrator must turn on FileVault using the FileVault page of the Security pane, as shown in Figure 7–16. OS X generates a recovery key, shown in Figure 7–17, when you turn on FileVault. It is a fail-safe for when a user forgets a login password. Be sure to copy down the recovery key and store it in a safe place. You only need one recovery key on each computer.

FIGURE 7–15 View and change the Gatekeeper settings by selecting one of the options under *Allow applications downloaded from:*

WARNING!

If you walk away from your computer while logged on, anyone can come along and access all your files. Be sure to use a strong password on your account and log out before walking away.

WARNING!

If you forget your password and do not know the recovery key, you will not be able to access your startup drive and any data stored on it. Copy down the recovery key and store it in a safe place.

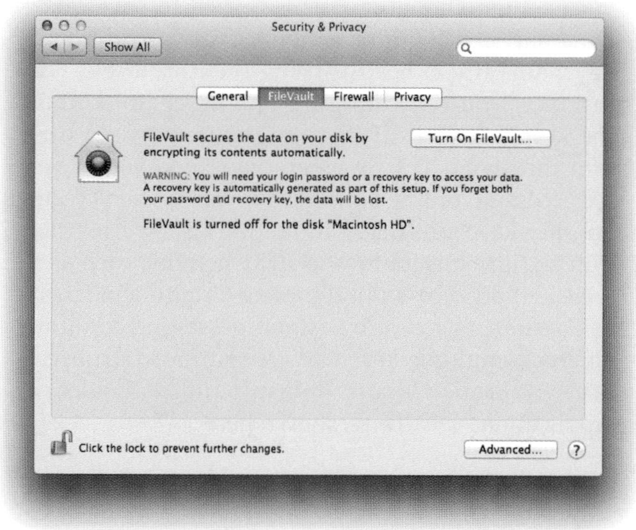

FIGURE 7–16 Click the *Turn On FileVault* button in the FileVault page of the Security preferences pane.

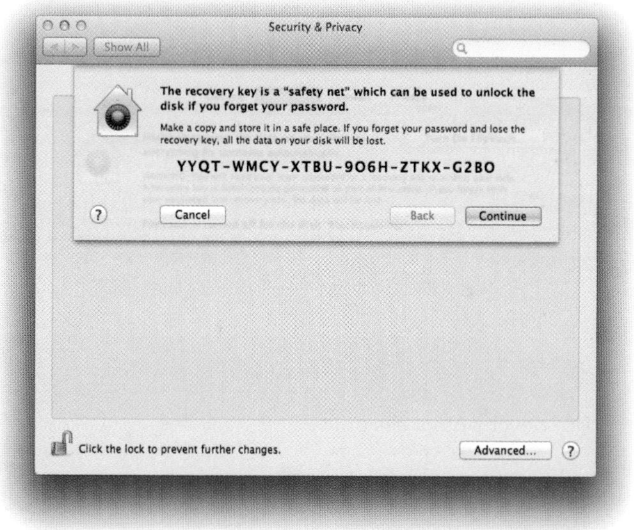

FIGURE 7–17 Carefully write down the recovery key and put it in a safe place.

Secure Virtual Memory

OS X uses a swap file, much as Windows does. The swap file is disk space the OS uses as if it is memory so they call it virtual memory. All multitasking operating systems use virtual memory to allow you to have several applications open. While you are actively using your word processor, most other open applications are just waiting for you to switch back to them. Therefore, it temporarily saves at least part of the code and data for these other apps to the swap file. Clever hackers can access the swap file, so Apple includes a feature in OS X called Secure Virtual Memory, which encrypts the swap file. Before OS X Mountain Lion, when you turned on FileVault it turned on Secure Virtual Memory, but beginning with Mountain Lion, this feature is on by default, without a way to turn it off in System Preferences.

Keychain

The keychain is part of a credentials management system using the name "keychain" as a metaphor for a physical keychain. The password to the keychain gives the user access to all the passwords or "keys" on that keychain. Each keychain is a secure database of a user's passwords, collected the first time it asks you to supply a user name and password to something, such as shared folders on your school or work network, at websites, FTP sites, and more.

Two default keychains, System and System Roots, belong to the OS. The first time you log in, OS X creates your first keychain, called login, using your account password as a master password for the keychain. Then as you go about your business, logging in to various servers to access email and other resources, as well as various websites, the credentials you supply are saved in your keychain, provided you respond to a prompt asking if you want to save the password. Although some websites have login programs that will not allow this, many do, and if you save the password for a website in your key chain, it will complete the login boxes (a process called AutoFill in Safari) each time you reconnect to one of these sites.

Safari turns AutoFill on by default, and you can turn it off if you do not want keychain to remember your credentials. Look for a setting similar to AutoFill, or one that mentions remembering passwords in any Internet browser to enable keychain with that browser.

For most of us, the login keychain is sufficient for all our needs, but you can create multiple keychains, each with a separate purpose, such as for your online shopping or as a place to save your personal credit information. Create additional keychains if you need varying security levels. For instance, you can configure one keychain so that the keychain locks if there is idle time over a certain threshold. This is where you keep your keys for accessing online banking accounts. Then create another keychain that will not have such a restriction because it is for low-security activity, such as a website you access purely for entertainment, such as Pandora, or for your instant messaging account. To create multiple keychains for various purposes, use Keychain Access, a utility found in Finder | Applications | Utilities, shown here.

The Keychain Access utility.

Managing Local User Accounts

OS X supports multiple local user accounts. At home, school, or work, you can set up a single computer with multiple accounts so that each person is restricted to his or her own home folder, preserving preferences from one session to another. As in Microsoft Windows, two users can log in to the same computer at the same time, but only one can have control of the "console," the keyboard, screen, and mouse, at any given time. OS X preserves each account's session in memory and users can switch back and forth using fast user switching. Alternatively, users can log in and log out when they finish working or step away.

Parental Controls

You access Parental Controls in System Preferences through the Parental Controls pane or through the settings for individual users in the Users and Groups pane. Parental Controls have four categories of restrictions you can apply to a Standard or Guest account. They are:

Note: You cannot apply Parental Controls to an administrator-type account.

- **Apps**—The desktop (Finder) for ease of use and/or to restrict which apps the user can open. Allow or deny the ability to modify the Dock.
- **Web**—Restrict access to adult websites or allow access only to certain websites.
- **People**—Control access to multiplayer games through Game Center, or limit mail and/or messages to a list of allowed contacts.
- **Time Limits**—Assign time limits during weekday and/or weekend and prevent access during defined times.

When you turn on Parental Controls for an account, it becomes a managed account.

Types of Users and Privileges

There are several types of user accounts; two of them, Administrator and Standard, are like the Windows account types of the same name. The others are Sharing Only, Guest account, and Root account. We describe the main functionality of the account types here.

Administrator Account. The Administrator account type, also simply called "admin," is for advanced users or for the person who will administer this computer, add more users, install software, and the like. The first account created during installation is an administrator. Open the Accounts preferences pane from System Preferences and view the local accounts on a Mac. Right after installation, it should have only one active account, the account created during installation. Notice the description "Admin" on the left under the account name in Figure 7–18. This level allows you to do the following:

- Change all system preference settings and install software in the main application and library folders.
- Create, modify, and delete user accounts.

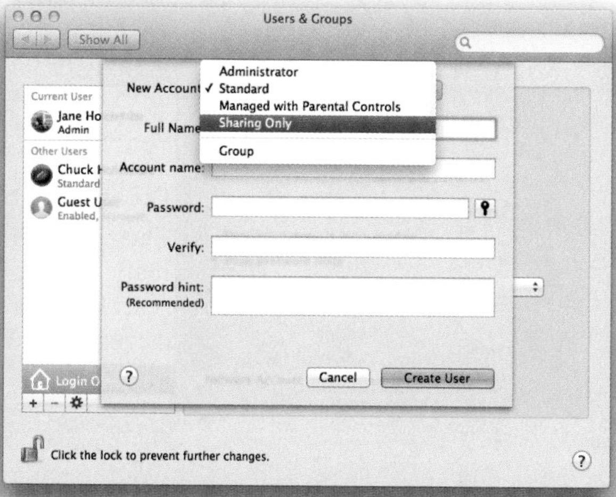

FIGURE 7–18 The Users & Groups preferences pane.

Standard Account. This account type is for ordinary users, those whom tech support typically need to save from themselves on a regular basis. A Standard account type gets into far less trouble because of these restrictions:

- File access is limited to only the user's Home folder and the Shared folder (/Users/Shared/) that is accessible to other users without restriction.
- Access is denied to higher-level system preferences, such as network settings, sharing, software update settings, user setup, and date and time settings.

Sharing Only Account. You can create a Sharing Only account for someone who only needs to access shared folders on your Mac over a network. With a Sharing Only account type someone can connect remotely and log in with the local account, but will not have her own set of Home folders on the local computer. A person with a Sharing Only account cannot log on locally at the computer where the Sharing Only account resides.

Guest Account. Guest is an account type with very limited access, but OS X no longer allows you to assign this account type to a new user. Instead, it creates a single Guest account, called Guest User. This account does not require a password, has access only to the Guest Home folder, and when a guest logs out, all files and folders created during that session in the Guest's Home folder are deleted. Enable the Guest Account in the Users & Groups preferences pane. To further restrict the Guest account, turn on Parental Controls, described previously.

Root Account. The Root account, often called a super-user account, exists mainly for the use of the OS. It is not enabled for interactive users in the standard installation of OS X. Root is only for people familiar with the inner workings of UNIX, and changing things on your computer using this account can result in serious system dysfunction and lost data. We will not describe how to enable it. Root gives you complete control over all folders and files on the Mac.

You rarely will require the amount of control over OS X system files that the Root account allows. Apple specifically organized OS X to limit the need to change the system files and folders.

Automatic Login

Automatic Login bypasses the login page and logs into the selected user account when the computer powers on. With Automatic Login turned off (the recommended setting), OS X prompts a user to enter passwords to log in. In recent versions of OS X an administrator configures automatic login by selecting the Login Options at the bottom of the Users & Groups preferences pane. This opens a page where you can enable or disable Automatic Login for individual local users, as well as modify the appearance of the login window (if Automatic Login is disabled).

Creating and Deleting User Accounts

The first user account is set up when you install OS X. This account is automatically an administrator-type account and it is automatically associated with the user's Apple account. After the installation process is complete, you can create additional user accounts, as described in Step-by-Step 7.04. We recommend that you take an additional step and enable an option on the user account page for the first user labeled, *Allow user to reset password using Apple ID*. This setting will make life easier for you if you should forget your password for this account, which we discuss later.

> **WARNING!**
>
> Only use Automatic Login in a very safe environment, such as your home, where the convenience outweighs any threat to your data.

Step-by-Step 7.04

Creating a New User/Deleting a User Account

In this exercise, you will add a new user to your computer. To complete this exercise, you will need the following:

- A Mac computer with OS X installed.
- An administrator account and password that will allow you to log on to your computer.

Step 1

Begin the process of creating a new user by opening the Users & Groups preferences pane. In the Users & Groups pane click the button with the plus sign at the bottom left.

Step 2

Type the full name and press the TAB key. This will create the account name based on the full name. You can change the full name and password later, but the account name is permanent. The user can log in as either. Both are case-sensitive. Enter the user password twice. A password can be anything, even blank, for any user not needing administrator access. Enter a password hint, and then click Create User.

Step 3

The new user appears in the sidebar of Users & Groups, and the settings for that user display on the right. The new user automatically becomes a Standard User. If you want to change this account to an administrator-type account, select that option on this page. If the new user is a child, it should be a Standard User, and you may want to enable Parental Controls.

To delete a user account select it in the sidebar of Users & Groups and then click the minus button (–) at the bottom of the sidebar. When prompted, select an option for saving or deleting the user's Home folder, and then click *Delete User*.

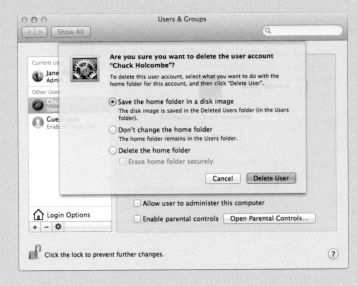

LO 7.5 | Troubleshooting Common Mac OS Problems

In this section you learn where to find basic help and a guide to the system utilities and keyboard shortcuts that can help you get out of trouble. You'll also learn how to handle the larger files that you'll encounter in today's computing environment.

Note: COMMAND+SHIFT+? opens the Help menu.

Where to Find Help

When problems arise, where do you go to find general help in OS X or from within an application?

Help with the OS

If you have questions about how the OS works, the first port of call is the help feature built into the OS. From the Finder, go to the Help menu and select *Help Center*. Now either click one of the blue links or enter a keyword in the Spotlight search box. If Help Center does not answer your questions and solve your problem, connect to the Internet and visit Apple's support center at **www.apple.com/support/**. Information there is well organized, and Apple's Knowledge Base, manuals, and related discussion groups are all fully searchable.

Alternatively, members of the network of Apple user groups around the world can get support from other users and learn more about their computers. Apple user groups are a useful and affordable way to increase your knowledge of your system and the software you choose and use. For more information, see **www.apple.com/usergroups/**.

OS X Help Center window with the Spotlight Search box on the top right.

If self-help fails and your computer is still under warranty, contact Apple directly, using the information that came with your computer. Technical support is expensive if your computer is outside its warranty period. Novice users who use their computers enough to increase the likelihood of multiple requests for support should consider signing up for an AppleCare service and support package to keep technical support costs down. Find more information at www.apple.com/support/products/.

Note: COMMAND+Q quits the open app. OPTION+COMMAND+ESC opens the Force Quit Applications box.

Help within Applications

If a problem with an open application persists, click the Help menu from the menu bar. In many cases, there will be a local help utility and an option to find online help for the application. Search through the help utility to find an answer to your problem or search the software publisher's website or the Web at large using a brief description of the problem or a part of the error message in the search string. Figure 7–19 shows the Safari help utility.

When to Quit

When you finish working with an app, you can quickly quit the app by pressing COMMAND-Q or by opening the app's menu (shown here) and selecting Quit. If an open application is behaving strangely—maybe it freezes, displaying the "busy" icon for no apparent reason—quit the application and restart it. This will resolve many transient problems.

FIGURE 7–19 The Safari Help utility.

Sometimes an application will not politely quit; that's when you must use Force Quit—either from the Apple menu or with the key combination of COMMAND+OPTION+ESC. This will bring up the Force Quit Applications box, shown here. It shows you all the running applications, so you can select the correct one. A force quit allows you to safely remove an application from memory without requiring a restart of your computer and without adversely affecting the rest of the programs running in memory.

OS X Failure to Quit

Sometimes, when you attempt to shut down, log off, or restart, you see a message that you haven't been logged out because an application has failed to quit, like the one shown here. Return to the app and close it out properly. If that does not work, use the Force Quit tool. If the application still refuses to quit, do a hard power-down by pressing and holding the power button for several seconds.

An application's Quit option.

Forgotten Password

The majority of calls to help desks are for forgotten passwords. Here we describe your options for recovering from this minor disaster.

Resetting a Password in OS X Snow Leopard or Older

The first-created user account on your computer is automatically designated an administrator. If you happen to forget or lose the administrator password, and

Select the application from the Force Quit Applications box.

Help to the Rescue!

If you're in OS X and can't remember the keyboard shortcuts for escaping a program freeze or some other action, jog your memory with OS X Help Center. Try this:

1. Click the desktop or the Finder icon on the Dock to make sure you're in the Finder.
2. Select the Help menu and select Help Center.
3. Type "Freeze" in the Help Center Search box and press ENTER.
4. Choose Shortcuts for Freezes.

if you have OS X Snow Leopard (10.6) or older, reset the password with the help of the installation disc. To do this insert the DVD and from the Install screen choose Utilities | Reset Password. Select the hard drive that contains the System folder, and use the first pop-up menu to select the name of your account. Enter your new password twice. You should keep the DVD in a safe place, because anyone with the OS X DVD can gain complete access to your system.

Note: If you *change* a password, OS X lets you keep your login keychain and assigns the new password to the keychain. When you *reset* a password, OS X creates a new login keychain for that user, and you will need to manually enter passwords and allow them to be saved in the new keychain.

Note: There is a difference between the Change Password and Reset Password features in Users & Groups. The *Change Password* button appears on the account page for the currently logged-on user, and that user must provide his or her current password before entering a new password. When you choose *Reset Password*, which an administrator can do for another user, you need to provide only the new password.

Resetting a Password in OS X Lion or Newer

With OS X Lion (10.7) or newer there is no official installation disc, so how you reset a password depends on the scenario.

You are logged in with an administrator account. If OS X is running and you are logged in with an administrator account and wish to reset the password for another account, open System Preferences | Users & Groups. If the lock is in the locked position, click it and enter your password. Select the user in the Users and Groups sidebar, and then select *Reset Password*. Enter a password, verify it by entering it a second time, provide a password hint, and then click *Reset Password*.

You have forgotten your password and cannot log in and FileVault is off. If you cannot get into OS X because you have forgotten your password, and if you don't have FileVault turned on, then at the login screen when you enter a wrong password, the Password Hint box will pop up. If the hint doesn't help, or if there is no hint, click Reset password with Apple ID. The Reset Password box will display, and you can enter your Apple ID and password, and then click Reset Password. Follow the instructions from there.

You have forgotten your password and cannot log in and FileVault is turned on. If FileVault is enabled on your computer, you may be able to use the FileVault recovery key to reset your login password. For detailed instructions, you will need to go to another computer and search support.apple.com for the article titled "If you forget your login password and FileVault is on."

The article cited walks you through the necessary steps. In short, you will first have the opportunity to attempt to login again. If that fails, and you cannot reset the password using your Apple ID, select the option to "reset it using your Recovery Key." Then enter your recovery key and reset the password. Be sure to save the new password in a safe location. Or memorize it.

Disappearing Sidebar Items

Our mantra is "Disaster is only a mouse-click away." We could write an entire book on the foibles of blithely moving objects around in any GUI. One minor but annoying problem we have had in OS X is the disappearance of Applications in the Finder Sidebar. Here is a simple solution to standard items disappearing from the Sidebar: Simply open the Finder menu, select *Preferences*, and then click *Sidebar* in the button bar. In the list of items, ensure that all the items you wish displayed have a check mark, and then close Finder preferences.

Control what appears in the Sidebar.

The Disk Utility.

Useful System Utilities

The utilities described here for OS X are useful for basic troubleshooting. As with any situation, if you find yourself in deep water, seek expert advice. Here is a quick guide to OS X's hard disk and network software utilities.

Disk Utility

Found in the OS X Utilities folder (Applications | Utilities), Disk Utility offers summary and usage statistics for all volumes attached to the computer. The utility also includes Disk First Aid, which enables you to verify or repair Mac OS Standard, Mac OS Extended, and UFS formatted disks, including hard disks and CD-ROMs. The software also works as a one-stop shop for erasing and partitioning volumes.

Network Preferences

Have you ever had a problem with your home Internet connection and found yourself talking to a help desk person from your Internet service provider (ISP)? The help desk often wants you to provide information about your network connection, such as the IP address and other configuration settings. To do that in OS X, open the Network pane in System Preferences, select the network connection in the sidebar, click the Advanced button, and then click the Hardware tab in the drop-down box. The MAC Address shows as five pairs of hexadecimal values.

Note: If your system is crashing a lot, one of the reasons may be damage to the hard disk. Running a diagnostic test with Disk Utility will reveal if there is damage.

Advanced page of the Network preferences pane.

Chapter 7 REVIEW

Chapter Summary

After reading this chapter and completing the Step-by-Step tutorials and Try This! exercises you should understand the following facts about Mac OS:

OS X History and Versions

- Stephen Wozniak, Steven Jobs, and Ronald Wayne started Apple Computer, now Apple Inc., in April of 1976 with the Apple I. The company introduced the Apple II one year later. In 1983 Apple introduced Lisa, the first production computer with a GUI.
- Apple introduced the Macintosh in 1984, the first affordable personal computer with a GUI.
- Apple introduced Mac OS X Server 1.0 in 1999 and the desktop version Mac OS X 10.0 in 2000. OS X has a UNIX core, known as Darwin.
- Apple has introduced several major versions of OS X—some within a year of the last version. It also has released many interim minor versions (10.8.1, 10.8.2, etc.).
- Find the version information on the Apple menu's *About This Mac* option.

Installing and Upgrading OS X

- OS X installs only on proprietary Apple hardware, which normally comes with the OS preinstalled.
- Before upgrading, check the version of the installed OS; you may need to upgrade to another version before upgrading to the latest version.
- Hardware requirements have not increased since OS X Leopard (10.5). You cannot upgrade some older Mac computers to the latest version. If the model is upgradable, check the firmware and make sure it has enough RAM and disk space.
- Disable disk encryption before upgrading. Decide where (which drive) to install OS X.
- Beginning with OS X 10.8 Mountain Lion, you can no longer buy OS X on DVD; you must do an online upgrade or download the installation image and burn it to DVD or USB flash drive if you want to do a clean installation.
- If you buy a new Mac, you complete the personalization of the installation with the help of the OS X Setup Assistant.
- After the installation, if you disabled disk compression or any other component or app, enable it. If you did a clean installation, you will need to

install and update apps and personalize the computer to your own preferences.
- The online installation of OS X includes all the latest updates, so you no longer need to immediately update the OS.

Navigating and Managing the OS X Desktop

- The OS X desktop has a menu bar across the top containing general functions as well as the drop-down menus for the current app.
- The Apple menu opens when you click the Apple icon in the upper left of the OS X window. Use this menu to shut down, restart, or log out, and a few other tasks.
- The Finder in OS X is the GUI face of OS X with a variety of file management tools.
- Each person who logs on to an OS X computer has a Home folder identified in the Finder windows with a house icon and the user's name. The Documents folder in Home is the default location used by many apps for each user's data files.
- System Preferences is the OS X equivalent of the Windows Control Panel.
- Switch between apps using the Dock or the Heads-Up Program Switcher.
- Drag icons on and off the Dock and configure it to be on the left side, right side, or bottom of the screen.
- See icons for all your installed programs using Launchpad, which can hold multiple screens of icons. Group program icons together in folders.
- Declutter the desktop with Mission Control, which lets you create and manage desktop Spaces.
- Notification Center displays messages about important events, such as new email and text messages or the availability of a new update at the top right of the screen. Open Notification Center to see all messages.
- Menu Extras are icons you can install at the top right of the menu bar; they open menus or controls.
- Most printers install automatically, appearing in any applications Print menu.
- If a printer does not automatically install, use the Print box, click Add Printer, and it will attempt to detect the printer.
- Use AirPlay to send local media files through an Apple TV device to a high-definition (HD) TV via Wi-Fi.

Managing Local Security in OS X

- The OS X Firewall is enabled by default. If you install or enable services on your Mac that require incoming traffic (not initiated from within), it will configure the Firewall to allow this type of traffic.
- Gatekeeper limits sources from which you can download apps. The most restrictive setting limits program downloads to the App Store. The next less-restrictive setting limits downloads to the App Store and identified developers. The Anywhere setting turns off Gatekeeper altogether.
- Using ASLR, OS X loads the kernel into random locations in memory.
- OS X apps are digitally signed and sandboxed, meaning that an app cannot access any code or devices it is not authorized to access.
- If you have important and sensitive information on your Mac, ensure that you securely encrypt your startup drive with FileVault. Additionally, use a strong password and never leave your computer unattended without logging out. When you turn on FileVault, it also encrypts your swap file, a feature called Secure Virtual Memory.
- The keychain is a secure database of a user's passwords. By default, OS X creates a keychain for you the first time you log in, using your account password as a master password for the keychain.
- OS X supports multiple local user accounts.
- The first user account in OS X is automatically designated an administrator.
- The types of user accounts in OS X are Administrator, Standard account, Sharing Only account, Guest account, and Root account.
- The Administrator account type can create new accounts, change all system preference settings, and install software in the main application and library folders.
- The Standard user account type can only access files in the user's home folder and the Shared folder (/Users/Shared/).

- The Sharing Only account type gives a remote user access to shared folders on the local computer, but this account cannot log on locally and does not have a set of local home folder.
- You cannot assign the Guest account type to any user other than the Guest User account created by OS X by default. It does not require a password, only has access to the Guest Home folder, and when the Guest logs off, the folder contents are deleted.
- The Root account has complete control over all folders and files on the Mac. Only the OS uses this account and it is disabled for interactive users by default. It seldom needs enabling.
- Automatic Login bypasses the login page and logs into the designated user account when the computer powers on. You should keep this turned off unless the computer is in a very safe environment.

Troubleshooting Common OS X Problems

- When you need help with OS X, first search through Mac Help or the Help utility for an application if you have narrowed the problem to one application.
- If an application freezes, press COMMAND-OPTION-Esc to force it to quit. OS X handles this extreme measure very well.
- A user can change his own password using Users & Groups. If a user forgets a password an administrator can reset the password, but the user will have a new, empty keychain associated with the new password. An administrator should configure her account so that she can reset her password using an Apple account. Then if the administrator forgets the password she can use the Apple account, through the login page, to reset the password.
- Use the Finder preferences pane to make folders display in the Finder sidebar.
- Erase and partition volumes and repair a damaged disk with Disk First Aid in the Disk Utility.

Key Terms List

address space layout randomization (ASLR) *(279)*

AirPlay *(277)*

Apple menu *(258)*

Automatic login *(282)*

Darwin *(254)*

Dock *(259)*

Finder *(264)*

Gatekeeper *(278)*

Guest User *(282)*

Home folder *(264)*

keychain *(280)*

Keychain Access *(280)*

Launchpad *(273)*

Mac OS X Server *(254)*

Menu Extras *(275)*

Mission Control *(274)*

Notification Center *(275)*

OS X *(255)*

OS X Setup Assistant *(257)*

recovery key *(279)*

sandboxed *(279)*

Secure Virtual Memory *(280)*

Shared folder *(281)*

Sharing Only account *(282)*

Spaces *(274)*

Spotlight *(264)*

Standard account *(281)*

System Preferences *(271)*

Time Machine *(257)*

Key Terms Quiz

Use the Key Terms List to complete the sentences that follow:

1. In a safe environment, such as your home, you can avoid entering your password at login by enabling _____.

2. To search for files use _____, a feature found in the desktop menu bar and at the top of every Finder window.

3. A user's passwords for logging on to various servers and websites are saved in a secure database called a/an _____.

4. At the core of OS X is a powerful UNIX system called _____.

5. The _____ screen displays icons for all installed apps.

6. The _____ account does not require a password, and any file or folder it creates is deleted when this user logs out.

7. _____ is to OS X as File Explorer is to Windows 8.

8. The _____ is a GUI object on the OS X desktop that holds program icons for fast launching, as well as icons for open applications you can use for task switching.

9. The _____ limits the online sources from which you can download programs.

10. The _____, accessed through a small icon at the extreme top left of the OS X screen, sounds like something the hostess hands you in a vegetarian restaurant.

Multiple-Choice Quiz

1. When did the first Mac OS appear?
   a. 1976
   b. 1983
   c. 1999
   d. 1984
   e. 2000

2. What major revision of OS X was released in the fall of 2013?
   a. Leopard
   b. Cheetah
   c. Snow Leopard
   d. Mavericks
   e. Lion

3. When you first power up a new Mac, what program starts automatically and prompts you for information?
   a. Dock
   b. Safari
   c. OS X Setup Assistant
   d. iChat
   e. System Preferences

4. Complete this sentence: In OS X, forced quits of applications . . .
   a. often cause other applications to fail.
   b. always require a restart of the OS.
   c. is not an option.
   d. usually cause a system crash.
   e. rarely affect the performance of the rest of the computer's functions.

5. Where will you quickly find version information about your OS X installation?
   a. Recent items
   b. Window menu
   c. Help menu
   d. Apple menu
   e. Finder

6. Which of the following is one of the four views available in Finder windows?
   a. Date
   b. Cover Flow
   c. Reverse
   d. Finder
   e. Jukebox

7. The Applications folder has disappeared from the Finder Sidebar. Where in the GUI can you go to put the Applications folder back into the Sidebar?
   a. System Preferences | General
   b. Utilities
   c. Sidebar | Preferences
   d. Finder | Preferences
   e. Windows | Restore

8. In addition to having an upgradable version of OS X running on one of the compatible models of Apple computer, you should also check to see if this (another system requirement) is up-to-date before upgrading to a new version of OS X.
   a. Apple ID
   b. Video drivers
   c. Firmware
   d. FileVault
   e. Gatekeeper

9. Which all-powerful account is used by the operating system, but is disabled for interactive users?
   a. Standard
   b. Group
   c. Administrator
   d. Root
   e. Global

10. You have an external hard drive from another Mac, and you would like to remove all the data on it and use it as backup for your new Mac. What will you use to prepare this disk for use?
   a. Finder
   b. Boot Camp Assistant
   c. System Preferences
   d. Tools
   e. Disk Utility

11. What type of service should you disable as a precaution before beginning an upgrade OS X?
   a. Networking
   b. Launchpad
   c. Mission Control
   d. Sharing
   e. Disk encryption

12. What keyboard shortcut can you use to force an application to quit?
   a. COMMAND-POWER key
   b. SHIFT-ESC

   c. SHIFT-RETURN
   d. COMMAND-OPTION-ESC
   e. Press C during startup

13. A Sharing Only type of account is not allowed to do which of the following?
   a. Connect over a network.
   b. Access shared folders.
   c. Log in locally.
   d. Enter a password.
   e. Enter a user name.

14. This account is automatically created by OS X; it does not require a password associated with it, has limited local access, and when this user logs out, the contents of its Home folder are deleted.
   a. Sharing Only
   b. Administrator
   c. Root
   d. Guest User
   e. Standard Account

15. Which of the following preference panes allows you to configure settings for Spaces, Dashboard, and shortcuts?
   a. Finder
   b. Mission Control
   c. Desktop & Screen Saver
   d. Dock
   e. Notifications

Essay Quiz

1. Research the significance of the UNIX core of OS X and write a few sentences describing your findings.

2. Your Mac laptop has both personal financial information and files for all your in-process school projects, including data from research for a major project in one of your classes. This laptop has two equal-sized partitions on the hard drive, and is always with you at home, at school, and at work. Describe how you will ensure the security of your valuable data.

3. Your copy of Microsoft Word suddenly freezes in midsentence. Describe the best way to regain control of your Mac.

4. When you brought your new iMac home and completed the information in the Mac OS Setup Assistant, you did not have Internet access. You have signed up for Internet access and the setup instructions from your ISP request the hardware address (MAC address) of your Wireless network card. First research and then explain where you will find this information within the OS X GUI and describe how it represents this value.

5. Describe the purpose of the Dock.

Lab Projects

LAB PROJECT 7.1

One of the users on your network, Helen Bandora, married Jon Moz, and changed her name to Helen Moz.

While it is simple enough to log into OS X as an administrator and alter her long user name to reflect her name change, changing her short name is not possible in OS X because it was used to create the

Home directory *hbandora*. Her Home directory is not particularly full, with some Microsoft Word files in the Documents folder and some MP3s in her Music folder.

You decide that it would be polite to change both login names. What do you do to give her a correctly named account?

You will need a computer with OS X installed on which you have administrator rights.

You will need to do the following:

1 Research the solution for setting up Mrs. Moz with a correctly named account.

2 Find Helen's Home directory on the hard drive.

3 Implement your solution on the lab computer.

LAB PROJECT 7.2

The manager of your department has asked you to set up a Mac with two USB printers attached and to teach a user how to print something on each of the two printers.

You will need a computer with OS X installed on which you have administrator rights, plus two USB printers. You can substitute network printers, if available. To make this lab true to life, it would be useful if one printer were a black-and-white laser printer and the other a color printer so there's a good reason someone might switch between the two.

You will need to do the following:

1 Install and check that both printers are working on your lab computer.

2 Find a willing volunteer.

3 Show the volunteer how to use the Print menu from any application to switch between printers.

LAB PROJECT 7.3

If you ever find yourself the administrator of a large network, you would want to minimize your network's electricity consumption by instituting good energy practices.

You will need a computer with OS X installed and do the following:

1 Go into the Energy Saver preferences pane and assess the various options you have for controlling the display and hard disk sleep features. Your goal is to reduce the display and hard disk sleep times to the minimum possible without causing the display to dim or the hard disk to spin down intrusively for users.

2 This is a chance to be creative and aware of the types of users of your network, and how they interact with the lab environment. Are computers used constantly, requiring a generous display or hard disk sleep time? Is the amount of RAM sufficient for working with files in memory or does the hard disk need to be accessed constantly? What kinds of software do your users use: processor and hard drive-intensive programs such as image manipulation and multimedia programs, or email and word processing software?

chapter

8

Linux on the Desktop

"But at the end of the day, the only thing that matters is actual code and the technology itself and the people who are not willing to step up and write that code, they can comment on it and they can say it should be done this way or that way or they won't, but in the end their voice doesn't matter. The only thing that matters is code."

—Linus Torvalds

In an interview conducted by Jim Zemlin, executive director of the Linux Foundation, January 2008

Learning Outcomes

In this chapter, you will learn how to:

LO **8.1** Describe Linux and its origins, and list benefits and drawbacks.

LO **8.2** Select, acquire, and install a distribution of Linux for the desktop.

LO **8.3** Identify certain features and utilities in a Linux GUI for customizing it and performing common tasks.

LO **8.4** Demonstrate the use of shell commands to accomplish common tasks.

LO **8.5** Secure a Linux desktop by creating user accounts, assigning passwords, and applying file and folder permissions.

Linux, a free operating system with many of the same qualities as UNIX, has the potential to save corporations millions of dollars. To grasp how important a free operating system is, think of an operating system as the engine of your computer. Then consider the engine in your car. An engine costs thousands of dollars, but if a company started making and distributing free engines, the cost of your new car would drop dramatically, requiring just the cost of the chassis, electrical system, radiator, passenger heater and air conditioner, radio, and many other components. Of course, the Linux community offers many of the additional software components for the OS free.

In this chapter, learn the basics of Linux on the desktop with one of the many GUIs available. Linux is far too broad a topic to give a detailed exploration here, but you will learn why Linux is growing in popularity. You will learn where to obtain Linux to test on your computer and basic configuration and navigation tasks in a Linux environment. If you have never worked with Linux before, this chapter will serve as an introduction to this OS and perhaps inspire you to study it further. ✸

LO 8.1 | Linux Overview

Linux is an open-source operating system based on UNIX. In this section discover why you should learn Linux, the features and benefits of Linux, and how and why Linux is used today.

Why Learn Linux?

Learning Linux can be very beneficial to your future career because of its growing importance on all types of computers. Like Windows and Mac OS X, you will find Linux on both desktops and servers.

Qualifying for a Job

If you are interested in a job in Information Technology (IT) or a related field, you should familiarize yourself with Linux. Because it is similar to UNIX, learning Linux prepares you for working with UNIX. Both Linux and UNIX are used recognized as stable server OS and used on servers worldwide. You are advertising your intelligence, initiative, and computer ability. A potential employer reviewing your résumé would see Linux knowledge as a big plus for an employee in many technology-related areas. Their reasoning is simple—if you can learn Linux, then you should quickly learn the idiosyncrasies of an organization's internal computer systems.

Improving Your Skills

Another reason to learn Linux is to improve your computer skills for working in a non-GUI environment, thus forcing you to be precise. Any OS is unforgiving when given the wrong instructions, but it doesn't take precision to browse a GUI and select the correct graphical object, which is how a GUI buffers users from the precision required by the operating system. The command-line interface (CLI) does not offer that buffer. In the IT networking environment the typical router or switch is managed using shell commands in a CLI.

The Evolution of Linux

In the early 1970s, Ken Thompson, a developer working at Bell Labs, was criticized for playing a computer game on company equipment. Thompson's response to the criticism was to find an unused computer and write an operating system that would run his game. This operating system became the foundation of UNIX, which has gone on to power the computers of many universities, corporations, and governments of the world. UNIX has become a powerful, stable, and fast system. While UNIX is not Linux, the latter does owe its existence to individuals like Thompson who looked at what he had done with UNIX and decided to create something similar. Below are just some of the important milestones in the evolution of Linux.

1984

In 1984, interested persons created the **GNU** organization to develop a free version of a UNIX-like operating system (GNU is a recursive acronym

Note: Learn more about GNU at **www.gnu.org**

for GNU's Not Unix). Since its founding, GNU members have developed versions of Linux, as well as thousands of applications that run on UNIX and Linux platforms. Some of these apps are bundled with distributions of Linux.

1988

In 1988, a group of UNIX licensees formed the Open Systems Foundation (OSF) to lobby for an "open" UNIX after AT&T formed a partnership with Sun Microsystems to develop a single proprietary UNIX with the best features of many versions. In response, AT&T and other licensees formed UNIX International to oppose the OSF. The trade press called the maneuverings of these two groups the "UNIX wars."

1991

In 1991, Linus Torvalds wanted to write a better, open-source version of MINIX, a UNIX-like operating system. Open-source software is distributed with all of its source code, which is the uncompiled program statements that can be viewed and edited with a text editor or special programming software. Linux is written in the C language as one or more text files, and then compiled, using a program called a C compiler, into binary object code. The object code is, essentially, an executable program in yet another language that can be interpreted by a computer's CPU or operating system and loaded into memory as a running program. A compiled program cannot be edited, but source code can be, allowing developers to customize the software as necessary.

In return for access to source code, developers commit to freely distributing the modified code. Torvalds and a team of programmers succeeded in his original goal, but he receives no direct financial gain because he does not own Linux—just the name—and the open-source community could easily decide to rename it. But we don't believe that will happen because of Torvalds's fame and the very nature of the Linux community.

1994

Because the software was open source, many individuals and several companies modified the kernel. Two of the versions available in 1994 were the Slackware and Red Hat kernels, both written in the C++ language; both with TCP/IP functionality for communicating on the Internet as well as primitive Web servers. To obtain a copy, one simply went to an Internet site and selected the distribution to download. This is true today, with many more sources for the code.

Note: The kernel is the core of the operating system. It contains all of the program code needed to allow the user to interact with the computer. The Linux kernel's code is freely available to any who wish to download it. Along with a great deal of other information, you can find the latest version of the Linux kernel at www.kernel.org. However, that alone is not what we download and install on our computers in this chapter; we download the kernel, plus drivers, services, and apps, all bundled together in a single ISO image.

Linux Today

The open-source movement has gained credibility in part because vendors such as Novell and IBM integrated open-source software into their product mix. The notion of free and open software, with no one entity owning the source code, thrives today and has the support of many organizations that

try this!

Research the Open-Source Debate

View the current arguments in the open-source debate. Try this:

1. Use your favorite Internet search engine to find recent articles on "open-source debate."
2. Look at the arguments on the pro-open-source side and the pro-proprietary side.
3. Who appear to be the major players on each side?

Note: The World Wide Web (WWW) (also called the Web) is the graphical Internet consisting of a vast array of documents located on millions of specialized servers worldwide. Hypertext Transfer Protocol (HTTP) is the protocol for transferring the files that make up the rich graphical Web pages we view on the Web. Using HTTP commands, a Web browser requests Web pages from a Web server to display on the screen of a local computer.

Note: Terminology for Linux is a little different from other OSs. When you buy or download a version of Linux you get a distribution, sometimes called a "distro," that includes the Linux kernel and a whole set of programs that work together to make a functioning version of Linux. Most distributions include a number of Linux applications. There are many distributions of Linux!

previously opposed it. Linux is the best example of this phenomenon and its popularity is growing. Manufacturers that previously featured mostly UNIX servers added Linux to their server lines. These vendors offer inexpensive Linux servers running the open-source Apache HTTP Server, often simply called "Apache." This Web server software was originally written for UNIX but also runs on Linux. In the past, separate versions have been available for other operating systems, including Windows. Apache is one of the most widely used Web servers due to its stability, security, and cost (free).

Benefits of Linux

There are several benefits to using Linux on your desktop computer.

Linux Is Free

The first benefit of Linux is cost. You may freely download many versions of Linux from the Web. Many sites, such as www.linuxlookup.com, offer Linux distributions in convenient ISO images. If you don't want to download these distributions, you may purchase prepackaged versions of Linux online or in computer stores for modest cost.

Canonical is the company behind the open-source Ubuntu Linux distributions, updating the OS frequently. In addition, they are involved in other open-source projects and offer consulting services, which is how they pay their employees and keep the lights on and the servers running.

The Fedora Project is the organization founded in 2003 by Red Hat and other contributors. The resulting Fedora Linux distributions are open source, and also the basis for Red Hat's commercially available Red Hat Enterprise Linux (RHEL).

Linux Can Run on Old Equipment

In addition to being free or inexpensive, Linux can run on old equipment. A nonprofit organization could provide computers for its employees with donated or very inexpensive equipment. There are countless situations in which computers too underpowered to run even an outdated version of Windows, continue to run reliably for years—as Web servers! The requirements for the latest version of the Ubuntu Linux Desktop Edition are:

- 700 MHz processor.
- 512 MB RAM.
- 5 GB of free space on a hard drive, USB thumb drive, or external hard drive.
- VGA compatible video adapter capable of 1024 × 768 screen resolution.
- A CD or DVD drive or a USB port if using USB-attached installation media.

Linux Is Fast

While Linux runs respectably well on old computers, it is even faster on newer computers. This is because Linux programs are very lean and efficient. They use as few resources as possible, graphics use in Linux is optional, and many Linux applications use few, if any, graphics. Graphics can slow a system's response time, making it seem slower than it truly is.

Linux Can Have a GUI

Unlike Windows, Linux was not intended to have a GUI, but rather just a text-only shell. A shell is the user interface to an OS; it accepts commands and displays error messages and other screen output. The traditional Linux shell

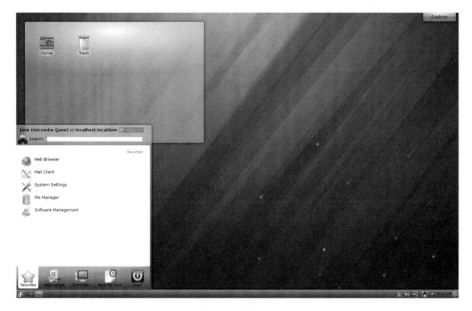

FIGURE 8–1 The KDE GUI in a Fedora installation.

is a command-line interface (CLI), such as the BASH shell. The term shell command is most often applied to text commands entered through a CLI shell.

Many distributions of Linux, especially those for desktop computers, come with a GUI shell created to a standard for Linux, X Window System. This standard was developed in 1984 at MIT for use with UNIX. An interested group formed the X Consortium in 1986 to continue the development of the X Window System (commonly called X Window or simply "X"). The Open Group then continued the work, beginning in 1997.

Many Linux GUIs are available today, including, but not limited to GNOME (usually pronounced "nome") and KDE. These competing Linux GUIs have improved over the years and various groups have developed their own GUIs, targeting different types of users. We find them as easy to work with as the Microsoft Windows or Mac OS X GUIs, after some practice. Figure 8–1 shows the KDE GUI bundled with a Fedora distribution. It has a bar across the bottom, much like the Windows taskbar, as well as a Fedora button (with a script "f" on it) on the far left of the bar. This button opens Kickoff Application Launcher. Figure 8–1 shows the result of clicking this button.

Linux Is Stable

Linux code is well written, which increases the speed at which Linux runs and improves the stability of the operating system. Linux is next to impossible to crash. If an application crashes, you can simply remove the program from memory and restart it (the program). This is why people use Linux on Web servers where stability is crucial.

Linux Is Secure

Linux is a secure operating system with all the appropriate security options, as well as the benefit of not being as much of a hacker target as Windows operating systems are. As open-source software, Linux has the advantage of having legions of programmers working to make it a better and more secure OS.

Linux Is Open Source

Finally, Linux is open-source software. This means users can read the source code and modify it as needed. This probably means little to the average user of the final version of a Linux kernel. However, during development, "beta" releases of the kernel are available to developers who download the code and test it thoroughly, searching for problems and correcting the code. This process helps to ensure an as-well-written-as-possible final release of the kernel.

Once they release a final version, developers can adjust the kernel as needed. We know a developer who modified his kernel to be more usable for vision-impaired users. He added better support for large-print output and a command-line narrator that reads the information on the command line out loud. Open source allowed the developer to modify his code to suit his needs.

Drawbacks of Linux

Even though Linux is widely used on corporate servers, websites, and large-scale networking environments, you still won't find many people using it on their home desktop computers. There are several reasons for this.

Lack of Centralized Support

No system is 100 percent secure; however, Microsoft products do have extensive documentation and support. Microsoft releases service packs and frequent updates to fix discovered vulnerabilities. Linux does not have this centralized support. When you purchase Linux from vendors it is often supported by vendor-provided documentation and user groups, but support and documentation for free Linux can be spotty. A user who downloads Linux from the Internet may receive only a downloadable manual and access to online help pages. It is true that the Linux community is growing, and there are many active user groups, but one must search them out and expend considerable time and effort to get questions answered.

Choice of GUIs Is Confusing

The fact that you can choose from various GUIs is confusing. Users want what they know, and the Linux GUIs, while responding to most of the same mouse and keyboard shortcuts as Windows and OS X, are still different from both Windows and each other, requiring some exploration and self-training. For instance, the desktop shown in the Ubuntu example in Figure 8–2 shows the new Unity desktop with a menu bar across the top, similar to OS X, and a Launcher bar along the side, unlike the GUIs for either OS X or Windows. However, the GUI shown in a Fedora distribution with a KDE GUI in Figure 8–1 has an entirely different look that is closer to the Windows Desktop with a bar across the bottom and a menu that opens from a button on the far left similar to the Windows Start Menu. Need we say more?

Limited Software Selection

People purchase computers to run applications—whether for business or for pleasure. There are important titles for Windows that are not available for Linux, so you need to check the software selection before moving to Linux on the desktop. But more titles are becoming available for Linux every year—even some very well-known titles. For example, consider Internet browsers. The most popular browsers, Mozilla Firefox, Google Chrome, and Microsoft Internet Explorer, are available for Linux, as are other browsers.

You are also limited in your choice of word processors. The most popular word processor is Microsoft Word. Chances are good that every desktop computer in your school uses Word. But Word is not available for Linux, although there are open-source programs that allow Word to work under Linux in certain circumstances. Various distributions of Linux have bundled excellent substitutions, including LibreOffice and Apache OpenOffice. Each of these is an applications suite that contains a word processor and other office productivity tools.

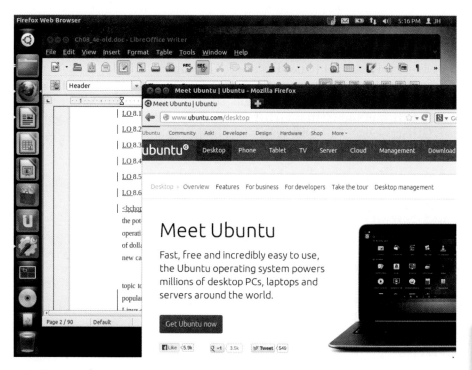

FIGURE 8–2 The Unity GUI desktop in an Ubuntu installation.

Note: Contrary to the rumors, Microsoft Office is not available for Linux, and an available version is not on the horizon. We urge you to try out the third-party office suites for Linux.

However, although both are very nice products, a proficient Microsoft Office user would have to learn how to use one with the same level of proficiency.

Figure 8–3 shows the Ubuntu Software Center, where you can search for software for an Ubuntu installation. This is similar to what Apple and Microsoft offer for their OS platforms.

Note: Versions of both LibreOffice and Apache OpenOffice are available for OS X and Windows as well as Linux.

Limited Hardware Support

Not all hardware products work with Linux, but we see this situation improving. Linux vendors work very hard to support the more common devices by providing drivers for them. Having the correct driver is crucial. If you have a new or unusual device, you may need to search the Internet for a driver. Maybe the vendor has not created a Linux driver for your new device, but there is great support among Linux users who create drivers and make them available on the Internet.

Complexity

The last block in the wall between Linux and greater success as a desktop OS is Linux's difficulty of use at the command shell, which continues to be where advanced tasks must be done. Only a limited subset of users care to invest the time and effort to learn its intricacies. Linux, like UNIX, assumes that you know what you are doing, and it assumes that you know the consequences of every command you type.

Notification Center icon

Menu bar

Notifications and Menu Extras

Dock

Trash

FIGURE 8–3 The Ubuntu Software Center.

Even with the new, improved GUI shells for Linux, it is not as easy to use as the more common operating systems. So if you implement Linux as a desktop OS, be prepared to spend time configuring Linux and providing training for other users who might need to use your computer.

Don't let this discourage you, however. By now, you have spent sufficient time working with operating systems so that you know the basic theory. You'll do fine in Linux. In this chapter we will explore how to work in Linux in a GUI as well as the basics of working in the Linux terminal window.

LO 8.2 | Linux on Your Desktop

So now that you know some of the history of Linux and its benefits and drawbacks, how will you experience it? Do you have a computer to dedicate to Linux so that you can install it? Do you plan to install it in a dual-boot configuration and continue to boot into another OS? Do you have a computer with a hypervisor in which you can create a virtual machine for testing Linux? In this section, we will describe the sources of Linux distributions for desktop computers and test an option you may not have considered for experiencing Linux: a live image.

Acquiring Linux for the Desktop

There are many distributions of Linux, and many sources for them. The most important criterion to keep in mind before selecting one is the role you wish the Linux computer to play—will it be a server or a desktop? When selecting a source, select one that meets your support needs. Are you a developer who wants to participate in the further development of Linux and Linux apps? If so, you can join a community of like-minded people at one of many websites where they gather. Since this is a survey class, we will assume that most students reading this are only interested in getting acquainted with Linux to understand its place in the world.

Our criteria for a distribution to feature in this chapter was for a desktop version of Linux that we can download and use quickly and easily. We selected two: Ubuntu and Fedora. Learn more about each of these distributions at the following websites:

- Ubuntu (**www.ubuntu.com**)
- Fedora (**www.fedoraproject.org**)

While we have downloaded and installed Linux from both sources, we chose Ubuntu Desktop Edition for most of our examples in this chapter mainly because we had worked with it with some success in the past. Both sources provide an ISO file that allows you to create a bootable disc. When you boot from the disc, you choose to install Linux onto the local computer or to boot into a live image of Linux. A live image is a bootable image of the operating system that will run from disc or other bootable media without requiring that the OS be installed on the local computer. This feature is sometimes called a Live CD, but that term is becoming somewhat outdated by the fact that you can now create a bootable CD, DVD, or solid-state drive (flash drive). Many system administrators create custom live images that include both an OS and handy utilities. When an OS fails, an administrator can boot up with the live image and use the utilities for diagnostics, troubleshooting, and data recovery. After downloading an ISO file, burn it to a disc or install it on a flash drive and you can then boot up the OS.

The Ubuntu distribution we selected includes a complete software bundle: the Unity GUI desktop and a number of GUI applications including LibreOffice, Firefox, and software selections for many other functions, such as email, chat, social networking, music streaming, photo management and editing, and more. The download for this edition is 700 MB.

The various versions of Linux have many things in common, so what you learn about one version will carry over to another version.

Step-by-Step 8.01

Downloading Linux and Creating a Live Image

This step-by-step exercise takes you through downloading a distribution of Linux and burning the image to a disc, which you can then use in the remainder of the class. The instructions and illustrations are for using a Windows 7 computer to download an Ubuntu Linux ISO file and to create a bootable DVD. You can complete this exercise using another distribution of Linux, and the steps will be similar. To complete this exercise you will need:

- A Windows 7 computer (if using another OS, the steps and screens will differ from those shown here).
- An optical drive capable of burning a disc.
- Broadband Internet access.
- A blank DVD disc.

Step 1

Use your browser to connect to **www.ubuntu.com**. Browse to the Download page by clicking the *Download* link at the top of the Ubuntu home page. If the website has changed and no longer shows this link, search for an appropriate link.

Step 2

Click the red link labeled *Ubuntu Desktop* (next to the down arrow). On the Download Ubuntu Desktop page read the information about the choices available. In our case, we picked the first choice, but also made sure to select the 64-bit version. Click the button to download, which in this case is the large button labeled *Ubuntu 12.04 LTS*.

Step 3

Before the download begins, it will ask you to contribute money, but this is not mandatory. Contribute if you wish and then download or scroll to the bottom of the page and follow the instructions to start the download.

Step 4

This illustration shows the dialog box you will see when using Firefox to download. If you are using Internet Explorer, a slender box will display along the bottom of the window, with basically the same choices. Choose to save the ISO file and click OK (Firefox) or Save (Internet Explorer). With either browser, the file will be saved in your Downloads folder.

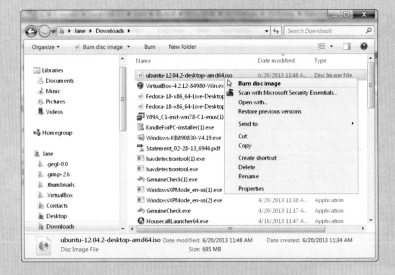

Step 5

Create the bootable disc by using the ISO image you downloaded. To do that in Windows 7 browse to the Downloads folder, right-click on the Ubuntu file, and select *Burn disc image*.

Step 6

Now test the disc by rebooting the computer with the disc inserted. After a brief delay during which you will see text on a black background, the Ubuntu Welcome screen displays. You have successfully downloaded Ubuntu Linux, created a bootable DVD, and are ready either to boot into Linux and explore it as a Guest or to proceed with an installation. Stay at this screen as you continue.

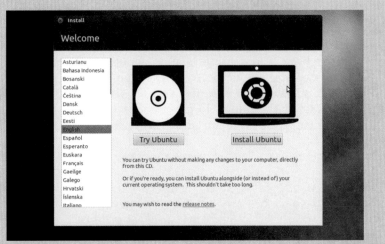

Installing Linux or Using a Live Image

If you completed Step-by-Step 8.01, you should be at the Welcome screen. If so, select a language, and then click *Try Ubuntu* if you just want to try out Ubuntu without installing it, using the live image. If you run the live image, you will not need to log in, as you will be automatically logged in with the Guest account.

Only select the second option, *Install Ubuntu*, if you are ready to install it on the same computer. If you plan to install it to another location, click the System (gear) icon in the upper right (not shown in the illustration in step 5), select *Shut Down* from the System menu and remove the disc before selecting *Shut Down* again in the confirmation box.

There are several possible scenarios for installing Linux. Just a few include a clean installation on a spare computer, a clean installation onto a second drive on a computer running another OS to create a dual-boot configuration, or an installation into a virtual machine. We installed both distributions of Linux into virtual machines on Windows 7 and Windows 8 computers. We also did clean installs onto a spare computer. We used VirtualBox as our hypervisor on both Windows 7 and Windows 8 and found Ubuntu simply worked better without tweaking it in the virtual machine, while Fedora, which was quirky in the virtual machine, ran and installed beautifully on the spare computer. Your experience may be different, as may the distribution you select.

If you did the exercises in Chapter 3 and installed a hypervisor, you only need to create a virtual machine for Linux, insert the disc you created, and start the virtual machine. If the virtual machine does not see the disc, you may need to modify the machine settings for the virtual machine to include the disc. If it recognizes the disc, the VM should start up and boot into the Ubuntu Welcome screen.

For the remainder of this chapter, leave Linux open—either using the live image or from an installation of Linux. If you choose to install it, you will find the installation is very similar to a clean installation of OS X or Windows, and shortly after you install Linux, you will see a notice that updates are ready to install. If you have time, follow the instructions for installing the updates.

We installed Linux distributions from two sources, and after each installation, there were more than 100 updates. We were not surprised, since the distributions we selected had been available for several months, and there were simply many updates. If you are installing Linux in a school lab and have limited time, do not install the updates at this point; wait until you have the time for them to install. Plan on restarting after installing the updates.

> *Note:* We recommend that you create a virtual machine for Linux, even if you plan only to boot into the live image because when you use a live image in a virtual machine you will still have access to your computer and can take notes, browse the Web, or take screen shots of the contents of the virtual machine.

LO 8.3 | Exploring a Linux GUI

In this section you will practice certain tasks in Linux using a GUI, beginning with logging in, exploring the GUI Desktop, locating tools for changing settings, modifying the desktop, and ending a Linux session.

Logging In to Ubuntu Linux

If you are running a live image of Linux, you are logged in as a Guest; but if you installed Linux, you will log in with the username and password you provided during installation. Normally, a login box will display, as shown in Figure 8–4. If you configured the Automatic Login, which is an option during the Ubuntu installation, you will not need to enter a password and will go directly to the desktop when you turn on your computer.

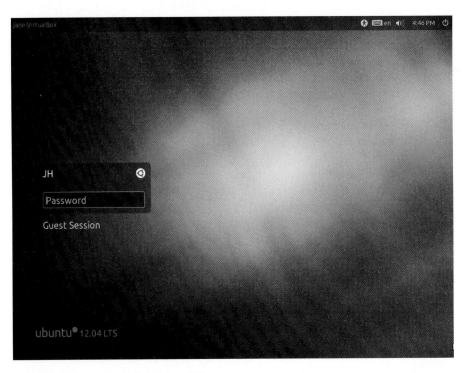

FIGURE 8–4 Log in to the Linux GUI.

In our example, the login page displays the full username we provided, which was simply uppercase initials, although full username implies both first and last names. The login username in this case is "jane" in all lowercase letters, but it is not displayed in the GUI. Whether it has a GUI or not, Linux is pervasively case-sensitive, so while the full username can include a mixture of upper and lower case, the installation program will only accept all lower case for the login username.

Notice in Figure 8–4 that you can also select *Guest Session* and log in as a Guest with no password. In that case, you will have more limited access than other users, but you will still be able to experience Linux.

The Ubuntu Unity Desktop

The Ubuntu Unity desktop has a bar across the top, which behaves much like the menu bar at the top of an OS X desktop. When no program is open on the desktop, the bar is titled *Ubuntu Desktop* on the far left and has a notification area containing various menu icons on the far right. If you simply move the cursor to the bar, a menu will display on the left with the desktop drop-down menus named *File*, *Edit*, *View*, *Go*, and *Help*.

The Ubuntu Desktop bar displays at the top of the screen in the Unity GUI.

Move the cursor to the Desktop bar to show the menus.

FIGURE 8–6 The Dash search utility displays recently used apps and files when it opens.

FIGURE 8–5 The Launcher with icons labeled.

The Ubuntu Unity desktop includes the Launcher, a bar on the left side of the screen that serves the same purpose as the OS X Dock or the pinned items feature on the taskbar on the Windows Desktop. Simply pause the mouse cursor over one of the icons on the Launcher and a title will pop out. Figure 8–5 is a screenshot we modified with a photo editor to show all the titles for the standard set of Launcher icons.

Searching in the Ubuntu Unity Desktop

The Dash is your search tool for finding apps and all types of files. To open it, click the Dash button on the Launcher or simply press the WINDOWS key. Notice that the Dash also displays recently used apps and files or folders, as shown in Figure 8–6. Clicking on the file named Ch08-4e-old.odt launches the LibreOffice Writer with that file open in it. Dash anticipates that a user may often need to search for a recently used app or file and therefore presents that information without requiring a search.

To search for a file or app, enter a search string into the Search box, shown in Figure 8–6. Dash shows matching app results in one row and file results in another row. The Try This! exercise will walk you through a search. Control where Dash searches using the icons across the bottom of the screen. When you select the house-shaped icon Dash searches your Home directory; if you select the next icon Dash searches Applications—both those that are installed and those available for download in the Ubuntu Software Center. The middle icon (resembling a document) tells Dash to

Note: Use the WINDOWS key to quickly toggle the Dash open or close.

try this!

Use a Linux GUI Search Tool

Whether you are using the Ubuntu Unity desktop or another GUI, it will have a search utility. If it is not apparent to you how to open the Search utility, use the Help utility for your distribution of Linux, which should be readily available from a menu. Try this:

1. Locate and open the Search utility.
2. In the Search box enter a search string and press the ENTER key.
3. What were the results? Did it find both apps and files that matched the search string?
4. Compare your results to others in your class.

search files and folders; selecting the musical note icon selects a search of music files; and the last icon, resembling the play button, searches for videos or movies.

Browse Directories in the GUI

Before browsing directories in either the GUI or the CLI take time to learn about the Linux directory hierarchy. It contains two types of directories. The first type consists of directories in which an ordinary user can make changes. We call these home directories. Every user has a home directory, the one place in Linux where a user has full control over files and directories without requiring elevated privileges. The second category consists of directories that the user cannot change: system directories, such as /etc and /bin, or home directories for other users.

To work with Linux directories you should understand how to use paths. A path is a description that an operating system uses to identify the location of a file or directory. In Windows, a full path to a file or directory begins with the drive designator (letter plus colon) and you build it using the backslash (\) character as separators between the drive and root directory (first backslash) and then between each of the subsequent directories in the path. Thus, a valid Windows path is C:\Winnt\System32. In Linux, you do not use a drive letter, but you use a forward slash (/) at the beginning of a path to represent the root and a forward slash (/) to separate directories in a path. A valid path is **/etc/gtk**. In Linux everything is a file identified within the file system. Files represent drives and other devices, as well as directories and files.

When you log in to Linux, your home directory becomes your current (working) directory. If you installed Linux with the defaults, your home directory path is **/home/*username***, where *username* is the user name for the account you used to log in. The default installation includes several other directories. The **bin** directory within your home directory contains many of the Linux commands. The **/etc** directory resides in the root and contains settings and configuration data for your Linux installation. Table 8–1 shows some of the default directories with brief descriptions.

Now that you know something about the directory structure on your Linux computer, find a tool in the Linux GUI for browsing the Linux

Note: Every user on a Linux computer has a home directory.

Note: While working in a GUI, you will not normally need to type in a path, nor will you often even see this notation in the GUI, but you should understand Linux paths as you navigate. You will need to understand paths if you decide to work in Linux at the CLI.

Note: While Linux is case-sensitive, Windows is case-aware, meaning that it will preserve the case used for the characters in a file name when you create it, but it does not require the correct case when retrieving or managing the file.

TABLE 8–1 Linux Default Directories

Directory	Purpose or Contents
/	The top, or root directory
/bin	Linux commands
/boot	Files to be loaded during Linux boot up
/dev	Files that represent physical devices
/etc	Linux system configuration files
/home	Home directories for each user
/lib	Shared libraries for programs and commands to use
/mnt	Mount points for removable devices
/opt	Optional (add-on) software packages
/proc	Current status of OS processes
/root	Root account home directory
/sbin	System commands and binary files
/tmp	Temporary files
/usr	Secondary hierarchy
/var	Several directories containing variable data

directories and explore the directories on your computer. A big advantage of working in a GUI is that you do not need to carefully type the names of files and directories—a fact made more important, since Linux is `case-sensitive`, meaning that it preserves the case used in the characters of a file name when created, and requires that you enter the correct case to open or manage the file. Step-by-Step 8.02 will guide you through the process of browsing the Linux directory structure. Notice that some directories have upper and lower case. You will want to remember that later when you explore Linux directories from the CLI.

Step-by-Step 8.02

Browsing the Linux File System in a GUI

In this exercise, use a GUI to browse the Linux directory structure. You will need the following:

- A computer running Linux with a GUI.
- The username and password for a user account.

Step 1

Log in to a Linux installation with a GUI. In our case, we logged in to Ubuntu Linux with the Unity GUI.

Step 2

The Unity GUI has an icon on the Launcher titled Home Folder (shown previously in Figure 8–5). Click it and a window opens focused on the currently logged-on user's home directory. This home directory contains directories created during the installation of this distribution of Linux, and it also contains directories created by the user.

Step 3

Browse through the directories in the home directory, then return to the home directory, and click the item on the left labeled File System. This opens focused on the root (the top level of the file system), which is two levels above the current user's home directory.

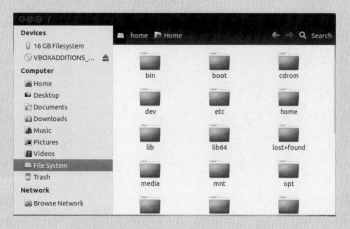

In File System double-click on the home folder to open the top-level home directory. A home directory should display for each user.

When you are finished browsing the directories, close the window.

Updating Ubuntu from the Unity Desktop

When updates to Ubuntu are available, the Update Manager icon appears in the Launcher displaying the number of updates, as shown here where the icon indicates that there are 10 updates available. Click it to open the Update Manager and install the updates.

The Update Manager icon appears on the Launcher.

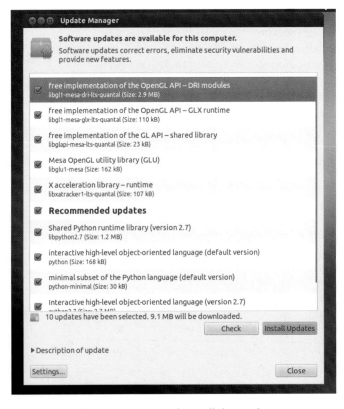

Open the Update Manager and install the updates.

System Settings

Launch System Settings from the System (gear) icon on the Launcher. Like the Control Panel in Windows and System Preferences in OS X, System Settings includes icons representing a number of settings, organized here by category. And, like the other OSs, you can call up the various control panels by other actions. Like OS X System Preferences, once you open a panel, such as Appearance, you can return to the main System Settings page by selecting *All Settings* from the bar at the top of the window.

Modify the Desktop

Modify the desktop to suit your personal tastes. As with Windows you can access desktop background settings by locating these settings through something like Control Panel, called System Settings (shown here) or right-click on the desktop and select *Change Desktop Background* to open the Appearance page, to make changes as described in Step-by-Step 8.03.

Unity's System Settings window serves the same purpose as Windows' Control Panel and OS X's System Preferences.

Step-by-Step 8.03

Modifying the Desktop

You will need the following:

- A computer with Ubuntu installed. The steps are written for Ubuntu with the Unity GUI.

- The username and password of an administrator account for this computer.

Step 1

Right-click on an empty space on the desktop to open a context menu. Select *Change Desktop Background*.

Step 2

In the Appearance control panel select a wallpaper. As you click on a wallpaper selection on the right, the small screen on the left shows the wallpaper, and it also displays behind the window.

Click on the Behavior tab to see the changes you can make to the Launcher's behavior. If you wish to change it, click the Off button, and then you can choose to auto-hide the Launcher, decide where the hot spot will be for opening the launcher, and adjust the hot spot sensitivity. Auto-hide may not work in a virtual machine.

No need to click an OK button; changes are made as soon as you select them. In our case, we selected a new wallpaper but did not change the behavior of the Launcher.

Return to System Settings and open Brightness and Lock. Here you can select the amount of time your computer can be inactive before the screen turns off. If Lock is off, then a simple key press or mouse motion will wake up the screen. You can also turn on Lock and require a password to wake the computer from suspend. Return to All Settings when you finish with this window.

Step 6

In All Settings, select *Displays*. This is where you can modify display settings. This example shows the display in a virtual machine. Return to All Settings.

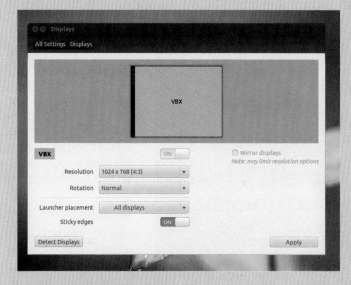

Step 7

Select *Universal Access*. This is where you can customize the Unity desktop to make it more accessible to someone who needs adjustments made for viewing the screen, listening, typing, or using a pointing device. When you are finished close the window.

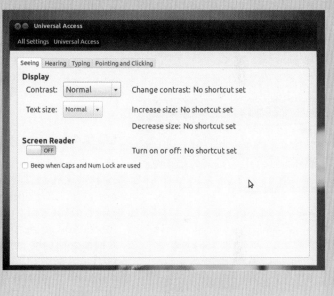

Ending a Linux Session from the GUI

As with Windows and OS X, you have choices for ending your session in Windows. You can simply log out, which is a reasonable choice if you are sharing a computer with someone else. You can shut down, which will both log you out and shut down your computer. You can restart Linux.

Logging Out of a Linux GUI Session

When you log out of Linux it ends your session, giving you an opportunity to save files before closing down all apps (and your desktop if in a GUI), but does not turn off the computer. After logging out, another user can log in, as Guest or using another account on that computer. How you log on or off a Linux GUI session depends on which GUI you are using.

If you are using the Ubuntu Unity desktop click on the System (gear) icon in the upper-right corner to open the drop-down menu shown in Figure 8–7. Then select *Log Out*. You will need to respond to the "Are you sure" to continue with Log Out. Then the session will end and after a delay a log-in page similar to the one shown back in Figure 8–4 will display.

FIGURE 8–7 The Ubuntu Unity System menu.

The **Switch User Accounts** menu.

Note: The switch users feature is also available in Windows and OS X.

Select **Shut Down**.

Note: If Ubuntu Linux with the Unity GUI is installed on a computer that supports Suspend, it will be an option from the System menu.

Note: Type the **exit** command to leave (log off) the Linux CLI. If you are using a terminal window, this closes the window—only ending that session, it does not shut down the Linux GUI in which the terminal window resides. Use the command **sudo shutdown now** from the CLI. In a terminal window, this command will shut down the computer.

Switching Users

If you have multiple accounts on a Linux computer you can take advantage of switch users, a feature that allows the currently logged-on user to leave their apps and data open in memory, switching away so that another user can log in to a separate session. Each user's session is protected, requiring a password to access again.

To switch users in Unity GUI in Ubuntu, open the Switch User Accounts menu by clicking the user icon on the right of the Desktop bar. Then either select another user to log on or click on **Switch User Account** at the top of the menu. This opens a login screen where you can select a local account and enter a password to switch to another account.

Shutting Down, Restarting, or Suspending a Linux GUI

When you shut down a Linux computer, you are logged out and the operating system closes all files and powers off the computer. When you select restart on a Linux computer, you are logged out and the operating system closes all files and then issues a restart command to the computer, without turning the power off. The operating system is then restarted and the log-in screen displays.

The option to Shut Down a computer from a Linux GUI is usually on the same menu as the Log Out option. When you select this choice in Ubuntu Unity, the Shut Down dialog box, shown here, displays. From here you can choose to *Restart, Cancel, Suspend,* or *Shut Down.*

LO 8.4 | Linux Command-Line Interface

The native Linux user interface is the command-line interface (CLI). Many installations of Linux, especially on servers, have only a CLI. Although there are great GUI options for working in Linux, system administrators still do much of the real work of supporting and managing Linux from the CLI, which forces you to be precise when entering commands. Any OS is unforgiving when given the wrong instructions, but it doesn't take precision to browse a GUI and select the correct graphical object, which is how a GUI buffers users from the precision required from a command prompt. Acquiring the habit of being precise now will help you succeed in future computer work.

To learn the commands, you must enter them at a Linux prompt. Sit at a Linux computer while reading the following sections because, as we examine various commands, you will have frequent opportunities to try them. Feel free also to experiment on your own. Note that your screen may not look exactly like the examples shown.

The Terminal Window in Linux

If you installed Linux with a GUI or are running it from a live image booted into a GUI, you can open a terminal window, equivalent to a Windows Command Prompt window, where you can experience the Linux CLI. How you do this depends on the GUI. For instance, in the Ubuntu Unity GUI, click on the Dash search tool and enter "terminal." Then select *Terminal* from the results list. That will open a terminal window, similar to the one shown in Figure 8–8.

When you open a terminal window you will see the $ prompt, which consists of the name of the currently logged-on user and the computer name. These are separated by the @ sign, which in turn is followed by a tilde (~) representing the path to your home directory. When you start a session at the $ prompt the current directory is your logged-on user's Home directory. The prompt ends with the dollar sign ($).

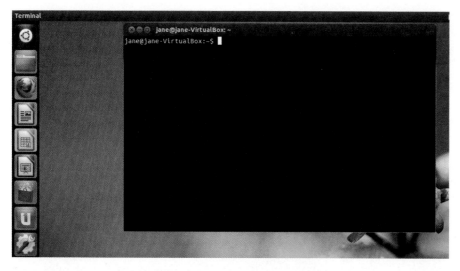

FIGURE 8–8 A terminal window in the Ubuntu Unity GUI.

If you make another directory current, the name of the current directory will be included in the $ prompt. The appearance of the $ prompt may vary somewhat among Linux versions. The blinking cursor that follows the $ prompt indicates that it is awaiting your command.

Using Linux Shell Commands

The most important thing to learn and remember about working in the Linux shell (in a terminal window or in Linux without a GUI) is that it is case-sensitive. Commands are entered in lowercase, and so are most options.

Linux Shell Command Syntax

When working at the CLI, the Linux shell command syntax follows these rules:

- All lines start with a Linux command (the first string of characters).
- A space must follow the command.
- Next come options, specific to the command, that modify its behavior. Most options are short options using a single character, while more recent options may be long (more than one character).
- Order of options is usually of little importance.
- Use a space between each option.
- Short options are preceded by a hyphen (-d); long options are preceded by two hyphens (--help).
- If you want to use multiple short options for a command you can combine them into one long option with a single hyphen at the beginning.
- Some commands are followed by what we call a parameter, which is a file name, directory, or device name. A parameter is the object that the command action targets.

try this!

Test Case Sensitivity in Linux
Test Linux case sensitivity. Try this:

1. At the Linux $ prompt enter the following command in all caps:

   MAN LS

2. Notice the resulting error message.

3. Now reenter the command in all lower case. The result is that the Linux user manual will open to the page on the command **ls**, which is the **list directory contents** command.

4. Use the SPACEBAR and UP and DOWN arrow keys to move through the manual page.

5. To quit a manual page, press **q**.

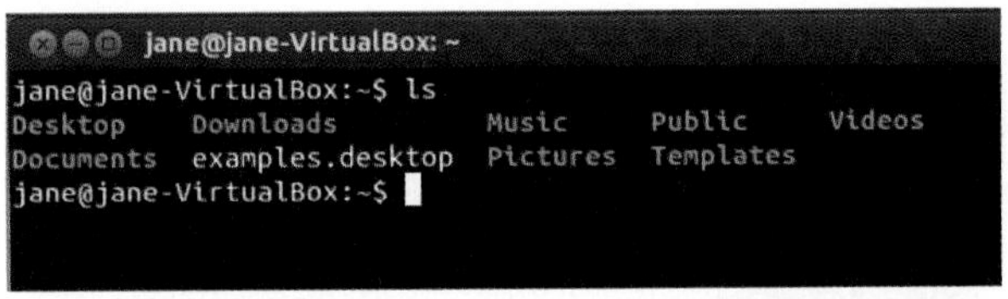

FIGURE 8–9 The **ls** command showing a simple listing of the current directory.

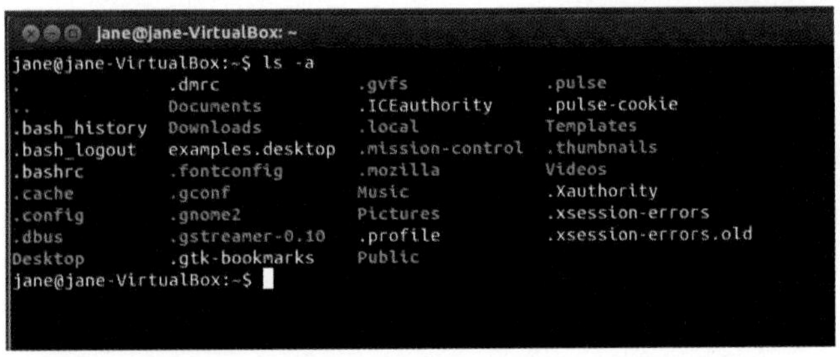

FIGURE 8–10 The **ls -a** command showing a listing of all items in the current directory.

FIGURE 8–11 The **ls** command using two options (**-a** and **–l**) showing a listing of all items in the current directory and the "long" information on each item.

In general, the command syntax in Linux follows this format:

```
command –option parameter
```

Combining Options

Now let's practice combining options. Consider the **ls** command, which lists contents of a directory, as shown in Figure 8–9, in which the command is run without any options or parameters.

It has several options, two of which are **a** (all files including hidden files) and **l** (lowercase "L") for long format listing that will include permissions, owner, size, modification time, and more. Figures 8–10 and 8–11 show the use of each of these commands alone. To use **ls** with the **a** option enter **ls –a**, which will simply list the files, as shown in Figure 8–10, but give no information about them, other than the color coding for the type of file, explained later. To use both options at once, enter **ls –al** or **ls –la**, as shown in Figure 8–11. Either will work. When too much text displays for the size of the terminal window, a scroll bar appears on the side, and you can use it to scroll through the results.

try this!

Using Multiple Options

Practice using **ls**. Run the command with a single option and then with multiple options. Try this:

1. Enter the command **ls**.
2. Notice that **ls** defaults to a column output (four across).
3. To get a long listing of this directory, enter **ls -l**. This runs the -l option on the current directory.
4. Now use multiple options. Enter **ls -la**. This provides a long listing for all files, including hidden files, in the current directory.

Note: The screen (or terminal window) gets pretty cluttered. To clear the screen and return the $ prompt to the top of an empty screen enter the **clear** command. If the screen has unusual characters on it that do not disappear with the **clear** command, use the **reset** command for a more thorough reset of the terminal window.

The Help Manual

Help is always at hand in the form of the online user manual, accessed with the **man** command. Type **man** *command* where *command* is the shell command you wish to learn more about. Figure 8–12 shows the result of entering **man ls**. This is the first page of the explanation for the **ls** command. Notice the instructions in white at the bottom of the screen. Press *h* to see an explanation of how to move through the manual. Press *q* to quit the **man** command. You can even see the documentation for the **man** command itself by entering **man man** at the $ prompt.

Command-Line History

Linux saves the shell commands you enter for the duration of the session (called command-line history), and you can scroll through these commands while at the $ prompt. Simply use the up and down arrow keys to move through the history. When you find the command you would like to reuse, you can edit the command by moving back and forth through it with the left and right arrow keys. When you are ready to use the command, simply press ENTER. Linux saves these commands in a file called .bash_history, but you do not need to know anything about this file to take advantage of this feature.

Command Completion

As you enter a command at the $ prompt, experiment with the command completion feature. Enter the command name and a few more characters of the options, then press the TAB key. Linux tries to guess what you intend to type next, and is especially clever at doing this when it looks like you are entering a directory name, indicated by the forward slash (/), but you need to give it more information than just the forward slash. For instance, when using the **cd** (change directory) command, if you enter **cd /e** and then press the TAB key, it will guess that you intended to type "etc/" and will complete it that way so that it reads **cd /etc/**. A more general term for this feature, when used in applications and search engines, is *autocompletion*.

Linux Feedback

When it comes to feedback, Linux commands are actually similar to Windows Command Prompt commands, in that they all provide cryptic feedback, communicating with you only if there is a problem. A Linux BASH command does not report when it is successful, though you'll get an error message if the command is incorrect. In this example, we first tried to change to the documents directory using the command **cd documents**. The second line shows an error. We then ran the **ls** command (third line) to see the contents (fourth and fifth lines) that showed the directory was actually named "Documents." We entered it again (sixth line), using the correct case: **cd Documents**. No message resulted from this command, although it is clear that we changed directories because the dollar prompt on the seventh line now shows Documents as the current location.

Like Windows, Linux relies heavily on a directory structure that has several predefined directories created by default during installation. Some hold important system files, and others hold user data. Linux is very similar. It has several directories for system files and a home directory for each user. You have already been introduced to a few of the file and directory management tools: **ls** and **cd** while learning the basics of working with shell commands. In this section you will use these and other commands to explore the default directories and learn more about working with Linux at the CLI.

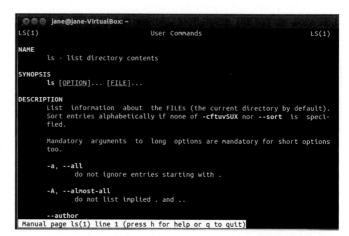

FIGURE 8–12 Enter the **man ls** command to see the manual page for the **ls** command.

What Time Is It?

Practice entering the date and calendar commands. Try this:

1. Type the command **date** and press ENTER. This will display the current date, along with the day of the week and time.
2. Now type the command **cal** and press ENTER. This will display the calendar for the current month with the day highlighted.

The **date** and **cal** commands.

A message appears only if a command causes an error.

Using Shell Commands for the Linux File System

A shorthand for this path both at the $ prompt and in a shell command is the tilde (~). Use the **ls** command to see other directories. Some have rather strange names.

In Linux everything is a file, even physical objects like a hard drive or other storage devices. Therefore, Linux shows each drive and other device simply as a part of the file system and gives it a path that begins at the root of the file system (/). Drives and other devices have assigned names, such as **/dev/sda0**, the first hard drive on an SCSI interface (indicated by **sda**); or **/dev/hda1**, the first hard drive on an IDE interface (**hda**).

Practice using shell commands to work with files and directories on your computer. Table 8–2 provides a list of basic file management commands for your reference.

You were introduced to the **ls** command earlier in this chapter and Figure 8–12 showed the use of the **man ls** command to display the manual page for this command. Table 8–3 lists and explains the commonly used options for **ls**. Recall that Linux is case-sensitive, so pay attention to the case of each option. By itself, **ls** provides only the names of visible files in the current directory, and the **–a** option that you learned about earlier lists all files and directories, even hidden files. Hidden files have names that begin with a period (.).

Listing the Contents of a Specified Directory. If you do not specify the directory you want **ls** to work on, it uses the current directory. To point ls to another directory, use the directory name as a parameter in the command. Figure 8–13 shows the result of typing **ls /etc**. The colors of the names tell you more about that file or directory.

- Blue = directory
- Green = program or binary data file such as jpeg
- Light blue or aqua = link to files in a different directory
- Pink = image file

TABLE 8–2 Basic Shell Commands for File Management

Command	Description
cd	Changes to another directory
chmod	Changes the mode or file permissions
cp	Copies a file
ls	Lists contents of a directory
mkdir	Makes a directory
more	Displays a text file, one screenful at a time
pwd	Prints the working directory
rm	Deletes a file

TABLE 8–3 Commonly Used Options for the ls Command

ls Option	Description
-a	Lists all files in the directory, including the hidden files. Files are hidden in Linux by making the first character a period, like this: **.bash_profile**
-l	Displays a long listing of the directory contents with all file attributes and permissions listed
-F	Classifies the listed objects. In particular, directory names have a / character after the name
-S	Sorts the output by size
-t	Sorts the output by time

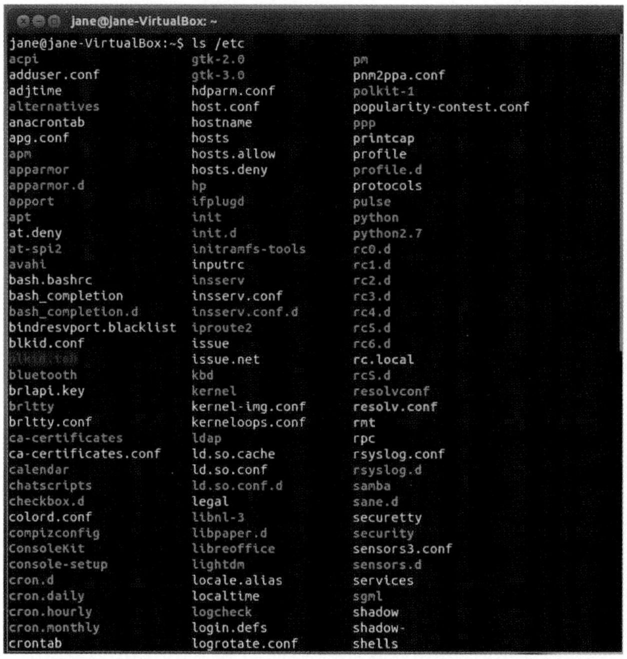

FIGURE 8-13 A listing of the **/etc** directory.

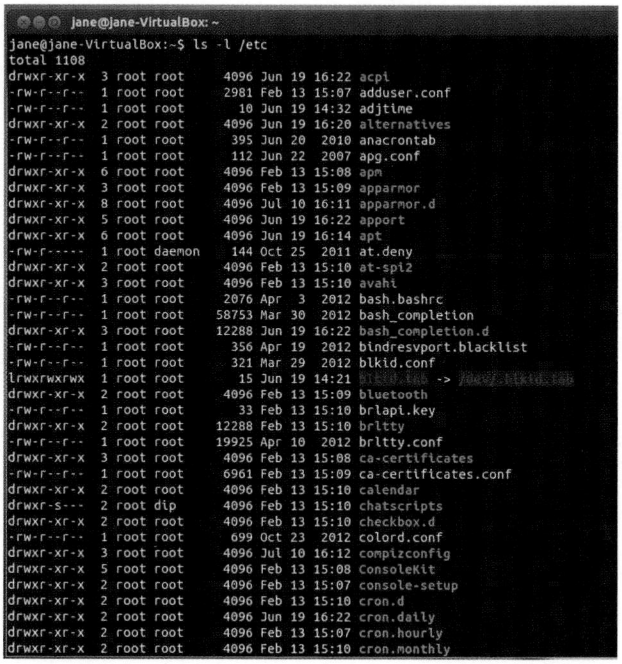

FIGURE 8-14 A listing of the **/etc** directory with more details.

- Red = compressed archive file
- White = text file
- Yellow = device

To view more details of the files in the **/etc** directory enter the command **ls -l /etc;** the output will be similar to that shown in Figure 8–14. This listing does not include hidden files because we did not use the **–a** option to see hidden files, as we did back in Figure 8–12.

In the results from using the **-l** option the first column is 10 characters wide and lists the attributes on the file or folder, which you will examine a little later in this chapter. The next column indicates the type of file. The number 1 indicates a normal file, and 2 is a directory. Higher numbers mean that the file is either a special system file or a link. The next two columns list the owner (normally the user who created the file) and last modifier of the file, respectively. The next number indicates the size of the file. The next columns indicate the file creation date and time. Lastly, it shows the name of the file. If a file is a link (light blue or aqua), it next lists the link location; the file after the arrow is the original file.

Changing the Current Directory. The command to change the current directory in Linux is **cd**. The **cd** command was used in previous examples in this chapter to illustrate the command completion feature and the need to pay attention to letter case. Let's focus on this command for itself now.

The **cd** command requires one parameter: the directory to change to. If the directory is a child of the current directory, then you only need the name to change to this directory. For example, suppose that in your home directory you have a child directory called private. To change to this directory, you enter **cd private**. If the directory is not a child of the current directory, you will need to enter the path to the directory. An absolute path will start with / (the root directory). Each directory in the path is listed after the / and separated from the next by another /. For example, to change to the **sbin** directory under the **/usr** directory, you would enter **cd /usr/sbin**. It is called an absolute path because you clearly provide its location beginning with the top level, which in Linux is the root directory.

WARNING!

To avoid seeing error messages in place of results, whenever you need to use a shell command to perform an operation on a hidden file or directory, be sure to include the (.) at the beginning of the name.

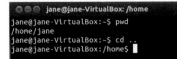

```
jane@jane-VirtualBox: /usr/sbin
jane@jane-VirtualBox:~$ cd /usr/sbin
jane@jane-VirtualBox:/usr/sbin$
```

FIGURE 8–15 Changing to the /usr/sbin directory.

```
jane@jane-VirtualBox: ~
jane@jane-VirtualBox:~$ cd /usr/sbin
jane@jane-VirtualBox:/usr/sbin$ cd ~
jane@jane-VirtualBox:~$
```

FIGURE 8–16 Changing to the Home directory using the tilde (~).

When you correctly use **cd** to change to a different directory, it rewards you with a change in your prompt. In Figure 8–15 the user started in the Home directory of the user jane, as indicated by the tilde (~) in the $ prompt, and changed to the /usr/sbin directory. The prompt changed to reflect the new directory. You can quickly change back to your personal home directory from any directory by entering **cd ~**. Figure 8–16 shows the result of entering this command.

Where Am I? Unfortunately, the Linux prompt does not (by default) show the entire path to the current directory. If you are unsure of where you are, use the command **pwd**, which stands for print working directory. It does not send anything to your printer; rather it displays (prints) the path to the working (current) directory on your screen, as shown here where the **pwd** command shows the path to the current directory (/home/jane) on the second line and then returns to the $ prompt on the third line.

```
jane@jane-VirtualBox: ~
jane@jane-VirtualBox:~$ pwd
/home/jane
jane@jane-VirtualBox:~$
```

Use the **pwd** command to display the path to the current directory.

try this!

Display the Contents of a File

Use the **more** command to display the contents of a file on the screen. Try this:

1. If a terminal window is not open, open it now.
2. If the prompt does not include a tilde (~), enter **cd ~** to ensure that you are in the Home directory.
3. Enter the command: **more .bash_history**. This will display the contents of the hidden file .bash_history, pausing after the screen is full.
4. Press the ENTER key (repeatedly) to scroll one line at a time or press the SPACEBAR to scroll one screenful at a time. Continue to the end of the output.

Relative Path. Linux allows you to use commands to navigate directories, using special symbols as shorthand for moving to directories that are relative to your current directory. For instance, the command **cd ..** will change the current directory to the next directory up in the hierarchy. If you are in your personal home directory, this command will move you to the home directory, one level up. In Figure 8–17 the first two lines show the **pwd** command and its result, showing that the /home/jane directory is current. The third line shows the command **cd ..** followed by the resulting $ prompt on the fourth line in which the /home directory is current. The /home directory is the parent directory of all the home directories on a Linux computer.

Place the .. characters between forward brackets (/) to move up additional levels. In addition, throw in a specific directory that exists at that level. For example, the command **cd ../../etc** moves up two levels and then to the etc directory. Be sure you know where you want to go, and remember, using one of these characters is supposed to save you typing. Rather than use the command string **cd ../../etc**, it is shorter to type **cd /etc**. Another special symbol is the single dot (.), which refers to the current directory.

```
jane@jane-VirtualBox: /home
jane@jane-VirtualBox:~$ pwd
/home/jane
jane@jane-VirtualBox:~$ cd ..
jane@jane-VirtualBox:/home$
```

FIGURE 8–17 Use the command **cd ..** to move to the parent directory of the current directory.

try this!

Using Relative Path Statements

A little practice with relative paths is helpful. Try this:

1. Type the command: **cd ..**
2. Return to your home directory by typing: **cd ~**
3. Now move to the /etc directory using a relative path: **cd ../../etc**
4. Return to your home directory by typing: **cd ~**

Wildcards. Linux supports the use of wildcards. A wildcard is a symbol that replaces any character or string of characters in a command parameter. It is also supported in other CLIs for other OSs. The use of the asterisk (*) as a wildcard in a file name or directory name replaces all the characters from the point at which you place the asterisk to the end of the name. For instance **ls bi*** would list all files or directories that begin with "bi."

Linux wildcard support is flexible. You can enter a range of characters as a wildcard. For instance, if you enter **ls [c-d]*** the **ls** command will display all files in the current directory that begin with the letters *c* through *d*. The bracket symbols ([]) are part of a Linux feature called regular expressions. Linux also allows you to use the dollar sign ($) to represent a single character within a file name, a feature also supported by DOS and the Windows Command Prompt. We considered ourselves very experienced DOS users (back in its heyday), and we found that using the dollar sign was rarely worth the bother.

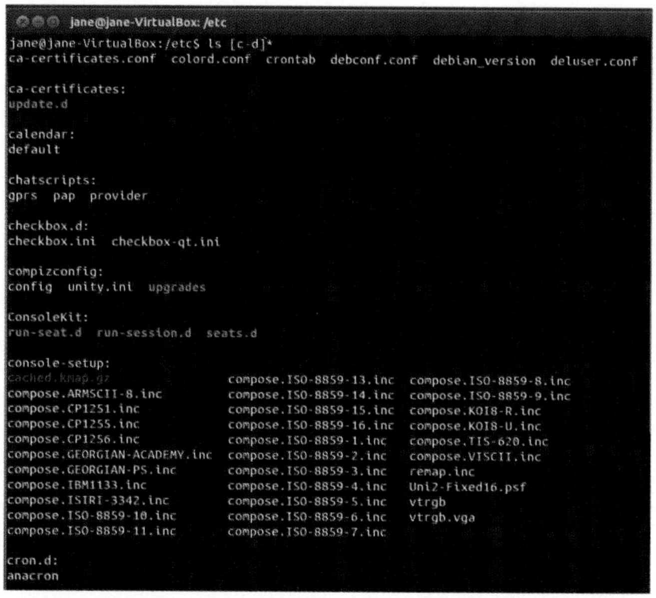

When a parameter for the **ls** command is the name of a directory the result will include the contents of that directory. Therefore, if you try the command in the example given in the previous paragraph from within the **/etc** directory the **ls [c-d]*** command will result in a long listing because each of the items that begins with either a "c" or "d" that is also a directory will cause **ls** to list the contents of that directory. Figure 8–18 shows just a portion of the output from running this command with the /etc directory current. Each line that ends with a colon is for a directory and the following line or lines display the contents of that directory. No wonder GUIs are so popular!

FIGURE 8–18 A portion of the results of the command **ls [c-d]*** when run from the **/etc** directory.

try this!

Using Wildcards

1. Change to the /etc directory (enter **cd /etc**).
2. Enter the command **ls e***. You'll see all files that begin with the letter *e*.
3. Now enter the command **ls [c-d]* /etc**.

Creating Directories

Create a directory in Linux with the **mkdir** command, which requires at least one parameter: the name of the directory to create. For example, to create a directory called junk within the current directory, enter the command **mkdir junk**. Because Linux gives you no feedback after you create a directory, use **ls** to verify that it built the directory.

If you list more than one parameter, then it will create a directory for each. Therefore, to create two directories named "sales" and "marketing" with one command, enter the command **mkdir sales marketing** (see Figure 8–19).

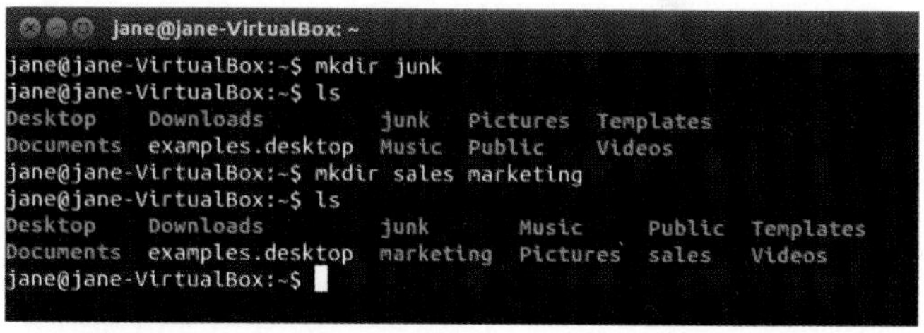

FIGURE 8–19 Use **mkdir** to create directories and **ls** to confirm that they were created.

Copying Files in Linux

The command to copy files is **cp**. We recommend you make a copy of a file before you change it. This allows you to recover from any changes you make.

The **cp** command requires two parameters. The first is the source file, which can be a file in the current directory or a file in another

try this!

Create Directories

Create directories in your home folder. Try this:

1. Enter the command **mkdir data**.
2. Use the **ls** command to confirm that it created the data directory.
3. Make several directories by entering the **mkdir** command followed by two or more names for new directories.
4. Use the **ls** command to confirm that it created the new directories.

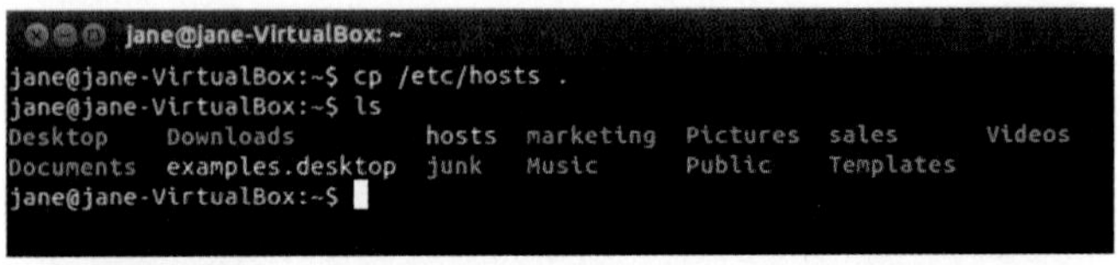

FIGURE 8–20 Copying the hosts file from the **/etc** directory to the user's home directory.

directory, as long as you provide the correct path. The second parameter is the target, which can be a target location to copy to and/or a name for the file. This makes more sense after you practice using the command.

As you can see in Figure 8–20, the file named hosts was copied from the /etc directory to the current directory. (The period at the end of the command represents the current directory.) This is just a copy, leaving the original hosts file in the /etc directory. Notice that Linux does not report that it copied a file. The figure also shows that we used the **ls** command to verify a successful copy of the file.

LO 8.5 | Securing a Linux Desktop

Linux is a very secure OS—whether you are using a GUI or a CLI. It is important to know how to configure a computer for the needs of its users. This includes managing user accounts and applying security to directories.

Managing Users

Linux allows several users to use one computer, but each user should have a unique account. When you create a user account, Linux also creates a home directory within the **/home** directory, using the user's name for the directory name. This is the place in the Linux file system where an ordinary user account has full control over directories and files. The user can both save files and create new subdirectories. Users can further protect files from other users by changing the permissions on files and folders in their home directories.

The Linux Root Account

Each installation of Linux has a root account, an all-powerful account that is only used when absolutely necessary to do advanced tasks. Ubuntu Linux comes with this account disabled in a way that no one can log in directly with the account, but there is a way to temporarily use it whenever you need it for tasks, such as creating or deleting users. However, you must be logged on with an administrator-type account to do this. You can do this from within a GUI or at a CLI in Linux. You will practice this when you create a user account in the next section.

Creating a User Account in a GUI

Step-by-Step 8.04 describes how to temporarily take on the power of the root account and add a new user in the Ubuntu Unity GUI. If you are using a different GUI, you will need to locate the GUI tool for administering user accounts. In Unity for Ubuntu, this is User Accounts.

Step-by-Step 8.04

Add a New User for User Accounts in Unity for Ubuntu

If you are adding no more than a few users to a desktop installation of Ubuntu, a GUI tool is the easiest to use. In this example we use the User Accounts tool in Unity for Ubuntu.

To complete this exercise you will need:

- A computer running Ubuntu with the Unity GUI.
- The username and password of an administrator-type account for this computer.

Step 1

Open *System Settings* in the Ubuntu Unity GUI and select *User Accounts* (on the bottom right) to open the User Accounts window. In this example there are two users. The first user created in Ubuntu, in this case JH, is automatically an administrator-type account. This user can perform administrative functions by temporarily borrowing the use of a root account. Standard users cannot do this.

Step 2

Before you can add a user you need to unlock the advanced settings in User Accounts. Do that by clicking on the Unlock icon on the top right of the User Accounts window. This opens the Authenticate dialog box. Enter your password and click the Authenticate button. This elevates your effective permissions to root, but only temporarily.

Step 3

After entering your password, you are returned to the User Accounts window. Notice that the icon on the top right has changed to a closed lock. Pause the cursor over it until the tool tip pops up with an explanation.

Step 4

To create a new user click the plus (+) button under the list of users to open the Create new account dialog box. Enter the Full name, and Linux will automatically create a Username, using the full name in all lower case with all illegal characters removed, such as the space. You can shorten the Username, if you want, as we did here.

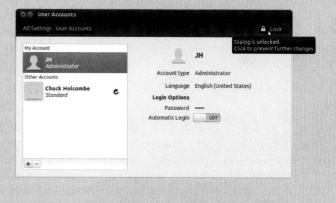

Step 5

The new user is added to the list of user accounts. To add a password for this user, click in the Password box.

Step 6

Enter a password twice and click Change.

Step 7

In the User Accounts dialog box click the close button in the upper left. The next time you open User Accounts, it will automatically be locked again.

Note: When you enter a password in a Linux CLI the characters you enter do not show on the line as you enter them. In fact nothing shows. The cursor does not move. Don't forget to press ENTER at the end of the password.

Managing User Accounts with Shell Commands

When adding many users to either a Linux desktop or server, an advanced Linux administrator will add users by creating a special script that will create a list of users much faster than using a GUI. We believe that if you need to create only a few users on a few computers, it is easier to work through the GUI. However, if you need to manage users on a Linux computer without a GUI, you will need to know how to work with shell commands. Table 8–4 lists useful commands for managing users with shell commands.

When working from a Linux CLI, temporarily assign root account privileges to the currently logged-on user (who must be an administrator-type

TABLE 8–4 Shell Commands for User Management

Command	Description
useradd	Adds a user to the system
userdel	Removes a user from the system
passwd	Changes a user's password
finger	Finds a username

account) by preceding the command you wish to run with the **sudo** command. When you use **sudo** it will prompt you to enter your password (not the root password). Then, for the next five minutes (by default) you will be able to run **sudo** without requiring a password. After this time has passed, if you run **sudo** again, you will need to enter your password. The following includes examples of using the **sudo** command to run administrative commands, beginning with the installation of software to add a command to Linux.

WARNING!

There is a good reason the **finger** command is not automatically installed. It is considered a security risk. However, you can choose to install it, and then disable it when you do not need it.

The **finger** command allows you to look up user information, but some installations of Linux (including Ubuntu) do not automatically install it. Therefore, if you want to experiment with the **finger** command, you must install the finger daemon. A daemon is a program that runs in background until it is activated by a command. Once installed, the **finger** daemon is activated by running the **finger** command. Install the **finger** daemon with this command: **sudo apt-get install finger.** This should result in the output shown here.

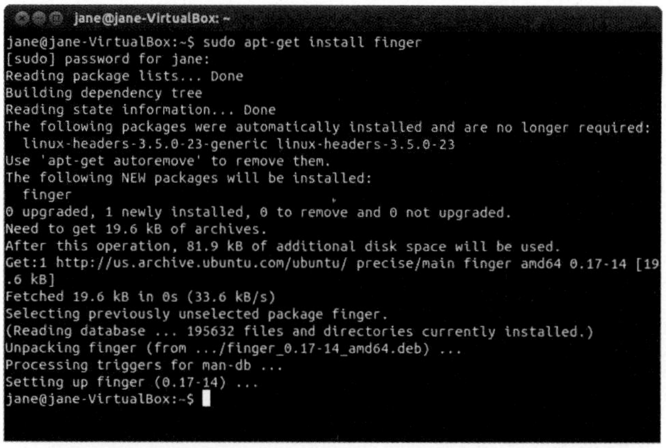

Installing the **finger** daemon.

From the command shell, use the **useradd** command preceded by **sudo** to create a user. This command requires at least one parameter, the username you want to add. If you want to create a password for this user in the same operation, use the **useradd** option **–p** followed by the password. For instance, to create an account for Ashley Phoenix using the username of aphoenix with the password pa22w0rD, enter the command **sudo useradd –p pa22w0rD aphoenix**. To verify that it created the user account, use **finger aphoenix** (see Figure 8–21).

Changing User Passwords

Changing a user's password involves the command **passwd**. Entering **passwd** without any additional parameters will let you change your own password. Any user can change his or her own password, but only a user with root privileges can change the password on other user accounts. For example, enter **sudo passwd aphoenix** to change the password for the aphoenix account. The administrator doing this does not need to know the current password for the account before changing it to the new one, but can simply enter the new password twice. Note that, as always, Linux doesn't display passwords.

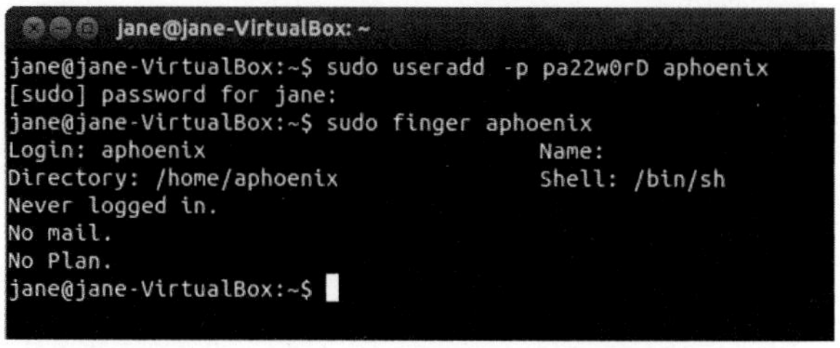

FIGURE 8–21 Create a user with the **useradd** command. Confirm its creation with the **finger** command.

Deleting Users

In any organization, employees leave. For security reasons, you should remove these accounts from the system shortly after the employee leaves. The command **userdel** allows you to remove a user from a Linux account.

The syntax for userdel is similar to that for **passwd** and **useradd**. For example, you can remove the aphoenix account with the command **userdel aphoenix**.

try this!

Creating New Users

Practice creating user accounts for Ashley Phoenix (aphoenix), Jose Martinez (jmartinez), Kiesha Olson (kolson), and Beverly Chung (bchung). Try this:

1. Precede each command with **sudo**. Start by creating one user, Ashley Phoenix.
2. Enter the command **sudo useradd –p** *password* **aphoenix**. Provide a password in place of *password*.
3. Confirm that Linux added the account by entering the command **finger aphoenix**.
4. Now add accounts for the other three people.

Recall that every user has a home directory in which to store his or her files. When you delete a user you do not remove this directory—you must remove these files manually. The long explanation for doing this is to delete the files contained in the user's home directory first; then delete the user's home directory itself. It will have the user's name. However, if a directory has subdirectories, you first need to switch into each subdirectory and delete all files in those as well. Once you have deleted the files, you change the directory to one level above and use the **rmdir** command. The syntax for **rmdir** is as follows: **rmdir *directoryname*.**

Now, for the quicker method for deleting a directory and its contents. The **rmdir** command can only remove empty directories, but the **rm** command removes a file or a directory and its contents. Use the **rm** command with the -r (remove) and -f (force) type **rm -rf** *directory-or-file-name* to remove a directory and everything below it.

WARNING!

The **rm** command is very dangerous. Be very careful, and check your spelling before hitting the ENTER key.

File and Folder Permissions

To implement security for a file or folder, you must first understand Linux file and folder attributes. When you use the **-l** option with the **ls** command you will see the attributes listed in a column of 10 characters on the far left. Each character is significant in both its placement (first, second, etc.) and in what each single character represents. The first character at the far left indicates whether the entry is a file (-), directory (**d**), or link (**l**). The next nine characters show the permissions on the file or folder for three different entities. Figure 8–22 shows a listing of a directory using both the **-l** option to show all the attributes of nonhidden entries. To decode the permissions, use the following list:

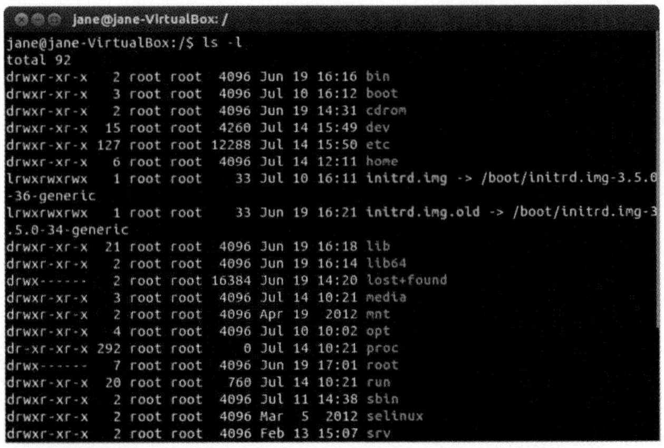

FIGURE 8–22 A sample listing showing attributes.

r = read

w = write

x = execute

- = disabled

Notice the set of permissions for the link named **initrd.img**. The attributes r (read), w (write), and x (execute) repeat three times. Linux is not repeating itself; it is listing permissions for three different individuals or groups. The first set of three permissions applies to the user who owns the files. Normally, if you create a file, then you are the owner.

The second set of three permissions applies to the group the user belongs to. We use groups to organize users, joining those with similar needs and access privileges. For example, a school may group all faculty members into a single group. This will allow instructors to create files that other instructors can read, but that students cannot read.

The third set of three permissions applies to all others. So the read, write, and execute permissions on initrd.img apply to the owner (root, in this case), the owner's group, and all others. Look at the permissions for the first entry, **bin**. The permissions on this directory are set so that the owner has read, write, and execute permissions, but the owner's group and all others have only read and execute permissions, meaning only the owner can change or delete the file.

Note:
To remember the order of the groups, think of the name UGO. UGO stands for User, Group, Other.

The command to change a file's or a directory's permissions is **chmod** (called change mode). The **chmod** command requires two options. The first option is the access mode number. The second option is the file to change.

TABLE 8–5 Access Mode Numbers

Permission	Value
Read	4
Write	2
Execute	1

There is a small calculation to perform to determine the access mode number. In Figure 8–22, the link named **initrd.img** has access mode number 777, and the directory **bin** has access mode number 755. You can calculate this number by using the values in Table 8–5. Determine the permission for each user or group by adding the values together. Thus, if the owner needs to read, write, and execute a file, the first number is $4 + 2 + 1 = 7$. If the group is also to read, write, and execute the file, the second number is also 7. If a user has permission only to read and execute a file, the value is $4 + 1 = 5$.

WARNING!

Always be sure the file owner has at least an access mode number of 6 for a file, which allows for read and write permissions. If the mode for the owner drops below 6, on some Linux installations any future access to this file is blocked. You should rarely have a file with permissions of 777 because it means that anyone can change the file.

Step-by-Step 8.05

Working with Directories

Imagine that a marketing firm that uses Linux as its primary OS hired you. You will work with a group of users. You need to create a series of directories that the group can see as well as a private directory that no one else but you can see. The following steps will allow you to create directories and set permissions on the directories. You will create these directories in your own home directory.

You will need the following:

- An account on a Linux computer with or without a GUI. If you log in to a GUI, open the terminal.
- Read access to the /etc directory.

Step 1

First create the directories needed to work. Use **mkdir** to create two directories, called wineProject and private, entering this command: **mkdir wineProject private.**

Step 2

Use the command **ls -l** to verify that Linux created the directories and to view the permissions assigned to the directories by default.

```
[jh@classlab01 wineProject]$ ls -l
total 8
-rw-rw-r--    1 jh        jh              70 Dec   3 10:11 busplan2006
-rw-rw-r--    1 jh        jh             178 Dec   3 10:10 instructor_letter
[jh@classlab01 wineProject]$ cd ~
[jh@classlab01 jh]$ ls -l
total 216
-rw-rw-r--    1 jh        jh              70 Dec   3 08:14 busplan2006
-rw-rw-r--    1 jh        jh             178 Dec   2 19:51 instructor_letter
-rw-r--r--    1 jh        jh            9283 Dec   2 22:03 mailcap
-rw-r--r--    1 jh        jh             112 Dec   2 22:03 mail.rc
-rw-r--r--    1 jh        jh            4426 Dec   2 22:03 man.config
-rw-r--r--    1 jh        jh           36823 Dec   3 06:49 mime-magic
-rw-r--r--    1 jh        jh           99960 Dec   2 22:03 mime-magic.dat
-rw-r--r--    1 jh        jh           12786 Dec   2 22:03 mime.types
-rw-r--r--    1 jh        jh            1110 Dec   2 22:03 minicom.users
-rw-r--r--    1 jh        jh             311 Dec   2 22:03 modules.conf
-rw-r--r--    1 jh        jh             281 Dec   2 22:03 modules.conf~
-rw-r--r--    1 jh        jh               0 Dec   2 22:03 motd
-rw-r--r--    1 jh        jh             242 Dec   2 22:03 mtab
-rw-r--r--    1 jh        jh            1913 Dec   2 22:04 mtools.conf
drwxrwxr-x    2 jh        jh            4096 Dec   3 10:10 private
drwxrwxr-x    2 jh        jh            4096 Dec   3 10:11 wineProject
[jh@classlab01 jh]$
```

Step 3

You are now the owner of these directories. Set the permissions on the private directory so that only you can access it, and on the wineProject directory give yourself read, write, and execute permissions, only read and write permissions to users in your group, and no permissions for others. To set the permissions appropriately enter these two commands: **chmod 700 private** and **chmod 760 wineProject.**

Step 4

Confirm the new permissions using **ls -l.**

Step 5

Populate the wineProject directory by copying two files into it from your home directory, using the **cp** command. For instance, to copy the file named "letter" type **cp letter wineProject.**

Step 6

Change to the wineProject directory by entering the command **cd wineProject.** Confirm that the files are there and view the permissions on the files. They do not inherit the permissions of the directory. You will need to modify the permissions on the files if you wish permissions more restrictive than those assigned to the directory. However, any restrictive directory permissions will keep users from accessing the contents of the directory.

Chapter 8 REVIEW

Chapter Summary

After reading this chapter and completing the Step-by-Step tutorials and Try This! exercises, you should understand the following facts about Linux:

Linux Overview

- Linux, originally created by Linus Torvalds, is free, open-source software that is like UNIX in stability and function.
- Many versions of Linux exist for all types of computers, and people often use Linux on Web servers.
- Linux benefits include cost (it is free or inexpensively bundled), the ability to run on old hardware, speed, and stability.

- Drawbacks of Linux include lack of centralized support, choice of GUIs is confusing, limited software selection, limited hardware support, and complexity.

Linux on Your Desktop

- There are many sources of Linux distributions: just two are Ubuntu (www.ubuntu.com) and Fedora (fedoraproject.org).
- Software distributions are available with GUIs and a complete software bundle of apps.

- Download a distribution as an ISO file and create a bootable DVD for installing. Popular distributions include a live image from which you can boot and run Linux without having to install it.
- As with other OSs you can install Linux as a clean installation on a spare computer, as a dual boot configuration on a computer already running another OS, or into a virtual machine.
- After installing Linux, initiate updates, as you would with Windows.

Exploring a Linux GUI

- If you boot into a live image of Linux, you are logged in as a Guest, but if you install Linux, you will log in with the username and password you provided during the installation.
- In a GUI, or at the CLI, Linux is case-sensitive.
- A Linux distribution with a GUI will have graphical objects similar, but not identical, to those in Windows and OS X.
- The Ubuntu Desktop bar displays at the top of screen in the Unity GUI, similar to the menu bar at the top of an OS X desktop.
- The Ubuntu Unity desktop includes the Launcher, a bar on the left side of the screen that serves the same purpose as the OS X Dock and the pinned items feature on the taskbar on the Windows Desktop.
- The Ubuntu Unity desktop has a search tool named Dash that lets you search for files and applications.
- Every user on a Linux computer has a home directory, the one place in Linux where a user has full control over files and directories without requiring elevated privileges. Users cannot normally change system directories, such as /etc and /bin or the directories of other users.
- A path is a description that an operating system uses to identify the location of a file or directory. In Linux you do not use a drive letter and you use a forward slash (/) character at the beginning of a path to represent the top level (root) of the file system.
- The path to a user's home directory is **/home/**_username_, where username is the username for logging in with the account.
- The **bin** directory within each user's home directory contains many of the Linux commands.
- The **/etc** directory resides in the root of the file system and contains settings and configuration data for a Linux installation.
- It is far easier to browse the Linux directory structure in a GUI than in a Linux CLI.

- The Unity GUI on Ubuntu includes an Update Manager utility for downloading and installing updates.
- Unity's System Settings window serves the same purpose as Windows' Control Panel and OS X's System Preferences.
- Modify the Unity Desktop using GUI tools similar to those in Windows and OS X.
- End a Unity Ubuntu Linux session with the Shutdown command, which will log out the currently logged-on user and turn off the computer. You can also choose to restart or suspend.

Linux Command-Line Interface

- The Linux native user interface is the CLI, and many installations, especially on servers, only have a CLI.
- If you installed Linux with a GUI or are running it from a live image booted into a GUI, you can open a terminal window, the equivalent to a Windows Command Prompt window, where you can try the Linux CLI.
- You can combine short options and precede them with a single hyphen (-).
- Some options are followed by a parameter, such as a file name, directory, or device name that the command action targets.
- The command syntax in Linux follows this format:

  ```
  command -option parameter
  ```

- The **reset** command clears the screen and returns the $ prompt to the top:
- The **man** command gives you access to the Linux manual. For instance, **man ls** displays the documentation for the **ls** command.
- Linux saves the shell commands you enter for the duration of the session, and you can scroll through these commands while at the $ prompt. Simply use the up and down arrow keys to move through the history.
- Linux has a command completion feature in which it tries to guess what you want to type next.
- The **date** command displays the day, date, and time. The **cal** command displays the calendar for the month with the current day highlighted.
- Linux gives very little feedback at the CLI, but it does issue error messages when you enter something wrong.
- Certain shell commands are useful when managing the file system. They are **cd**, **chmod**, **cp**, **ls**, **mkdir**, **more**, **pwd**, and **rm**.

- When you list the contents of a directory, the items are color coded to identify different types of entries.
- Linux allows you to use commands to navigate directories, using special symbols as shorthand for moving to directories that are relative to your current directory.
- The wildcard asterisk (*) is a symbol that replaces any character or string of characters, in a command parameter.
- Create a directory in Linux with the **mkdir** command, which requires at least one parameter: the name of the directory to create. Use multiple parameters to create multiple directories with one command.
- Use the **cp** command to copy files. It requires a parameter for the source file, and one for the target location and/or name of a file.

Securing a Linux Desktop

- If multiple people need to use one computer, each should have a unique account.
- When you create a Linux account, it also creates a home directory for the account using the user's name for the directory name.
- The **root account** is an all-powerful account that is only used when absolutely necessary to do advanced tasks. Ubuntu Linux comes with this account disabled in a way that no one can log in directly with the account, but there is a way to temporarily use it whenever you need it for tasks, such as creating or deleting users.
- Create an account using a GUI tool or by using the **useradd** command at the CLI. The **userdel** command will delete specified users, **passwd** is used to change a user's password, and the

finger daemon will confirm that a user has been created.
- Temporarily assign root account privileges to the currently logged-on user by preceding the command you intend to run with the **sudo** command. **Sudo** will prompt you to enter your password (not the root password). Then, for the next five minutes (by default) you will be able to run **sudo** without requiring a password.
- The **rmdir** command can only delete empty directories, while the **rm** command will delete a directory and its contents. This is a very dangerous command.
- When you use the **ls** command with the **-l** option it lists files and directory details. The first 10 characters are attributes. The first character is the type of entry: file (**-**), directory (**d**), or link (**l**). The next nine characters show the permission on the file or folder for three different entities (owner, group, and others).
- The characters that represent permissions are **r** for read, **w** for write, **x** for execute, and **-** for disabled.
- The command to change a file's or a directory's permissions is **chmod**. The first option for the **chmod** command is the access mode number. The second option is the file to change.
- Access mode values are 4 for read, 2 for write, and 1 for execute. These are added together to create the access mode number. If the owner, group, or other has read (4), write (2), and execute (1) permission to a file, the access mode number for that entity on that file is 7. Turning it around, an access mode number of 5 means that the entity has read and execute permissions on a file.

Key Terms List

$ prompt *(312)*

absolute path *(317)*

access mode number *(324)*

Apache HTTP Server *(296)*

BASH *(297)*

burn *(300)*

case-aware *(306)*

case-sensitive *(307)*

command completion *(315)*

command-line history *(315)*

daemon *(323)*

GNOME *(397)*

GNU *(294)*

home directory *(306)*

Hypertext Transfer Protocol (HTTP) *(296)*

Kickoff Application Launcher *(297)*

Launcher *(305)*

Linux *(294)*

live image *(300)*

object code *(295)*

open-source software *(295)*

owner *(324)*

path *(306)*

Red Hat Enterprise Linux (RHEL) *(296)*

root account *(320)*

shell *(296)*

shell command *(297)*

source code *(295)*

switch users *(312)*

terminal window *(312)*

Ubuntu *(296)*

Web *(296)*

wildcard *(318)*

World Wide Web (WWW) *(296)*

X Window *(297)*

X Window System *(297)*

Key Terms Quiz

Use the Key Terms List to complete the sentences that follow. Not all terms will be used.

1. To access the CLI in the GNOME GUI, you open a _____.

2. GNOME is an example of a/an _____ GUI.

3. At the CLI you enter commands at the _____.

4. When you create a user in Linux, the OS creates a _____ on disk for that user.

5. When you write digital data to an optical disc, you are said to _____ it.

6. A/an _____ is a program that runs in background until it is activated by a command.

7. The _____ organization was created in 1984 to develop a free UNIX-like operating system.

8. A/an _____ is a command that you must enter at the CLI.

9. Linux is an example of _____, because it is software that is distributed with all of its source code, which allows the purchaser to customize the software as necessary.

10. The most powerful account in Linux is the _____.

Multiple-Choice Quiz

1. Linux is modeled on which operating system?
   a. Windows
   b. UNIX
   c. NT
   d. VMS
   e. CP/M

2. If the access mode number for the owner of a file or directory drops below this on some Linux installations, any future access to this file is blocked.
   a. 5
   b. 8
   c. 1
   d. 7
   e. 6

3. Who was the initial developer responsible for Linux?
   a. Ken Thompson
   b. Linus Torvalds
   c. Steve Jobs
   d. Dennis Ritchie
   e. Fred Linux

4. Which user has the most power and privileges in Linux?
   a. Administrator
   b. Admin
   c. Absolute
   d. Root
   e. Linus

5. What is the command a user invokes to log off when working at the Linux shell?
   a. exit
   b. shutdown
   c. bye
   d. log off
   e. quit

6. What is the Linux shell command to copy a file?
   a. cpy
   b. rm
   c. mv
   d. copy
   e. cp

7. What option for the **ls** command lists all files in a directory, including the hidden files?
   a. -S
   b. -F
   c. -l
   d. -a
   e. -t

8. What is the shell command (and option) to turn off a Linux computer immediately?
   a. sudo down
   b. sudo shutdown now
   c. exit stat
   d. off now
   e. power off

9. What feature preserves your open apps and data, but allows another user to log in to his or her own session on the same computer?
   a. daemon
   b. lock screen
   c. live image
   d. switch users
   e. Guest

10. What organization formed in 1988 to lobby for an "open" UNIX after AT&T formed a partnership with Sun Microsystems to develop a single proprietary UNIX?

   a. GNU

   b. Apache

   c. Ubuntu

   d. BASH

   e. OSF

11. Which command displays a text file one page (screenful) at a time?

   a. mkdir

   b. more

   c. pwd

   d. cd

   e. rm

12. What command can you use at the CLI to temporarily borrow the privileges of the most powerful account in a Linux system?

   a. sudo

   b. root

   c. rm

   d. switch users

   e. chmod

13. Which Linux command can you use to change file permissions?

   a. cd

   b. ls

   c. more

   d. chmod

   e. rm

14. Why would an advanced Linux administrator use shell commands rather than a Linux GUI when creating many users at once?

   a. The shell commands are more intuitive.

   b. Linux GUIs are too cryptic.

   c. Shell commands are faster.

   d. The Linux CLI is more secure.

   e. You cannot create users from a Linux GUI.

15. When in the terminal window, which command would return you to your Home directory, no matter what directory is current?

   a. cd ..

   b. cd ~

   c. cd /

   d. chmod ~

   e. cd.

Essay Quiz

1. List and explain the reasons that Linux has not yet taken over the desktop OS market.

2. Discuss how your school or work could use Linux.

3. Discuss how open-source software can benefit an organization.

4. The Helping Hand, a charitable organization, has asked you to set up its computer systems. The organization has a very limited budget. Describe how Linux can allow users to be productive while costing very little.

5. Explain the merits of **sudo**, as implemented in Ubuntu Linux.

Lab Projects

LAB PROJECT 8.1

The Unity GUI includes workspaces, a feature not described in this chapter, although a button for using it was shown on the Launcher in Figure 8–5. Research the workspaces and write a few sentences describing the notion of workspaces in Linux.

LAB PROJECT 8.2

When installing Ubuntu Linux the **Who are you?** page has an option entitled **Require my password to log in**, and below that is another option entitled **Encrypt my home folder**. Research this last option and describe another option you should not enable after you have selected this option, along with the reason not to. Hint: locate the Getting Started with Ubuntu 12.04 manual.

LAB PROJECT 8.3

Research and describe the Suspend and Hibernate options sometimes available from the Unity Shutdown menu (accessed from the icon on the far right of the menu bar).

9 The Command-Line Interface

Who cares about the command-line interface (CLI) anyway? Why should you need to learn about using an interface that, as mentioned in Chapter 1, requires memorization of commands? One reason to do this is because Windows, OS X, and Linux OSs each still have a command-line interface for running text-based utilities; and because all of these operating systems have certain administrative utility programs that are available only from a CLI. In fact, Linux runs quite well without a GUI, and OS X is a GUI built on top of the Darwin UNIX core.

The CLI is the preferred interface for many Linux server administrators who run Linux without a GUI interface. The Linux CLI is so important that we chose not to separate it from the Linux chapter, devoting significant space in Chapter 8 to appropriate Linux commands for security settings and file management.

Developing command-line skills will increase your comfort level with a non-GUI interface anywhere you encounter one. To that end, this chapter describes and compares the CLIs in Windows 7, Windows 8, and OS X and gives you an opportunity to learn and practice your CLI skills. The beauty of working with a windowed command-line interface in a GUI environment is

Learning Outcomes

In this chapter, you will learn how to:

LO **9.1** Open the Windows 7 or Windows 8 Command Prompt in the context of a Standard user or Administrator.

LO **9.2** Use various techniques to use commands at the Windows Command Prompt.

LO **9.3** Enter CLI commands in OS X's Terminal window.

that you can have more than one window open at a time—perhaps showing the syntax in one window while you practice using the command in another.

The first section of this chapter describes the various types of Command Prompts you can open in Windows, followed by a section on running Windows Command Prompt commands. Then we move on to the CLI in an OS X Terminal.

Finishing this chapter will prepared you well for Chapter 10, which covers the client side of networking in which we use command-line commands to troubleshoot networking problems. We did not include those commands in this chapter because they will have more value to you after learning more about networking desktop computers. ✳

LO 9.1 | Introduction to the Windows Command Prompt

The Windows Command Prompt is a command-line interface launched from within Windows or from a recovery environment. The Windows Command Prompt, in all its iterations, is text-based, both in its user interface as well as in its input and output. Command Prompt commands can get some real work done, especially in working with files and disks. In this section we describe the various methods for opening Command Prompts in Windows beginning with running it from within Windows as a Standard user, then as an Administrator, and finally we explore how to open a Command Prompt from a recovery environment.

The Windows Command Prompt Is Not MS-DOS

The Windows Command Prompt runs in its own window, and defaults to a Command Prompt of simple white characters on a black background. In spite of the visual similarities between the Windows Command Prompt and Microsoft's three-decade-old CLI, MS-DOS, the Windows Command Prompt is not MS-DOS and the differences are more than skin (user interface) deep.

MS-DOS was a small OS with no security features and no native GUI and it was written for the features found in Intel CPUs of the 1980s. This limited MS-DOS to 16-bit processing and only a megabyte of address space, a large portion of which was not available for RAM memory. That is a tiny fraction of the memory installed in modern computers and used by newer operating systems and their programs. Further, MS-DOS did not support multitasking. The MS-DOS component that supported the Command Prompt and interpreted commands was a little program called command.com.

The Windows Command Prompt command interpreter, cmd.exe, provides a CLI to either 32-bit or 64-bit Windows and is subject to the security features of the Windows OS in which it runs. You will not be able to run commands requiring an Administrator unless you run the Command Prompt as an Administrator, which we will describe later.

The Windows Command Prompt Is Not Windows PowerShell

PowerShell is a CLI scripting environment for advanced users. Administrators of large Active Directory domains find PowerShell to be a more effective tool for some tasks than the GUI administrative tools that come with the Server editions of Windows. Like the Command Prompt, PowerShell runs in the 32-bit or 64-bit mode of the Windows installation. It accepts some of the same commands used at the Windows Command Prompt, but it also works

Note: DOS is an acronym for disk operating system. MS-DOS was Microsoft's DOS, arguably the most successful DOS. Microsoft has not sold or licensed MS-DOS in many years. There are other DOS operating systems for those who want a small, limited operating system, such as FreeDOS (www.freedos.org).

Note: If you expect to open the Command Prompt frequently, pin it to the Windows taskbar. Do this in both Windows 7 and Windows 8.

with three other categories of commands. It comes with Windows 7 and Windows 8, but you need to look for it if you are interested. In Windows 7, open Start, type **powershell** in the Search box, and select *PowerShell* from the results. One way to open it in Windows 8 is to open Applications and search for it. As with the Windows Command Prompt, you can run PowerShell as a Standard user or as an Administrator.

Whereas the Command Prompt only accepts text input and creates text output, PowerShell can also accept software objects, as defined in object-oriented programming. A software object has fields that define its state, and each object has a set of behaviors. Much modern programming, even in operating system code, uses object-oriented programming.

Using PowerShell is beyond the scope of this book. If you are comfortable working at the Windows Command Prompt and ready for more advanced challenges, such as creating scripts for advanced tasks in Windows 7 or Windows 8, you will find more information on PowerShell at Microsoft.com and a series of free tutorials at www.powershellpro.com. That's all we're going to say on that subject. Let's return to the Windows Command Prompt.

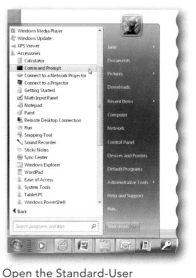

Open the Standard-User Command Prompt from the Accessories folder on the Windows 7 Start Menu.

Opening Windows 7 Command Prompts

Open the Windows 7 Command Prompt from within Windows in the context of a Standard user or in the context of an Administrator. If Windows is unstable or not working at all you may still be able to open a Command Prompt in Safe Mode or boot with the Windows 7 disc and locate a menu in which one option is a System Recover Command Prompt. In the following, you'll practice each of these methods for opening a Windows 7 Command Prompt.

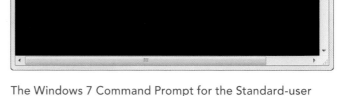

The Windows 7 Command Prompt for the Standard-user context.

The Windows 7 Standard-User Command Prompt

One way to open a Windows 7 Command Prompt is to open the Start menu, select *All Programs,* and locate Command Prompt in the Accessories folder. Once opened, the title bar for the Standard-user context simply says "Command Prompt." Within the Command Prompt window you will see the Windows version and copyright information, which is visible only at the beginning of a session. Once you fill up the window with commands and results, this information disappears. Below that is the prompt, which, by default, consists of the path to the currently logged-on user's home directory followed by a blinking cursor. A path, as defined in Chapter 8, is a description that an operating system uses to identify the location of a file or directory. You will see this on your computer when you do the Try This!

Open the Command Prompt in Windows 7

If you have access to a Windows 7 computer, open an instance of the Command Prompt, pin it to the taskbar, and leave it open while you read this chapter. Try this:

1. Open Start Menu | All Programs | Accessories | Command Prompt.
2. With the Command Prompt open, right-click on its icon in the taskbar and select **Pin this program to taskbar**.
3. Leave it open as you read through the chapter.

The Windows 7 Administrator Command Prompt

To open the Windows 7 Command Prompt in the security context of an Administrator, locate the Command Prompt in the Accessories folder (as described earlier). This time, right-click on Command Prompt and select

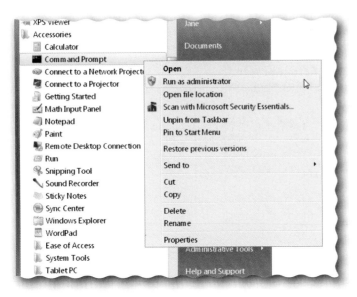

FIGURE 9–1 Select **Run as administrator.**

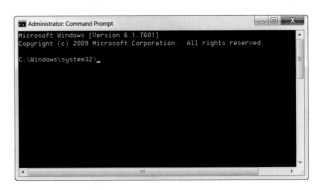

FIGURE 9–2 The Windows 7 Administrator Command Prompt.

Note: Another way to open the Windows 7 Command Prompt is by entering "cmd" at the Search box on the Start menu. Select **cmd.exe** from the results.

Note: If you are unable to open an Administrator Command Prompt it may be because the computer you are using has been configured to not allow this. This is not unusual in school labs.

WARNING!

It is not a good idea to make a habit of using the Administrator Command Prompt every time you need to run a Command Prompt command. Recall the rule of least privilege described in Chapter 2. If you run a command that requires elevated privileges you will get this message: "Error: Logged-on user does not have administrative privilege." At that point open an Administrator Command Prompt, respond to the User Account Control dialog box, and repeat the command.

Run as Administrator as shown in Figure 9–1. You will need to respond to a User Account Control dialog box before the Command Prompt will open. Figure 9–2 shows the Windows 7 Administrator Command Prompt identified in the title bar of the window. The prompt is also different from the Standard user Command Prompt in that it shows the path to the System32 directory that contains many important CLI tools.

Windows 7 Safe Mode with Command Prompt

Safe Mode with Command Prompt is a startup mode in which Windows starts without using all of the drivers and components that would normally be loaded and opens an Administrator Command Prompt window against a black background with the words "Safe Mode" in each corner of the screen, as shown here. To open it, restart a Windows 7 computer, press F8 before Windows loads, and when the Advanced Boot Options menu displays, select *Safe Mode with Command Prompt.* Because it will come up in the Administrator security context, it will prompt you to authenticate before Safe Mode with Command Prompt opens.

Windows 7 System Recovery Command Prompt

The Windows 7 System Recovery Command Prompt requires the use of the Windows 7 installation disc. Boot the computer with the Windows 7 disc as you would to install the OS. At the first screen select language, time, and currency format, and keyboard or input method and click *Next.* On the second screen, shown in the second illustration on page 335, select **Repair your computer**. This opens the System Recovery Options screen where you select the top radio button to select **Use recovery tools** . . . Click *Next* and a list of System Recovery Options displays. Select **Command Prompt** from this list and the Windows 7 System Recovery Command Prompt will display as shown in Figure 9–3. Notice that this is an Administrator Command Prompt within the recovery environment. In this Command Prompt, the focus is X:\sources. The X drive is actually a RAM disk, a disk volume created in RAM memory

Windows 7 Safe Mode with Command Prompt.

Select **Repair your computer** to access Recovery Options.

using a special driver loaded during startup. The drive letter is not significant because the software could have assigned any drive letter not required by installed hardware when creating the RAM disk. The Recovery software created the drive and the **sources** directory and then copied some program and support files to sources, perhaps because a RAM disk is very fast.

Note: We also call a RAM disk a RAM drive.

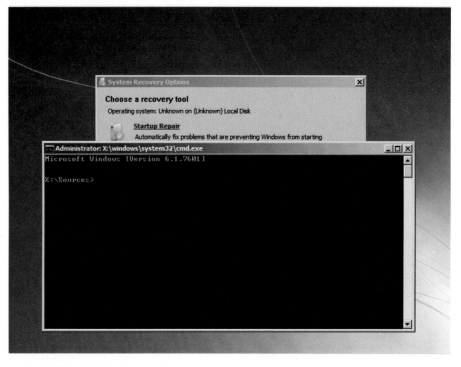

FIGURE 9–3 The Windows 7 System Recovery Command Prompt.

Select **Command Prompt** from the Power User Menu.

The Windows 8 Standard-User Command Prompt.

The Windows 8 Command Prompts

The Windows 8 Command Prompt is nearly identical to the Windows 7 Command Prompt. In this section learn how to open the Windows 8 Standard-user and Administrator Command Prompts as well as the Safe Mode and Recovery Mode Command Prompts.

Standard-User and Administrator Command Prompts

In Windows 8, open the Power Users Menu (WINDOWS KEY + X). Notice the two choices: Command Prompt and Command Prompt (Admin). The first opens the Standard-User Command Prompt, while the second opens the Administrator Command Prompt. Once opened, the prompt in the Standard-User Command Prompt resembles that in Windows 7. In this example, the currently logged-on user's home directory is C:\Users\janeh_000. The Administrator Command Prompt in Windows 8 (See Figure 9–4) is similar to that in Windows 7. You will need to respond to a User Account Control dialog, and then The Administrator Command Prompt opens focused on the System32 directory. The Try This! describes the steps to open the Windows 8 Standard-User Command Prompt.

Safe Mode and Recovery Mode Command Prompts

Windows 8 has a Safe Mode with Command Prompt. Step-by-Step 6.05 in Chapter 6, titled Exploring Windows 8 Advanced

try this!

Open the Command Prompt in Windows 8

If you are sitting at a Windows 8 computer while reading this chapter, open an instance of the Command Prompt, pin it to the taskbar on the Desktop, and leave it open while you read this chapter. Try this:

1. Open the Power User Menu with WINDOWS KEY + X and select Command Prompt.
2. With the Command Prompt open, right-click on its icon in the taskbar and select **Pin this program to taskbar**.
3. Leave it open as you read through the chapter.

FIGURE 9–4 The Windows 8 Administrator Command Prompt.

Options, includes a description in step 7 of how to open the Windows 8 Safe Mode with Command Prompt, which runs as Administrator at the Command Prompt.

Windows 8 also has a Recovery Mode Command Prompt, shown in Figure 9–5. The Windows 8 Recovery Mode does not require the use of the installation disc. If Windows 8 cannot start up normally it will start in Safe Mode or in Recovery Mode and you can access recovery tools including the Recovery Mode Command Prompt.

If you can start Windows 8, you can open the Recovery Mode through PC Settings. If you have a Windows 8 computer, practice opening this Command Prompt by following the steps in the Try This!

try this!

Open the Recovery Options Command Prompt

Explanation. Try this:

1. Open the Settings bar (WINDOWS KEY I) and select **Change PC Settings**.
2. On the PC Settings page select **Update & Recovery**.
3. On the Update and Recovery page select **Recovery**.
4. Under **Advanced startup** click or tap the **Restart now** button.
5. After the restart the Choose an option page displays. Select **Troubleshoot**.
6. On the Troubleshoot page select **Advanced Options**.
7. On the Advanced Options page select **Command Prompt**.
8. On the blue Command Prompt page select the account you will sign in with, and then enter your password and click Continue. An Administrator Command Prompt will open against a plain blue background, as shown in Figure 9–5.

FIGURE 9–5 The Windows 8 Recovery Command Prompt.

LO 9.2 | Success at the Windows Command Prompt

Up to this point, you may have done a few things at the Windows Command Prompt without much instruction. Were you successful? Or did you receive an error message? The most common reason for error messages at the Command Prompt is a typo in the command line. If you enter the wrong command name, the error will read " *'name'* is not recognized as an internal or external command, operable program, or batch file." Other error messages are associated with typos at the command line, too. For instance, if you enter a valid command name but an incorrect switch (also known as an "option") or other parameter, the error is, "The syntax of the command is incorrect." Use the up arrow to see the command-line history and check for a typo.

Success in this case means correctly entering commands and getting results that make sense. To help you have success at the Command Prompt the following sections describe:

- How the Command Prompt uses letter case.
- How the Command Prompt interprets a command.
- How it locates a program after you enter it at the prompt.
- Which command will accomplish the task you have in mind.
- Where to find the correct syntax for a command.
- How to interpret the syntax to correctly enter a command at the Command Prompt.
- How to use redirection operators.
- How to run a batch file from the Command Prompt.
- How to do file management at the Command Prompt.

Armed with this knowledge you will be able to do simple tasks at the Command Prompt.

How Does the Command Prompt Use Letter Case?

Recall that you learned in Chapter 8 that, because Linux is case-sensitive, you must be careful about letter case at the command line. How does the Windows Command Prompt work with letter case? Windows is case-aware, meaning that it will pay attention to letter case when creating files. But it is not case-sensitive, so you can open the same file without matching the letter case of the actual file. Another example of its case insensitivity is that the Command Prompt does not differentiate between uppercase and lowercase letters used in commands and file names. So, at the Command Prompt, "dir" is the same as "DIR." But if you successfully create a directory named **MYDIR** and then try to create a directory name **mydir** in the same location, you will get an error message, "A subdirectory or file mydir already exists." Experiment with case awareness in the Try This! exercise.

try this!

Test Case Awareness and Case Insensitivity

Test case awareness and case insensitivity in the Windows Command Prompt. Try this:

1. Open a Standard-User Command Prompt.
2. Type the command **DIR** (using the same case, as indicated) and press ENTER.
3. Repeat the same command in all lower case. It should run the same both times, demonstrating that the Windows Command Prompt is not case-sensitive.
4. Type **md MYDIR** and press ENTER.
5. Type **dir** and ensure that it created the directory with all uppercase letters. This indicates case awareness.
6. Try to create a directory named **mydir** in all lower case. You should receive an error message, which demonstrates case insensitivity.

How Does the Command Prompt Interpret a Command?

Learn how the Command Prompt interprets a command so that you will understand why some commands fail. As an example, consider a simple command, the **dir** command, that lists directory contents. The command interpreter interprets what you enter at the Command Prompt. It receives commands, finds the actual program code for the command, loads the program code into memory, and passes along any additional instructions from the command line. For instance, if you enter the command **dir c: /a**, the command interpreter would pass the additional parameters **c: /a** to the command **dir**.

Some commands have no additional instructions. For instance, the **ver** command displays only the Windows version and does nothing else, but most commands have several options you can use. The list of such commands is quite long; a small sample includes **del**, **md**, **ren**, and **xcopy**. Figure 9–6 shows the screen output after running the **ver**, **del**, **md**, **ren**, and **xcopy commands** without any command parameters. Notice that only the **ver** command works successfully without any further instructions.

Parsing the Command Line

Let's look at this process more closely. When you type something into the command line and press ENTER, the command interpreter kicks into action behind the scenes. It takes what you entered and parses it. In this context, parse means to divide what is entered at the command line into components in preparation for interpreting the command. The command interpreter parses the components of your entry based on special delimiter characters. A delimiter character marks the boundary between parameters. The most important delimiter character to remember is the space character (the result of pressing the space bar). When parsing a command line we call the components parameters. For instance, **dir c: /a** has three parameters: **dir**, **c:**, and **/a**. The first parameter must be the command; the other parameters must be valid options that the command understands. A parameter that begins with a forward slash (/) is called a switch.

```
Command Prompt

Microsoft Windows [Version 6.1.7601]
Copyright (c) 2009 Microsoft Corporation.  All rights reserved.

C:\Users\Jane>ver

Microsoft Windows [Version 6.1.7601]

C:\Users\Jane>del
The syntax of the command is incorrect.

C:\Users\Jane>md
The syntax of the command is incorrect.

C:\Users\Jane>ren
The syntax of the command is incorrect.

C:\Users\Jane>xcopy
Invalid number of parameters
0 File(s) copied

C:\Users\Jane>_
```

FIGURE 9–6 Command Prompt errors.

Using Spaces within a Parameter

Windows allows file and directory names to contain spaces, but when you use one of these names at the command line, each space will be treated like a delimiter. Therefore, whenever you need to type a file or directory name that includes a space, surround it with quotes, as in **xcopy "my list.txt" c:\data**.

How Is a Program Found and Loaded?

The next job for the command interpreter is to find and load the command program, matching it with the first parameter at the beginning of the command line. It searches in paths described in the registry. Let's say you entered the command **chkdsk**. You have not provided a file name extension with the command (which is quite normal), so the command interpreter will first check in various locations for the command code. First it searches its own list of internal commands. An internal command is one that resides within the operating system code and is not stored as a separate file on disk. If it finds the command name in that list, the command interpreter doesn't search any further, loads the code into memory, and passes on any other parameters that were on the command line.

Our example command, **chkdsk**, is not an internal command, which the command interpreter will discover after checking the list of internal commands. Now it will look for an external command that matches. A Command Prompt external command is a file stored on disk that contains instructions and has one of the following extensions: **.com**, **.exe**, **.bat**, or **.cmd**. (Typing **chkdsk.exe** on the command line would have told the command interpreter earlier that this was an external command.) Because we didn't include the file name extension, it is still not sure about the exact file. Now it will look for a match, using those extensions.

But wait! Where does the command interpreter look for external commands? It first looks in the current directory, and then it consults a list stored in the OS called the search path. A search path is a list of paths created and maintained by the operating system. The OS uses the search path when looking for programs and their components before loading them into memory. By simply entering **path** on the command line you will see the Windows search path for your computer. The result of running this on a Windows 8 computer was three lines, shown here.

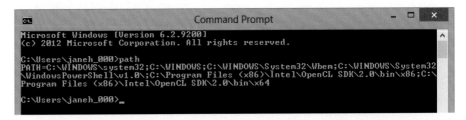

The result of using the **path** command in Windows 8.

> **Note:** There are dozens of internal commands, but you will use only a handful, such as **cd, cls, copy, date, dir, md, move, more, tree, path, echo, rem, rd, set, time, type, ver**, and **vol**. Use the HELP program (an external command) to learn more about these commands.

try this!

View the Windows Search Path

On any Windows computer, try this:

1. Open the Command Prompt.
2. Type **path** and press ENTER.
3. The result shows the Windows search path.

The external Command Prompt commands are all in one location: C:\Windows\System32. This is the first path in the search path, so if you enter a command name that the command does not find in that location (ending in .com, .exe, .bat, or .cmd), the command interpreter will continue to search in all those other locations before issuing an error message. This happens quickly. What about the other locations? Windows and installed programs use them. In fact, the System32 directory contains many graphical Windows utilities, such as Regedit, which you used in Chapter 6. You can launch some of these, including Regedit, from within a Command Prompt, but they run in their own window.

Using Redirection Operators

A command-line redirection operator is a symbol, such as the greater-than sign (>), double greater-than sign (>>), or the vertical bar (|), that affects the behavior of commands. The greater-than sign (>) redirection operator takes command output and sends it to a device (such as a printer) or to a file with the name you provide to the right of the operator. In the case of a file, if the file doesn't exist it creates the file. If a file by that name does exist, it overwrites the existing file. However, if you want to append output from a command to an existing text file, use the double greater-than operator (>>).

If you place a vertical bar, commonly called a pipe, between two commands, the command interpreter will redirect the output from the first command as input to the second command. This is called piping and is available in most (if not all) CLIs. A good use of this feature is when you discover that the output of a command scrolls out of view. You can scroll the window up to see what does not fit in the window because, by default, it saves up to 300 lines of the current session, but that's a lot of scrolling. So simply run the command again, adding the vertical bar plus the **more** command. The command you enter looks like this: *command* | **more.** The **more** command filters the input it is given and displays the first screen or window of data. The message ".. More .." displays at the bottom. You get no clue that you only need to hit SPACEBAR to advance one window at a time or press ENTER to advance one line at a time. If you want to cancel the **more** command (or any command that continues to run), simply press CTRL-C. Step-by-Step 9.01 will demonstrate the use of redirection.

Which Command Will Accomplish the Task?

To discover which command will accomplish the task you have in mind, you must do some detective work. One readily available source is the **help** command. Learn to use it. Many command names give you clues to their function. At the Command Prompt, simply type **help**, and you will get a listing of Windows Command Prompt commands with descriptions. Of course, you will need some help getting started with this, because entering **help** by itself simply sends the list to the screen, and before you know it you are staring at the end of the list. Step-by-Step 9.01 will walk you through using the Help command along with a few tips on getting command output into a usable form using redirection.

Note: Check out the command-line references available online. Enter Windows command-line reference into a search engine. The authoritative one is at Microsoft's website, but Tim Fisher at About.com has several lists that we like to use, so look for **about.com** in the search results.

Note: Press CTRL-C to cancel a command.

Step-by-Step 9.01

Using the Help Command with Redirection

In the following steps you will learn how to send the output of the **help** command to a file so that you can browse through the various commands and see a brief description. To complete this exercise, you will need a Windows computer.

Open a Standard-User Command Prompt. Type **help** and press ENTER. On a fast computer, you'll be unaware that many lines of text went by, and you're left looking at the end of the list of commands.

```
SC                Displays or configures services (background processes).
SCHTASKS          Schedules commands and programs to run on a computer.
SHIFT             Shifts the position of replaceable parameters in batch files.
SHUTDOWN          Allows proper local or remote shutdown of machine.
SORT              Sorts input.
START             Starts a separate window to run a specified program or command.
SUBST             Associates a path with a drive letter.
SYSTEMINFO        Displays machine specific properties and configuration.
TASKLIST          Displays all currently running tasks including services.
TASKKILL          Kill or stop a running process or application.
TIME              Displays or sets the system time.
TITLE             Sets the window title for a CMD.EXE session.
TREE              Graphically displays the directory structure of a drive or
                  path.
TYPE              Displays the contents of a text file.
VER               Displays the Windows version.
VERIFY            Tells Windows whether to verify that your files are written
                  correctly to a disk.
VOL               Displays a disk volume label and serial number.
XCOPY             Copies files and directory trees.
WMIC              Displays WMI information inside interactive command shell.

For more information on tools see the command-line reference in the online help.

C:\Users\janeh_000>_
```

This time repeat the command and pipe it to **more**. Type **help | more** and press ENTER. Then press the SPACEBAR to scroll one window full at a time or press ENTER to display one line at a time. If you want to end the command before you come to the end of the list, press CTRL-C to cancel.

```
C:\Users\janeh_000>help | more
For more information on a specific command, type HELP command-name
ASSOC             Displays or modifies file extension associations.
ATTRIB            Displays or changes file attributes.
BREAK             Sets or clears extended CTRL+C checking.
BCDEDIT           Sets properties in boot database to control boot loading.
CACLS             Displays or modifies access control lists (ACLs) of files.
CALL              Calls one batch program from another.
CD                Displays the name of or changes the current directory.
CHCP              Displays or sets the active code page number.
CHDIR             Displays the name of or changes the current directory.
CHKDSK            Checks a disk and displays a status report.
CHKNTFS           Displays or modifies the checking of disk at boot time.
CLS               Clears the screen.
CMD               Starts a new instance of the Windows command interpreter.
COLOR             Sets the default console foreground and background colors.
COMP              Compares the contents of two files or sets of files.
COMPACT           Displays or alters the compression of files on NTFS partitions.
CONVERT           Converts FAT volumes to NTFS.  You cannot convert the
                  current drive.
COPY              Copies one or more files to another location.
DATE              Displays or sets the date.
DEL               Deletes one or more files.
DIR               Displays a list of files and subdirectories in a directory.
DISKCOMP          Compares the contents of two floppy disks.
-- More  --
```

Repeat the command and send its output to a text file so that you can browse through the commands. To do this type **help > help.txt** and press ENTER. Then to confirm it created the file type **dir help.txt** and press ENTER.

```
C:\Users\janeh_000>help > help.txt

C:\Users\janeh_000>dir help.txt
 Volume in drive C is OS
 Volume Serial Number is B4F0-FD5F

 Directory of C:\Users\janeh_000

07/21/2013  09:09 AM            5,866 help.txt
               1 File(s)          5,866 bytes
               0 Dir(s)  396,104,884,224 bytes free

C:\Users\janeh_000>
```

Now open the file in Notepad. At the Command Prompt type **notepad help. txt**. This demonstrates opening a Windows app from within the Command Prompt.

Browse through the list of commands. Leave the Notepad window open while you continue through this chapter. You can return to it when you need a definition of a command.

```
help.txt - Notepad
File  Edit  Format  View  Help
For more information on a specific command, type HELP command-name
ASSOC          Displays or modifies file extension associations.
ATTRIB         Displays or changes file attributes.
BREAK          Sets or clears extended CTRL+C checking.
BCDEDIT        Sets properties in boot database to control boot loading.
CACLS          Displays or modifies access control lists (ACLs) of files.
CALL           Calls one batch program from another.
CD             Displays the name of or changes the current directory.
CHCP           Displays or sets the active code page number.
CHDIR          Displays the name of or changes the current directory.
CHKDSK         Checks a disk and displays a status report.
CHKNTFS        Displays or modifies the checking of disk at boot time.
CLS            Clears the screen.
CMD            Starts a new instance of the Windows command interpreter.
```

What Is the Correct Syntax?

The **help** program will help you find a command that will accomplish a task, but you also need to know how to tell the command exactly what to do. This requires that you know the syntax of the command. Command syntax is a set of rules for correctly entering a specific command at the command line. This includes the command name and the parameters that act as instructions to the command. A quick way to see the syntax for a command is enter the command name followed by **/?**, as shown in Figure 9–7. Here again, you may want to use the pipe symbol (|) and **more** command to view the information one window at a time.

```
Command Prompt
C:\Users\janeh_000>xcopy /?
Copies files and directory trees.

XCOPY source [destination] [/A | /M] [/D[:date]] [/P] [/S [/E]] [/V] [/W]
                           [/C] [/I] [/Q] [/F] [/L] [/G] [/H] [/R] [/T] [/U]
                           [/K] [/N] [/O] [/X] [/Y] [/-Y] [/Z] [/B] [/J]
                           [/EXCLUDE:file1[+file2][+file3]...]

  source       Specifies the file(s) to copy.
  destination  Specifies the location and/or name of new files.
  /A           Copies only files with the archive attribute set,
               doesn't change the attribute.
  /M           Copies only files with the archive attribute set,
               turns off the archive attribute.
  /D:m-d-y     Copies files changed on or after the specified date.
               If no date is given, copies only those files whose
               source time is newer than the destination time.
  /EXCLUDE:file1[+file2][+file3]...
               Specifies a list of files containing strings.  Each string
               should be in a separate line in the files.  When any of the
               strings match any part of the absolute path of the file to be
               copied, that file will be excluded from being copied.  For
               example, specifying a string like \obj\ or .obj will exclude
               all files underneath the directory obj or all files with the
               .obj extension respectively.
  /P           Prompts you before creating each destination file.
  /S           Copies directories and subdirectories except empty ones.
  /E           Copies directories and subdirectories, including empty ones.
               Same as /S /E. May be used to modify /T.
  /V           Verifies the size of each new file.
  /W           Prompts you to press a key before copying.
  /C           Continues copying even if errors occur.
  /I           If destination does not exist and copying more than one file,
               assumes that destination must be a directory.
  /Q           Does not display file names while copying.
  /F           Displays full source and destination file names while copying.
  /L           Displays files that would be copied.
  /G           Allows the copying of encrypted files to destination that does
               not support encryption.
  /H           Copies hidden and system files also.
  /R           Overwrites read-only files.
  /T           Creates directory structure, but does not copy files. Does not
               include empty directories or subdirectories. /T /E includes
               empty directories and subdirectories.
```

FIGURE 9–7 The **xcopy** command syntax.

Note: Practice using the **copy**, **xcopy**, and **robocopy** commands in Step-by-Step 9.02.

It won't come as a surprise to you that the syntax is cryptic. Let's look at the syntax of the **xcopy** command. This command is aware of directories, unlike the ancient **copy** command, and while more advanced commands are available at the Windows Command Prompt, we still find **xcopy** to be a handy command to use for general file and directory copying. To correctly enter this command, you must first type **xcopy** followed by the optional and required parameters in the order shown. All optional parameters are in square brackets with required parameters shown without brackets. Of course, you don't use the brackets in the actual command line. For the **xcopy** command the source is the only required parameter, and it is the file or files to copy. You can include the path to a file or a directory, as in **c:\data**, which is a directory. The destination is not required, but if you don't provide it, the command interpreter will assume you want to copy to the current directory.

To copy the **c:\data** directory and all its contents, including files and directories (both occupied and empty) to drive F, type **xcopy c:\data f: /e**.

Batch Files at the Command Prompt

The Windows Command Prompt supports batch files. A batch file is a text file that contains commands you could enter at the Command Prompt but choose

The **robocopy** command syntax.

to put in a batch file to automate running the commands. When run, the commands in a batch file are executed in the order in which they appear in the file. This is quite handy when you want to run several commands and need to do this on a regular basis, such as a daily backup. We sometimes refer to a batch file as a script.

Note: All the CLIs discussed in this book support batch files—each in its own way.

While you can schedule backups through the GUI with either Windows 7's Backup and Restore or Windows 8's File History, perhaps you have a special need. For instance, you want to back up certain directories to a thumb drive before leaving the office to go to a meeting. You could create a batch file and run it as you prepare for the meeting so that you can take the thumb drive with you.

To create a batch file, open a text editor, such as Notepad, type in the commands—one line per command, just as you would enter the commands at the Command Prompt. When you are finished, save the file with a meaningful file name, and give it a **cmd** extension. This is the correct extension for Windows batch files. MS-DOS and very old versions of Windows used the **bat** extension, and Windows will still run files with that old extension, but without some advanced features. It is better to use the **cmd** extension that Microsoft added in Windows NT and has improved with newer versions of Windows, adding more capabilities to this type of batch file.

Once created, run a batch file from the Command Prompt by entering its file name or run it from the GUI by double-clicking (or tapping) the file name.

Working with Files and Directories

There are many tricks to using the Command Prompt, but the few described previously should get you started. Now it's time to practice more Windows Command Prompt commands for working with files and directories.

File and Directory Basics

When you work at the Windows Command Prompt, you follow the same rules for naming files as you do in the GUI; you just do not have the convenience of seeing information through the GUI. If you attempt to create a file name that breaks the rules, you will know soon enough via an error message. So let's look at the basic rules.

Do Not Use Reserved Characters in a Directory or File Name. A reserved character is a non-alpha-numeric character reserved for a special purpose by the operating system, in this case Windows. When you see the list, you will recognize many of the characters, because you have already used them at the command line. Keep your file and directory names simple. If you want to use a character to make the name more readable, as between words, use the hyphen (-) or underscore (_) character. The reserved characters are:

- Less than (<)
- Greater than (>)
- Colon (:)
- Double quote (")
- Forward slash (/)
- Backslash (\)
- Vertical bar or pipe (|)
- Question mark (?)
- Asterisk (*)

Do Not Use Names Reserved by Windows. Windows uses certain names to refer to devices, such as serial and parallel ports and the screen:

- AUX
- COM1 through COM9
- CON
- LPT1 through LPT9
- NUL
- PRN

Use Meaningful, but Not Overly Long Names. Windows supports long file names, but there is a limit, and you reach it quicker for files that are several directory levels below the root. The maximum length of a path is 260 characters. That includes three characters for the volume, such as **c:**, and one more for a normally invisible null character that follows the file name and extension. That leaves 256 characters for a file at the root of the volume and less for files within subdirectories, because it counts the characters in all the directory names in the path as well as the backslashes separating each component.

So the takeaway concerning naming files and directories is to use meaningful, but brief, names. If you attempt to create a file or directory that exceeds the limit, you will see an error message that you have exceeded the maximum path limit. Consider that, in Windows, user files are by default saved in the **c:\users**_username_ directory so you already have several characters in the path for files you save in this location.

Do Not Delete Existing File Name Extensions. A file name extension helps to identify the file type to Windows so that it knows whether the file is program code or if it is a data file. That's how it knows how to treat the file. A file name extension for a file that it can open is associated in Windows with one or more programs that can open that file. You created text files earlier using the text output of a Command Prompt command. Since this output was text, without any extraneous formatting or programming code, the files created were text files and the **.txt** extension was correct. You were able to open the file using Notepad, which is a text-file editor. Not to belabor the point, but be careful that you do not overwrite or delete existing file name extensions when you work with files at the Command Prompt.

When you work with files in the Windows GUI, it protects you from making certain mistakes regarding file name extensions. By default, Windows Explorer (File Explorer in Windows 8) hides file name extensions, and when you rename a file in the GUI, it protects the extension so that you actually have to go to some trouble to overwrite it. That is not true at the Command Prompt. Basically, although you work with files at the Command Prompt in this chapter as a learning tool, we do not recommend doing file management from the Command Prompt.

WARNING!

Renaming files at the Command Prompt is a task that is fraught with opportunity for mistakes. Avoid overwriting file name extensions by not renaming files at the Command Prompt unless it is absolutely necessary.

Use Wildcards. You can use the asterisk (*) and question mark (?) as wildcard characters; the asterisk is the more useful of these two. You can use the asterisk to replace all characters from that point to the end of the file name or all characters to the end of the extension. For example, ***.doc** refers to all files with the DOC extension. Similarly, **read*.*** refers to all files beginning with READ and with any extension. This wildcard is very powerful and useful. For instance, if you wanted to copy all files from the current directory to a target directory on drive **c:** named **backup**, you could simply type the command **copy *.* c:\backup**.

The question mark replaces a single character for each instance of the question mark. This had more value a few decades ago when file names were only eight characters long. For instance, **diskco??.*** refers to all files that match the provided characters and have any characters in the seventh or eighth place of the file name.

Note: If you are looking for files that vary only by certain characters, and not necessarily at the end of the file name, use the **?** wildcard.

Understand File Attributes. In addition to file types, it helps to understand the basic file attributes saved in each file or directory entry. Each file attribute describes some characteristic of a file. There are actually many types of attributes associated with a file or directory on an NTFS volume, but we will only concern ourselves with the basic file attributes. These determine how the operating system handles the file. For instance, if the file attribute for directory is on, or *set*, then the file entry is for a directory, which acts as a container for files and directories. The basic file attributes are as follows:

- **Read-only**—An attribute that indicates that a file may not be modified or deleted. Windows automatically puts this attribute on certain files as a small measure of protection. Anyone using a program that ignores this attribute, or using a program that permits turning off this attribute, can delete the read-only file, depending on the permissions assigned to the file.

- **Archive**—An attribute that, when turned on, indicates a file was created or modified since the last backup. Windows places this attribute on all new or changed files. Most backup programs also can turn off this attribute for each file backed up, allowing the program to keep track of the backed-up files.

- **System**—A special attribute that indicates that a file is a critical part of the operating system.

- **Hidden**—An attribute that will cause a file or directory to be hidden from programs that pay attention to this attribute, such as the **dir** command.

- **Volume label**—An attribute used for a special root directory entry that saves the name of a disk volume, provided someone named the volume.

- **Directory**—An attribute that indicates that the entry is a directory, not a file.

These basic file attributes are used in many file systems in various OSs such as NTFS for Windows. If you are working at the Command Prompt, it's important to understand the read-only and hidden attributes because someday the first one may keep you from editing a file and the second one may keep a file from displaying in a directory listing. Use the **attrib** command to view file attributes and to change some of the attributes. Figure 9–8 shows the result of running the **attrib** command on the Documents directory showing the Archive (A), System (S), and Hidden (H) attributes on certain files.

try this!

Make a File Read-Only

Use the **attrib** command to make a file read-only. Try this:

1. If you created the file **help.txt** in Step-by-Step 9.01, it should be in your home directory. Open a Standard user Command Prompt and type the command **dir *.txt** to ensure that the file is there. If it is not, but another text file is present, use it for this exercise.

2. At the Command Prompt, type **attrib +r help.txt** and press ENTER.

3. Confirm that the file is now read-only with the **attrib** command: Type **attrib *.txt** and press ENTER.

4. If an *r* is displayed by the file name, it is read-only. Try deleting this file: type **del help.txt**.

5. Remove the read-only attribute: type **attrib -r help.txt**.

```
C:\Users\janeh_000\Documents>attrib
A            C:\Users\janeh_000\Documents\Ch05w.docx
A            C:\Users\janeh_000\Documents\chkdsk.txt
A      H     C:\Users\janeh_000\Documents\Default.rdp
A      SH    C:\Users\janeh_000\Documents\desktop.ini
A            C:\Users\janeh_000\Documents\help.txt
A            C:\Users\janeh_000\Documents\robocopy.txt
A            C:\Users\janeh_000\Documents\xcopy.txt

C:\Users\janeh_000\Documents>
```

FIGURE 9-8 The **attrib** command showing attributes for files in the Documents directory.

Step-by-Step 9.02

Managing Files and Directories

Practice working with files and directories from the Command Prompt. Copy files from one directory to another directory, navigate directories, create a directory, and compare the results of using three different commands to copy files (**copy**, **xcopy**, and **robocopy**).

Step 1

At the Command Prompt, type **dir** and press ENTER to see a listing of files and directories in the home directory.

```
C:\Users\janeh_000>DIR
Volume in drive C is OS
Volume Serial Number is B4F0-FD5F

Directory of C:\Users\janeh_000

07/22/2013  08:52 PM    <DIR>          .
07/22/2013  08:52 PM    <DIR>          ..
06/30/2013  09:03 PM    <DIR>          .VirtualBox
07/22/2013  08:50 PM             2,405 chkdsk.txt
07/22/2013  08:47 PM            16,832 cls
07/10/2013  06:24 PM    <DIR>          Contacts
07/10/2013  06:24 PM    <DIR>          Desktop
07/18/2013  11:35 AM    <DIR>          Documents
07/18/2013  08:02 PM    <DIR>          Downloads
07/17/2013  05:10 PM    <DIR>          Favorites
07/21/2013  09:09 AM             5,866 help.txt
07/10/2013  06:24 PM    <DIR>          Links
07/10/2013  06:24 PM    <DIR>          Music
07/22/2013  08:52 PM    <DIR>          MYDIR
07/21/2013  09:07 AM    <DIR>          Pictures
04/26/2013  12:55 AM    <DIR>          Roaming
07/22/2013  06:56 PM             7,469 robocopy.txt
07/10/2013  06:24 PM    <DIR>          Saved Games
07/10/2013  06:24 PM    <DIR>          Searches
07/22/2013  09:22 AM    <DIR>          SkyDrive
07/10/2013  06:24 PM    <DIR>          Videos
06/27/2013  12:39 PM    <DIR>          VirtualBox UMs
07/22/2013  06:56 PM             3,496 xcopy.txt
               5 File(s)         36,068 bytes
              18 Dir(s)  396,194,779,136 bytes free

C:\Users\janeh_000>
```

Step 2

Copy all the text files from the home directory to the Documents directory. Type **copy *.txt documents** and press ENTER. A list of the copied files displays on the left.

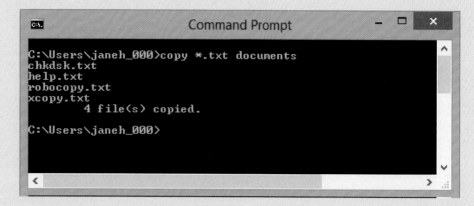

Step 3

To move down one level into the Documents directory, type **cd documents** and press ENTER.

```
C:\Users\janeh_000>cd documents

C:\Users\janeh_000\Documents>
```

Step 4

Check that it copied the files successfully. Type **dir** and press ENTER. Look for the files with **txt** extensions. If the files scroll out of the window reenter the command with a parameter. Type **dir *.txt** and press ENTER.

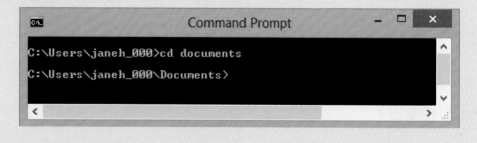

Step 5

Create a directory in the Documents directory. Type **md manuals** and press ENTER. Use the **dir** command to confirm that the new directory is in your Documents directory.

```
C:\Users\janeh_000\Documents>md manuals

C:\Users\janeh_000\Documents>dir
 Volume in drive C is OS
 Volume Serial Number is B4F0-FD5F

 Directory of C:\Users\janeh_000\Documents

07/23/2013  02:21 PM    <DIR>          .
07/23/2013  02:21 PM    <DIR>          ..
07/05/2013  08:12 PM         8,738,207 Ch05w.docx
07/22/2013  08:50 PM             2,405 chkdsk.txt
06/30/2013  01:06 PM    <DIR>          Custom Office Templates
07/18/2013  05:04 PM    <DIR>          Dell Downloads
07/21/2013  09:09 AM             5,866 help.txt
07/23/2013  02:21 PM    <DIR>          manuals
07/22/2013  06:56 PM             7,469 robocopy.txt
07/22/2013  06:56 PM             3,496 xcopy.txt
               5 File(s)      8,757,443 bytes
               5 Dir(s)  396,158,951,424 bytes free

C:\Users\janeh_000\Documents>
```

To create a new directory named **mybackup** and to copy the contents of the **manuals** directory into the **mybackup** directory at the same time, use the **xcopy** command. Type **xcopy manuals mybackup** and press ENTER.

When asked if the target (**mybackup**) is a file name or directory type **d** for directory and the command will proceed, showing the list of files copied on the left.

```
                                        Command Prompt                    _  □  ✕
C:\Users\janeh_000\Documents>xcopy manuals mybackup
Does mybackup specify a file name
or directory name on the target
(F = file, D = directory)? d
manuals\chkdsk.txt
manuals\help.txt
manuals\robocopy.txt
manuals\xcopy.txt
4 File(s) copied

C:\Users\janeh_000\Documents>
```

To confirm that the **mybackup** directory was created, type **dir mybackup** and press ENTER.

Now try an advanced command, **robocopy,** for a very simple task, copying the **mybackup** directory into a directory named **newbackup** (that **robocopy** will create). Type **robocopy mybackup newbackup**. Notice the full report created by **robocopy**.

```
                                        Command Prompt                    _  □  ✕
C:\Users\janeh_000\Documents>robocopy mybackup newbackup
-------------------------------------------------------------------------------
  ROBOCOPY     ::     Robust File Copy for Windows
-------------------------------------------------------------------------------

  Started : Tuesday, July 23, 2013 4:03:55 PM
   Source : C:\Users\janeh_000\Documents\mybackup\
     Dest : C:\Users\janeh_000\Documents\newbackup\

    Files : *.*

  Options : *.* /DCOPY:DA /COPY:DAT /R:1000000 /W:30

------------------------------------------------------------------------------

            New Dir          4    C:\Users\janeh_000\Documents\mybackup\
100%        New File        2405       chkdsk.txt
100%        New File        5866       help.txt
100%        New File        7469       robocopy.txt
100%        New File        3496       xcopy.txt

------------------------------------------------------------------------------

            Total    Copied   Skipped  Mismatch    FAILED    Extras
  Dirs :        1         1         0         0         0         0
  Files :       4         4         0         0         0         0
  Bytes :   18.7 k    18.7 k         0         0         0         0
  Times :  0:00:00   0:00:00                       0:00:00   0:00:00


  Speed :              620516 Bytes/sec.
  Speed :              35.506 MegaBytes/min.
  Ended : Tuesday, July 23, 2013 4:03:55 PM

C:\Users\janeh_000\Documents>
```

Now see what was copied into **newbackup**. Type **dir newbackup** and press ENTER. Notice that the directory **mybackup** was not copied in, just the contents of the **mybackup**.

```
                                        Command Prompt                    _  □  ✕
C:\Users\janeh_000\Documents>dir newbackup
 Volume in drive C is OS
 Volume Serial Number is B4F0-FD5F

 Directory of C:\Users\janeh_000\Documents\newbackup

07/23/2013  04:00 PM    <DIR>          .
07/23/2013  04:00 PM    <DIR>          ..
07/22/2013  08:50 PM             2,405 chkdsk.txt
07/21/2013  09:09 AM             5,866 help.txt
07/22/2013  06:56 PM             7,469 robocopy.txt
07/22/2013  06:56 PM             3,496 xcopy.txt
               4 File(s)         19,236 bytes
               2 Dir(s)  397,176,803,328 bytes free

C:\Users\janeh_000\Documents>
```

Robust Copying with Robocopy

The **robocopy** command, known as the robust copier, is a sophisticated copy utility that has been included in Windows since Windows Vista. When you use it, **robocopy** displays a detailed report of the results, as shown in step 9 of Step-by-Step 9.02. Flip back to that step and look at the illustration. We used a very simple **robocopy** command in order to show the basics of this report. Notice that at the end of the report it has columns that list how many directories and files it copied, if there are any problems such as skipped or mismatched files or directories, and if any failed to copy. The column labeled Extras refers to files or directories that exist in the destination, but not in the source. This can occur when you copy into an existing directory and is not a problem if you want to keep files that exist in the destination.

When you use the **robocopy** command you indicate the source and destination in the form *drive:\path* or *\\servername\share\path*. It will then assume that it should copy all files within the source (or *.*). You cannot use file names in the directory source and destination parameters, but you can use them elsewhere on the **robocopy** command line to specify what files to copy. You can do this, and even use wildcards in the file names, but file names must follow the source and destination and precede the options unless they are part of an option.

Consider a scenario in which we want to copy a directory that contains almost 300 MB of subdirectories and files. We know that Microsoft Word backup files with the **wbk** extension occupy a good bit of space in the source. We want to copy these files as an archive, but do not want to copy over the **wbk** file. Both the **xcopy** command and the **robocopy** command can do this, but the **robocopy** command is faster and gives us a report of the entire operation. The command **robocopy c:\projects e:\projects /xf *.wbk /e** will copy all the files in **c:\projects** to **e:\projects** with the exception (**/xf**) of any file with the **wbk** extension (***.wbk**). The **/e** option tells **robocopy** to copy all subdirectories, including empty ones, and it will create the **projects** directory on the destination drive if it does not already exist. As a test, we ran the command as described. It ran without errors, skipped 25 files (the **wbk** files), and the resulting files and directories took up 88 MB less space on the destination than on the source.

This explanation describes just a few capabilities of the **robocopy** command that comes with Windows, and we have not even mentioned similar third-party utilities that many IT professionals prefer to use. If you are interested in more than this survey level, enter "robocopy" into a search engine and see what various sources have to say. For instance, the Microsoft technical forums discuss the pros and cons of many such file copy tools.

LO 9.3 | Using Terminal in OS X

OS X has a CLI in the form of Terminal, a window where you can get in touch with OS X's UNIX roots. As with the Command Prompt in Windows, the OS X security applies to your activities while working in Terminal. Terminal shares other features with the other CLIs described in this book: internal and external commands, the use of delimiter characters, a command interpreter (several are available, but the one we use for our example is BASH). It also uses search paths, supports batch files, and uses command-line options. In this section we give an overview of Terminal features and several opportunities for you to practice using the commands in Terminal. You will find that it includes many of the same commands you used for Linux in Chapter 8.

try this!

Open a Terminal Window in OS X

Open a Terminal window in OS X. Try this:

1. Open a Finder window by clicking on the Finder icon on the Dock and browsing to **Applications | Utilities | Terminal**.
2. Double-click **Terminal** to launch it.
3. With Terminal open, right-click on its icon in the Dock and select **Options | Keep in Dock**.
4. Leave it open as you read through the chapter.

Launch Terminal

Launch Terminal from the Utilities folder below the Applications folder, shown here. This gives you a doorway to the UNIX underpinnings of OS X via a BASH shell complete with the $ prompt you learned about in Chapter 8. In this discussion and our examples, we assume you are using the default BASH shell. Consider adding Terminal to the Dock so that it is easy to quickly launch. See how in the Try This!

The default Terminal $ prompt, as shown in Figure 9–9, begins with the computer name followed by a colon (:) with a tilde (~) representing your home directory. These are followed by the user name of the currently logged-on user and the $ sign. After opening Terminal notice that just like all other

Open Terminal from the Utilities folder.

Add the Terminal to the Dock.

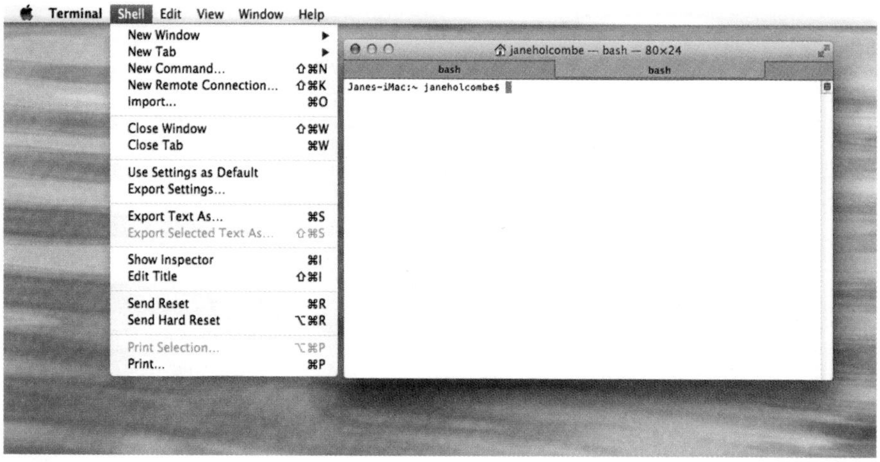

FIGURE 9–9 The Terminal Shell menu.

windows in OS X, it has its own menu at the top of the screen, (Figure 9–9). Use the **Shell** menu to launch a new Terminal window so that you can have multiple windows open at once. The Terminal window also supports multiple tabs. Select **New Tab** to open a new tab in the current Terminal Window, also shown in Figure 9–9. Or close the current tab or window, or select another option from the Shell menu.

Shell Commands in Terminal

There are well over a thousand commands available in Terminal, and one way to quickly see a complete list is to use the command completion feature. We described this as a Linux feature in Chapter 8, where we only described one aspect of the feature: typing one or more characters at the $ prompt, followed by the TAB key. Terminal, like Linux, will try to guess what you are typing, completing the command for you. If you press the TAB key twice at an empty Terminal Command Prompt, it will first pause and prompt you by asking if you want it to display all the possibilities. Press **y** to proceed or **n** to cancel. If you let it proceed, it will display all commands, as shown in Figure 9–10 which has two windows to show both the command line and the output. This would normally all happen in one window. Move the scroll bar up to see the commands that scrolled out of the window area, and press the space bar to have it send more commands. This is not a very satisfying way to see the commands, but it gives you a sense of the quantity of commands.

Before you start typing commands at the $ prompt you should understand that like Linux (and UNIX), OS X Terminal is case sensitive and case-aware. Commands are (mostly) in lower case, but options may vary, and whenever you type a directory or file name in Terminal, pay attention to case just as you would in Linux. Figure 9–11 shows the Terminal window (at top) with the result of running the **ls** (list) command on the user's Home directory. The Finder window overlaying the Terminal window shows the GUI version of this list. In both cases, the names are in upper and lower case, exactly as created, and anytime you refer to these names in Terminal, you must use the correct case.

Note: For a short list of frequently used commands see the *UNIX Command Summary* at www.bsd.org/unixcmds .html.

Working with Manual Pages

Once you know the name of a command that you want to use, tap into the power of the **man** command to learn how to use that command. As in Linux, you view the manual page, called a `manpage` (usually many "pages") of a command by entering the **man** command followed by the name of the command.

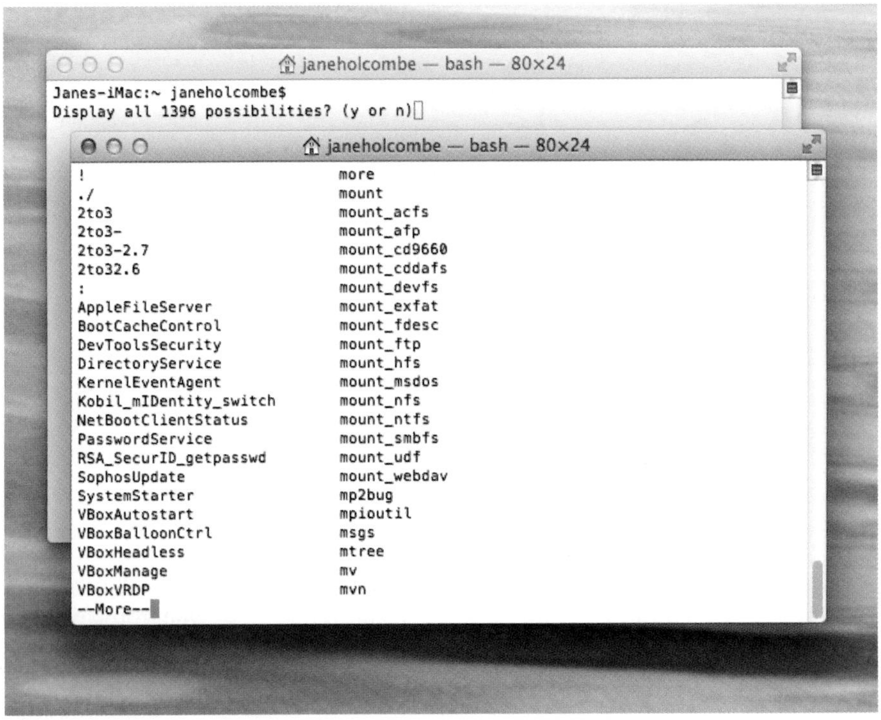

FIGURE 9–10 Press the TAB key twice; then type **y** to see the complete command list.

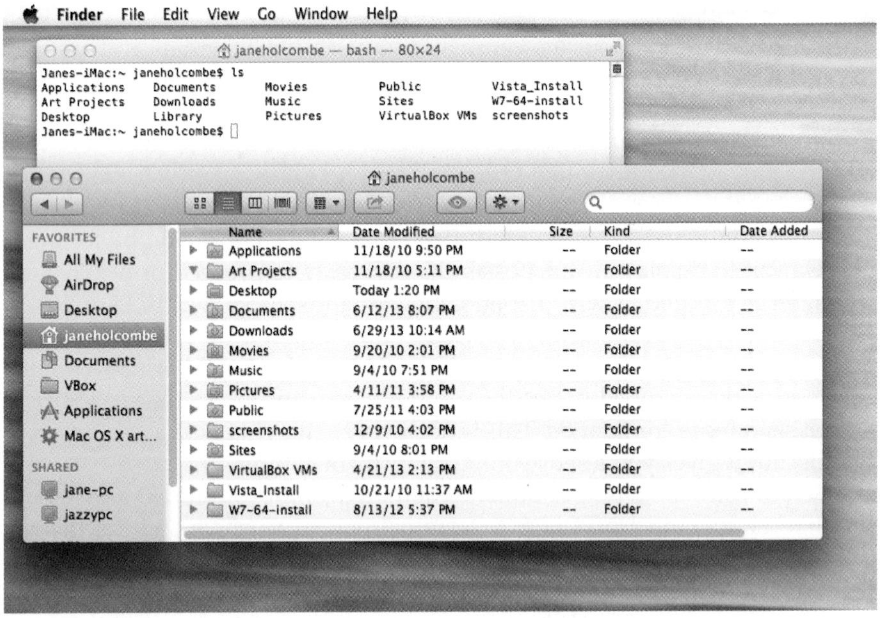

FIGURE 9–11 A Terminal window (at top) overlaid by the Finder window.

For instance, to see the manual page for the **ls** command type **man ls**. The documentation for the command will display one screen buffer at a time. A colon (:) and a blinking cursor displays on the last line of the window, indicating that there is more of the manpage to display. When you are ready to move to the next screenful of the manpage press the spacebar (or press RETURN to advance one line at a time). To go back up, press the up arrow or the B key. When it gets to the end of the manpage "(END)" replaces the colon. You can quit a manpage at any time by pressing the **q** key. Practice in Step-by-Step 9.03.

Note: Whenever the screen gets too cluttered, simply use the **clear** command.

Using the Man Command

Open two Terminal Windows in OS X and practice using the **man** command in one window as a guide for working in a command in the second window.

Step 1

At the $ prompt type **man ls** and press ENTER.

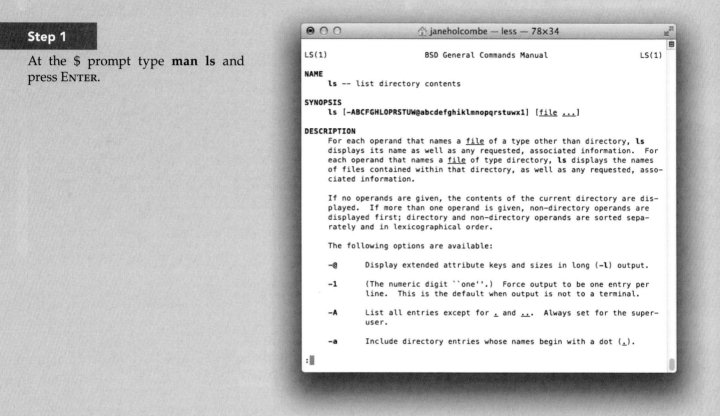

Step 2

Notice what the manpage says will occur if no operands (options) are entered at the command line. Test this by opening a second Terminal window, while leaving the one with the manpage open. To do this, click the **Shell** menu and then select **New Window**.

Step 3

Use the **ls** command without any options. In the new window type **ls** and press ENTER. This displays a list of the nonhidden files and directories in the current directory.

Back in the first Terminal window, the first page of the **ls** manpage describes the **-a** option. In the second Terminal window add the **-a** option to the **ls** command to see a list that includes both hidden and nonhidden files and directories. Type **ls -a** and press ENTER. All the normally hidden entries appear. They are the files and directories that begin with a period (**.**).

```
● ○ ○                ⌂ janeholcombe — bash — 80×24
Janes-iMac:~ janeholcombe$ ls -a
.                        .lesshst              Music
..                       .nchsoftware          Pictures
.CFUserTextEncoding      .webex                Public
.DS_Store                Applications          Sites
.Trash                   Art Projects          VirtualBox VMs
.Xauthority              Desktop               Vista_Install
.adobe                   Documents             W7-64-install
.bash_history            Downloads             commandlist.txt
.cups                    Library               screenshots
.fontconfig              Movies
Janes-iMac:~ janeholcombe$
```

You know which entries are hidden and which are not, but so far, it is not clear which is a file and which is a directory. The second page of the **ls** manpage describes the **-F** option. To see all entries (as in step 4), and to also see directories identified with an ending slash (/), type **ls -aF** and press ENTER. Be sure to type the correct case.

```
● ○ ○                ⌂ janeholcombe — bash — 80×24
Janes-iMac:~ janeholcombe$ ls -aF
./                       .lesshst              Music/
../                      .nchsoftware/         Pictures/
.CFUserTextEncoding      .webex/               Public/
.DS_Store                Applications/         Sites/
.Trash/                  Art Projects/         VirtualBox VMs/
.Xauthority              Desktop/              Vista_Install/
.adobe/                  Documents/            W7-64-install/
.bash_history            Downloads/            commandlist.txt
.cups/                   Library/              screenshots/
.fontconfig/             Movies/
Janes-iMac:~ janeholcombe$
```

The output of the **ls** command with the **-aF** identifies all the directories with the forward slash (/). Notice the **.** and **..** entries. The single period (**.**) represents the current directory and the double period (**..**) represents the parent directory—the directory above the current directory.

In the window where you have been experimenting with the **ls** command, use the **cd** (change directory) command to move up to the parent directory. Type **cd ..** and press ENTER. This changes the current directory to the parent directory.

```
● ○ ○                📄 Documents — bash — 80×24
Janes-iMac:~ janeholcombe$ cd ..
Janes-iMac:Users janeholcombe$ cd ~
Janes-iMac:~ janeholcombe$ cd Documents
Janes-iMac:Documents janeholcombe$
```

Return to the Home directory: Type **cd ~** and press ENTER.

Change to the Documents directory: Type **cd Documents** and press ENTER.

When you are finished with the **ls** manpage in the first window press **q** to quit.

Command-Line History

You can avoid retyping the same command during a Terminal session by using Terminal's command-line history feature, which is the same as that described for Linux in Chapter 8. Terminal saves the commands you enter for the duration of the session, and you can scroll through these commands. Simply use the up and down arrow keys to move through the history. When you find the command you want to reuse, you can edit it by moving back and forth through it with the left and right arrow keys. When you are ready to use the command, simply press ENTER. Like Linux, Terminal (using the BASH shell) saves these commands in a file called bash_history, but you do not need to know anything about this file to take advantage of this feature.

Note: Like Linux, UNIX-based OS X Terminal provides for the temporary use of the root account security context by preceding a command with the **sudo** command and providing your password. As in Linux, this works only if you have logged in as an Administrator. It also explains why Terminal does not need an option to "Run as administrator" that the Windows Command Prompt uses.

Command Completion

You already know that pressing the TAB key (twice) will (after you respond **y** to a prompt), display the names of all the Terminal commands. You can also use the TAB key for command completion. As you enter a command at the $ prompt, experiment with the command completion feature. Enter the command name and a few more characters of the options, and then press the Tab key. BASH tries to guess what you want to type next, but doesn't do it in the same way as the example given for Linux in Chapter 8. For instance, when using the **cd** (change directory) command, as in step 7 of Step-by-Step 9.03, you could enter **cd D** and then pressed the TAB key twice. If there is only one match for a directory beginning with an uppercase **D**, command completion completes the line with that name, but if there are several matches, it shows all directory entries in the current location that begin with an uppercase D, as shown on the second line in the top Terminal window in Figure 9–12. It also opens the dollar prompt with your command showing (in this case **cd D** on the third line). All you need to do is type in a few more characters of the directory name, such as **oc** and then press TAB, and it completes the line to read **cd Documents/**. The bottom Terminal window in Figure 9–12 shows this. When the line contains the command you want, move the left and right arrow keys to make changes to the line before running it, or simply press ENTER to run the command line as is. The $ prompt in the bottom window in Figure 9–12 shows the change to the Documents directory.

More Common Commands

Among the most common commands in Terminal are those for creating and navigating directories. They have the same names as commands used in Linux and some of them match commands used at the Windows Command Prompt. To create a directory in Terminal use the **mkdir** command. To create a directory in the current (working) directory simply type **mkdir** *dirname*. To change to a directory just below the working directory type **cd** *dirname*. The

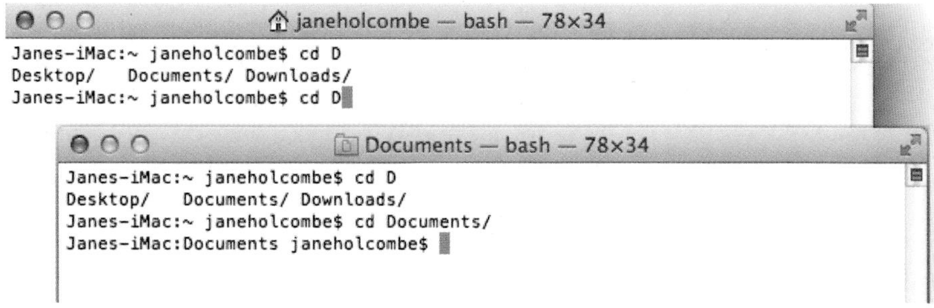

FIGURE 9–12 An example of command completion.

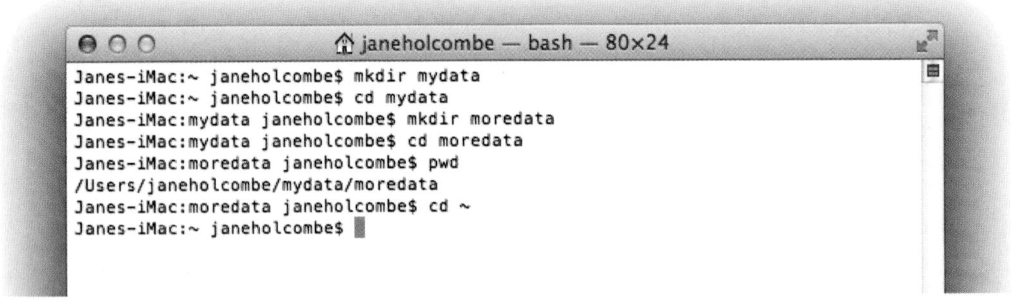

```
●  ●  ●                ⌂ janeholcombe — bash — 80×24

Janes-iMac:~ janeholcombe$ mkdir mydata
Janes-iMac:~ janeholcombe$ cd mydata
Janes-iMac:mydata janeholcombe$ mkdir moredata
Janes-iMac:mydata janeholcombe$ cd moredata
Janes-iMac:moredata janeholcombe$ pwd
/Users/janeholcombe/mydata/moredata
Janes-iMac:moredata janeholcombe$ cd ~
Janes-iMac:~ janeholcombe$ █
```

FIGURE 9–13 A Terminal window showing a series of commands for creating and navigating directories.

Note: As with Linux, if you are logged on with an Administrator account you can use the **sudo** command (see Chapter 8) to temporarily borrow root privileges to complete a task.

prompt changes to reflect the current directory, but it does not give the full path. To see where you are in the directory tree use the **pwd** (print working directory) command. Figure 9–13 gives an example of a series of commands: The numbered lines below correspond to each line in Figure 9–13.

1. The command **mkdir mydata** creates the directory **mydata** below the working directory (the user's home directory).
2. The command **cd mydata** changes the working directory to the new directory.
3. The command **mkdir moredata** creates a new directory within **mydata**.
4. The command **cd moredata** changes the working directory to **moredata**.
5. The command **pwd** requests "print working directory."
6. The full path to the working directory displays.
7. The command **cd ~** changes the working directory to the user's home directory.
8. The $ prompt is ready and waiting for the next command.

Chapter 9 REVIEW

Chapter Summary

After reading this chapter and completing the exercises, you should understand the following facts about the Windows Command Prompt and Terminal in OS X:

Introduction to the Windows Command Prompt

- The Windows Command Prompt is a CLI launched from within Windows or from a recovery environment.
- The Windows Command Prompt is not MS-DOS (a 16-bit OS), but a CLI to 32-bit or 64-bit Windows.
- The Windows Command Prompt is not PowerShell, a very powerful Windows CLI that also runs in the 32-bit or 64-bit mode of Windows and accepts some Command Prompt commands.

PowerShell goes beyond the text-based Command Prompt command because it accepts other types of commands including the ability to work with software objects.

- Windows 7 and Windows 8 both allow you to open the Command Prompt from within Windows in either the Standard user context (the default) or in the context of an Administrator.
- For troubleshooting and repairing the OS, both Windows 7 and Windows 8 have on option for Safe Mode with Command Prompt.
- Windows 7 and Windows 8 each also have a special Recovery Command Prompt. You need the Windows 7 installation disc for its version, but you can access the Windows 8 Recovery Command Prompt without the installation disc.

Success at the Windows Command Prompt

- The Windows Command Prompt is case-aware, but not case sensitive.
- The Windows Command Prompt interprets commands by parsing the command line into its parts separated by delimiters.
- Windows searches the search path for commands.
- When used at the Command Prompt, the greater than (>) redirection character sends the output of the command on the left to the file named on the right.
- When used at the Command Prompt, the vertical bar (|) character sends the output of the command to the left of it to a device (such as a printer) or to a file with the name you provide to the right of the operator.
- The **more** command is a filter that holds screen output and sends it one screenful at a time. Pressing the SPACEBAR will advance one screenful, and pressing the ENTER key advances one line.
- The **help** command lists commands with a brief description.
- Enter a command name followed by the **/?** parameter to see the syntax of the command.
- The Windows Command Prompt supports batch files. A batch file is a text file with a **cmd** extension that contains commands that you could enter at the Command Prompt, but choose to put in a batch file to automate running the commands.
- File names cannot include reserved characters (< > : " /\ | ? *) and cannot be certain names used by Windows for devices.
- The maximum length of a path is 260 characters, including three characters for the volume (such as **c:**) and one normally invisible null character at the end of the file name. In between are all the directory names, backslashes (\), and the file name and extension.
- Do not delete existing file name extensions.
- Use the wildcard character asterisk (*) to replace a group of characters. Use the wildcard character dollar sign ($) to replace a single character.
- The basic file attributes are read-only, archive, system, hidden, volume label, and directory. Become familiar with working with the read-only and hidden attributes at the Command Prompt.
- There are several Command Prompt commands for copying files. The simplest is **copy**, and **xcopy** has added support for directories. The much more advanced robust file copy, **robocopy**, copies directories and their contents; it will not act on a file name. It also provides a full report after it completes a copy.

The Terminal CLI in OS X

- The OS X CLI is the Terminal window where you can run OS X's UNIX commands at the $ prompt.
- Open a Terminal window from the Utilities directory.
- If you need to open Terminal frequently, open it, right-click its Dock icon, and select **Options | Keep in Dock.**
- You can open multiple Terminal windows, and each window can have multiple tabs open.
- The default Terminal $ prompt begins with the computer name followed by a colon and a tilde (~) to represent the home directory. These are followed by the user name of the currently logged-on user and the $ sign.
- The Terminal window has a menu at the top of the OS X screen. Use the Shell menu to open new windows and/or new tabs within an open Terminal window.
- At the $ prompt press the Tab key twice and respond to the resulting message with a **y** to see a list of all command names (without descriptions).
- OS X Terminal is case-sensitive. Commands are usually in lower case, but options can vary, as do directory and file names.
- Scroll through command-line history with the up and down arrow keys. Use left and right arrow keys to move back and forth through a command line to edit it.
- Use the TAB key for command completion, pressing it when you have a portion of a command line typed and it will provide hints or complete the line.

Key Terms List

batch file (344)

cmd.exe (332)

command.com (332)

Command Prompt (332)

delimiter character (339)

external command (340)

file attribute (347)

internal command (340)

manpage (353)

MS-DOS (332)

parse (339)

piping (341)

PowerShell (332)

RAM disk (334)

redirection operator (341)

Safe Mode with Command
    Prompt (334)

search path (340)

switch (339)

syntax (343)

System Recovery Command
    Prompt (334)

Terminal (351)

Key Terms Quiz

Use the Key Terms List to complete the sentences that follow. Not all terms will be used.

1. _____ is the Windows Command Prompt command interpreter.

2. A set of rules for correctly entering a specific command and its options at the command line is called the command's_____.

3. A character that separates the components on a command line is a/an _____.

4. The _____ feature of a CLI command interpreter takes the output from one command and sends it as input to another command.

5. A command interpreter must _____, or divide into components, what is entered at the command line before it can load the program and pass the options from the command line to the program.

6. The _____ is a list of locations used by the command interpreter to locate a program to load into memory.

7. _____ is the CLI window in OS X.

8. A/an _____ for a Terminal command shows its syntax.

9. The Windows CLI is called the _____.

10. Create a _____, a text file containing command-line commands, when you want to automate tasks from a CLI.

Multiple-Choice Quiz

1. When you open Windows Command Prompt from Safe mode or in Recovery mode it runs in this security context.
   a. Standard user
   b. Guest
   c. Administrator
   d. Power user
   e. Superuser

2. An Administrator of a large Active Directory domain can automate advanced tasks using this Windows scripting environment that supports object-oriented programming.
   a. Command Prompt
   b. Terminal
   c. Manpage
   d. PowerShell
   e. System Recovery Command Prompt

3. To open a Windows Administrator Command Prompt you must respond to this.
   a. The Windows sign-in screen.
   b. A User Account Control dialog box.
   c. An "Are you sure…?" prompt.
   d. A survey from Microsoft.
   e. The $ prompt.

4. In Windows 8 the Command Prompt is available on the Power Users Menu. What shortcut keys will open this menu in Windows 8?
   a. WINDOWS KEY + X
   b. WINDOWS KEY + F1
   c. WINDOWS KEY + P
   d. WINDOWS KEY + Q
   e. WINDOWS KEY + I

5. What do you need before you can open a Windows 7 System Recovery Command Prompt?
   a. The Guest account must be enabled.
   b. A flash drive.
   c. A working installation of Windows 7.
   d. You must first log on to Windows 7 as Administrator.
   e. The Windows 7 installation disc.

6. What directory copy command provides a detailed report of the results each time you use it?
   a. copy
   b. xcopy
   c. robocopy
   d. path
   e. attrib

7. Which of the following is a redirection operator? Select all correct answers.
   a. ?
   b. *
   c. |
   d. "
   e. >

8. Of the CLIs you studied in this chapter, which CLI window supports multiple tabs?
   a. Windows Command Prompt
   b. PowerShell
   c. Windows 8 Recovery Command Prompt
   d. OS X Terminal
   e. None of them supports tabs.

9. At the OS X Terminal $ prompt, what key do you press for command completion?
   a. TAB
   b. RETURN
   c. COMMAND
   d. CAPS LOCK
   e. CTRL

10. Which of the following characters can you use in a file name in Windows?
    a. $
    b. (
    c. \
    d. -
    e. *

11. What can you learn from the syntax of a command?
    a. The command's file attributes.
    b. The rules for entering that command and its options at the command line.
    c. The list of possible errors created by the command.
    d. The version of the command.
    e. How much memory a command uses.

12. You want to run a single command in OS X Terminal, but it requires elevated privileges. What should you do?
    a. Open Terminal in the root security context.
    b. Precede the command with the **sudo** command.
    c. Log in to OS X with the root account.
    d. Precede the command with the **runas** command.
    e. You cannot do this in OS X Terminal.

13. Where does the OS X Terminal BASH shell store command-line history?
    a. Desktop/
    b. Documents/
    c. bash_history
    d. In a tabbed window
    e. In Terminal

14. Which of the following is the name of the OS X CLI that runs in a window and accepts UNIX commands?
    a. Command Prompt
    b. System Recovery Command Prompt
    c. Terminal
    d. PowerShell
    e. Cmd.com

15. You entered a command at the Windows Command Prompt, but received the error message: "The syntax of the command in incorrect." What is the most likely cause of the error?
    a. Typo in the command name.
    b. Incorrect versions of MS-DOS.
    c. Insufficient permissions.
    d. You do not have Administrator rights.
    e. Typo in one or more parameters.

Essay Quiz

1. Having heard technicians with long experience talk about "opening a DOS prompt" in Windows, you are surprised to hear that the "Windows Command Prompt is not MS-DOS." Use your own words to explain why this last statement is true.

2. Explain the difference between case-aware and case sensitive, in reference to the CLIs you studied in this chapter, along with an example.

3. Define the term "search path" and describe how you can quickly see the entire search path at the Command Prompt.

4. Describe the parts of the default OS X Terminal $ prompt.

5. Were you able to do the exercises in this chapter in at least one version of the Windows Command Prompt as well as the OS X Terminal? If so, compare your experience with the Windows Command Prompt versus Terminal.

Lab Projects

LAB PROJECT 9.1

Research how to use the Windows Command Prompt **shutdown** command to restart your computer. Create a shortcut on the Windows desktop, test it, and demonstrate it. Explain how you did it.

LAB PROJECT 9.2

You work in a small office where 10 users with Windows 7 computers need to have the same directory structure. Each computer must have a **customer** directory and a **sales** directory in the user's **Documents** directory. Further, the **customer** directory must contain directories named **whlsale** and **retail**. The **sales** directory must contain three directories: **ads**, **promos**, and **plans**. Therefore, you have decided to automate this task.

1. To automate the process of creating several directories on 10 computers, create a batch file similar to the listing that follows, and name the batch file with a name, such as **newdirs.cmd**. You can distribute this batch file to each user via email, with instructions for copying the file onto their Desktop and running it from there in the GUI.

```
@ECHO OFF
ECHO This batch file will create subdi-
   rectories in the Documents directory.
PAUSE
cd %homepath%\documents
md customers sales
md customers\whlsale
md customers\retail
md sales\ads
md sales\promos
md sales\plans
ECHO The directories have been created.
PAUSE
```

2. Test the batch file by clicking on it from the GUI or by opening a Command Prompt, changing to the location of the batch file and enter the name in the Command Prompt. The output from this command should look like this:

```
This batch file will create subdirecto-
   ries in the Documents directory.
Press any key to continue...
The directories have been created.
Press any key to continue...
```

3. Did the batch file run correctly for you? If not, open it again in Notepad and look for typos. Then run it again.

4. After you have succeeded in running the batch file, explain what each line of the file is doing. If you do not understand how a command line works, research it using the help file, Internet searches, and any other sources. Then insert a comment line above each line of the batch file, explaining what each command does. Create a comment line by beginning the line with the colon (:). A comment is not executed, and if echo is turned off, it will not display during the execution of the batch file.

LAB PROJECT 9.3

Research Apple OS X Terminal's use of batch files in the BASH shell and report on the file type you must use, the file name extension for Terminal, and how you have it recognized by the OS for launching.

10

Connecting Desktops and Laptops to Networks

"Several principles are key to assuring that the Web becomes ever more valuable. The primary design principle underlying the Web's usefulness and growth is universality. When you make a link, you can link to anything. That means people must be able to put anything on the Web, no matter what computer they have, software they use or human language they speak and regardless of whether they have a wired or wireless Internet connection."

—Tim Berners-Lee

In an essay in Scientific American, November 22, 2010

A stand-alone PC—one with no connection whatsoever to a network—is a rare thing today. Most of us can find some reason or need to connect to a network, whether it is a small home network, a corporate intranet, or the Internet. Without a network connection, a PC is like a remote island where the inhabitants have resolved to be isolated from civilization. And it does take resolve today to be so isolated because there are means by which a computer in even the most remote location can connect to the Internet or another network. The heart and soul of all networks are the computers that provide the services we, as clients, seek on a network. These services are as simple as those that give us access to files and printers, Web pages, applications, and much more. Each of these services provides an important role on a network.

At work, at school, and at home, computer users depend on client software components that connect to services—whether for online research, playing games, engaging in a community through social media, using email, or downloading and uploading files.

Learning Outcomes

In this chapter, you will learn how to:

LO **10.1** Configure a client for a TCP/IP network.

LO **10.2** Connect to the Internet.

LO **10.3** Work with basic Internet clients.

LO **10.4** Configure File and Printer clients.

LO **10.5** Troubleshoot common network client problems.

In this chapter you will study the client side of networking. Because a client cannot interact with network servers unless you properly configure it to communicate on a network, we begin with an overview of TCP/IP, the most popular set of rules for transporting information over all types of networks. Learn how to configure network connection settings on a client computer, and learn about the file and printer clients used most often on private networks. Then move on to the Internet, first examining methods for connecting to the Internet, and then examining the most common Internet clients. Finally, practice methods for troubleshooting common connection problems. ✹

LO 10.1 | Configuring a Network Connection

In the computer technology world a protocol is a set of rules, usually formalized in a standard published by one of many standards organizations. We also call a software implementation of a protocol a protocol, although some protocols define hardware. For instance, the Institute of Electrical and Electronics Engineers (IEEE) defines standards under its wide umbrella, and a number of IEEE standards describe how our wired and wireless networks connect and work at the hardware level and firmware level. These network standards all have the prefix 802 followed by a decimal point and the number of a section that began life as the IEEE's 802 project ("80" for 1980 and "2" for February). For instance, standards for the wired Ethernet networks that have connected networks for three decades are IEEE 802.3 standards, while the wireless Wi-Fi networks most of us use in many venues are IEEE 802.11 standards.

A different set of standards define the software our computers use to communicate over these wired and wireless networks. This software must work together, and it is bundled together in what we call a protocol stack. The most important protocol stack is TCP/IP.

Understanding the TCP/IP Protocol Suite

TCP/IP is a group of protocols that evolved from the work of the Defense Advanced Research Projects Agency (DARPA); the Internet Engineering Task Force (IETF) now oversees TCP/IP development. TCP/IP is the underlying protocol suite of the Internet and nearly all private networks, regardless of the network medium (wired or wireless).

Each software implementation of a component of TCP/IP is a protocol, regardless of whether it is a driver, a service, or an application. Further, every computing device you use must have the proper TCP/IP protocols installed to communicate on a network. So, in computer networking, a protocol is both the set of rules for doing some task as well as the software that accomplishes it. In this section we will work at understanding the TCP/IP protocol suite.

The TCP/IP protocols work together to allow both similar and dissimilar computers to communicate. You need this protocol suite to access the Internet, and it is the most common protocol suite used on private intranets. It gets its name from two of its many protocols: Transmission Control Protocol (TCP) and Internet Protocol (IP)—the core protocols of TCP/IP. If, during Windows installation, Windows detects a wired or wireless network adapter it will install a driver for that adapter card and the TCP/IP protocol will automatically install.

TCP/IP is a subject of epic proportions! We offer only an introduction to TCP/IP, in which we attempt to arm you with useful information, but not overwhelm you with detail. Our goal is to give you an overview of TCP/IP, and familiarize you with the settings that you may need to enter or modify for your desktop or laptop computer. Of course, this knowledge should also

Note: For an entertaining overview of TCP/IP and the workings of network devices (routers, switches, and firewalls), check out YouTube video *TCP/IP the Movie* (Parts 1 and 2).

help you with your mobile devices, the subject of Chapter 11. Most computers and mobile devices need little or no help in acquiring the address they need to connect to a network, but knowing more about how this works is very helpful when things don't work as they should.

Transmission Control Protocol

Transmission Control Protocol (TCP) is the protocol responsible for the accurate delivery of messages, verifying and resending any pieces that fail to make the trip from source to destination. Several other protocols act as subprotocols, helping TCP accomplish this.

Internet Protocol

Internet Protocol (IP) is the protocol that delivers each IP **packet** (a small "package" containing chunks of data) from a source to a destination over a network on an **Internetwork** (a network of networks connected through routers). Special routing protocols use a destination IP address to choose the best route for a packet to take through a very complex internetwork. IP has subprotocols that help it accomplish its work, but we will not discuss the subprotocols.

Presently there are two versions of Internet Protocol: IPv4 and IPv6, each with its own addressing scheme. Both protocols are present on the Internet, as it slowly transitions away from the older **IPv4** (the standard since 1983) to IPv6. A lot of attention is focused on the differences in addresses used by these two protocols, but there are many reasons for the Internet's move to **IPv6**.

The short (and simple) list of why IPv6 is better than IPv4 includes:

- IPv6 has many more addresses.
- IPv6 works better with mobile devices using a subprotocol, Mobile IP.
- IPv6 automatically assigns addresses to devices in a very reliable and no-fuss way.
- IPv6 manages addresses better.
- IPv6 has subprotocols that support better security.

It is important for you to learn about IP addresses because you cannot participate on a TCP/IP network without a valid IP address.

IP Addressing Fundamentals

Perhaps you have never been involved in anything requiring knowledge of IP addressing, so you might think this section is not necessary or you can ignore it. However, whether you're a junior networking associate, a power user in a company, or at home as a customer of an Internet service provider (ISP), you might have to look up an IP address on a computer. Why? Perhaps you suddenly cannot connect to a network, and you call a help line for help. The help desk person may ask for information about how your computer is configured to connect. Be prepared for such a scenario by becoming familiar with IP addressing and where you can find the network configuration information on your computer. Then you can give help desk personnel the information needed to quickly resolve your network problem.

Let's explore the basics of IP addressing. First, an IP address is not assigned to a computer but to each network interface card (NIC) on a TCP/IP network, whether wired (Ethernet) or wireless (Wi-Fi). A modem (whether it is a cable modem, DSL modem, or an old analog modem) also has an address when you use it to connect to the Internet. If your computer has multiple network connection devices connected to different networks, such as an Ethernet network adapter connected to a LAN and a Wi-Fi or cellular connection, each must have an address when it connects to a network.

Note: A local area network (LAN) is a network that covers a building, home, office, or campus. It can be wireless or wired. A Wi-Fi network is a wireless LAN (WLAN). The typical maximum distance covered by WLAN signals or LAN cabling is in the hundreds of feet. Learn more about Wi-Fi later in this chapter.

Note: The title bar in Figure 10–1 reads: "Local Area Connection Properties." "Local Area Connection" is simply the default name Windows 7 gives an Ethernet connection. In Windows 8, the default name for this connection is "Ethernet" and the same dialog box is "Ethernet Properties."

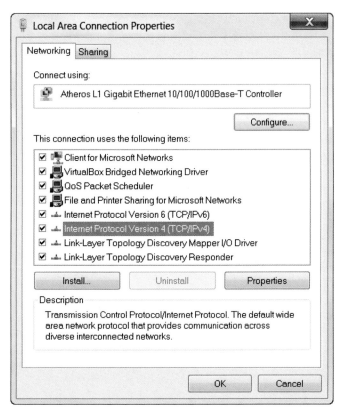

FIGURE 10–1 The Windows 7 Local Area Connection Properties dialog box.

That is why you see the Internet Protocol as a component of a connection in Windows (see Figure 10–1). The Connect Using box near the top of the Local Area Connection Properties dialog box identifies the connecting device to which these settings apply. Figure 10–1 shows that Windows supports both IPv4 and IPv6. Next, learn about IP addresses.

An **IP address**, along with a subnet mask (explained later) identifies your computer (a "host" in Internet terms), and the network on which it resides. An IP address, when added to a message packet as the destination address, allows the message to move from one network to another until it reaches its destination. At the connecting point between networks, a special network device called a router uses its routing protocols to determine the route to the destination address, before sending each packet along to the next router closer to the destination network. Each computer that directly attaches to the Internet must have a globally unique IP address. Both versions of IP have this much, and more, in common. Following are short explanations of IPv4 and IPv6 addresses.

IPv4 Addresses. IPv4 has been used on the Internet and other internetworks for the past three decades. With 32-bit addressing, calculated by raising 2 to the 32nd power (2^{32}), IPv4 offers almost 4.3 billion possible IP addresses, but the way in which they were initially allocated to organizations greatly reduced the number of usable addresses, and we have now run out of IPv4 addresses.

An IPv4 address is 32 bits long in binary notation, but it usually appears as four decimal numbers, each in the range of 0–255, separated by a period. See examples of IPv4 addresses in Figures 10–2, 10–3, and 10–4. Figure 10–2 shows the Windows 7 Network Connection Details with the address of the

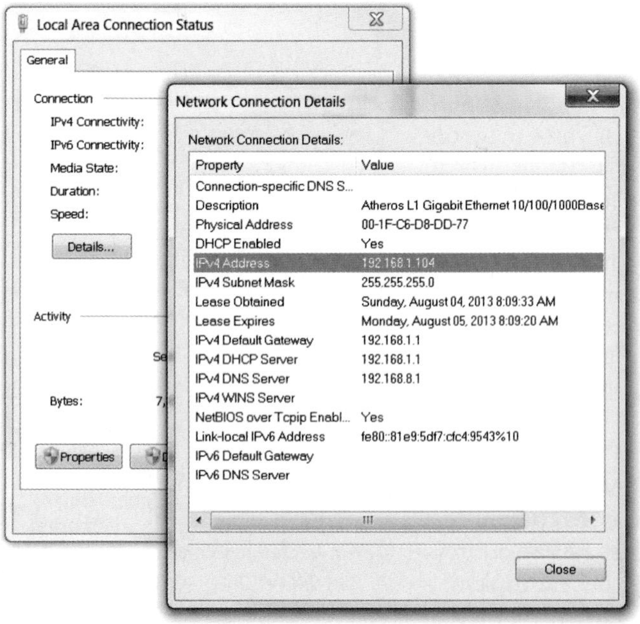

FIGURE 10–2 The Windows 7 Network Connection Details box.

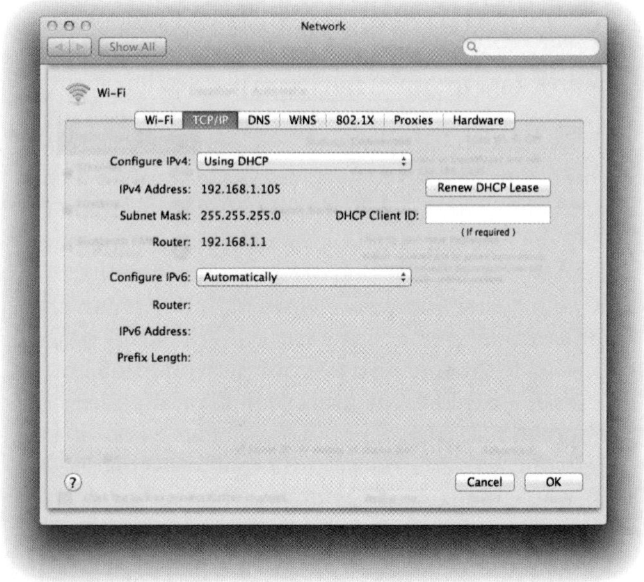

FIGURE 10–3 The OS X Network preferences pane.

local connection set as 192.168.1.104. The other IP addresses shown are to other network devices.

In the OS X Network preferences pane, shown in Figure 10–3, the Wi-Fi device (called AirPort in earlier versions of OS X) has an IPv4 address of 192.168.1.105. Figure 10–4 shows the Network dialog box from Ubuntu's Unity GUI with an IPv4 address of 10.0.2.15. Because this is a very simplified explanation, we will not go into the exact rules for these addresses, just an overview. And, as you can see, there is more to an IP configuration than the address of the device itself, but we will tell you more about IP addresses before we discuss these other settings.

FIGURE 10–4 The Network dialog box in the Ubuntu Linux Unity GUI.

IPv6 Addresses. The Internet is currently transitioning to Internet Protocol version 6 (IPv6) with a new addressing scheme that provides many more addresses. For many years, manufacturers and standards organizations worked toward the day when they could fully support IPv6 on the Internet. In fact, the World IPv6 Launch Day was June 6, 2012. On that day, however, the Internet world did not become an IPv6-only world. What did happen was that many important Internet service providers and websites became available to computers using either IPv4 or IPv6. They include Bing, Facebook, Google, Yahoo! and many more. For the near future (perhaps decades), IPv4 and IPv6 will coexist on the Internet and on all the connected private and governmental internetworks of the world. Recent versions of operating systems and virtually all new networking equipment come with support for IPv6 built in, as you saw in some of the earlier figures in this chapter.

IPv6 has 128-bit addressing, calculated by raising 2 to the 128th power (2^{128}), which supports a huge number of unique addresses—340,282,366,920, 938,463,463,374,607,431,768,211,456 to be exact. An IPv6 address appears as eight groups of four hexadecimal digits separated by colons. You will often see an IPv6 address shortened by eliminating leading zeros in a group, and if there are all zeros between a set of colons, the zeros won't show and you will see just two colons together. If two or more groups of all zeros are adjacent there will still only be two colons. In Figure 10–5 an IPv6 address is first shown in full hexadecimal notation, then with leading zeros removed, and finally as eight groups of binary numbers.

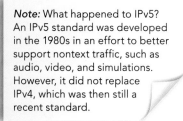

Note: What happened to IPv5? An IPv5 standard was developed in the 1980s in an effort to better support nontext traffic, such as audio, video, and simulations. However, it did not replace IPv4, which was then still a recent standard.

Note: What progress has the Internet community made in moving toward an IPv4-free world? Check out the website **www.worldipv6launch.org** to see where things stand in the IP protocol world.

An IPv6 Address in hexadecimal notation:

2002:0470:b8f9:0000:020c:29ff:fe53:45ca

The same address in hexadecimal notation with leading zeros removed:

2002:470:b8f9::20c:29ff:fe53:45ca

The same address in binary notation:

0010000000000010	0000010001110000	1011100011111001	0000000000000000
0000001000001100	0010100111111111	1111111001010011	0100010111001010

FIGURE 10–5 An IPv6 address expressed in both hexadecimal and binary notation.

Which Addresses Can You Use?

While we described both IPv4 and IPv6 addresses above, our discussion here centers around IPv4 because it will be around for a long time and you are more likely to need help resolving a problem with an IPv4 address than with an IPv6 address. There are billions of addresses, so how do you pick an address to use? Of course, the answer is—it all depends. Will you be using the address on a public network (the Internet) or on a private network? A central organization decides how to allocate all these addresses for use on the public Internet. They also understand that organizations need to use IP addresses within their private networks, and long before allocation of all the IPv4 addresses, schemes were developed to slow down the depletion of addresses. One of those schemes involved dividing the possible IP addresses into two broad categories: public addresses and private addresses.

Public Addresses. Public IP addresses are designated for hosts on the Internet. In IP terminology, a host is any computer or device that has an IP address. To communicate over the Internet, you must send your message from an IP address that is unique on the entire Internet, and your message must go to a unique IP address. The centrally responsible organization for allocation of public IP addresses is the Internet Assigned Numbers Authority (IANA). This organization allocates numbers to various Regional Internet Registries (RIRs), which have the task of allocating IP addresses to Internet service providers. The largest ISPs, in turn, allocate addresses to other ISPs. You, or your school or employer, receive addresses for each Internet connection from your ISP. The addresses provided are from selected portions of those many billions of possible addresses specifically used on the Internet.

Private Addresses. A private IP address is an address from one of three ranges of IPv4 addresses designated for use only on private networks, so they are unusable on the Internet. All the IPv4 addresses in Figures 10–2, 10–3, and 10–4 are private addresses. In fact, many organizations use these addresses on their private IP networks, and you do not need to get permission to do so.

If a computer with a private address connects to the Internet, it will not be able to communicate because Internet routers will not forward packets with private addresses. Therefore, the same private address can be in use on thousands of private networks, thus relieving some of the pressure on the limited supply of IPv4 addresses. Table 10–1 shows the three ranges used as private IPv4 addresses. All other IPv4 addresses either have specialized uses or are public addresses valid for computers and devices that are on the Internet. So how is it possible for you to communicate over the Internet if your computer's network card has a private IPv4 address? Read on to learn how this is done.

If a computer user on a private network using private IP addresses wishes to connect to the Internet, a device between the local network and the Internet must intercept, repackage, and give a public IP address as its source address to each data packet before it goes onto the Internet. Then, if there is a response, each returning packet will go through the same process before returning to the private address.

TABLE 10–1 IPv4 Private IP Address Ranges

Private IPv4 Address Ranges
10.0.0.0 through 10.255.255.255
172.16.0.0 through 172.31.255.255
192.168.0.0 through 192.168.255.255

If you are connecting to the Internet from home, or through your school or work, there is a device between your computer and the ISP that substitutes (or translates) your actual IP address to a unique Internet IP address. There are a couple of methods for doing this. One involves a special network service called a proxy server, and another involves a special service called network address translation (NAT), which a NAT router provides. These are services that your ISP or network administrator manages for your school or organization. Such services also exist in the devices now commonly sold in consumer electronics stores called Internet routers, which allow home or small-office computers to connect to the Internet, usually through a cable or DSL connection.

How Does a NIC Get an IP Address?

A NIC gets an IP address in one of two ways: static address assignment or automatic address assignment. Automatic address assignment is the most common method used today and automatic IP address assignment itself has two methods.

Static Address Assignment. A static IP address is manually configured by an administrator for a host and can, therefore, be considered semipermanent—that is, it stays with the device until someone takes action to change it. Manually configuring an IP address involves manually entering the IP address and other necessary IP settings. Most organizations do static IP addressing only on servers, network printers, and network devices such as routers that are required to have static addresses.

Where will you find this information in the rare event that you are required to use a static address on your desktop or laptop computer? Actually, unless you are setting up your own TCP/IP network (a very advanced task!), you will be given the IP addressing information by a network administrator if you are connecting to a LAN at school or work, or by your Internet service provider if you are configuring an Internet connection. But most ISPs automate all the configuration of home Internet connections.

If you find yourself having to do this, be sure to carefully enter the numbers given to you, and double-check them! In Windows, you will enter these in the TCP/IP properties found in the properties dialog box for the network connection.

Automatic Address Assignment. One nearly universal method is used for assigning IP addresses to computers: automatic IP addressing. Another method is used as a sort of fail-safe: Automatic Private IP Addressing (APIPA).

- Most organizations use automatic IP addressing for their desktop computers. It requires a special server or service on the network, called a Dynamic Host Configuration Protocol (DHCP) server, which issues IP addresses and settings to computers configured to obtain an IP address automatically, thus making them DHCP clients. The news gets even better since the default configuration of TCP/IP on a Windows, Mac, or Linux (depending on the distribution) computer is to obtain an IP address automatically. Look for the line in Figure 10–2 that shows that DHCP is enabled for Windows 7, and in Figure 10–3 the Mac OS X Network preferences dialog box shows that it is using DHCP to configure IPv4. However, in the Ubuntu Linux Network dialog box in Figure 10–4, you would need to click the Options button and bring up the Editing Wired connection 1 dialog box (not shown) to learn how the network card receives an IP address.

> **WARNING!**
> Incorrect IP configuration settings can make your network connection useless. Modify IP configuration settings only if a network administrator or your ISP provides you with settings and tells you to. Then, take great care to be accurate!

Note: Flip back to Figure 10–2 showing the Network Connection Details. The third line from the bottom contains the link-local IPv6 address fe80::81e9:5df7:cfc4:9543%10. In this case, the NIC assigned this address to itself because it did not receive an address. This NIC communicates on the network using the IPv4 address.

- Do not confuse *automatic* with *automatic private*. Most operating systems will enable a feature of DHCP—**Automatic Private IP Addressing (APIPA)**, whereby a DHCP client computer that fails to receive an address from a DHCP server will automatically give itself an address from a special range that has 169.254 in the first two octets of the IPv4 address. This is also called a link-local address, and IPv6 uses addresses that begin with fe80::. If a computer uses a link-local address, it will only be able to communicate on the local network segment, and even then only with other devices and computers that use the same network ID.

APIPA allows a novice to set up a small TCP/IP network without needing to learn about IP addressing. Each computer would use APIPA to assign itself an address, first testing that no other computer on the LAN is also using that same host ID. Theoretically, two or more computers on the same network using this method could do file-and-printer sharing.

IP Configuration Settings

If you must manually configure IPv4, you will need to understand the other settings to enter in addition to the IP address. Refer to the Internet Protocol Version 4 Properties dialog box in Figure 10–6 while reading the following descriptions of the various IP settings.

Subnet Mask. When a network device gets an IP address, it must also get a subnet mask. The subnet mask for an IPv4 address is as critical as the address itself because it takes what looks like a single address and divides it into two addresses by masking off part of the address. It is a little like your house address. The house number gives the address on the street, but you also need

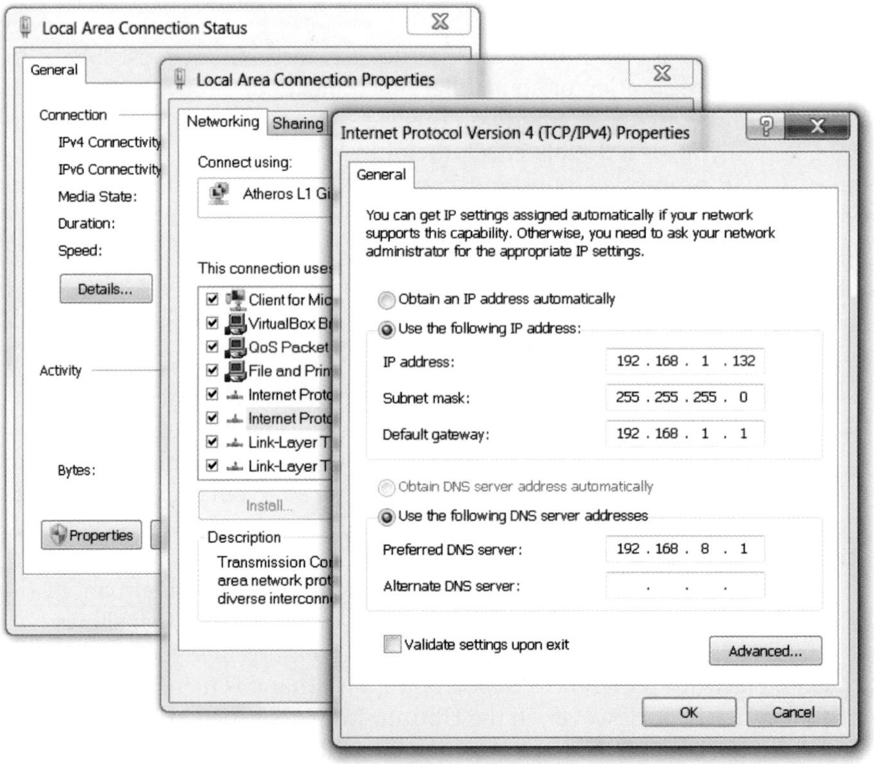

FIGURE 10–6 Manually configure TCP/IP in Windows using the Internet Protocol Version 4 (TCP/IPv4) Properties dialog box.

the street name. If you look at the Properties dialog box in Figure 10–6, the address 192.168.1.132 has a mask of 255.255.255.0. The IP protocol now knows that this network device has the host address of 132 (its house number) on network 192.168.1 (its street name). The host address is the host ID, and the network address is the net ID.

Let's take a brief look at how masking works. Technically, it is done using binary math (base-2 math that uses only 0s and 1s), but you do not have to be a binary math whiz to understand the concept of masking; just look at the IP address and the mask in its binary form. You can use the scientific setting of the Calculator program that comes with Windows to convert each octet (a group of eight binary digits) of an IP address from binary to decimal or vice versa. Using an IP address of 192.168.100.2, if you convert this address to binary, it looks like this:

11000000.10101000.01100100.00000010.

If you convert the mask of 255.255.255.0 to binary, it looks like this:

11111111.11111111.11111111.00000000.

If you lay the mask on top of the IP address, the ones cover (mask) the first 24 bits (short for binary digits). What falls under the ones of the mask is the network address, and what falls under the zeros of the mask is the host address. Figure 10–7 should make this concept clearer.

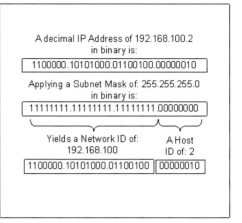

FIGURE 10–7 A subnet mask covers a portion of an IP address.

Default Gateway. The next entry shown back in Figure 10–6 is the default gateway. This is the IP address of the router connected to your network. The router is the network device that directs traffic to destinations beyond the local network. The net ID of the gateway address should be identical to the net ID of your NIC. Without a properly configured router, as well as the correct address (Default Gateway) for reaching this router, you cannot communicate with computers beyond your network. In our example in Figure 10–6, the router connects network 192.168.1 to other networks. Anytime your computer has a packet destined for a network with a network address other than 192.168.1, IP will send the packet to the gateway address to be forwarded to a host on another network.

DNS Servers. The last two settings are addresses of Domain Name System (DNS) servers. DNS is a distributed online database containing registered domain names mapped to IP addresses. Thousands of name servers on the Internet maintain this distributed database. When you attempt to connect to a website, such as www.mhhe.com, your computer's DNS client queries a DNS server to determine the IP address for that website.

You may enter two addresses in the Microsoft Properties dialog shown in Figure 10–6—a primary DNS server and a secondary DNS server. The primary DNS server is the server the DNS client on your computer contacts any time you make a request to connect to a server using a domain name rather than an IP address. The DNS server will attempt to resolve the name to an IP address. The DNS client contacts the second DNS server only if there is no response from the first DNS server, but it does not use the second DNS server when the first DNS server responds that it cannot resolve the name. This is when you see an error similar to: "DNS query for www.*somedomainname*.com failed: host not found."

The Internet Corporation for Assigned Names and Numbers (ICANN), a California nonprofit corporation, currently oversees the Domain Name System, after having replaced an organization called InterNIC. The U.S. government sanctions ICANN, which reports to the U.S. Department of Commerce.

Anyone wishing to acquire a domain name contacts one of the roughly 200 domain name registrars of top-level domains (.com, .org, .pro, .info, .biz, and so on) accredited by ICANN. Once registered with ICANN, each domain name and its IP address go on the Internet Domain Name Servers so that users can access Internet services offered under those domain names.

Step-by-Step 10.01

Examine a Connection's IP Configuration in a GUI

In this step-by-step exercise, you will examine a connection's IP configuration in the Windows GUI. The illustrations are from Windows 7, but this also works in Windows 8. You will need:

- A computer with Windows 7 or Windows 8.
- A user account and password for the computer.

Step 1

Open Control Panel and under Network and Internet click View network status and tasks. This opens the Network and Sharing Center.

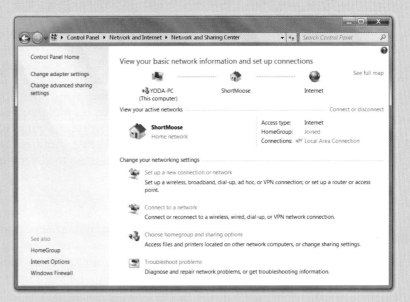

Step 2

In the Network and Sharing Center click **Change adapter settings** in the task list on the left. This opens the Network Connection window. Our example has only one network connection device, but you may have more than one listed.

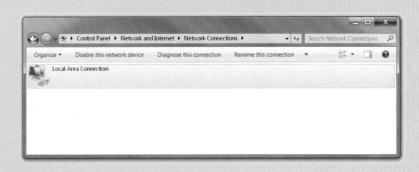

Step 3

Double-click on the network connection you wish to examine. This opens the Status dialog box for the connection.

Step 4

Click the Details button. This will open the Network Connection Details box, as shown back in Figure 10–2. This is a good place to see the IP address of your NIC in the GUI.

Step 5

If you wish to make changes to the configuration, click the Close button to return to the Status dialog box. Then click the Properties button on the Status page to open the properties for this connection.

Step 6

Keep in mind that only an advanced user should make changes to the network configuration. To look at the Properties dialog box for IPv4 for this connection double-click Internet Protocol Version 4 (TCP/IPv4).

Step 7

When you have examined the configuration, click Cancel to close each open box without making changes. Then click Close to close the connection you examined, and then close the Network Connections window.

```
D:\Windows\system32\cmd.exe

D:\Users\Yoda>ipconfig /all

Windows IP Configuration

   Host Name . . . . . . . . . . . . : Yoda-PC
   Primary Dns Suffix  . . . . . . . :
   Node Type . . . . . . . . . . . . : Hybrid
   IP Routing Enabled. . . . . . . . : No
   WINS Proxy Enabled. . . . . . . . : No

Ethernet adapter Local Area Connection:

   Connection-specific DNS Suffix  . :
   Description . . . . . . . . . . . : Realtek PCI GBE Family Controller
   Physical Address. . . . . . . . . : 00-27-19-CD-2F-C2
   DHCP Enabled. . . . . . . . . . . : Yes
   Autoconfiguration Enabled . . . . : Yes
   Link-local IPv6 Address . . . . . : fe80::607f:c2b:3650:edcb%11(Preferred)
   IPv4 Address. . . . . . . . . . . : 192.168.1.134(Preferred)
   Subnet Mask . . . . . . . . . . . : 255.255.255.0
   Lease Obtained. . . . . . . . . . : Sunday, November 21, 2010 7:05:43 AM
   Lease Expires . . . . . . . . . . : Monday, November 22, 2010 7:05:51 AM
   Default Gateway . . . . . . . . . : 192.168.1.1
   DHCP Server . . . . . . . . . . . : 192.168.1.1
   DHCPv6 IAID . . . . . . . . . . . : 234891033
   DHCPv6 Client DUID. . . . . . . . : 00-01-00-01-14-2D-C9-A0-00-27-19-CD-2F-C2

   DNS Servers . . . . . . . . . . . : 192.168.8.1
   NetBIOS over Tcpip. . . . . . . . : Enabled
```

FIGURE 10–8 The output from running the command ipconfig /all.

Viewing an IP Configuration from a Command Prompt

You can view the IP configuration of a Windows, Linux, or Mac OS X computer from a Command Prompt using either IPCONFIG (Windows) or **ifconfig** (Linux and Mac OS X).

In the Windows Command Prompt use the **ipconfig** command without any command-line switches to have it display only the IP address (both IPv4 and IPv6, when present), subnet mask, and default gateway for each NIC that is connected to a network. Using the command with the **/all** switch will display much more information for each NIC. For instance, without this switch no detail is listed under Windows IP Configuration, but with the **/all** switch, as shown in Figure 10–8, several lines display, beginning with the Host Name. Then, for each adapter, in addition to the basic IP address, subnet mask, and default gateway, all the IP configuration information for each NIC displays. This includes the physical address, several lines of information pertaining to DHCP, and one or more DNS server addresses, if available, as well as the status of NetBIOS over TCP/IP, a protocol used for downward compatibility in networks with older Windows versions.

try this!

View Your IP Configuration from a Windows Command Prompt

Check out your current IP configuration using the **ipconfig** command. Try this:

1. Open a Command Prompt.
2. At the prompt type **ipconfig**.
3. After viewing the results of the command, type the command again with the **/all** switch: **ipconfig /all**.
4. Notice the additional information the **/all** switch provides.

The equivalent of the Windows **ipconfig** command in the Mac OS X Terminal window or at a $ prompt in Linux is the **ifconfig** command. Open a Terminal window in OS X or access the $ prompt in Linux and enter the **ifconfig** command with the **-a** switch to see all information about all network interfaces in that computer. The results for a Mac OS X Terminal window are shown in Figure 10–9 and from the $ prompt in Linux Ubuntu in Figure 10–10. Notice that the information in OS X and in Linux is more difficult to decipher than it is in Windows. For instance, in both Figures 10–9 and 10–10 the lines labeled "inet6" refer to IPv6, while those beginning with "inet" refer to IPv4. You'll find the physical addresses of installed NICs in Figure 10–9 on lines beginning with "ether." In Figure 10–10 the line containing the physical address of the Ethernet NIC is in the first line of the section labeled eth0.

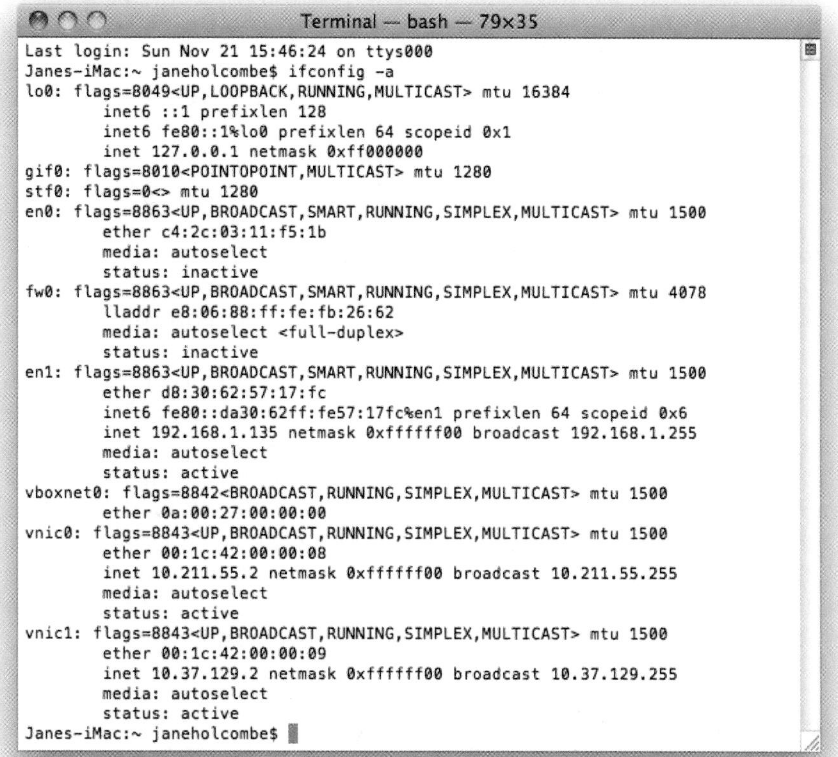

```
● ● ●                    Terminal — bash — 79×35
Last login: Sun Nov 21 15:46:24 on ttys000
Janes-iMac:~ janeholcombe$ ifconfig -a
lo0: flags=8049<UP,LOOPBACK,RUNNING,MULTICAST> mtu 16384
        inet6 ::1 prefixlen 128
        inet6 fe80::1%lo0 prefixlen 64 scopeid 0x1
        inet 127.0.0.1 netmask 0xff000000
gif0: flags=8010<POINTOPOINT,MULTICAST> mtu 1280
stf0: flags=0<> mtu 1280
en0: flags=8863<UP,BROADCAST,SMART,RUNNING,SIMPLEX,MULTICAST> mtu 1500
        ether c4:2c:03:11:f5:1b
        media: autoselect
        status: inactive
fw0: flags=8863<UP,BROADCAST,SMART,RUNNING,SIMPLEX,MULTICAST> mtu 4078
        lladdr e8:06:88:ff:fe:fb:26:62
        media: autoselect <full-duplex>
        status: inactive
en1: flags=8863<UP,BROADCAST,SMART,RUNNING,SIMPLEX,MULTICAST> mtu 1500
        ether d8:30:62:57:17:fc
        inet6 fe80::da30:62ff:fe57:17fc%en1 prefixlen 64 scopeid 0x6
        inet 192.168.1.135 netmask 0xffffff00 broadcast 192.168.1.255
        media: autoselect
        status: active
vboxnet0: flags=8842<BROADCAST,RUNNING,SIMPLEX,MULTICAST> mtu 1500
        ether 0a:00:27:00:00:00
vnic0: flags=8843<UP,BROADCAST,RUNNING,SIMPLEX,MULTICAST> mtu 1500
        ether 00:1c:42:00:00:08
        inet 10.211.55.2 netmask 0xffffff00 broadcast 10.211.55.255
        media: autoselect
        status: active
vnic1: flags=8843<UP,BROADCAST,RUNNING,SIMPLEX,MULTICAST> mtu 1500
        ether 00:1c:42:00:00:09
        inet 10.37.129.2 netmask 0xffffff00 broadcast 10.37.129.255
        media: autoselect
        status: active
Janes-iMac:~ janeholcombe$ █
```

FIGURE 10–9 The result of running the **ifconfig -a** command in a Terminal window in OS X.

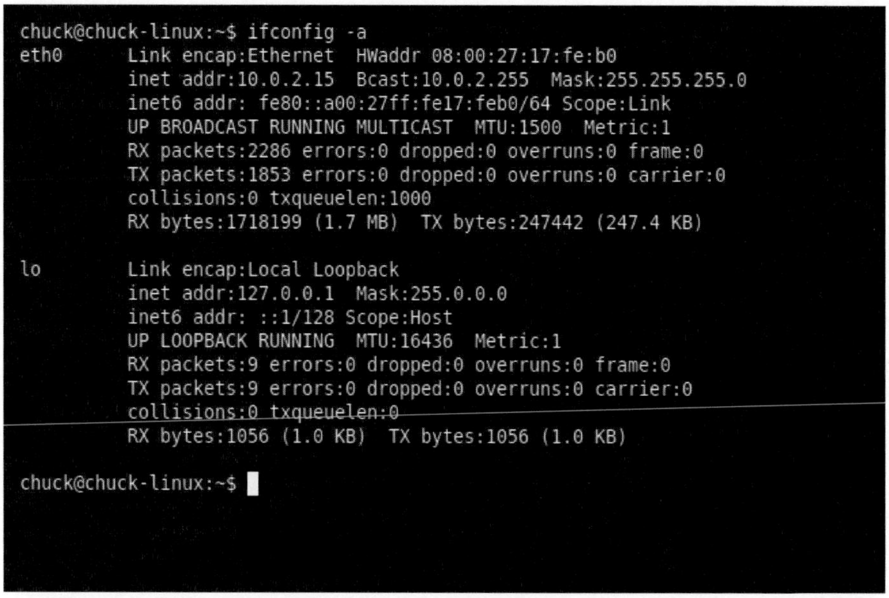

```
chuck@chuck-linux:~$ ifconfig -a
eth0      Link encap:Ethernet   HWaddr 08:00:27:17:fe:b0
          inet addr:10.0.2.15  Bcast:10.0.2.255  Mask:255.255.255.0
          inet6 addr: fe80::a00:27ff:fe17:feb0/64 Scope:Link
          UP BROADCAST RUNNING MULTICAST  MTU:1500  Metric:1
          RX packets:2286 errors:0 dropped:0 overruns:0 frame:0
          TX packets:1853 errors:0 dropped:0 overruns:0 carrier:0
          collisions:0 txqueuelen:1000
          RX bytes:1718199 (1.7 MB)  TX bytes:247442 (247.4 KB)

lo        Link encap:Local Loopback
          inet addr:127.0.0.1  Mask:255.0.0.0
          inet6 addr: ::1/128 Scope:Host
          UP LOOPBACK RUNNING  MTU:16436  Metric:1
          RX packets:9 errors:0 dropped:0 overruns:0 frame:0
          TX packets:9 errors:0 dropped:0 overruns:0 carrier:0
          collisions:0 txqueuelen:0
          RX bytes:1056 (1.0 KB)  TX bytes:1056 (1.0 KB)

chuck@chuck-linux:~$ █
```

FIGURE 10–10 The result of running the **ifconfig -a** command at the $ prompt in Ubuntu Linux.

LO 10.2 | Connecting to the Internet

A connection to the Internet is a wide area network (WAN) connection. A wide area network (WAN) is a network that covers a very large geographic area. A WAN connection is a connection to a network over a long distance (miles). There are several WAN technologies to choose from. Some of these are wired technologies, and some are wireless. You must initiate some connections every time you wish to connect to the Internet. Most connection methods described here remain available 24/7, in which case, Internet access is as simple as opening your browser or sending an email. The connections include a wide range of speeds. In this section, we will compare the various means of connecting a network or computer to the Internet and discuss the most common methods for doing so from home or a small business so that you can make a decision for yourself. This will also help you to understand something about how you are connecting to the Internet from school or work, although we will not discuss the very expensive high-speed WAN services for connecting a large enterprise (commercial, government, or educational) to the Internet.

The choice of physical means of connecting to the Internet closely relates to your choice of an organization that will give you access to the Internet. This section includes an overview of these organizations first. Then you will consider the differences between a direct computer-to-Internet connection versus a computer-to-LAN-to-Internet connection. And finally, you will learn about the technologies used at the connection point to the Internet, regardless of whether it is a single computer or a LAN connection. Most of the screenshots used as examples in this section are Microsoft Windows 7, but all OSs surveyed in this book have capabilities similar to those described here.

Internet Service Providers

An Internet service provider (ISP) is an organization that provides individuals or entire companies with access to the Internet. For a fee, an ISP provides you with this connection service and may offer other Internet-related services, such as Web-server hosting and email. Many ISPs provide proprietary software for Web browsing, email management, and accessing other Internet services. Some ISPs specialize in certain connection types. For instance, HughesNet and dishNET are both ISPs that specialize in satellite Internet services. T-Mobile (www.tmobile.com), Verizon, and AT&T all provide ISP services for their cellular customers; and your local telephone company may provide ISP services for dial-up, DSL, and even cable customers. Virtually all cable TV providers also provide Internet service.

try this!

Find Internet Service Providers

You can use the Internet to find ISPs you might want to use. Try this:

1. Use your Web browser to connect to your favorite search engine, search on "Internet Service Provider," and brace yourself for a *long* list of ISPs and sites related to ISPs.

2. To find ISPs that specialize in satellite connections, for example, search on "Internet Satellite Data Service Provider."

3. Then, further refine your search to just one country by entering a country name in the search by results box.

Computer-to-Internet versus LAN-to-Internet

Almost any computer will first connect to a LAN or WLAN, which in turn connects to a router on its way to the Internet. There is usually at least one router between your computing device and the Internet.

At the point of connection at home, you will have some sort of modem (cable, DSL, or analog). One port of the modem connects to a WAN connection

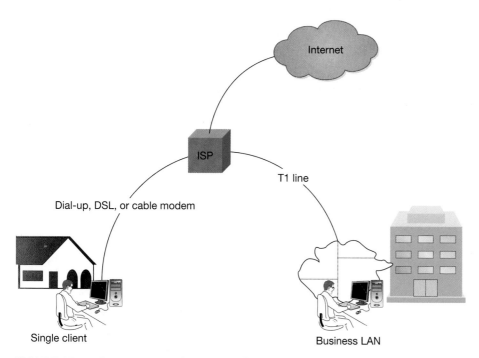

FIGURE 10–11 Connecting to the Internet from a single computer or from a LAN.

and then to an ISP. The other port may connect directly to a computer or, most often, to a router that in many cases is also a wireless access point (WAP) and an Ethernet switch. At school or work, client computers connect to a LAN or WLAN, which ultimately connects through a router to a high-speed Internet connection. Figure 10–11 shows these two scenarios.

Wired Connectivity Technologies

Many wired WAN technologies for connecting to the Internet utilize the telecommunications infrastructure of the telephone system—either in its traditional state or with upgrades and equipment added to that infrastructure. Another private network often used for wired Internet connections belongs to the cable TV companies, which provide Internet access for their customers.

Dial-up Connections Using Analog Modems

A technology that clearly takes advantage of the traditional phone system is dial-up, an inexpensive choice available to anyone with a standard phone line and an analog modem. At one time every laptop came with an internal analog modem.

Analog modems as standard equipment in laptops have gone the way of the buggy whip. Never heard of buggy whips? That's our point. Maybe you haven't heard of modems, either, which further supports our opinion of modems. However, dial-up is the only low-cost means of connecting to the Internet in some areas of the world, including within the United States, and millions still use dial-up, so we will devote some space to this topic.

The longtime speed standard for dial-up is 56 kilobits per second (Kbps). The dial-up connection at 56 Kbps is very slow compared to a LAN running at 100 megabits per second (Mbps) or 1 gigabit per second (Gbps). In addition to a standard phone line (what we often call a "land line") you also need to subscribe to an Internet connection service from an ISP. The cost of the ISP subscription should be your only cost in addition to your phone service. But it is an either/or situation—you may either use the modem *or* use the phone *or*

Note: Who still uses dial-up? Apparently millions of Americans still do. A line in AOL's second-quarter 2013 earnings report listed over 2.5 million Domestic AOL-brand access subscribers. This category appears to be mainly their dial-up ISP services. According to Brian Fung of *The Washington Post*'s *The Switch* blog, around 17 percent of dial-up users live where no broadband is available, and 35 percent of dial-up users say the price needs to fall before they will switch to broadband.

use a fax machine. When using an analog modem you may not use the phone line simultaneously for voice or fax.

In a dial-up connection to the Internet, your computer uses its modem to dial a telephone number provided by the ISP (hence the term *dial-up connection*). One of many modems maintained by the ISP at its facility answers your computer's call; a server maintained by the ISP for authenticating customers authenticates you, and then the ISP routes traffic between your computer and the Internet for that session. Like a voice phone conversation, the connection is only temporary and ends when either your PC or the ISP's server ends the call. Most ISP servers disconnect a dial-up connection automatically after a certain period of inactivity.

High-Speed Wired Access

If multiple users need to share an Internet connection, the connection between the network and the ISP must be adequate to simultaneously carry the traffic created by all the users at peak usage times. The authors presently have a Wi-Fi router connected to a DSL modem. Through that wireless router we connect four desktop computers (two Windows PCs, one Linux computer, one iMac), one Windows 8 laptop, two Kindles, two smartphones, an iPad, and a Samsung Galaxy tablet. That's 11 devices for just two people. Many families exceed that number. For this you need high-speed WAN connections, such as the four wired options we describe here, or one of the wireless options detailed later.

Integrated Services Digital Network. Integrated services digital network (ISDN) is a digital telephone service that simultaneously transmits voice, data, and control signaling over a single telephone line. ISDN service operates on standard telephone lines but requires a special modem and phone service, which adds to the cost. An ISDN data connection can transfer data at up to 128,000 bits per second (128 Kbps). This seems extremely slow to most of us with faster options. While rarely used in homes in the United States, ISDN may be all that is available for a wired WAN connection in some areas, especially outside of the United States.

The benefits of ISDN (beyond the faster speed compared to a dial-up connection) include being able to connect a PC, telephone, and fax machine to a single ISDN line and use them simultaneously.

ISDN has fallen out of favor in many areas where there are higher performance options, such as cable and DSL. In remote parts of the world, another optional broadband service, satellite communications, may be a more viable option than ISDN because it does not require the wired infrastructure needed by ISDN.

Digital Subscriber Line. Digital subscriber line (DSL) service is similar to ISDN in its use of the telephone network, but it uses more advanced digital signal processing to compress more signals through the telephone lines. Because you can use DSL only within a few miles of the central office, it requires component changes in the telephone network before they can offer it. Like ISDN, DSL service can provide simultaneous data, voice, and fax transmissions on the same line. It gives you a dedicated circuit from your home or office to the central office and the service can usually guarantee consistent upload and download speeds.

Several versions of DSL services are available for home and business use. Each version provides a different level of service, speed, and distance, and each normally provides full-time connections. The two most common are asynchronous DSL (ADSL) and synchronous DSL (SDSL). ADSL is the type of service normally available to home users. Other versions include high-data-rate DSL (HDSL) and very high-data-rate DSL (VDSL). The abbreviation often used to refer to DSL service in general begins with an *x* (*x*DSL), reflecting the varied first character in the DSL implementations.

Across the DSL services offered by various ISPs, data transmission speeds range from 128 Kbps for basic DSL service through 24 Mbps for high-end service. When describing DSL speeds, they usually refer to the speed of traffic flowing "downstream"—that is, from the ISP to your computer. For instance, the authors subscribe to a rural phone company's ADSL service, which provides a downstream speed of 10 Mbps, but an upstream speed of 1 Mbps. While SDSL provides the same speed in each direction, it is much more expensive and not widely available. Most home users require only the higher speeds for downloads (browsing the Internet, downloading multimedia files, and so on), so SDSL service is only practical for customers who must upload a great deal of data. If you have a Web server on your network, it uploads data every time an Internet user accessed it so it would benefit from SDSL service. Additionally, you would also want a static IP address for this server, a second expensive option. As a rule, if you require a website for a small business or hobby, the cheapest and most reliable way to do this is to use a web-hosting service that will host your website on their servers, on fast networks, and provide a wide range of optional services.

Although the various Internet servers must upload a great deal of data in response to user requests, commercial Internet servers are normally hosted on much faster links than those discussed here.

Cable. Many cable television companies now use a portion of their network's bandwidth to offer Internet access through existing cable television connections. They call this Internet connection option cable modem service because of the need to use a special cable modem to connect.

Cable networks use coaxial cable, which can transmit data as much as 100 times faster than common telephone lines. Coaxial cable allows transmission over several channels simultaneously. Internet data can be on one channel while transmitting audio, video, and control signals separately. A user can access the Internet from his or her computer and watch cable television at the same time, over the same cable connection, without the two data streams interfering with one another.

The biggest drawback to cable modem service is the fact that the subscribers in a defined area share the signal. As the number of users in an area increases, less bandwidth is available to each user. Therefore, while cable providers advertise higher speeds than DSL, they cannot guarantee consistent speeds.

Wireless Connectivity Technologies

Like wired communications, wireless has moved from analog to digital over the years. Today, you can connect to the Internet through cellular networks, wireless wide area networks (WWANs), wireless LAN (WLAN) connections (if the WLAN ultimately connects to the Internet), and by satellite.

Smartphones support both voice and high-speed cellular data service, allowing users to surf the Internet from any location offering the required signal. Cellular Internet companies usually meter their connections, meaning that your plan allows only a predetermined amount of downstream data per month. Extra charges apply if you exceed the permitted amount.

In addition, modern smartphones also come with Wi-Fi. This allows users to configure their phones to use a Wi-Fi connection, when available, for connecting to the Internet, thus saving on connection and data charges from their cellular provider.

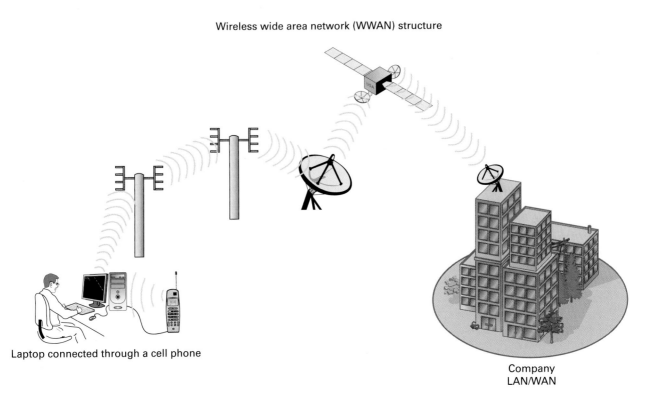

Wireless wide area network (WWAN) structure

Laptop connected through a cell phone

Company
LAN/WAN

FIGURE 10–12 A WWAN includes devices that retransmit the wireless signal.

Tablets optionally have cellular communications features as well as Wi-Fi, allowing Web browsing, and communicating by email and other features.

Wireless WAN Connections

A wireless wide area network (WWAN) is a digital network that extends over a large geographical area. A WWAN receives and transmits data using radio signals over cellular sites and satellites, which makes the network accessible to mobile computer systems. At the switching center, the WWAN splits off into segments and then connects to a public or private network via telephone or other high-speed communication links. The data then links to an organization's existing LAN/WAN infrastructure (see Figure 10–12). The coverage area for a WWAN, normally measured in miles or kilometers, makes it therefore more susceptible to environmental factors, such as weather and terrain, than are wired networks.

A WWAN is a fully bidirectional wireless network capable of data transfer at speeds in excess of 100 Mbps for a cost comparable to most DSL services. Usually, basic WWAN services offer connection speeds between 1 and 10 Mbps. With dedicated equipment, the speeds can reach 100 Mbps. A WWAN system requires an antenna tuned to receive the proper radio frequency (RF).

A cellular Internet connection is an example of a WWAN. Many cellular services offer Internet access. That access may be directly from a smartphone, in which case, special software is included in the phone to provide a user interface. Some cellular providers also allow for the use of cellular modems with a desktop or laptop computer. Most cellular services sell a cellular modem card.

Satellite

Satellite connections are as suitable for large businesses as for small offices, cybercafés, individuals, homes, and the armed forces. Satellite is the WAN of choice when it is not possible or practical to use a wired connection and when cellular WAN services are not available or are too slow or costly. Satellite Internet providers offer several levels of service based on speed and they offer either stationary installations or mobile installations. The hardware cost for a mobile satellite installation is considerably higher than that for a stationary installation, and the ongoing service fees are higher, too.

Satellite Internet Connection Speeds. Like ADSL, satellite data communication is usually faster downstream than upstream. The discrepancy can be huge, as we found when we had our own mobile satellite system installed on our motor home in 2003. During our three years of living and working on the road, we often achieved download speeds of 400 Kbps to 800 Kbps (and occasionally more), but upload speeds were only in the range of 25 to 45 Kbps. While these speeds seem minimal compared to the mobile satellite options available today, the system worked well for us because, like most Internet users, our greatest need was for fast downloads as we browsed the Internet or downloaded files. At the time, cellular service was slow or simply did not exist in most locations, and so we found a mobile satellite connection was the best solution as long as we were careful not to park under trees or other obstacles to the satellite signal.

Satellite Internet Connection Costs. Today, the price of consumer-grade mobile satellite equipment and the basic monthly service fees are four times more expensive than they were in 2003. But the base plan speeds from our former provider are much faster, at 3 Mbps down and 1 Mbps up. If you are willing to spend the money on the appropriate equipment and service, you can have mobile satellite speeds of up to 5 Mbps down and 2 Mbps up.

Satellite Internet Connection Latency. However, satellite communications tend to have a higher latency, or lag. Think of watching a news broadcast that includes a foreign correspondent reporting over a satellite link. The news anchor in the studio asks a question, and you see the correspondent on the screen with a frozen smile while he or she waits to hear the question in its entirety. While it is barely noticeable when someone is reporting the news, such latency is very undesirable for real-time Internet applications, such as online games. Many IT professionals consider satellite connections unreliable, but it can be the best solution for Internet communications in remote areas.

When individuals or organizations contract with an ISP for satellite service, they install an Earth-based communications station. It usually includes three parts: a transceiver (a combined transmitter and receiver), a device that for simplicity we call a modem, and the satellite dish on its mount. You place the satellite dish outdoors in direct line-of-sight of one of several data satellites in geostationary orbit around the Earth. The modem connects the other components to the computer or LAN. A mobile installation (on a land- or water-based vehicle) is generally much more expensive than a stationary installation because the mount must allow for moving the dish to align on the satellite, and therefore requires controlling circuitry and a costly motor-driven mount to achieve this with precision. The monthly service plans for mobile satellite communications are also more expensive than those for stationary installations.

Because a satellite traveling in a geostationary orbit moves at the same speed as the Earth's rotation it hovers over the same location on the Earth—therefore you can align a satellite dish antenna precisely on the satellite. The satellite links the user's satellite dish to a land-based satellite operations center, through which the signal goes to the Internet (see Figure 10–13).

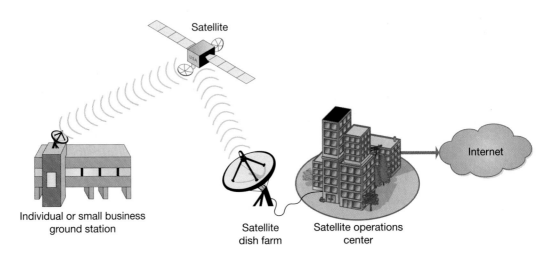

FIGURE 10–13 Accessing the Internet through a satellite WAN connection.

WLAN Connections

A wireless LAN (WLAN) is a local area network, usually using one of the standards referred to as Wi-Fi (for wireless fidelity). The Wi-Fi standards of the Institute of Electrical and Electronics Engineers include 802.11a, 802.11b, 802.11g, 802.11n, and 802.11ac listed from oldest to newest. The maximum distance covered by a WLAN is a few hundred feet rather than miles. Therefore, this is not a technology that connects directly to an ISP (as a WWAN or satellite connection will) but can be used to connect to another LAN or device with a WAN connection. This is the technology of Internet cafés, wireless laptops, tablets, and smartphones. With enough wireless hubs, called wireless access points (WAPs), an entire community can offer wireless access to a shared Internet connection.

Many of us have one of the high-speed WAN technologies described above and connect multiple devices to them through a device that is both a wireless access point (WAP) and an Internet router. The authors presently have a Wi-Fi router connected to an ADSL connection. Through that wireless router we connect all our computing devices to the Internet.

The latest IEEE 802.11 standards are both faster and more secure owing to encryption technology. Therefore, we regularly replace our Wi-Fi devices with newer ones that are up to the new standards.

Using a Virtual Private Network

Mobile users and remote offices often need to connect to a corporate intranet through the Internet using any of the connection technologies discussed earlier. You can make such a connection more secure by connecting through a virtual private network (VPN), over an existing WAN connection. Think of a VPN as a simulated private network that runs inside a "tunnel" from end point to end point. When an individual connects from a computer or mobile device we call this connection a remote access VPN (see Figure 10–14). When two networks connect by VPN, we call it a site-to-site VPN.

One end is a computer connected to the Internet, while the other end is a VPN server in the private network. The tunnel effect is the result of encapsulating each data packet sent at one end of the tunnel and removing it from the encapsulation at the receiving end. Because the encapsulation itself provides only a very small amount of protection we need to apply other measures to protect the data, such as encrypting the data, and requiring authentication at both ends of the tunnel.

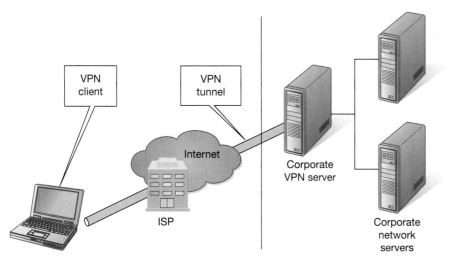

FIGURE 10–14 A remote access VPN.

LO 10.3 | Using Internet Clients

The growth in the number and type of Internet services has increased the number of client types required to access those services. We will limit our discussion of Internet clients to Web browsers, email clients, and FTP clients. Many services are accessible through Web browsers. Email may be the most important service on the Internet—many people, who have no other use for the Internet, use email. And finally, the File Transfer Protocol (FTP) remains an important file transfer method for large files on the Internet.

Web Browsers

While the World Wide Web (the Web) is just one of many services that exist on the Internet, it alone is responsible for most of the huge growth in Internet use that began after the Web's introduction in the early 1990s. Web technologies changed the look of Internet content from all text to rich and colorful graphics, and made it simple to navigate the Web by using a special type of client called a Web browser.

The Web browser's ease of use hides the complexity of the Internet, as protocols help to transfer the content of a Web page to the user's computer. There the Web browser translates the plain-text language into a rich, colorful document that may contain links to other pages—often at disparate locations on the Internet. Today, the popular free Web browsers come in versions for Mac OS X, Microsoft Windows, and Linux. Beyond the desktop, you'll find versions of these and other Web browsers with scaled-down screens for smartphones and other hugely popular mobile devices. In short, just about any electronic device that can connect to the Internet and has a display has some kind of browser.

Web browsers are free; Apple's Safari is bundled with OS X and Internet Explorer is bundled with Microsoft Windows. Are they the best browsers to use on those OSs? You will want to try different browsers and see for yourself.

Online reviews rate Google Chrome, Mozilla Firefox, and Microsoft Internet Explorer as the top three. We will not provide a source for these reviews because the most up-to-date review site we found had a problem. When one of the authors downloaded and installed Google Chrome from a link at the review site, the resulting Chrome installation had very annoying adware installed with it, as did the other two browsers on that computer. She finally succeeded in installing Chrome using a link at Google.com. Of course, she had broken her own rule that you always download programs directly from the source—not from a download service.

Common Browser Features

Popular browsers share many of the same features for both general browsing and security. General browser features found in most browsers include:

- Add-ons
- Autofill
- Automatic updates
- Bookmarks
- Integrated search engine
- Password manager

- RSS feeds
- Save tabs
- Search within page
- Synchronization
- Tabbed browsing
- Zoom

Google Chrome

Google Chrome is software from the Chromium open-source project and other sources. It is in its 28th major version at this writing and has a clean look with no menu bar, but a small button on the right called the Chrome button that opens the Customize and Control menu (shown in Figure 10–15). From this menu you can access any feature you would find in a menu bar. The Settings option opens your personal settings page (saved with your Google account). The Help option connects to Chrome's online help.

Mozilla Firefox

Mozilla Firefox, a product of the Mozilla Foundation, is a longtime favorite, currently at version 23, shown in Figure 10–16. The Firefox add-on, FireFTP, is our workhorse FTP client (discussed later in this chapter). Firefox has a menu bar with important options and settings. If it is not visible, press the ALT key to open it whenever you need it. If you wish to keep the menu bar visible, press ALT, select the View menu (see Figure 10–17) and select Toolbars. Then click to place a check by Menu Bar and any other toolbar you want to stay visible. To find other important settings open the Tools menu and select Options

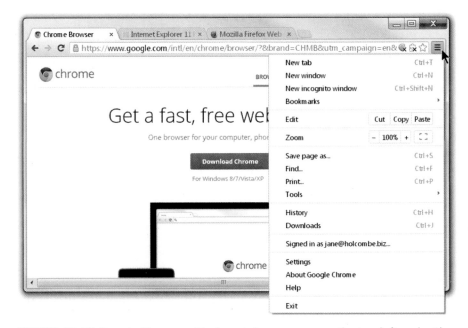

FIGURE 10–15 Google Chrome with three tabs open across the top left and with the Chrome menu open on the right.

FIGURE 10–16 Mozilla Firefox.

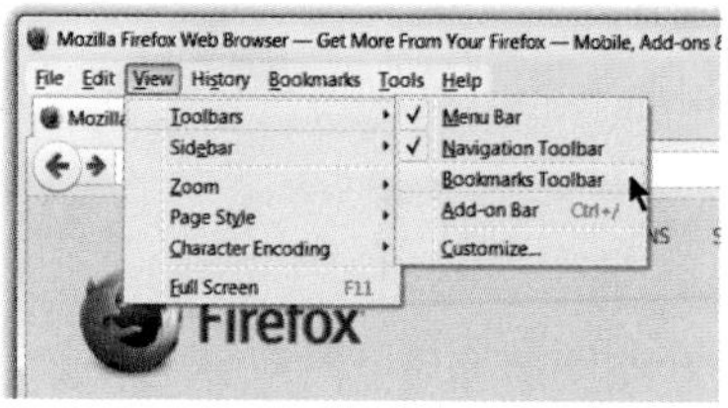

FIGURE 10–17 The Firefox View menu.

(see Figure 10–18) to open the Options dialog box where many important settings are located.

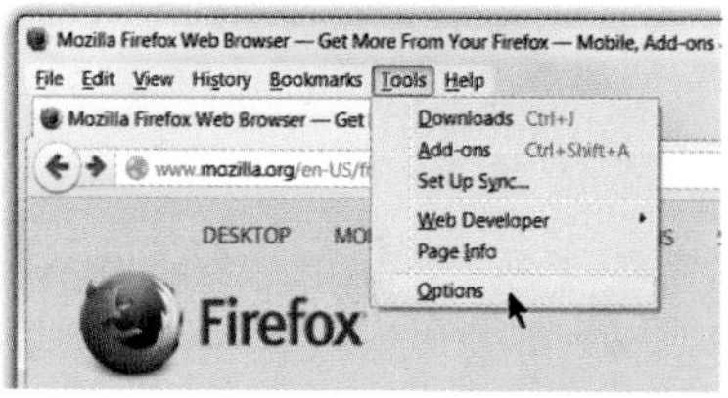

Internet Explorer

Microsoft introduced the Internet Explorer (IE) Web browser with the Windows 95 operating system, and IE is still bundled with Windows and available for free for Windows and Mac OSs at the Microsoft website. Figure 10–19 shows the open Tools menu for IE version 11 on the Windows 8.1 desktop. As with Firefox, the IE menu bar is hidden until you press the ALT key. And, like Firefox, you can use the View options to select what toolbars you want to stay visible in IE.

FIGURE 10–18 The Firefox Tools menu.

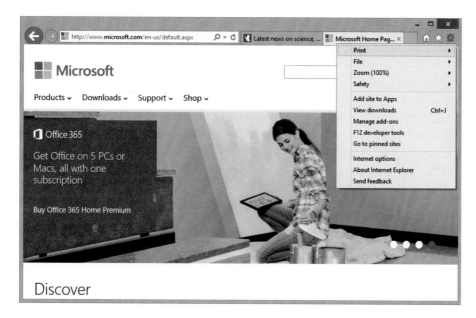

FIGURE 10–19 Internet Explorer with the Tools menu open on the right.

The Opera Web browser logo.

The Apple Safari browser logo.

Other Browsers

While Chrome, Firefox, and IE are rated the top three Web browsers, alternatives include Opera (www.opera.com) and Apple Safari (www.apple.com/safari) for OS X and Windows PCs.

Security and Web Browsers

Rather than dive into the details of every security setting in your Web browser, we'll define certain security threats and describe how to manage them through modern Web browsers.

Cookies. As you learned in Chapter 2, cookies are good—mostly. Under some circumstances people can use them for the wrong purposes, but for the most part, their benefits outweigh the negatives. Normally, only the website that creates the cookies can access them. However, some advertisers on websites have the browser create so-called third-party cookies, which other sites that include this advertiser can use. Look for options to manage cookies when configuring a Web browser. Figure 10–20 shows the Content settings where you can change how Chrome handles cookies.

try this!

Disable Third-Party Cookies in Chrome

Locate the settings for Cookies in the Chrome browser. Try this:

1. In the Chrome browser click the Chrome button on the far right of the menu bar to open the Chrome menu and select Settings.
2. On the Settings page scroll down to the bottom. If the last item is Hide Advanced Settings, skip to step 3. If the last item on the Settings page is Show Advanced Settings, click it.
3. Locate the Privacy category and click the Content Settings button.
4. The Cookies category shows your current settings for cookies. If it is not selected, click to place a check in the box labeled **Block third-party cookies and site data**.

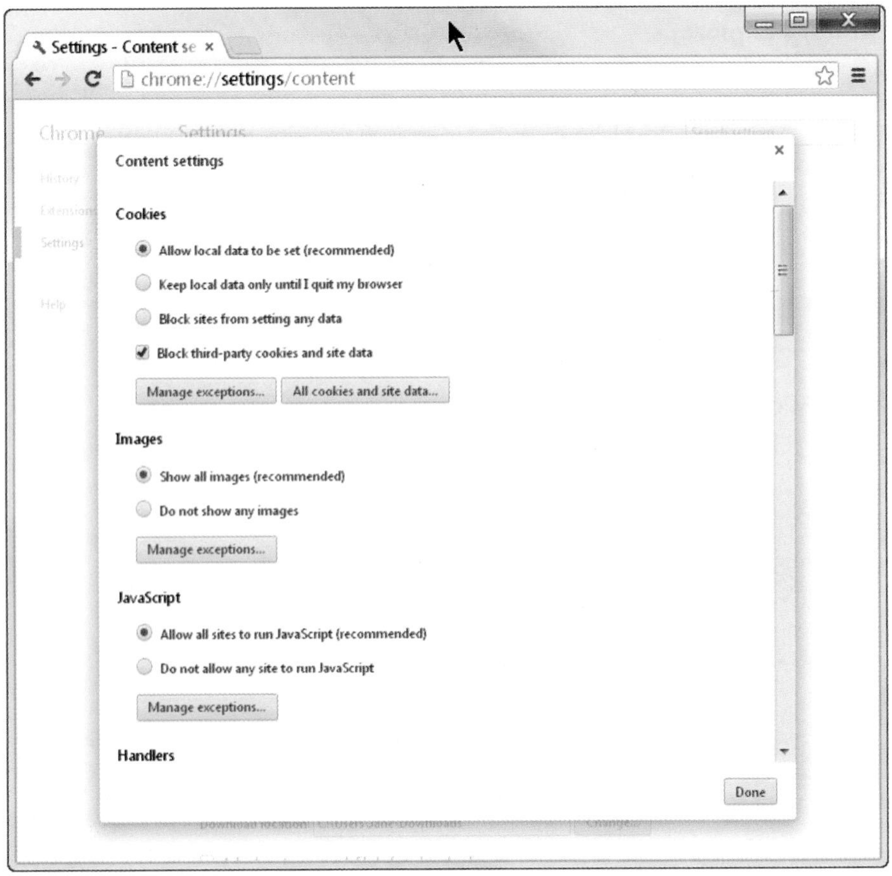

FIGURE 10–20 The Chrome Content Settings page includes settings for cookies.

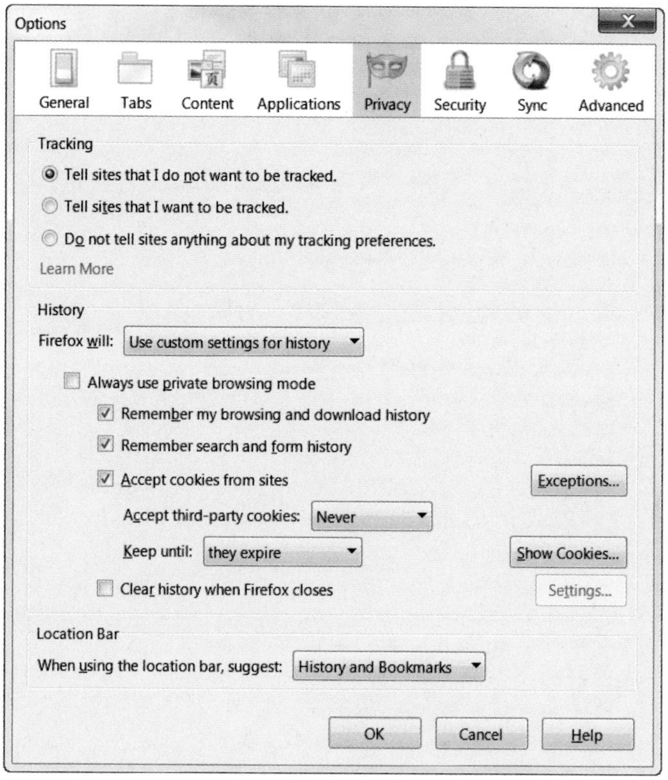

FIGURE 10–21 The Firefox privacy page with settings to protect you while browsing.

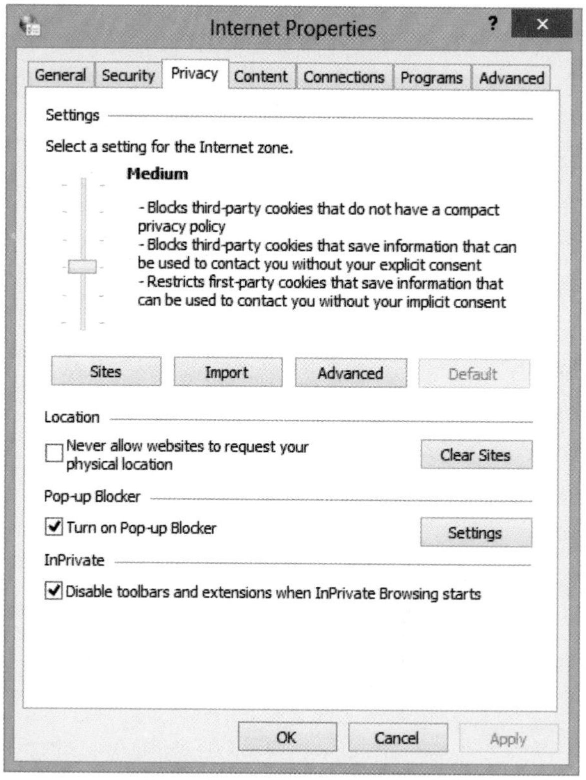

FIGURE 10–22 The Internet Explorer privacy page with settings to protect you while browsing.

Figure 10–21 shows the Firefox Privacy page with the settings for cookies. Notice that we configured it to accept only first-party cookies (those directly from a site). In IE, you need to dig a little deeper to find the settings for cookies. Open the Privacy page in Internet Options and click the Advanced button. On the Advanced Privacy Settings dialog box you can manage first-party and second-party cookies, with options to accept, block, or prompt you for each type of cookie.

To see the Internet Explorer options open the Tools menu and select Internet Options. In the Internet Properties dialog box select the Privacy tab (Figure 10–22). Notice the vertical slider bar on the left. It is set at the Medium setting for browsing the Internet (the Internet zone). In Internet Explorer a zone may be an area such as the Internet or local intranet or a list of sites grouped together, as in trusted sites and restricted sites. The description to the right of the slider describes what this setting blocks and restricts.

Browsing History. Your browsing history is useful information to marketers and others who want to learn more about you. At the same time, this information also makes life a bit easier for you when you return to favorite sites. While your browser does not divulge this information, a system compromised by spyware or malware could reveal this information to the wrong persons. Additionally, if you leave your computer unattended but logged on with your account, anyone with access to your computer could look at your browsing history; system administrators or others who have administrative access to your computer can do the same. Once again, your security needs may be at odds with your need for convenience on the Web. Therefore, Web browsers allow you to manage your browsing history.

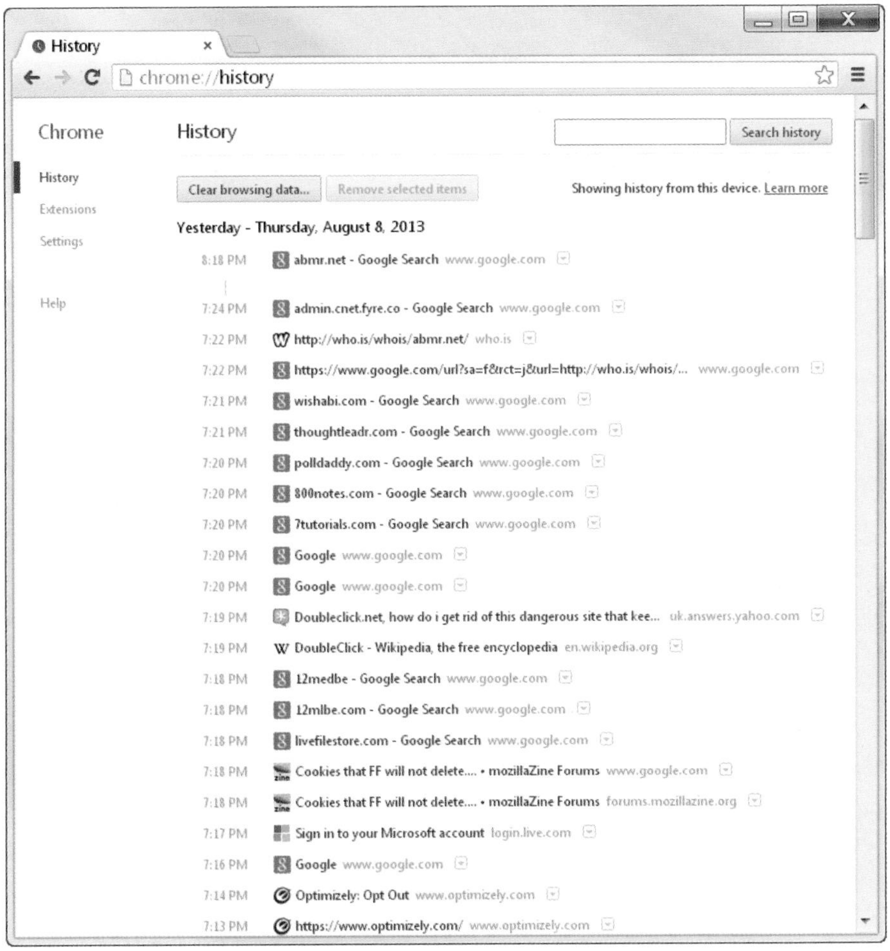

FIGURE 10–23 The Chrome History page.

Access the Chrome browser History page by selecting History from the Chrome menu. Figure 10–23 shows the History page. Click the Learn More link on the top right to learn how to manage browser history in Chrome.

In IE if you want to quickly delete all browsing history, open the Tools menu and select **Delete browsing history**. If you want to configure how long to save browsing history, open Internet Options and on the General tab click the Settings button under Browsing History. This opens the Website Data Settings dialog box, Click the History tab and on the History page, shown in Figure 10–24, set the number of days to save browser history. The other two tabs have settings for temporary Internet files and caches and databases. These three tabs include three types of files saved locally as you use your Internet browser.

In Firefox, manage browsing history settings on the Privacy page in the Options dialog box, shown previously.

Private Browsing. Private browsing is a security feature available in browsers that allows you to browse the Web without saving any history on the local computer of the sites visited. Chrome, Firefox, and Internet Explorer offer private browsing. When you turn on private browsing you open a new window, and your protection exists as long as you remain in that window, even as you open new tabs within the window. Always use private browsing when you use a shared computer, as in a library or school lab.

FIGURE 10-24 The History page of the Website Data Settings dialog box.

Chrome's name for private browsing is incognito. To start a private browsing session in Chrome select **new incognito window** from the Chrome menu or use the shortcut CTRL-SHIFT-N. Then notice the icon in the upper-left corner, shown here, resembling a man with dark glasses and hat peering down on your folders. As long as this is present you are browsing incognito in Chrome.

Firefox simply calls the feature Private Browsing, and to use it open the File menu from the menu bar and select **New Private Window** or use the shortcut CTRL-SHIFT-P. The Firefox Private Browsing window is clearly marked, both on the left and on the right (the purple mask) of the window, as shown here.

Internet Explorer calls private browsing InPrivate Browsing. To use it open the Tools menu and select InPrivate Browsing (or CTRL-SHIFT-P). When you open an InPrivate window in Internet Explorer, the address box is clearly labeled, as shown here. It opens a page that alerts you that InPrivate is turned on and provides a link to online information about this feature, which opens in a new InPrivate browsing window. When you are ready to continue browsing, simply enter a universal

While a Chrome incognito window is open, this character at the upper left watches over the window.

The Firefox Private Browsing window.

The Internet Explorer InPrivate Browsing window

resource locator (URL) in the address box or click the Home button on the IE menu bar to open your home page.

Passwords. Do you like to have your browser remember your password to websites, or would you rather enter your user name and password every time you access a site? While it is convenient to have the browser remember passwords, this practice is a security risk if your computer is not protected with a strong password, or if you leave your computer unattended while you are logged in. Configure the browser password settings that work best for you.

In Chrome open the Chrome menu and select Settings. In Settings enter **password** in the search box. The resulting search results will resemble Figure 10–25, which brings together all the settings having to do with passwords in Chrome. The first one is for synchronizing your settings across your devices, a handy feature if you sign in to Chrome with a Google account and want all your Google preferences synchronized across your devices. If you click on the **Clear browsing data** button under Privacy, a dialog box opens that allows you to select what browsing data to clear, allowing you to avoid deleting saved passwords while removing the data that tracks your browsing habits. The last section in the Search results for password is the section Passwords and forms. The first setting allows you to enable Autofill with information such as your mailing address, so if you start typing this into a form in the Chrome browser, it will complete it. This information is collected automatically once you enable this option. Click the **Manage Autofill settings** link to see what has been saved. Finally, the last item includes the link **Manage saved passwords**. Click on this to see what passwords are saved and to delete those you no longer want to save.

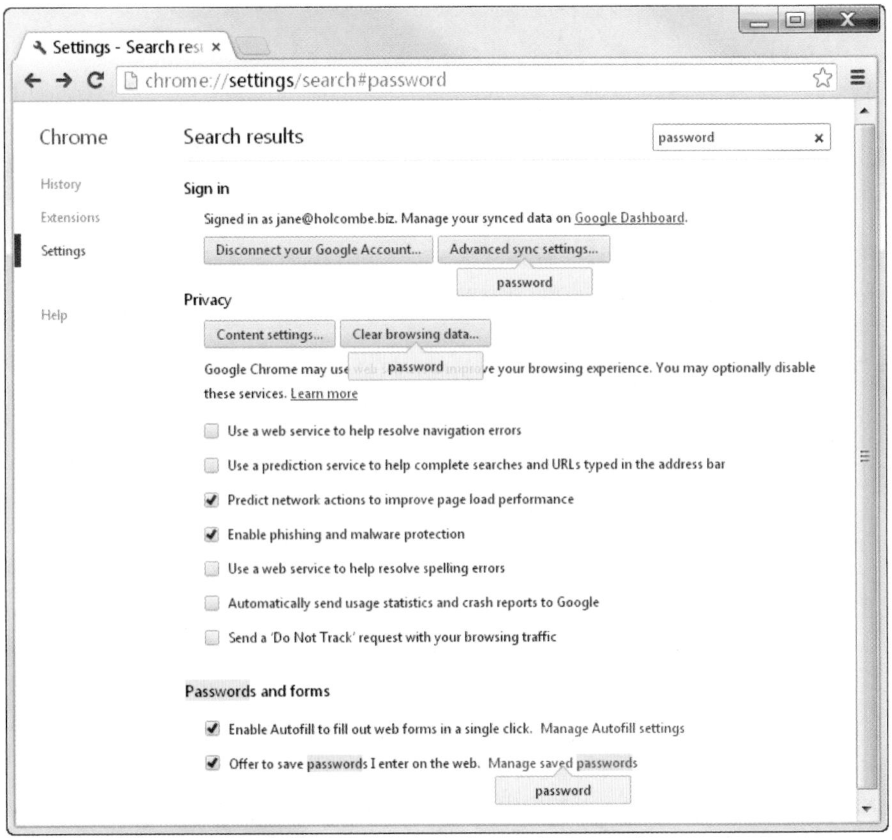

FIGURE 10–25 The Search results from searching on **password** in Chrome Settings.

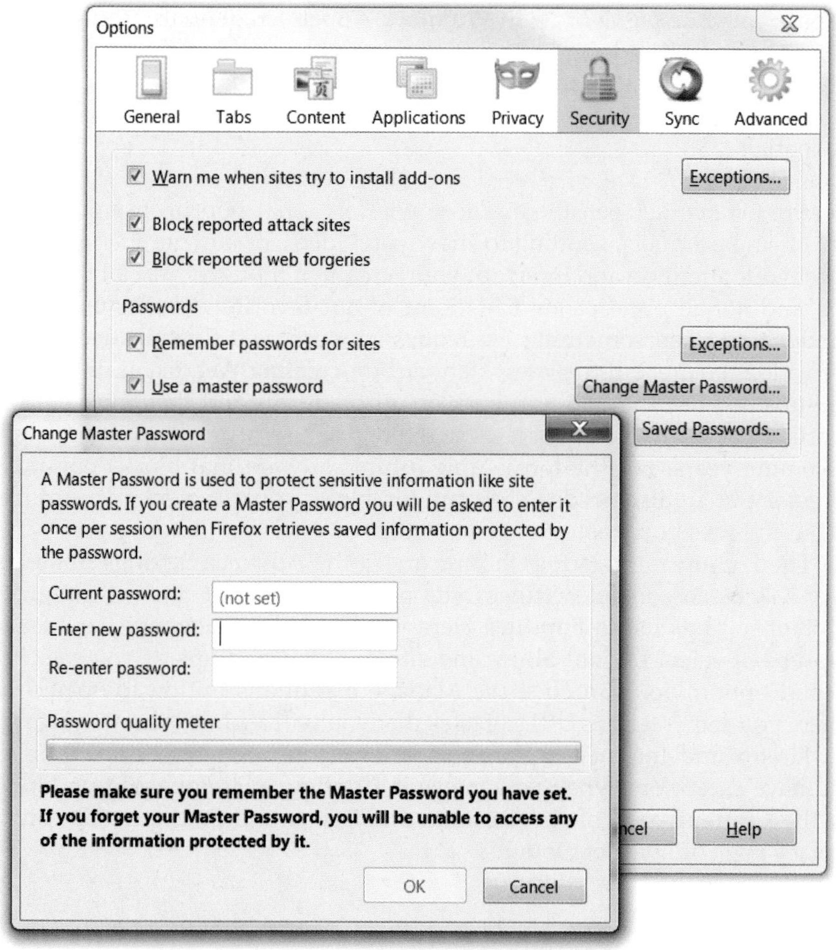

FIGURE 10–26 The Firefox Security Options with the Change Master Password dialog box open.

Manage passwords in Firefox on the Security page of the Options dialog box, where you can add a master password to your password list by clicking to place an "X" by **Use a master password**. That opens the dialog box shown in Figure 10–26. If you decide to set a password, it will prompt you to enter it once per Firefox session in which Firefox retrieves a password for a website. Back in the Security dialog box click on the Saved Passwords button to see and manage the saved passwords.

Internet Explorer also saves passwords and other information you enter at websites. To turn this on enter the search string "Internet Options" in either Start Search in Windows 7 or Windows 8 Search. Select Internet Options from the results. In Internet Options open the **Content** tab and then select **Settings** under AutoComplete. Figure 10–27 shows the AutoComplete Settings dialog box in Windows 8. In both Windows 7 and Windows 8 you can select the types of entries you want to use AutoComplete to save.

Internet Options in Windows 7 only has the Delete AutoComplete History button; it does not have the Manage Passwords button that is available in Windows 8. This button in Windows 8 opens Credentials Manager, where you can

FIGURE 10–27 The Internet Explorer AutoComplete Settings dialog box.

manage all your passwords. In Windows 7 open Credentials Manager from Start Search. In Windows 7 you can change a password in Credentials Manager, but not see the current password. Credential Manager in Windows 8 allows you to both change and view a password, if you provide administrator credentials.

Pop-Ups. We've all seen them. Those windows that pop up from a website advertising products, wanting to show you videos, or any number of excuses to get your attention and interrupt your stream of thought. We call them pop-ups, and not all pop-ups are bad. Some of our favorite websites use pop-up windows to open something we requested, such as a downloaded page or even a login page, but the latest standard for creating Web pages discourages pop-ups because they do not work on all platforms and they interfere with assistive browsing technologies. Therefore, the use of pop-ups should wane in coming years. For the foreseeable future software that blocks pop-ups is necessary, but it also needs to be configurable so you can block pop-ups from all but the sites you trust.

The Pop-up settings for Chrome are in the Advance Settings under Privacy. Click the content settings button and then scroll down through the Content settings list to **Pop-ups**. Here you can either allow all sites to show pop-ups or select **Do not allow any site to show pop-ups**. If you select the second option, you can click the Manage exceptions button to open a box where you can enter the URLs of sites that you will allow to show pop-ups.

Firefox and Internet Explorer also allow you to enable/disable pop-ups and have exceptions when you enable it. Configure Firefox's pop-up blocker on the **Content** page of the **Options** dialog box and configure IE's on the Privacy page of Internet Options.

Email Clients

The scope of Internet email has made several major jumps in the past decades. It evolved from a service used by academics and government workers, through the period when early PC users accessed services such as CompuServ, to today's casual PC users, numbered in the billions, who joined the Internet since the advent of the World Wide Web in 1991. Because of the explosion in the use of the Internet, email has long been the most compelling reason to own a PC—but today you do not even need to use a PC to participate in personal email. Many people access their personal and business email from their mobile devices. Further, you do not even need to own the device you use for Internet access.

An email client used in a school or corporate network may be specific to the private mail servers the user connects to, such as Microsoft Exchange, or the client may be one of several that you can use for different types of mail servers. Many users have access to email client software such as Microsoft Outlook, Windows Live Mail, Mozilla Thunderbird, Eudora, or Pegasus. Users who subscribe to Web mail or free email services such as Gmail, MSN, or Yahoo! can use a Web browser rather than special email client software. Regardless of the type of client software, they all accomplish the task of sending and receiving in the same way.

The client software will show a list of all of the messages in the mailbox by displaying information it reads from the message headers. The message header is information added to the beginning of the message that contains details such as who sent it and the subject, and also may show the time and date of the message along with the message's size. Then the user may click on a message to open it and read the body of the email. Users can then respond to the message, save the message, create a new message, add attachments, and/ or send it to the intended recipient.

Email clients have become much easier to use, even to the point of automatically detecting and configuring the underlying settings for connecting to an email server, given your personal account information. They also will import your email and contact information from other accounts.

Types of Email Accounts

There are three types of email accounts: POP, IMAP, and Web mail. The first two are protocols, while the third describes email that you access via the Web, and therefore, the protocol is HTML. When you configure an email client, you need to know the address and type of server, defined by the account type.

POP. Post Office Protocol (POP) is a protocol that enables email client computers to pick up email from mail servers, so that you can open it and read it in your email client. When it picks up a message, it deletes it from the POP server. The current version is POP3. This has been very popular with ISPs because it minimizes the amount of disk space required on the email server for each account. The user is responsible for maintaining and backing up messages. When the client computer does not connect to the email server, the user can still access all the locally stored messages.

IMAP. Internet Message Access Protocol (IMAP) is a protocol that will allow users to maintain the messages stored on an email server (usually on the Internet) without removing them from the server. This type of account allows you to log in and access your message store from any computer. Of course, the message store is not available to you when you are offline, and you may run out of allotted disk space on the mail server, at which point it rejects new messages.

Web Mail. Web mail is a generic term for using a Web browser (and therefore, either HTTPS or HTTP) to retrieve email, replacing the traditional email client, such as Microsoft Outlook. You can use Web mail to connect to Web-based email services such as Hotmail, Gmail, and Yahoo! that keep your messages stored on the Internet. If you wish to connect to one of these services using an email client, you will need to enable IMAP for your account before you can successfully add your account to the client. To do that, consult the Help utility at the provider.

> *Note:* Most mail servers with POP accounts give you the option to connect using Web mail so that when you are away from your desktop computer and your email client software, you can connect using any Web browser from any computer. Of course, you will need to authenticate using your email address and password. If you are planning to do this, be sure to access it at least once beforehand to make sure you know how to use it!

Outlook

Outlook is Microsoft's email client that is part of the Microsoft Office suite. You can use it as a client to any of the three types of accounts. It offers core email features, such as an address book and folders for organizing mail, plus additional personal productivity features such as an appointment calendar, a to-do list, and scheduling. It supports the use of more than one email account.

Windows Live Mail

Windows Live Mail is an email client available as a free download from Microsoft's Windows Essentials page. It does not have all the features of the commercial Outlook product. For instance, you can only use it for Internet email accounts, but like Outlook, Windows Live Mail will manage multiple email accounts.

Configuring and Using an Email Client

Whether you use Outlook, Windows Live Mail, or one of many third-party email clients, you will need to know the same information to configure your email client. This includes:

- The type of mail server you are accessing (POP3, IMAP, HTTPS, or HTTP).
- Your account name and password.
- The DNS name of the incoming mail server.
- If you are preparing to connect to a POP3 or IMAP server, you will also need to know the name of an outgoing mail server.

If you do not have this information, ask your ISP, in the case of a private account, or ask a network administrator if your mail server is a corporate mail server. ISPs often provide email configuration information on their websites. Check this out before configuring your email client because it will help you avoid certain pitfalls. For instance, when configuring a client using a cell data connection you may have to configure it to authenticate to a certain mail server in the home service area.

Step-by-Step 10.02

Connecting a Client to an Email Account

To complete this step-by-step exercise you will need a PC with an Internet connection and Windows 7 with Windows Live Mail, although the basic steps are similar in other email clients. To complete the exercise you will need the following information:

- The type of account.
- Your account name, password, and email address.

- The DNS names of the outgoing and incoming mail server.
- The DNS name or IP address of an incoming mail server for POP3, IMAP, or HTTP.
- The DNS name or IP address of an outgoing mail server (SMTP).
- If using a provider, such as Gmail, you will need to enable IMAP first.

Step 1

If you have just installed Windows Live Mail, then when you click the Close button at the end of the installation, it will open to the **Add your email accounts** page.

Step 2

Open Windows Live Mail, click on the Accounts tab, and then click the button labeled **Email** on the far left.

Step 3

In the **Add your email accounts** page enter all the information for logging on to your email account. If your information is correct, Live Mail will be able to automatically connect to your account, so do not turn on the manual option shown at the bottom. Unless you see a message, click Next. If you see a message, follow the instructions and then return to this page and click Next.

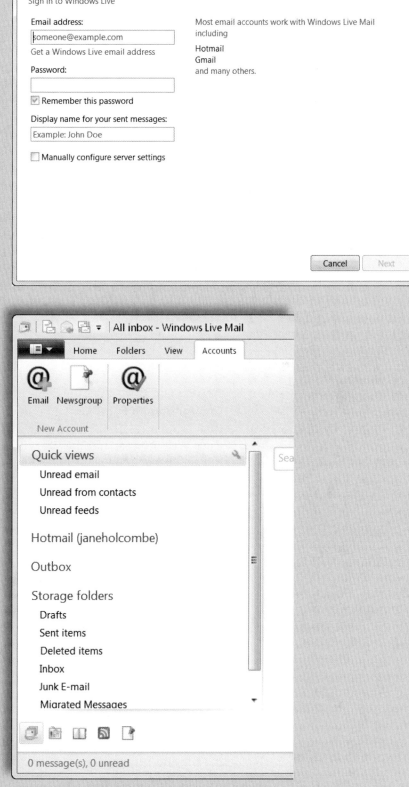

Step 4

Live Mail now displays your new account. Close the Windows Live Mail window when you are finished.

FTP Clients

You use File Transfer Protocol to transfer files between a computer running the FTP server service and an FTP client. It is a preferred method of transferring files over a TCP/IP network, especially the Internet, because it is simple and fast. Before the advent of the World Wide Web and the use of GUI tools for working on the Internet, people used character-mode FTP clients because that was all there was. Because of the tremendous growth in the number of Internet and Web users, we now have a variety of GUI FTP client programs. You can even use some of the popular Web browsers as FTP clients, although programs designed specifically as FTP clients are usually easier to use and allow you to save the connection settings, including (but not limited to) the URL for the site, user name, and password.

Anonymous FTP

If an FTP site does not require a user name and password, it is said to allow anonymous connection, which means that all users connecting are using the Anonymous account, which may mean they can only read and copy the files from the FTP site but cannot copy files to the site. We call an FTP site that allows anonymous connections an anonymous FTP site. It is simple to connect to such a site using your browser by entering the URL, including the protocol suffix, **ftp**. You can download by selecting and copying files from the site, but we don't recommend that you do this from an unfamiliar FTP site. Schools and some employers use FTP sites for transferring files to and from students and employees.

Configuring an FTP Client

When connecting to a site that requires a user name and password, you can use a Web browser and the site will prompt you to log in. A Web browser is fine for connecting to an FTP site you will visit only once, but when you wish to save the site settings, or manage settings for many FTP sites, you should find a free or commercial FTP client that suits your needs. A quick search of "FTP client" using an Internet search engine will yield a long list of clients. The free Mozilla FireFTP, an add-on to Mozilla Firefox, is a favorite of ours. To configure an FTP client you will need:

- The host name of the FTP server.
- A user ID and password (if applicable).

You may also need to know if the FTP server allows passive mode connections and/or secure (SSL) connections. Figure 10–28 shows FireFTP. The left pane is open to the local hard drive, while the right pane shows the contents of a folder on the FTP site.

LO 10.4 | Sharing Files and Printers

File and printer sharing allows users to share and access files and printers over a network. All the OSs discussed in this book have methods for allowing file and printer sharing. There are two sides to file and printer sharing: the server side and the client side, and before you implement either side of this equation, take a few minutes to understand how they interact. Both sides

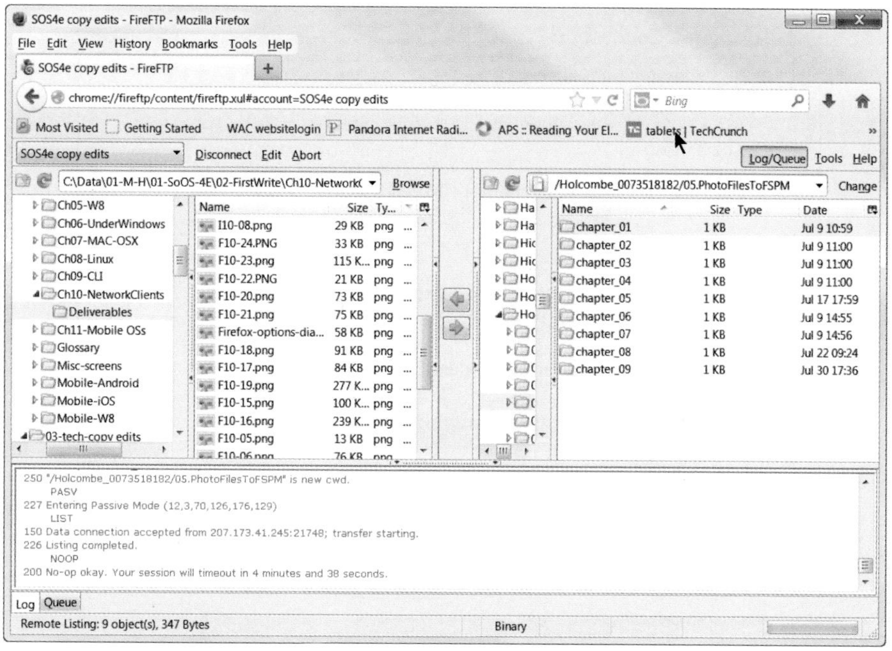

FIGURE 10–28 The user interface of FireFTP, an FTP client.

must use complementary file and printer services that can talk to each other. Then, you can implement sharing on the server side (even on a desktop computer) and users can access it from the client side. For our examples we'll use Microsoft Windows 7.

The Server Side of File and Printer Sharing

A **file and printer server** (often simply called a file server), is a computer that gives client computers access to files and printers over a network. The actual folder or printer being shared acts as a connecting point on the server and is called a **share**. A share is visible as a folder over the network, but it is a separate entity from the disk folder or printer to which it points. Like other file-sharing services, the one installed with Windows allows you to share both files and printers. This service is installed and enabled by default, although it is up to you to decide how to use it. On a Windows desktop computer, look for File and Printer Sharing for Microsoft Networks in the Properties dialog box for a network connection, as shown in Figure 10–29.

The Client Side of File and Printer Sharing

A file and printer client includes both the user interface and the underlying file-sharing protocols to access its matching file-sharing server service on a network server. The client for Microsoft file and printer sharing is installed and enabled by default. With the client installed, you can use the Windows GUI to see those Microsoft computers on the network that have file and printer sharing turned on. You can see both dedicated Windows network servers and Windows desktops that have this service turned on. Your ability to connect to any shares on those computers depends on the permissions applied to each share. Figure 10–30 shows four computers that are visible because they have the file and printer service turned on.

With appropriate permissions, you will be able to browse to the shared folders on a server and perform file operations, such as copying, moving, deleting, and opening files in your locally installed applications.

Note: As a rule, a desktop computer should not have File and Printer Sharing turned on, especially if the computer is a member of a domain and connects to dedicated servers for file and printer services. The exception to this is when a desktop computer is participating in a HomeGroup or work group and must share local files and printers with other computers. This is common in the small office/home office (SOHO) situation.

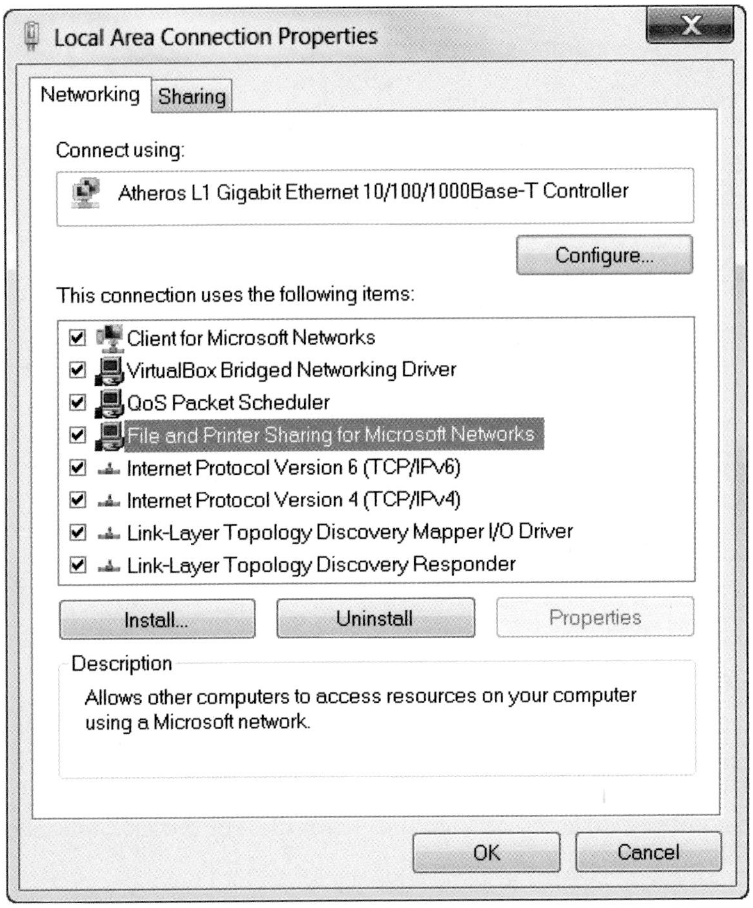

FIGURE 10–29 File and Printer Sharing for Microsoft Networks is listed for a network connection.

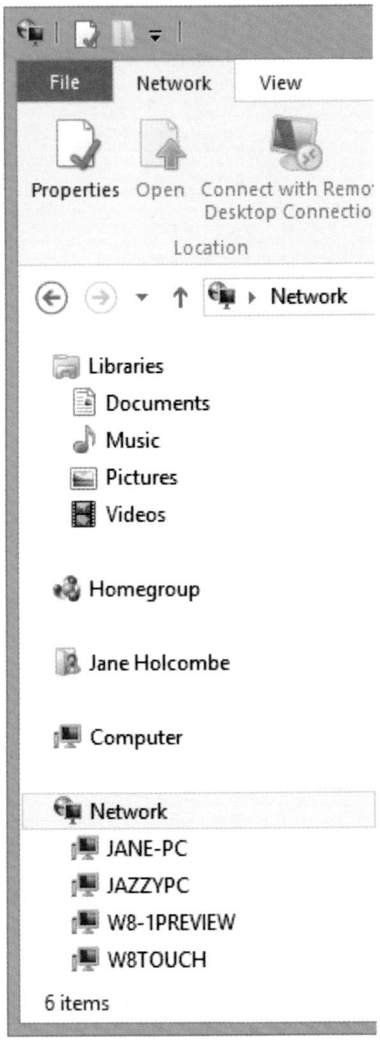

FIGURE 10–30 The computers listed at the bottom under Network have File and Printer Sharing turned on.

Sharing Files and Printers in Windows 7 and Windows 8

To illustrate how to share files and printers from your Windows desktop we will use two methods. The first is HomeGroup, a feature introduced in Windows 7 and included in Windows 8. The second is the sharing of the Windows Public folder, supported in both versions of Windows.

try this!

Find Microsoft File and Printer Servers

You can use Windows Explorer in Windows 7 or open File Explorer on the Windows 8 Desktop to look for the file and printer servers on your network. Try this:

1. Open Windows Explorer/File Explorer.
2. Browse to the Network folder in the left pane.
3. View the icons in the contents pane. In both Windows 7 and Windows 8 the icons resembling a computer with a blue screen are file and printer servers.
4. If any file and printer servers are visible, double-click one to access it and browse. If you do not have permissions, you will see a Network Error message. If you have permissions to a server, you will be able to browse the folders to which you have permissions.

Sharing with HomeGroups

HomeGroup is an easy-to-configure implementation of Microsoft's file and printer sharing, with only a single password protecting the Home-Group shares on all Windows 7 computers that join a HomeGroup. You only have to enter the password once on every client computer in the HomeGroup when the client first joins the HomeGroup. You can configure a Windows 8, Windows 8 Pro, Windows RT, or Windows 7 computer running any edition of this OS to be a client in a HomeGroup. Windows 8, Windows 8 Pro, and Windows RT can also create and host a HomeGroup, but only certain editions of Windows 7 can create and host a HomeGroup. Those versions are Windows 7 Home Premium, Professional, Ultimate, and Enterprise editions. Beyond this, there are several requirements and restrictions:

- Only Windows 7 and Windows 8 computers can participate in HomeGroups.
- A Windows 7 or Windows 8 computer can belong to only one HomeGroup at a time, and only one HomeGroup can exist on one LAN or WLAN.
- Windows 7 or Windows 8 computers that are part of a Windows Active Directory Domain cannot create a HomeGroup but they can join one.
- To create or join a HomeGroup a Windows 7 computer must connect to a Home network location (see Figure 10–31). A Windows 8 computer must connect to a Private network (the new name for the same location).
- You must enable IPv6 for a Windows 7 or Windows 8 computer and all firewalls between HomeGroup computers must support IPv6 and allow file and printer sharing for the computer to participate in a HomeGroup. IPv6 is enabled by default in both versions of Windows, as well in the Windows Firewall.
- When you join a HomeGroup you decide what, if any, local libraries and printers you will share with the HomeGroup.

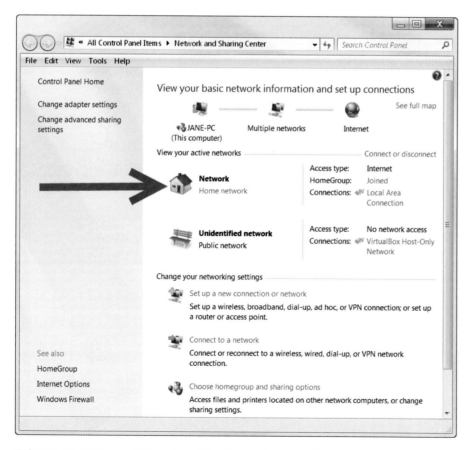

FIGURE 10–31 Open Network and Sharing and ensure that your computer is a member of a Home network (Windows 7) or a Private network (Windows 8).

Creating and Joining a HomeGroup

Create a HomeGroup to share your local files and printers with others on your home or small business network. To complete this exercise you will need the following:

- Windows 7 Home Premium, Professional, Ultimate, or Enterprise edition.
- The Windows 7 computer must connect to a Home network (Open Network and Sharing Center to confirm).

Step 1

From the Start menu enter HomeGroup in the Search box and select HomeGroup from the results list. On the HomeGroup page click Create a HomeGroup.

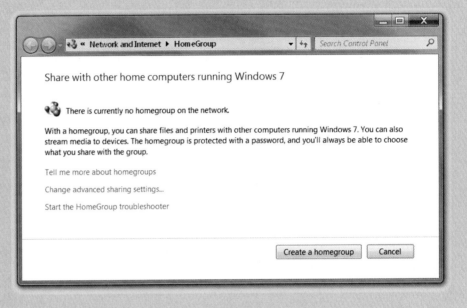

Step 2

The first page of the Create a HomeGroup wizard lists your personal folders and any local printer with checks for those that are shared and empty check boxes for those that are not shared. By default, Windows does not share your Documents folder. Select what you would like to share, and click Next.

Windows will generate a password for your HomeGroup. Write it down or use the link to print the password and instructions. You will need to enter the password on the other computers on your network as you join them to the HomeGroup. After writing down or printing out the password, click the Finish button. Note, if you lose the password you can open Home-Group on any computer that has successfully joined and view it.

Go to another Windows 7 computer on your network, and from the Start menu enter "homegroup" in the Search box. Then click Join now and follow the instructions to enter the HomeGroup password.

Sharing the Public Folder

If you have a Windows 7 computer and one or more older version of Windows including those older than Windows 7 on a home or small business network, then HomeGroup is not an option if you want all the computers to participate.

First look at the Public folders on a Windows 7 computer. The master Public folder is located under the Users folder on the drive on which Windows 7 is installed. This folder is, by default, shared to anyone on the network who has an account in the local accounts database. In fact, if a user on the network has logged on to a Windows computer using an account that matches (same user name and password) the one you create on your "server" computer, then the user can connect to the Public share without going through a logon screen. The Public folder has several subfolders, shown in Figure 10–32. These folders have a special relationship with the default Libraries for each user.

By default, no user data resides in the Public folder. You have to copy or move files into the Public

FIGURE 10–32 The Public folder and its contents.

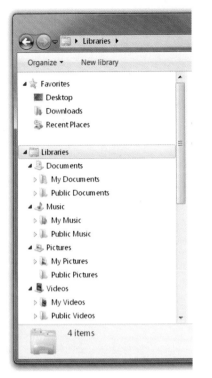

FIGURE 10–33 The Public folders within each Library.

folder, and the way you do that in Windows 7 is through the Libraries. If you look at the contents of the Libraries on a Windows 7 computer, you will see that each Library has a Public folder, in addition to the base folder for that library, as shown in Figure 10–33. Recall what you learned about Libraries in Chapter 4. A library does not contain the folders that appear in the library, but rather pointers to the locations for those folders. So, the My Documents folder in the Documents library points to the currently logged-on user's Documents folder, located in a folder with that user's name, which holds the user's folders and preferences (also called the profile). Similarly, the Public Documents folder in the Documents library points to the Public Documents folder under the Public folder.

So, simply drop files and folders into one of these public folders in your libraries, and people on the network who have local accounts on your computer can connect and access these files and folders. Be sure to add the users to your local accounts by following the instructions in Step-by-Step 4.05 in Chapter 4. If the user name and password do not match the account with which a user logs on at her computer, she will need to supply a user name and password to access the Public folder.

LO 10.5 | Troubleshooting Common Network Client Problems

If you are unable to access another computer on the network, several command-line utilities will help in pinpointing the source of a problem and arriving at a solution. In this section you will learn to troubleshoot common client connection problems using each of these utilities, as indicated by the symptoms. Each utility provides different information and is most valuable when used appropriately. For instance, you should first view the IP configuration using the **ipconfig** utility and verify that it is correct for the network to which you are connected. If you discover any obvious problems when you view the IP configuration, correct them before proceeding. Then test the ability to communicate using the **ping** command. Here you will practice this procedure and a few others.

Built-In Network Diagnostics

Each of the operating systems surveyed in this book has a variety of utilities for diagnosing network problems. From the command-line utilities discussed later in this section to GUI tools that combine the functions of several tools into one broad-stroke diagnostics tool, each generation of OS brings improvements in these tools. In Windows 7 and Windows 8, the Windows Network Diagnostics, the Windows 7 version shown in Figure 10–34, will diagnose the problem area (the broadband modem in this example) and instruct you on how to solve the problem. Similarly, if your Internet connection fails, the Network Diagnostics window will display and attempt to diagnose the problem. This is true in both Windows 7 and Windows 8.

FIGURE 10–34 The Windows 7 Network Diagnostics tool.

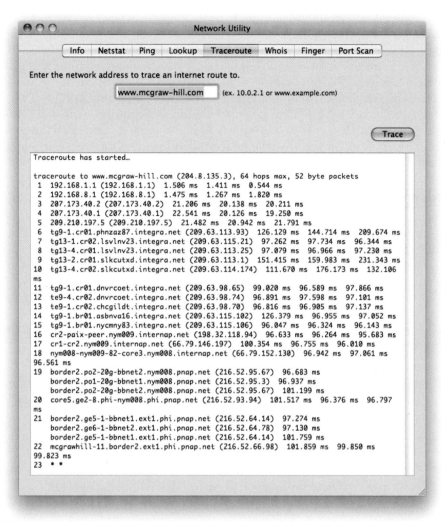

FIGURE 10–35 The Mac OS X Network Utility at work (notice the various network diagnostic tools listed across the top).

The Network Utility in Mac OS X, shown in Figure 10–35, requires more knowledge of the individual tools, but it does spare you from entering the commands from Mac OS X Terminal window.

Testing IP Configurations and Connectivity

When the TCP/IP suite is installed on a computer, it includes many protocols and many handy little programs that network professionals quickly learn to use. You should learn two right away, for those times when you find yourself sitting at your computer and talking to a network professional while trying to resolve a network problem. These are commands you enter at a command line. In Windows these commands are **ipconfig** and **ping**. In Mac OS X and Linux they are **ifconfig** and **ping**. Learn about these commands below, and then do Step-by-Step 10.04, in which you will use both of these commands to test a network connection.

Verifying IP Configuration with ipconfig

The **ipconfig** command will display the IP configuration of all network interface cards, even those that receive their addresses and configuration through DHCP. Using this command shows whether the IP settings have been successfully bound to your network adapter. *Bound* means that there is a linking relationship, called a binding, between network components—in this case, between the network protocol and the adapter. A binding establishes the order in which each network component handles network communications. When troubleshooting network connectivity problems on an IP network, always use the **ipconfig** command to verify the IP configuration.

If the **ipconfig** command reveals an address beginning with 169.254, it is a symptom of a failure of a Windows DHCP client to receive an IP address from a DHCP server (for whatever reason). Troubleshoot the DHCP server on your network (such as the DHCP service in a broadband router).

Troubleshooting Connection Errors with the ping Command

The **ping** command is useful for testing the communications between two computers. The name of this command is actually an acronym for packet Internet groper, but we prefer to think (as many do) that it was named after the sound of underwater sonar. Instead of bouncing sound waves off surfaces, the **ping** command uses data packets, and it sends them to specific IP addresses, requesting a response (hence the idea of pinging). This is a great test to see if you can access a certain computer.

To use the **ping** command, give it an address and it sends packets to the specified address, "listens" for a reply, and then displays the results.

1. Pinging the IP address of the computer's own NIC and receiving a successful response indicates that the IP protocol and the local address is working. Using the example in Figure 10–36, from Host_1-1 you would type: **ping 192.168.1.101** to ping the local NIC.

2. Then ping another computer on the same network to test the ability to communicate between the two computers. Again, from Host_1-1 you would type **ping 192.168.1.102** to ping Host_1-2, a computer on the same network.

3. Next, ping the gateway address to ensure that your computer can communicate with the router. Again, working from Host_1-1 in Figure 10–36, type **ping 192.168.1.1** to ping the gateway address for Network 1, which is the address of the router interface (NIC) connected to Network 1.

4. Finally, ping an address beyond your network, to test the router and the ability to communicate with a computer via the router. Using Figure 10–36, from Host_1-1 type **ping 192.168.2.101** to ping the address of Host_2-1 on Network 2.

Now the bad news about the **ping** command. First, a firewall can block specific types of traffic or configure an individual computer not to respond to

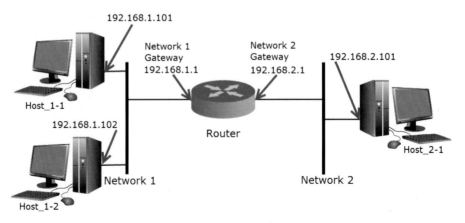

FIGURE 10–36 Two networks connected by a router.

a ping. Hence, you may not be able to ping a computer, even if you can communicate with that same computer in other ways such as by Web browsing or downloading email. Nonetheless, it is still worth learning to use the **ping** command for testing a connection because it will often work and give you good information

The reason firewalls or individual computers block or ignore the requests from a **ping** command is because people can use this command in malicious ways—most notoriously in a denial of service (DoS) attack, in which someone sends a large number of ping requests to an address, thus making the server unavailable to accept other traffic.

Step-by-Step 10.04

Testing an IP Configuration

In this step-by-step exercise, you will look at the IP configuration settings to determine whether they are automatic or static, then you will test the current configuration. The first test will let you confirm that you can communicate with a computer on your network, and the second test will confirm that you can communicate with a router on your network. The last test will confirm that you can communicate with a computer beyond your network. To complete this exercise, you will need the following:

- A computer with Windows.

- A working connection to the Internet.
- The IP address of another computer on your local network (use this when a step asks for *NearbyIPaddress*). Enter this in the appropriate line in step 3.
- The IP address of a computer beyond your local network (use this when a step asks for *RemoteIPaddress*). Enter this in the appropriate line in step 3.
- The user name and password of an account that is a member of your computer's Administrators group.

Step 1

Check out your current IP configuration using the IPCONFIG command. To do that, first open a Command Prompt by selecting Start | Run, and in the Open dialog box, type "CMD" and press ENTER. Type **ipconfig /all** at the Command Prompt.

```
C:\Documents and Settings\Jane>ipconfig /all

Windows IP Configuration

        Host Name . . . . . . . . . . . . : Wickenburg
        Primary Dns Suffix  . . . . . . . :
        Node Type . . . . . . . . . . . . : Hybrid
        IP Routing Enabled. . . . . . . . : No
        WINS Proxy Enabled. . . . . . . . : No

Ethernet adapter Local Area Connection:

        Connection-specific DNS Suffix  . :
        Description . . . . . . . . . . . : Realtek RTL8139/810x Family Fast Eth
ernet NIC
        Physical Address. . . . . . . . . : 08-00-46-A7-29-3B
        Dhcp Enabled. . . . . . . . . . . : No
        IP Address. . . . . . . . . . . . : 192.168.100.48
        Subnet Mask . . . . . . . . . . . : 255.255.255.0
        Default Gateway . . . . . . . . . : 192.168.100.1
        DNS Servers . . . . . . . . . . . : 192.168.100.1

C:\Documents and Settings\Jane>
```

Step 2

If the current settings show an IP address other than 0.0.0.0, IP has successfully bound an IP address to the network adapter. If the current settings include DHCP enabled = **Yes**, and shows an IP address for a DHCP server, then your network adapter is configured to receive an address automatically and has received its address from the DHCP server whose address is listed. If your DHCP Enabled setting = **No** and your computer has a set of values for the IP address and subnet mask, then it has a static IP configuration that is successfully bound to the network adapter.

Gather the information from the **ipconfig /all** command and fill in the first three lines provided below. Your instructor will give you the last two items, *NearbyIPaddress* and *RemoteIPaddress*. You will need these addresses in the following steps.

IPaddress: _____

Default GatewayIPaddress: _____

DNSServerIPaddress: _____

NearbyIPaddress: _____

RemoteIPaddress: _____

At the Command Prompt, enter **ping** *IPaddress*, where *"IPaddress"* is the address of your computer from step 3. You should receive four replies if your computer is properly configured. If you receive an error message or fewer than four replies, report this to your instructor.

At the Command Prompt, enter **ping** *NearbyIPaddress*, where *"NearbyIPaddress"* is the address of another computer on your same network. You should receive four replies if your computer is properly configured and if the other computer is also powered up and properly configured. If you receive an error message or fewer than four replies, report this to your instructor.

```
C:\Documents and Settings\Jane>ping 192.168.100.48

Pinging 192.168.100.48 with 32 bytes of data:

Reply from 192.168.100.48: bytes=32 time<1ms TTL=128
Reply from 192.168.100.48: bytes=32 time<1ms TTL=128
Reply from 192.168.100.48: bytes=32 time<1ms TTL=128
Reply from 192.168.100.48: bytes=32 time<1ms TTL=128

Ping statistics for 192.168.100.48:
    Packets: Sent = 4, Received = 4, Lost = 0 (0% loss),
Approximate round trip times in milli-seconds:
    Minimum = 0ms, Maximum = 0ms, Average = 0ms

C:\Documents and Settings\Jane>_
```

If the last test was successful, and if your computer has a gateway address, test this address now. Return to the Command Prompt and enter **ping** *Default gatewayIPaddress*, where *"Default gatewayIPaddress"* equals the Default Gateway address recorded in step 3. You should receive four replies if your computer is properly configured and if the default gateway is active on your network.

```
C:\Documents and Settings\Jane>ping 192.168.100.1

Pinging 192.168.100.1 with 32 bytes of data:

Reply from 192.168.100.1: bytes=32 time<1ms TTL=128
Reply from 192.168.100.1: bytes=32 time=1ms TTL=128
Reply from 192.168.100.1: bytes=32 time<1ms TTL=128
Reply from 192.168.100.1: bytes=32 time<1ms TTL=128

Ping statistics for 192.168.100.1:
    Packets: Sent = 4, Received = 4, Lost = 0 (0% loss),
Approximate round trip times in milli-seconds:
    Minimum = 0ms, Maximum = 1ms, Average = 0ms

C:\Documents and Settings\Jane>
```

If your IP configuration includes the address of a DNS server, you should test connectivity to the DNS server now. Return to the Command Prompt and enter **ping** *DNSServerIPaddress*, where "*DNSServerIPaddress*" equals the DNSServer address recorded in step 3. You should receive four replies if your computer is properly configured and if the default gateway is active on your network.

If you were given the address of a computer beyond your local network, test this address now by returning to the Command Prompt and entering **ping** *RemoteIPaddress*, where "*RemoteIPaddress*" is the address of the remote computer.

Troubleshooting Connection Problems with tracert

You may have situations in which you can connect to a website or other remote resource, but the connection is very slow. If this connection is critical to business, you will want to gather information so that a network administrator or ISP can troubleshoot the source of the bottleneck. You can use the **tracert** command to gather this information. **tracert** is a command-line utility that traces the route taken by packets to a destination. When you use this command with the name or IP address of the target host, it will **ping** each of the intervening routers, from the nearest to the farthest, as shown in Figure 10–37. You see the length of the delay at each router, and you will be able to determine the location of the bottleneck. You can then provide this information to the people who will troubleshoot it for you. Consider a scenario in which your connection to the Google search engine (www.google.com) is extremely slow. You can use this command to run **tracert** and save the results to a file: **tracert www.google.com tracegoogle.txt.**

> *Note:* For a more thorough treatment of this topic, search the Microsoft TechNet site for the article "How to Troubleshoot Basic TCP/IP Problems."

try this!

Use tracert

You can use **tracert** to determine where a problem is occurring. Try this:

1. Open a Command Prompt.
2. Type **tracert www.google.com**
3. If the command runs successfully, you will see output similar to Figure 10–37, but with different intervening routers.

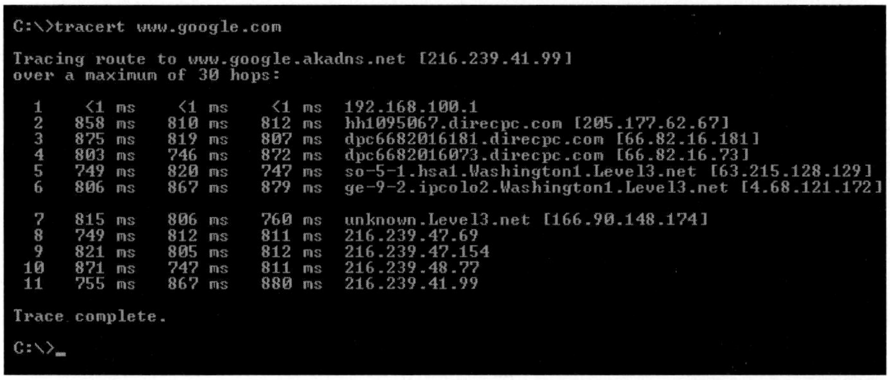

```
C:\>tracert www.google.com

Tracing route to www.google.akadns.net [216.239.41.99]
over a maximum of 30 hops:

  1    <1 ms    <1 ms    <1 ms  192.168.100.1
  2   858 ms   810 ms   812 ms  hh1095067.direcpc.com [205.177.62.67]
  3   875 ms   819 ms   807 ms  dpc6682016181.direcpc.com [66.82.16.181]
  4   803 ms   746 ms   872 ms  dpc6682016073.direcpc.com [66.82.16.73]
  5   749 ms   820 ms   747 ms  so-5-1.hsa1.Washington1.Level3.net [63.215.128.129]
  6   806 ms   867 ms   879 ms  ge-9-2.ipcolo2.Washington1.Level3.net [4.68.121.172]

  7   815 ms   806 ms   760 ms  unknown.Level3.net [166.90.148.174]
  8   749 ms   812 ms   811 ms  216.239.47.69
  9   821 ms   805 ms   812 ms  216.239.47.154
 10   871 ms   747 ms   811 ms  216.239.48.77
 11   755 ms   867 ms   880 ms  216.239.41.99

Trace complete.

C:\>_
```

FIGURE 10–37 The **tracert** results.

> *Note:* If you want to save a copy of the information displayed by a command-line command (such as **tracert**), you can send the screen output of this command to a text file, using the command-line redirection symbol (>). You can use any file name and any path to which you have write access. For instance, type **tracert www.google .com >tracegoogle.txt.** No output will appear on the screen.

Troubleshooting DNS Errors Using ping, netstat, and nslookup

Have you ever attempted to browse to a Web page, only to have your browser display an error message such as "Cannot find server or DNS Error"? This may be a name resolution problem because the fully qualified domain name (FQDN) portion of a URL, such as www.google.com, must be resolved to an IP address before a single packet goes to the website.

Using the ping Command to Troubleshoot DNS

One way to test if the problem is a connectivity problem or a DNS error is to first test for connectivity by either pinging the IP address of the website or using the IP address in place of the FQDN in the URL. If you cannot reach the website by using its IP address, then it is a connectivity problem and you should resolve it by contacting your network administrator or ISP and telling them the symptoms and the results of the **ping** test.

If you can reach the website by pinging the IP address but cannot access it through your browser, then it is a name resolution problem. A simple test to see if DNS name resolution is working is to ping the FQDN. Figure 10–38 shows the result of pinging the FQDN www.google.com. Notice that this displays the IP address of the website, confirming the DNS name-to-IP address resolution is working.

Using the netstat Command to Troubleshoot DNS

When you are troubleshooting networking problems, it is very helpful to have a second computer that does not display the same problems. Then you can use the second computer to discover the IP address of a website by using your browser to connect. Once connected, you can use the **netstat** command to discover the IP address of the website. **netstat** displays network statistics, protocol statistics, and information about current TCP/IP connections. Figure 10–39 shows the result of running the **netstat** command after connecting to a website with a browser. The IP address for this website, www.google.com,

FIGURE 10–38 Pinging the FQDN www.google.com reveals the IP address.

FIGURE 10–39 The **netstat** command displays the IP address and protocol information of current connections.

is shown under Foreign Address, and the protocol used to connect to the website, http, is shown after the colon.

Using the nslookup Command to Troubleshoot DNS

Finally, the classic command for troubleshooting DNS, used for many years on the Internet and other TCP/IP networks, is **nslookup**. The NS in this command name stands for "name server." This command allows you to send queries to a DNS name server directly and see the results. It is a very powerful command, but you can use it to test your DNS setting without learning all of its subcommands. Running **nslookup** in a Command Prompt without any additional command-line parameters will cause it to attempt to connect to the name server address in your IP configuration. Then it displays the **nslookup** prompt, a greater-than sign (>). You may enter subcommands at this prompt. If it cannot connect to the DNS server, it will display an error, as shown in Figure 10–40. If you see this error, contact your network administrator or ISP. Type **exit** at the **nslookup** prompt to exit from the command. Then type **exit** again to exit from the Command Prompt.

Note: To learn more about the **nslookup** command, search on **nslookup** in the Windows Help program.

```
C:\>nslookup
*** Can't find server name for address 192.168.100.1: Non-existent domain
*** Default servers are not available
Default Server:  UnKnown
Address:  192.168.100.1

> _
```

FIGURE 10–40 The **nslookup** command reveals a DNS problem.

Chapter 10 REVIEW

Chapter Summary

After reading this chapter and completing the Step-by-Step tutorials and Try This! exercises, you should understand the following facts about networking:

Configuring a Network Connection

- A protocol is a set of rules, usually formalized in a standard published by one of many standards organizations. A software implementation of a protocol is also called a protocol.
- TCP/IP is the protocol suite needed to access the Internet.
- Transmission Control Protocol (TCP) and Internet Protocol (IP) are the core protocols of TCP/IP.
- An IP address assigned to a network adapter or modem connects it to a network.
- IPv4, an old version of the protocol, is slowly being replaced by IPv6. An IPv4 address is 32-bits long and usually expressed in dotted decimal form, such as 192.168.1.1. An IPv6 address is 128-bits long, expressed in eight groups of hexadecimal numbers separated by colons, such as 2002:0470:b8f9:0000:020c:29ff:fe53:45ca.

- Public IP addresses are for hosts on the Internet and each address must be unique on the entire Internet.
- A private IP address is one of three ranges of IP addresses designated for use only on private networks. They are not for use on the Internet, and you do not need to obtain permission to use these addresses on a private network.
- Computers on a private network using private IP addresses get access to the Internet through a specialized device, usually a router.
- Each host on a TCP/IP network must have an IP address. A host receives an address by two general methods: automatically as a DHCP client via a network DHCP server (or a self-assigned APIPA address), or as a static address, which involves someone manually assigning an address to the host.
- In addition to the IP address there are several IP configuration settings including subnet mask, default gateway, DNS server, advanced DNS settings, and WINS settings.

Connecting to the Internet

- A connection to the Internet is a wide area network (WAN) connection.
- An Internet service provider is an organization that provides individuals or entire companies access to the Internet.
- Common wired WAN technologies include dial-up, ISDN, DSL, and cable.
- ISDN is a digital telephone service that simultaneously transmits voice, data, and control signaling over a single telephone line and can transfer data at up to 128,000 bits per second (128 Kbps).
- Digital subscriber line (DSL) service is similar to ISDN in its use of the telephone network, but it uses more advanced digital signal processing to compress more signals through the telephone lines and so is much faster than ISDN.
- Many cable television companies now offer Internet access through existing cable television connections using special cable modems.
- Wireless options for connecting to the Internet include cellular networks, wireless wide area networks (WWANs), wireless LAN (WLAN) connections (if the WLAN ultimately connects to the Internet), and satellite.
- Mobile users and remote offices often need to connect to the corporate intranet through the Internet using any of the connection technologies discussed previously, with the addition of a virtual private network (VPN) for security.

Using Internet Clients

- Web technologies changed the look of Internet content from all text to rich and colorful graphics, and made it simple to navigate the Web by using a special type of client called a Web browser.
- The top Web browsers are Google Chrome, Mozilla Firefox, and Internet Explorer.
- Both Firefox and IE have a large number of configuration settings that range from GUI preferences to settings critical to protecting your privacy and maintaining security for your computer and personal data.
- An email service and client are defined by the protocols they use, which are POP3, IMAP, and Web mail (HTML protocol).
- While some email services require dedicated clients, some email clients can interact with a variety of email server types.

- To configure any email client you need a specific set of information. This includes:
  - The type of mail server you are accessing (POP3, IMAP, or HTTP).
  - Your account name and password.
  - The DNS name of the incoming mail server.
  - If you are preparing to connect to a POP3 or IMAP server, you will also need to know the name of an outgoing mail server.
- File Transfer Protocol (FTP) is a protocol used to transfer files between a computer running the FTP server service and an FTP client. It is simple and fast.
- An FTP site that allows anonymous connections is an anonymous FTP site.
- If a site requires a user name and password, it will prompt you, whether you are using a Web browser to connect or an FTP client.
- A Web browser is fine for occasionally connecting to FTP sites, but use an FTP client to save settings for FTP sites you visit repeatedly.
- To configure an FTP client you will need the following, including:
  - The host name of the FTP server.
  - User ID and password (if applicable).
  - Account (if applicable).

Sharing Files and Printers

- A file and printer sharing protocol allows a computer to share files and printers with compatible clients.
- A file and printer client includes both the user interface and the underlying file-sharing protocols to access a file-sharing system on a network file and printer server.
- Windows installs with both the server and client components for file and printer sharing.
- Windows 7 and Windows 8 computers have the HomeGroup feature that allows sharing with other Windows 7 and Windows 8 installations that only require that you enter a password the first time the computer connects to the HomeGroup.
- To join or create a HomeGroup a Windows 7 computer must be connected to a Home network location; a Windows 8 computer must be connected to a Private network location. Same location; different names.
- To join or create a HomeGroup, a Windows 7 or Windows 8 computer must have IPv6; all firewalls between HomeGroup computers must also support IPv6 and must allow file and printer sharing.

- To share files on a Windows 7 or Windows 8 computer with an older version of Windows, add local accounts for the users with whom you want to share the contents of your Public folder.

Troubleshooting Common Network Client Connection Problems
- All the OSs surveyed in this book have GUI-based Network Diagnostics that combine many functions.

- Several command-line commands help in diagnosing and solving network client connection problems. These utilities include:
  - **ipconfig**
  - **ping**
  - **tracert**
  - **netstat**
  - **nslookup**

Key Terms List

anonymous FTP site *(396)*

automatic IP addressing *(369)*

Automatic Private IP Addressing (APIPA) *(370)*

default gateway *(371)*

dial-up *(377)*

digital subscriber line (DSL) *(378)*

Domain Name System (DNS) *(371)*

Dynamic Host Configuration Protocol (DHCP) server *(369)*

file and printer server *(397)*

File Transfer Protocol (FTP) *(396)*

fully qualified domain name (FQDN) *(408)*

host ID *(371)*

integrated services digital network (ISDN) *(378)*

Internet Protocol (IP) *(365)*

Internet service provider (ISP) *(376)*

internetwork *(365)*

IP address *(366)*

IPv4 *(365)*

IPv6 *(365)*

local area network (LAN) *(365)*

net ID *(371)*

octet *(371)*

packet *(365)*

private browsing *(388)*

private IP address *(368)*

protocol *(364)*

protocol stack *(364)*

public IP addresses *(368)*

remote access VPN *(382)*

router *(371)*

share *(397)*

site-to-site VPN *(382)*

static IP address *(369)*

subnet mask *(370)*

TCP/IP *(364)*

Transmission Control Protocol (TCP) *(365)*

virtual private network (VPN) *(382)*

Web browser *(383)*

Web mail *(393)*

wide area network (WAN) *(376)*

wireless LAN (WLAN) *(382)*

wireless wide area network (WWAN) *(380)*

zone *(387)*

Key Terms Quiz

Use the Key Terms List to complete the sentences that follow:

1. _____ are used for hosts on the Internet.

2. _____ is the version of the Internet Protocol that is slowly replacing the version that has been in use since 1983.

3. IE uses a/an _____ to assign security settings for selectively restricting browsing.

4. An IPv4 address beginning with 169.254 is a/an _____ address.

5. A/an _____ is not used for hosts on the Internet.

6. A/an _____ is an organization that provides individuals or entire companies with access to the Internet.

7. In an IPv4 address, each grouping of decimal numbers is called a/an _____ because it represent eight bits

8. Among IP configuration settings, the _____ is the IP address of the router used to send packets beyond the local network.

9. _____ is a term for a group of wired high-speed technologies offered through the phone company, and capable of much greater speeds than ISDN.

10. Most organization use a _____ to assign IP addresses to desktop computers.

1. The IPv4 address 192.168.30.24 is an example of one of these.
   a. DNS server address
   b. Public IP address
   c. Private IP address
   d. Automatic private IP address
   e. WINS server address

2. A computer requiring access to file and printer services on a network server running a Windows operating system must have a Microsoft file and printer client installed. Where can you find this?
   a. It is included with Windows and must be installed after setup.
   b. It is included with Windows and installed during setup.
   c. It is not included with Windows and you must download it from the Microsoft website.
   d. It can be downloaded from the Novell website.
   e. It must be installed and configured in the Connection properties dialog box.

3. In the chapter, which form of DSL is described as having the same speed upstream as downstream?
   a. ADSL
   b. xDSL
   c. VDSL
   d. HDSL
   e. SDSL

4. Your neighbor tells you that he has to initiate a connection to the Internet and complains that the connection is much slower than the connection he enjoys at work—and he is disconnected if there is a period of inactivity. From his description, which type of connection do you believe he has?
   a. ISDN
   b. Dial-up
   c. ADSL
   d. SDSL
   e. Cable

5. What appears in the Windows Connect Using box in the connection properties dialog box?
   a. A connection device
   b. An ISP name
   c. A user name
   d. A password
   e. A phone number

6. Which of the following is obviously *not* a valid IPv4 address?
   a. 192.168.100.48
   b. 10.0.33.50
   c. 172.300.256.100
   d. 30.88.29.1
   e. 200.100.99.99

7. You have two email clients installed on your computer. Where can you configure Windows to use one of them as your default email client?
   a. Control Panel | Internet Options | Programs
   b. Control Panel | Network Connections
   c. Start | Run | CMD
   d. Control Panel | Internet Options | Advanced
   e. Start | All Programs | Outlook Express

8. What command can you use to view the status of current connections, including the IP address and protocol used for each connection?
   a. ipconfig
   b. cmd
   c. ping
   d. netstat
   e. tracert

9. Which of the following is an example of an IPv6 address with the leading zeros removed?
   a. 2002:0470:b8f9:0000:020c:29ff:fe53:45ca
   b. 192.168.1.1
   c. 10.0.0.1
   d. 2002:470:b8f9::20c:29ff:fe53:45ca
   e. 0.0.0.0

10. Which command would you use as a test to see if a DNS server will respond to a request to resolve a name?
    a. ping
    b. nslookup
    c. ipconfig
    d. netstat
    e. tracert

11. This IPv4 configuration setting defines the two parts of an IP address: the Host ID and the Net ID.
    a. Gateway
    b. Subnet mask
    c. DNS
    d. DHCP
    e. Host name

12. Where in Internet Options can you configure how IE manages cookies?
    a. General page
    b. Security page
    c. Tabs page
    d. Advanced Privacy Settings dialog box
    e. Exceptions button

13. Your neighbor, a retiree on a modest fixed income, has asked your help in acquiring an Internet connection for his computer, a desktop computer running Windows 7. His only interest in Internet access is to use email to keep in touch with his children, who live in other states. He has a reliable phone connection. Based on this information, which service will you recommend?
    a. Cable
    b. ISDN
    c. Dial-up
    d. DSL
    e. Satellite

14. If you wanted to see the IP configuration from the $ prompt on a MAC, Linux, or UNIX system, which command would you use?
    a. ipconfig
    b. netstat
    c. nslookup
    d. ping
    e. ifconfig

15. What protocol is responsible for the accurate delivery of messages, verifying and resending pieces that fail to make the trip from source to destination?
    a. Internet Protocol
    b. Transmit Control Protocol (TCP)
    c. Secure Sockets Layer (SSL)
    d. File Transfer Protocol (FTP)
    e. Transmission Control Protocol (TCP)

Essay Quiz

1. Your computer was recently connected via a network adapter to a LAN that includes a router through which traffic passes to the Internet. You know the adapter was configured to use TCP/IP, and you need to test its ability to communicate with computers on the LAN and on the Internet. In your own words describe the steps you will take.

2. Your school uses an FTP site where each instructor posts documents, such as course assignments, white papers, and schedules for students to download. In addition, for each course, every student has a folder and is expected to upload class assignments to his or her folder. Each student has a user name and password to access the FTP site and must connect to a specific folder for each course. Would you use a Web browser or would you use an FTP client program? In your own words, explain your choice, including why it is the right choice for you.

3. A state agency that dispatches mobile units to disaster areas to monitor the disaster sites for hazardous chemical and biological contamination requires reliable Internet access for these units from any location in the state. They need to keep up-to-date with technical information via postings on federal websites and to upload their data to state and federal FTP sites. Which Internet connection option is the best fit for their needs? Explain your answer.

4. Describe the Windows 7 and Windows 8 HomeGroup feature.

5. Explain subnet masking in simple terms, including why a subnet mask is required when an adapter is configured with an IP address.

Lab Projects

LAB PROJECT 10.1

Survey your classmates, co-workers, and other acquaintances to determine the following:

1 What percentage of them has Internet access from home?

2 Of those who have Internet access from home, what percentage has had it for 10 years or more?

3 Of those who have Internet access from home, what percentage has had it for five years or more?

4 Of those who have Internet access from home, what percentage has had Internet access for less than one year?

5 Why is home Internet access important to those who have it?

6 Discuss the results with your classmates.

LAB PROJECT 10.2

This project requires the use of a Windows, Linux, or Mac computer that has Internet access. Using methods you learned in this chapter, find the answers to the following questions:

1. Does the lab computer have its own connection to the Internet or does it connect to the Internet through a LAN?

2. How is an IP address assigned to the lab computer?

3. Record the IP configuration settings for the lab computer below:
   a. IP address
   b. Subnet mask
   c. Default gateway
   d. DNS server

LAB PROJECT 10.3

Interview the IT staff at your school, place of work, or another organization and determine what Internet services they offer to students (Web pages, email, FTP, etc.). The list will usually go beyond the basic services studied in this chapter. Create a list of these services and the clients they require.

11 Mobile Operating Systems

"In May 2009, mobile Internet traffic only accounted for 0.9% of total Internet traffic. Today, however, it accounts for a whopping 15%. And the trend suggests that number will be close to 30% by the end of next year."

—From an article entitled "The Six Most Fascinating Technology Statistics Today," published on the *Daily Reckoning* (dailyreckoning.com) in July 2013, reporting on a presentation by Mary Meeker and Liang Wu at the Internet Trends D11 Conference, May 29, 2013.

Mobile computing in the 21st century has evolved from two branches of the technology tree: the telephony branch and the personal computing branch. Today's mobile devices only remotely resemble their awkward ancestors because today's devices are remarkably tiny and powerful, more like fictional *Star Trek* communicators than any 20th century phones or computers. The versatility and widespread consumer appeal of today's mobile devices exceeds the extraordinary imagination and vision of *Star Trek* creator Gene Roddenberry, at least in their use by consumers. Perhaps no one could have predicted three decades ago how tiny and powerful computing and communicating devices would become, and that they would be so common that individuals would insist on using them at work.

Chapter 1 introduced mobile devices and mobile operating systems. Before reading this chapter, we urge you to review the Chapter 1 section titled "Today's Mobile OSs." The coverage includes a description of the hardware features of popular smartphones and tablets. They include cameras, speakers, speaker jacks, adapters for a growing number of wireless technologies, and several types of sensors. Sensors include the accelerometer (described in the

Learning Outcomes

In this chapter, you will learn how to:

LO **11.1** Describe the benefits and challenges of personal mobile devices in the workplace.

LO **11.2** Configure wireless connections on mobile devices.

LO **11.3** Configure email, apps, and synchronization on mobile devices.

LO **11.4** Secure mobile devices.

overview of mobile devices in Chapter 1), GPS, magnetometer, proximity sensor, compass, and ambient light sensors.

In this chapter, we first explore the issues surrounding employees using their personal mobile devices at work and then we describe common configuration tasks for your mobile device and finally we look at security for mobile devices. ✹

LO 11.1 | From Luggable to BYOD

Mobile computing was once something only certain business travelers did using computers that were just luggable versions of the PCs they left at the office. Mobile computing has evolved, and in just the last few years the mobile computing market has been flooded with tiny and powerful mobile devices. Now consumers in every walk of life practice mobile computing, children carry smartphones to preschool, and teachers uncrate boxes of iPads preloaded with student coursework. The "mobile" aspect seems to mean we are not tethered to power and data lines, even as we practice mobile computing at home and everyplace else we go day or night.

In this section, you'll peek at the past of mobile computing, which wasn't very mobile, rarely connected, and involved little computing power. Then you'll examine the issue of using personal mobile devices in the workplace.

Mobile Computing Then and Now

In a span of 30 years mobile computing devices went from a few heavy underpowered devices to today's large number of mobile devices that fit nicely in the hand and whose weight is measured in ounces rather than in tens of pounds. Hence, personal mobile devices are rarely out of reach of their owners who have come to depend on them at home, school, work, and play. Some of us have lived through this history.

Sometime in the mid-1980s our friend Amber was waiting in the baggage area of an airport as a gray plastic bin rose into view at the center of the baggage carousel and made a precarious slide down to the moving stainless-steel track. She recognized its clattering contents as the components of a Compaq portable computer, its cracked case the size of a 21st century gaming tower.

Obviously some road warrior had wearied of lugging 28 pounds of technology and checked it as baggage. Amber smugly snatched up her own suitcase and placed it on top of her luggage cart that already contained her carry-on: a 16-pound Zenith Data Systems Z-180 Portable PC. She had spent the flight with her feet resting uneasily on the portion of the laptop that did not fit under the passenger seat in front of her, while the luggage cart rode in the overhead compartment. There was no way she could actually put the laptop on her lap and get real work done. Amber's laptop was valuable to her as an always-configured-correctly instructor's computer for the classes she taught on PC hardware and supporting the DOS operating system. Computer professionals like Amber, rather than the typical consumer of the time, were the target market for portable computers. To quote the Welcome page of the Zenith Data Systems Z-180 Owner's Manual:

> *This Owner's Manual is for you, the new computer user. In the first part of this manual, you will learn how to set up and operate your new computer for the first time. In the second part, you will learn about the firmware of the computer and how to program it. In the third part, you will learn about the hardware and how to use the programmable registers in the computer.*

Programmable registers? Times have changed. Three decades later we no longer expect or need a manual for a new tablet or smartphone. Another big change is that modern mobile devices are almost always connected to some network, whereas the old devices did not connect to any network while in transit. Amber had to wait until she arrived in a classroom with a connection to a local area network (LAN) or hotel room that included a "modem line" for a slow dial-up connection. The more expensive the hotel, the more they charged for this service. Today's travelers demand that hotels provide free high-speed Internet access, and many of them have cellular data plans so that their mobile devices can wirelessly connect to the Internet 24/7.

And consider what they do with those connections! Mobile device users collectively upload and share hundreds of millions of photos every day. They upload an estimated one hundred hours of video to YouTube per minute. And this type of traffic is increasing as more and more mobile users stay in touch, sharing their thoughts and opinions via social media, and keeping up with work and personal email. This pervasiveness of mobile devices has led to a phenomenon in the workplace that we explore next.

The home screen on an Android smartphone.

Mobile Devices and BYOD

Smartphones and tablets present a challenge for schools and employers because many individuals come to school or work armed with a pocket or a backpack full of technology. And they don't care to spend any time separated from these devices. Many demand to be able to use these devices for accessing work email, text messages, and data. This practice is called bring your own device (BYOD), and it occurs in many organizations, whether or not they officially condone it.

There are variations of policies (or lack of them) governing BYOD in the workplace. Here are just a few examples:

- Companies may reimburse an employee who uses their own device for cellular voice and data usage. This is important, because cellular voice charges are usually by the minute, and cellular data services are metered, with the cost going up with the amount of data downloaded. Charges can quickly mount up for someone using their personal device for work.

- In a form of shared ownership, an employer subsidizes the purchase of an employee's personal mobile device, giving the employee the option of buying a more expensive device than budgeted.

- An employer may allow or require use of personal mobile devices but not compensate the employee or have any clear policies regarding how to protect work data.

Advantages of BYOD to Employers

There are many advantages to employers of BYOD; a short list includes:

- Quicker response by the employee to communications.
- It saves the employer the cost of the device.
- Some jobs either require, or at least benefit from, the use of mobile devices.
- Acceptance of employees' use of mobile devices attracts tech-savvy people.
- Employees are inclined to work outside of normal work hours.
- You can deliver important job training to mobile devices that employees can use when needed.

An Apple iPad home screen.

Disadvantages of BYOD to Employers

There are risks to allowing employees to access email and corporate data using their personal mobile devices. A few of the issues with BYOD include:

- It may conflict with corporate security policy.
- It may violate government regulations for employees to have certain data on their mobile devices.
- If a device is lost or stolen, it puts the employer at risk.
- Employees may leave a job and still have sensitive work-related data on devices.
- Normally intellectual property created as part of a job belongs to the employer. It is unclear who owns the intellectual property if it is created on the employee's device.

Risks of BYOD to Employees

There are risks and concerns for the employee. Consider these issues:

- Who will pay for the cost of the device?
- Who will pay for added voice and data usage due to business use?
- What protects the employee's if the employer's policy mandates monitoring BYOD devices?
- Can an employer or law enforcement agency confiscate an employee's device for any work-related reason?

Note: According to a 2013 survey sponsored by Acronis of 4,374 IT professionals in eight countries, 58 percent of enterprises did not have adequate policies in place to manage BYOD practices. In their survey they included the use of personally owned smartphones, tablets, and PCs. Only 21 percent responded that they would remotely wipe data on mobile devices of employees leaving the company.

Basic BYOD Policies

Basic BYOD policies should address these areas:

- Who owns intellectual property created on an employee's device—the employee or the employer?
- What security requirements should there be and how should they be enforced, including, but not limited to passwords, encryption, and remote wipe (remotely deleting data from a lost or stolen device)?
- How and when does the employee back up the employer's data?
- Will video- and audio-recording features in BYOD devices be allowed in the workplace?
- Will the employer take advantage of location services on devices to monitor an employee's location during working hours? A location service is one that allows an app to track your location, using one or more methods, often with the help of the Internet.

Managing BYOD

Managing BYOD begins with company policies covering work behavior, security, and employee reimbursement. Existing policies may cover the use of personal devices in very broad terms and need updating. Employers have many options for managing BYOD to protect themselves and their employees. They also want to make the mobile devices more useful to the employees.

Employers' awareness of BYOD and the need to manage it varies. Therefore some experts on security and BYOD promote a bottom-up approach, seeking to educate the employees so that they will be aware of the risks to themselves and request more clarity in BYOD policies from their employers.

In addition to modifying policies for BYOD, employers can enforce those policies and manage mobile devices using a category of software called mobile device management (MDM). Companies such as Citrix, VMware, Sophos, MobileIron, Acronis, and Microsoft offer such products—sometimes integrated into existing suites of products. Mobile device management is a broad term for the variety of features offered and the different approaches by the vendors of this type of software.

Some employers use products that include some form of virtualization. That may be in the form of a virtual machine running on the remote device or some variation of application virtualization—with processing occurring either on the mobile device or on remote servers.

Others prefer to create a Web-based portal to work apps and data, making this available to a wider range of devices, since the only required client software is a browser.

try this!

Research BYOD

In the spring of 2013 Dan Lohrmann, Chief Security Officer of the State of Michigan, published an inexpensive e-book titled *BYOD for You: The Guide to Bring Your Own Device to Work*, available on Amazon for $2.99. He and others have published very informative articles on this topic that are available on the Web. Research BYOD, using these or other sources, and see if there is something you can apply to your own use of mobile devices at work or school. Try this:

1. Open an Internet search engine and search on **BYOD**. Look for articles that are available without asking you to provide personal information. Avoid these because they are targeted to people who are shopping for products to manage mobile devices in corporations. Look for sources like ZDNet and other technical publications.

2. Read at least three articles on this topic.

3. Did you learn anything that will change how you will use mobile devices?

4. Discuss your research and conclusions with your classmates.

LO 11.2 | Configuring Accounts and Wireless Connections on Mobile Devices

Chapter 1 described some of the wireless options for mobile devices and Chapter 10 described and compared networking technologies. In this section we first describe the accounts required for each of the mobile operating systems discussed in this chapter. Then we detail how to configure your mobile operating system to connect your device to four types of wireless networks: cellular data networks, Wi-Fi WLAN networks, Bluetooth connections for connecting to nearby devices, and another type of wireless connection over very short distances, called Near Field Communication (NFC).

Your Mobile Device Account

All popular smartphones and tablets require a user account. That includes Apple's iPhone and iPad, Android devices, and Microsoft Windows 8 and Windows Phone 8 devices.

Google Account

A Google account is an account that gives you access to Google services. A Google account is free and you can have more than one. To create a Google account, connect to accounts.google.com, shown on the next page. You can use/create a Google Gmail account or use any existing email account. If you wish to use an account other than a Gmail account, simply click on the blue

The Create a new Google Account page.

link titled **I prefer to use my current email address** located under the **Choose your username** box.

Apple ID

An Apple ID is your account as a customer of Apple for Apple services and products. Like a Google account, an Apple ID is a free account, although some of the services may be fee-based. The credentials include an email address (any working email address) and a password for the Apple ID—*not* the password for using the email account.

If this is your first Apple product, you will create a new account at the time of purchase. This account is associated with their iTunes account and the credit card used for purchasing music for the iPod. Therefore, many think of it as an iTunes account, but you can use this one account for all your Apple devices and services, such as iCloud and Apple Online Support. For security reasons consider creating a second Apple ID without an associated credit card

The **My Apple ID** page where you can log in to manage an existing account or create a new Apple ID.

that you use for downloading free apps from the Apple store and for synchronizing data across devices. Connect to the My Apple ID page, shown on the previous page, where you can log in with an existing account and manage it, or create a new Apple ID account.

Another reason for having multiple accounts is for more iCloud data storage because each account has a free data storage limit. A family with multiple devices may want a separate account for each member. Or an individual with multiple devices may want one account for a device used mostly for work and another account just for personal use.

Microsoft Account

A Microsoft account is a free account that gives the subscriber access to Microsoft services, such as Hotmail, Messenger, SkyDrive, Windows Phone, Xbox Live, and Outlook.com. Although the account is free, some of the services may be fee-based. To sign up for a Microsoft account, connect to signup.live.com, shown here, and provide the required information.

Microsoft account	Sign in

Already have a Microsoft account? If you use **Hotmail**, **SkyDrive**, **Xbox LIVE** and want to claim a new email address, sign in, and then rename your account or create an alias.

Who are you?

Name

First   Last

Birth date

Month   Day   Year

Gender

Select one

How would you like to sign in?

Microsoft account name

someone@example.com

Or get a new email address

Create a password

Create a new Account at the **Microsoft account** page.

Connecting to Cellular Networks

When preparing to buy a smartphone, first shop for the cellular provider, such as Verizon, AT&T, Sprint, T-Mobile, Cricket, or U.S. Cellular. Look for the best service and options in your area. Having only one or two providers with coverage in your area narrows down the choices, but if you live in an area with coverage by several cellular providers, you may want to visit several stores or websites to compare plans and costs before making your final choice.

After selecting the carrier and the plan you would like, select the device. Once you have selected the device that fits your needs and budget, you normally sign a contract for a certain level of service before you gain possession of the device. While there are many plans, they generally charge you a flat rate for up to a certain number of voice minutes, and a separate flat rate for a certain amount of cellular data usage. Research this and read customer reviews of cellular data plans before you buy because reviews will tell you a lot about other customers' experiences with the provider.

Before you receive the phone the cellular service provider will program it for your cellular account. This process often includes inserting a card called a Subscriber Identity Module (SIM) into the device. If you purchase the device over the Internet, the SIM card may come with the device, with instructions

The **Welcome** screen on a Windows Phone 8 smartphone.

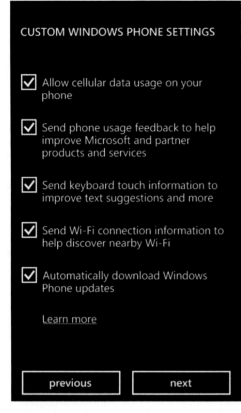

CUSTOM WINDOWS PHONE SETTINGS

☑ Allow cellular data usage on your phone

☑ Send phone usage feedback to help improve Microsoft and partner products and services

☑ Send keyboard touch information to improve text suggestions and more

☑ Send Wi-Fi connection information to help discover nearby Wi-Fi

☑ Automatically download Windows Phone updates

Learn more

| previous | next |

FIGURE 11–1 The custom Windows Phone Settings screen.

on installing it and activating the phone. If you purchase a smartphone in a bricks-and-mortar store, you will usually configure the cellular connection while still in the store, or the salesperson may do it for you.

The first time you power up a new smartphone that has not been prepared or one that has the basic configuration but still needs your personal settings, a setup screen will display and lead you through the process. For instance, a Windows Phone 8 smartphone starts up with a welcome screen, shown on the previous page. Tap the **get started** button and it will lead you through selecting a language, accepting the terms of use, reading the privacy statement, and other steps for setting up your phone. Figure 11–1 shows a Windows Phone 8 screen with all the custom Windows Phone settings selected.

Cellular data communications is optional in a tablet, adding a premium to the cost of the device because of the required internal cellular modem as well as the ongoing cost for the cellular data plan. As with a smartphone, the cellular provider will either configure the device or give you special instructions. The device may come preconfigured for connecting to the cellular network, and the first time you start it up, you personalize it by going through a menu, similar to the one shown for a Windows Phone 8 smartphone.

Connecting to Wi-Fi Networks

To connect to a Wi-Fi network for the first time, open the Settings app on your device. Then select the option for Wireless (or Wi-Fi) and turn on Wi-Fi, if necessary. It will then scan for Wi-Fi networks and list detected Wi-Fi networks, using the SSID of each network. A **Service Set ID (SSID)** is a network name used to identify a wireless network. Consisting of up to 32 characters, the SSID travels with the messages on a Wi-Fi network, and all wireless devices on a WLAN must use the same SSID in order to communicate.

In the list of available cellular networks, select one and enter the required password. It will remember this network and the password, maintaining a list of Wi-Fi networks it has successfully connected to and automatically providing the password you entered the first time you connected. If you travel, you will need to do this for each new Wi-Fi network you connect to. Figure 11–2 shows an iPad Wi-Fi Settings page with a successful connection to a Wi-Fi network named ShortMoose.

In some cases, the hotspot administrator turns off broadcasting of the SSID, so that the network name will not show in the list of networks. In that case, the administrator gives authorized users the name of the network and credentials to enter. On an iOS device, select Other Network to open the drop-down box shown in Figure 11–3.

There is an important money-saving feature that is enabled by default in some mobile devices with both cellular and Wi-Fi connections. If the device connects to a Wi-Fi network, it will use that rather than the cellular network for data. So, when you open your browser, the device will automatically use the Wi-Fi network. If a Wi-Fi network is not available, when you open your browser or other app requiring Internet access the device will connect using an available cellular data network. Your device may

try this!

Enable or Disable Wi-Fi

If you have a mobile device, it should have a setting for enabling or disabling Wi-Fi networking. Try this:

1. Open the Settings utility in your mobile device.
2. Search for the Wi-Fi settings.
3. Enable or disable Wi-Fi.
4. Test the setting by opening an app that requires Wi-Fi access.
5. Return the Wi-Fi setting to its previous configuration.

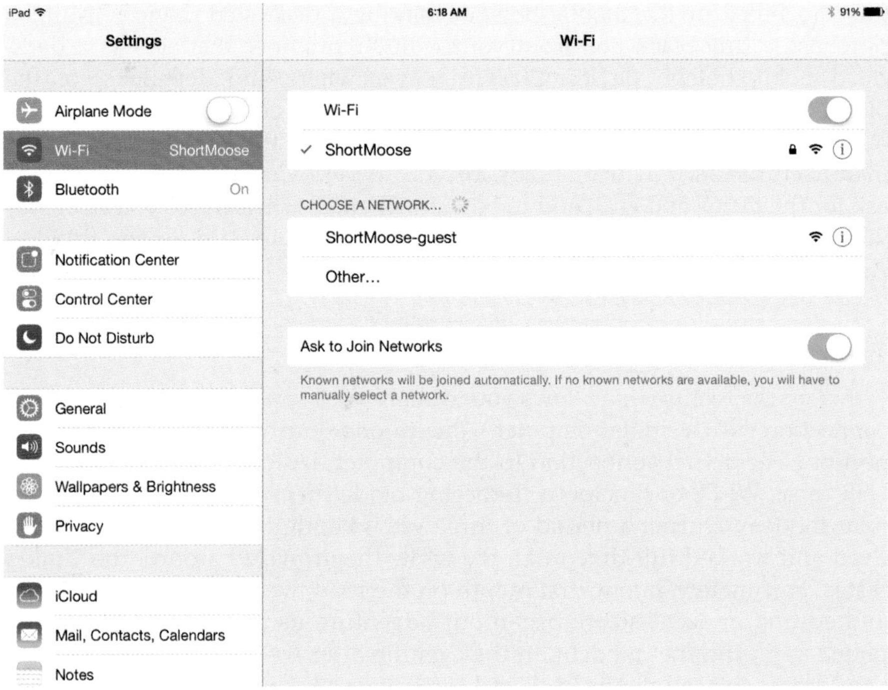

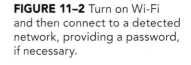

FIGURE 11-2 Turn on Wi-Fi and then connect to a detected network, providing a password, if necessary.

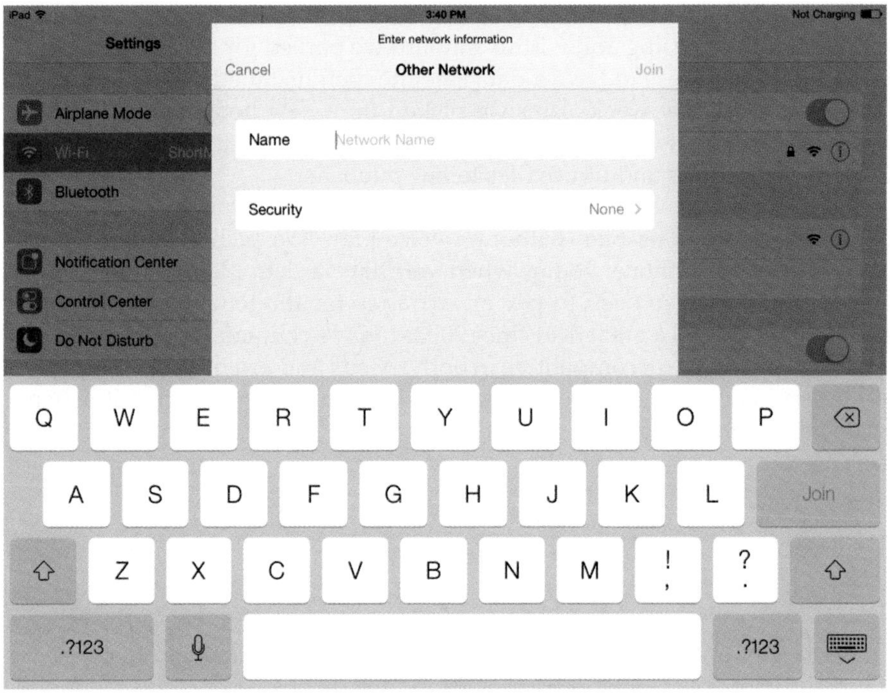

FIGURE 11-3 If the network name (SSID) is not visible, enter the network name and required credentials.

include an option for not allowing cellular access for Internet browsing or other data connections, such as transferring files or email.

Mobile Hotspots

A **mobile hotspot** shares its data cellular connection with nearby devices connected via Wi-Fi. The device at the core of the mobile hotspot is a cellular wireless router. This may be a smartphone or tablet with cellular access and

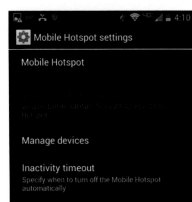

FIGURE 11–4 The **Mobile hotspot settings** screen on an Android smartphone.

Note: Tethering is also used to describe a connection between your mobile device and another mobile device or computer for the sake of synchronizing or backing up data.

WARNING!

Disable Bluetooth when you do not absolutely need it. The Bluetooth pairing process is a security vulnerability, allowing someone with a Bluetooth-enabled device to connect and install malware, listen to your conversations, make phone calls, and more. Turn it off manually, or install a battery management app that will turn it off when you disconnect a Bluetooth device.

this capability, or the mobile hotspot may be a dedicated device. You also purchase a tiny black box from your cellular provider that acts as a dedicated mobile hotspot device. Carry this everywhere, and, depending on the plan you purchased, share your cellular broadband connection with several other devices. Novatel has a trademarked name for the hotspot device they manufacturer: MiFi, which stands for "my Wi-Fi." Contact your provider to ask for the terms and cost, and to have them enable the service you select for your account. Figure 11–4 shows the Mobile Hotspot settings page from an Android smartphone.

Tethering

Tethering is a feature that allows you to share your smartphone's cellular data connection with a single computer—one-to-one sharing of your Internet connection. The actual connection to the computer, laptop, or tablet can be via USB cable, Wi-Fi, or Bluetooth. Tethering mode turns your phone into a cellular modem. During a period of three years beginning in 2003 the authors lived and worked full-time in an RV while they traveled around the United States. Fortunately, in our first month on the road, we were between writing and editing projects, so we began our adventure using a single mobile cell phone as an Internet modem. In the evening after we parked for the day we would pass the cell phone back and forth across the aisle that separated our two "offices" to take turns connecting to each computer, mainly for accessing email.

Our cellular modem in 2003 operated at about 56 Kbps, so we did very little Internet browsing and within a month we parked for two days in a business park in San Jose to have a data satellite dish installed on the roof of the motor home. A few weeks later we picked up a new book contract and we were ready with the high-speed Internet access required for research and for uploading chapters and figure files to our publisher.

Back in 2003, we purchased that cell phone just to use it as a cellular modem; it had a data plan without a voice plan. We each already carried a conventional cell phone. Today, when you have a data plan for your smartphone you may also need to pay an extra fee for the tethering service. The world has changed a great deal since 2003. Today's cellular devices offer much faster speeds, and are competitive in both speeds and pricing with mobile satellite service. However, tethering may not be your best option, and it may not even be an option from your carrier. It may be included with a mobile hotspot service.

Connecting to Bluetooth Devices

Bluetooth is a wireless standard used for communicating over very short distances. The most common implementation of Bluetooth connects devices at a distance of up to one meter. You might want to use Bluetooth to connect a Bluetooth headset or keyboard to your mobile device, or to connect a mobile device to a PC or Mac to synchronize data. Bluetooth consumes battery power, so it is disabled by default. To connect devices via Bluetooth, first open the Settings app on your mobile device and enable Bluetooth. Then enable it on the computer or Bluetooth device you wish to connect to so that they can discover (find) each other, which they will attempt to do as soon as you enable Bluetooth. We call a connection between two Bluetooth devices a pairing.

When connecting two computing devices, such as an iMac and an iPhone or iPad tablet, go to the Settings screen on each one and select the other device for pairing. After a short pause a message will display with a pairing code (also called a PIN code), as shown in Figure 11–5 showing the message on an

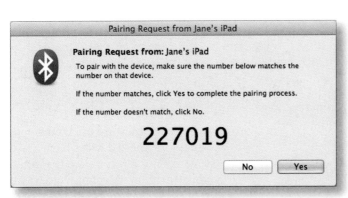

FIGURE 11–5 Pairing an iPad with an iMac.

FIGURE 11–6 Pairing a Bluetooth keyboard with an iPad.

iMac when pairing with an iPad. Then you may simply need to confirm that the same pairing code shows on the screen for both devices and click or tap the Yes button.

When connecting a Bluetooth device without a screen (such as a headset or keyboard) to a computer or mobile device, turn on the device and allow the smartphone, tablet, or PC to discover it. Figure 11–6 shows the message that appears on an iPhone when it discovers a Bluetooth keyboard. Enter the code at the keyboard to complete the pairing. After this, you will not need to enter the code each time they pair, but you will need to turn on Bluetooth if you turn it off after using it.

Finally, test connectivity between the devices. We have found that just entering the pairing code on a keyboard is not enough confirmation that the connection is working. So in the case of a keyboard, open an app, such as an Internet browser, tap on a box requiring text (such as an address box), and then start typing on the keyboard. If it does not work you may not have confirmed the pairing on both sides (not always necessary). We have also found that a failure to connect is often a case of impatience, so a short wait is in order. However, if you have a problem with the pairing, disable Bluetooth on both devices and start over again.

> *Note:* On devices that we have tested, the order for setting up a Bluetooth connection is: (1) enable Bluetooth, (2) find a device for pairing, (3) enable pairing, (4) enter PIN code, and (5) test connectivity.

try this!

Pair Two Devices with Bluetooth

Connect your mobile device to a computer or peripheral using Bluetooth. Try this:

1. Open the Settings utility in your mobile device.
2. Locate the Bluetooth setting and turn it on.
3. Turn on your Bluetooth device.
4. The mobile device should show that it is searching, connecting, and pairing.
5. It if is a keyboard, enter the code that appears on the mobile device.
6. Test the connection: for instance, play music to test a Bluetooth headset.
7. Disable Bluetooth when you are finished.

Connecting with Near Field Communications

Some newer mobile devices include a special chipset that supports **Near Field Communication (NFC)**. With this enabled and configured, you can position your phone very close to another that also has NFC enabled and share data and even pay for purchases at locations using this type of device. The Windows 8.1 implementation of NFC, as described in Chapter 5, is Tap to Send. This feature is not widely available, and at this time it appears that Apple has no plans to support NFC in their mobile devices.

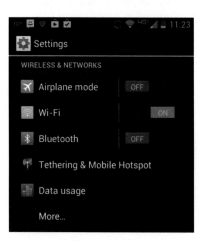

FIGURE 11–7 The **Settings** screen for Wireless connections on an Android smartphone.

Note: Enable and disable several features in iOS 7 by swiping up from the bottom of the screen to open the **control center**. Features you can turn on or off from here include **Airplane Mode**, **Wi-Fi**, **Bluetooth**, **Do Not Disturb**, and **Mute**. **Control center** also has screen controls for video, sound, and brightness, and you can also launch **Camera** and the **Clock** (World Clock, Alarm, Stopwatch, and Timer) from this handy tool.

Airplane Mode

When traveling on a commercial airliner you are required to turn off radio frequency (RF) signals from all personal devices for all or part of the flight. At one time this required powering down cell phones, but modern mobile devices are actually useful to their owners, even when they are not connected. Therefore, these devices have a feature called Airplane mode. When you Turn on Airplane mode all radios in your device are turned off, including cellular, Wi-Fi, Bluetooth, and NFC, but you can continue calculating your expense account or playing Angry Birds, as long as you don't require a wireless connection. Look for it in the Settings app. Figure 11–7 shows the settings screen on an Android smartphone containing the switch for enabling or disabling Airplane mode as well as Wi-Fi, Bluetooth, and Tethering and Mobile Hotspot.

LO 11.3 | Email, Apps, and Synchronization

Once you know how to work with your mobile device's connection settings, you will want to configure email, acquire new apps, and enable synchronization.

Configuring Email

In order to use your mobile device to access your email, begin by adding the account. Mobile devices support several types of accounts for email, social networking, data backup, and more. And you can configure a single device to use several accounts. Mobile operating systems know the basic connection information for many types of accounts. Therefore, for many accounts, you only need to provide your personal login information to the account, which is usually an email address and password. Figure 11–8 shows a list of account types supported on an iPad. Chapter 10 described email account types as well as the settings required to connect to an email account.

Online Email Accounts

For online email accounts, such as Hotmail or Gmail, you do not have to specify a sending and receiving server. All you need to enter is your user name and password. All the mobile OSs described here work with online email accounts.

Accounts Requiring IMAP, POP, or SMTP Settings

If you want to use an account type other than an online email service, you will need server addresses obtained from your mail server administrator. To receive mail you will need an address for a Post Office Protocol 3 (POP3) or an Internet Message Access Protocol 4 (IMAP4) server that receives your incoming mail and forwards it to you. An email client uses one or the other of these. To send mail you usually need the address of your Simple Mail Transfer Protocol (SMTP) server that accepts your outgoing mail and forwards it to the recipient's mail server.

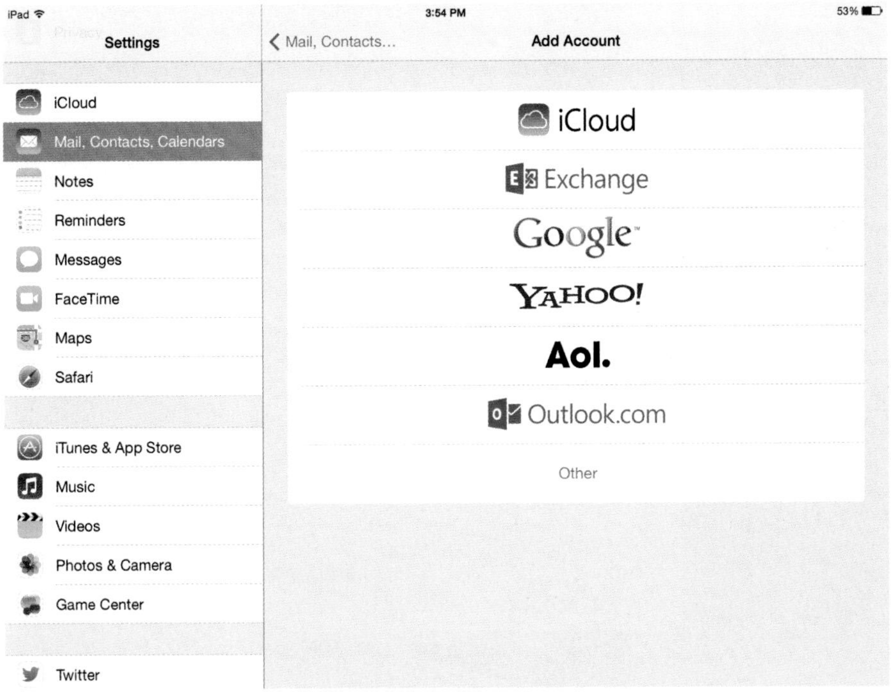

FIGURE 11–8 Mobile OSs allow you to use many types of accounts for email and social networking.

Note: The name of the server for sending and/or receiving email will not always match the domain name seen after the @ in the email address. The name of the server is irrelevant, as long as it points to the correct mail server.

The addresses for these servers are not numerical. A POP3 address will simply be the name of a mail server in an Internet domain, and may resemble this: pop.domainname.com; while the address for an IMAP4 server might look something like this: imap.domainname.com. Then, we probably don't need to say this, but the SMTP address might look like this: smtp.domainname.com. These are just examples, and you need to get the actual addresses for these servers from your email administrator.

Armed with the needed information, locate the email settings on your mobile device and carefully enter the information. On an iPad, open the Settings app and tap **Mail, Contacts, Calendars**. Then, in **Accounts** category in the right pane tap **Add Account**. Does the list include the type of email account you need to use? If it does, tap it and continue. If not, tap **Other** at the bottom of the list and then tap **Add Mail Account**. The **New Account** dialog box will display, along with the virtual keyboard (unless you have an external keyboard connected). Enter your name (not a user account name), email address, password for that email account, and a description for the email account that will identify it for you in the list of accounts. Tap **Next**, and follow the instructions, using the addresses you obtained from your mail server administrator. Figure 11–9 shows the settings for a POP account named "Personal" by the user. If you slide the green button to the right of "Account" you can disable the account without deleting it. If you scroll down in this list of settings, you will find another button that allows you to delete the account.

On an Android device you will have a Google account for accessing Google services and Gmail. To add another type of account in Android, open **Settings**. Then under the **Accounts** category select **Add Account**. This opens the **Add an Account** screen that lists a variety of account types, not just email accounts but social networking sites, photo sharing sites, data backup sites, and other accounts added as you install certain apps. For example, the current list on one of our Android phones is Corporate (Exchange Server), Email, Facebook, Google, and Visual Voice Mail.

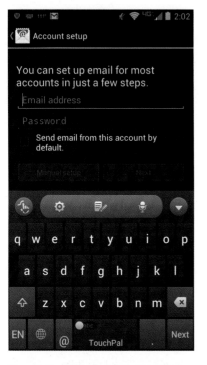

The Android **Account setup** screen.

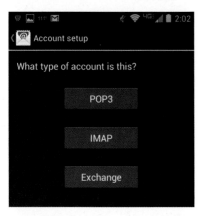

Select the type of account.

FIGURE 11–10 Click **add an account** to add a new account to Windows Phone 8.

FIGURE 11–9 The settings for a POP email account.

From the **Add an account** screen add a new email account to an Android device by tapping **Email.** This may open directly to the **Account Setup** screen. If this opens the **Synchronize Account** screen, tap **Other** and it will open the **Account Setup** screen, shown in the top of the margin. Enter the email address and password for the account, which should enable the two buttons (**Manual setup** and **Next**). If you want this to be the default email account for sending emails, before moving from this screen tap to place a check in the box in the middle of the screen. Then tap **Next** to display the screen shown at left where you select the type of account: POP3, IMAP, or Exchange. Select the type, and then enter the information from your email administrator in the following screens.

In Windows Phone 8, your Microsoft account is your first email account as well as your account for accessing Microsoft services. You can add other accounts as well. As with Android and iOS, these other accounts include email accounts and social networking accounts. The Mail app for Windows Phone 8 only works with cloud-based email accounts, relying on an Internet-based email service to store email data, rather than save all your saved messages on your smartphone.

To add accounts to Windows Phone 8, open **Settings | System | email+ account** (Figure 11–10). You may see a different list of accounts, depending on what accounts you have added to your phone. To add a new account of any type click **add an account**. Then on the **Add an Account** screen select from the accounts listed. This screen lists both email and social networking accounts. The email account types supported by Windows Phone 8 include Outlook (actually Exchange ActiveSync), Hotmail, Yahoo! Mail, and Google (Gmail). Select one of these options and enter your email address and the password for using that email account. Then tap **sign in** and Mail will attempt to detect other settings required for the connection, and you may be prompted to enter more information.

Select **other account** at the bottom of the screen (not shown) to configure an email service using IMAP or POP. Again, enter your email address and password for the account and attempt to sign in. Then use the **advanced setup** option only if Mail fails to detect the correct settings and you need to enter mail server settings manually.

Configuring an Exchange Client

Many organizations use internally maintained Microsoft Exchange mail servers for employee email accounts and for email within the organization as well as over the Internet. Also, many hosting services for Internet domain names offer Exchange email hosting services to their clients. Exchange gives the organization full administrative control, while providing users with a central location for their email history, contacts, tasks, and many collaborative tools.

If you need to connect your device to an Exchange server, first open Accounts from Settings. All the mobile OSs described in this chapter list Microsoft Exchange as an account type. Select it and enter the email address, user name, password, and a description for the list of accounts.

Note: The organization owning the Exchange server and domain, such as a company or university, centrally manages and owns all Exchange accounts stored in one Exchange accounts database. Google and Microsoft centrally maintain and administer the individual accounts stored in Gmail and Hotmail, respectively. Due to the complexity and cost of managing large numbers of email accounts, organizations are increasingly outsourcing email services to companies like Google and Microsoft.

Mobile Apps

It's all about the apps. Apps are what make your mobile device the high-tech version of a Swiss Army knife. All mobile devices come with some built-in apps, but everyone installs more apps. Whatever mobile OS you select, you can choose from among hundreds of thousands of mobile apps. Apps are OS specific, so you must find apps that work with your OS and device. The major mobile operating systems differ in how the apps are available and what apps are available. The home screens on these mobile devices will normally have an icon for connecting to an online retail site for buying apps for that mobile OS and (sometimes) device type.

When you find an app that sounds like what you need, read through the description, paying close attention to the requirements. An app may require certain services in order to work as advertised. For instance, you may need to give the app full control of your device or turn on the location service and/or global positioning system (GPS) service.

Apps for Android

Play Store is an Android app that connects you to the Google Play online app store, the official source for Android apps, but since this is an open OS, there are other sources in the open-source market, such as AndroidPIT at www.androidpit.com. Pay very close attention to the specs for an app, as there are many versions of Android, with features that are only supported on some devices. Figure 11–11 shows a small sampling of the Android apps at the Google Play store.

Apps for Apple iOS

Apple's online App Store or the brick-and-mortar Apple stores are the only app sources for Apple devices of any type. They sell only Apple-sanctioned software from many publishers. Because of the screen size differences some apps display best on the device for which they were written. Tap the App Store on the home page of your iOS device to connect to the App Store; the first time you connect from a device you will need to provide your Apple ID and password. Figure 11–12 shows the App Store. You update apps through the App Store, and when one or more updates are ready, the number of updates will appear on the App Store icon, as shown on the next page. When you open the App Store, the updates will display, and if you decide to update or download an app, you will need to enter your Apple ID and password before continuing.

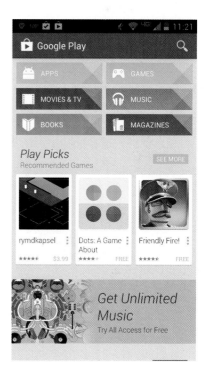

FIGURE 11–11 A small sampling of apps at the Google Play online app store.

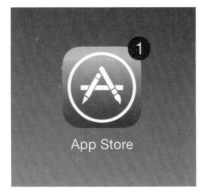

The number on this App Store icon indicates that one update is available.

FIGURE 11-12 The Apple online App Store.

Apps for Microsoft Windows

The Microsoft Store has apps from many publishers for all their Windows OSs on all devices, including those for mobile devices running Windows 8, Windows RT, or Windows Phone 8. Some are free, but there is a charge for most of them. The Microsoft model is, in part, like the Apple model. You must purchase apps written for the new Windows 8 GUI (regardless of the device for which it is intended) or Windows Phone exclusively through the Microsoft Store; apps written for traditional Windows or the Windows 8 Desktop GUI are available at the Microsoft Store and through other sources that sell software.

Synchronization

Some of us have multiple computing devices. The authors each have a desktop PC, a laptop, and a smartphone. In addition, Jane has an iMac and iPad and Chuck has an Android tablet. With so many devices (and we know people with more), it is a challenge to keep track of our data. Therefore, we **synchronize** certain data between devices. When data is synchronized between two locations, the files are examined and newer files replace the older files—sometimes, but not always, in both directions so that the contents match. Synchronizing can be to another computer or mobile device or to a cloud-based service to ensure against data loss if the device is lost or stolen.

We don't do this between the two users, but each of us synchronizes our own data between mobile devices and PCs and between mobile devices and a cloud service.

Connecting Mobile Devices for Syncing

You can synchronize your smartphone or tablet with your computer, using a USB cable, Wi-Fi, Bluetooth, or over the Internet using a cloud-based service. If you choose a cable, use the USB cable that came with the smartphone; it

Note: Depending on the device and the options available to you, you can synchronize data using four connection types: USB cable, Wi-Fi, Bluetooth, or cellular data network.

is usually attached to an alternating current (AC) adapter for charging. Disconnect it from the AC adapter and connect the end previously connected to the power supply (usually a standard USB connector) to the computer and connect the other end to the device. On smartphones, this will usually be a micro USB connector; on iPad and some other tablets, it is a proprietary 30-pin connector. On some devices, this connection will cause two programs to run on the PC—one from your cellular provider (if the device has cellular service) for configuring your online account (if you already have one, you simply log in). The second program will be device-specific to aid in transferring files.

Syncing Android Devices

When you connect an Android device to your computer it is treated like an external drive, and you can copy files back and forth once you figure out the directory structure and locate the files you want to copy or back up. Strictly speaking, this isn't syncing. There are individual solutions for various types of data. For instance, when you create a contact in Android it asks you to pick an account to store (or back up) the contact information. The choices are Google or one provided by your cellular carrier. Select Google and they will be automatically backed up and synced to Google over the Internet, either through a cellular connection or via Wi-Fi. Who do you expect to have the longest relationship with, Google or your cellular provider? We use Google to back up our contacts because it will be available to use if we cancel the contract with the cellular provider.

Syncing an iOS Device with a Mac or PC

Use Apple iTunes for syncing an iOS device with a Mac or PC. It comes with all Apple computers and is a free download for Windows PCs. You can synchronize apps, several types of audio content, books, contacts, calendars, movies, TV shows, photos, notes, documents, and ringtones. At this time, to install iTunes on a PC the requirements are:

- A PC with 1 GHz Intel or AMD processor.
- 512 MB of RAM.
- Windows XP Service Pack 2 or later or 32-bit editions of Windows Vista, Windows 7, or Windows 8.
- The 64-bit editions require the 64-bit iTunes installer (Apple will detect and download the correct installer).
- 400 MB of available disk space.
- A broadband Internet connection for connecting to the iTunes store.

If you have a Mac, you may still need to update to the latest version of iTunes. The current requirements for installing the latest version of iTunes to an Apple computer are:

- A Mac with an Intel Core processor.
- OS X version 10.6.8 or later.
- 400 MB of available disk space.
- Broadband Internet connection for connecting to the iTunes store.

Whether you are using a PC or Apple Mac computer, download and install the latest version of iTunes. To do that connect to the iTunes page at the Apple website (currently at www.apple.com/itunes/download/).

There are other requirements for playing music and video through iTunes on a PC, but we are only concerned with the requirements to synchronize your contacts, email, pictures, music, and videos from the device to the Mac or PC. You cannot copy files from the Mac or PC to the mobile device. You can also back up (not sync) your apps using iTunes.

Another option that is more of a backup than a synchronizing option is iCloud, an Apple Internet-based service for backing up your data from any Apple device to the iCloud service. This data is available to all devices from any location with Internet access.

Step-by-Step 11.01

Configuring Synchronization in iOS using iTunes

This step-by-step exercise goes through the steps for synchronizing your iPad or iPhone data using iTunes. To complete this exercise, you will need the following:

- The latest version of iTunes on your Mac or Windows PC.
- An iPhone or iPad as well as the USB cable that came with the device.

Step 1

Open iTunes on your Mac or Windows PC. Connect the USB cable to the iPad and the computer. The first time you do this on a Windows PC there will be a slight delay while it installs the driver. Then the iPad will synchronize with the computer.

Step 2

Click the **Device** button (in this case, "iPad") on the right to open the summary page for your device.

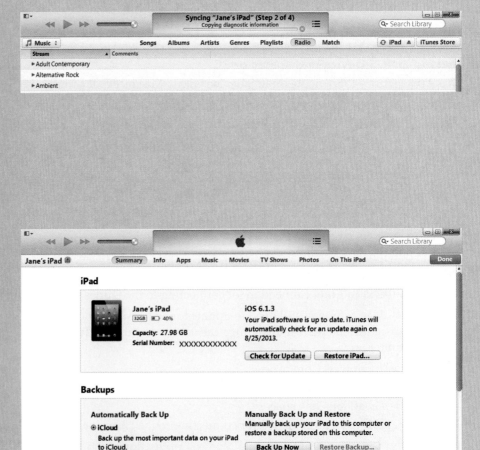

Step 3

Click the various tabs to select items to be synchronized. For instance, clicking **Info** in iTunes on a Windows PC gave us the options for synchronizing with Outlook (contacts, calendar, email, and accounts). It also included options for synchronizing Internet Explorer bookmarks and Outlook notes.

Step 4

Return to the summary page and scroll down to Backups. You can configure the device to back up to iCloud or to the computer. If you select **This computer** and also select the checkbox labeled **Encrypt local backup**, it will back up account passwords from the iPad.

Step 5

If you would like to initiate a backup now, click **Back Up Now**. This message will display while it is backing up (with the name of your device).

Step 6

When you have finished configuring synchronization and backup, click the **Done** button in iTunes. If you have made changes, this dialog box will appear in Windows. Click **Apply** and it will return you to the page in iTunes that was open when you first connected the iPhone or iPad.

Step 7

Close iTunes when you are done.

SETTINGS   4:44

backup

Backups help you guard against mishaps
by saving certain info to the cloud.

What gets backed up?

app list+settings
backup off

text messages
backup off

photos
auto upload off

FIGURE 11–13 On the **Backup** page select each type of data and enable backup.

iOS 7.0
Your software is up to date.

The iOS **Software Update** status message.

This Windows Store tile shows three updates ready to download and install.

Syncing Windows Phone

In Windows Phone 8 you have several ways to synchronize different types of data. You can sync email accounts, podcasts from iTunes, and you can synchronize your Windows Phone 8 data with the cloud and with your PC.

If you sign in to your Windows Phone 8 device with a Microsoft account you can back up your settings, text messages, photos, and videos to SkyDrive. You can Enable Backup during the initial Windows Phone setup or later by opening Settings | Backup. On the Backup page (Figure 11–13) select what you want backed up. You need to turn Backup on for each type of data.

LO 11.4 | Securing Mobile Devices

How do you protect a mobile device from malware? How do you keep the wrong people from logging on to a device they stole or found? How do you keep mobile operating systems up to date? How can you find lost devices?

Security Software for Mobile Devices

Many security programs are available for each of the mobile operating systems. They include such features as antivirus, antispam, browsing protection, and privacy features that will alert you if an app attempts to access your private information (for example, location, contacts, and messages). These free or inexpensive security suites may also include backup and missing device features. If a device is missing, you can use this software to locate it over the Internet (if you previously enabled location services), initiate a loud alarm on the device, and/or do a remote wipe (deleting all contents), making it effectively unusable by anyone who steals or finds it. We describe remote wipe later in the chapter.

Mobile OSs also have built-in security features. We will describe the steps you can take to make your mobile device more secure with built-in settings.

Patching and OS Updates

As with any computer, you need to keep your device updated with operating system patches and security updates. All the mobile OSs described here are automatically updated. You can check on the status for each OS.

Presently, Android has updates turned on by default. You can see the status of updates on your Android device by opening **Settings**. Then scroll down and tap **About device** (or **About phone**). This opens a list of information about your device. Locate and tap **Software update** (or System updates) included in this list. This will give you the status of updates, and on some devices you can disable or enable this setting. We recommend that you leave it turned on.

To check the status of updates on an Apple iOS device, open Settings, then tap General, and on that page locate and tap Software Update to see the current state. Figure 11–14 shows the General page from the iPad's Settings app. Tap on Software Update and it will give the status, shown here. Later we will discuss several security settings on the General page.

Windows 8, Windows RT, and Windows Phone 8 all update automatically, as do their apps, through the Windows Store. The Store tile will display the number of app updates waiting to download and install. Simply tap the tile and the first screen will be the update screen. You can select apps individually or choose to update all of them.

Securing Lock Screens on Mobile Devices

A mobile device has a lock screen that keeps you from accidental touch actions, such as inadvertently "pocket dialing" your boss when you are at lunch. Mobile devices usually have a setting for a passcode lock that keeps the

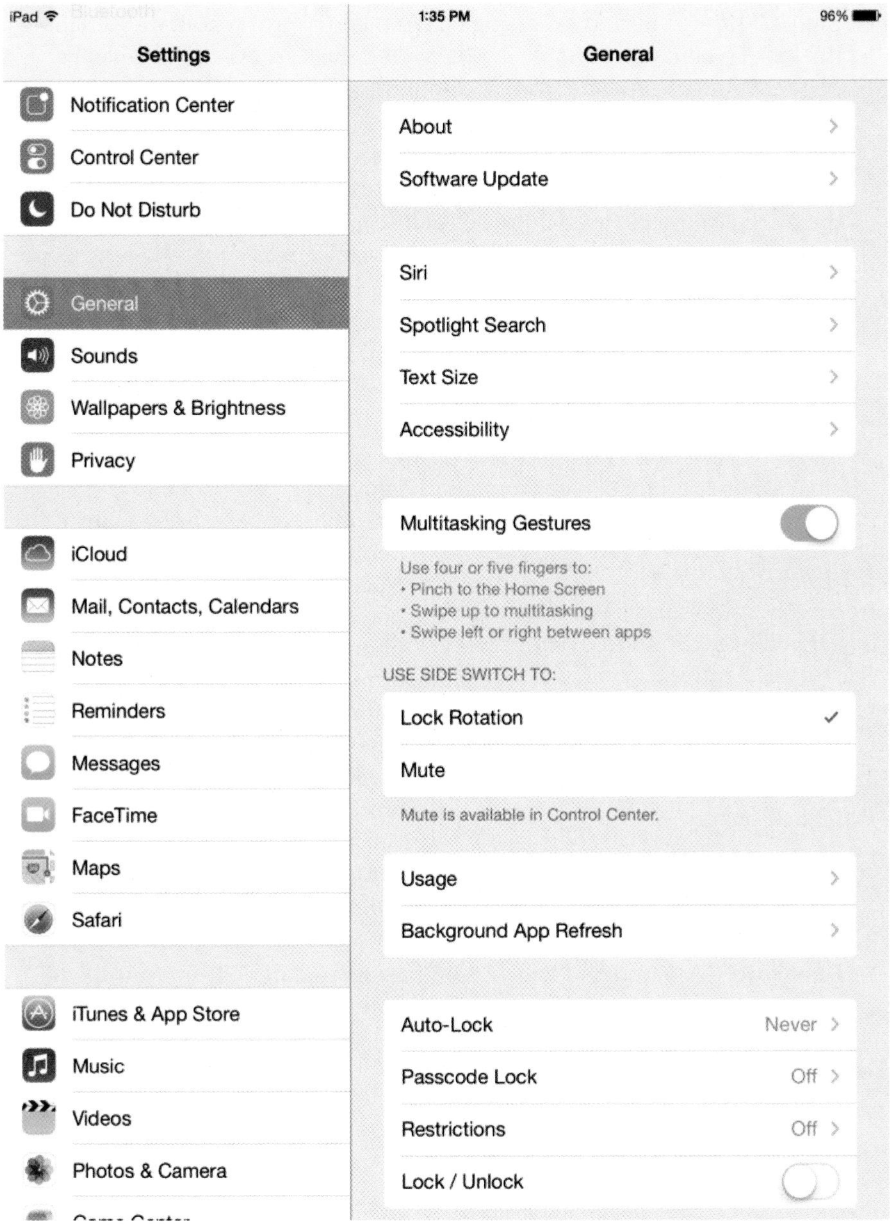

iPad 📶 Bluetooth	1:35 PM	96% 🔋
Settings	**General**	

Settings
- Notification Center
- Control Center
- Do Not Disturb

- **General**
- Sounds
- Wallpapers & Brightness
- Privacy

- iCloud
- Mail, Contacts, Calendars
- Notes
- Reminders
- Messages
- FaceTime
- Maps
- Safari

- iTunes & App Store
- Music
- Videos
- Photos & Camera

General

| About | > |
| Software Update | > |

Siri	>
Spotlight Search	>
Text Size	>
Accessibility	>

| Multitasking Gestures | ⬤ |

Use four or five fingers to:
- Pinch to the Home Screen
- Swipe up to multitasking
- Swipe left or right between apps

USE SIDE SWITCH TO:

| Lock Rotation | ✓ |
| Mute | |

Mute is available in Control Center.

| Usage | > |
| Background App Refresh | > |

Auto-Lock	Never >
Passcode Lock	Off >
Restrictions	Off >
Lock / Unlock	◯

Note: The iPhone 5S includes a new method for unlocking the device, a fingerprint scanner built into the home button. Apple calls this feature "touch ID." In addition to letting you unlock your phone with your fingerprint, you can also use it in place of the Apple ID password at Apple' App and iTunes stores.

FIGURE 11–14 The **General** page of the iPad's Settings app.

lock screen in place until you perform some action, such as entering a code or password. Without a passcode lock a simple swipe closes the lock screen and gives anyone access to the device. Android, iOS, Windows 8, Windows RT, and Windows Phone 8 all include this feature, although they use different terms to describe it as well as different options.

Android Screen Lock

The Android tablet and phones used for research for this chapter are all up to date, but the settings, screens, and options vary slightly between the tablet and the phones. The Lock screen settings on the tablet include None, Swipe, Face unlock, Pattern, PIN, and Password. The Lock screen options on our Android phones uses the term "Slide" in place of "Swipe." Here is a brief summary of these settings:

- **None**—No lock screen. This is a risky setting for a mobile device because you have no protection from pocket dialing or other touch actions.

- **Swipe/Slide**—These two settings have the identical result: they enable the lock screen, but a simple swipe (slide) gives access to the tablet or phone. While it protects from accidental touch actions, it is low security.

- **Face Unlock**—This setting uses facial recognition to identify you. To configure it, select this setting and follow the instructions. You may need to move the phone away from your face until your image is enclosed by the oval. It will also ask you to select a secondary option for when you cannot unlock your phone with face unlock. This is generally less secure than using a pattern, PIN, or password.

- **Pattern**—This medium security option has you tap at least four dots in an array of nine. It will ask you to repeat this pattern to unlock the lock screen.

- **PIN**—An Android **personal identification number (PIN)** is a numeric code that the user selects and uses for the lock screen. On the authors' Android smartphones a PIN can be from 4 to 17 characters long. PINs are not terribly secure because many people use predictable patterns (such as 1234) or a significant personal number, such as a phone number or Social Security number. If a hacker has access to information about a person, they have a good chance of guessing the PIN. In this case, the security level of your PIN would be low. If you use a PIN that is not based on a number associated with you, it will not be easy to guess, raising the security level the PIN.

try this!

Choose a Screen Lock Setting for Android

Mobile operating systems change frequently, so these steps and options may change by the time you read this. If you have an Android smartphone and want to make it more secure by assigning a screen lock PIN or password. Try this:

1. Open **Settings**.
2. Scroll through the settings and select **Security & Screen Lock,** or under the Personal category select **Lock screen**.
3. Tap **Screen lock**.
4. Select a lock screen option to make your device more secure.

- **Password**—An Android lock screen password can be from four to sixteen alphanumeric characters. Generally, the more characters, the higher the security. As with a PIN, the best password is one that cannot be associated with you. Review the information in Chapter 2 on creating secure passwords.

Passcode Lock for iOS

The iPad has **Passcode Lock** as an option on the General page of Settings. Tap it to open the **Passcode Lock** settings page, shown in Figure 11–15. Notice the two messages below the Erase Data setting. One begins with "Erase all data on this iPad." All data will *only* be erased after 10 failed passcode attempts, *if* you turn on **Erase Data.** However, the second statement, "Data protection is enabled," is true because the iOS data protection feature is enabled when you turn Passcode on. In iOS **data protection** encrypts mail messages and attachments on the device, using the passcode as the encryption key.

In iOS a simple passcode is only four digits long. To be more secure turn off Simple Passcode (see Figure 11–15), With this turned off you can enter a very long passcode using any combination of numbers, letters, special characters, and punctuation. Figure 11–16 shows the passcode keypad that displays when you turn the Passcode Lock on and have simple passcode enabled.

The Auto-Lock option that appears above Passcode Lock on the General page only sets the amount of time of inactivity before a device locks, but this does not, on its own, require a passcode. If you don't

1:57 PM	93%
‹ General	**Passcode Lock**

Turn Passcode Off

Change Passcode

Require Passcode   Immediately ›

Simple Passcode

A simple passcode is a 4 digit number.

ALLOW ACCESS WHEN LOCKED:

Siri

Erase Data

Erase all data on this iPad after 10 failed passcode attempts.

Data protection is enabled.

FIGURE 11–15 The iOS **Passcode Lock** settings.

FIGURE 11–16 The **Passcode keypad** displays on the iPad **Lock** screen.

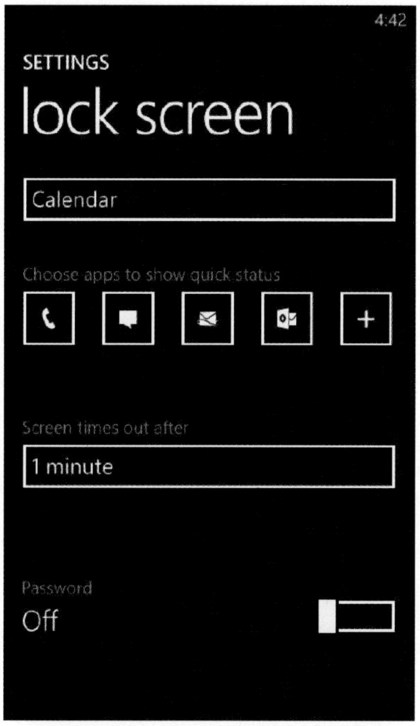

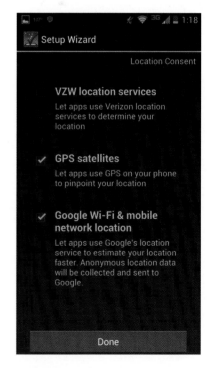

FIGURE 11–17 Enable Windows Phone 8 Lock Screen password by moving the **Password** slider to the **On** position.

require a passcode, you simply use a swipe to close the lock screen and access the device.

Windows Phone 8 Lock Screen Password

When you use a Lock screen password in Windows Phone 8, a password entry screen displays after you swipe on the Lock screen. Configure a Lock screen password by opening Settings | Lock Screen. Then locate the Password option at the bottom of the Lock Screen page (Figure 11–17) and move the slider to **On**. Then in the **Create a password** page enter a code of four digits or more and tap Done.

After you create a password, the Lock Screen settings include two new options: **Change password** and **Require a password after**. The first allows you to change the password. You will be required to enter the old password before you can change it. The second option controls how often you need to enter a password. The default is **Each time**. You can change this to a screen time set in minutes (1, 3, 5, 15, or 30). Securing your Windows Phone 8 device with a password will still allow you to make an emergency call (911 in the United States) without entering a password.

Location Settings

Locator applications have a variety of uses, such as allowing you to find your lost or stolen mobile device from another device or computer, plotting driving directions to it from your current location, and much more. For these apps to work you need to enable a location service on your device.

On an Android device, the Setup Wizard, shown in Figure 11–18, may have several location service sources. In this case, there is one from Google

FIGURE 11–18 Locator services on an Android device using the Verizon cellular network.

Enable or Disable Location Services

If you have a mobile device, it should have a setting for enabling or disabling location services. Try this:

1. Open the Settings utility in your mobile device.
2. Look for a setting for location and tap it.
3. If you do not see a setting for location, look for "privacy."
4. Once you find it, disable it and test it by opening a mapping program and trying to find your location. It will fail if you turned the location service off, and it will succeed if you turned it on.

Note: Remember that any locator app first requires that the location service on the device be turned on. On an iOS device, this service is called Location Services, and on an Android device there may be multiple location services.

that uses Wi-Fi and mobile network, one based on the device's GPS feature, and another from the cellular provider. The cellular location service may incur a charge. You can also open Settings and tap Location access to see that the Emergency 911 (E911) location service is enabled by default and cannot be disabled on a mobile cellular phone.

On an iPad, open **Settings**, select **Privacy**, then tap **Location Services** to open the list of settings shown here. Notice that you can enable or disable location services for various components and apps on this device.

On a Windows 8, Windows RT, or Windows Phone 8 device look for a Privacy setting or Location setting. Then enable or disable it in the individual apps that request location services.

The iOS **Location Services** settings.

Lost or Stolen Devices

Mobile devices are easily stolen and lost. Therefore, take steps ahead of time to protect your data and to help you locate the lost or stolen device. This will usually involve enabling a locator service on the device that tracks its location.

Android Device Manager

Beginning in August 2013 Google quietly enabled a service, previously available only to business accounts, to all Google accounts with Android devices. This service is called Device Manager and it will help you locate your device, change the lock screen settings, and even remotely wipe all the data if necessary.

To enable this service, open **Settings** and then select **Security** (or **Security & Screen Lock**). Locate and tap **Device Administrators** to open the page shown in Figure 11–19. Then tap **Android Device Manager** to open the Android Device Manager page, shown in Figure 11–20. To enable this service tap **Activate** at the bottom of the page.

After enabling Android Device Manager you can manage your Android smartphone from any computer by connecting to **https://www.google.com/android/devicemanager**. Sign in with the Google account associated with your device, and the **Android Device Manager** page will display. After a short display the map will show the location of your device, as shown in Figure 11–21. If you have simply misplaced the device at home, select **Ring** and the device will ring until you turn it off and on again. If it is stolen, but appears to be physically near you, selecting **Ring** will alert you to who has the phone. You can also remotely erase all the data from the device by selecting Erase Device.

Apple iCloud Find My iPhone

On an Apple OS X or iOS device you can enable a free feature that uses iCloud to locate a lost or stolen iMac, iPad, or iPhone and then select from several actions, including a remote wipe if your device is lost or stolen. On an iOS device open Settings and select iCloud. Then enable **Find My iPhone** (or iPad or iPod). Tap **Allow** in the confirmation message that displays.

Once enabled, you can connect to www.icloud.com from another computer and log in with your Apple ID. On the iCloud home screen select **Find My iPhone** (that is the name of this service, whether you have an iPhone or not). You will need to log in with your Apple ID to **Find My iPhone.** Then on the next screen a map will display with the location of your devices.

Select All Devices at the top left of this page to open a menu of your devices. Select

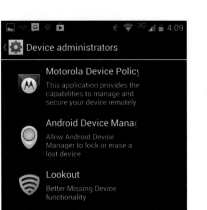

FIGURE 11–19 Open **Device Administrators** and tap **Android Device Manager.**

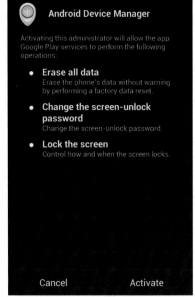

FIGURE 11–20 Tap **Activate** to enable remote management with Android Device Manager.

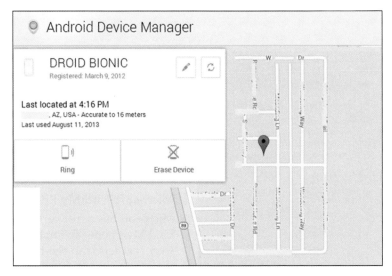

FIGURE 11–21 Android Device Manager shows the location of your device and allows you to ring the device or remotely erase all the data.

FIGURE 11–22 Use this box in iCloud to play a sound, send a message, or erase the data on a lost or stolen device.

the lost or stolen device, and **All Devices** changes to the name of the selected device and a box opens for that device, as shown in Figure 11–22. This box tells you the battery life of the device (see the upper-right corner of Figure 11–22) and lets you take some action. Clicking **Play Sound** causes a sound on the device, and it will display the message "Find My iPad Alert," on the device. Select **Lost Mode** and enter a passcode to lock the device (this appears if the device does not already have a passcode) and a phone number where you can be reached. You can also modify the message that will display with your phone number on the lost device. Phone number and message to display on the device. The default message is "This iPad has been lost. Please call me." The message and phone number will display on the device. Once the passcode is entered, the device is no longer in Lost Mode and can be used. The last option is **Erase iPad**. Select this if you are convinced it is stolen.

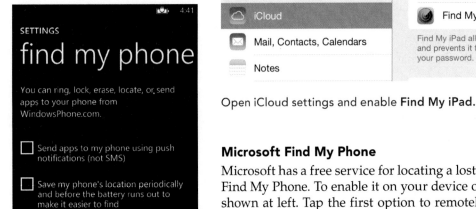

Microsoft's **Find My Phone** settings.

Open iCloud settings and enable **Find My iPad.**

Microsoft Find My Phone

Microsoft has a free service for locating a lost or stolen Windows Phone called Find My Phone. To enable it on your device open **Settings** | **Find My Phone**, shown at left. Tap the first option to remotely ring, lock, erase data, or send apps to the phone from Microsoft's Windows Phone website, WindowsPhone.com. Tap to place a check in the second box and Windows Phone will save its location to SkyDrive until the battery runs out.

Chapter Summary

After reading this chapter and completing the Step-by-Step tutorial and Try This! exercises, you should understand the following facts about mobile operating systems.

From Luggable to BYOD

- Just 30 years ago mobile computing involved lugging heavy computers that could not connect to a network when in transit. They were not meant for the typical consumer, but for technically savvy persons.
- Today's mobile devices are popular consumer devices that are tiny, powerful, and connected 24/7.
- People bring their personal mobile devices to school and work, a practice called bring your own device (BYOD).
- Most employers do not have an adequate policy for BYOD to address the many issues of security, ownership, and cost.
- Mobile device management (MDM) is a category of software for managing mobile devices.

Configuring Accounts and Wireless Connections on Mobile Devices

- All popular smartphones and tablets require a user account.
- An Android device has a Google account associated with it for accessing Google services. The Google account can be your Gmail account or you can associate it with another existing email account.
- An Apple ID is a customer account for accessing Apple services and products. Any working email address will do as the account name, and then create a password for the Apple ID.
- You only need one Apple ID, but since the free iCloud storage has a set limit per account, a person with many devices and/or many family members sharing the account may want to have multiple accounts in order not to run out of free storage space.
- A Microsoft account is a free account that gives the subscriber access to Microsoft services.
- A smartphone requires a cellular connection from a cellular provider.
- A cellular data connection is an extra option for a tablet, adding a premium to the cost of the device, plus requiring a cellular data plan.

- All popular mobile devices offer Wi-Fi connections, which you can enable and connect to hotspots using appropriate credentials. Using Wi-Fi for data when it is available saves on cellular data costs.
- A mobile device with a cellular connection may be able to share that connection, turning the device into a mobile hotspot. Cellular providers charge a service fee for allowing you to do this.
- You can purchase a separate device to use as a dedicated mobile hotspot. Novatel calls their mobile hotspot device MiFi.
- Tethering is a feature that allows you to share your smartphone's cellular data connection with a single computer.
- Near Field Communication (NFC) is a special chipset in some mobile devices that allows you to position your device close to another that also has NFC enabled and share data, pair with a Bluetooth device, or pay for purchases.
- Airplane mode is a feature of mobile devices that, when enabled, turns off all radio frequency (RF) signals. It complies with commercial airline requirements.

Email, Apps, and Synchronization

- Any popular mobile device can support multiple accounts of different types at once.
- Mobile operating systems understand the basic connection information require for many types of accounts, so you may only need to enter the personal login information for the account and it will attempt to connect.
- Sometimes when configuring an email account you may have to provide more information, such as the name of POP, IMAP, or SMTP servers.
- Each mobile OS has some service for synchronizing data between the mobile device and other devices or to the cloud.

Securing Mobile Devices

- There are security apps available for mobile devices that are free or inexpensive.
- Mobile OSs also have some security features built in.

- By default, mobile operating systems have updates enabled, so that security patches and updates of the OS are downloaded and installed automatically.
- A mobile device has a lock screen to prevent accidental touch actions. You can protect a lock screen with various security measures so that a simple swiping gesture does not give the wrong person access to the device.
- Android Screen Lock has several options for securing the lock screen including Face Unlock, pattern, PIN, and password.
- Passcode Lock is the lock-screen feature on iOS.
- Windows Phone 8 has a Lock-screen password feature. When you enable this it requires a password of at least four digits before you can get past the Lock screen.
- There are many locator applications, such as mapping programs or an app or service for finding your lost or stolen mobile device. They require a location service. Your device may have multiple location services available.
- Android Device Manager is a free service from Google that will help you locate and manage a lost or stolen device, remotely wipe the device, and cause it to ring.
- Apple iCloud has the free Find My iPhone service. Enable it through iCloud settings on your device.
- Enable Microsoft's Find My Phone on a Windows Phone 8 device and it will save your phone's location to SkyDrive until the battery runs out. Then, before the battery runs out and using another computer, connect and sign in to windowsphone.com and you can cause the lost or stolen phone to ring, lock, erase data, and show you its location. This feature also lets you send apps to your phone from windowsphone.com.

Key Terms List

Airplane mode (426)	MiFi (424)	personal identification number (PIN) (436)
Apple ID (420)	mobile device management (MDM) (419)	remote wipe (434)
Bluetooth (424)	mobile hotspot (423)	Service Set ID (SSID) (422)
bring your own device (BYOD) (417)	Near Field Communication (NFC) (425)	Subscriber Identity Module (SIM) (421)
data protection (436)	pairing (424)	synchronize (430)
Google account (419)	passcode lock (434)	tethering (424)
location service (418)		

Key Terms Quiz

Use the Key Terms List to complete the sentences that follow:

1. If you turn on the _____ feature of a cell-enabled mobile device the device serves as a cellular modem for an attached computer.

2. Turn on _____ to turn off all radios in your mobile device.

3. The list of available Wi-Fi networks that display on your device or computer are each identified by a/an _____.

4. The practice of people using their own mobile devices at work is called _____.

5. One company uses the trademarked name of _____ to identify their line of small devices that act as dedicated mobile hotspots.

6. A connection between two Bluetooth devices is called a _____.

7. Some organizations use a type of software called _____ to manage mobile devices used by their employees.

8. If your device is stolen, be prepared to protect it by learning what you need to do to cause a/an _____, which will delete all your data on the device.

9. A/an _____ secures the lock screen on a mobile device.

10. Your mobile device may include the option to share your cellular wireless connection, turning your smartphone or tablet into a _____.

Multiple-Choice Quiz

1. Which of the following is *not* true concerning BYOD?
   a. Employees may personally incur higher voice and data costs when they bring their own devices to work.
   b. A lost or stolen device can put the employer at risk.
   c. It is unclear who owns intellectual property created.
   d. An employee's private data on their personally owned device may be at risk.
   e. Most organizations have adequate policies in place for BYOD.

2. Which of the following is not a type of wireless communications?
   a. NFC
   b. USB
   c. Wi-Fi
   d. Cellular
   e. Bluetooth

3. Which of the following is an account required for using an Android smartphone?
   a. Apple ID
   b. Microsoft account
   c. Yahoo!
   d. Google account
   e. Hotmail

4. Which type of connection is the primary connection type for a smartphone?
   a. NFC
   b. USB
   c. Wi-Fi
   d. Cellular
   e. Bluetooth

5. Which type of connection is an option for a tablet that adds cost to the hardware as well as a fee for data usage?
   a. NFC
   b. USB
   c. Wi-Fi
   d. Cellular
   e. Bluetooth

6. Which feature, if available, allows you to share your smartphone's cellular data connection with just a single computer?
   a. Mobile hotspot
   b. Tethering
   c. MiFi
   d. SSID
   e. BYOD

7. Which mode turns off all radio frequency (RF) signals on a device?
   a. Tethering
   b. Mobile hotspot
   c. Airplane mode
   d. Synchronization
   e. Data protection

8. What wireless connection feature, if available in your phone, would allow you to pay for purchases by simply positioning the device very close to another device with this feature?
   a. NFC
   b. USB
   c. Wi-Fi
   d. Cellular
   e. Bluetooth

9. Without this type of feature on a mobile device, a simple swipe gives anyone access to the device. What is the term for this feature?
   a. Location service
   b. Passcode lock
   c. Updates
   d. Screen saver
   e. Device manager

10. What Android Screen Lock option does not require that you use something you memorized? You could say that it requires that Android memorize something.
    a. PIN
    b. Password
    c. Face Unlock
    d. Pattern
    e. Passcode Lock

11. What free Google service is available to all Google accounts, allowing them to locate their lost or stolen Android mobile devices?
    a. iCloud
    b. Find My Phone
    c. Android Device Manager
    d. Find My iPhone
    e. Google Play

12. Use this Apple service to synchronize your iOS device with a Mac or PC.
    a. iCloud
    b. Apple ID
    c. Find My iPhone
    d. iTunes
    e. iMac

13. What Apple service allows you to back up your data from any Apple device so that it is available to all your devices?
   a. iCloud
   b. Apple ID
   c. Find My iPhone
   d. iTunes
   e. iMac

14. What type of card inserted into a mobile device programs it for a user's cellular account information?
   a. NFC
   b. SSID
   c. MDM
   d. SIM
   e. MiFi

15. This name identifies a Wi-Fi network.
   a. NFC
   b. SSID
   c. MDM
   d. SIM
   e. MiFi

Essay Quiz

1. Describe your ideal mobile device, whether it exists or not.

2. What options do you have for cellular service in your area? Write a paragraph listing the cellular providers who service your area and which one you would choose if you were shopping for a mobile device today. Explain your choice.

3. Take a poll of your fellow students or co-workers. What mobile operating systems are on their mobile devices? Record the results of your poll and compute the percentage using Android, iOS, and Windows.

4. What is the US Federal Aviation Administration policy for the use of electronic devices on an airliner? If you live in another country, research the policy of the equivalent agency in your country. Does this policy allow for Airplane mode?

5. Has this chapter influenced your attitude toward mobile devices? Explain your answer and discuss with your instructor and fellow students.

Lab Projects

LAB PROJECT 11.1

Research mobile device management (MDM) software products by searching for recent product reviews and answer the following questions.

① What mobile operating systems did the majority of the MDM products you found support?

② How many of the reviewed products included support for desktop OSs in addition to mobile OSs? List the OSs and the number of MDM products you found that supported them.

③ How many of the MDM products reviewed included a feature that would block devices from accessing email if MDM policies were violated?

LAB PROJECT 11.2

An organization that hosts email services for clients does not need to view the content of the messages in order to provide this service. They can deliver messages by simply examining the header information of the packets that comprise each message. Storing email messages on servers also does not require scanning the content.

Two popular email service providers, Microsoft (hotmail.com and outlook.com) and Google (Gmail), both include advertising next to your messages in their web-based email GUIs. Research this practice by these two providers and see if you discern any difference in their use of advertising. Write up your findings and share them with your instructor or class.

LAB PROJECT 11.3

This book describes mobile devices at a point in time: summer of 2013. What do you see as the most significant change in mobile devices since then? Is it a new type of mobile device or a revolutionary new app? Is this change a law concerning mobile devices? Discuss this change with your classmates, and tell why you believe it is the most significant change.

Securing and Troubleshooting Windows XP

In this appendix we have provided information for securing and troubleshooting Windows XP, with an emphasis on Windows XP Professional, which has more tools for both tasks.

Microsoft introduced two editions of Windows XP, Professional and Home Edition, in October 2001. Windows XP did not have a viable replacement (in the minds of computing professionals) until the advent of Windows 7 in 2009. Windows XP still exists on many desktops and you should be prepared to work with it. This appendix describes how to configure security for Windows XP and includes some preventive maintenance and troubleshooting tips. All the examples are for Windows XP Professional edition; some of the features described may not be available in other editions of Windows XP. ⬤

Securing Windows XP Professional

Here we look at some of Windows XP's security features including required logon, the NTFS file system, and code signing/driver signing. We'll also explore the basics of managing local security accounts in Windows XP.

Required Logon

As described in Chapter 2, a logon to Windows is mandatory, and you must perform this logon from an account that is a member of a security database—either the local security accounts database built into Windows XP Professional on the local computer or a network-based security database, such as an Active Directory domain. When you install Windows XP, it gives you an opportunity to create an automatic logon so that you will not have to manually enter your user name and password. In a casual environment in which security is not an issue, this is a good thing, but in any situation in which you need computer security, do not automate the logon. It defeats the purpose of the required logon, which is to prevent unauthorized access to your computer.

NTFS

The security features in the NTFS file system in Windows XP include support for file encryption, but you can turn this on for a file or folder only if you do not have file compression also turned on. This is an either/or situation. The most important NTFS feature is the support of permissions on files and folders. These permissions can apply to individual users or groups belonging to either the local or domain-based accounts database.

Code Signing/Driver Signing

Microsoft digitally signs the Windows XP program code before releasing it, and Windows XP checks for this signature to ensure that the code suffered no damage or tampering. A subset of this is driver signing; Microsoft certifies Windows XP drivers before the vendor ships the product. We call a certified driver a signed driver. Microsoft provides the vendor with a digital signature incorporated into the driver file. Signed drivers are supposed to eliminate hardware conflicts and unnecessary delays. Figure A–1 shows a network card driver with a digital signature.

Windows XP Account Management

If a Windows computer is a member of a Windows NT or Active Directory domain, administrators will mainly do management of users and groups at the domain level, and each user who logs onto the local computer will use a domain user account. But if a computer is a stand-alone computer or a member of a work group (as you will often see in very small organizations), administrators will have to manage users and groups on each computer. For that reason, it is good practice to create users on a desktop computer. You are also working with the same concepts on a small scale that an administrator must work with in a domain. First, we'll look at the tools for local account management, and then you will create a local account using one of those tools.

Windows XP Professional has two user management tools—a simpler tool intended for home and small business use and an advanced tool for professional administrators.

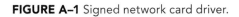

FIGURE A–1 Signed network card driver.

Simple Account Management in Windows XP Professional

In Windows XP, a simple user management tool, the User Accounts Control Panel applet, simplifies the user management tasks. The User Accounts applet hides the complete list of users, using a simplistic reference to account types that is actually a reference to its group membership. They call an account that is a member of the local Administrators group a computer administrator account, while an account that only belongs to the Local Users group is a limited account. The users it displays depends on the currently logged-on user. When an administrator logs on, she will see both types of accounts as well as the Guest account, a low-privilege account that, if enabled, is available to users that don't have an account defined and need occasional access to a computer. Users logging on using the Guest account can access local data and applications but can't install software or hardware. By default, the Guest account is disabled and isn't password-protected.

Note: Control Panel in Windows XP has two views: the default category view with just a few categories listed and Classic (Windows 9x) view, with all choices listed.

When a limited account user logs on, only that user's account is visible in User Accounts. This tool may be sufficient for managing accounts on a desktop or laptop computer at home or in a very small business with low security requirements.

Windows XP Professional User Accounts.

Advanced Account Management in Windows XP Professional

You will find Local Users and Groups, an advanced tool for managing local security accounts in Windows XP Professional, in the Computer Management console (see Figure A–2). A knowledgeable administrator will choose to create and manage users through Local Users and Groups, which reveals all existing users and groups.

To open the Computer Management console, right-click on My Computer and select Manage from the context menu. In addition, you can find this console and others in the Administrative Tools folder located in Control Panel. In Windows XP you can customize the Start menu to add the Administrative Tools folder to the All Programs menu.

FIGURE A–2 The Windows XP Computer Management console.

try this!

Add Administrative Tools to the Windows XP Professional Start Menu

Administrative Tools is a special folder containing helpful tools for administration. Make it handy by adding it to your All Programs folder now. Try this:

1. Right-click Start Menu, select Properties, select the Start Menu tab, and then click the Customize button next to the words "Start Menu."

2. In the Customize Start Menu dialog box, select the Advanced tab, and scroll the list under Start Menu Items to the bottom to System Administration Tools. Then select the radio button next to Display on the All Programs Menu.

3. Click *OK* twice to close the Customize Start Menu dialog box as well as the Taskbar and Start Menu Properties dialog box.

4. Confirm that Administrative Tools now displays on the All Programs list. You will use Administrative Tools in upcoming step-by-step exercises in this appendix.

Note: To create and manage users, you log on as the Administrator or a member of the local Administrators group. Be sure to assign a password to the Administrator account so that only authorized users can access this all-powerful account.

Note: When you create new user accounts on your own computer, create both a computer administrator account and a limited account for yourself. Use the administrator account whenever you need to install new software or make changes to the computer. Use the limited account for your day-to-day work. This protects your computer from viruses that might use the elevated privileges of your administrator account to cause damage.

Note: Encryption is a very advanced feature that you should use only after studying it carefully. It would take more than a chapter just to talk about encryption in depth!

Creating a New User

Creating a new user account enables that user to log in with a user name and password. This allows an administrator to set the rights and permissions for the user.

Creating users in User Accounts is a straightforward process. You need to provide a user name and an initial password. The user can change the password later. You also need to know the type of account to create: computer administrator or limited.

Unless otherwise specified by an administrator, you should create one limited account (member of the Users group) per user of the computer and one account that is a member of the local Administrators group (in addition to the Administrator account created during installation). The reason for creating two administrator accounts is so that if one administrator is not available, or is not able to log on to the computer, another one can. It's simple redundancy. Windows XP actually reminds you to do this; the first time you try to create a local account after installing Windows XP it will only allow you to create a computer administrator account. After that, it will allow you to create limited accounts.

Password Reset Disk

Windows XP Professional allows the currently logged-on user to create a Password Reset disk to use in case of a forgotten password. This is very important to have because if you forget your password, and an administrator resets the password using User Accounts or Local Users and Groups, then when you log on using the new password, you will find that you will lose access to some items, including files that you encrypted when logged on with the forgotten password. When you reset a password with a Password Reset disk, you can log on using the new password and still have access to previously encrypted files.

Best of all, with the Password Reset disk, users have the power to reset their own passwords. You only have this power if you think to create a Password Reset disk before you forget the password! If you need to create a Password Reset disk for a computer on a network (domain), search the help system for "Password Reset Disk" and follow the instructions for a computer on a domain.

The Password Reset disk is both a convenience and a threat. You only have to create the disk once, regardless of how many times you may later change the password. It is a convenience in that you only have to make it one time and it will always work. It is a threat in that it will always work on your machine, no matter who has it and uses it!

Creating User Accounts and a Password Reset Disk in Windows XP

This exercise describes how to create new user accounts in Windows XP Professional. First, you will create a new account that is a member of the administrators group, and then you will create a limited account. If you are working with Windows XP Home Edition, you will already have an account, in addition to the built-in Administrator, that is an administrator type. After creating the new accounts, you will log on with one of the new accounts and create a password reset disk.

To complete this step-by-step exercise you will need the following:

- A computer with Windows XP Professional installed.
- A USB flash drive or a floppy disk if the computer has a floppy disk drive.
- The password for the Administrator.
- A blank formatted floppy disk.

In this exercise the assumption is that no new accounts were created since creating the Administrator account during installation.

Step 1

Log on as Administrator and open Control Panel. Select the User Accounts applet. Click CREATE A NEW ACCOUNT. On the Name the New Account page enter the first letter of your first name, followed by your last name and click NEXT.

Step 2

On the Pick the Account Type page, the option for limited is grayed out (unavailable) if this is the first account you have created since installation. The first new account (in addition to the Administrator account) can only be a computer administrator. Notice the tasks a computer administrator can do, then click CREATE ACCOUNT.

Step 3

After creating the account, you automatically return to the main page of User Accounts where you should see your new account.

Step 4

Now you can create one or more limited accounts. In this case, you'll create one. Follow the steps you used to create the previous account, creating a user name consisting of your entire first name and the first letter of your last name. *Be sure to read the description of the limited account type on the Pick an Account Type page.* The illustration shows several accounts.

Step 5

Back on the main page, the newest account will appear as a limited account, and each of these new accounts has a blank password. Create a password for each account beginning with the computer administrator account. In User Accounts select Change an account. On the Pick An Account To Change page, select the new computer administrator you created above.

Step 6

On the following page, select Create a Password. Before creating a password, click on each of the items in the Learn About list to learn how to create a secure password as well as a good password hint, and a message about what to do when you forget your password. Then, use what you learn to fill in the text boxes for the new password and a password hint, and then click CREATE PASSWORD.

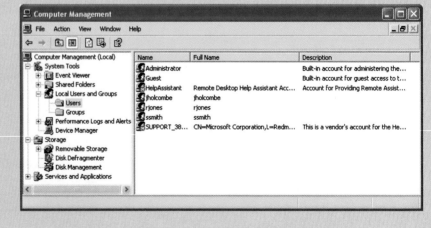

Step 7

Use the BACK button to go back to the Pick an Account to Change page, select each of the accounts you created, and create a password and password hint. When you have created passwords for your accounts, close the User Accounts Pick an Account to Change page.

Step 8

While you were able to create accounts and to create passwords, you were not able to place users in any group accounts other than Administrators or Users or add any additional information. If you want to go beyond the capabilities of the User Accounts tool, you need to open the Computer Management Console. Do that now. Right-click on My Computer and select Manage.

Step 9

In the Computer Management console, select Local Users and Groups and click on Users. The users you created in the previous steps will display, as well as users not shown in User Accounts.

Step 10

Double-click the limited account you created to open the Properties for this user account. The User Accounts tool used the user name you entered as both the user name and full name. Change the full name to your full name and add a description (such as "student" or "manager").

Step 11

Select the Member Of tab and click the Add button. In the Select Groups box, click the Advanced button to bring up another Select Groups box that will allow you to view all the local groups in a list from which you can make a selection.

Step 12

Select Power Users from the list. Then click OK three times to close the three open dialog boxes. When you return to the Computer Management console you may have to refresh the Users node by selecting the Users folder and pressing the F5 key. The full name and description for the limited account should now show. Close Computer Management.

Step 13

Now create the Password Reset disk. First insert a blank, formatted flash drive into a USB port or insert a blank formatted floppy disk into drive A:. Then open User Accounts and on the Pick A Task page select the account that you are currently logged in on as (Administrator). On the next page select *Prevent a forgotten password* from the list of *Related Tasks* (on the left). Read the Welcome page of the Forgotten Password Wizard, and then click Next.

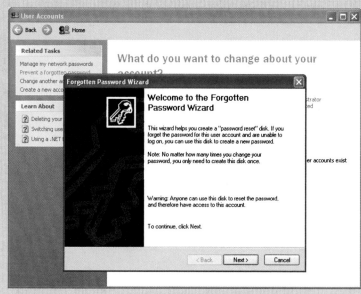

On the Create a Password Reset Disk, select the drive and click next. On the Current User Account Password page enter the current user account password and click NEXT. The Creating Password Reset Disk page will show a progress bar while creating the disk. When it completes, click NEXT, then click FINISH to close the wizard. Remove the flash drive or disk. Make sure you properly label the flash drive or disk, including the account name and computer, then store it in a safe and secure place.

Applying Security to Files, Folders, and Printers

Windows XP Professional fully supports the use of permissions to protect files, folders, and printers. Permissions for files and folders depend on the use of the NTFS file system, as does file encryption. Printer permissions are supported regardless of the file system in use. In this section you will explore NTFS permissions for files and folders and encryption on NTFS volumes.

Securing Files and Folders on an NTFS Drive

Windows XP supports the NTFS file system that allows you to control who has access to specified files and folders by assigning permissions. These permissions restrict access to local users and groups as well as to those who connect to these resources over the network. However, in the case of those connecting over a network, the share permissions (not related to NTFS permissions) take effect first and may block access to the underlying files and folders. Only NTFS volumes allow you to assign permissions to files and folders. In this section, we will focus on the security features of NTFS in Windows XP, including file and folder permissions and encryption.

File and Folder Permissions. On a volume formatted with the NTFS file system, each folder and file has a set of security permissions associated with it. Each file and folder on an NTFS volume has an associated access control list (ACL), which is a table of users and/or groups and their permissions to the file or folder. Each ACL has at least one access control entry (ACE), which is like a record in this tiny ACL database that contains just one user or group account name and the permissions assigned to this account. An administrator, or someone with the permissions to create ACEs for the file or folder, creates the ACEs. To view the ACEs in an ACL for a file or folder, open the properties dialog box and select the Security tab. Figure A–3 shows the Security page for a folder named *spreadsheets*. Notice the list of permissions for the user jholcombe. This is an ACE.

FIGURE A–3 The list of permissions for a folder.

The permissions you can set on folders differ slightly from those that you can set on files. In both cases, there are standard permissions, each of which is composed of several special permissions. For example, the standard file permission called Read permission consists of the following special permissions: Read Data, Read Attributes, Read Extended Attributes, Read Permissions (the permissions on the file), and Synchronize.

The standard file permissions are follows:

- Full Control
- Read
- Modify
- Write
- Read and Execute

Note: Most of the time, standard permissions are all you need.

The standard folder permissions are the same as the standard file permissions with the added permission of List Folder Contents.

Folders that contain sensitive information, such as payroll files, should be protected from unauthorized access. To do this you can assign permissions to certain users and groups, and you can keep others out, implicitly or explicitly. This is possible because each of the standard permissions and each of the special permissions has three states: Allow, Deny, or implicit denial. You can check only one box at a time for any permission. If both the Allow and Deny boxes are clear, that permission does not apply at all—it's implicitly denied. Checking the Allow box allows that permission, and checking the Deny box denies that permission—it's explicitly denied. Why have these three-state permissions? If you leave a user account off the permissions list, thus implicitly denied access to a file or folder, you can give that user access to the file and folder through membership in a group that has access. On the other hand, an administrator can explicitly grant access to a group or explicitly restrict access to a member of the group using the Deny state of a permission. This will override the permission to the file or folder that was granted to the group.

try this!

Research Special Permissions

It is important to understand permissions so that you can protect resources from unauthorized access or damage. Don't try to memorize them—remember that help is just a few mouse clicks away. Use the Windows XP Help and Support Center now to see the list of special permissions that make up each of the standard permissions listed here. Try this:

1. Start Help and Support from the Start menu. In the Windows XP Help and Support Center, use the search box to find articles on special permissions.

2. In the Search Results list, open article *How to set, view, change, or remove special permissions for files and folders in Windows XP* and read the descriptions of each of the special folder permissions.

3. When you have completed your research, close Help.

Note: During installation, the Windows setup program sets default permissions on the folders it creates that allow the OS to function but that keep ordinary users from harming the OS. You can cause harm to the OS if you change these default settings. You should change NTFS permissions only for data files and folders that you create for data files.

Permissions Assigned to Personal Folders. When a new user logs on to Windows the operating system will create personal folders just for that user. In addition, if the local drive is an NTFS partition, it will assign a default set of permissions to those folders designed to keep other users out of those folders. Now you will explore the default permissions set on these folders.

NTFS Permission Inheritance. The folders and files on a disk volume are in a hierarchy, with the drive itself at the top, followed by the root folder and subfolders. A newly created folder or file inherits the permission settings of the parent folder, unless you choose to block this inheritance, which is an option in the Security dialog of the file or folder. When you view permissions on a file or folder, the permissions inherited from the parent will be grayed out, and you will not be able to modify those permissions at that level. You can assign new permissions, but you cannot alter inherited permissions. You can modify them in the folder in which they originated. You can choose to block inheritance on a folder or file to which you wish to assign different (usually more restrictive) permissions. If you block inheritance, Windows XP will prompt you with the option to copy the previous inherited permissions.

Step-by-Step A.02

Viewing Permissions on Personal Folders

In this step-by-step exercise, you will explore the NTFS permissions automatically assigned to personal folders. To complete this step-by-step exercise, you will need the following:

- A computer with Windows XP Professional installed.

- The user accounts created in Step-by-Step A.01.
- Drive C: set up as an NTFS partition (per the instructions in the installation step-by-step exercise).

Step 1

Log on as the limited account you created in Step-by-Step A.01. Open My Computer, browse to C:\Documents and Settings, and notice the folders. There will be one for each logged-on user, plus one titled All Users.

Step 2

Open the folder for the account with which you logged on and view the contents that make up the user profile for the user. Created the first time that user logged on, they contain the files that hold that user's desktop files, favorites, the Start menu, and several other important folders and files. Windows creates these folders on any file system that Windows supports, even FAT16 or FAT32.

Step 3

When a user first logs on to a computer that has NTFS on the boot drive (the drive in which the system files are installed), Windows sets permissions on the personal folders it creates for the user. To view these permissions, right-click the folder named for your user account, select Properties, and then click the Security tab. Click the Permissions button, and you will see the list of users and groups that have permissions to the folder. Notice that the Everyone group is not on the list.

Step 4

By default, the Security page shows only the standard permissions and lets you assign only the standard permissions. Notice the Allow and Deny check boxes for each standard permission. To see the special permissions, click the Advanced button and then click the View/Edit button to see the special permissions assigned to the selected user. You will rarely need these special permissions. Click Cancel three times to close the Properties dialog box.

Step 5

Try to open a folder named for another account. You will not be able to do this, because the user account you are using does not have permissions to access the personal folder of another user. Log off.

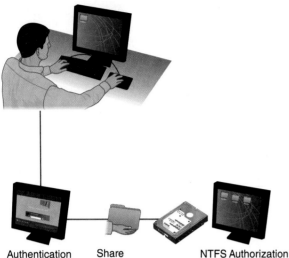

Authentication   Share   NTFS Authorization
Authorization

Accessing an NTFS file or folder through a network share.

Combining NTFS and Share Permissions

Anyone sitting at your computer who logs on can access files and folders on an NTFS volume if the permissions allow. You might say that person has to go through two security "doors": the authentication door (during logon) and the authorization door in which the security system checks the ACL on each file or folder for NTFS permissions for that user.

If you share a folder on that same NTFS volume, it is visible to network users, and anyone coming over the network comes through three doors. Only this time the authentication door is between the computer and the network (yes, even though it is not apparent, an incoming user authenticates). Then there are two authorization doors: one at the share point (the shared folder) at which Windows checks permissions to see if the incoming user is authorized to have access and another at the NTFS file and folder level where it checks the NTFS permissions.

NTFS File and Folder Encryption

Windows XP Professional allows you to make individual files or folders even more secure using the Encrypting File System (EFS), a component of the operating system, to encrypt files and folders saved on an NTFS volume. See how this works in the following scenario.

Jaime is a financial planner who carries his laptop to meetings with his clients. On his hard drive he has files containing confidential data on each of his clients. He needs to be sure to keep this information secure from prying eyes, and he worries that if someone steals his laptop this information would fall into the wrong hands. To guard against this, Jaime has four good practices:

1. He encrypts all confidential data files on his laptop, which is running Windows XP Professional.
2. He makes sure that he always uses a complex password that would be difficult to guess.
3. He changes his password frequently and never reuses old passwords.
4. He always uses the Lock Computer option in the Windows Security dialog box whenever he leaves his computer unattended—even briefly.

Encrypting a File or Folder. Jaime has encrypted a folder on his laptop that he calls Data. While the folder itself is not actually encrypted, all files in this folder are now encrypted and any new files he saves into that folder are automatically encrypted. This may sound rather high tech and inconvenient, but it was quite simple to do, and once Jamie turned on encryption for this folder, he never had to think about it again. As long as he logs on with the same account that he used when he turned on encryption, he simply opens the encrypted files using his normal applications. The security components of the OS verify his authorization to access these files *and* that he is the person who encrypted them. Someone logged on to his computer with a different account will not be able to open these files, even if the person uses an account with Full Control permission to the files.

To encrypt a file or folder, simply open the Properties dialog box, click the Advanced button, and place a check mark in the box labeled *Encrypt contents to secure data.* When you click OK to close the Properties dialog box you must make a decision. In the case of a folder, you must decide whether to encrypt

Accepting the default will encrypt the current and future contents of a folder.

the current contents of the folder and all new contents or to encrypt only the new contents. In the case of a file located in an unencrypted folder, a Warning message asks you to choose between encrypting the file and the parent folder or encrypting only the file. If you move or copy an encrypted file to an NTFS volume, it will retain its encryption, even if it is moved to a folder that does not have encryption turned on. Conversely, moving an unencrypted file into an encrypted folder using a drag-and-drop operation will not result in the file being encrypted. Be sure to only use cutting and pasting (or saving from within an application) to move files into encrypted folders. Further, if you move or copy an encrypted file to a non-NTFS volume it will be decrypted.

Decrypting Files and Folders. The only person who can decrypt a file or folder is the person who encrypted it or a member of a special group called recovery agents. By default, only the local Administrator is a member of this group. Recovery is not the same as being able to directly access the data; it is a very advanced task, described in Windows XP Professional Help and Support.

The warning message when encrypting a file.

Securing a Local Printer

In addition to setting permissions on files and folders, you may set permissions on your local printer. A printer has a single set of permissions that affect both the locally logged-on user and users accessing the printer as a share on the network. Printer permissions are simple compared to NTFS permissions. Printer permissions consist of

- Print—permission to send documents to the printer.
- Manage Printer—permission to print plus permission to pause and restart the printer, change spooler settings, share the printer, assign printer permissions, and change printer properties.

Note: If you use a Windows XP Professional computer at school or work, you may discover that encryption isn't available when you look at the Advanced Properties of a file or folder on an NTFS volume. This is because it is possible for a knowledgeable administrator to turn off encryption.

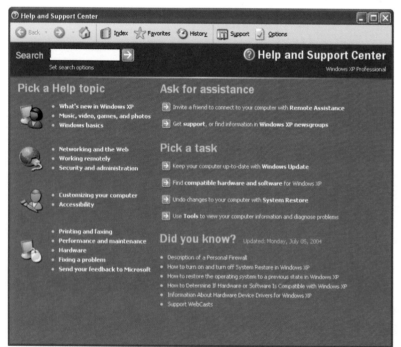

FIGURE A–4 The Advanced button on the printer properties page shows printer permission details.

- Manage Documents—permission to pause, resume, restart, cancel, and rearrange the order of documents submitted by all users. This permission does not include the print or manage printer permission.

When you add a printer driver, the default permissions allow any user to print; a special group called Creator Owner has Manage Documents permission, but only members of the Power Users and Administrators groups get all of the permissions. Creator Owner refers to anyone printing a document, giving each user the right to manage just their own documents. Figure A–4 shows the default permissions for a printer named Accounting.

While all users are assigned the print permissions through the Everyone group, an administrator can assign more restrictive permissions, if needed. One way to do that is to remove the Everyone group and explicitly assign permissions to users and groups. Another method is to leave the Everyone group as is, but to explicitly deny print permission to a single user or group.

Troubleshooting Common Windows XP Problems

If life were perfect, then your computer would work all the time, with no problems. However, no matter how hard you work, your computer will find new ways to annoy you. In this section, we will review some features for being prepared for problems and troubleshooting. We will introduce you to the Windows XP Help and Support Center and to proactive tasks that you can perform with the Backup Utility and System Restore.

Where to Find Help

Launch Windows XP Help and Support Center from Start | Help and Support, and you'll see a large menu of options for troubleshooting. From here you can invite someone to connect to your computer and remotely access your desktop to help you correct a problem. You can connect to Microsoft's support site or to a newsgroup to research a problem or to seek help and advice. We won't detail all the choices, but don't overlook this program when you need to troubleshoot or when you simply wish to learn more about Windows.

The Help and Support Center should be the first place you look for answers.

Perform Proactive Maintenance Tasks

Someone once said that the best offense is a good defense. Don't wait for problems to occur before you take action. Have a defense strategy in which you take steps to avoid problems. Include backing up data, disk defragmenting, and periodic housekeeping of the files and folders. Be prepared to use the System Restore and Automatic System Recovery features. You should install and configure an antivirus program.

Creating Backups and Automated System Recovery Disks

Yes, we know you've heard it repeatedly. You need to actually back up your data files on removable media, on an external hard drive, or to a network server. This is extremely important! Do it often and do it right. Windows XP Professional, like previous versions, has the Backup Utility, available through Start | All Programs | Accessories | System Tools.

Windows XP Professional has a recovery feature, Automated System Recovery (ASR), which creates a backup of the entire system partition (where the OS is installed) and therefore provides a more holistic repair, restoring your operating system to a certain point in time. ASR requires some planning. You must use the Advanced Mode of the Backup Utility (NTBACKUP. EXE) to create an ASR backup set, which includes an ASR diskette to initiate a boot-up into the ASR state, and a system partition backup to media, such as tape, another local hard disk, or a network location that is accessed via a drive letter (a "mapped" drive). Figure A–5 shows the Advanced Mode of the Backup Utility with the option for running the Automated System Recovery wizard to create an ASR set. An ASR backup set does not include a backup of other partitions, nor does it allow you to select data folders. Therefore, your Windows XP Professional backup strategy should include the occasional creation of an ASR set and frequent backups to save data and changes to the OS since the last ASR set.

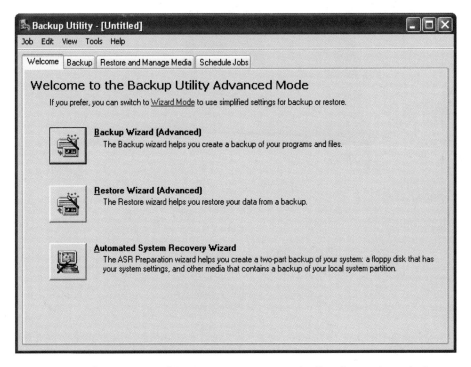

FIGURE A–5 The Automated System Recovery wizard will walk you through the creation of an ASR disk set.

Explore the Backup Program (NTBACKUP)

The backup program NTBACKUP is the tool provided with Windows XP Professional for creating backups, ASR backups, and ASR diskettes. You should familiarize yourself with this program. To complete this step-by-step exercise, you will need the following:

- A computer with Windows XP Professional i.
- A user name and password for an account that is a member of the Administrators group.

Step 1

Log on as an Administrator. First, run the Backup Utility and examine the Automated System Recovery Preparation wizard. Open the Backup program quickly by entering the command NTBACKUP in the Run box (from Start | Run). In the Welcome page of the Backup Or Restore wizard, click Advanced Mode.

Step 2

In the Welcome page of Advanced Mode, click on the Automated System Recovery Wizard button. This will open the Automated System Recovery Preparation wizard. Click Next.

Step 3

On the Backup Destination page, notice the Backup Media Type box. In the very unlikely chance that your system includes a tape backup system it will give you a choice between tape and file. If the Backup Media Type box is grayed out (like the illustration), you can only back up to a file (rather than to tape), and you must provide a destination for this file on any local hard drive or network location available to you.

Step 4

Cancel the Automated System Recovery wizard, and explore the Backup page of Backup Utility. In the left pane, notice the check boxes that allow you to select drives and folders to back up. Click on the words "System State," and the contents of System State will display in the right pane. Placing a check in the box to the left of System State will back up all these items. The grayed-out boxes show you that you can back up all the components of System State, or none of them, but you cannot select individual System State components.

Step 5

Click on the words "Local Disk (C:)" in the left pane, and the right pane will reveal the contents. Now click on the check box to the left of "Local Disk (C:)," and notice that all the check boxes in the right pane are selected *except* pagefile.sys. This is a special file used by the system for virtual memory and should *not* be backed up; it cannot be selected for backup in the Backup Utility.

Step 6

Click some of the folders on drive C:, and notice that you can move around in them, much as you can in My Computer, selecting and deselecting folders to include in a backup. When you have explored the folders, close the Backup Utility.

Create Restore Points for System Restore

Windows XP has a great System Restore, which solves some major problems with a few mouse clicks. If you make a change to a Windows XP computer that results in problems, you can restore it to its previous state, as long as you can start Windows—either normally or in Safe Mode (we describe Safe Mode in Chapter 6). System Restore saves complete Windows configuration information from discrete points in time. Each of these discrete points is a restore point. Some restore points are set automatically. For instance, by default, every time you install new software, System Restore creates a restore point. Thus, if installation of a program causes your computer to malfunction, simply restore the system to a point before that installation and the computer should work.

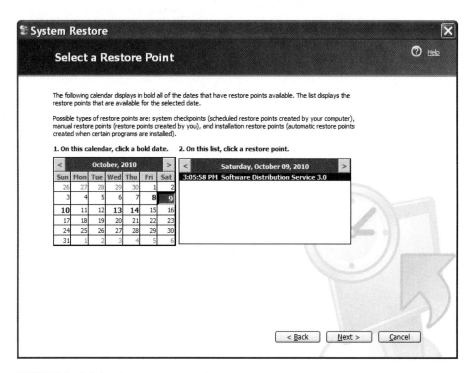

FIGURE A–6 Selecting a restore point.

Note: Learn more about the registry in Chapter 6.

During the restore process, only settings and programs are changed. No data is lost. Your computer will include all programs and settings as of the restore date and time. This feature is invaluable for overworked administrators. A simple restore will fix many user-generated problems.

To restore to a previous point, you start the System Restore wizard by choosing Start | All Programs | Accessories | System Tools | System Restore. Select the first radio button, Restore My Computer To An Earlier Time, and then click Next.

The second screen shows a calendar with restore points. Any day with a boldface date has a restore point. These points are created after you add or remove software, or install Windows updates, and during the normal shutdown of your computer. Figure A–6 shows a program installation restore point. Select a date to restore to and click Next.

The last screen before restoring the system is a warning. It advises you to close all open programs and reminds you that Windows will shut down during the restore process. It also states that the restore operation is reversible. Thus, if you go too far back in time, you can restore to a more recent date.

You don't have to count on the automatic creation of restore points. You can open System Restore at any time and simply select Create A Restore Point. This is something to consider doing before making changes that might not trigger an automatic restore point, such as directly editing the registry.

System Restore turns on by default and uses some of your disk space to save information on restore points. To turn System Restore off or change the disk space usage, open the System Properties applet in Control Panel, and select the System Restore tab, where you will find these settings. Disabling System Restore is now a common part of cleaning off many virus infections to make sure

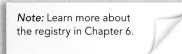

System Restore settings.

that a virus isn't hiding in the restore files, but be warned that turning System Restore off, even for a moment, deletes all old restore points.

The Blue Screen of Death (BSOD)

The Stop screen, often referred to as the Blue Screen of Death (BSOD), will appear if the OS detects that a fatal error has occurred. A fatal error is one that causes too much instability to guarantee the integrity of the system and still prevent loss of data in open files. A stop error is such an event.

Preparing for Stop Errors in Windows XP

To prepare for a BSOD, you should decide how you want your computer to behave after a stop error. You do this by modifying the System Failure settings on the Startup and Recovery page. These settings can be found by opening the System applet in Control Panel, selecting the Advanced tab, and clicking the Settings button under Startup And Recovery.

- *Write An Event To The System Log* causes Windows to write an event to the system log, which is one of several log files you can view using Event Viewer (found under Administrative Tools). We highly recommend this setting because it means that even if the computer reboots after a Stop screen, you can read the stop error information that was on the screen in the system log.

- *Send An Administrative Alert* is a setting that sends an alert message to the administrator that will appear on the administrator's screen the next time the administrator logs on. This is a useful setting to alert a domain administrator if your computer is part of a domain.

- *Automatically Restart* is a setting we recommend, as long as you have also selected the first option, which preserves the stop error information in the system log file.

- *Writing Debugging Information* contains one drop-down list, a text box, and a check box. The drop-down list allows you to control the existence

The default System Failure settings on the Startup and Recovery page.

and the size of a dump file that will contain debugging information. The settings include None, Small Memory Dump (64 KB), Kernel Memory Dump, and Complete Memory Dump. A complete memory dump contains an image of the contents of memory at the time of the fatal error. You can send this file to Microsoft for evaluation of a problem, but this amount of effort and cost (Microsoft charges for these services) is normally only expended on a critical computer, such as a network server. For a desktop computer, select None. This will gray out the second text box, the location of the dump file, and the check box labeled "Overwrite any existing file."

Troubleshooting a Stop Error

Eric, a colleague of ours, experienced a stop error in Windows XP. He was present when it occurred and he scanned the first few lines on the screen for a clue. The system rebooted while he was viewing the screen, but this was not a problem to him. After the reboot, he logged on and opened the system log in Event Viewer. He saw the message "STOP [several sets of numbers in the form 0x00000000] UNMOUNTABLE_BOOT_VOLUME." A search of *support.microsoft.com* using just the last part of this message (UNMOUNTABLE_BOOT_VOLUME) described how to determine the cause and the action to take by examining the values that preceded it. Eric discovered that the solution to his problem was to restart Windows using the recovery console and to run a command from the command line.

An Old Application Will Not Run

You have a new Windows XP computer. You need to run a program that worked nicely on your now-defunct Windows 95 computer. However, when you start the program in Windows XP, it doesn't perform correctly. Maybe the screen doesn't look quite right, or perhaps the program frequently hangs. To solve this problem, Windows XP allows you to trick the program into thinking that the OS is actually Windows 95 by using compatibility options. You

The Program Compatibility Wizard walks you through assigning settings to allow an older program to run under Windows XP.

can set these options by running the Program Compatibility wizard from the Help and Support Center or by setting the options manually from the properties of the shortcut or program file.

To run the Program Compatibility wizard, select Start | All Programs | Accessories | Program Compatibility Wizard. Following the instructions, you may choose to have the wizard display a list of all installed programs from which you can select your problem program. Then you can move through the wizard, selecting settings for emulating earlier versions of Windows and/or modifying the display settings for the program. Then test the program to see if there is an improvement.

Alternatively, you can set compatibility settings manually. On the Start menu, locate the shortcut for the offending program. Right-click and select Properties. Select the Compatibility tab. On this page, place a check in the box under Compatibility Mode, and then select Windows 95 in the drop-down list below it (see Figure A–7). Click OK and test the program. If it still has problems, go back to the Compatibility page, and tweak the Display Settings and/or turn off advanced text services. If you need help, click the Program Compatibility link at the bottom of the page.

FIGURE A–7 Use the Compatibility page to make manual settings.

Appendix B

Windows Mouse and Keyboard Shortcuts

Mouse Action or Mouse+Key Combination	Result in Windows 7 and Earlier	Result in Windows 8
ALT + PRNTSCR	Captures the current window and saves it in the Clipboard.	
CTRL + −	Zoom out (where supported in the GUI).	
CTRL + +	Zoom in (after a zoom out and where supported in the GUI).	
CTRL + A	Select all.	
CTRL + F1	Expand or minimize the ribbon in an app with the ribbon. (Includes File Explorer in Windows 8).	
CTRL + Roll middle scroll wheel	Semantic zoom (in and out).	
CTRL + SHIFT + ESC	Opens Task Manager.	
CTRL-ALT-DELETE	Opens the CTRL-ALT-DELETE menu.	
Double left-click	Selects or activates the object, performing the default command. If the pointer is in a document, this action selects the word at the insertion point, and a third click selects the sentence or paragraph (depending on the application and the version of the application). The third click for selecting an entire paragraph disappeared from Microsoft Word several versions ago.	
Drag and drop	After pointing at a graphic object, hold the primary pointing device button down while moving the pointing device to visually drag the object. At the destination, release the button to drop the object.	
F1	Opens context-sensitive Help where supported.	Opens context-sensitive Help where supported on the Desktop. It does not work in Modern apps or the Start screen.
Hover	The object the mouse pointer hovers over will display a tooltip, infotip, or similar information, if enabled for the object.	
PAGE DOWN	Depending on context, moves cursor/current screen to next screen.	
PAGE UP	Depending on context, moves cursor/current screen to previous screen.	
PRNTSCR	Captures the screen and saves it in the Clipboard.	
SHIFT key + single left-click	For selectable objects, this action contiguously extends the selection.	
Single left-click	Selects or activates an object, depending on the current context and location of the pointer. For instance, if the pointer is in a document, this action sets the insertion point.	
Single right-click	Selects the object and displays its context menu.	
WINDOWS KEY + F1	Opens Windows Help and Support window.	Opens Windows Help and Support window on the Desktop.
WINDOWS KEY ALONE	Opens the Start menu.	Returns to Start screen or returns to previous app from Start screen.

Mouse Action or Mouse+Key Combination	Result in Windows 7 and Earlier	Result in Windows 8
WINDOWS KEY + PRTSCN	Captures the screen and saves it in the Clipboard.	Captures the screen and saves it in a folder named *Screenshots* in the Pictures folder.
WINDOWS KEY (hold) + TAB KEY (repeat)	Cycles through open apps using Flip 3D, showing previews of each open window.	Cycles through Modern app history in the task switcher bar on the left of the screen. Desktop apps appear as one "app."
WINDOWS KEY + SHIFT + LEFT ARROW KEY	On dual display system, switches contents of windows.	On dual display system moves desktop window to left display.
WINDOWS KEY + SHIFT + RIGHT ARROW KEY	On dual display system, switches contents of windows.	On dual display system moves desktop window to right display.
WINDOWS KEY + +	Opens Magnifier to magnify all or part of the screen.	
WINDOWS KEY + ESC	Closes Magnifier.	
WINDOWS KEY + , (COMMA)	N/A	Peek at the Desktop. Release to return to previous screen or Desktop window.
WINDOWS KEY + HOME	Minimize nonactive desktop windows.	
WINDOWS KEY + LEFT ARROW KEY	Snaps current desktop window to left.	
WINDOWS KEY + RIGHT ARROW KEY	Snaps current desktop window to right.	
WINDOWS KEY + UP ARROW KEY	Maximizes current desktop window.	
WINDOWS KEY + DOWN ARROW KEY	Restores/minimizes current desktop window.	
WINDOWS KEY + PGUP KEY	Same as PGUP KEY alone.	Moves Start screen to left monitor.
WINDOWS KEY + PGDN KEY	Same as PGDN KEY alone.	Moves Start screen to right monitor.
WINDOWS KEY + 1–9	Opens desktop app at the given position on the task bar.	
WINDOWS KEY + C	N/A	Opens Charms bar.
WINDOWS KEY + D	Minimizes all open windows and displays the desktop.	From Desktop, same as Windows 7. From Start screen or Modern app, opens the Desktop.
WINDOWS KEY + E	Opens a Windows Explorer window.	Opens a File Explorer window on the Desktop.
WINDOWS KEY + F	Opens a Search window.	Opens Search focused on files.
WINDOWS KEY + H	N/A	Opens the Share bar allowing Modern apps to share data (if they support this feature).
WINDOWS KEY + I	N/A	Opens the Settings bar.
WINDOWS KEY + J	N/A	When using Snap, switches focus between apps.
WINDOWS KEY + K	N/A	Opens the Devices bar.
WINDOWS KEY + L	Locks the PC displaying the Sign-In screen.	Locks the PC displaying either the Lock screen (if enabled) or the Sign-In screen.

Mouse Action or Mouse+Key Combination	Result in Windows 7 and Earlier	Result in Windows 8
WINDOWS KEY + M	Minimizes all windows.	Minimizes all Desktop windows.
WINDOWS KEY + O	N/A	Toggles the device orientation of mobile devices on and off in portrait or landscape.
WINDOWS KEY + P	Opens projection/second monitor options.	
WINDOWS KEY + Q	N/A	Opens the Apps Search bar.
WINDOWS KEY + R	Opens the Desktop Run box.	
WINDOWS KEY + T	Cycles through open Desktop apps.	
WINDOWS KEY + U	Opens Ease of Access Center.	
WINDOWS KEY + W	N/A	Opens Settings Search.
WINDOWS KEY + X	N/A	Opens Power User menu.
WINDOWS KEY + Z	N/A	When in Start screen or a Modern app, opens Apps bar on bottom of screen.

Glossary

The number at the end of the entry refers to the chapter where the term is introduced.

$ prompt (Pronounced "dollar prompt.") The Linux command prompt displayed in the BASH shell or in a terminal window when you are logged on as an ordinary (nonroot) user. (8)

absolute path A directory path that begins with the top level. in Linux, an absolute path begins with a forward slash (/) to indicate the root directory. (8)

accelerometer A component of a mobile device that detects the physical tilt and acceleration of the device, allowing the device to change the screen orientation for readability. (1)

Access Control Entry (ACE) An entry in an Access Control List, containing just one user or group account name and the permissions assigned to this account for that file or folder. (4)

Access Control List (ACL) A table of users and/or groups and their permissions to access the file or folder associated with the ACL. (4)

access mode number A value assigned to a file permission in Linux. The user (owner), group, and others each have a different access mode number calculated using the following values: read = 4, write = 2, and execute = 1. (8)

Action Center A Windows feature, represented by the small flag icon on the right of the toolbar; it will briefly display a message balloon when there is a problem with security programs or backup. (4)

activation A method of combating software piracy, intended to ensure that each software license used solely on a single computer. (4)

Add Printer wizard A series of onscreen instructions that guide you through the installation of a printer's driver and utilities. (4)

address space layout randomization (ASLR) A security feature of OS X Mountain Lion and newer that loads the core operating system code, the kernel, into random locations in memory, rather than loading into the same memory addresses every time. This prevents malware from accessing operating system functions based on where they are known to be in memory. (7)

administrator account type An account type in the OSs surveyed in this book. A user logged on with an administrator account type can perform systemwide tasks such as changing computer settings and installing or removing software and hardware. (2)

adware A form of spyware software downloaded to a computer without permission. It collects information about the user in order to display targeted advertisements, either in the form of inline banners or pop-ups. (2)

Aero Shake A Windows Aero feature that lets you quickly minimize all but one window by giving that window a quick shake. (4)

Aero Snap A Windows Aero feature that lets you manipulate windows quickly. To maximize a window drag it until its title bar touches the top edge of your display. Restore a maximized window by dragging it away from the top of the display. (4)

Airplane Mode A feature of mobile devices that turns off all wireless communications (cellular, Wi-Fi, Bluetooth, and NFC) without powering off the device. (11)

AirPlay A feature that was first introduced in iOS, and later added to OS X in Mountain Lion for connecting to an Apple TV, which acts as an intermediary device for sending iTunes songs, video, pictures, and other data from the computer to a high definition (HD) TV via Wi-Fi. (7)

anonymous FTP site An FTP site that does not require a user name and password, but allows anonymous connection, which means that all users connecting are using the Anonymous account. As such, a user only has the permissions assigned to the Anonymous account. (10)

Apache HTTP Server Open source Web server software, originally written for UNIX, runs on Linux. (8)

Apple ID A free account that identifies the holder as a customer of Apple for all Apple services and products. (11)

Apple menu A pop-up menu opened by clicking on the Apple icon in the upper left of the OS X desktop. (7)

application Software that allows a computer user to perform useful functions such as writing a report or calculating a budget. (1)

application virtualization Virtualization of an application whereby a user connects to a server and accesses one or more applications rather than an entire desktop environment. (3)

AppLocker A new feature in Windows 7 for controlling which applications each user can run, reducing the chance of malware running on the user's computer. Administer AppLocker with Group Policy, centrally managed through a Windows Active Directory domain. (4)

Assigned Access A feature added in Windows 8.1 that allows an administrator to assign a single user account to run just one app. (5)

authentication Validation of a user account and password that occurs before the security components of an OS give a user access to the computer or network. (2)

authorization The process of both authenticating a user and determining the permissions that the user has for a resource. (2)

automatic IP addressing A method by which a host can be assigned an IP address and all the additional configuration settings automatically. (10)

Automatic login In OS X (and other operating systems), a setting that bypasses the login page and logs into the selected user account when the computer powers on. (7)

Automatic Private IP Addressing (APIPA) A method by which a DHCP client computer that fails to receive an address from a DHCP server will automatically give itself an address from a special range that has the value 169 (base-10) in the first octet (eight binary digits) of the IP address. (10)

Automated System Recovery (ASR) A Windows XP recovery tool replaced by System Image Recovery in Windows 7. (4)

avatar An animated computer-generated human used in a virtual world to represent an individual. (3)

back door A way to use software to bypass security and gain access to a computer. (2)

Back tip In Windows 8, a thumbnail image of the previous active app that appears when the user points a mouse in the upper left corner. (5)

BASH An acronym for Bourne Again Shell; the Linux component (shell) that provides the character-mode user interface for entering and processing commands, issuing error messages, and other limited feedback. (8)

batch file A text file that contains commands that automate running the commands. (9)

binary file A file that contains program code, as opposed to a file containing data. (6)

BitLocker A feature in the Enterprise and Ultimate editions of Windows Vista and Windows 7 for encrypting the drive on which the Windows OS resides and (in Windows 7 and continuing in Windows 8) other drives beyond the system drive. BitLocker is off by default. BitLocker works with a Trusted Platform Module chip in the computer so that if the drive is removed, it cannot be decrypted. (4)

BitLocker To Go An enhanced feature in Windows 7 and Windows 8 BitLocker that includes encryption of removable devices. (4)

bloatware Slang for the software added to a computer when it is purchased with Windows preinstalled. Some of these programs are useful, but most of it is annoying or may be free trial software that you can try, but must purchase to use after the trial period (often 30 days) expires. (5)

bluesnarfing The act of covertly obtaining information broadcast from wireless devices using the Bluetooth standard. (2)

Bluetooth A wireless standard for using radio waves to communicate over very short distances between devices. The most common implementation of Bluetooth wirelessly connects devices at a distance of up to one meter. (11)

bootloader OS startup code that must be loaded into early in the startup process. The Windows Vista, Windows 7, and Windows 8 bootloader is a file named BOOTMGR. (6)

bootstrap loader A firmware program that uses hardware configuration settings stored in nonvolatile memory, commonly called CMOS, to determine what devices can start an OS and the order in which the system will search these devices while attempting to begin the OS startup process. It then loads the bootloader program. (6)

botherder Someone who initiates and controls a botnet. (2)

botnet A group of networked computers that, usually unbeknown to their owners, have been infected with programs that forward information to other computers over the network (usually the Internet). (2)

Bring Your Own Device (BYOD) The practice of using personal mobile devices at work. (11)

browser hijacking Malware installed on a computer that causes the Internet Explorer home page to always point to a specific site, often advertising something. Hijackers make it very difficult to defeat the hijack by modifying the registry so that every time you restart Windows or Internet Explorer the hijack reinstates. (2)

burn To write digital data just once to a disc. Traditionally this term refers to the writing of data to a disc (CD-R, DVD-R, or BD-R) that can only be written to once in any given area of the disc. Once full, you cannot add data to the disc. It is "write-once." The source files can be individual files or an ISO file. (8)

case-aware In an operating system, a feature that allows the OS to preserve the case used for the characters in a file name when creating it, but does not require the correct case when opening or managing the file. (8)

case-sensitive In an operating system, a feature that allows the OS to preserve the case used for the characters in a file name when creating it, and requires the correct case to open or manage the file. (8)

central processing unit (CPU) An integrated circuit (chip) that performs the calculations, or processing, for a computer. See also *microprocessor*. (1)

charm Shortcut-like object that appears on the Charms bar in Windows 8. This bar slides out from the right side of the screen. (5)

Charms bar A bar that displays on the right side of a Windows 8 screen and contains charms. (5)

clean installation An installation of an OS onto a completely empty hard disk or one from which all data is removed during the installation. (4)

client A software component on a computer that accesses services from a network server. (1)

cmd.exe The Windows Command Prompt command interpreter. (9)

code signing A practice Microsoft introduced in Windows 2000 in which all of the operating system code is digitally signed to show that it has not been tampered with. See also *driver signing*. (6)

cold boot A method of starting up a computer and operating system by turning on the power switch. (5)

command.com The MS-DOS command interpreter. (9)

command completion A feature of Linux (and OS X Terminal UNIX) that completes what is entered at the command line with a command name or file or directory name. (8)

command-line history The Linux and UNIX (and OS X Terminal) feature that saves command-line history in a file named bash_history. (8)

command-line interface (CLI) A user interface that includes a character-based command line that requires text input. (1)

Command Prompt In Windows, the command-line interface that is launched from within Windows or in Safe Mode or as a Recovery option. (9)

computer. A device that calculates. (1)

Connected Standby A power-saving mode in Windows 8 that allows specially designed apps to perform small tasks in background, such as email and notifications, with very little power usage. (5)

Consent Prompt Part of the User Account Control security feature since Windows Vista, this prompt appears when a user is logged on as an administrator and a program attempts to perform a task requiring administrative permissions The task is allowed to complete only if the user selects the Yes button. (6)

content filter In an Internet browser, software that blocks content. (2)

cookies Very small text files an Internet browser saves on the local hard drive at the request of a website. Cookies may contain user preferences for a specific site, information entered into a form at a website (including personal information), browsing activity, and shopping selections made at a website. (2)

Credentials Prompt Part of the User Account Control security feature since Windows Vista, this prompt appears when a user is logged on as a standard user and a program attempts to perform a task requiring administrative permission. The prompt will ask the user for an administrator password to continue. (6)

cursor In a command-line interface (CLI), the cursor is merely a marker for the current position where what you type on the keyboard will go. In a GUI the cursor is sometimes replaced by a graphical pointer that can have a variety of shapes you can move around by manipulating a pointing device. (1)

cybercrime Illegal activity performed using computer technology. (2)

daemon In Linux, software that runs in background until it is activated. (8)

Darwin The name of the core operating system on which OS X is based. A product of the open-source community. (7)

data protection In iOS a feature that is turned on when you enable the Passcode Lock that encrypts mail messages and attachments on the device, using the passcode as the encryption key. (11)

data type In the Windows registry, a special data format. There are several registry data types, such as REG_BINARY, REG_DWORD, and so forth. (6)

data wiping The permanent removal of data from a storage device. (2)

default gateway The IP address of the router connected to your network. The net ID of the default gateway address should be identical to that of your NIC. The router is a network device that sits between networks and directs traffic to destinations beyond the local network. (10)

delimiter character A characters, such as a space that marks the boundary between CLI parameters in the Windows Command Prompt. (9)

desktop virtualization The virtualization of a desktop computer into which you can install an operating system, its unique configuration, and all the applications and data used by a single person. (3)

device driver Software that is added to an OS to control a physical component (device). A component-specific device driver is needed for each unique hardware device connected to a computer. (1)

device management An OS function that controls hardware devices through the use of device drivers. (1)

Device Manager A Windows recovery tool that aids in troubleshooting device problems. This Windows Control Panel applet displays the list of hardware and the status and properties of each device. Use this to disable a device or to update or roll back a device driver. (6)

Device Stage A feature introduced in Windows 7 that, if the device supports it, will bring up a page from which you can make many choices for managing the device; it often includes an accurate image of the device. (6)

dial-up An inexpensive WAN option available to anyone with a phone line and a standard analog modem (the long-time standard runs at 56 Kbps). (10)

digital certificate A special file stored on a computer that may hold a secret key for decrypting data. (2)

digital signature In Windows, encrypted data that can be unencrypted by Windows in a process called file signature verification. (6)

digital subscriber line (DSL) A WAN service similar to ISDN in its use of the telephone network, but using more advanced digital signal processing to compress more signals through the telephone lines. (10)

directory A special file that can contain files as well as other directories. This term is most often used with non-GUI operating systems, while *folder* is most often used when describing a directory in a GUI. (1)

distribution A bundling of the Linux kernel and software—both enhancements to the OS and applications—such as word processors, spreadsheets, media players, and more. (1)

DMZ A network between the internal network and the Internet with a firewall on both sides. (2)

Dock A floating bar on the OS X desktop that holds icons for commonly used programs, as well as icons for open applications. A single click on an icon launches the program. (7)

Domain Join A feature that allows a Windows computer to join a Microsoft Active Directory Domain. (5)

Domain Name System (DNS) A distributed online database containing registered domain names mapped to IP addresses. Thousands of name servers on the Internet maintain this distributed database. When you attempt to connect to a website, your computer's DNS client queries a DNS server to determine the IP address of the website. (10)

drive-by download A program downloaded to a user's computer without consent. Often the simple act of browsing to a website or opening an HTML email message may result in such a surreptitious download. A drive-by download may also occur when installing another application. (2)

driver signing Code signing of device drivers that indicates two things: the integrity of the file or files, and that the device driver has passed Microsoft's tests for compatibility. (6)

dual-boot A multiboot configuration with just two choices of operating systems. (4)

dumb terminal A device consisting of little more than a keyboard and display with a connection to a host computer (mainframe or minicomputer) and having no native processing power of its own. (3)

Dynamic Host Configuration Protocol (DHCP) server A server that issues IP addresses and settings to computers that are configured to obtain an IP address automatically, thus making them DHCP clients. (10)

Early Launch Anti-Malware (ELAM) A Windows 8 security feature that examines all device drivers before they are loaded into memory, preventing suspicious drivers from loading. (6)

edge gestures Touch gestures that begin close to the bezel of the screen on a Windows 8 computer. (5)

edition A packaging of a Windows version. (1)

email spoofing Forging of the sender's address in the email message's header (the information that accompanies a message but does not appear in the message) so that an incorrect address appears in the "from" field of an email message. (2)

embedded OS An operating system stored in firmware, as in a mobile device (1)

Encrypting File System (EFS) An NTFS file encryption feature for encrypting selected files and folders (not entire drives). (2)

encryption The transformation of data into a code that can be decrypted only through the use of a secret key or password. (2)

exploit A malware attack (2)

external command A command program stored on disk, rather than within the operating system code. The command interpreter looks for an external command program in the search path on disk if it cannot find it in memory. (9)

Fast Boot A feature of Windows 8 startup that takes advantage of the hibernated kernel (if the last shutdown was a Hybrid Shutdown), bringing the hibernated system session out of hibernation, saving all the work of the Kernel Loading phase. In addition, on a computer with multiple CPU cores, the cores work in parallel when processing the hibernation file. Fast Boot is the default when you power up your computer. (6)

FAT file systems Several related file systems based on the original FAT file system. They include FAT12, FAT16, FAT32, and exFAT. Each has a logical structure that includes a file allocation table (FAT) and a directory structure. (4)

file and printer server A network server that gives client computers access to files and printers. Also simply called a file server. (10)

file attribute A characteristic of a file or directory that is recorded in an entry for that file or directory. (9)

File Explorer Previously named Windows Explorer, the name of the Windows file management tool beginning with Windows 8. (5)

file management An operating system function that allows the operating system to read, write, and modify data and programs organized into files. (1)

file signature verification The process by which Windows unencrypts a digital signature and verifies that the file has not been tampered with. (6)

file system The logical structure used on a storage device for the purpose of storing files, as well as the code within an operating system that allows the OS to store and manage files on a storage device. (1)

File Transfer Protocol (FTP) A protocol used to transfer files between a computer running the FTP server service and an FTP client. It is a preferred method of transferring files over a TCP/IP network, especially the Internet, because it is simple and fast. (10)

FileVault A feature in Mac Os X that, in earlier versions of OS X, encrypted the Home folder. In recent versions, it encrypts the entire startup disk. (2)

Finder The foundation of the OS X GUI and the equivalent to Windows Explorer, the Windows file management tool. (7)

firewall A firewall is either software or a physical device that examines network traffic. Based on predefined rules, a firewall rejects certain traffic coming into a computer or network. The two general types of firewalls are network-based firewalls and personal firewalls that reside on individual computers. (2)

firmware Software resident in integrated circuits. (1)

first-party cookie A cookie that originates with the domain name of the URL to which you directly connect. (2)

Flip 3D A Windows Aero feature that lets you switch through your open windows as if they were in a stack of cards or photos. (4)

folder A special file that can contain files as well as other directories. This term is most often used with GUI operating systems, while *directory* is most often used when describing a directory in a non-GUI. (1)

forged email address An address that appears in the "from" field of an email address because the sender address was modified in the email message's header (the information that accompanies a message but does not appear in the message). This type of forgery is also called *email spoofing*. (2)

formatting The action of an operating system when it maps the logical organization of the file system to physical locations on the storage device (most often a conventional hard disk drive or solid-state drive) so that it can store and retrieve the data. (1)

fraud The use of deceit and trickery to persuade someone to hand over money or other valuables. (2)

fully qualified domain name (FQDN) The human-readable TCP/IP name corresponding to the TCP/IP address of a host, as found on a computer, router, or other networked device. It includes both its host name and its domain name. (10)

gadget A small program represented by an icon on the Windows Vista Sidebar, or, in Windows 7, anywhere on the desktop. A gadget performs some small function—usually involving keeping information handy in a small screen object. (4)

Gatekeeper A security feature of OS X that limits sources from which you can download apps. (7)

GNOME An acronym for GNU network object model environment, a Linux GUI that uses the Linux X Windows system. (8)

GNU An organization created in 1984 to develop a free version of a UNIX-like operating system. GNU, a recursive acronym for GNU's Not UNIX, has developed thousands of applications that run on UNIX and Linux platforms. Many are distributed with versions of Linux. (8)

Google account A free account that gives the account holder access to Google services. (11)

graphical user interface (GUI) A user interface that takes advantage of a computer's graphics capabilities to make it easier to use with graphical elements that a user can manipulate to perform tasks such as system and file management and running applications. (1)

group account A security account that may contain one or more individual accounts. In some security accounts databases, it may contain other groups. (2)

Group Policy A set of configuration settings that can be centrally managed and applied to each computer and logged-in user in a Microsoft Active Directory domain. (5)

guest account A special account used when someone connects to a computer over a network but is not a member of a security account recognized on that computer. That person connects as a guest (if the guest account is enabled) and will only have the permissions assigned to the guest account. (2)

guest OS An operating system running within a virtual machine. (3)

Guest User An account created by OS X that does not require a password, has access only to the Guest Home folder, and when this account logs out, all files and folders created during that session are deleted. Disabled by default; enable it in the Users and Groups preferences pane. (7)

header The information that accompanies a message but does not appear in the message. (2)

hibernate A Windows power or shutdown option that, if enabled, saves both the system state and the user session in a file named hiberfil.sys. (6)

hive The portion of the Windows registry represented in one registry file. (6)

home directory In Linux, a directory created for a user, using the user's login name, and located under the /home directory. This is the one place in Linux where an ordinary user account has full control over files without logging in as the root account. (8)

Home folder A folder created by OS X for a user that displays in the Finder when that user is logged on, identified in the sidebar by a house icon and the user's name. Certain folders are created by the OS in Finder including Desktop, Documents, Downloads, Movies, Music, Pictures, and Public. The user can create new folders and save all their data in this set of folders. (7)

honey pot A server created as a decoy to draw malware attacks and gather information about attackers. (2)

host ID The portion of an IP address that identifies the host on a network, as determined using the subnet mask. (10)

host key A key or key combination that releases the mouse and keyboard from a virtual machine to the host OS. In VirtualBox on a Mac, it is the left Command key, while in Virtual PC it is the right Alt key. (3)

Host OS The operating system installed directly on the computer. A Type II hypervisor runs on this OS. (3)

hotspot A Wi-Fi network that connects to the Internet through a router. (2)

Hybrid Shutdown The default when you select Shutdown from the Windows 8 Power menu: (1) Windows sends messages to all running apps to save data and settings, and then shuts down the apps, (2) Windows closes the session for each logged-on user, and (3) Windows hibernates the Windows session and saves it in a file. It does not hibernate the User session. (6)

Hypertext Transfer Protocol (HTTP) The protocol for transferring the files that make up the rich graphical Web pages we view on the World Wide Web (WWW). It includes the commands a Web browser uses to request Web pages from a Web server to display on the screen of a local computer. (8)

hypervisor The software layer that emulates the necessary hardware for an operating system to run in. It is the hardware virtualization that lets multiple operating systems run simultaneously on a single computer, such as a network server. (3)

identity theft This occurs when someone collects personal information belonging to another person and uses that information to fraudulently make purchases, open new credit accounts, or even obtain new driver's licenses and other forms of identification in the victim's name. (2)

image An exact duplicate of the entire hard drive contents, including the OS and all installed software, that is used to install copies of an OS and associated applications on multiple computers. (4)

input/output (I/O) Anything sent into a computer (input); anything coming out of a computer (output). Every keystroke you enter, all files read in, and even voice commands are input. Output can include a printed page, what you see on the screen, and even sounds. (1)

integrated circuit (IC) A small electronic component made up of transistors (tiny switches) and other miniaturized parts. (1)

integrated services digital network (ISDN) A digital telephone service that simultaneously transmits voice, data, and control signaling over a single telephone line. ISDN service operates on standard telephone lines, but requires a special modem and phone service, which adds to the cost. An ISDN data connection can transfer data at up to 128,000 bits per second (128 Kbps). (10)

internal command A program that resides within the operating system code and is not stored as a separate file on disk. (9)

Internet Protocol (IP) The core TCP/IP protocol that delivers communications in chunks, called packets. This protocol allows your computer to be identified on an internetwork by a logical address called an IP address. Special routing protocols can use a destination IP address to choose the best route for a packet to take through a very complex internetwork. IP also has subprotocols that help it accomplish its work. (10)

Internet service provider (ISP) An organization that provides individuals or entire organizations access to the Internet. For a fee, an ISP provides you with this connection service and may offer other Internet-related services such as Web server hosting and email. (10)

internetwork A network of interconnected networks. (10)

IP address The logical address used on a TCP/IP network to identify a network interface card (NIC). (10)

IPv4 The version of the Internet Protocol in use since 1983 (with updates). (10)

IPv6 The latest version of the Internet Protocol that is gradually replacing IPv4. (10)

ISO image A copy of the entire contents of a CD or DVD that can be easily transferred to a writeable CD or DVD with ISO image copy software. (5)

job management An operating system function that controls the order and time in which programs are run. For example, an operating system's print program can manage and prioritize multiple print jobs. (1)

Jump List In Windows, a list of recently opened items such as files, folders, and websites that appear when you right-click on a program on the Start menu or taskbar. (4)

kernel The main component of an operating system that always remains in memory while a computer is running. (1)

key In the Windows registry, a folder object that may contain one or more sets of settings as well as other keys. (6)

keyboard shortcut A key combination that performs an assigned action, saving you several mouse or keyboard actions. (5)

keychain A database in which OS X saves encrypted passwords. The first keychain, login, is created for each user and associated with the user's login password. (7)

Keychain Access The OS X utility for managing the keychain. (7)

keylogger See *keystroke logger*. (2)

keystroke logger A hardware device or a program that monitors and records a user's every keystroke, usually without the user's knowledge. Also called a keylogger. (2)

Kickoff Application Launcher A GUI object on the KDE GUI bundled with Fedora that, when clicked, opens a menu (similar to the Windows Start menu) for launching programs. (8)

Last Known Good (LKG) Configuration A Windows start-up option for start-up failures due to a configuration change. It lets you restore the system to a single restore point (not called that), and you only have a narrow window of opportunity in which you can use LKG—on the first reboot after making a configuration change, and *before* logging on. (6)

Launcher A GUI object (a bar) on the left side of the Ubuntu Unity desktop that serves the same purpose as the OS X Dock and the pinned items feature on the taskbar on the Windows Desktop. (8)

Launchpad A feature new in OS X Mountain Lion that resembles the home screen on Apple iOS devices. It consists of one or more screens holding icons for all installed apps. Apps can be grouped together and/or launched from the Launchpad. (7)

library A feature introduced in Windows 7, in which a library is a special folder with pointers to disk folders that can be in many locations, but will all appear to be in the same library. (4)

limited account An account type in Windows XP that is a simplistic reference to an account that only belongs to the Local Users group. (2)

Linux An open source operating system based on UNIX that was developed by Linus Torvalds and others beginning in 1991. (8)

Live File System A file format used by Windows 7 to burn discs that will only be used on newer Apple Macs and newer PCs (Windows XP or newer OS). Using Live File System you can directly copy items to the drive without requiring extra hard drive space. You can copy items individually, over time—either by leaving the disc in the drive or reinserting the disc multiple times. (4)

live image A bootable image of the operating system that will run from disc or other bootable media without requiring that the OS be installed on the local compute. (8)

live tile A rectangle on the Windows 8 Start screen that when tapped with a finger or clicked with a mouse launches an app. The "live" part of the name is due to each tile's ability to display active content related to the app without requiring that you launch the app. (5)

local area network (LAN) A network that covers a building, home, office, or campus. It can be wireless or wired.

A Wi-Fi network is a wireless LAN (WLAN). The typical maximum distance covered by WLAN signals or LAN cabling is measured in hundreds of feet. (10)

local security The security options available and limited to a local computer. In Windows, this includes local security accounts and local security for files and folders, Windows BitLocker drive encryption, Windows Defender antispam protection, and Windows Firewall. (4)

location service A service on a computer or mobile device that allows an app to track your location, using one or more methods, often with the help of the Internet. (11)

Lock screen A screen that displays at start up of a Windows 8 computer, when Windows is locked, or when a period of inactivity triggers the screen saver. You must use a swiping motion (with finger or mouse) to close the Lock screen and access either the Sign-in screen or the Start screen. (5)

logon phase A phase of Windows startup during which a user is authenticated, the service control manager starts, logon scripts run, startup programs run, and noncritical services start. Plug-and-play detection occurs during this startup phase. (6)

Mac The product name for Apple's computers. (1)

Mac OS X Server The first of the Mac OS X line designed for Mac Server computers. It was introduced in 1999, shipping preinstalled on Mac Server. Today you can only buy it as an add-on to OS X; you must have OS X to install Mac OS X Server. (7)

malware A shortened form of "malicious software" that covers a large and growing list of threats such as viruses, worms, Trojan horses, or spam. (2)

manpage In Linux, UNIX, and the OS X Terminal window, a manual page is the documentation for a command, accessed with the **man** command. (9)

Mastered When burning a disc in Windows this option allows you to use the burned CD or DVD in a conventional CD or DVD player or in any computer (older Apple Macs or PCs). The downside is that each item you select to copy to the PC is stored temporarily in available hard disk space (in addition to the space used by the original file) and then all files are copied in one operation. (4)

master file table (MFT) The main logical structure of the NTFS file system that is expandable and uses transaction processing to track changes to files. (4)

Measured Boot. A UEFI firmware feature that logs the startup process. Antimalware software can analyze this log to determine if malware is on the computer or if the boot components were tampered with. (6)

memory The physical chips that store programs and data. There are two basic types: random-access memory (RAM) and read-only memory (ROM). (1)

memory management An operating system function that manages and tracks the placement of programs and data in memory. Advanced operating systems, such as Windows, Linux, and Mac OS X, use memory management to make optimal use of memory. (1)

Menu Extras Icons on the right side of the OS X menu bar that give quick access to some System Preferences settings. (7)

microcomputer A computer built around a microprocessor. (1)

microprocessor An integrated circuit (chip) that performs the calculations, or processing, for a computer. Also called a processor or central processing unit (CPU). (1)

Microsoft account A free account with Microsoft that gives the subscriber access to Microsoft services, such as Hotmail, Messenger, SkyDrive, Windows Phone, Xbox LIVE, and Outlook.com. (5)

Microsoft Product Activation (MPA) Microsoft's method of combating software piracy, intended to ensure that each software license is used solely on a single computer. After installing Microsoft software, MPA will attempt to contact Microsoft's site to confirm the product is authentic. Normally, during activation the user is prompted to enter a product code, found on the packaging. Many other software vendors require activation. See *activation*. (4)

Microsoft Security Essentials (MSE) A free security app from Microsoft includes general malware protection and free, automated updates. Available for Windows Vista and Windows 7 at www.microsoft.com/security_essentials. MSE was replaced in Windows 8 by Windows Defender. (4)

Microsoft Store The name for brick-and-mortar stores and an online site that sell hardware and software compatible and approved by Microsoft. (5)

MiFi Novatel's trademarked name for the hotspot device they manufactured. It stands for "my Wi-Fi." (11)

Mission Control A screen in OS X where you can create and organize Spaces. (7)

mobile device management (MDM A category of software for enforcing policies and managing mobile devices. (11)

mobile hotspot A mobile device that shares its data cellular connection with nearby devices connected via Wi-Fi. (11)

motherboard The central circuit board of a computer to which all other devices connect. (1)

mouse A pointing device that you move with your hand on a level surface to manipulate objects on the computer screen. (5)

MS-DOS Microsoft's 1980's era CLI OS that they have not licensed or sold in many years. (9)

MSCONFIG The System Configuration Utility, a Windows tool for modifying system startup, allows you to modify and test start-up configuration settings without having to alter the settings directly. It allows you access to settings that are buried within the registry and allows you to make the changes temporary or permanent. (6)

multiboot An installation that leaves an old OS in place, installing a new OS in a separate location. This allows you to select the OS you want to boot into every time you start the computer. (4)

multitasking Two or more programs (tasks) running simultaneously on a computer. (1)

multitouch. The ability to interpret multiple simultaneous touch gestures, such as the pinching gesture in which fingers first touch the device (screen, touch mouse, or touch pad) at separate locations and then pinch them together. (5)

Near Field Communication (NFC) A chipset that supports a short-distance wireless standard that requires two devices to touch before communicating. (11)

net ID The network portion of an IP address, as determined through the subnet mask. (10)

network virtualization A network addressing space that exists within one or more physical networks, but which is logically independent of the physical network structure. (3)

Notification Center An OS X feature that displays important status messages, notifying the user of important events, such as a new email or text message or that an update is available. (7)

NTFS The preferred Windows file system that is expandable and uses a transaction processing system to track changes to files, so that it can roll back incomplete transactions. It also includes several other features: file compression, file encryption, file and folder security, and indexing. (4)

object code An executable program, the result of compiling programming statements, that can be interpreted by a computer's CPU or operating system and loaded into memory as a running program. (8)

octet A group of eight binary digits. (10)

on-screen keyboard A virtual keyboard that is available as an accessibility option. It also displays in Windows 8 on devices without a keyboard when you need to enter alphanumeric characters on a device that lacks a keyboard. (5)

open source software Software distributed with all its source code, allowing developers to customize it as necessary. (8)

operating system (OS) A collection of programs that provides a computer with critical functionality, such as a user interface, management of hardware and software, and ways of creating, managing, and using files. (1)

OS X The Apple desktop operating system. (7)

OS X Setup Assistant In a new computer with Mac OS X preinstalled, the OS is not configured, so the first time it is powered up, this program prompts you for the user preferences information. (7)

Out of Box Experience (OOBE). A feature on a new computer with Windows 8 preinstalled. When you take it out of the box and turn it on, you will be greeted with this last phase of Windows installation where you personalize the GUI and configure how you will sign in. (5)

owner In Linux, the user account that creates a file or directory. This term is also used in Windows. (8)

packet A piece of a message packaged by the Internet Protocol. In addition to the portion of a message, each packet is given a header that contains information including the source address (local host address) and the destination address. (10)

pairing A connection between two devices using the Bluetooth wireless standard. (11)

Parental Controls A feature in Internet Explorer that allows parents using a password-protected administrator account to protect their children from harm by setting specific Parental Controls for a child's user account. Apple OS X uses the same name for this type of feature. (2)

parse The action of a command interpreter of dividing the text entered at a command line into its components, based on special delimiter characters, such as the space character. (9)

partition (n) An area of a physical hard disk that defines space used for logical drives. (1)

passcode lock A string of characters (or gestures) that a user enters to close the lock screen and access a device. (11)

password A confidential string of characters that a user enters (along with a user name) in order to be authenticated. (2)

password cracker A program used to discover a password. (2)

path A description that an operating system uses to identify the location of a file or directory. (8)

PC Settings screen A Windows 8 screen containing several panels for configuring Windows 8 settings. (5)

permission A level of access to an object, such as a file or folder, that is granted to a user account or group account. (2)

personal computer (PC) A microcomputer that complies with the Microsoft/Intel standards. (1)

personal folders In Windows, a set of special folders saved on disk for each user who logs on. (4)

personal identification number (PIN) A type of password of four or more numeric characters. (11)

phishing A fraudulent method of obtaining personal financial information through Web page pop-ups, email, and even paper letters mailed via the postal service. Often purports to be from a legitimate organization, such as a bank, credit card company, or retailer. Phishing is a form of social engineering. (2)

pinning A feature introduced in Windows 7 that allows you to place icons for applications and destinations on the taskbar and Start menu. Once pinned, an item's icon remains on the toolbar regardless of whether the program is open or closed. The user clicks it to open the application or destination. (4)

piping A feature of a CLI command interpreter that takes the output from one command and sends it as input to another command. (9)

plug and play The ability of a computer to detect and configure a hardware device automatically. To work, the computer, the device, and the OS must all comply with the same plug-and-play standard. (6)

pop-up An ad that runs in a separate browser window you must close before you can continue with your present task. (2)

pop-up blocker A program that works against pop-ups. (2)

pop-up download A program that is downloaded to a user's computer through the use of a pop-up page that appears while surfing the Web. (2)

portable operating system An operating system that you can use on a variety of computer system platforms, with only minor alterations required to be compatible with the underlying architecture. (1)

power-on self-test A series of tests of system hardware that runs from firmware when a computer starts up. (6)

PowerShell A Windows CLI scripting environment for advanced users and administrators. (9)

Power User menu A Windows 8 menu that opens when you use the WINDOWS KEY+X shortcut. This menu contains many handy utilities. (5)

private browsing A security feature available in browsers that allows you to browse the Web without saving any history on the local computer of the sites visited. (10)

private IP address An address from one of three ranges of IP addresses designated for use only on private networks and not to be used on the Internet. The private IP address ranges are 10.0.0.0 through 10.255.255.255, 172.16.0.0 through 172.31.255.255, and 192.168.0.0 through 192.168.255.255. (10)

processes Components of a program that are active in memory. (1)

processor See *microprocessor*. (1)

Program Compatibility Troubleshooter A wizard that you run from Help and Support to set compatibility options for an older application that will "trick" the older program into thinking that the OS is actually the earlier version of Windows required by the application (such as Windows XP). (4)

protocol In the computer technology and networking world a set of rules, usually formalized in a standard published by one of many standards organizations. This is also the term for the software that implements a certain set of rules. (10)

protocol stack A group of bundled programs based on networking protocols and designed to work together. (10)

public IP addresses IP addresses assigned to hosts on the Internet. (10)

RAM disk A disk volume created in RAM memory using a special driver loaded during startup. (9)

random-access memory (RAM) Memory in a computer that acts as the main memory for holding active programs. (1)

read-only memory basic input output system (ROM BIOS) The original system-level PC firmware replaced in recent years by firmware that complies with a newer standard. See *Unified Extensible Firmware Interface (UEFI)*. (1)

Recovery Key A code generated by OS X when it encrypts the start disk with FileVault. (7)

Red Hat Enterprise Linux (RHEL) Red Hat's commercially available version of Linux. (8)

redirection operator A symbol, such as the vertical bar (|) and the greater-than sign (>), that affects the behavior of commands, sending the output somewhere other than the screen (to a file or as input to another command). (9)

registry A database of all configuration settings in Windows. (6)

remote access VPN A connection between an individual computer or mobile device using a VPN over a WAN connection. (10)

Remote Desktop A feature that allows a user at one computer to connect to another and view and work in its desktop. (5)

Remote Desktop client A feature in some editions of Windows that allows a Windows computer to connect to a Remote Desktop host on a remote computer. (5)

Remote Desktop host A feature in some editions of Windows that allows a Windows computer to host incoming Remote Desktop sessions. (5)

remote wipe A feature that allows someone to delete the contents of a mobile device over the Internet. (11)

restore point A snapshot of Windows, its configuration, and all installed programs. If your computer has nonfatal problems after you have made a change, you can use System Restore to roll it back to a restore point. (4)

ribbon A feature of recent versions of Microsoft Office also found in File Explorer in Windows 8. (5)

root account In Linux, an all-powerful account that is used only when absolutely necessary to do advanced tasks. Ubuntu Linux comes with this account disabled in a way that no one can log in directly with the account, but there is a way to use it temporarily whenever you need it for tasks, such as creating or deleting users. (8)

root key In the Windows registry, each of the top five folders is a root key, sometimes called a subtree in Microsoft documentation. Each of these root keys is the top of a hierarchical structure containing folders called keys. (6)

rootkit Malware that hides itself from detection by antimalware programs, by concealing itself within the OS code or any other program running on the computer. (2)

router A network device that sits between networks and directs (routes) traffic to destinations beyond the local network. (10)

Safe Mode A start-up mode in which Windows starts without using all of the drivers and components that would normally be loaded. Use Safe Mode when your Windows computer will not start normally. (6)

Safe Mode with Command Prompt A start-up mode in which Windows starts without using all of the drivers and components that would normally be loaded and opens an Administrator Command Prompt window against a black background with the words "Safe Mode" in the four corners of the screen. Use Safe Mode when your Windows computer will not start normally. (9)

sandboxed A feature in OS X that isolates an app so that it cannot access any code or device it is not authorized to access. (7)

scareware A vector technique that uses threatening messages, such as a message offering to fix problems it claims to find and asking for payment. Or it may state that you must complete a survey or it will delete critical files. (2)

screen acceleration. A feature of mobile operating systems that takes advantage of the built-in hardware accelerometer by rotating the image on the screen to accommodate the position and allow you to read the screen. (1)

screen rotation A feature of mobile operating systems that takes advantage of the built-in hardware accelerometer by rotating the image on the screen to accommodate the position and allow you to read the screen. (1)

Search bar A bar that opens on the right of the screen in Windows 8 after you click or tap the Search charm on the Charms bar. It contains a search box for entering key words to search for all types of data in many locations. (5)

search path A list of paths created and maintained by the operating system in which it searches for programs and their components before loading them into memory. (9)

secret key A special code that can be used to decrypt encrypted data. (2)

Second-Level Address Translation (SLAT) A feature found in many newer Intel and AMD CPUs and required by some hypervisors. (3)

Secure Boot A UEFI firmware feature that loads only trusted operating system bootloaders. This is one of the UEFI security features required on computers that come with Windows 8 preinstalled. (6)

Secure HTTP (HTTPS) A form of the HTTP protocol that supports encryption of the communications. HTTPS uses the Secure Sockets Layer (SSL) security protocol. (2)

Secure Sockets Layer (SSL) A security protocol for encrypting network data. (2)

Secure Virtual Memory An OS X feature that encrypts the swap file. (7)

security An operating system function that provides password-protected authentication of the user before allowing access to the local computer. Security features may restrict what a user can do on a computer. (1)

security account In a security accounts database, a security account is a listing of information about a user, group, or computer. A user or computer account used for authentication; both user and group accounts are used for authorization with assigned permissions. (2)

security ID (SID) A unique string of numbers preceded by *S-1-5* that identifies a security principle in a Windows security accounts database. (6)

semantic zoom A feature in the Windows 8 Metro-style GUI that shrinks objects on the screen. (5)

server A computer that plays one or more of several important roles on a network. In all of these roles, the server provides services to other computers (clients). (1)

server virtualization When a single machine hosts multiple servers, each of which performs tasks independently from the others as separate physical machines would. (3)

Service Set ID (SSID) A network name that identifies a Wi-Fi network. (11)

Settings bar. In Windows 8 a bar containing charms that opens various settings utilities. It opens on the right of the screen when you swipe from the bottom right or use the WINDOWS KEY + I shortcut. (5)

share A connecting point to which network clients with the correct permissions may connect. It is visible as a folder over the network, but it is a separate entity from the disk folder to which it points. (10)

Shared folder A folder, created by OS X in each user's Home folder. It is accessible to other users without restriction. (7)

Sharing Only account In OS X, an account that allows a user to login remotely and access shared folders, but that does not have a Home folder and cannot be used to login locally on that computer. (7)

shell The operating system component that provides the character-mode user interface—processing commands and issuing error messages and other limited feedback. (8)

shell command A command entered through a CLI shell. (8)

shortcut An icon that represents a link to an object, such as a file or program. Activating a shortcut (by clicking on it) is a quick way to access an object or to start a program from any location without having to find the actual location of the object on your computer. (4)

Sleep A Windows power down option that leaves the computer in a very-low-power mode in which the system state and user session (applications and data) are saved in RAM, but the screen turns off. (6)

site-to-site VPN A VPN connection between two networks. (10)

smartphone A cell phone that also connects to the Internet and runs a variety of apps for entertainment, education, and work. Modern smartphones have high-quality touch screens. (1)

SmartScreen A feature introduced in Internet Explorer 9 that prevents the downloading of suspicious programs during Web browsing. It was expanded in Windows 8 so that it is no longer limited just to the Internet Explorer browser and is now called *Windows SmartScreen*. (5)

Snap A feature of Windows 8 that allows two apps to share the screen with a vertical division between them. (5)

social engineering The use of persuasion techniques to gain the confidence of individuals—for both good and bad purposes. People with malicious intent use social engineering to persuade someone to reveal confidential information or to obtain something else of value. (2)

social media A service (Internet-based or other) that provides a place where people can interact in online communities, sharing information in various forms. (2)

social networking The use of social media. (2)

social networking site A website that provides space where members can communicate with one another and share details of their business or personal lives. (2)

solid-state drive (SSD). A storage device that uses integrated circuits, which can be written to and read from much faster than conventional hard disk drives and optical drives. (1)

source code The uncompiled text program statements that can be viewed and edited with a text editor or special program software. (8)

Spaces An OS X feature in which a space is a virtual screen; OS X supports up to 16 Spaces. Use Spaces for separating categories of files, such as those for work, play, and school projects. (7)

spam Unsolicited email. This includes email from a legitimate source selling a real service or product, but if you did not give permission to send such information to you, it is spam. (2)

spam filter Software designed to combat spam by examining incoming email messages and filtering out those that have characteristics of spam, including certain identified keywords. (2)

spear phishing Targeted phishing attacks that often target high-value individuals. (2)

spim An acronym for Spam over Instant Messaging; the perpetrators are called spimmers. (2)

Spotlight A Mac OS X search utility that, much like Search in Windows, is a live search, so it starts presenting results as soon as you start typing. (7)

spyware A category of software that runs surreptitiously on a user's computer, gathers information without permission from the user, and then sends that information to the people or organizations that requested the information. (2)

Standard account In OS X, an account type that can only access files in that user's Home folder and the Shared folder and is denied access to higher-level system settings. (7)

standard user account An account for an "ordinary" user without administrator status. (2)

Start button A button on the Windows 7 taskbar that opens the Start menu. In Windows 8.1 the Start button has been returned to the Desktop taskbar, but only returns you to the Start screen. It also displays in the Smart screen when a mouse is pointed at the bottom left corner. (5)

Start screen The Windows 8 home screen that contains rectangular tiles that you tap with a finger (on touch screens) or click with a mouse to launch the related apps. These tiles replace the old desktop shortcuts and are called live tiles. (5)

Startup Repair A Windows recovery tool that will scan for problems with missing or damaged system files and attempt to replace the problem files. (4)

static IP address An IP address that is manually configured for a host and can, therefore, be considered semipermanent—that is, it stays with the device until someone takes action to change it. (10)

storage virtualization Utilizing many hard drives as though they are one. (3)

subkey In the Windows registry, a key that exists within another key. (6)

subnet mask An important IP configuration parameter as critical as the address itself, because it takes what looks like a single address and divides it into two addresses by masking off part of the address. (10)

Subscriber Identity Module (SIM) An integrated circuit card that, when inserted into a mobile device, programs it for a customer's use on a cellular network. (11)

switch A Windows Command Prompt command-line parameter that begins with a slash (/). (9)

Switcher A black bar containing thumbnail images of all active apps that slides out of the left edge of the screen after a mouse drag from edge corner. (5)

switch users A feature of most operating systems that allows the currently logged-on users to leave their apps and data open in memory, switching away so that another user can log in to a separate session. (8)

synchronize To match the contents of two locations, sometimes in both directions, so that the contents match. (11)

syntax A set of rules for correctly entering a specific command at the command line. The rules include the placement of the command name and the parameters that you can use to modify the behavior of the command. (9)

System Image Recovery A Windows recovery tool that will let you restore a complete PC Image backup, provided you created one. This is a replacement for the Automated System Recovery (ASR) tool previously found in Windows XP. (4)

System Preferences The OS X equivalent of the Windows Control Panel. (7)

System Recovery Command Prompt A command prompt accessed by starting a computer from the Windows 7 disc and navigating through the menus to the Recovery Options screen and select Command Prompt. (9)

System Restore A recovery tool that creates restore points, which are snapshots of Windows, its configuration, and all installed programs. If your computer has nonfatal problems after you have made a change, you can use System Restore to roll it back to a restore point. (4)

tablet A mobile computing device with a touch screen, usually no integrated keyboard, and is larger than a smartphone and much more portable than a laptop. (1)

Tap to Send A Windows 8 feature that sends data wirelessly to a compatible nearby device when the user taps on a special area on the exterior of the device. The device must include a Near Field Communication (NFC) chipset. (5)

task management An operating system function in multitasking OSs that controls the focus. The user can switch between tasks by bringing an application to the foreground, which gives the focus to that application. (1)

Task Manager A program for removing errant programs. This Windows utility allows you to see the state of the individual processes and programs running on the computer and to stop one of them, if necessary. (4)

TCP/IP A suite of protocols that work together to allow both similar and dissimilar computers to communicate. This protocol suite is needed to access the Internet and is the most common protocol suite used on private intranets. It gets its name from two of its many protocols: Transmission Control Protocol (TCP) and Internet Protocol (IP)—the core protocols of TCP/IP. (10)

Terminal A window in the OS X GUI that provides a command-line interface (CLI) for entering UNIX shell commands. The default Terminal shell is BASH. (9)

terminal client Software on a computer that establishes a connection to a terminal server. (3)

terminal services Software running on servers to which user connect from their desktop PCs using terminal client software. (3)

terminal window A window in a Linux GUI that provides a command-line interface (CLI) for entering Linux shell commands. (8)

tethering A. feature that allows you to share your smartphone's cellular data connection with a single computer. The actual connection to the computer, laptop, or tablet can be via USB cable, Wi-Fi, or Bluetooth. Tethering mode turns your phone into a cellular modem. (11)

thin client A minimally configured network computer. (3)

third-party cookie A cookie that originates with a domain name beyond the one shown in the URL for the current Web page. (2)

thumbnail A small graphic image representing a larger object, such as an open app or screen. (5)

Time Machine An OS X backup utility that automatically backs up files to a dedicated drive that is always available when the computer is turned on. (7)

token A physical device that can be used in authentication, either alone or together with a user name and password. (2)

touch mouse A mouse pointing device that responds to touch gestures on the surface of the mouse, in addition to the typical mouse features. (5)

touchpad A pointing device that responds to finger touch gestures. They are in most laptops and come as separate wireless and USB devices. (5)

Transmission Control Protocol (TCP) The protocol responsible for the accurate delivery of messages, verifying and resending pieces that fail to make the trip from source to destination. Several other protocols act as subprotocols, helping TCP accomplish this. (10)

Trojan horse A program that is installed and activated on a computer by appearing to be something harmless, which the user innocently installs. This is a common way that a virus or a worm can infect a computer. (2)

Trusted Boot A Windows 8 feature that examines each of the system files loaded during the boot process before it is loaded into memory. (6)

Type I hypervisor A hypervisor that can run directly on a computer without an underlying host operating system—sometimes called a bare-metal hypervisor. (3)

Type II hypervisor A Type II hypervisor requires a host operating system. (3)

Ubuntu A group of Linux distributions supported by a company named Canonical. (8)

Unified Extensible Firmware Interface (UEFI) A system firmware standard that replaced the three-decades-old ROM BIOS. (1)

Upgrade An installation of an OS that installs directly into the folders in which a previous version of was installed, preserving all your preferences and data. (4)

Upgrade Advisor A compatibility checker that you can run from the Microsoft website and run before upgrading to a new version of Windows. (4)

user account A record in an accounts database that represents a single person and that is used for authentication. (2)

User Account Control (UAC) A security feature that prevents unauthorized changes to Windows. A user logged on with a privileged account with administrative rights only has the privileges of a standard account until the user (or a malicious program) attempts to do something that requires higher privileges. (2)

user interface (UI) The software layer, sometimes called the shell, through which the user communicates with the OS, which, in turn, controls the computer. (1)

user right In Windows, the privilege to perform a system-wide function, such as access the computer from the network, log on locally, log on to a computer from the network, back up files, change the system time, or load and unload device drivers. (2)

value entry A setting within a Windows registry key. (6)

vector A mode of malware infection, such as email, code on websites, Trojan horses, searching out unprotected computers, sneakernet, back doors, rootkits, pop-up downloads, drive-by downloads, war driving, and Bluesnarfing. (2)

version A unique level of an operating system or other software. (1)

virtual desktop infrastructure (VDI) Hosting and managing multiple virtual desktops on network servers. (3)

virtual keyboard An onscreen image of a keyboard with labeled keys that you can tap. (1)

virtual machine A software simulation of a computer. In Windows, when a DOS application is launched, the OS creates a DOS virtual machine that simulates both the hardware of a PC and the DOS operating system. When a 16-bit (Windows 3.*x*) Windows application is launched, Windows creates a virtual machine that includes the Windows 3.*x* OS. (3)

virtual machine monitor (VMM) Another name for hypervisor. A software layer that emulates the necessary hardware for an operating system to run in. (3)

virtual memory A system of memory management in which the OS moves programs and data in and out of memory as needed. (1)

virtual private network (VPN) A virtual tunnel created between two end points over a real network or internetwork. This is done by encapsulating the packets. Other security methods are also usually applied, such as encryption of the data and encrypted authentication. When set up in combination with properly configured firewalls, a VPN is the safest way to connect two private networks over the Internet. (10)

virtual reality When a virtual environment includes three-dimensional images and involves other senses, giving the participant a feeling of actually being present in that time and space. (3)

virtual world An online simulated communal environment within which users, often using an animated computer-generated human (avatar), can interact with one another and create and use various objects. (3)

virtualization The creation of an environment that seems real, but isn't. (3)

virus In the broadest sense, a virus is the term used for all malware, as it is a program that is installed and activated on a computer without the knowledge or permission of the user. At the least the intent is mischief, but most often it is genuinely damaging in one way or another. (2)

war driving The act of moving through a neighborhood in a vehicle or on foot, using either a laptop equipped with Wi-Fi wireless network capability or a simple Wi-Fi sensor available for a few dollars from many sources. War drivers seek to exploit open hotspots, areas where a Wi-Fi network connects to the Internet without the use of security to keep out intruders. (2)

warm boot Restarting a computer without a power-down and power-up cycle. (5)

Web An acronym for the term World Wide Web (WWW). (8)

Web-based installer An online installer, available through the Microsoft website for upgrading to Windows 8. (5)

Web browser A special type of client software used to navigate the Web. Examples include Firefox, Chrome, Safari, and Internet Explorer. (10)

Web mail A generic term for Web-based email services such as Hotmail, Gmail, and Yahoo! that keep your messages stored on the Internet, allowing you to access them via a Web browser from any computer. (10)

wide area network (WAN) A network that covers a very large geographic area (miles). (10)

wildcard A symbol that replaces any character or string of characters as a parameter in a CLI command. (8)

Windows 8.1 An update to Windows 8 released in late 2013. (5)

Windows 8 *Basic* One of two Windows 8 editions designed for the traditional Intel/AMD computer architecture. This edition is comparable to Windows 7 Home or Home Premium editions, containing features the typical home user would need. *Basic* is not officially part of the name, but used in this book to distinguish this edition from the Windows 8 version in general. (5)

Windows 8 Pro Comparable to Windows 7 Professional and Windows 7 Ultimate, this edition is aimed at individuals with more advanced needs, at home or in a small office. (5)

Windows Aero Microsoft's name for a group of GUI desktop features and visual themes introduced in Windows Vista. (4)

Windows Defender A free built-in antispyware product now integrated into the Windows 7 Action Center where you can configure spyware scanning and updates. In Windows 8, this is an improved product with added capabilities that make it a multifunction security program. (4)

Windows Easy Transfer (WET) A utility that will transfer your data, email, and settings for the Windows desktop and your applications from an old installation of Windows to Windows 7. (4)

Windows Explorer The primary tool for copying, moving, renaming, and deleting files in Windows. (4)

Windows Flip A feature of Windows that is activated when you press and hold the ALT KEY while tapping the TAB KEY. It displays a rectangle across the middle of the screen that shows all running apps, including individual Desktop apps. (5)

WINDOWS KEY (⊞) A key located near the bottom left of most keyboards that displays a Windows logo and is used in combination with other keys to create keyboard shortcuts. (5)

Windows Media Center (WMC). A Microsoft app for managing and playing several forms of digital media including DVDs. (5)

Windows Media Player (WMP). A Microsoft app for managing and playing several forms of digital media, but does not play DVDs. (5)

Windows Memory Diagnostic Tool A Windows recovery tool that tests the system's RAM because RAM problems can prevent Windows from starting. (4)

Windows Preinstallation Environment (Windows PE) A scaled-down Windows operating system. Much like the old Windows Setup program, it has limited drivers for basic hardware and support for the NTFS file system, TCP/IP, certain chipsets, mass storage devices, and 32-bit and 64-bit programs. Windows PE supports the Windows Setup GUI, collecting configuration information. (4)

Windows Recovery Environment (Windows RE) A powerful group of Windows diagnostics and repair tools that runs in the Windows Preinstallation Environment (Windows PE). (6)

Windows RT A Windows 8 edition that does not run on the traditional Intel/AMD computer architecture, but comes preinstalled on tablets based on the ARM processor architecture. (5)

Windows setup The traditional program for installing and upgrading Windows. (5)

Windows SmartScreen A feature based on the SmartScreen feature of Internet Explorer 9. No longer just part of the Internet Explorer browser, it runs at the OS level so that it protects against malicious downloads from any source, such as browsers, email, and even your local network or locally attached drives. SmartScreen uses special sensing features, as well as an online service to determine if software is malicious. (5)

Windows Store An online retail site that sells Windows 8 and Windows 8 apps. (5)

Windows Update A Windows program that can automatically connect to the Microsoft site and download and install updates. (4)

Windows XP Mode Introduced in Windows 7; Windows Virtual PC with a free and legal Windows XP VM preinstalled. (3)

wireless LAN (WLAN) A local area network using one of the standards referred to as Wi-Fi (for wireless fidelity). The Wi-Fi standards of the Institute of Electrical and Electronics Engineers (IEEE) include 802.11a, 802.11b, 802.11g, 802.11n, and 802.11ac. The distance covered by a WLAN is measured in a few hundred feet rather than miles. (10)

wireless wide area network (WWAN) A digital wireless network that extends over a large geographical area. (10)

World Wide Web (WWW) The graphical Internet consisting of a vast array of documents located on millions of specialized servers worldwide. (8)

worm A self-replicating computer virus. (2)

X Window See *X Window System.* (8)

X Window System The program code used as the basis for many GUIs for Linux or UNIX. (8)

zero-day exploit An exploit that a software vulnerability in an operating system or application such as those we study in this book is found that is unknown to the publisher of the targeted software. (2)

zombie An individual computer in a botnet. (2)

zone In Internet Explorer, an area that contains one or more websites to which you can assign restrictions that control how Internet Explorer handles cookies. A zone may be an area such as the Internet or local intranet or a list of sites grouped together, as in trusted sites and restricted sites. (10)

Photo Credits

Chapter 1

Opener: © Fuse/Getty Images; p. 2: Courtesy of Hewlett-Packard; p. 4 (top): Courtesy of Toshiba; p. 4 (bottom): © Joseph Branston/MacFormat magazine via Getty Images; p. 10 (mouse): Computer History Museum; p. 10 (researchers): Courtesy of Alcatel-Lucent; p. 10 (Xerox): © Xerox/Getty Images; p. 10 (Altos): © Mark Richards/ZUMAPRESS/Newscom; p. 11 (processor): CPU collection Konstantin Lanzet; p. 11 (MITS), p. 11 (Apple I): © SSPL/Getty Images; p. 11 (Jobs and Wozniak): © DB Apple/picture-alliance/dpa/Newscom; p. 11 (Gates and Allen): © Microsoft/ZUMApress/Newscom; p. 12 (Apple II): © Time & Life Pictures/Getty Images; p. 12 (CD): © Howard Kingsnorth/Getty Images; p. 12 (IBM PC): © Bettmann/Corbis; p. 13 (Macintosh): © INTERFOTO/Alamy; p. 13 (IBM PC): © imago stock&people/Newscom; p. 14 (IBM Convertible), p. 17 (PalmPilot): © SSPL/Getty Images; p. 17 (iMac): AP Photo/HO; p. 18 (Jaguar), p. 19 (Tiger): Courtesy of Apple; p. 20 (Jobs with iPhone): © Tony Avelar/AFP/Getty Images; p. 20 (Snow Leopard): Courtesy of Apple; p. 20 (iPad): © Simon Lees/PC Plus Magazine via Getty Images; p. 21 (Surface): © FocusDigital/Alamy.

Chapter 2

Opener: © Chad Baker/Ryan McVay/Getty Images; p. 41: © Carol and Mike Werner/Alamy; p. 44: Courtesy of www.keycobra.com; p. 48: © Henrik Kettunen/Alamy; p. 50: © Troy Aossey/Getty Images; p. 51 (thief): © Image Source/Getty Images; p. 51 (spill): © R and R Images/Photographer's Choice/Getty Images; p. 53: © Comstock Images/Getty Images; p. 54: © artpartner.de/Alamy.

Chapter 3

Page 85: Rutherford Appleton Laboratory and the Science Technology Facilities Council.

Chapter 4

Opener: © Eloy Alonso/Reuters.

Chapter 5

Page 169: © Jane Holcombe.

Chapter 6

Opener: © Jan Stromme/The Image Bank/Getty Images.

Chapter 7

Opener: © Brian Kersey/Stringer/Getty Images.

Chapter 8

Opener: © Image Source/Corbis.

Chapter 10

Opener: © Yuriy Panyukov/Alamy.

Appendix A

Opener: © Reuters/Corbis.

Index

Note: Figures and tables are indicated by *f* or *t* following a page number.

Symbols

$ prompt, 312–313, 353
.. (double dot), 318
>> (double greater-than sign), 342
/ (forward bracket), 318
> (greater-than sign), 342, 409
. (single dot), 318
~ (tilde), 316
| (vertical bar), 342
* (wildcard), 319, 347
? (wildcard), 347–348

Numbers

32-bit OS, 9
64-bit OS, 9

A

Absolute paths, 317
Accelerometers, 30, 31
Access Control Entry (ACE), 155, 454
Access Control List (ACL), 155, 454
Access mode numbers, 324–325, 325*t*
Accidents, protecting against, 51–52
Account pictures, 192
Action Center, 135, 135*f*
Activation, 121–122, 173
Add Printer wizard, 145
Address space layout randomization
    (ASLR), 279
Administrative Tools, 450
Administrator accounts, 153
Administrator account type, 67, 281
Administrator Command Prompt,
    334, 336
Administrators
    passwords of, 71
    security issues, 42, 46, 55, 62–64, 68
    troubleshooting security, 76
Advanced Boot Options Menu, 235–238,
    236*f*
Adware, 45
Aero Shake, 131
Aero Snap, 131
Airplane mode, 428
AirPlay, 277
Allen, Paul, 11, 13

AMD, 166, 170
AMD Virtualization, 86
Analog modems, 379–380
Android, 5, 30, 429–430, 431, 433, 437–441
Anonymous FTP sites, 398
Antivirus software, 60
Apache HTTP Server, 296
Apache OpenOffice, 298
Apple
    founding of, 254
    OSs for, 16–17, 254 (*see also* OS X)
    security threats to, 277
Apple App Store, 431, 432*f*
Apple Boot Camp, 106–107, 254
Apple I, 11, 254
Apple II, 3–4, 11, 12, 14, 254
Apple ID, 422–423
Apple iOS, 5, 431, 433–435, 438–439
Apple Lisa, 16, 254
Apple Macintosh, 13, 16, 254
Apple menu, 258, 264, 264*f*
Apple operating systems, 4
Apple Safari. *See* Safari
Apple Time Capsule, 257
Apple TV, 277
Applications (apps)
    defined, 2
    installing, 145, 197–198, 198*f*
    killer, 14, 15–16
    managing, 197–199
    mobile devices, 32, 33*f*, 431–432
    moving between, 192–193
    OS X, 262–263, 272
    quitting, 285
    removing, 146
    switching, 272
    updating, 145, 199
    Windows 7, 145–146
    Windows 8, 192–193, 192*f*, 197–199
Application virtualization, 84–85
AppLocker, 137
Archive, 348
ARM architecture, 166, 169–170
ARPANET, 10, 12
Asimov, Isaac, 1
Assigned Access, 204
Asynchronous digital subscriber line
    (ADSL), 380–381
AT&T, 295

Atkins, Sharon, 83
Attachments, 48
attrib command, 348–349, 349*f*
Authentication, 64–65
Authorization, 64–65
Autocompletion, 315
Automated System Recovery, 139,
    461, 461*f*
Automatic address assignment, 371–372
Automatic login, 65, 282
Automatic Private IP Addressing
    (APIPA), 371–372
Avatars, 84

B

Back doors, 42
Background, Windows 8, 192
Back tips, 193
Backup images, 187
Backups
    OS X, 257–258
    purpose of, 51–52
    registry, 217–220
    Windows 8, 187–188
    Windows XP Professional,
        461–465
Ballmer, Steve, 117
Banner ads, 50
Bare-metal hypervisors, 86
BASH shell, 297, 353, 358
BASIC computer language, 13, 15
Batch files, 345–346
BCD. *See* Boot Configuration Database
    (BCD)
BCDedit, 226
Bell Labs, 10, 11, 12
Berkeley Software Distribution, 11, 12
Berners-Lee, Tim, 15, 365
binary files, 213
Binary math, 373
Binding, 406
Bing, 193
BitLocker, 72–73, 137, 157–158, 170, 171
BitLocker Drive Encryption, 157–158
BitLocker To Go, 73, 137, 157, 170, 171
Bloatware, 187
Blue Screen of Death (BSOD), 465–466
Bluesnarfing, 43

Bluetooth, 31, 43, 426–427
Boot Configuration Database (BCD), 214, 226
Booting up, 6
Bootloader, 223
Boot logging, 237
Bootstrap loader, 223
Botherders, 45
Botnets, 45
Brin, Sergey, 17
Bring your own device (BYOD), 419–421
Broadband routers, 57
Browsers. *See* Web browsers
Browsing history, 389–390
Built-in user accounts, 66
Burning, 300
BYOD. *See* Bring your own device (BYOD)

C

Cable/DSL routers, 57
Cable modem service, 381
Caps lock, 75
Case awareness, 306, 339, 354
Case insensitivity, 339
Case sensitivity, 304, 307, 313, 354
cd command, 317–318, 359
cd private, 317
CD-ROM File System (CDFS), 137
CDs, burning, 150–151
Cellular Internet connectivity, 382
Cellular providers, 423
Central processing units (CPUs), 2
Certificates, 72
Change Password, 286
Charms, 185
Charms bar, 185
Child accounts, 203
Chinese People's Liberation Army, 40
Chips, 2
chmod command, 324
Chrome, 385, 386*f*, 388, 388*f*, 390–392, 390*f*, 392*f*, 394
Cisco Wireless-N Router, 57*f*
Citrix, 85–86, 88
Clean installations, 121
Clear command, 314, 355
CLI. *See* Command-line interface (CLI)
Click kiddies, 54
Client Hyper-V, 102–105, 170
Clients, 5
cmd.exe, 332, 334
CMOS, 223
Coaxial cable, 381
Code, malware in, 41
Code signing, 229, 448
Cold boot, 180
Column view, in Finder, 267, 268*f*
command.com, 332
Command completion, 315, 354, 358

Command-line history, 314, 358
Command-line interface (CLI), 6, 17, 294, 331–359
    Linux, 312–320
    OS X, 352–359
    reasons for learning/using, 331–332
    Windows, 332–352
Command processor, 6
Command Prompts, 332–352
    errors, 340*f*
    IP configuration examined from, 376–377
    tips for success, 339–352
    Windows 7, 333–336
    Windows 8, 336–338
Commands
    canceling, 342
    interpretation of, 340–341
    Linux, 313–320, 316*t*
    OS X, 354–359
    syntax, 344–345
    Windows, 340–341
Commodore PET, 4, 11
Compact discs, 12
Compatibility
    checking, 122
    program, in Windows 7, 137–138, 143
    program, in Windows 8, 175–177
    program, in Windows XP Professional, 466–467
Computer accounts, 68
Computer management, Windows 7, 139–140
Computer professionals (techs), 17
Computers
    defined, 2
    old, Linux compatible with, 296
    security threats to, 40–54
config, 213, 213*f*
Connected Standby, 169
Connectivity, 31
    wired, 379–381
    wireless, 381–384
Consent Prompt, 69, 229
Content filtering, 63
Control button, 195
Control center, 428
Control Panel, 146
Cookies, 50, 62, 388–389
Cooper, Martin, 10
Copy, 269
Coughlin, Tom, 74
Cover Flow view, in Finder, 268, 268*f*
cp command, 319–320
Crackers, 53
Crashes, system, 287
Credentials, 280
Credentials Prompt, 69, 229
csrss.exe, 224

Cursors, 6
Cybercrimes, 40

D

Daemons, 323
Darwin, 254
Dash, 305, 305*f*
Dashboard, 274
Data management. *See* File management
Data protection, 438
Data synchronization, 33
Data transmission speed, 379–383
data types, 217
Data wiping, 73–74
Debugging Mode, 238
Default gateway, 373
DEFAULT hive, 214, 214*f*
Default save location, 149
Defense Advanced Research Projects Agency (DARPA), 366
Definition files, 60
Delete, 269
Deleted files, restoring, 196–197
Delimiter characters, 340
Denial-of-service attacks, 54, 407
Desktop
    Windows 7, 130–135, 140–145
    Windows 8, 194–197, 194*f*
Desktop computers, 4
    OSs for, 12–25
Desktop virtualization, 84
Detect and Configure hardware, 223
Developers, 6
Device drivers, 3, 8–9
    installing, 229–230
    managing, 230–234
    security, 225
    signed vs. unsigned, 229–230
    Windows 8, 178, 183–184
Device management, 8–9
Device Manager, 231–234, 245–246, 246*f*, 247*f*, 441
Devices, 245–246, 246*f*
Devices and Printers Control Panel, 144*f*, 230–231, 230*f*
Device Stage, 231, 231*f*
Dial-up connectivity, 379–380
Digital certificates, 72
Digital Equipment Corporation, 11
Digital signatures, 229, 279
Digital subscriber line (DSL), 380–381
Directories, 8
    Linux, 306–308, 306*t*, 315–318, 325–326
    Windows Command Prompt, 346–352
Directory Services Restore Mode, 238
Disable automatic restart on system failure, 238

Disabled components, 263
Disable driver signature enforcement, 238
Disasters, protecting against, 51–52
Disk Management, 139–140, 139f
Disk operating system (DOS), 332
Disk Utility, 287
Display resolution, 140–142
    See also Screen resolution
Display settings, 140–143
Distributions, 29
DMZ, 58
DNS errors, 410–411
Dock, 259, 272, 353
Domain Join, 171
Domain Name System (DNS), 373–374
DOS, 17, 332
DOS prompt, 6, 6f
Double greater-than sign (>>), 342
Drive-by downloads, 42
Drivers. *See* Device drivers
Driver signing, 229–230, 238, 448
Dual-boot installations, 120
Dumb terminals, 85
DVDs, 17, 150–151
Dynamic Host Configuration Protocol
    (DHCP) server, 371–372

E

Early Launch Anti-Malware (ELAM),
    225, 229
Edge gestures, 192
Editions, 19
Email, 394–397, 428–431
Email spoofing, 48
Email vectors, 41
Embedded OSs, 4
Encrypted authentication, 57t
Encrypting File System (EFS), 72, 72f,
    170, 458
Encryption, 71–74
    OS X, 258, 279
    Windows 7, 157–158
    Windows XP Professional,
        458–459
Engelbart, Douglas, 10
etc directory, 317f
Ethernet, 367
Exchange mail services, 431
Exit command, 312
Exploits, 40
explorer.exe, 237
Exposé, 274
Extended File Allocation Table (exFAT)
    file system, 136
External commands, 341

F

Facebook, 40–41
Family Safety, 203, 204f

Fast Boot, 225
Fatal errors, 465
FAT file systems, 136, 140
Federal Trade Commission Bureau of
    Consumer Protection, 52, 52f
Fedora, 296–298, 300, 303
Feedback, in Linux, 315
File allocation table (FAT), 136
File and printer servers, 399–400
File and print service, 5
File attributes, 348, 349f
File Explorer, 184, 195–196, 195f, 196f
    See also Windows Explorer
File extensions, 148
File history, 187–188, 188f, 197
File management, 8
    Linux, 316–320
    OS X, 264–265
    Windows 7, 146–150
    Windows 8, 195–196
    Windows Command Prompt,
        349–351
File name extensions, 347
Files
    security, 155–157, 454–460
    sharing, 398–404
    Windows Command Prompt,
        346–352
File servers, 5
File signature verification, 229
File systems, 8, 316–319
File Transfer Protocol (FTP), 398
FileVault, 73, 73f, 258, 279, 279f
Finder, 264–268, 266f
Find My Phone, 441–442
finger command, 323
Firefox, 385, 386–387, 387f, 389–391, 389f,
    393, 393f, 394
FireFTP, 386, 399f
Firewalls, 56–60
    network-based, 56–58, 58f
    OS X, 278, 278f
    personal, 59–60, 159
    router, 159
    technologies, 57t
    Windows 7, 159
FireWire, 257
Firmware, 3, 223, 258
First-party cookies, 50
Fisher, Tim, 342
Flash drives, 8
    encryption, 157
    file systems, 136
    malware on, 42
Flat-panel displays, 184
Flip 3D, 130–131, 131f, 193
Floppy disks, 10, 42, 137
Floppy drives, 13
Folders, 8
    creating and managing, in OS X,
        270–271, 273

Linux, 316
    security, 155–157, 454–460
Force Quit, 285
Forged email addresses, 48
Formatting, 8
Fraud, 46
FreeBSD, 300
FreeDOS, 332
Freezing, of apps, 285, 286
FTP. *See* File Transfer Protocol (FTP)
Fully qualified domain name (FQDN),
    410, 410f
Fung, Brian, 379

G

Gadgets, 143
Garman, Steven R., 1
Gatekeeper, 278–279, 279f
Gates, Bill, 1, 11, 13, 15
Gimmes, 48
GNOME GUI, 297, 298
GNU, 294–295
GNU C Compiler, 29
Google, founding of, 17
Google accounts, 421–422
Google Android. *See* Android
Google Chrome. *See* Chrome
Graphical user interface (GUI), 7f, 294
    IP configuration examined in,
        374–375
    Linux, 6, 296–298, 297f, 303–312
    Windows 8, 27–28, 165–168
Greater-than sign (>), 342, 409
Group accounts, 67–68, 68f
Group Policy, 171
Guest accounts, 66, 282
Guest OSs, 85

H

Hackers, 52–53
hardware
    detecting and configuring, in
        startup phase, 223
    major changes to, 121
    standards, 366
hardware abstraction layer (HAL), 223
Headers, 48
Heads-up program switcher, 272
Health Insurance Portability and
    Accountability Act (HIPAA), 40
Help Center, for OS X, 284
Help command, 342–344
Help manual, 314
Hibernate, 222
Hidden files and extensions, 213, 348
Hidden icons, 134
Hives, 213
Hoaxes, 48
Home directories, 306

Home folders, 264–265, 265f
HomeGroups, 399–403
Host ID, 373
Host keys, 87
Host OS, 85
Hosts, 370
Hotspots, 42–43
Hughes, Gordon, 74
Hybrid Shutdown, 222, 225
Hypertext Transfer Protocol (HTTP), 296
Hypervisors, 86–88, 303

I

IBM, 10, 295
    OS/2, 18–19
IBM PCs, 15
iCloud, 422, 423, 441–442
Icon view, in Finder, 266, 266f
Identity theft, 48–49
ifconfig command, 376–377, 377f, 405
Images, 121
IMAP email account, 395, 428–429
Inappropriate/distasteful content, 49
Incognito, 391
Information Technology
    professionals, 294
In-place installations, 120
InPrivate Browsing, 391–392
Input/output (I/O), 2–3
Installation
    applications, 145, 197–198, 198f
    device drivers, 229–230
    Linux, 300, 303
    OS X, 257–262
    printers, 144–145, 276
    Windows 7, 118–129
    Windows 8, 171–183
Institute of Electrical and Electronics
    Engineers (IEEE), 366, 384
Integrated circuits (ICs), 2
Integrated services digital network
    (ISDN), 380
Intel, 10, 166, 170
Intel Virtualization Technology for
    x86, 86
Interactive users, 152
Internal commands, 341
Internet
    computer-to- vs. LAN-to-,
        378–379
    connecting to, 378–384, 379f
    firewalls, 159
    term first used, 12
Internet Assigned Numbers Authority
    (IANA), 370
Internet clients, 385–398
    email, 394–397
    FTP, 398
    Web browsers, 385–394

Internet Corporation for Assigned
    Names and Numbers (ICANN),
    373–374
Internet Engineering Task Force (IETF),
    366
Internet Explorer, 61–62, 62f, 385, 387,
    387f, 389–394, 389f, 393f
Internet Message Access Protocol
    (IMAP), 395, 428–429
Internet Protocol (IP), 367–377
        addressing fundamentals,
            367–372, 369f
        configuration settings, 372–377,
            372f
        IPv4, 367–371
        IPv6, 367, 369
        overview, 367
Internet routers, 371
Internet servers, 381
Internet service providers (ISPs), 378
Internetwork, 367
"In the wild," 45
Invasion of privacy, 49–50
iPad, 20, 429, 440
IP addresses, 368–371
ipconfig command, 376, 404–406
IP configurations, testing, 405–409
iPhone, 20
iPod Touch, 30
IP packet filter, 57t
IPv4, 367–371
IPv5, 369
IPv6, 367, 369, 369f
ISO images, 179
iTunes, 422, 433–435

J

Job management, 6–7
Jobs, Steve, 11, 12, 16, 253, 254
Journals, for recording configuring or
    troubleshooting process, 235
Jump drives, 8
Jump Lists, 131–134, 132f

K

Kapor, Mitch, 13
KDE GUI, 297, 297f
Kernel, 6, 279, 295, 298
Kernel loading, 223–224
Keyboards. See On-screen keyboards
Keyboard shortcuts, 168, 469–471
Keychain Access, 280
Keychains, 280, 286
Keys, 216
Keystroke loggers, 44
Kickoff Application Launcher, 297
Kildall, Gary, 11
Killer apps, 14, 15–16
Kiosk computers, 204

L

LAN Manager, 21
LANs. See Local area networks
    (LANs)
Laptops, 4
Laser printers, 14
Last Known Good (LKG)
    Configuration, 237–238
Latency, in Internet connections, 383
Launcher, 305
Launchpad, 273, 273f
Libraries, 135, 136f, 148–149
LibreOffice, 298
Limited accounts, 66–67
LinkedIn, 41
Link-local address, 372
Linux, 15, 28–29, 29f, 293–326
    acquiring, 300–301
    authentication and authorization,
        64–65
    benefits of, 293, 294, 296–298
    browsers, 298
    command-line interface, 312–320
    commands, 313–320, 316t
    copying files, 319–320
    desktop modification, 309–311
    devices compatible with, 4
    directories, 306–308, 306t,
        315–318, 325–326
    downloading, 301–302
    drawbacks, 298–300
    ending sessions from GUI,
        311–312
    feedback in, 315
    file and folder permissions,
        324–325
    file system, 316–319
    firewall, 59
    folders, 316
    GUI for, 6, 296–298, 297f, 303–312
    Help manual, 314
    history of, 294–296
    installing, 300, 303
    logging in, 303–304
    options, 313–314, 316t
    overview, 294–300
    search function, 305–306, 306f
    security, 66–69, 297, 320–326
    speed of, 296
    system settings, 309
    updating, 308
    user management, 320–325, 322t
    virtual machines, 303
    word processors, 298
List view, in Finder, 267, 267f
Live File System, 151
Live images, 300–303
Live tiles, 167
Local accounts, 173–174, 181–182,
    201–202

Local Area Connection, 367, 368f
Local area networks (LANs), 31, 367, 378–379
Local security
    defined, 152
    files and folders, 155–157
    OS X, 277–284
    Windows 7, 137, 152–159
    Windows 8, 183
Location services, 420, 439–440
Lockout, 75–76
Lock screens, 189–190, 436–439
LOG, 214
Logging in, to Linux, 303–304
    See also Logon, to Windows XP
        Professional; Signing in,
        to Windows 8
Logging out, of Linux, 311
Logical drives, 8
Logon, to Windows XP Professional, 448
    See also Logging in, to Linux;
        Signing in, to Windows 8
Logon phase, 224
Logon problems, 75–76
Lohrmann, Dan, 421
Lotus 1-2-3, 13, 15, 16
Low-resolution video, 237
LSASS.EXE, 224
ls command, 314, 314f

M

Mac App Store, 259, 279
Macintosh, 4, 13, 16, 254, 277
Mac OS, 254
Mac OS X. See OS X
Mac OS X Server, 254
Mainframes, 12
Malware, 40–46, 76
man command, 314, 354–357
man ls command, 315f, 355
Manpage, 354–355
Mastered format, 151
Master file table (MFT), 137
Measured Boot, 225
Memory, 3
    OS use of, 9–10
    virtual, 8, 280
Memory dump, 466
Memory management, 8
Menu bar, 263
Menu Extras, 275, 276, 276f
Menulets, 276
Message headers, 394
Messaging services, 5
Metro GUI, 165
Microcomputers, 2
    origins of, 10
    OS functions, 5–9
    See also Personal computers (PCs)
Microprocessors, 2

Microsoft
    activation, 121–122
    founding of, 11
    registration, 121–122
    virtualization, 86, 88
Microsoft accounts, 173–174, 181–182, 201–202, 423
Microsoft Active Directory Domain, 174
Microsoft Enterprise Desktop
    Virtualization (MED-V), 93
Microsoft operating systems, 4
Microsoft Product Activation
    (MPA), 121
Microsoft Security Essentials, 99, 128, 159
Microsoft Software Assurance plan, 119
Microsoft Store, 170, 432
Microsoft Support Lifecycle, 25
Microsoft Virtual PC 2007, 88–93
Microsoft Windows. See entries
    beginning with Windows
MiFi, 426
MINIX, 295
Mission Control, 274, 275f
Mistakes, protecting against, 51–52
MITS Altair 8800, 13
mkdir command, 319, 358
Mobile device management (MDM), 421
Mobile devices, 4–5
    apps, 32, 33f, 431–432
    cellular networks, 423–424
    hardware features, 30
    history of, 418–419
    hotspots, 425–426
    lost or stolen, 441–442
    security, 32–33, 74, 436–442
    synchronization, 33
    tethering, 426–427
    updating, 436
    Wi-Fi networks, 424–425
    Windows 8 support for, 169
    in the workplace, 419–421
    See also Smartphones
Mobile hotspots, 425–426
Mobile operating systems, 4, 30–33, 30f
    connectivity, 31
    email, 428–431
    features, 31–33
    mobile device hardware, 30
    synchronization, 432–436
    user accounts and wireless
        connections, 421–428
Modems, 367, 379–380, 381, 383
more command, 318, 342
Motherboards, 3
Motorola, 10
Mouse, 10, 13, 167
Mouse actions, 167
Mouse shortcuts, 469–471
Mozilla Firefox. See Firefox

MSCONFIG, 245
MS-DOS, 17, 18f, 332
Multiboot installations, 120
Multiple displays, 142–143
Multitasking, 7
Multitouch, 166–167, 172

N

Names, for files and directories, 347
    See also Renaming
Near Field Communication (NFC), 169, 427
Negroponte, Nicholas, 211
Net ID, 373
netstat command, 410–411
Network access
    icons indicating, 134–135
    verifying, 128
Network address translation (NAT), 371
Network Diagnostics (Windows), 404
Network interface card (NIC), 178, 367, 371
Network operating system (NOS), 21
Network preferences, 287
Networks, 365–411
    configuring, 366–377
    connection to Internet, 378–385
    Internet clients, 385–398
    mobile devices, 423–426
    sharing files and printers, 398–404
    troubleshooting, 404–411
Network Utility (OS X), 405
Network virtualization, 84
New Virtual Machine Wizard, 89, 91, 104
NIC. See Network interface card (NIC)
Notification areas, 134–135, 135f, 263–264
Notification Center, 275, 275f
Novatel, 426
Novell, 21, 295
nslookup command, 411, 411f
NTBACKUP, 462–463
NTFS file systems, 22, 72, 72f, 136–137, 140, 155–157, 448, 454–459
ntoskrnl.exe, 223
ntuser.dat hive, 214

O

Object code, 295
Octets, 373
Online accounts, 71
Online virus scan, 76–77
On-screen keyboards, 168, 168f, 169
Open architecture, 211
Open-source software, 295–298
Open Systems Foundation, 295
Opera, 388

Operating systems (OSs)
  Apple, 16–17
  current, 26–29, 26t
  defined, 2
  embedded, 4
  finding type of, 9, 10
  functions, 5–9
  history of, 10–25
  IBM PC, 15
  memory, 9–10
  for mobile devices, 4, 30–33, 30f, 421–436
  portable, 11
  for servers, 5
  for smartphones, 4–5
  for tablets, 5
  virtualization of, 85
Optical discs
  burning, 150–151
  file management, 149–150
  file systems, 137
Optical drives, writing to, 137
Options, in Linux, 313–314, 316t
Oracle, 88
Oracle VirtualBox, 105, 107–112
Organized crime, 52
OS/2, 18–19
Osborne, Adam, 12
OSs. See Operating systems (OSs)
OS X, 28, 29f, 253–287
  applications, 262–263, 272
  authentication and authorization, 64–65
  backing up, 257–258
  changing settings, 271–272
  command-line interface, 352–359
  desktop, 264f
  devices compatible with, 4
  encryption, 73
  firewall, 59
  installing/upgrading, 257–262
  introduction of, 17
  locked dialog boxes, 69, 70f
  navigating and managing, 263–277
  post-installation tasks, 262–263
  printers, 276–277
  recommended system requirements, 257–258
  security, 66–69, 277–284
  troubleshooting, 284–287
  UNIX foundations of, 11, 12, 28, 254, 353
  upgrading, 258–262
  utilities, 287
  versions, 255–257, 255t
  virtual machines, 106–112
  Windows 7 on, 86, 86f
OS X Cheetah, 255
OS X Firewall, 278
OS X Lion, 286

OS X Mavericks, 28, 255, 258, 265
OS X Mountain Lion, 28, 255, 258, 259, 273, 274, 277–280
OS X Setup Assistant, 257
OS X Snow Leopard, 257, 258, 285–286
Outlook, 395
Out of Box Experience (OOBE), 180–183
Owners, file, 324, 325

P

Packet monkeys, 54
Packets, 367
Page, Larry, 17
pagefile.sys, 224
Pairing, 426–427, 427f
Palm webOS, 5
Palo Alto Research Center (PARC), 10, 12
Parallels, 88
Parameter, 313
Parental controls, 62–63, 63f, 281
Parsing, 340
Partitions, 8, 85, 106–107
Passcode lock, 436–439
Password crackers, 44
Password Reset disk, 450
Passwords
  best practices, 69–71
  defined, 43
  keychains, 280
  Linux, 323
  resetting, 285–286, 450
  security measures, 55, 65–66, 70–71
  stealing, 43–44
  strong, 55, 66, 70–71
  Web browsers, 392–394
  Windows XP Professional, 450
Paste, 269
Patching, 436
path command, 341
Paths, 306
PC DOS, 17
PC Settings screen, 186
Permissions
  assigning, 69
  defined, 65
  device drivers, 229
  files and folders, 155–157, 156f, 156t, 324–325, 454–458
  inheritance of, 455
  Linux, 324–325
  NTFS, 155, 157, 454–458
  printers, 459–460
  Windows XP Professional, 454–458
Personal computers (PCs)
  defined, 4
  introduction of, 15
  See also Microcomputers

Personal digital assistants (PDAs), 17
Personal folders, 147
Personal identification number (PIN), 438
Phishing, 46–48
Phone phreaking, 53
Picture Tools, 196f
ping command, 405, 406–407, 410
Pinning, 131–134, 132f
Pipe symbol (|), 342
Piping, 342
Plug and play, 229, 230
Plug-and-play detection, 224
Pocket dialing, 189–190, 436
POP email account, 395, 428–429
Pop-up blockers, 61, 61f, 394
Pop-up downloads, 42
Pop-ups, 42, 394
Portable operating systems, 11
Post-installation tasks
  OS X, 262–263
  Windows 7, 128–129
  Windows 8, 183–189
Post Office Protocol (POP), 395, 428–429
power-on self-test (POST), 3, 223
PowerShell, 332–333
Power usage/saving, 166, 169, 221–222
Power User menu, 171f, 189
Printers
  default, 231, 231f
  installing, 144–145, 276
  local, 144
  network, 144–145
  OS X, 276–277
  security, 459–460
  sharing, 398–404
  See also Devices and Printers Control Panel
Print Queue, 277
Print servers, 5
Privacy
  invasion of, 49–50
  protection of, 61–62
Private browsing, 390–392
Private IP addresses, 370, 370t
Processes, 7
Product key, 169f, 173, 174, 179–180
Program Compatibility Troubleshooter, 137–138
Program Compatibility wizard, 466–467
Programmers, 6
Program startup, 224
Protocols, 366
Protocol stack, 366
Proxy service, 57t, 371
Public folders, 403–404
Public IP addresses, 370
Public networks, 159, 159f
pwd command, 318, 359

Q

Quick Access toolbar, 195–196

R

Radio frequency (RF) signals, 428
Radio Shack TRS-80, 4
RAM disk, 335–336
Random-access memory (RAM), 3, 139
Read-only, 348
Read only memory basic input output
  system (ROM BIOS), 3, 223
Recovery keys, 279, 279f
Recovery Mode Command
  Prompt, 338
Recovery Tools, 138–139, 235–245
Recycle Bin, 196–197
Red Hat, 295, 296
Red Hat Enterprise Linux, 296
Redirection operators, 342, 409
Refresh recovery option, 244, 244f
Regedit, 215–217, 216f, 220
Regional Internet Registries (RIRs), 370
Registration, 121–122
Registry, 212–220
    automatic changes, 212
    backing up, 217–220
    components, 216f
    data types, 217t
    defined, 212
    files and folders, 213–215
    hives, 215, 215t
    root keys, 216f, 217t
    temporary portion, 215
    viewing and editing, 215–217
Registry locations, 216
Relative paths, 318
Remote access VPN, 384
Remote Desktop, 170
Remote Desktop client, 170
Remote Desktop host, 171
Remote wipe, 436
Remove everything option, 244
Removing
    applications, 146
    software, 187
Renaming, 269
Repair Your Computer, 235
Reserved characters, 346
Reserved names, 347
Reset command, 314
Reset Password, 286
Restart, 222
Restore points, 138–139, 200–201,
  217–220, 463–465, 464f
Restoring deleted files, 196–197
Return to OS Choices Menu, 238
Ribbon, 196
rm command, 324
robocopy command, 345, 352

Roddenberry, Gene, 417
ROM BIOS. See Read only memory
  basic input output system
  (ROM BIOS)
Root accounts, 282, 320
Root keys, 216
Rootkits, 42
Routers, 159, 368, 371, 373, 384, 406f
Rule of least privilege, 69, 334
Run as Administrator, 334, 334f

S

Safari, 265, 280, 385, 388
Safe Mode, 236–240
Safe Mode with Command Prompt, 237,
  334, 338
Safe Mode with Networking, 237
SAM hive, 215
Sandboxed, 279
Sarbanes-Oxley Act, 40
Satellite connectivity, 382–383, 384f
SAV, 214
Scareware, 41
Screen resolution, 184
    See also Display resolution
Screen rotation/acceleration, 31, 32f,
  33f, 169
Screen sharing, 199
Scripted installations, 121
Script kiddies, 53
Sculley, John, 253
Search
    Linux, 305–306, 306f
    Windows 8, 193, 194
Search paths, 341
Second-Level Address Translation
  (SLAT), 102
Secret keys, 71–72
Secure Boot, 225
Secure Erase, 74
Secure HTTP (HTTPS), 72
Secure Sockets Layer (SSL), 72
Secure Virtual Memory, 280
Security, 9, 39–77
    defenses, 54–74
    gadgets as threat to, 143
    Linux, 297, 320–326
    mobile devices, 32–33, 74,
      436–442
    physical, 74
    printers, 459–460
    software for, 55–56
    threats, 40–54
    troubleshooting, 74–77
    Web browsers, 388–394
    Windows 8, 200–204
    Windows XP Professional,
      448–460
    See also Local security
Security accounts, 66–69

Security certificates, 72
SECURITY hive, 215
Security patches, 41
Security policies, 55
Security software, 55–56, 56f, 128
Semantic zoom, 191
Sensor devices, 169
Servers, 5
    See also Internet servers
Server virtualization, 84
Service Set ID (SSID), 424
SERVICES.EXE, 224
Settings bar, 185
Shared folders, 281
Shares, 399
Sharing files and printers, 398–404
Sharing Only accounts, 282
Shell commands
    Linux, 297, 313–320, 316t,
      322–323
    OS X, 354–359
Shells, 6, 12, 29
Shortcuts
    desktop, 130, 130f
    mouse and keyboard, 469–471
Show Hidden Icons, 134
Shutdown, 220, 221f, 222, 312
Sidebar items, disappearance of, 286
Signing in, to Windows 8, 173–174,
  181–182, 182f
    See also Logging in, to Linux;
      Logon, to Windows XP
      Professional
Simple Mail Transfer Protocol (SMTP),
  428–429
Site-to-site VPN, 384
Slackware, 295
Sleep, 221
Smartphones
    cellular networks, 423–424
    connectivity of, 31, 381
    operating systems for, 4–5, 30
    See also Mobile devices
SmartScreen, 203
Snap, 168, 199
Sneakernet, 41–42
Social engineering, 46–48
Social media, 40–41
Social networking, 40–41
Social networking sites, 40
Social Security numbers, 71
Software
    Linux capabilities, 298
    standards, 366
SOFTWARE hive, 215
Software updates, 263
Software versions, 13–14
Solid-state drives (SSDs), 8
Source code, 295
Spaces, 274
Spam, 46

Spam filters, 60
Spear phishing, 47–48
Speed. *See* Data transmission speed;
   Linux: speed of
Spim, 46
Spotlight, 264
Spreadsheets, 14, 16
Spyware, 45
Standard account type, 281
Standard user accounts, 66–67
Standard-User Command Prompt, 336
Start button, 171, 171*f*
Start menus, Windows 7, 131–132
Start screen, Windows 8, 27*f*, 167, 167*f*,
   182, 183*f*, 190–192, 190*f*
Startup
      modifying, 225–228
      troubleshooting with modified,
         235–238
      Windows 7, 222–224, 226–228,
         235–238
      Windows 8, 223, 225, 226,
         241–245
      Windows Vista, 235–238
Startup Repair, 138
Start Windows Normally, 238
Static address assignment, 371
Stop errors, 465–466
Storage virtualization, 84
Subkeys, 216
Subnet masks, 372–373, 373*f*
Subscriber Identity Module (SIM),
   423–424
Subtrees, 216
sudo command, 323, 358, 359
Sudo shutdown now, 312
Sun Microsystems, 295
Super-user accounts, 282
Swap files, 280
Switcher, 193
Switches, 340
Switching users, 221, 312
Switch Users, 152
Synchronization, of data, 432–436
Synchronous digital subscriber line
   (SDSL), 380–381
Syntax, 344–345
System, 280
System Configuration Utility
   (MSCONFIG), 245
System Failure settings, 465–466
SYSTEM hive, 215
System Image Recovery, 139
System Preferences, 271, 271*f*
System Recovery Command Prompt,
   334–336
System Restore, 138–139, 217–220, 237,
   463–465, 464*f*
System Roots, 280
System Settings, 309
System trays, 134–135

T

Tablets, 5, 31, 424
Tap to Send, 169
Task bars, 131–132
Task management, 7
Task Manager, 138
Tasks, how to view, 7
TCP/IP, 13, 366–367
      See also Internet Protocol (IP)
Techs. *See* Computer professionals
   (techs)
Terminal (OS X), 352–359
Terminal clients, 85
Terminal services, 85
Terminal window (Linux),
   312, 313*f*
Tethering, 426–427
Theft
      hardware, 51
      identity, 48–49
      mobile computing, 74
Thin clients, 85
Third-party cookies, 50, 388
Thompson, Ken, 294
Threats, security
      accidents, mistakes, and
         disasters, 51–52
      defenses against, 54–74
      identity theft, 48–49
      keeping up-to-date on, 52, 63–64
      to Macs, 277
      malware, 40–46
      people behind, 52–54
      privacy issues, 49–50
      social engineering, 46–48
      theft, 51
      types, 40–54
      warning signs, 54–55
Thumb drives, 8
Thumbnails, 193
Thunderbolt, 257
Time Machine, 257–258
Tokens, 65
Torode, John, 11
Torvalds, Linus, 15, 28–29, 293, 295
Touch gestures, 167
Touch mouse, 167
Touchpads, 167
Touch screens, 31
tracert command, 409
Transceivers, 383
Transfer, of data and settings,
   122–123
Transmission Control Protocol (TCP),
   367
Trojan horses, 41
Troubleshooting
      device problems, 245–247
      log-on problems, 75–76
      with modified startups, 235–238

network client problems, 404–411
   OS X, 284–287
   security, 74–77
   Windows, 235–247
   Windows XP Professional,
      460–467
Trusted Boot, 223, 225
Twitter, 41
Type I hypervisors, 86
Type II hypervisors, 86–87

U

Ubuntu, 296, 298, 300, 303, 308, 311,
   320–322
Ubuntu Desktop, 304–305
Ubuntu Software Center, 299, 299*f*
UEFI. *See* Unified Extensible Firmware
   Interface (UEFI)
Undeleting, 73
Unified Extensible Firmware Interface
   (UEFI), 3, 223, 225
Uninstall. *See* Removing
Unity GUI, 298, 299*f*, 304–305, 308, 311,
   312, 313*f*, 320–322
Universal Disk Format (UDF), 137
UNIX, 10, 11–12, 28, 254, 294–295, 353
UNIX International, 295
Unprotected computers, 41
Updateability, 32
Updates
      applications, 145, 199
      installation, 128–129
      Linux, 308
      mobile operating systems, 436
Upgrade Advisor, 122
Upgrade Assistant, 174, 175, 177–178
Upgrades
      OS X, 258
      Windows 7, 119–120
      Windows 8, 172, 174–175,
         177–178
U.S. Department of Commerce, 373
User Account Control (UAC), 68–69,
   137, 155
User accounts, 66, 67*f*
      creating/deleting, 282–284
      Linux, 320–325
      mobile devices, 421–423
      OS X, 280–284
      Windows 7, 152–155
      Windows 8, 201–203
      Windows XP Professional,
         448–454
User interface (UI), 6
User logon, 224
User names, 70
User rights, 65
Users
      interactive, 152
      security threats to, 40–54

V

Value entries, 216
Vectors, 40–43
Versions, 13–14
Vertical bar (|), 342
Video Graphics Array (VGA), 14
VirtualBox, 303
Virtual desktop infrastructure (VDI), 85–86
Virtualization, 83–112
  current situation, 85–88
  defined, 84
  history of, 85
  mobile device management, 421
  OS X, 106–112
  overview, 84–88
  types, 84–85
  Windows desktops, 88–106
Virtual keyboards, 31, 32f
Virtual machine additions, 129
Virtual machine monitors (VMMs), 86
Virtual machines, 84
  Linux, 303
  OS X, 106–112
  Windows 8, 187
  Windows desktops, 88–106
Virtual memory, 8, 280
Virtual private network (VPN), 57t, 384, 385f
Virtual reality, 84
Virtual worlds, 84
Viruses, 15, 44–45, 76–77
  See also Antivirus software
VisiCalc, 12, 14, 16
VMware, 85–86, 88
Volume labels, 348
VPN. See Virtual private network (VPN)

W

War driving, 43
Warm boot, 180
Wayne, Ronald, 254
Web-based installers, 174
Web browsers, 16, 385–394
  browsing history, 389–390
  Chrome, 386
  common features, 386
  cookies, 388–389
  hijacking, 45–46
  Linux, 298
  passwords, 392–394
  pop-ups, 394
  private browsing, 390–392
  security, 388–394
Web-hosting services, 381
Web mail, 395
Webservices, 5
Websites, malware in code on, 41

White-hat hackers, 53
Wide area networks (WANs), 31, 378
Wi-Fi networks and connectivity, 31, 42–43, 367, 381, 384, 424–425
Wildcards, 318–319, 347–348
Wilson, Ray, 447
Windows, 19–25
  authentication and authorization, 64–65
  command-line interface, 332–352
  device drivers, 229–234
  editions, 19
  firewall, 59
  power options, 221–222
  recovery tools, 235–245
  registry, 212–220
  security, 66–69
  troubleshooting, 235–247
  troubleshooting security, 76
  user options, 221
  versions, 19
  virtual machines, 88–106
Windows 1–3, 20
Windows 3.0, 20
Windows 3.1, 20, 21f
Windows 7, 26–27, 27f, 117–159
  32- vs. 64-bit, 9
  Command Prompts, 333–336
  compatibility check, 122
  customizing and managing, 139–151
  default file locations, 147, 148f
  desktop, 130–135, 140–145
  display settings, 140–143
  editions, 118–119
  encryption, 72–73
  features, 130–139, 130f, 146, 147
  file management, 146–150
  file system support, 136–137
  Home Basic edition, 119
  installing, 118–129
  installing/removing applications, 145–146
  logon screen, 224f
  memory limits, 9t
  OS X, 86, 86f
  post-installation tasks, 128–129
  program compatibility, 137–138
  recommended system requirements, 118, 118t
  recovery tools, 138–139, 138f
  Safe Mode, 238–240
  security, 137, 152–159
  sharing files and printers, 399–404
  Starter edition, 119
  startup, 222–224, 226–228, 235–238
  updating, 122, 128–129
  upgrade paths, 119–120, 119t
  User Account Control, 68–69
  user accounts, 152–155

  user and power options, 220–222
  Windows Virtual PC, 93–94, 100–102
  Windows XP Mode, 93–99
Windows 8, 165–204
  Advanced Startup options, 241–245
  Client Hyper-V, 102–105
  Command Prompts, 336–338, 337f
  desktop, 28f, 194–197, 194f
  Devices page, 232f
  drivers, 178, 183–184
  editions, 169–171
  encryption, 72–73
  features, 166–169
  file management, 195–196
  GUI for, 27–28, 165–168
  installing, 171–183
  managing apps, 197–199
  memory limits, 9t
  mobile device hardware, 169
  Modern vs. Desktop, 27–28, 165, 167–168
  navigating and configuring, 189–199
  on-screen keyboard, 168, 168f, 169
  post-installation tasks, 183–189
  recommended system requirements, 172
  removing software, 187
  Restart, 222
  search function, 193, 194
  security, 183, 200–204
  sharing files and printers, 399–403
  shutting down, 188–189
  signing in, 173–174, 181–182, 182f
  Start screen, 27f, 166f
  startup, 223, 225
  updated drivers, 178
  update to, 171
  updating, 184–186
  upgrade paths, 172, 172t
  User Account Control, 68–69
  user accounts, 201–203
  user and power options, 220–222
  virtual machines, 187
  Web-based setup, 178–179
Windows 8.1, 171, 194, 194f, 337
Windows 8 Basic, 170
Windows 8 Pro, 170–171
Windows 95, 22
Windows 98, 22–23, 23f
Windows 2000, 4, 24f
Windows Aero, 130–131
Windows Defender, 137, 159, 183, 200–201, 201f
Windows Easy Transfer, 122–123, 123f
Windows Enterprise editions, 119
Windows Explorer, 147–148, 149f
  See also File Explorer

Windows Firewall, 59–60, 59*f*, 60*f*, 159, 200
Windows Flip, 193
    See also Flip 3D
Windows for Workgroups, 20–22
Windows Live Mail, 395–397
Windows Me (Millennium Edition), 23–24
Windows Media Center (WMC), 170, 171
Windows Media Player (WMP), 170
Windows Memory Diagnostic Tool, 139
Windows NT, 22
Windows NT 3.5, 22
Windows NT 4.0, 22, 23*f*
Windows OS, 4
Windows Phone, 5
Windows Phone 8, 165, 169, 430–431, 436, 439, 440
Windows Preinstallation Environment (PE), 123–124, 235
Windows Recovery Environment (Windows RE), 235
Windows RT, 169–170
Windows Server 2003, 24
Windows setup, 179
Windows SmartScreen, 203–204, 204*f*
Windows Store, 170, 173, 197–199, 198*f*
Windows Update, 63–64, 64*f*, 122, 129, 184–186
Windows Virtual PC, 93–94, 100–102

Windows Vista, 25, 26*f*
    encryption, 72
    Microsoft Virtual PC 2007 installation, 89–90
    recommended system requirements, 118
    resistance to, 117
    Safe Mode, 238–240
    similarities to Windows 7, 117
    startup, 235–238
    upgrade to Windows 7, 119
    User Account Control, 68–69
Windows XP, 24–25, 25*f*
    Help, 460
    Microsoft Virtual PC 2007 installation, 89–90
    running old applications, 466–467
Windows XP Mode, 93–99
Windows XP Professional, 447–467
    account management, 448–454
    backing up, 461–465
    file, folder, and printer permissions, 454–460
    security, 448–460
    troubleshooting, 460–467
WINLOAD.EXE, 223
WINLOGON.EXE, 224
Wired connectivity, 379–381
Wireless access points (WAPs), 384
Wireless connectivity, 381–384, 424–428
Wireless LAN (WLAN), 367, 378–379, 384

Wireless wide area networks (WWANs), 381, 382, 382*f*
WLAN. *See* Wireless LAN (WLAN)
WordPerfect, 13
Word processors, for Linux, 298
WordStar, 12
Workplace, mobile devices in, 419–421
Workstations, 22
World IPv6 Launch Day, 369
World Wide Web, 15, 296, 365
Worms, 45
Wozniak, Stephen, 11, 16, 254

X

xcopy command, 345
Xerox, 10
X Window System, 297

Y

Yahoo!, 16
YouTube, 19

Z

Zero-day exploits, 40
Zombies, 45
Zones, 389
Zooming, 191